PUBLIC AND NONPROFIT MARKETING: CASES AND READINGS

Christopher H. Lovelock
Harvard University

Charles B. Weinberg
The University of British Columbia

The Scientific Press
Palo Alto, California

John Wiley & Sons
New York   Chichester   Brisbane
Toronto   Singapore

PUBLIC AND NONPROFIT MARKETING:
    CASES AND READINGS
        Christopher H. Lovelock
        Charles B. Weinberg

ISBN 0-471-88578-9

Case material is made possible by the cooperation of organizations
who may wish to remain anonymous by having names, quantities,
and other identifying details disguised while maintaining
basic relationships. Cases are prepared as the basis for
class discussion rather than to illustrate either effective
or ineffective handling of administrative situations.

Cover design by Ann Renzi
Illustrations by Rogondino & Associates
Typography by The Scientific Press
Printed in the USA

10 9 8 7 6 5 4 3 2 1

To our mothers

Clare Lovelock and Sylvia Weinberg

and in memory of our fathers

Colin Lovelock and Samuel Weinberg

Contents

Preface   ix

Studying and Learning from Cases   xi

I. OVERVIEW   1

Cases   1. University Arts Program   3
Patrick Hanemann & Charles B. Weinberg

2. The 911 Emergency Number in New York   15
Jeffrey S. Kahn & Christopher H. Lovelock

3. Sierra Club Publishing Division   21
Arthur Segel & Charles B. Weinberg

Readings   4. Public and Nonprofit Marketing Comes of Age   33
Christopher H. Lovelock & Charles B. Weinberg

5. An International Perspective on Public Sector Marketing   43
Christopher H. Lovelock

6. Marketing Communications in Nonbusiness Situations   57
Michael L. Rothschild

7. Advertising and Publicity Programs in the Executive Branch   67
of the National Government: Hustling or Helping the People?
Dean L. Yarwood & Ben M. Enis

II. DEVELOPING A CONSUMER PERSPECTIVE   77

Cases   8. City of Dallas   79
Christopher H. Lovelock

9. Water Conservation in Palo Alto   91
Peter T. Hutchison, Don E. Parkinson, & Charles B. Weinberg

10. Seville Community College   105
Christopher H. Lovelock

11. The Golden Gate Corridor Busway   Amtrak   107
Charles B. Weinberg & Barton H. Weitz

12. The Birds, the Bees, and the Bugs   117
Robin B. Dow & Michael R. Pearce

Readings   13. Nonprofits: Check Your Attention to Customers   131
Alan R. Andreasen

14. Diffusion of Innovations   137
Everett M. Rogers & F. Floyd Shoemaker

15. Preventive Health Care and Consumer Behavior: 147
Towards a Broader Perspective
John A. Quelch & Stephen B. Ash

III. STRATEGIC ISSUES   **155**

Cases 16. Beth Israel Hospital, Boston   157
            Terrie Bloom, Christopher H. Lovelock, & Penny Pittman Merliss

        17. Amtrak   169
            Christopher H. Lovelock

        18. The Richardson Center for the Blind   185
            Roberta N. Clarke & Benson P. Shapiro

Readings 19. Consumer Energy Conservation Policy in Canada: 197
            Behavioural and Institutional Obstacles
            Gordon H. G. McDougall & Randolph B. Mank

        20. Competing for Scarce Resources   207
            Ellen Greenberg

IV. THE MARKETING MIX   **213**

Cases 21. Museum Wharf   215
            Roger Davis & Christopher H. Lovelock

        22. Wessex College   231
            Christopher H. Lovelock

        23. Montecito State College: Division of Extension Studies   233
            Christopher H. Lovelock

        24. American Repertory Theatre   243
            Penny Pittman Merliss & Christopher H. Lovelock

Readings 25. Marketing Mix Decisions for Nonprofit Organizations: 261
            An Analytical Approach
            Charles B. Weinberg

        26. The Mass Media Family Planning Campaign   271
            for the United States
            Richard K. Manoff

        27. The Baptists Want You!   277
            William Martin

        28. Evaluating Social Persuasion Advertising Campaigns: 287
            An Overview of Recent C.O.I. Experience
            John Samuels

V. IMPLEMENTATION   **295**

Cases 29. United States Postal Service   297
            L. Frank Demmler & Christopher H. Lovelock

        30. Stanford University: The Annual Fund   307
            Christopher H. Lovelock

        31. Ethical Problems in Marketing Research   321
            Charles B. Weinberg

        32. London Goodwill Industries Association: Used Bookstore   325
            Judith Marshall & David Burgoyne

33. Rapid Transit in Los Angeles 335
Christopher H. Lovelock & L. Frank Demmler

Readings 34. Strategies for Introducing Marketing into 353
Nonprofit Organizations
Philip Kotler

35. Should Not-for-Profits Go into Business? 361
Edward Skloot

36. Marketing National Change: Decimalization in Britain 367
Christopher H. Lovelock

Preface

Public and Nonprofit Marketing: Cases and Readings is an updated and combined version of our two earlier books, *Cases in Public and Nonprofit Marketing* and *Readings in Public and Nonprofit Marketing,* both pub-lished by The Scientific Press. This new book is organized to complement our text, *Marketing for Public and Nonprofit Managers,* but can also be read and studied independently.

Development of these books reflects our belief—discussed more fully in the first reading—that public and nonprofit marketing has now come of age. In both the cases and articles, we have tried to show the state of art in research and practice as these apply to marketing among public agencies and nonprofit organizations. The materials assembled here, we believe, provide relevant case histories as well as conceptual insights, stimulate and challenge as well as inform, and demonstrate the value of new method-ological approaches as well as that of tried and tested man-agerial policies. The book can be used for self-study as well as a text in classes and seminars.

Public and Nonprofit Marketing: Cases and Readings comprises a total of thirty-six chapters: twenty cases and sixteen readings. All the cases have been pretested through classroom use. Of the sixteen readings, five are retained from our previous volume and eleven are new. All but three articles were published in 1978 or later, four were either spe-cially prepared for this edition or were published in 1982–83.

Of the twenty cases, thirteen are carried over from the previous edition (two are revised) and seven are new. Six of the cases included in this book have been reviewed and

"recommended" by the editorial board of the Public Policy and Management Program for Case/Course Development. These six are: Beth Israel Hospital, Golden Gate Corridor Busway, The 911 Emergency Number in New York, Uni-versity Arts Program, United States Postal Service, and Water Conservation in Palo Alto.

The book is divided into five parts, corresponding to the organization of *Marketing for Public and Nonprofit Man-agers.* These five parts are entitled Overview, Developing a Consumer Perspective, Strategic Issues, The Marketing Mix, and Implementation.

In our experience, managers in different types of non-business organizations often believe that their field of activity is so different and so specialized that they can learn little from studying the operations of organizations in other fields. We suggest that this is a mistaken view. Developing a profes-sional sense of management entails the ability to distinguish the specific from the generalizable; to recognize the value of certain concepts, tools, and strategies for problem solving across a wide range of situations; and to apply these in ways that recognize the distinctive nature of the specific problem under review.

Accordingly, we have combined materials involving general discussion of marketing's value for nonbusiness organizations with cases and articles covering a broad range of specific applications. These include health care, public transportation, the performing and visual arts, education, and energy conservation. We invite readers to compare and contrast the different situations presented, with a view to developing their own conceptual insights and evaluating the transferability of specific marketing strategies and analytical procedures.

ACKNOWLEDGEMENTS

We would like to express our thanks to all those who have contributed to the development of this book, as well as its predecessors. Casewriting tends to rely heavily on field research, and we particularly appreciate the cooperation extended by the management of those organizations (sometimes disguised) who were the subjects of field visits and willing to share their experience with us and other casewriters.

We also wish to thank our fellow authors whose cases and articles (and the author's present affiliation, where known) will be found on the first page of each case selection. We are also indebted to the original publishers of the works included, as listed on the first page of each selection. To all, we say, "thank you."

In selecting materials for inclusion in this book, we have relied on our own and others' classroom experience, including executive education seminars as well as graduate and undergraduate programs. In addition to colleagues who offered suggestions, we also had the benefit of responses to a survey of users of the earlier books. We are grateful for their help and encouragement and hope that they will be pleased with the selection of materials we made.

Many people have been involved in bringing this book into print and it is not possible to mention them all by name. However, we would like to acknowledge especially the secretarial help provided by Patricia Morison and Beverly Outram, as well as the staffs of the Word Processing Centers at the Harvard Business School and the University of British Columbia, who struggled through reading our notes and typing numerous versions of many of the articles and cases. Publication of this book would not have been possible without the special efforts of Richard Esposito of John Wiley & Sons, Inc., and Paul Kelly of The Scientific Press, both of whom we thank heartily.

Financial support for our work was generously provided at Harvard by the Associates of the Harvard Business School, and at UBC, in part, through grants from the Social Sciences and Humanities Research Council of Canada.

Finally, we wish to thank our students, whose critical analysis in classroom discussions has served to sharpen and refine the cases and to help us select the articles included in this book.

Christopher H. Lovelock
Charles B. Weinberg

Studying and Learning from Cases

Dealing with cases is very much like working with the problems that men and women encounter in their jobs as managers. In most instances, you will be identifying and clarifying problems facing a nonbusiness organization, analyzing qualitative information and quantitative data, evaluating alternative courses of action, and then making decisions about what strategy to pursue for the future.

Reflecting the uncertainty of the real-world managerial environment, the information presented in a case is often imprecise and ambiguous. The goal in using the case method is not to develop a set of "correct" facts, but to learn to reason well with available data. You will find—and perhaps be frustrated by the fact—that there is no one right answer or correct solution to a case. Instead, there may be a number of feasible strategies management might adopt, each with somewhat different implications for the future of the organization, and each involving different trade-offs.

As a teaching approach, the case method can only be successful if you accept the role of an involved participant in the case, as opposed to that of a disinterested observer. Unlike lectures and textbooks, the case method of instruction does not present students with a body of tried and true knowledge about how to be a successful manager. Instead, it provides an opportunity to learn by "doing."

If you are using this book in a course or seminar, you will be exposed to a wide range of different management situations within a relatively short space of time. Yet, these cases collectively provide a much broader exposure than most marketing managers experience on the job in many years. Recognizing that the problems with which managers must deal are not unique to a particular institution (or even to a specific field, such as education or health care) forms the basis for developing a professional sense of management.

CASES AND THE REAL WORLD

In spite of the realism that casewriters try to build into their cases, it's important to recognize that they differ from "real-world" management situations in several important respects. First, the information is "prepackaged" in written form. By contrast, practicing managers accumulate their information through such means as memoranda, meetings, chance conversations, research studies, observations, news media reports, and other externally published materials—and, of course, by rumor.

Second, cases tend to be selective in their reporting because most of them are designed with specific teaching objectives in mind. Each must fit a relatively short class period and focus attention on a defined category of management problems within a given subject area. To provide such a focus—and to keep the length and complexity of the case within reasonable bounds—it may be necessary to omit information on problems, data, or personnel that are peripheral to the central issue(s) in the case.

In the real world, management problems are usually dynamic in nature. They call for some immediate action, with further analysis and decisions delayed until some later time. Managers are rarely able to wrap up their problems, put them away, and go on to the next "case." In contrast, a case discussion in class is more like a "snapshot" taken at a particular point in time. However, sometimes a sequel case provides a sense of continuity and the need for future decisions within the same organization.

A final contrast between case discussions and the realities of real-world management is that participants in case discussions are not responsible for implementing their decisions, nor do they have to live with the consequences. This does not mean, however, that you can be frivolous when making recommendations in class. Your instructor and classmates are likely to be critical if your contributions are not based upon a careful analysis and interpretation of the facts.

PREPARING A CASE

Just as there is no one right solution to a case, there is no single "correct" way of preparing a case. However, the following broad guidelines may help familiarize you with the job of case preparation. With practice, you should be able to establish a working style with which you feel comfortable.

Initial Analysis. First, it's important to gain a feel for the overall situation, by skimming quickly through the case. Ask yourself:

- What sort of organization is the case about?
- What is the nature of the field (broadly defined)?
- What is going on in the external environment?
- What problems does management appear to be facing?

An initial fast reading, without attempting to make notes or to underline, should provide you with some sense for what is going on and what information is being presented for analysis. Then you will be ready to make a very careful second reading of the case. This time, seek to identify key facts so that you can develop a situation analysis and clarify the nature of the problem(s) facing management. Make some notes as you go along in response to such questions as:

- What decisions need to be made and who will be responsible for making them?
- What are the objectives of the organization itself and of each of the key players in the case? Are they mutually compatible objectives? If not, can they be reconciled or will it be necessary to redefine the objectives?
- What resources and constraints are present which will help or hinder attempts by the organization to meet its objectives?

You should make a particular effort to establish the significance of any quantitative data presented in the text of the case, or, more often, in the exhibits. See if new insights may be gained by combining and manipulating data presented in different parts of the case. But don't accept the data blindly. With cases, as in real life, not all information is equally reliable or equally relevant. On the other hand, casewriters do not deliberately misrepresent data or facts to "trick" you.

Developing Recommendations. At this point, you should be in a position to summarize your evaluation of the situation and to develop some recommendations for management. First, identify the alternative courses of action that the organization might take. Next, consider the implications of each alternative, including possible undesirable outcomes, such as discouraging customers from using the product, provoking involvement by politicians or stimulating responses from competing organizations. Ask yourself how short-term tactics fit with longer-term strategies. Relate each alternative back to the objectives of the organization (as defined or implied in the case, or as redefined by you). Then, develop a set of recommendations for future action, making sure that these are supported by your analysis of the case data.

Your recommendations will not be complete unless you give some thought to how the proposed strategy should be implemented:

- What resources—human, financial and other—will be required?
- Who should be responsible for implementation?
- What time-frame should be established for the various actions proposed?
- How should subsequent performance be measured?

Small Group Discussions. The best results in the early stages of case preparation are generally achieved by working alone. But a useful step, prior to class discussion, is to discuss the case with a small group of classmates. These small groups facilitate initial "testing" of ideas, and help to focus the discussion on the main considerations. Within such a discussion group, present your arguments and listen to those of other participants. The aim of such a meeting is not to reach a consensus, but to broaden, clarify, and redefine your own thinking—and to help others do likewise.

Effective management of marketing involves adjusting the organization's resources to the changing character of the marketplace; this is different from just applying knowledge about "what works" and "what doesn't work" in marketing. Accordingly, the focus of small group discussions should be on analysis and decision making: What are the facts? What do they mean? What alternatives are available? What specifically should management do, how, and when?

CLASS DISCUSSIONS

In class, you may find that the role played by an instructor teaching the case method differs significantly from that of a lecturer. The instructor's role in case discussions is often similar to that of a moderator—calling on students, guiding the discussion, asking questions, and periodically synthesizing previous comments.

Responsibilities of Participants. The role of participants is similarly different. Instead of being a passive note-taker, you will be expected to become an active participant in class discussions. Indeed, it is essential that you participate; for if nobody participated, there would be no discussion! If *you* never join in the debate, you will be denying the other participants the insights that you may have to offer. Moreover, there is significant learning involved in presenting your own analysis and recommendations and debating them with your classmates—who may hold differing views or else seek to build on your presentation. But don't be so eager to participate that you ignore what others have to say. Learning to be a good listener is also an important element in developing managerial skills.

A few last words of general caution may be helpful. Avoid indiscriminate "rehash" of case facts in your presentation—the instructor and the other participants have already read the case, too. Work towards building a coherent class discussion, rather than making random comments.

Before making a contribution, ask yourself if the points you plan to make are relevant to what has gone before, or if they will result in a significant redirection of the discussion.

Occasionally, it may happen that you are personally familiar with the organization depicted in a case. Perhaps you are privy to additional information not contained in the case, or perhaps you know what has happened since the time of the case decision point. If so, keep this information to yourself unless, and until, the instructor requests it. There are no prizes for 20–20 hindsight, and injecting extra information that nobody else has is more likely to spoil the class discussion than to enhance it.

Learning comes through discussion and controversy. In the case method of instruction, participants must assume responsibility not only for their own learning, but also for that of others in the class. Thus, it is important that you be well-prepared, willing to commit yourself to a well-reasoned set of analyses and recommendations, and receptive to constructive criticism. If you do not accept this challenge, you are likely to find the case method aimless and confusing. On the other hand, if you do accept it, then you'll experience in the classroom that sense of excitement, challenge, and even exasperation that comes with being a manager in real-world situations.

PART I
Overview

Cases

1. University Arts Program   **3**

2. The 911 Emergency Number in New York   **15**

3. Sierra Club Publishing Division   **21**

Readings

4. Public and Nonprofit Marketing Comes of Age   **33**

5. An International Perspective on Public Sector Marketing   **43**

6. Marketing Communications in Nonbusiness Situations   **57**

7. Advertising and Publicity Programs in the Executive Branch   **67**
of the National Government: Hustling or Helping the People?

1

University Arts Program

Patrick Hanemann
Charles B. Weinberg

In late March 1975, Andre Williams, Director of Mardi Gras University's Office of Public Events, was trying to determine the scope and policies of the University Arts Program for the next academic year (1975–76). He had just reviewed two persuasive reports. One, a consultant's report (Appendix 1), suggested reducing the number of performances by one-third and increasing the average ticket price by $1.00 in order to come closer to the Program's goal of breaking even. The other, prepared by a student intern (Appendix 2), advocated a policy of audience expansion, which would require Mr. Williams to develop special programs to achieve the desired increase in audience size. In designing the Program for 1975–76, Mr. Williams intended to consider carefully these two reports, which conflicted in a number of areas.

During the course of its 1974–75 season, the University Arts Program was scheduled to present 31 performers or groups in 42 performances of classical music, theatre and dance. Twenty-seven of these performances were given during the first six months of the season. Seating capacity for these performances was 32,783; total attendance was 14,383, or approximately 44% of capacity (see Exhibit 1). Expenses amounted to $84,000, while income on ticket sales totaled $46,700 (see Exhibit 2). Grants from the National Endowment for the Arts increased this figure to $52,500, leaving a net deficit of $31,500. Mr. Williams expected that the deficit for the entire season would approximate $50,000. Any losses incurred by the Program were underwritten by the University, which did not require the Program to make a profit. However, a deficit of this magnitude would not be tolerated on a continuing basis. (See Exhibit 3 for results of previous years.)

The University. Founded in 1885, Mardi Gras University was a private, coeducational institution located in New Orleans, Louisiana. During the 1974–75 academic year, the University had enrolled approximately 6,500 undergraduates and 5,000 graduate students. There were 1,100 faculty members and 5,900 staff members. A high proportion of the students and faculty lived on campus. Most others lived in neighboring communities.

While Mardi Gras was a leading private university in the area, there were numerous other colleges and universities in this metropolitan region, which had a total population of approximately 1.5 million. Other private institutions included Tulane University, Sophie Newcomb College, Loyola University, and Holy Cross College. The University of New Orleans and Southern University of New Orleans were also located in town. There were also two so-called "black" colleges, Xavier and Dillard.

Patrick Hanemann is a member of the Stanford MBA Class of 1974; Charles B. Weinberg is Professor of Marketing, University of British Columbia.

EXHIBIT 1
Ticket Sales by Category, First Six Months 1974—1975

Performing Group	Reserve	Student Discount	Student Rush	Group	Season	Special Series	Total Seats Sold
1 Inner City I	80	75	116	0	14	15	300
2 Inner City II	152	139	203	0	30	45	569
3 New York Chamber Soloists I	121	34	60	0	48	18	281
4 New York Chamber Soloists II	108	25	42	0	18	13	206
5 Gustav Leonhard	81	44	84	0	20	15	244
6 Modern Jazz Quartet	393	380	202	0	54	30	1,059
7 Gary Graffman	208	75	172	0	40	16	511
8 Les Menestriers	243	158	168	0	62	63	694
9 Siobhan McKenna	473	167	0	0	72	22	734
10 Harkness Ballet	863	547	70	0	59	60	1,399
11 Emlyn Williams	187	54	72	0	68	22	403
12 Elly Ameling I	185	29	41	0	25	15	295
13 Elly Ameling II	312	60	90	0	50	19	531
14 Dorothy Stickney	199	18	49	0	36	23	325
15 Lotte Goslar Troupe I	70	25	27	0	18	12	152
16 Lotte Goslar Troupe II	109	121	106	0	59	49	444
17 Lotte Goslar Troupe III	210	305	9	0	—	—	524
18 Speculum Musicae	34	7	43	0	23	10	117
19 Anthony Newman	85	78	101	0	44	10	318
20 Secolo Baroco	148	58	69	25	64	62	426
21 I Musici	445	165	69	30	99	33	841
22 Jacob Lateiner	182	42	94	0	31	15	364
23 Repertory Dance Theatre I	98	81	89	0	40	37	345
24 Repertory Dance Theatre II	80	132	29	0	0	0	241
25 Repertory Dance Theatre III	112	38	78	0	39	23	290
26 P.D.Q. Bach	697	652	134	70	63	32	1,648
27 Music from Marlboro	97	14	14	0	56	27	208
Totals	5,972	3,523	2,201	125	1,132	689	13,639
Per Cent of Audience	44%	26%	16%	1%	8%	5%	100%
Total Attendance	14,383						

Mardi Gras University was located on an attractively landscaped, 700-acre campus in Chartrain, a suburb of New Orleans some ten miles from the city center. The University was quite well served by major highways, but public transportation services to the campus ceased at 7 p.m. on weekdays.

The Performing Arts in New Orleans. Cultural offerings in the New Orleans area took several forms. The New Orleans Opera House Association had a six-week season each year at the 2,300-seat New Orleans Theatre of the Performing Arts, while the New Orleans Philharmonic Symphony Orchestra performed during a 38-week season at the same location. Other permanent offerings included a year-round season at the 350-seat Beverly Dinner Playhouse and Black drama at the 120-seat Free Southern Theatre. Visiting performing arts companies often used the facilities at New Orleans' Municipal Auditorium and Rivergate Convention Center. Additional cultural events included those sponsored by other colleges and universities in the New Orleans area, although none of these institutions offered as extensive an arts program as that of Mardi Gras University.

The Program. As Director of Mardi Gras's Office of Public Events, Andre Williams was responsible for administration of the University Arts Program. He had set a number of objectives for the Program, although he had not weighted them in terms of importance. Among these, Mr. Williams included the following:

Present a self-supporting series of top-quality professional performing events.

Keep prices as low as possible in order to make performances widely accessible.

Augment academic offerings in the theory and practice of the arts.

Contribute positively to the extracurricular educational experience of the Mardi Gras students.

Contribute to the University's position within the New Orleans community as a cultural and intellectual resource.

EXHIBIT 2
Ticket Revenues by Category, First Six Months, 1974—1975

Performing Group	Reserve	Student Discount	Student Rush	Group	Season	Special Series
1 Inner City I	$ 319.00	$ 211.00	$ 232.75	—	$ 49.84	$ 49.80
2 Inner City II	619.00	421.00	408.25	—	107.37	141.40
3 New York Chamber Soloists I	544.50	127.50	120.00	—	162.24	56.70
4 New York Chamber Soloists II	486.00	93.75	84.00	—	60.84	40.95
5 Gustav Leonhard	364.50	165.00	168.00	—	67.60	47.25
6 Modern Jazz Quartet	1,568.75	1,170.00	406.25	—	192.24	102.80
7 Gary Gaffman	936.00	281.25	344.00	—	135.20	50.40
8 Les Menestriers	1,093.50	592.50	336.00	—	209.56	226.80
9 Siobhan McKenna	2,128.50	626.25	—	—	243.36	79.20
10 Harkness Ballet	3,486.25	1,479.00	140.00	—	211.94	192.00
11 Emlyn Williams	841.50	202.50	144.00	—	229.84	79.20
12 Elly Ameling I	832.50	108.75	82.00	—	84.50	47.25
13 Elly Ameling II	1,404.00	225.00	180.00	—	169.00	59.85
14 Dorothy Stickney	895.50	67.50	98.00	—	121.68	82.80
15 Lotte Goslar Troupe I	297.50	92.00	54.00	—	64.08	40.80
16 Lotte Goslar Troupe II	451.75	368.00	229.25	—	211.94	153.40
17 Lotte Goslar Troupe III	683.00	729.25	18.00	—	—	—
18 Speculum Musicae	153.00	26.25	86.00	—	77.74	31.50
19 Anthony Newman	382.50	292.50	202.00	—	148.72	31.50
20 Secolo Baroco	666.00	217.50	138.00	$ 90.00	216.32	195.30
21 I Musici	1,844.75	484.00	144.75	90.00	352.44	103.95
22 Jacob Lateiner	819.00	157.50	188.00	—	104.78	47.25
23 Repertory Dance Theatre I	408.50	263.00	178.00	—	143.54	118.20
24 Repertory Dance Theatre II	236.00	224.00	58.00	—	—	—
25 Repertory Dance Theatre III	458.00	112.00	156.00	—	113.12	75.40
26 P.D.Q. Bach	2,667.75	1,811.00	268.00	266.00	224.28	110.40
27 Music from Marlboro	400.50	48.50	28.00	—	189.28	85.05
Totals	$24,987.75	$10,596.50	$4,491.25	$446.00	$3,891.45	$2,249.15
Per Cent of Revenue	53%	23%	10%	1%	8%	5%
Total Receipts	$46,662.10					

EXHIBIT 3
Results of Previous Years

	Number of Performances	Capacity	Audience	Audience as % of Capacity	Students as % of Audience
1972–73 Season	20	25,972	14,726	56.7%	36.8%
1973–74 Season	26	39,602	20,133	50.8%	39.1%
Fall 1974	10	16,132	8,492	52.6%	39.3%
Fall 1974*	9	10,132	7,448	73.5%	36.2%
Winter 1974	8	16,132	8,542	53.0%	NA
Spring 1974**	8	7,338	3,099	42.2%	35.6%
1974–75 Season First 27 Performances	27	32,783	14,383	44.0%	42.0%

* The first performance of the year was the Utah Symphony in the 6,000 seat Amphitheater which was attended by 1,044. This row excludes that performance.

** There was considerable student unrest on campus during the spring concerning the denial of tenure to three popular faculty members.

Contribute to Mardi Gras's national and international prestige by presenting a program qualitatively commensurate with other offerings of the University.

Help solidify the importance of the arts in social development and, hopefully, to thereby insure the future of the arts.

In addition, Mr. Williams had exclusive responsibility for artist selection and scheduling. Of the first 27 performances offered during 1974–75, there were 13 performances of instrumental music, 9 of dance, 3 of drama, and 2 of vocal music.

Offerings covered a broad spectrum of the classical repertoire and featured some of the finest touring artists of the United States and Europe. Fourteen performances were held in Lafitte Auditorium, a 720-seat concert hall at the center of campus. Twelve performances were given in Memorial Hall, a 1,694-seat multi-purpose facility which also served the University as a lecture hall and convocation center. The remaining performance was presented off-campus in the 975-seat auditorium of a high school.

Other facilities on campus which were often used for theatrical and musical performances included the University Church (1,000 seats), Rittle Theater (192 seats), and the Amphitheater (capacity 6,000 persons).

Promotional Activities. The Program was advertised in three major ways: (1) direct mailing, (2) newspaper advertising, and (3) posters and flyers.

The direct mailing consisted of the University Arts brochure, a 32-page booklet featuring pictures and brief descriptions of the season's offerings, together with ticket information and a presentation of the programs scheduled by the Music and Theatre Departments of the University. Thirty thousand copies of the brochure were produced. Of these, 20,000 were distributed at the beginning of the fall quarter according to a mailing list, with additional copies available upon request. The 20,000 figure included 12,000 locally-based supporters of the Program and 8,000 Mardi Gras alumni who were selected on the basis of their proximity to the University. This alumni mailing excluded those living in New Orleans, however, because it was felt that interested alumni in the immediate vicinity of the University would learn of the Program through local newspaper advertising. The list had been compiled from a number of different sources over the past several years, and efforts had been made during the summer of 1974 to eliminate duplications. Mr. Williams conceded, however, that he had no way of determining the impact of the brochure on Program attendance levels, nor indeed any way of knowing what percentage of names on the list were still in the area or had any interest in receiving the brochure. In addition to this mailing, which generally went to non-students, there was an on-campus dis-

tribution of *The Season*, a listing of the year's performance schedule.

Over the first six months of the season, costs for the brochure amounted to $2,200 (allocated on a performance basis for twenty-seven of the scheduled forty-two performances), with *The Season* and the *Winter Almanac* accounting for an additional $213. Including mailing expenses (approximately $540), the costs of the direct mail promotion for the six-month period totalled $2,950, or 24% of the total promotional budget for this period.

A second element of promotional activity, newspaper and publication advertising, accounted for 62% of the period's advertising budget, and was distributed as follows:

The Times Picayune	$2,460
New Orleans States-Item	2,420
Mardi Gras Daily	1028
Clarion Herald	814
Alumni Almanac	728
Student Life	54
Total	$7,504

With the exception of the *Student Life*, where advertising appeared only quarterly in the form of a listing of the quarter's events, newspaper advertising copy was fairly uniform, consisting of the University Arts logo and a brief description of each of the events scheduled over the next few days, together with relevant information regarding time, place and ticket prices (see Exhibit 4).

The third area of promotional activity, constituting 14% of the period budget, was devoted to posters, flyers and "table tents." Posters were used both on-campus (on kiosks, bulletin boards and at the Jackson box office) and off-campus (at remote Ticketron outlets and in heavily-traveled, consumer-oriented areas such as the Shopping Center). Flyers were generally used for student distribution, and "table tents" were displayed on tables in the Jackson Union and in the dining rooms of campus housing facilities.

Pricing. Standard prices for reserved seating generally were $4.75, $3.75 and $2.75 in Memorial Hall, and $4.50 in Lafitte Auditorium. A discount of $.75 per reserved ticket was offered to all under 18 years of age and to anyone who held a current student body card. Student rush tickets were sold, at a price of $2.00 per ticket, for all seats which were still available fifteen minutes prior to scheduled curtain time. A discount of 20% was offered to groups of twenty or more people attending the same performance. In addition, there were seven separate series ticket plans. The "Choose Your Own" plan enabled the patron to select any ten performances during the year at a savings of 23% to 28% off the individual ticket prices. The remaining six series—Dance, Theatre, Keyboard, Early Music, Connoisseur and

EXHIBIT 4
Two Sample Newspaper Advertisments, Spring 1975

THE ARTS AT MARDI GRAS UNIVERSITY

TONIGHT | **THE** | *EARLY MUSIC SERIES*
8:00 p.m. | NEW | The liturgical drama of the Spanish Renais-
University | YORK | sance Mass "Missa Ave, Maris Stella" by
Church | PRO | Cristobal de Morales will be magically re-
| MUSICA | created *in Mardi Gras's University Church as*
part of the Pro Musica's last concert. The secular music of sixteenth century Spain comparable in its richness, variety, musicality and artistry to that of Italy and France will also be performed.
TICKETS: $4.75, 3.75, 2.75 / students $4, 3, 2 (Student Rush, if available, $2.)

TONIGHT | **THE** | *DRAMA DEPARTMENT PRODUCTIONS*
8:00 p.m. | ARCHITECT | A brilliant, inventive and exhilarating experi-
MAY 8-12 | AND THE | ence in "the theater of panic." EXTRA
& 15-19 | EMPEROR OF | MIDNIGHT PERFORMANCES: May 10,
6 *Midnight perfs.* | ASSYRIA | 11, 12 and 17, 18, 19.
Rittle | *by* | *TICKETS: AT DOOR ONLY 7:30 p.m. &*
Theater | ARRABAL | *11:30 p.m.*
PRICES: $2 / students $1.
TIME 8:00 p.m. and midnight.

8:00 p.m. | THE Mardi Gras | *MUSIC DEPARTMENT SERIES*
Saturday | GLEE CLUB | A happy musical revue of show tunes, popu-
MAY 12 | Robert MacKinnon, | lar songs, and folk music, featuring the Axi-
Lafitte | Director | dentals.
Auditorium | | *TICKETS: $2.00 / students $1.00*

8:00 p.m. | THE | *MUSIC DEPARTMENT SERIES*
Sunday | FRANCESCO | Guest artists: Marie Gibson, soprano, and
MAY 13 | TRIO | Paul Hersh, viola and piano. Shostakovich:
Lafitte | | *Seven songs on poems by Alexander Blok,*
Auditorium | | *for soprano and trio, Op. 127,* Dvorak: *Piano Quartet, Op. 87, in E flat major;* Villa-Lobos: *Duxchoros, for violin and cello;* Schubert: *Fantasy in F minor, Op. 103, for one piano, four hands.*
Tickets: $2.00 / students $1.00

ckets at Jackson Box Office, Maison Blanche Box Office and all area CKETRON agencies. By mail send s.a. envelope with check or money der payable to Jackson Box Office, Mardi Gras University. Phone 1-2300, X4317. Discount tickets available at Jackson Box Office only.

THE ARTS AT MARDI GRAS UNIVERSITY

LAST WEEK | **THE** | *DRAMA DEPARTMENT PRODUCTIONS*
8:00 p.m. | ARCHITECT | A brilliant, inventive and exhilarating experi-
MAY 15-19 | AND THE | ence in "the theater of panic." EXTRA
3 *Midnight perfs.* | EMPEROR OF | MIDNIGHT PERFORMANCES: May 17, 18
Rittle | ASSYRIA | & 19.
Theater | *by* | *TICKETS: AT DOOR ONLY 7:30 p.m. &*
| ARRABAL | *11:30 p.m.*
PRICES: $2 / students $1.
TIME: 8 p.m. and midnight.

8:00 p.m. | THE | "Bouyant ensemble playing and vibrant solo
Saturday | NEW | work" by Paula Hatcher, Charles Forbes and
MAY 19 | YORK | Glenn Jacobson of the New York Camerata
Lafitte | CAMERATA | will ensure an evening of artistic excellence.
Auditorium | | Program: Boismortier, Trio Sonata in E minor, Op. 37, No. 2, for flute, viola da gamba and continuo; Bach, Suite in G for solo cello; Handel, Flute Sonata; Scarlatti, Music of the English Renaissance for recorders and harpsichord, Two Sonatas for harpsichord; Rameau, Piece en concert for flute, cello and harpsichord.
TICKETS: $4.50 / students $3.75. (Student Rush, if available, $2.)

7:45 p.m. | ADVENTURE | *DISCOVERY '72 TRAVEL FILM SERIES*
Monday | ACROSS SOUTH | Let genial adventuring trubadour Rudi
MAY 21 | AMERICA | Thurau take you to the open air Indian
Memorial | *produced and* | market at Huancayo, the spectacular Inca
Hall | *narrated by* | Feast of the Sun at Cuzco, the romantic
| RUDI THURAU | Iguazu Falls in Brazil, and to Ushuaia, the southernmost city on earth, as he travels across South America with his two companions. The visual diary of a thrilling adventure.
TICKETS: $1.75 / students $1.

Tickets at Jackson Box Office, Maison Blanche Box Office and all area TICKETRON agencies. By mail send s.a. envelope with check or money order payable to Jackson Box Office, Mardi Gras University. Phone 321-2300, X4317. Discount tickets available at Jackson Box Office only.

Celebrity—provided discounts ranging from 20% to 30% on particular groupings of performances.

Consultant Report. In response to the increasing deficit which developed during the course of the year, Mr. Williams requested in February of 1975 that the Management Studies Office, an in-house Mardi Gras consulting group, examine the Program's operations and make recommendations for improvement. After conducting a breakeven analysis on the Program's revenue and expense data for the first six months of the 1975–76 season, Mr. James Finster of the Management Studies Office proposed two basic modifications for the 1975–76 season:

1. Reducing the number of performances from 42 to 28.

2. Increasing the average regular (reserved) ticket prices by $.75 for all seats in Memorial Hall, and by $1.00 for all seats in Lafitte Auditorium. (See Appendix 1 for full report.)

Next Year. Mr. Williams had to submit a plan for 1975–76 by the end of March. By then he had to decide how many performances the University Arts Program would have next year in order to finalize contractual arrangements with the artists. To make that decision, he would have to evaluate both Mr. Finster's report and one prepared by Mr. Seth Granger, an MBA student from the Tulane Graduate School of Business, who had been working as an intern in the Public Events Office (Appendix 2). In conversations with Mr. Granger, Mr. Williams had heard repeated arguments showing a need for an aggressive policy of audience expansion. On the other hand, the low attendance for the current year, less than 50% of capacity, was a major problem. Any audience expansion plan must first be able to explain these low attendance levels.

Although some had suggested that Mr. Williams expand his programming to include such events as rock concerts, this was not possible. Aside from his belief that such programming did not fit within the objectives of the Arts series, the student government already had a series of rock and folk concerts on campus.

Mr. Williams turned his attention to the following questions:

1. Why was attendance averaging less than 50% of capacity? What could be done to increase audience size?

2. What would be the advantages and disadvantages of having 25 performances as Mr. Finster suggested? Of raising prices?

3. What plan should he develop? Why?

Appendix 1

Management Studies Office Report

To: Andre Williams
From: James Finster
Subject: Program Pricing and Promotion

This memo summarizes and expands some of our earlier discussions.

Let me begin by suggesting an operating guideline. As we discussed, Special Events is a deficit operation during the academic year. For example, the total cost of the performances in Lafitte during 1973–74 exceeded what the total revenues would have been if every performance had sold out. If the maximum ticket price for Lafitte were substantially higher, say $5.50, it would still be necessary to sell in excess of 80% of the seating capacity to break even, assuming that the average cost of a performance in Lafitte is about $2,600. *Therefore, as a guideline you should assume that a good promotion program and an optimal pricing policy will continue to result in a net deficit.*

You can think of this overall deficit as an average deficit per performance. In 1973–74 there were 26 performances and a total deficit of about $27,000, or an average deficit of about $1,000 per performance. In 1974–75 a deficit of $50,000 is projected for 42 performances, or an average deficit of about $1,200 per performance. With 28 performances in 1975–76 and assuming a deficit goal of no more than $11,000, *your financial objective would be to reduce the average deficit to about $400 per performance. This objective, I believe, will be difficult to achieve, and the only assistance I can offer comes in the form of suggestions to try out, rather than sure-fire remedies.*

Pricing. The previous summary demonstrates in part the value of breakeven analysis. A breakeven analysis determines the point at which costs equal revenues when any of three factors are varied:

1. Ticket prices
2. Number of tickets sold
3. Cost of the performance

The three are interrelated on the basis of what is called "contribution margin," and this relationship is described in detail in the appendix to this memo.

The average contribution margin (average C.M.) in 1974–75 for ticket sales in Memorial Hall ranges from $3.00 to $3.25 per ticket. For Lafitte the average C.M. is about $3.50 per ticket sold. Using the formula given in the appendix, you can check the average contribution margin for each performance from the Ticketron printout. The average C.M. varies as the distribution of sales varies by the price category. If the performance has a low turn out, the proportion of regular ticket sales will probably be significantly lower than average and the average C.M. will correspondingly be low. For planning purposes, however, I would use the average C.M. listed previously.

In 1973–74 the average cost of a performance was about $2,700 in Lafitte and $4,000 in Memorial Hall. For breakeven at the present price structure, about 770 tickets or 107% of capacity, would have to be sold for each performance in Lafitte, and about 1,230 tickets, or 73% of capacity, for each performance in Memorial Hall. A 10 percent reduction in performance cost for Lafitte would reduce the breakeven point also by 10% to 694 tickets sold, whereas a 10 percent increase in the average C.M. would reduce the breakeven point to 701 tickets sold, not a significant difference.

I suggest that the average regular ticket prices be increased by $.75 for all seats in Memorial Hall and by $1.00 for seats in Lafitte for 1975–76. If the distribution of ticket sales by price category remains constant, the average C.M. will increase by approximately 95% of the price increase. The net effect of a price increase depends upon how elastic the demand is for tickets. As a hedge against adverse decreases in demand, I suggest that the price increases be varied in proportion to the popularity of the performance. *The most popular attractions and performance nights should absorb the highest increases in ticket price.* I suggest the following price ranges:

High price and Lafitte: $4.95–5.95
Medium price: 3.95–4.95
Low price: 2.95–3.95

Series and season ticket specials should all have discounts in the range of 30 percent to encourage commitment to greater numbers of performances.

In 1973–74 the average cost of talent was about 50% of the total performance cost for the dance attractions (because of the reimbursement of talent cost) and about 65% for all other attractions. You can determine percentages for particular attractions or types of attractions, and then use these percentages to project total performance costs from the contract price of the talent. The total performance cost projection and your estimation of popularity can be used as the basis for determining ticket prices for the performance.

Performance cost can be significantly decreased by having more consecutive performances by an attraction. You mentioned the constraints of this approach but it does offer the best potential for cost reduction. For popular attractions demand should be sufficient to support multiple performances.

Promotion. I can only offer personal suggestions here. You will have to continue to experiment with various promotion strategies on the basis of subjective evaluation. I would advise that you seek to establish an information system to obtain a more objective means of evaluating promotional expenditures. For example:

1. Questionnaire surveys can be conducted through the Mardi Gras Daily or distributed in the lobby during a performance.

2. A short questionnaire can be given to persons who buy tickets at the box office, to be completed on the spot and returned to a box at the box office.

3. A survey can be sent to the names on the mailing lists, either in the University Arts brochure or separately.

Other suggestions:

1. Devise a system to record the names and addresses from checks and the particular performance for which purchased when tickets are purchased from the box office.

2. The "Choose Your Own" season tickets can be promoted as long as there are sufficient remaining performances. Maybe a choose your own half-season ticket can be offered after fall quarter for the remaining performances.

3. The University Arts could be done in a less expensive format and the savings could be used for additional mailings during the year.

Conclusion. *I believe that the greatest potential for reducing the deficit depends upon reducing the number of performances (for example, about 25 per year), increasing the ratio of number of performances to number of*

popular attractions, and pricing each performance on the basis of projected demand and breakeven analysis. Improvement of promotional strategy will remain subjective and will occur only gradually as you develop more selective information on who your customer is, why he attends Public Events' performances, and how he can be reached.

CONTRIBUTION MARGIN

Contribution Margin (C.M.) is defined as the dollar contribution made by a ticket sale to the total cost (talent, allocated promotion, technical, house, and hospitality costs) of a performance. The C.M. is the sale price of a ticket less any direct ticket sale costs, such as commissions to the Jackson box office (5% of ticket price) and Ticketron charges (10 cents per ticket issued at box office, 25 cents per ticket issued at remote location). For a performance the C.M. for each price category of tickets must be averaged to produce the average contribution margin per ticket sold (average C.M.). The average C.M. will vary as the distribution of ticket sales varies by price category.

Calculation of Average C.M.

$$\text{Average C.M.} = \frac{\text{Total Ticket Receipts} - \text{Direct Ticket Sales Costs}}{\text{Total Tickets Sold} - \text{Complimentary Tickets}}$$

Direct Ticket Sales Costs:

.05 (Ticket Receipts)   [Jackson]
.25 (Number Remote Tickets)   [Ticketron]
.10 (Number Box Office Tickets)   [Ticketron]

Example	Issued	Sold	Receipts
Total Sales, Box Office	532	522	$1,839.85
Total Sales, Remote	44	44	198.00
Grand Total	576	566	$2,037.85

$$\text{Average C.M.} = \frac{\$1,839.85 + \$198.00 - .05(\$1,839.85) - .25(44) - .10(532)}{566 - 35^*} = \$3.54$$

Relationship of C.M. to breakeven sales or costs. C.M. $\times$ Estimated Ticket Sales = Projected Breakeven Performance Cost. For example, if C.M. = $3.50 and estimated ticket sales = 600, then the cost of the performance cannot exceed $3.50 $\times$ 600, or $2,100 if a profit or breakeven is desired.

As another example, if C.M. = $3.50 and projected performance cost is $2,500, then to meet breakeven ticket sales would have to be no less than $2,500 divided by $3.50 or 714.

---

*Assuming number of complimentary tickets is 35.

Appendix 2
Audience Analysis and Recommendations

Excerpts from report by Mr. Seth Granger

The goals underlying the initiation of the University Arts Program were presumably two-fold: (1) to service the expressed need for classical entertainment on campus and in the surrounding community (to satisfy the existing demand), and (2) to foster the development of an appreciation for classical entertainment among those whose prior exposure has been inadequate or non-existent. This second function, in particular, serves to differentiate the Mardi Gras Program from other commercial concert series. Missionary work in any field involves a long-term investment in hopes of future returns; to attract new audiences for the performing arts requires a process of exposure and education of indefinite length. . . .

Audience segmentation has been defined as the "process by which a firm partitions its prospective customers (the market) into subgroups or submarkets (segments). The objective of segmentation is to group individual prospects so that their responses to marketing inputs will be similar." I would like to suggest a division of the New Orleans population into groups determined by interest level (current patrons, likely prospects, and unlikely prospects) and by professional status (student and non-student). While this initial segmentation is necessarily general, it provides us with a means of selecting promotional messages and media to appeal more directly and effectively to groups whose information channels and promotional needs are quite different. Interest level in the performing arts largely predetermines the promotional needs of the various subgroups. Promotional needs of current patrons are primarily informational; that is, details regarding time, place and content of scheduled performances, delivered in time to permit a decision and close enough to the performance date to inspire action. Likely, though uncommitted, prospects require somewhat more; in addition to informational details, they also need some exhortation, some indication of the pleasure and excitement which can be derived from an evening of classical entertainment. Un-

likely prospects, as might be expected, may not be susceptible to any sort of promotional activity without a prohibitively intense program of education and development; for this reason, this segment, in both its student and non-student forms, will not be considered a primary target for the initial program of audience expansion proposed here. . . .

Having established these four segments—current student patrons, likely student prospects, current non-student patrons, and likely non-student prospects—as primary targets for our audience expansion efforts, I would recommend that efforts be made to acquire information regarding the behavior of each of their responses to various advertising channels, their decision patterns, their alternative entertainment preferences, and their reactions to the Program's content and promotion. A preliminary attempt in this direction was made during this past year, when an audience questionnaire [see Exhibit 6] was designed and distributed to a near-capacity audience at a performance given by the New York Pro Musica in the University Church. Approximately 400 completed questionnaires were returned; from this number a random sample of 50 questionnaires was selected and subjected to examination via the SPSS program at the Mardi Gras University computer facility.

The questionnaire sought to provide information concerning personal characteristics (income, place of residence, profession, etc.), programming and scheduling preferences, and information channels utilized by current patrons. Although time constraints precluded adequate pre-testing, resulting in ambiguity in certain questions, and although the small sample size reduced the pure statistical validity of the findings, the survey results proved interesting on a number of points.

The bulk of the respondents (64%) were in an age range between 23 and 45 years, 12% were below age 23. At least 68% of the respondents lived within a three-mile radius, while only 8% came from residential areas on the far side of New Orleans. One third of the respondents

EXHIBIT 5
Audience Questionnaire

THE ARTS AT MARDI GRAS UNIVERSITY

This survey is being administered for planning purposes by the Mardi Gras Office of Public Events in hopes of better serving you, those who are interested in the performing arts. We would greatly appreciate your assistance by completing the following questionnaire.

Upon completion of the questionnaire, simply place it on the floor under your chair.

1) Age _____ 2) Sex _____ 3) Marital status: single ____ married ____ other _____

4) Profession: _____

5) Are you currently a Mardi Gras .... (check appropriate) student _____ staff _____
    faculty member _____ alumni _____ no association _____ other _____

6) Is a member of your immediate family currently a Mardi Gras .... (check appropriate) student _____
    faculty member ____ staff ____ alumni ____ no association ____ other _____

7) If a member of your immediate family is associated with Mardi Gras, what is their relationship to you?
    _____

8) Place of residency: Mardi Gras campus _____ other _____

9) How many other arts programs have you attended at Mardi Gras within the past year?
    0 _____ 1-3 _____ 4-10 _____ over 10 _____

10) In the space provided, please indicate the number of times you have attended any of the programs by the following groups or at the following locations within the past three months:
    _____ Flint Center   _____ Dollar Opera
    _____ Circle Star Theater   _____ Zellerbach Hall
    _____ Spring Opera   _____ Mardi Gras Music Department
    _____ Tulane Symphony   _____ Mardi Gras Drama Department
    _____ New Orleans Symphony   _____ City Opera

11) Did you receive the Arts at Mardi Gras brochure for the 1974-75 season? Yes _____ No _____

12) Through which of the following sources did you purchase your ticket for this performance?
    mail _____ Sears _____ at the door _____ Jackson Ticket Office _____
    Maison Blanche _____ Ticketron Box Office _____ Other _____

13) If you did not purchase your ticket on a discount plan, what was the price of your ticket for this performance? _____

14) Did you purchase any of the following ticket plans for the 1974-75 season?
    _____ The Theater Series   _____ Early Music Series
    _____ Keyboard Series   _____ Celebrity Series
    _____ Connoisseur Series   _____ Choose Your Own Season Ticket
    _____ Dance Series

15) If you purchased tickets using any of the ticket plans, please estimate the savings per ticket plan that you received over purchasing the tickets separately. _____

EXHIBIT 5 (continued)

16) Does current advertising provide sufficient information as to the following:

location   yes _____   no _____

time   yes _____   no _____

program content   yes _____   no _____

17) How long ago did you make your decision to attend this performance? 0-1 week _____ 1-4 weeks _____
1-3 months _____ over 3 months _____

18) Through which of the following sources did you first become aware of this performance?
friends _____   "Arts at Mardi Gras" brochure _____
news stories (paper?) _____
radio (station?) _____
advertising (what paper?) _____
posters and flyers (where did you see them?) _____
other (specify) _____

19) Which one of the following sources was most influential in your decision to attend this
performance? friends _____   "Arts at Mardi Gras" brochure _____
news stories (paper?) _____
radio (station?) _____
advertising (what paper?) _____
posters and flyers (where did you see them?) _____
other (please specify) _____

20) From which of the following sources do you usually seek information about performances of
the arts? (check as many as apply)
newspapers (which ones?) _____
radio (what stations?) _____
posters (where?) _____
friends _____
Other (specify) _____

21) Please indicate your preference as to the days on which performances are given by ranking
the following:(1 meaning most preferred, 7 least preferred)
Sunday _____ Monday _____ Tuesday _____ Wednesday _____ Thursday _____
Friday _____ Saturday _____

22) Please indicate the time at which you prefer the performances to begin. _____

23) Please give an indication of how you feel about the following statement: "I would enjoy attending
an arts performance at each of the following locations:" (please check only those with which
you are familiar)

	strongly agree	agree	uncertain	disagree	strongly disagree
Amy Auditorium	_____	_____	_____	_____	_____
Arena Stage	_____	_____	_____	_____	_____
Lafitte Auditorium	_____	_____	_____	_____	_____
Amphitheater	_____	_____	_____	_____	_____
Rittle Theater	_____	_____	_____	_____	_____
Memorial Hall	_____	_____	_____	_____	_____
University Church	_____	_____	_____	_____	_____

EXHIBIT 6
Occupation of Survey Respondents

Occupation	Number of Respondents
Student	9
Educator	8
Professional	8
Business	14
Housewife	2
Artistic	2
Other	4
No Response	3
Total	50

Source: Audience Survey.

listed their occupation as student or educator and 28% described theirs as business (Exhibit 6). Seventy-six percent of the respondents indicated that they had attended at least one prior performance offered by the Program during the past year, demonstrating the preponderance of what I have termed current patrons, as opposed to likely prospects, in the Program audiences. No such high prior attendance level was found for any of the other New Orleans cultural events or organizations listed. The effectiveness of promotional material in providing adequate information regarding location, time and content of performances was generally given a high rating, although satisfaction with content information was noticeably lower (58%) than with time (72%) or location (72%). Thirty percent of the respondents decided to attend the performance during the week preceding the performance, another 30% made its decision one to four weeks before the performance. Thirty-four percent acted on a decision which they had made over three months before the performance date, while only 6% decided to attend during the period from one to three months in advance. In cross-tabulating decision time by brochure receipt, it was found that over 47% of those who made a decision to attend more than three months in advance had been recipients of the brochure.

Perhaps most interesting were the ways in which respondents found out about the New York Pro Musica performance in particular, and about cultural events in New Orleans in general. Three sets of questions were posed, dealing with general sources of cultural information, information which made them aware of the Pro Musica concert, and information which was most important to their attending the performance. General information sources most frequently cited by respondents were newspaper advertising (78%) and friends—i.e., word-of-mouth advertising (32%). Information leading to awareness of the performance was derived predominantly from the brochure (34%), newspaper advertising (24%) and friends (24%). The most important factor leading to the actual decision to attend the performance, according to questionnaire respondents, was the reputation of the New York Pro Musica itself. This factor was cited by roughly 40% of the respondents, while the next most important factor—friends—accounted for only 20%. Aside from the obvious implication that, in classical as in popular entertainment, the best-known performers and groups are the easiest to sell, these findings suggest an interesting hypothesis. Carrying the preceding truism one step further, it might well be worthwhile to consider varying the intensity of the advertising campaign depending on the relative fame or obscurity of the performer involved. Certain of the performances offered this past year—notably PDQ Bach, the Harkness Ballet, and the New York Pro Musica—are self-selling to a considerable extent although other individual performers and groups, though possibly possessed of a comparable level of talent or skill, attract smaller audiences. This argument for promotional activity of variable intensity is also supported by an examination of the relative success, measured by attendance levels of the four basic elements of the Program's offerings (see Exhibit 7). While dramatic offerings generally played to average attendance levels of 63% of capacity, and vocal and instrumental music both averaged 53% capacity, the nine performances of dance offered during the first six months of the 1974–75 season drew only 31% of capacity. Excluding the single performance of the Harkness Ballet, this figure drops to 22% for the remaining eight performances. Although one could suggest that the dance portion of the Program's "product line" be dropped, classical and modern dance deserve an important place in the Program's efforts to augment academic offerings and to contribute positively to the extracurricular educational experience of students.

EXHIBIT 7
Attendance by Performance Category, First Six Months 1974—1975

	Number of Performances	Capacity	Paid Attendance	% of Capacity
Instrumental Music	13	13,437	7,243	53%
Harkness Ballet	1	1,694	1,635	97%
Other Dance	8	13,552	3,092	22%
Drama	3	2,460	1,565	63%
Vocal Music	2	1,649	880	53%

2

The 911 Emergency Number in New York

Jeffrey S. Kahn
Christopher H. Lovelock

"The calls were pouring in at an unusually high rate at Police headquarters yesterday about how hot it was, how the water wasn't running, how a big dog was after a cat again, and, occasionally, about a shooting or a suicide.

It was the fifth anniversary of the 911 system, the consolidation of the police, fire department and ambulance services through a single phone number, and it appeared that city residents by the thousands were ignoring Mayor Lindsay's appeal last week not to dial 911 except in a true emergency."[1]

So began a story in *The New York Times* in July 1973 describing some of the problems surrounding New York City's 911 emergency telephone number. Flooded with calls that were often quite inconsequential, the Police Department found itself unable to respond promptly to genuine emergencies.

Rising public criticism of such delayed responses had convinced Mayor John V. Lindsay and his advisers that a public education campaign should be developed to discourage use of 911 for non-emergency calls. The problem was how to devise a campaign which would differentiate emergencies from non-emergencies without reducing citizen confidence in the 911 system.

In March 1967, the President's Commission on Law Enforcement and Administration of Justice recommended that: Wherever practical, a single [emergency] number should be established, at least within a metropolitan area and preferably over the entire United States." By dialing a simple, easily-remembered series of digits, any citizen would be able to summon a quick response to an emergency.[2]

At that time, most American cities had innumerably different numbers for fire, police, and ambulance service. The St. Louis telephone directory listed 161 emergency numbers on a single page, Washington, D.C., had at least 45 emergency numbers, and Los Angeles County had 50 numbers for police alone. The existing numbers were hard to memorize and rarely duplicated in other cities.

Hence the suggestion for a simple, universal,

---

[1] "Calls to 911 Show that One Man's Vexation is Another Man's Dire Emergency," by Pranay Gupte, *New York Times,* July 10, 1973, pp. 43, 83.

This case was prepared from published sources. Jeffrey S. Kahn was a member of the Harvard MBA class of 1975 and is now a Director of the Kahn Companies. Christopher Lovelock is Associate Professor of Business Administration at Harvard University.

[2] "911—A Hot Line for Emergencies," by J. Edward Roush, *Readers' Digest,* December 1968, pp. 211–219.

emergency number. The concept was not new, having already been implemented in a number of other countries. Great Britain had used the number 999 ever since 1937 to call police, fire, or ambulance service. Although skeptics argued that the services desired could be reached just as simply by dialing 0 for the operator, studies showed that going through the operator took longer and that every second counted in achieving an effective response to emergencies.

The rising crime rate and civil unrest of the late sixties lent urgency to the Presidential Commission's recommendation. After some prodding, the American Telephone and Telegraph Company announced, in January 1968, that it would make the digits 911 available as the single emergency telephone number throughout the nation.[3] However, the decision on whether or not to use this number was left up to individual local governments.

IMPLEMENTATION IN NEW YORK

In New York City, which was often regarded as a magnification of the good and bad points of American city life, the 911 concept seemed ideal to the city administration and the police department. Mayor Lindsay's promise of a "Fun City" depended to a great degree on removing the fear of crime which affected resident and visitor alike. Although New York had had a single emergency police number since November 1964, the seven digits (440-1234) were less easily remembered than 911 and took longer to dial.

The idea of easy access to police protection and emergency help was viewed not only as a solution to lawlessness but also as a cure for citizen alienation. Anyone could "dial 911" and, because there would be no back-door to police help, all citizens would receive equal protection. Inspector Anthony Bouza (later Assistant Chief and Commander of the Police Communications Division) pointed out that 911 was to be ". . . a police-extended offer to participate in the solution of a citizen's problems . . . to overcome cultural and psychological barriers to these contacts [between citizen and policeman]."[4]

As the largest municipal police force in the nation, this reduction in citizen alienation was especially important to the New York City Police Department. With 32,000 well-paid officers protecting eight million New Yorkers in five boroughs, the department provided one of the highest police-to-citizen ratios in the world.

However, New York City continued to be regarded as a crime center. The organization of the force was divided along both functional and geographical lines. Functionally there were detective, public affairs, communications, and other divisions; while geographically the department split into 75 precincts and seven field service area commands (the five boroughs including Manhattan and Brooklyn divided north/south). Over the years the NYCPD had been responsible for a number of innovations in police methods and technology. Their initiation of the 911 system in the summer of 1968 was to have been the first of any major city, and the third among all cities in the nation.

From the Police Department's viewpoint, the major benefit desired was a reduction in crime, with more criminals being apprehended and many crimes being deterred. An important secondary benefit sought was greater community support of the police through citizen participation in crime detection and a resulting increased confidence in the force. In fact, the same President's Commission report that advocated 911 also included a Task Force Report that showed a significant relationship between police response time to a crime and the probability of an arrest. The initiation of a 911 system was therefore expected to yield a double bonus: technologically speeding the emergency response by police from the time of notification, and at the same time improving the probability that the police would be rapidly notified of emergencies through citizen initiative.

The Emergency Communications Center. A centralized communications system had been recommended several years earlier, but it was only after several "hot" summers and AT&T's announcement of 911 availability that the Mayor's Office gave the go-ahead for the multi-million dollar project.

Technologically the project was almost totally handled by the New York Telephone Company in coordination with the police. Previously there had been five geographically separate "communications centers" in each of the city's five boroughs. Each answered calls to the "old" police emergency number, 440-1234, dialed from its portion of the city, and each had its own method for dispatching officers to the scene. Now there was to be one communications center handling all emergency calls via "automatic call distributors" (ACDs) which would continuously and evenly feed incoming calls to 48 switchboard positions.[5] These positions would in turn be linked by a 12-channel color-coded conveyer belt to the radio dispatch consoles for each borough. An ACD operator would receive a call,

[3] "AT&T Units Plan '911' Emergency Number Nationwide: Cost Will Exceed $50 Million," *Wall Street Journal,* January 15, 1968, p. 3.

[4] "911 = Panacea or Nostrum?" by Anthony V. Bouza, *Bulletin* (Associated Public Safety Communications Offices), March 1972, pp. 8+.

[5] "Electronics in Law Enforcement," by Marce Eleccion, *IEEE Spectrum,* February 1973, pp. 33–40.

fill out the appropriately colored dispatch form, and place it on the belt where it would be whisked to the appropriate dispatcher.[6]

The dispatchers were linked to more than 500 radio motor patrol (RMP) cars and to an increasing number of walkie-talkie-equipped foot patrol officers through VHF radio antennas located atop the Empire State Building in midtown Manhattan. Additional backups were located at Police Headquarters downtown. Each dispatcher covered about a dozen precincts with a separate radio frequency for that area.

Later this entire system was to be augmented by the department's IBM 306 computer which, by providing automatic dispatch assistance, would further speed the process. While complex and expensive, the system would provide a far simpler and more efficient means of handling emergency calls than previous approaches.

Planning the Communications Campaign. No less complex was the problem of getting the message of 911 to the citizens of and visitors to New York City. It would do no good to have a highly efficient system ready to answer emergencies if the populace did not know of or care to make use of the system. The Mayor's Office, telephone company, and police department were to coordinate the "marketing" of 911. The Mayor would be in overall charge, as well as specifically initiating press releases at timed intervals. The police would furnish some material from their printing office, as well as specifically applying the message on all department forms and stationery and the large mobile "billboards" provided by the doors and trunks of their radio cars. The New York Telephone Company would, in coordination with their advertising agency, develop the marketing message and generally provide for its dissemination.

In view of the Mayor's desire for this effort to be a highly visible symbol of his administration's efforts on behalf of "law and order," and because the system was to be used by a citizenry that was highly diverse and of which many were poorly educated or of non-English-speaking backgrounds, the message had to be both bold and simple. After some discussion the campaign slogan became: "DIAL 911." This message, with the number written large inside a square logo, was to be endlessly repeated throughout the city, often in conjunction with an additional message (Exhibit 1).

Most critical was the timing of the campaign. To create the maximum awareness desired, it was felt that the campaign had to "hit" all at once, but if it was premature and people began using the system too early—before it was ready—then they might quickly condemn it as simply another publicity flop. And so, on the week of June 24, 1968, after the last of a series of publicity releases on the forthcoming project had been reprinted in the *Times, News,* and *Post,* the city received a publicity blitz. All telephone booths[7] received a bright red decal, police cars sported the symbol, subways and billboards urged the message too. Newspapers carried advertising, and end-of-the-month telephone bills displayed the logo. It was a saturation campaign.

Inauguration of the System. The following Monday, on July 1, 1968, Mayor Lindsay made the first "official" call inaugurating the system. After several false starts, caused by dialing 911 on an inside line, the Mayor fiinally got through, identified himself, and suggested that a squad car be sent to lock up the City Council. In his dedication speech, Mr. Lindsay said:

> This is, perhaps, the most important event of my administration as Mayor. The miraculous new electronic communications system we inaugurate this morning will affect the life of every New Yorker in every part of our city, every hour of the day. No longer will a citizen in distress risk injury to life or property because of an archaic communications system.[8]

After less than four weeks of operation, the Police Department reported that emergency telephone calls had risen from 12,000 daily under the old 440-1234 number to 18,000 (including 2,000 for ambulances and 200–300 for fire emergencies) for 911. "The big thing we're doing is building up the public's access to us," commented Deputy Chief Inspector William J. Kanz of the Communications Division. Officials claimed that police cars typically arrived at the scene of a complaint within two minutes of a telephone call, more than a minute faster than under the previous system.[9]

Despite several complaints of slow response, the initial reaction was generally one of jubilation and acclamation. The police officer was indeed the New Yorker's friend; after all, wasn't he being turned to in ever increasing numbers? It was felt that 911, by its success, was bringing about a better community relationship between citizen and government by overcoming the reluctance of many people to call the police. As Inspector Bouza later pointed out:

> The implication of . . . [overcoming inhibitions] is tremendous because it reveals that the police are not dealing with a known volume of work, but rather with a flexible volume, the size of which depends on the accessibility and efficiency of the police.[10]

---

[6] "Police Emergency Center Dedicated by Mayor," by David Burnham, *New York Times,* July 2, 1968, p. 43.

[7] Pay telephone booths were converted to make it possible to dial 911 without first inserting a dime.

[8] "Police Emergency Center Dedicated by Mayor," by David Burnham, *New York Times,* July 2, 1968, p. 43.

[9] "911 Busy Number, Police Here Find," *New York Times,* July 27, 1968, p. 25.

EXHIBIT 1
911 Symbol as Used in Print Advertising, Summer 1968

Concern Over Delayed Responses. Yet this "accessibility and efficiency" were the very points which, after the initial successful reaction, began to trouble both citizen and policeman alike, not to mention Mayor John Lindsay. The original criteria for 911 operations had involved a heavy emphasis on speed of answering. An efficient system required that over 90% of all calls be answered within 15 seconds of the first ring and 95% within 30 seconds. These figures were indeed not only met but exceeded. However, with 18,000 calls a day this still meant that almost a thousand calls took longer than half a minute for response; time during which a person hung up, became antagonized, or, more simply, lost confidence in the system.

As always, it was the bad news that gained the publicity. Articles began appearing in the city's three dailies questioning the efficacy of the 911 system or, more pointedly, the efficiency of the New York City

Police Department itself. 911 became the butt of some of the more typical "New York City life" jokes, drawing guffaws from local TV and radio personalities as they called the emergency number on the air for the amusement of their viewers and listeners.

In keeping with the complex technology of the system, the Police Department with the aid of telephone company consultants turned to improving the mechanics of the system. Operations analysis dictated that there no longer be a "secondary" pool of operators awaiting overflow calls, but that all operators be thrown into the breech to answer primary demand. Since there was an unexpectedly large number of Spanish-speaking callers, more bilingual operators were put on the line for transfers. Yet while the answering speed goals continued to be exceeded and improved, the criticism of police response continued.

Part of the problem resulted from the system centralization. Much of the souring of public response to 911 was due to the fact that people perceived the success or failure of the police in terms of *overall* re-

---

[10] "911 = Panacea or Nostrum?" by Anthony V. Bouza, *Bulletin* (Associated Public Safety Communications Officers), March 1972, pp. 8+.

sponse, which meant prompt arrival "on the scene." But the ever-increasing volume of calls at peak times (such as Saturday nights) meant an ever-increasing volume of "radio runs" in which cars were dispatched to callers; in many cases, callers who did not require a squad car and its two officers to solve their problem. Previously, for example, kindly Precinct Sergeant O'Reilly knew that Mrs. Smith called the precinct whenever her husband stayed out a little late for a drink with the boys, whereupon the sergeant managed to calm the situation over the phone. Now Mrs. Smith called 911, which, answering her call within 15 seconds, immediately dispatched a radio motor patrol car to her door.

Facing this type of problem, the Department first requested additional patrol cars from the Mayor. Communications also initiated a "screening" process that identified those calls that, in the operator's judgment, did not require a dispatch. Still another response to the need for improved service was the introduction in October 1969 of the SPRINT system, real-time computer direction of the entire call reception and car dispatching system by two IBM 360 computers. All these system improvements resulted in reductions in call-answering time and overall response time.

Yet as crime in the country at large—and in New York City in particular—continued to rise, people continued to make use of 911 in growing numbers. In 1972 the Department, having made continuous use of technology to keep up with demand, now began to wonder if, perhaps, another approach was needed. In particular, many involved with 911 felt that there should be some way of cutting down on the non-emergency calls that were entering the system; not only the "Mrs. Smith's husband" type of calls, which ought by rights still go to the precinct, but also those which the police had never handled and were not equipped to handle.

HOW TO ELIMINATE NON-EMERGENCY CALLS?

The situation finally came to a head in the summer of 1973, when hot weather sometimes helped push the total number of calls to well over 20,000 a day. Many of these calls were relatively inconsequential, such as requests for policemen to fix a malfunctioning air-conditioner. "What may be an emergency for a lot of people," said Sergeant Albert Lucci, a Supervisor in the Communications Center, "isn't necessarily an emergency for the police. A lot of people just don't realize this." [11]

As a result, the 48 emergency phone circuits were often jammed with non-emergencies. "Sometimes," added Sergeant Lucci, "it takes a while for people with real emergencies to get through to us." Out of a daily average of 18,000 calls, studies had shown that only 7,100 were real emergencies to which police cars were dispatched. Other calls concerned such diverse problems as Medicaid information, marriage licenses, open hydrants, street potholes and even VD information.

To an amazing degree, 911 had apparently won both the respect and disregard of the typical New Yorker, who took city services for granted. The communications system had in many respects become similar to the all-night talk shows on the popular city radio stations, but, better yet, 911 was free. Every pay telephone displayed the invitation to "dial 911," including the prominent notation that it was a free, "dimeless" call. Police cars, while perhaps not as omnipresent, still urged the citizens to dial 911. The emergency phone system was perhaps the only real city-wide "freebie" left in New York.

The rising volume of complaints about slow police response to the initial 911 call (delays of 5 to 45 minutes were cited) and subsequent tardy follow-up were a matter of serious concern to both the police and the city administration. The problem was particularly acute on weekends and on weekday evenings. [12]

The question was, what to do? An appeal by Mayor Lindsay in early July not to dial 911 except in a genuine emergency had no apparent impact. In an editorial, *The New York Times* argued that "it is too easy for New Yorkers to make use of the emergency system, it costs too little in time and trouble, and therefore the temptation to dial '911' for trivial reasons has apparently become more irresistible." The editorial thereupon suggested that dialing 911 be "made a little more bothersome"—perhaps by turning it into a seven digit number like 911-1000. [13] Others argued that the problem could be resolved by charging for 911 calls from pay phones.

After discussions between the Police Department, the Telephone Company, and Mayor's Office, it was eventually decided that some form of educational campaign was needed. At issue was the form the campaign should take. What organization(s) should sponsor it? At whom should it be directed? What media should it use? And what should the messages say?

Watching the situation in New York City with some interest was adjacent Nassau County on Long Island, which was about to introduce its own 911 service. The Nassau County Police Department was very anxious to avoid a repetition of the problems that had plagued New York City and wondered what strategy to employ.

---

[11] "Calls to 911 Show that One Man's Vexation is Another Man's Dire Emergency," by Pranay Gupte, *New York Times,* July 10, 1973, pp. 43, 83.

[12] "Delays are Cited on Calls to 911" by Pranay Gupte, *New York Times,* July 23, 1973, p. 1.

[13] "Emergency Calls . . ." *New York Times,* August 14, 1973, p. 32.

3

Sierra Club Publishing Division

Arthur Segel

Charles B. Weinberg

The Sierra Club was the oldest and largest conservation organization in the world. To many, the Sierra Club was virtually synonymous with conservation and environmental activism. The Club's board of directors had included over the years a number of nationally prominent political leaders, business people, educators, and conservationists.

In 1974, nearly 150,000 members participated in its outings, subscribed to its publications, and joined forces on environmental issues arising in cities and towns, state legislatures and in Congress.

THE PROBLEM

Jon Beckmann came to the Sierra Club's publishing division in early January 1974 from a small, high quality publishing house in Boston. As Editor-in-Chief of the Club's publishing business (over $500,000 in sales annually), he and a small staff were responsible for the day to day operations of the division as well as future planning. Mr. Beckmann had been hired by the Publishing Committee (PubCom), a group of Club members both in and outside the publishing industry who were appointed by the Club President to attend quarterly meetings to set policies. PubCom members included some of the most influential members at the Club.[1]

Arthur Segel is a member of the Stanford MBA Class of 1975. Charles B. Weinberg is Professor of Marketing, University of British Columbia. The assistance of Mr. Jon Beckmann is gratefully acknowledged.

[1]The PubCom Chairman in Mid 1974, Kent Gill, was later elected as President of the Sierra Club. His primary opponent, the Treasurer of the Club, was also a member of the PubCom (see Exhibit I).

EXHIBIT 1
Publishing Committee Members[1]

Donald Bradburn	Doctor
Paul Brooks	Writer, former editor-in-chief Houghton Mifflin Co.
Richard Cellarius	Professor
Michael Fox	Washington book store manager
Kent Gill	High School principal
Richard Grossman	Professor, former head Grossman Publishers
Dave Harris	Comptroller, Sierra Club
Holway Jones	Librarian
H. R. Kessel	Sales Manager University of California Press
Mort Levin	Vice President, Viking Press
Michael McCloskey	Executive Director, Sierra Club
Cliff Rudden	Comptroller for Publishing, Sierra Club
Paul Salisbury	Architect
Will Siri	Physicist
Paul Swatek (Treasurer of Club)	Massachusetts Audubon
William Webb	Publishers representative
Denny Wilcher	Fundraising, Sierra Club

[1]All members of the Committee, except for Mr. Holway Jones who was a recent appointee, had long been affiliated with the Club and most had served on the Publishing Committee for several years.

While the Committee was the final decision-making body for the Publishing Division, the Editor-in-Chief traditionally had a great deal of authority and his recommendations were seriously considered. Mr. Beckmann had a number of critical decisions to make for the next Committee meeting. The publishing industry traditionally sold its greatest volume during the Christmas season, and because more than a year was usually required for editorial work, printing, promotions and distribution, the Committee had to select new titles it wished to print for the following year at its next meeting. A June print run allowed a short time for a Fall promotional campaign followed by distribution to the bookstores in early October for Christmas. Specifically, Mr. Beckmann had a number of already researched manuscripts or books from members, writers, and photographers from which he had to select the types of books the Club wanted, the specific titles, and their selling prices. The Publishing Division had already contracted its calendars, photographic portfolios, posters and necessary reprints for the upcoming year. Although Mr. Beckmann was completely new to the organization, he was in a position to make decisions that would have an impact on the division's finances over several years. Obviously, he wanted to be as knowledgeable as possible for his appearance before the Pub-Com in three weeks.

CLUB BACKGROUND

The *Sierra Club Bulletin* of December 1967 pointed out that:

> John Muir, Scottish immigrant, farmer, inventor, sheep-herder, pre-med dropout, botanist, explorer, sawmill operator, historian, geologist, writer, wanderer and disciple of wilderness, might have difficulty today in recognizing the small, intimate Sierra Club he helped found seventy-five years ago.

The Club Bylaws, written in 1892 by Muir himself, were still relevant and stated the purposes of the Sierra Club as follows:

> To explore, enjoy and preserve the Sierra Nevada and other scenic resources of the United States and its forests, waters, wildlife and wilderness;
>
> To undertake and to publish scientific, literary and educational studies concerning them;
>
> To educate the people with regard to national and state forests, parks, monuments and other natural resources of special scenic beauty; and
>
> To enlist public interest and cooperation in protecting them.

The Club's first battle was a fight to save Yosemite Valley from being reduced by one-half and sold to developers. In 1912 Muir accompanied President Theodore Roosevelt on a pack trip through the region

with the purpose of turning Yosemite into a National Park, which was accomplished later that year. Other early efforts included pressing for the establishment of National Forests and creating trails. In 1901 the Club began its Outing Program; by 1974 it was sending members on expeditions all over the world. Its conservation efforts in California—to preserve Hetch Hetchy Valley in Yosemite and to extend natural park status to Kings Canyon (1935) gained the Club national support and recognition. Vigorous efforts to save Dinosaur National Monument on the Colorado-Utah border from a huge reservoir and power plant in 1950 initiated the Club's surge in national membership. Since that time, the Club had used its money, time and efforts to push for the North Cascades National Park in Washington, Redwood National Park in California, and to support smaller campaigns for Point Reyes and Cape Cod National Seashores and for Canyonlands, Guadalupe, Oregon Dunes Seashore and Great Basin, Prairies, Channel Islands and Kauai National Parks. The Club's legal confrontations over the Disney Corporation's proposed Mineral King development and its lobbying efforts against strip mining, the Alaskan pipeline and the supersonic transport (SST) in the late 1960's and early 1970's brought the Club national prestige at a time when environmental questions were first being raised by legislators and the public at large. In 1974, the Club had a reputation for political activism, expertise in hiking, camping and quality publications.

Club policies had not, however, been without their internal strife. For example, many members debated whether the Club should actively commit itself against the use of nuclear reactors as an alternative energy source. Others, although a minority, felt that the Club should discontinue its political activity altogether and concentrate its time and efforts on outings for its membership, trail guides for hikers, and photographic essay type books for the general public. In 1973, Club membership reached 142,000 spread geographically in the following way:

California	77,000
West	18,000
Midwest	14,000
Northeast	19,000
South	12,000
Foreign	2,000

One of the Sierra's Club membership recruitment brochures stated:

> Wherever nature needs defense, the Sierra Club wants to be on the scene . . . to rescue these untrammelled places from those who see them only as wasted space. The environment of the cities now also needs to be made fit for man: we must be more effective in combatting air and water pollution and the prevalence of chemical contaminants, noise, congestion, and blight. . . . Technology must be challenged to do a better job in managing the

part of the planet it has already claimed. The Club offers programs as diverse as the environmental challenges that man faces. Each offers an opportunity to become involved.

The Sierra Club had almost 50 regional chapters and more than 200 local groups which organized and presented a variety of talks, films, exhibits, and conferences. The Club offered a local and worldwide outing program which included wilderness outings, activity trips such as mountaineering and bicycling, local trips (walk, knapsack, or climb), and clean-up and trail maintenance trips. The Club also published a monthly magazine, *The Sierra Club Bulletin,* and a monthly chapter newsletter which were both distributed free to members, books available to members at a discount, and a calendar. And finally, the Club provided an opportunity to do conservation work.

The Sierra Club Bulletin. The *Bulletin* was published ten times a year and was distributed free to all members of the Sierra Club. It was lavishly illustrated with color photographs, reproduced to the highest standards. A typical issue of about forty pages would contain two stories about wilderness areas, two stories about battles to protect natural areas against encroachment by industrial or commercial developers, and a story about a person who had done battle for the environmental cause. In addition, a number of short articles appeared. Approximately ten of the pages in the center of the magazine were joined together in a section labeled "Commentary" which reported and commented upon news items thought to be of interest to club members. For example, the July–August 1972 issue included stories entitled "Club granted [legal] standing to sue in Mineral King case," "Coast initiative [to protect coastline] wins spot on California ballot," and "Canada rejects Village Lake Louise." The *Bulletin* usually contained a few pages of advertising from companies marketing to hikers and campers, and to readers of wilderness books; it also included a few pages of advertising about such Sierra Club offerings as foreign trips, calendars, and, of course, Sierra Club books.

PUBLISHING HISTORY

In 1964, the Club published a few expensive publications. Ten years later, some 80 publications were sold, ranging from expensive picture books to inexpensive trail guides. Membership growth seemed to have closely paralleled the Club's expanding publishing operations, and many attributed the Club's success and reputation to its quality books (see Exhibit 2).

EXHIBIT 2
Books Sold and Number of Members

Year	Number of Books Sold (000's)	Number of Members (000's)
1966	52	42
1967	118	58
1968	192	65
1969	151	81
1970	135	107
1971	144	135
1972	138	136

1965–1969: Years of Boom and Bust. In 1965, Dave Brower, long associated with the Club in almost every position, became Editor-in-Chief. It was during his tenure that publications grew enormously and also developed serious problems. Brower left in 1969 to start Friends of the Earth (F.O.E.) in a belief that the Sierra Club's increasing involvement in political issues was detracting from its purpose; however, Brower still served as an honorary vice-president.

Under Brower's leadership, the Club developed a large market in photographic-essay type books ("exhibit format") that successfully transmitted information and catalyzed concern in conservation issues. According to Congressmen active in the conservation cause, such books (especially ones on the Northern Cascades, Point Reyes and the Redwoods), played an important role in the establishment of new national parks. They also served to promote what members referred to as "the Sierra Club philosophy."

Brower sought out quality publishing firms in New York and Europe. In efforts to maintain the highest quality product, it was not unusual to send a single photograph back and forth to London several times until the picture was acceptable. Many books and calendars were printed in a remote town in Italy.

But expansion and quality had their costs. In only three out of the last 12 years had publishing activities resulted in a surplus. While this may have been offset by the volume and dollar gains in membership, publishing had generated hundreds of thousands of dollars of losses to the Club. In 1969 alone, publishing lost in the area of $250,000 (see Exhibits 3, 4, and 5 for financial data).

1970–1973. Brower's resignation eventually brought John Mitchell as Editor-in-Chief in 1970. Mitchell attempted to relieve Publishing's dollar burden on the Club and make his division "more business-like." Offices were moved from the head offices in San Francisco to New York. Scribners, who previously handled book distribution for the Club, enlarged its responsibilities and took over the accounts receivable—a problem which had begun to plague the Club to a serious degree. Scribners had a "big stick" with bookstores,

EXHIBIT 3
Historical Summary
Operating Surpluses and Deficits
(thousands of dollars)

Fiscal Year Ended	Surplus (deficit)	Comments
1973	$ 90.0	Estimated year-end results
1972	99.5	Reflects $100,000 bequest of of Katherine Squire
1971	(469.8)	
1970	84.8	
1969	(119.2)	Nine months due to change in fiscal year
1968	(158.9)	
1967	(65.6)	
1966	56.9	
1965	(28.2)	
1964	193.6	Reflects $200,000 bequest of Bertha Rennie
1963	(93.3)	
1962	43.9	
1961	(17.2)	
1960	(22.6)	

EXHIBIT 4
Expenditures by Department

	1972 Actual	1975 Budget
Outings	22.5%	22.2%
Conservation	21.1%	28.9%
Publications	19.9%	17.0%
Member Services	7.8%	8.4%
Bulletin	7.3%	6.5%
General Overhead	21.3%	16.9%
Total	$3,290,500	$4,310,800
Chapter Subventions	313,000	349,100
	$3,603,500	$4,659,900

namely its size and predominance in the publishing field, whereas the Sierra Club had little or no clout to effectively pursue receivables. The Club's staff was reduced accordingly.

As the Club's financial worries temporarily lessened, tensions emerged on another front. Mitchell had started publishing books on specific environmental issues or so-called "battle books." The battle books were successful in providing support for the Club's conservation efforts. On the other hand, they also became a source of conflict between the publishing staff and the conservation staff which directed the Club's political lobbying. Conservation people often became irritated with the technical quality of some of the books since books on oil spills or energy policy, for example, sometimes contained inaccurate information. Furthermore, coordination of efforts often floundered. For example, a book on clear-cutting of forests came out too

late to generate any effective support for a Congressional bill. This resulted in a strong desire for the publishing division to move back to San Francisco for greater coordination and control.

A serious rift developed in this regard. Mitchell, with the support of some committee members, felt that a professional operation could not be run outside of New York. Others, headed by the conservation people, felt that it was important that the Club remain "small-time" and "*un*professional." There was a fear of a bureaucratic bigness and, concomitantly, of becoming dysfunctional. Just prior to Beckmann's arrival in January, an upheaval occurred, resulting in Mitchell's leaving and a major reshuffling of positions in the Committee.

Publishing, January 1974. Beckmann had his own ideas on what was wrong. He focused his initial efforts on seeking out a small but professional staff. Next, he wanted to steer the Publishing Division toward a break-even situation. He recognized that, while quality was important, too often the Club had suffered enormous financial consequences in its mission to preach the conservation movement—enough losses at times to impair the Club's very existence. Through luck, fund-raising drives and gifts from estates, the Club had always managed to survive. But Beckmann did not want the Club to be hurt any further by exorbitant publishing losses. He perceived that this was particularly critical in light of the energy crisis recently sparked by the Arab oil embargo. He questioned whether the whole environmental cause might become less popular because of the newly realized quest for energy sources. Furthermore, the economy as a whole was showing serious signs of weakness as rapid inflation raged and recessionary fears mounted. It was at such a time that the Club should have been in its most robust financial state to keep environmental issues alive among legislators and the public.

He followed a different vein in discussing the uniqueness of the Sierra Club in publishing its own books:

> Publishing, by nature, is not terribly adaptable to short-run changes. The longer the time allowed for promotion of a book, the better the quality will be and a lower cost product will result. A book in a "normal" business takes about two years from start to finish. The Club has tried in the past to turn out books within a matter of nine or ten months in order to be responsive to conservation issues. This responsiveness, however, has its costs. As the span of time is reduced to churn out a book from a normal two-year cycle, there is an increased tendency to publish badly; that is, to lose control over the quality of the book or the costs or both. Furthermore, operating and selling expenses for the division are high compared to industry averages. A Club that is inherently short-sighted in a volatile short-sighted world of chang-

EXHIBIT 5
Income Statement
(thousands of dollars)

	Fiscal Year 1974 Budget		Fiscal Year 1975 Budget	
Revenue	Amount	% of Sales	Amount	% of Sales
Sales				
Trade	$304.6	53.4	$370.0	55.2
Chapter	40.4	7.1	50.0	7.5
Member	225.0	39.5	250.0	37.3
Net Sales	$570.0	100.0	$670.0	100.0
Subsidiary Income				
Subsidiary Rights[1]	$120.0		$140.0	
Less Costs and Royalties	35.0		20.0	
Net Subsidiary Income	$ 85.0		$120.0	
Miscellaneous Income	5.0		0	
Total Revenue	$660.0		$790.0	
Expenses				
Costs of Sales				
Production Costs	$264.0	46.3	$249.3	37.2
Inventory Write Down	15.0	2.6	15.0	2.2
Royalties	65.0	11.4	86.2	12.9
Total Cost of Sales	$344.0	60.3	$350.5	52.3
Editorial Expenses	40.0	7.0	40.0	6.0
Selling Expenses				
Sales and Distribution	$ 77.0	13.5	$ 92.4	13.8
Shipping and Warehouse	61.5	10.8	67.5	10.1
Total Selling Expenses	$138.5	24.3	$159.9	23.9
Promotion Expenses				
Advertising	$ 31.5	5.5	$ 40.0	5.9
Direct Mail	15.6	2.7	18.0	2.7
Catalogues	10.0	1.8	12.0	1.8
Review Copies (Gratis)	4.0	0.7	6.0	0.9
Exhibits	3.0	0.5	4.0	0.6
Total Promotion Expenses	$ 64.1	11.2	$ 80.0	11.9
Administrative Expenses				
Salaries and Related Costs	$ 77.7	13.6	$ 93.2	13.9
Travel	18.0	3.2	21.0	3.4
Interest	9.8	1.7	10.0	1.5
Meetings	8.6	1.5	8.6	1.3
Outside Services	2.6	0.5	4.0	0.6
Telephone	7.0	1.2	10.0	1.5
Rent—Office	5.8	1.0	6.0	0.9
Duplicating and Copier	4.0	0.7	4.0	0.6
Supplies	3.0	0.6	3.0	0.4
Legal Fees	1.0	0.2	2.0	0.3
Rent—Equipment	0.3	—	1.0	0.2
Equipment	0.5	0.1	1.0	0.2
Repairs and Maintenance	0.2	—	0.2	—
Membership, Dues and Subscriptions	0.4	—	0.5	0.4
Other	1.0	0.2	—	—
Total Administrative Expenses	$139.9	24.5	$164.5	24.6
Total Expenses	$726.5	127.5	$794.9	118.7
Surplus (deficit)	($ 66.5)		($ 4.9)	
Subsidies[2]	$124.0		$ 64.0	
Surplus (deficit) After Subsidies	$ 57.5		$ 59.1	

[1] Subsidiary income is considered by publishers as the only profit making area in the publishing industry. Most publishers break even and rely on subsidiary income for profits. Subsidiary income includes income from calendars and non-calendar items such as paper/hardcover reprints, book clubs, serial sales and foreign sales. Needless to say, subsidiary income had grown dramatically as calendar sales have increased. Industry wide subsidiary rights usually accounted for 14% of sales.

[2] The Publishing division traditionally received large amounts of subsidies from the Sierra Club Foundation. The Foundation met yearly to allocate its funds to specific projects, i.e., specific books in Publishing's case, within the Club. The Foundation was created as a separate legal entity in 1969 after the Club was refused tax deduction status for its contributions because of its political lobbying. The Foundation was set up to receive tax deductible gifts and operates independently of the Club.

EXHIBIT 6
Membership Data*

Length of Membership	Percent of Members
Less than 1 year	27%
1 to 2 years	26%
3 to 4 years	19%
5 to 7 years	12%
8 to 12 years	8%
13 years or more	9%

Occupation	Occupations of Club Members	Occupations of Main Wage Earners of the Households from Which Members Come
Managers and Executives	11%	17%
Lawyers, Doctors and Dentists	8%	12%
Other Professionals	7%	11%
College Teachers	7%	9%
Other Teachers	11%	9%
Clerical and Blue Collar Workers	7%	9%
Engineers	3%	7%
Technicians	5%	7%
Students	19%	6%
Homemakers	12%	1%
Other	10%	12%

Reasons for Joining (length of membership in years)

	Less than 1	1—2 yrs.	3—4 yrs.	5—7 yrs.	8—12 yrs.	13 yrs.	Average
A. To participate in outdoor activities	30%	30%	18%	30%	46%	61%	32%
B. To personally participate in conservation activities	24%	15%	10%	8%	6%	3%	14%
C. To show general support of Club's conservation activities	25%	43%	57%	55%	40%	17%	41%
D. A and B	5%	4%	4%	2%	3%	8%	5%
E. A and C	8%	4%	4%	4%	5%	3%	5%
F. Other	5%	3%	7%	2%	1%	7%	5%

* Based on a mail survey done in 1971 on a random sample of club membership. A total of 859 questionnaires were returned which represents a 56% response rate. Figures do not always add because of rounding error.

ing political constituencies is always in conflict with a sub-part of the organization that demands long-term planning for stability and growth.

This conflict is much more than psychological. Planning requires large dollar commitments long in advance of actual publication to explore new titles and pay for the development of new titles before the actual selling period. The percentage of funds going towards advances on future publishing projects is far below the industry average. If the Club wants to maintain the high quality of its publications and reduce the financial instability that publishing has encountered in the past, the Club must recognize this essential difference in Publishing's need for long-term funding and planning versus the Club's need to be continually responsive to member needs and conservation issues.

Beckmann did not feel that the Club in the past had made a commitment to its publishing program. The program expanded when the Club funds were plentiful and contracted when monies were lean. Beckmann continued:

A publishing program's health depends upon a combination of imprint identity, reliability, publishing activity,

and the staff skills to support these characteristics. A program in which these characteristics are fragmented or maintained erratically cannot publish to maximum advantage—that is, cannot inform, persuade, inspire—reach those people whom the program (or individual titles) is designed to interest.

Beckmann also spoke of the shift in product line:

We have an image as a gift or "coffee-table" book. But I wonder if the time for our large photographic books has gone by. On the other hand, while our efforts increasingly seem to be to generate technical and informational books, they don't always sell. We seem to be more and more dependent on our calendar market which might some day collapse. Maybe we need a few books like *On the Loose* and issue oriented lines. We need to strike a balance. People will be willing to read about some subjects in newspapers or magazines but wouldn't buy a book about them. Our goal is to remain a non-commercial publisher and produce books of quality with the environmental message. At the same time there would be no point in publishing books that did not really reach the public.

EXHIBIT 7
Geographic Distribution of Commercial Sales of Sierra Books: 1974

Area	No. of States	Percent of Sales	Selected States	Percent of Sales
Far West	3	29	California	25
Mid Atlantic	8	17	Massachusetts	8
North Central	6	13	New York	5
South	10	11	Illinois	5
New England	6	10	New Jersey	4
Mountain	8	9	Tennessee	3
Southwest	3	5	Colorado	3
Great Plains	5	2	Texas	3
Other[1]	2	4	Alaska	3

Source: Scribner State Sales Report Data on Sierra Club, May 31, 1974.

[1] Includes Alaska, Hawaii, plus Canadian and European sales.

THE MARKET FOR SIERRA CLUB PUBLICATIONS

Members accounted for less than 40% of present sales. They received 20% off on the retail book prices, and Beckmann expressed concern that the Club was actually losing money on membership sales. In theory, member sales should be less expensive than commercial sales, but the figures seemed to indicate that selling costs to members were abnormally high. Traditionally, members of the Club were outdoor enthusiasts, although the Club's political action on environmental issues had widened its membership base. Wage-earning members were largely composed of business executives, professionals, and teachers (see Exhibit 6). About one-half of the membership had belonged to the Club for more than three years. Sixty percent of sales were to commerical outlets. The proportion of member sales to commercial sales had been diminishing over the past two to three years; before 1965, the Club had sold almost entirely to its members.

Commercial outlets not only included book sellers but camping and sporting stores. Approximately 45% of "Tote Book" sales (hiking guides, etc.) were sold through camping stores in 1974. Since Sierra Club book purchasers were often campers and hikers who were either students or young professionals, Sierra Club purchasers had long been regarded by the Club staff as being highly price conscious. Because of this and because the Club had no capital for overprintings, a policy had been established to avoid remaindering books —particularly the high-priced "exhibit-format" (photographic essay-type) books. "Remaindering" involved selling left-over stock books that were not "moving," to booksellers at a reduced rate. Booksellers often used remaindered books for special sales. Thus far, remaindering had occurred only three or four times, and the Book of the Month Club had sometimes purchased remainders for their book dividends.

Forty-five percent of retail sales occurred between October 31 and December 31, or during the "Christmas rush." With this in mind, the Club had been severely hurt by timing problems in the past. If books ran late, if there were a dock strike or if stores failed to receive shipments in September and October, sales could be drastically affected for the year. The purchase of *new* books (or calendars) at Christmas also increased, perhaps because people were fearful of giving books that someone might already possess.

California, particularly the San Francisco Bay Area, had traditionally generated the greatest number of sales for the Club. As with the publishing industry as a whole, book sales were also strong up and down the Eastern urban corridor. Sales were very heavy for the Club in Massachusetts, New York and New Jersey. In states in which environmental issues were popular, such as in Alaska, Oregon, and Colorado, sales were also strong. Finally, the Club had witnessed surprising growth in book sales and in membership from the South, particularly the Southeast. Tennessee commercial book sellers, for example, sold as many volumes as Colorado book sellers for the first half of 1974 (see Exhibit 7).

Pricing. Pricing strategies in the publishing industry were complicated. Because the market was fickle, pricing was considered to be "more an art form than a science."

In the Sierra Club, a price was suggested to the Publishing Committee by the Editor-in-Chief. New books were examined for their (1) effects on cash flow, (2) relevance to book lists, (3) price to the consumer, and (4) type of production. In the industry there were standard pricing guidelines. A common "rule of thumb" was that a book should sell for about five times production costs, except when royalties and promotional monies were not required or if a substantial

EXHIBIT 8
Publishing Industry* Rules of Thumb

	% of Retail Sales Price
Discount to bookstores	46
Cost of Sales:	
Manufacturing	20
Royalties	8
Operating expenses:	
Editorial	3
Production	1
Marketing	9
Fulfillment	5
General and administrative	6

Source: 1973 Industry Statistics of the Association of American Publishers.

---

* See Exhibit 5, footnote 1 for a better understanding of "other publishing income" or what is known as "subsidiary rights." The above figures reflect that without "subsidiary rights" income, the publishing industry makes little or no profit.

EXHIBIT 9
Number and Type of Books Sold for Two Years
(thousands of units)

Book Type	1970—1971	1972—1973
Exhibit Format	42 (32%)	23 (17%)
Battle Books	20 (14%)	13 (10%)
Totes and Guides	42 (32%)	45 (33%)
Calendars	21 (16%)	49 (36%)
Other	8 (6%)	8 (4%)
Total	134 (100%)	138 (100%)

market appeal existed, then this figure could be four to one. In the past, Sierra Club books had been underpriced with the intention of subsidizing customers to promote a concern for conservation issues.[2]

Suggested Offerings. Specifically, Mr. Beckmann had to make recommendations on the following titles in each of the following categories:

Exhibit Format
1. *The Rockies* (color)
2. *Thoreau's Country* (b&w)

Totes
1. *Golden Gateway*
2. *Nature Photography*

Battlebooks
1. *Parks in Peril*
2. *Impact of the Military on U.S. Lands*

Underground
1. *Woodstoves*
2. *Better Homes and Garbage*

Each of these categories and titles, are explained in detail in the next few sections.

Exhibit Format. "Exhibit Format" or the large hard cover photographic-essay type books had been the trademark of the Club to much of the public. The Club usually had a first printing of 7,500 copies and followed up with reprintings when necessary. In the middle 1960's, when the Club was the first producer of these kinds of books, the book sizes were often too large

---

[2] For additional information on sales and costs of books, see Exhibits 8–11.

for normal presses or binding equipment. Machinery had to be specially adapted for printing; and binding was often done by hand. Quality was not sacrificed. One of the most successful of the prototype photographic conservation book series, *In Wildness*, sold 54,000 copies at $25 each, with a $7.00 cost of production. Although its success was attributed to its "name" photographer, its superior production and its uniqueness at the time, *In Wildness* sold 2,000 volumes in 1974. *On the Loose*, a similar idea but not quite an exhibit format book, due to its paper production and smaller size, exceeded all other book sales with its student-oriented nature photography and poetic text.

Others had been less successful. In fact, the great financial drag incurred by the Club during the late 1960's was caused by what the staff felt was an overemphasis on the Exhibit Format series. Furthermore, Exhibit Format books that didn't move were expensive to inventory. *Floor of the Sky*, published in 1972 at a production cost of $5.75 and a selling price of $19.75, sold only 4000 volumes in three years. Beckmann felt that the book failure was due to its subject matter—The Great Plains—which did not have wide appeal to Sierra Club book purchasers. Other staff members claimed that the topic was too broad and that there were insufficient people in the Great Plains States to constitute a market. *Slickrock* (1971) and *Everglades* (1970), both selling at $27.50 and costing about $7.50 to produce had similarly mediocre sales on only 5000 and 8000 volumes respectively. Another problem, in addition to lagging sales for the Exhibit Format series overall, was that material and production costs for high quality paper and photography—particularly color—had soared in recent months.

Thoreau's Country was a black and white photographic study based on the work of Herbert Gleason (1855–1937) of the landscapes—meadows, woods, farms, Walden Pond, Cape Cod, the Maine Woods—which inspired the writings of Henry David Thoreau. Gleason, an excellent photographer although largely unrecognized until the early 1970's, had taken these photographs in the early 1900's. The production cost of the book would be at least $7.50. The *Rockies* was a magnificently photo-

EXHIBIT 10
New vs. Old Books Sold[1]

	1970—71	1971—72	1972—73	1973 (Sept.—Dec.)
Total Number of Items Sold[2]	134,713	144,309	138,024	57,747
Number and (percent) of Old Items	76,170 (57)	82,257 (57)	82,021 (65)	39,186 (71)
Number and (percent) of New Items	58,441 (43)	61,982 (43)	48,777 (35)	16,663 (29)

Source: Sierra Club Memorandum, Publication Sales through December, 1973.

[1] A publisher is interested in how much of his new or old line books is selling. If the old line is selling well, inventory is depleted and the firm may consider reprinting popular volumes. If the new line is selling well, the new volumes may have "caught the market" and old volumes may have lost their appeal.

[2] Items include books and calendars. Some items are not classified as new or old in the Club's records.

graphed survey of the Rocky Mountains area in the United States and came within the traditional framework of Sierra Club exhibit format books. Its production cost would be substantially higher than that of either *Everglades* or *Slickrock*.

Totes. The "Tote book" series consisted of small, inexpensive paperbound books meant to be taken on hikes. List price for totes were $4.95, at a production cost of around $1.75. As production costs were increasing, more recent totes sold for $7.95. The Club usually had a first printing of 10,000 copies. The tote line actually began in 1971, although similar kinds of books had been printed earlier. Totes covered either specific trails—such as in the Tetons, Grand Canyon, Austrian Alps, Dolomite Alps and the Smokies—or more general subjects such as cooking, hiking, and backpacking. The general subject totes were, on the whole, much more successful than the specific trail guides. For example, a High Sierra guide published back in 1959 sold 67,000 copies and was still popular in 1974. A *Food for Knapsackers* tote sold nearly 50,000 copies since its publication in 1970. On the other hand, the *Survival Songbook* tote was considered a failure after sales of 21,000 copies since reprintings of the book had never "moved" after the year of its introduction to the market.

Guides to specific trails or areas of the country usually sold on a different magnitude. A *Climber's Guide to Yosemite* or *In the Smokies* each sold around 9000 volumes and were still selling well since their publication around 1972.

The Club's staff felt that totes enhanced the Club's reputation and provided a service. On the whole, Beckmann felt that "Totes do well over the long pull."

Beckmann also noted that "The totes are taking a different direction, more toward appreciation of the area's natural characteristics than a trail guide." The *Golden Gateway* was a guide to the area set aside in and around San Francisco, from Point Reyes in the North through Golden Gate Park to San Gregorio beaches in the South. The Gateway was the largest urban area park of its kind. The purpose of *Nature Photography* was self-explanatory.

Battlebooks. The Battlebooks Series were highly technical books on specific currently relevant subjects and usually had a 5,000 copy initial printing. They were published as paperbacks, with prices being kept low ($2.75) to encourage sales. Production costs were generally around $1.00 each. Books on *Clearcutting, Mercury, Energy, Stripping,* and *Oilspill* were attempts to respond quickly to important political issues and generally met with wide approval by Club members and the conservation community at large. It was this series, however, that had caused problems in 1973; a rush to publish had led to the subsequent discovery of technical errors, while some books appeared after Congressional action had already been taken.

Many volumes received wide acclaim for their substantive content. They provided an easy to read but informative format to the pressing issues of the day. *Energy* and *Ecotactics,* two of the most successful Battlebooks, sold around 19,000 copies each. Most sold from 5000 to 8000 copies. There was a strong feeling that the public expected an expert job be done. While the Club wanted to continue the Battlebooks, sales (except to libraries) were generally poor and inventories increased. However, the Club felt a responsibility to continue investigative reporting and to use Battlebooks as weapons to generate political support.

EXHIBIT 11
Sales Summary

	Pub. Date	Production Cost ($)	List Price ($)	Books in Inventory	Sales per Year									
					1966 & Prior	1967	1968	1969	1970	1971	1972	1973	1974 to Aug.	Total
Exhibit Formats														
Floor of the Sky	9/72	6.18	19.75	2,973	—	—	—	—	—	—	1,484	2,409	166	4,059
In Wildness	10/62	7.00	25.00	152	31,241	5,234	4,826	2,160	3,491	2,618	1,821	2,023	1,131	54,625
On the Loose	5/67	1.12	7.95	5,865	—	18,978	37,029	14,167	12,060	8,498	4,426	3,391	1,815	100,346
Everglades	10/70	7.56	27.50	1,470	—	—	—	—	—	6,347	1,044	305	268	7,964
Slickrock	9/71	7.34	27.50	1,592	—	—	—	—	—	1,860	2,215	596	296	4,967
Glacier Bay	5/67	7.80	17.50	651	—	4,090	1,011	362	587	487	249	245	537	7,568
Galapagos (2 volumes)	10/68	15.60	55.00	—	—	—	5,996	238	690	384	262	25	—	7,595
Baja	10/67	8.07	17.50	40	—	5,032	2,203	685	919	1,140	698	488	247	11,412
Totes														
Climbers Guide Yosemite	4/71	1.44	6.95	555	—	—	—	—	—	3,944	1,774	1,519	1,343	8,580
Food for Knapsackers	5/71	.67	2.45	691	—	—	—	—	—	9,586	18,839	11,647	7,892	47,964
Hiking Tetons	11/73	1.87	4.95	1,017	—	—	—	—	—	—	—	—	4,197	4,197
Smokies Guide	7/73	2.75	7.95	3,373	—	—	—	—	—	—	—	3,999	4,426	8,425
Survival Songbook	4/71	1.47	4.95	4,002	—	—	—	—	—	13,009	6,804	974	346	21,133
Battle Books														
Energy	1/72	.60	2.75	3,638	—	—	—	—	—	—	6,720	5,923	5,241	17,884
Clearcut	1/72	1.25	2.75	224	—	—	—	—	—	—	6,911	1,520	19	8,450
Oilspill	1/72	.82	2.75	432	—	—	—	—	—	—	4,927	981	496	6,404
Mercury	5/71	.57	2.75	412	—	—	—	—	—	5,441	2,160	288	(29)	7,860
Stripping	4/72	.73	2.25	2,504	—	—	—	—	—	—	2,736	1,583	781	5,100

Underground. The Sierra Club did not have an "Underground" series per se. However, Mr. Beckmann had received two manuscripts which he felt would start the Publishing Division on a different type of book. These essentially appealed to the "counter culture" and were in the nature of the *Whole Earth Catalogue*, which had met with considerable success over the past few years. Since the Club had not published anything like this before, Mr. Beckmann had no specific cost comparisons. He used his general knowledge about the industry and the Club's other experiences to make some calculations.

Specifically, the proposed book entitled *Woodstoves* consisted of hand-lettered descriptions, with handsome drawings and photographs of wood burning stoves found around the country. Beckmann felt the timing of such a book might fit perfectly if the energy crisis continued into the future. Furthermore, he felt that more and more people were appreciating rural life styles and antiques. He was met, however, with one objection by a staff member who claimed:

> I hope this book doesn't have the thrust that we should all go out and start burning wood. If any appreciable fraction of our 210 million population thinks that, the result would be horrendous.

Beckmann pondered over whether the book was consistent with the Club's philosophy.

The second possibility, *Better Homes and Garbage,* was a manuscript that had been prepared by several faculty members and students from Stanford University. Beckmann said:

> It's in the school of technical "how to" manuals that are being published more and more. Essentially *Better Homes . . .* is a reference book that is an attempt to summarize available information on a low impact technology that is useful in developing alternative life styles. If we do it, I see it selling in paper for around $8.95. It would appeal to those who have already left the cities and need specific information on how to get the most heat out of glass panels or whatever. I think it might also appeal to the secondary armchair market which the *Whole Earth Catalogue* did. The text is lucid and practical.

While *Better Homes . . .* was appealing, Mr. Beckmann was concerned that the book might be too different from the other books in the Club's line and might somehow damage the Club's quality image.

CONCLUSION

Beckmann reviewed the list once more. He was concerned about the future economic health of the Club and the role that this decision would play vis-à-vis the Club as a whole. Immediately pressing was the problem of what books to sell at what prices. Which books would be consistent with the Club's philosophy but not jeopardize the Club's ability to continue? Which books might best enhance the Club's image and spread the conservation cause?

He felt that these immediate questions could not be answered without examining longer range questions. For example:

> How might publishing become less dependent on calendar sales?
>
> Should members continue to receive significant discounts?
>
> How could the division reduce its backlist titles in inventory?
>
> How might publishing best use its clientele and the momentum it has generated from past successes?
>
> What new directions, if any, should the Publishing division undertake?

Underlying these questions was still a basic decision that the Club would have to make regarding its commitment to the Publishing division. Beckmann foresaw the need for a large initial capitalization for planning and researching future manuscripts. Unless the Club would be willing to make that commitment, Beckmann saw two alternatives, either "an erratic program which is crippled every two or three years and does not publish effectively or efficiently; or a packaging operation in which the Club lends its name to books to be published by other publishers, and in which case the Club ceases to be a publisher in the accepted sense of the word." Beckmann pondered these questions, and began to draft his thoughts for an agenda for the upcoming PubCom meeting.

4

Public and Nonprofit Marketing Comes of Age

Christopher H. Lovelock
Charles B. Weinberg

How are marketing theory and practice applied in nonbusiness marketing? This chapter reviews developments in public and nonprofit marketing in recent years, highlighting achievements (and a few failures) across a wide array of application areas. Particular attention is devoted to the role of marketing in the arts, health care, energy conservation, public transportation and higher education.

We believe that public and nonprofit marketing has come of age. Before the late 1960s, applications of marketing theory and practice outside the profit-making private sector were, if not unheard of, certainly very rare. Ten years later, a very different situation prevails.

As evidence of the maturation of nonbusiness marketing, we first review the historical development of the broadened concept of marketing. We show that, in addition to being widely written about, nonbusiness marketing is being taught in both academic and executive development programs. We highlight some of the public and nonprofit areas in which marketing tools and concepts are being actively employed by practicing managers. And, as evidence of nonbusiness marketing's newly adult status, we show how insights developed by researchers and practitioners in nonbusiness marketing contribute usefully to marketing activities in the business sector.

Christopher H. Lovelock is Associate Professor of Business Administration, Harvard University.

Charles B. Weinberg is Professor of Marketing, University of British Columbia.

HISTORICAL PERSPECTIVE

In 1969, Kotler and Levy [1] published their now classic article "Broadening the Concept of Marketing" in which they criticized the then prevailing view of marketing as "a function peculiar to business firms." They rebuked students of marketing for either ignoring marketing in such nonbusiness areas as politics, higher education, and fund raising, or for treating them cursorily as public relations or publicity activities. Instead, they argued, marketing thought and theory should be expanded to incorporate marketing activities in public and nonprofit organizations.

Their article was intended to be provocative. And, indeed, it stimulated a debate that continued for several years. For instance, Luck [2] argued that the marketing discipline should be confined to market transactions characterized by the sale and purchase of goods and services for money. So long as nonbusiness organizations sold their products, he wrote, they were engaging in marketing. But if there were no established terms of sale, then it was not marketing.

Despite—or perhaps because of—these debates, nonbusiness marketing became integrated into the mainstream of both marketing theory and practice in the 1970s. The dedication of the entire July 1971 issue of the *Journal of Marketing* [3] to marketing's changing social/environmental role was particularly influential. That issue included applications of marketing technology to fund raising, health services, population problems, solid waste recycling, and other aspects of "social marketing."

Shortly thereafter, Kotler [4] developed his "generic concept" of marketing, highlighting the evolution of marketing through several stages of "consciousness." Consciousness One conceived of marketing as essentially a business subject concerned with market transactions. Consciousness Two extended marketing's realm to include all transactions where "one can identify an organization, a client group, and products broadly defined." Finally, Consciousness Three argued that "marketing applies to an organization's attempt to relate to all of its publics, not just its consuming publics."

A survey of marketing educators published in 1974 [5] showed that an overwhelming majority of them agreed that marketing went beyond just economic goods and services and market transactions. Yet some authors still remained skeptical of the broadened concept. For instance, Bartels [6] expressed fears of an "identity crisis in marketing." He perceived several disadvantages in shifting marketing's emphasis from economic to social behavior. These included the diversion of attention from such pressing problems as physical distribution; teaching that emphasizes methodology at the expense of a practical knowledge of products, markets, and specific applications; and a trend toward an abstract, esoteric literature that cannot be understood by practitioners. However, Bartels also conceded some benefits. Among these were the transfer of knowledge to areas where little behavioral research had been done and the cross-fertilization of concepts developed by researchers in dissimilar fields.

We believe that the controversy over broadening the marketing concept is now over. But perhaps it is being replaced by a new debate. In 1976, Hunt [7] proposed a conceptual model of the nature and scope of marketing that included separate categories for the profit and nonprofit sectors. Subsequently, he defended this model against critics who argued that the profit/nonprofit dichotomy was unnecessary [8].

> My own belief [he wrote] is that the *similarities* between marketing in the profit sector versus the nonprofit sector greatly outweigh the *differences*. . . .
> [But] I suggest that the profit–sector/nonprofit–sector dichotomy will be useful until such time as (1) "broadening the concept of marketing" ceases to be controversial, (2) nonprofit sector marketing is completely integrated into all marketing courses (and not treated as a separate subject with separate courses), (3) administrators of nonprofit organizations generally perceive their organizations as having marketing problems, and (4) these administrators hire marketing people and, where appropriate, set up marketing departments.

In following sections, we review recent progress in the field of public and nonprofit marketing, in the academic

literature and elsewhere. We first explore the question of whether the differences between business and nonbusiness marketing are meaningful ones, and then examine five specific areas of application: the arts, health care, energy conservation, public transportation, and higher education. In the process, we address certain points raised by Hunt: (1) to what extent has nonbusiness marketing been integrated into the mainstream of marketing coursework and literature (rather than being treated separately), and (2) how much progress has been made by different types of nonbusiness organizations in accepting the validity of the marketing concept, employing marketing professionals, and making use of marketing tools and concepts? Future managerial and research needs also are considered. Because of space limitations, we seek to highlight issues rather than be comprehensive. However, the references cited in the footnotes should prove useful to those wishing to explore particular issues in greater depth.

IS PUBLIC AND NONPROFIT MARKETING REALLY DIFFERENT?

What, in fact, are the differences between business and nonbusiness marketing? Are they important, and do they aid or hinder integration? Four key differences are examined: the presence of multiple publics, a nonprofit orientation, a concern with services rather than physical goods, and public scrutiny and nonmarket pressures.

Multiple Publics. Shapiro [9] highlights the separation between resource attraction and resource allocation in the nonprofit organization. In profit-making enterprises, clients pay money for the products received. But in nonprofit organizations, the clients who receive services and the donors or taxpayers who provide funds are often unrelated groups. Thus, fund raising and service delivery may involve separate, but interrelated, marketing activities to two different publics. Although taxation may be thought of as involuntary, initiating new or increased taxes often requires marketing efforts. These marketing efforts involve individual taxpayers directly when the procedure followed includes a referendum on the issue. For example, only after the schools in Toledo, Ohio, had been closed indefinitely did a fifth attempt to pass a referendum for a property tax increase succeed in November 1977 [10].

This notion of two publics can be readily expanded to one of multiple publics including outside suppliers, employees, regulators, and many others [11]. But this concept of multiple publics is not confined to nonprofit organizations. Business firms engage in periodic resource attraction activities—separated from the sale of products—as they seek to sell new stock or bond issues or to negotiate loans from banks. Firms also have suppliers with whom they engage in market transactions. Many industries are increasingly regulated at the federal, state, or local level. In addition to their relationships with consumers, many companies are involved in ongoing relationships—often of an adversary nature—with citizen groups, formalized consumer organizations, and stockholders. Orchestration of the exchange relationships with each of these publics is necessary if a firm is to succeed in its central purpose of selling the goods and services that it produces.

There are, admittedly, differences between business and nonbusiness organizations in the emphasis they place on relating to publics other than consumers. But the concept of multiple publics *is* relevant for business marketers [12]. What is interesting, in relation to developments in marketing theory and practice, is that it was the study of nonbusiness organizations that highlighted the importance of these publics for marketers.

Nonprofit Objective. Because nonbusiness organizations do not normally operate for profit, it has been argued that their success or failure cannot be measured in strictly financial terms [13]. The lack of even a theoretical goal of profit maximization makes it more difficult to choose among strategic and tactical alternatives. This is a fundamental distinction. However, the fact that the bottom line tends to be colored red does not mean that financial performance is a meaningless measure for public and nonprofit marketers. Let us examine two implications of the nonprofit objective.

First, the presence of an operating deficit usually signals that the funds needed to balance operating revenues and expenses are coming from sources other than consumers. When the public treasury funds the deficit, the justification for tax-supported subsidies reflects a belief that the external economies or "social profit" resulting from providing a public service exceed its associated financial costs. This notion forces the public sector marketer to review the objectives of the organization, to develop marketing plans for achieving these objectives (within the prevailing financial constraints), and then to devise nonfinancial measures of performance which will allow management to evaluate later how well these objectives have, in fact, been achieved.

The second implication of a nonprofit orientation is actually very businesslike and applies to those public or nonprofit organizations that sell their services at a price. Although deficits may be accepted in such organizations, significant increases in current deficits may not be. When coupled with a distrust of marketing by top management, the possibility of incurring such deficits may make it difficult for nonbusiness marketing managers to enlarge their scope of operations. This problem has led some marketing personnel to adopt a strategy of incremental analysis, isolating the projected costs and revenues of specific actions. Approval for expansion of operations can be gained if costs do not exceed revenues. However, even if costs do exceed revenues, incremental "social profits" from the expanded programs that justify a deficit increase may be identified.

Incremental analysis has long been used by business marketers, but the concept of balancing financial profits against "social profits" is relatively new to the private sector. Devising appropriate measures—or social indicators—was first raised by Bauer et al [14]. The development of social indicators and their integration with marketing strategy are of concern to both public and private sector marketers [15, 16].

Services Rather than Physical Goods. Most nonbusiness organizations produce services rather than physical goods [13]. One might expect that public and nonprofit marketers could benefit from studying the marketing of consumer services in the private sector. But, in fact, the latter area received relatively little attention from marketing scholars until recently [17, 18].

The lack of private sector analogues has had two effects. First, it has made the successful transfer of the marketing tools, concepts, and strategies that have been developed by consumer goods firms more difficult because two hurdles had to be leaped, from the private to the public/nonprofit sector and from goods to services. Second, it has forced marketing theorists to radically rethink previous conceptions and definitions of marketing in order to make this double jump.

Recent conceptual and empirical research in services marketing is tending to include both business and nonbusiness services and, thus, is leading to a fruitful cross-fertilization between the two sectors [19]. In many service industries, such as higher education, public transportation, and utilities, the public/private and profit/nonprofit distinctions are blurred anyway.

Public Scrutiny and Nonmarket Pressures. Most public agencies are subject, at least in theory, to close public scrutiny because of their role in the provision of public services, an expressed desire for openness in government, and a need to prevent abuses of natural or legislated monopoly power. The review of proposed prices for mail services in the United States by the Postal Rate Commission exemplifies a particularly intensive form of public participation in the strategy formulation process.

Because public and nonprofit organizations do not have profit as an objective, and often are heavily subsidized, they are not constrained by the "discipline of the marketplace." Instead, they may be expected or even required (in the case of some public agencies) to provide services or serve market segments that a profit-making organization would find uneconomic. Political pressures, in particular, may force retention of inefficient services and economically suboptimal strategies. Examples include the requirement that the U.S. Postal Service maintain rural postoffices and that Amtrak provide rail passenger service on routes across thinly populated areas.

However, private firms also may be forced by political and other pressures to keep plants open that they would rather close, or to withdraw from the marketplace such profitable but unsafe or socially undesirable products as noisy machines, dangerous children's toys, and ''gas guzzling'' cars. Regulation is increasing in the private sector, and marketers in both private and public sectors must learn to work within the constraints that it imposes. Information disclosure requirements, meantime, have eliminated some of the traditional secrecy of private firms.

MARKETING APPLICATIONS
IN SPECIFIC FIELDS

Efforts to apply marketing and consumer research to nonbusiness organizations first appeared in number during the mid-1960s. They focused on specific areas, notably health, public transportation, and political topics. These efforts provided the necessary base for development of an integrated theory and conceptual organization in the late 1960s and early 1970s.

Most current work in nonbusiness marketing centers on application of marketing concepts and strategies in specific fields. However, as the level of sophistication rises, researchers in public and nonprofit marketing are ceasing simply to borrow and adapt tools and theories developed elsewhere and are themselves contributing to knowledge generation in marketing. In other words, a two-way traffic is emerging.

One example comes from market research involving a review of drop-off delivery techniques for self-administered questionnaires. The consumer surveys in which this methodology was used and progressively refined all had nonbusiness topics—politics, adult education, health behavior, and public transportation [20, 21].

We now review briefly developments in five specific application areas: the arts, health, energy, public transportation, and higher education. It is important to note that each of these fields includes both profit and nonprofit organizations and straddles both the public and the private sectors.

The Arts. The arts have established a good record of both theoretical and practical developments in the use of marketing. Baumol and Bowen's pathbreaking analysis [22] shows that labor intensity in the performing arts and the limited opportunity to substitute capital for labor make it unlikely that the performing arts could exist without subsidy and donation. This analysis has since been used in other public sector areas, such as higher education [23].

Morison and Fliehr's book *In Search of an Audience* [24] shows how a marketing approach helped build an audience for the Tyrone Guthrie Theater in Minneapolis. Many visual and performing arts groups have conducted surveys of their audiences, and some have developed strategies based on the results.

For example, a survey of subscribers to the American Conservatory Theatre (ACT) in San Francisco [25, 26]

showed that the 15% price discount (seven tickets for the price of six) was not one of the major benefits sought. The discount was discontinued, yet both renewal and new subscriber acquisition rates remained within the usual bounds. The most frequently cited benefit of subscriptions was to ''make me more certain to attend each play.'' This finding not only provided an interesting perspective on human behavior, but also suggested possible copy strategies to use in subscription campaigns. Attendance behavior before subscribing also was studied. It was found that as many as one-third of new subscribers had not attended an ACT performance in the previous five years. The size of this ''sudden subscriber'' group was surprising, because it was counter to the conventional wisdom that patrons gradually increase frequency of attendance before deciding to subscribe.

Most arts organizations are typically small and have relatively few management positions. Thus, bureaucratic procedures are limited and access to management generally implies access to top management. Development and implementation of a computer-assisted performance selection model with the Lively Arts at Stanford program [27] required intensive contact with the entire management structure, but was greatly facilitated by the fact that this structure consisted of only three people.

Many arts managers seem to be more receptive to new and creative approaches than are managers in other fields. ''We've never done it that way before'' is not often given as a reason for rejecting marketing. However, arts managers are particularly sensitive to the threat of diluting quality standards in order to appeal to mass markets. There may also be a conflict between satisfying artistic needs for creativity and self-expression and appealing to audience tastes. This conflict may necessitate persuasive communications to educate the audience.

Arts organizations have found it easy to undertake consumer research because it is relatively simple to identify a sample of users and to administer a questionnaire to them. A museum can readily interview visitors, and a performing arts organization can send questionnaires to samples selected from its mailing list. However, relatively few arts organizations survey people who do not already have a tie to the organization.

Health Care and Related Areas. Rising medical costs, excess capacity in many hospitals, and the development of new forms of health care delivery, such as health maintenance organizations (HMOs), have served to spur interest in marketing in the field of health care. At the same time, growing attention has been devoted to encouraging changes in behavior patterns which will lead to better health and/or broader societal benefits [28]. This effort was stimulated by the National Consumer Health Information and Health Promotion Act of 1976, which provided for a national program [29]. Areas of application include nutrition, alcohol and drug abuse, birth control, and immunization campaigns. Interest in health behavior marketing appears to predate that in health services marketing; several articles on the former topic appeared during the 1960s [30].

In terms of marketing, health provides an interesting contrast to the arts. The latter are seen by most people as a luxury, and the proportion of the population regularly attending or participating in arts-related activities is very small. Health, however, is of concern to everyone at some point or another, rich and poor alike. Though some people are extremely concerned about health matters, others are afraid to seek health care. The health care marketing task is further complicated by the fact that services often must be marketed in advance of need.

Marketing studies in health care have emphasized not only consumer research and communication, but also distribution systems. Bucklin and Carman [31] applied the theory of vertical market structures to the evaluation of alternative health care delivery systems. Developing alternative ways of delivering health care to provide better service to consumers at lower cost has been an important concern of health care planners in recent years. Marketing activity was greatly stimulated by passage in 1975 of the Health Maintenance Organization and Resources Act; it effectively requires all HMOs seeking federal certification and funding to give explicit attention to marketing.

HMOs have been instrumental in overturning long-standing professional prohibitions on the use of advertising in the health care field. Research by Richard et al [32] suggests that most HMOs recognize the need for marketing activities to achieve an adequate enrollment base, but marketing responsibilities in such organizations are often dispersed and lack focus. In an effort to develop strategies for diffusion of the HMO concept, Venkatesan [33] applied consumer behavior concepts to marketing this approach to health care delivery. Two applications of management science to marketing health care facilities were published in the 1976 volume of *Operations Research* [34].

Evidence of continued interest in health marketing is provided by academic and professional meetings devoted to this topic. For instance, in 1976, the University of Nebraska sponsored a symposium examining consumer behavior in the health marketplace from a variety of perspectives [35]. Also, many general management development courses for health professionals now include marketing modules.

Other aspects of health marketing have been treated in recent conference papers. The ''Patients Bill of Rights'' and marketing of blood donorship have been discussed at AMA [36]. Nutritional behavior and preventive medicine, antismoking, and antidrug abuse have been discussed at ACR [37, 38], and HMOs were among the topics discussed at AIDS in 1977 [39].

Energy Conservation. Energy conservation provides a good illustration of the premise that a crisis spurs innovation [40]. Before the crisis resulting from the Arab oil embargo of 1973–74, there had been limited recognition of the need for future energy conservation but minimal action directed toward achieving that end. Although oil prices rose sharply as a result of exporter-initiated price increases and several communication campaigns were launched to promote energy conservation, marketing applications in this field must generally be regarded as a failure in the United States. The greatest achievement to date probably represents a legalistic approach rather than a marketing one, consisting of an effort to enhance vehicle fuel efficiency by legislating rising minimum standards for U.S. produced cars.

Energy has been a popular topic for papers at recent AMA, ACR, and AIDS conferences. Twelve papers were presented in 1976–77, most of them emphasizing consumer attitudes, behavior patterns, and response to information programs [e.g. 41–46]. Yet Montgomery and Leonard-Barton's 1977 review of the literature [47] concluded that ''relatively little is known about several major dimensions of importance in the marketing of home energy conservation. Further, what literature exists is diffuse and often inaccessible. . . .'' These authors cited no U.S. examples of organizations that employed an articulated marketing program— starting from consumer research and leading to a positioning and marketing mix strategy designed to achieve specific objectives—though they found many consumer and market research studies and some examples of unidimensional use of marketing variables (they did not review in detail the British experience discussed later). Thus, utilities have employed price incentives to discourage consumption, but rarely integrated these with other marketing mix elements. As the authors point out, price is at best a necessary but not a sufficient condition to achieve conservation. For example, many Northern Californians reduced water usage in 1977 without direct price variation in response to general and specific campaigns based on the drought and the consequent need for water conservation.

Why has marketing had such limited impact on energy conservation in the United States? First, general concern with energy conservation probably dates only from the 1973 Mideast War, although several prominent ecologists had foreseen the need for conservation earlier. Second, there are few organizations whose primary purpose is to encourage energy conservation, in contrast to those that have been vitally concerned for many years with such social causes as preservation of the environment (such as the Sierra Club) and family planning (such as Planned Parenthood). Until the establishment of the Department of Energy in 1977, federal attention was spread across many different offices. The Federal Energy Administration employed several people with titles such as ''energy conservation marketing specialist,'' but political pressures confined its consumer marketing efforts to public service advertising involving such vague messages as ''Don't Be Fuelish.''

Regulated utilities, whose long-term strategy has been to pursue profit growth through increased consumption, are only now beginning to adapt their marketing programs to achieving profits through such strategies as smoothing demand for service on a time-of-day basis.

A third reason lies in the debate about whether the solution to the energy problem lies in technological (''hard'') solutions or in changing behavior patterns to conserve and reduce waste (''soft''). Because many technological solutions would be invisible to the user, some writers seem to focus on technology as the sole answer because it would be more convenient. Yet, Montgomery and Leonard-Barton [47] present many examples, especially from industry, in which electrical energy consumption has been dramatically reduced through conservation. A marketing approach would attempt to combine ''hard'' and ''soft'' solutions. For example, adopting solar energy will require identification of the needs of target segments and their responsiveness to alternative solar energy devices.

Fourth, because utilities are regulated profit-seeking companies, the primary focus of their marketing program has been price. But regulatory procedures often make it difficult for utilities to practice differential price strategies and to use price as a promotional device in conjunction with other marketing efforts.

In summary, little has been accomplished in the marketing of energy conservation in the United States. Yet it is a major societal problem that raises a classic public sector marketing challenge: How to maintain a behavior over time? The primary energy conservation problem is not to persuade people to adopt less wasteful behaviors in the midst of a crisis, but to do so continuously. The same problem also occurs, for example, in programs to encourage people to adhere to low cholesterol diets, to obey the 55 mph speed limit, and to stop smoking.

Rather more success in energy conservation has been achieved in Britain, where a 12-point program was introduced by the government in December 1974. It was directed at both individual and industrial users and included incentives, legal compulsion, economic pricing of energy, and a major communication campaign. This campaign, directed by the U.K. Department of Energy and firmly based on consumer research findings, began in January 1975 and continues in a new phase in 1977–78. It seeks to secure both immediate reductions in energy use and the longer term changes in public attitudes and habits needed to secure continuing economies. A wide range of paid media are used, supplemented by exhibitions, syndicated articles, and publicity campaigns by the various fuel industries. The approach has been not only to persuade people of the *need* to save energy, but also to demonstrate specifically *how* to do so (research findings showed that people were ignorant of such approaches as home insulation).

According to Phillips and Nelson [48], regular surveys of public attitudes, claimed behavior, and future intentions show significant gains from the original, precampaign baseline figures. Retail audits of sales of thermal insulation

materials provide encouraging confirmation that consumers are acting in accordance with campaign recommendations, not only to insulate but also to use a specific thickness of insulation.

Phillips and Nelson draw some important conclusions about energy conservation marketing from the British experience: (1) price alone will not lead directly to efficient energy saving (although economic pricing is a prerequisite of a credible conservation policy), (2) paid advertising should be supported by other publicity activity, (3) publicity support and cooperation by the fuel industries provides needed credibility to government programs, (4) point-of-sale follow-through is needed to achieve the objective of stimulating energy-saving durables, and (5) households may differ in their energy-saving priorities according to both household composition and circumstances, and thus a segmented strategy is required.

Public Transportation. Urban transit probably has received more attention from consumer researchers and marketing specialists than any other single public or nonprofit field. The seminal work on transit marketing was published by Schneider [49] in 1965. By the early 1970s, a significant number of research studies and demonstration projects had been undertaken by university researchers and consulting firms, many of them financed by federal agencies. Writing in 1972, Lovelock [50] attempted to coordinate and synthesize this previous work with his own research, and to develop some general strategic marketing recommendations for transit management.

Transit marketing has benefited from strong federal support. Since the early 1970s, a determined effort has been made by the Urban Mass Transportation Administration (UMTA), an agency of the U.S. Department of Transportation, to promote improved management skills in the transit industry. In part, this effort may have been a response to charges that the industry was poorly managed and too operations oriented, and that excessive emphasis was being given to developing new technology at the expense of improving the quality of management.

UMTA has given particular attention to marketing. In 1975, the agency sponsored a National Transit Marketing Conference in conjunction with the American Public Transit Association (APTA), the industry trade organization [51]. Subsequently, UMTA commissioned development of a *Transit Marketing Management Handbook* [52] from several consulting firms. Four volumes had been published by 1977 on the marketing plan, pricing, organization, and transit information aids. UMTA also has sponsored a two-week marketing management program and management courses which include a marketing component for transit personnel. In addition, UMTA has financed university research projects in marketing through its University Research and Training program. The findings of UMTA-financed studies are widely available through the National Technical Information Service, a U.S. Department of Commerce service.

UMTA's major investment in marketing to date has been its sponsorship of the Transit Marketing Project, described as "the first major commitment at the Federal level to define and demonstrate a basic methodology for transit marketing; to test and upgrade state-of-the-art techniques; and to develop new techniques" [53]. Initiated in 1975, the project began with consumer research studies in both Baltimore and Nashville. These studies sought to (1) define the consumer groups offering the greatest potential as a source of rider volume and (2) identify the most important benefits people desired from transportation for local trips, as well as their attitudes and behavior patterns in regard to alternative modes of transportation. Subsequently, marketing strategies were developed for both cities to enable their respective transit systems to tailor improved services to target market segments.

Although there is now greater awareness of marketing among transit managers and certain systems are engaged in sophisticated marketing efforts, others remain heavily operations oriented. For the latter group, marketing often is still equated with advertising and community relations. Pricing, scheduling, routing, vehicle design, driver training, and public information services have yet to be widely accepted as elements in an integrated marketing package.

Consumer research in transportation by marketing academics (often closely linked to the work of consulting firms) has extended traditional work by engineers and economists in modal choice modeling. Emphasis has been placed on developing better understanding of the consumer decision process, incorporating attitudinal concepts in modal choice research [54], and on relating transit objectives to market segmentation strategies [55].

Higher Education. At a 1972 conference, Kotler and Dubois [56] discussed marketing and the American education "industry" in broad terms. They examined three major problem areas (insufficient funds, lagging innovation, and unmotivated students) at both school and college levels. But nearly all marketing attention since then has focused on improving admissions for individual colleges. Though fund raising has been extremely important for higher education during the past few years, the limited literature on this topic has been directed at fund raising in a general rather than at a specifically educational context.

Interest in marketing has been spurred by the publicity given to noncontrollable demographic trends. Primary demand for a college education from students in traditional age groups is ceasing to grow and will soon start declining because of a fall in the birth rate that began in the 1950s. This change has led to a shift from a sellers' to a buyers' market in higher education. Many traditionally strong institutions now worry about their ability to attract students of the same academic caliber as in the past—a problem exacerbated by the national trend of declining SAT scores. Other institutions worry about their ability to attract sufficient students of almost any caliber. In an "industry" with heavy capital investments, failure to maintain or increase student enrollment levels at a time of rapidly rising costs can lead to a drastic shortfall between revenues and expenses.

As a result, admissions offices have shifted their emphasis from screening to recruitment; marketing has been seized upon—sometimes indiscriminately—as a means of improving a college's competitive position in recruiting students in traditional age groups. To a lesser extent, market and consumer research has been used to identify nontraditional students and develop offerings tailored to their needs.

Some schools have succumbed to the "majority fallacy." These schools, by lowering admissions standards and broadening their range (but not depth) of courses, have failed to appeal to any specific segment and, consequently, have intensified their admissions problems.

Among recent literature in higher education marketing is the proceedings of a 1976 colloquium on marketing and college admissions sponsored by the College Entrance Examination Board [57], which includes papers on analyzing the future market for college education and applications of marketing theory and positioning strategy to college admissions. It is interesting to compare Kotler's model of an applicant's college decision process [58]—a choice process which may extend over more than a year and have lifelong implications—with Lovelock's model of modal choice decision-making in transportation [59]—a frequently repeated and relatively low-risk decision.

Evidence of educational administrators' perceived interest in marketing is provided by advertisements for marketing workshops and seminars in the *Chronicle of Higher Education*. However, personal experience suggests that many top administrators are not especially interested in, or able to relate to, marketing; they appear to see it as a necessary tool for their fund-raising and admissions offices, but not necessarily as a fundamental concept underlying management of the entire institution. Possibly this disinterest reflects their own pressing involvement in such issues as faculty management, labor relations, and compliance with federal equal opportunity regulations.

WHAT NEXT FOR PUBLIC AND NONPROFIT MARKETING?

Several broad conclusions can be drawn about the state of the art in nonbusiness marketing. No serious controversy remains among academics as to whether or not nonbusiness marketing belongs in the general field of marketing. As with other marketing topics, personal interests, together with institutional priorities, will determine whether or not an individual does research in the area or an institution offers a course in it. The trend toward integration of nonbusiness material in basic texts and courses suggests, however, that this aspect of marketing is being accepted on its own merits.

It is clear that nonbusiness marketing has progressed beyond the stage of a topic discussed only between academics. Marketing tools and concepts are being widely discussed, written about, and promoted across a broad range of diverse application areas. To an increasing extent, marketing is the subject of articles in "trade" publications, is included in professional development courses, and provides the major topic of workshops and conferences sponsored by practitioner organizations. Marketing activities also are being promoted by government legislation as well as by research contracts and dissemination of findings.

When one looks at the record of marketing in a nonbusiness managerial context, however, the picture appears cloudy and the results have been mixed. As in the private sector, there have been failures in planning and execution, and even outright bungling (as in the case of the $2 bill reissue).[1] But there have been successes, too, in the arts, health care organizations (notably HMOs), public transportation, higher education, and other areas of application. And there is growing recognition that marketing techniques provide a new perspective and powerful new tools for tackling a range of difficult social welfare problems [61].

Successful applications of marketing by nonbusiness organizations also can be found outside the U.S. Several British public agencies have had a marketing orientation longer than their American counterparts. For instance, British Rail, the (British) Post Office, and London Transport all show a high level of sophistication in their use of marketing research and in strategic implementation of such concepts as market segmentation; they have been much studied by representatives of similar organizations in other countries. As a general policy, nonbusiness marketing managers should make a point of seeking insights from related organizations abroad as well as at home.

To further increase acceptance of marketing tools and concepts among public and nonprofit managers will require the *marketing of marketing itself*. The task is twofold. First, it must be demonstrated that marketing is applicable to their specific situations. Second, nonbusiness managers (like their business counterparts) must be educated to recognize the scope and complexity of marketing, and to realize that it extends far beyond just advertising and selling. Initially nonbusiness managers sometimes resist the use of marketing terminology. As a first step, it often helps to explain marketing concepts and strategies in terms with which these managers feel comfortable. However, in the long run, development of a professional marketing orientation and cross-fertilization of ideas are impeded if each area of application retains its own terminology.

---

[1] Although the Federal Reserve Board had the benefit of findings from an in-depth research study it had commissioned of bankers, retailers, and consumers, it appeared to make no use of these insights when reintroducing the bill, limiting its efforts to a low-level public relations program [60].

One practice which represents a double-edged sword is the use of outside marketing consultants. Although consultants can be a valuable educational resource and provide important analytical and strategic insights, any set of recommendations is only as good as the skills of the managers responsible for implementation. Continued use of consultants may deprive "in-house" personnel of the experience of on-the-job training. Consultants should be used as a supplement to, rather than a replacement for, an organization's own staff. If on-the-job training activities are limited, then participation in professional development programs may be valuable for fledgling marketing managers.

We see three specific areas in which nonbusiness managers need to develop their skills for the future. The first is the ability to understand and to analyze the impact of marketing variables. Decisions on allocating marketing resources among different variables and orchestrating the marketing mix to achieve desired objectives cannot be made effectively without this understanding and analytical skill.

The second need is for better understanding of consumer decision processes. It is difficult to develop strategies for influencing consumer behavior if one does not understand how consumers make decisions about their behavior patterns in the first place. Public and nonprofit organizations generally lack detailed data bases on which to identify problems and test decision alternatives.

Last, there is a need for a better understanding of marketing and a stronger consumer orientation among nonmarketing personnel. This need is especially pressing in service organizations, because services tend to be labor-intensive, there is a high degree of personal contact with consumers, and production and consumption often take place simultaneously. Too often, an operations orientation prevails, and marketing's role is limited to that of a communications appendage.

Future Research Needs. Overall, we see a need to coordinate and consolidate managerial learning, both within the nonbusiness area and between business and nonbusiness marketing. Business and nonbusiness services, in particular, may have much to learn from each other. Taken as a group, neither has historically had a strong marketing orientation, and thus each is developing expertise in marketing concurrently. In another area, computer and model based marketing decision aids, which have had increasing impact in the private sector, have had only limited use in the public sector [62].

More work also is needed on developing a rigorous taxonomy of marketing. One possibility is to consider splitting marketing by government agencies away from marketing by private nonprofit organizations. The rationale for this separation lies in the greater impact of nonmarket factors on the former group. An alternative approach would be to categorize marketing activities by all types of organizations into three major areas, according to the nature of the product being marketed—namely, physical goods, services, and behavior patterns (safe driving, for instance). One problem facing marketers in the third category is maintaining behavior over time (for example, preventing reversion to previous "bad" behavior once people have given up smoking, started to floss their teeth, and begun driving at 55 mph). Relatively little work on this topic is found in the social psychology literature, and marketers need to devote more attention to it.

Another area meriting further study involves the strategic implications of decision-making when profit is not the goal. Public and nonprofit organizations badly need to develop clearly defined and measurable objective functions that are appropriate to their particular missions. Without these, it is hard to formulate marketing strategies and harder still to assess whether or not they have been successful. Also needed is a mechanism to facilitate decisions on tradeoffs among multiple objectives.

A final area meriting research is marketing's role in government. Can marketing technology be brought to bear on transactions between federal and state or local governments? In particular, how should the federal government go about obtaining voluntary compliance with its policies (adoption of high technology waste disposal system, for example) as an alternative to trying to force compliance through legislation?

Even in the area of legislation, marketing insights may prove useful. People will not necessarily obey laws just because they are on the statute books. Consumer research is needed to help legislators frame laws that are realistic in their expectations of human behavior. Moreover, marketing efforts may also facilitate individual understanding of the rationale of new legislation, its impact, and what will be expected of citizens by way of compliance.

CONCLUSION

It is evident that nonbusiness marketing has come a long way in a relatively short period of time. The subject is taken seriously in academia, is having a growing impact on management practice in a diverse range of applications, and is contributing to general advancement of the field of marketing. These facts, we believe, justify our contention that public and nonprofit marketing has come of age. They in no way imply a lack of potential for future growth, improved judgment, or greater sophistication.

REFERENCES

1. Kotler, Philip, and Levy, Sidney J. "Broadening the Concept of Marketing." *Journal of Marketing* 33 (January 1969):10–15.
2. Luck, David J. "Broadening the Concept of Marketing—Too Far." *Journal of Marketing* 33 (July 1969): 53–55.
3. Kotler, Philip, and Zaltman, Gerald. "Social Marketing: An Approach to Planned Social Change." *Journal of Marketing* 35 (July 1971): 3–12.
4. Kotler, Philip. "A Generic Concept of Marketing." *Journal of Marketing* 36 (April 1972):46–54.
5. Nickells, William G. "Conceptual Conflicts in Marketing." *Journal of Economics and Business* 27 (Winter 1974): 140–43.
6. Bartels, Robert. "The Identity Crisis in Marketing." *Journal of Marketing* 38 (October 1974):73–76.
7. Hunt, Shelby D. "The Nature and Scope of Marketing." *Journal of Marketing* 40 (July 1976):17–28.
8. Hunt, Shelby D. "The Three Dichotomies Model of Marketing: An Elaboration of Issues." In *Macro-Marketing: Distributive Processes From a Societal Perspective*, edited by Charles C. Slater, pp. 52–56. Boulder: University of Colorado, 1977.
9. Shapiro, Benson P. "Marketing for Nonprofit Organizations." *Harvard Business Review* 51 (September–October 1973):123–32.
10. Stuart, Reginald. "Toledo Students Back in School After Tax is Approved." *The New York Times*. 10 November 1977, p. A-18.
11. Kotler, Philip. *Marketing for Nonprofit Organizations*, Chapter 2. Englewood Cliffs, NJ: Prentice-Hall, 1975.
12. Heskett, James L. *Marketing*, pp. 531–33. New York: Macmillan, 1975.
13. Lovelock, Christopher H., and Weinberg, Charles B. "Contrasting Private and Public Sector Marketing." In *1974 Combined Proceedings*, edited by Ronald C. Curhan, pp. 242–47. Chicago: American Marketing Association, 1975.
14. Bauer, Raymond A., ed. *Social Indicators*. Cambridge: MIT Press, 1966.
15. Clewett, Robert L., and Olson, Jerry C., eds. *Social Indicators and Marketing*. Chicago: American Marketing Association, 1974.
16. Hamburger, Polia Lerner. *Social Indicators—A Marketing Perspective*. Chicago: American Marketing Association, 1974.
17. Rathnell, John M. *Marketing in the Service Sector*. Cambridge, MA: Winthrop, 1974.
18. Lovelock, Christopher H. "Marketing Consumer Services: Insights from the Public and Private Sectors." In *Proceedings. Seminaire de Recherche en Marketing*. Aix-en-Provence, France: Institut d'Administration des Affaires, 1975.
19. Eigler, Pierre; Langeard, Eric; Lovelock, Christopher H.; Bateson, John E. G., and Young, Robert F. "Marketing Consumer Services: New Insights." Marketing Science Institute, Report #77-115, December 1977.
20. Stover, Robert V., and Stone, Walter J. "Hand Delivery of Self-Administered Questionnaires." *Public Opinion Quarterly* 37 (Summer 1974): 284–87.
21. Lovelock, Christopher H.; Stiff, Ronald; Cullwick, David, and Kaufman, Ira M. "An Evaluation of the Effectiveness of Drop-Off Questionnaire Delivery." *Journal of Marketing Research* 13 (November 1976): 358–64.
22. Baumol, William T., and Bowen, William G. *Performing Arts: The Economic Dilemma*. New York: Twentieth Century Fund, 1966.
23. Massy, William F. "A Dynamic Equilibrium Model for University Budget Planning," *Management Science* 23 (November 1976): 248–56.
24. Morison, Bradley G., and Fliehr, Kay. *In Search of an Audience*. New York: Pitman, 1968.
25. Ryans, Adrian B., and Weinberg, Charles B. "Consumer Dynamics in Nonprofit Organizations." *Journal of Consumer Research*, in press.
26. Weinberg, Charles B. "Building a Marketing Plan for the Performing Arts." *Association of College, University, and Community Arts Administrators Bulletin*, May 1977.
27. Weinberg, Charles B., and Shachmut, Kenneth M. "ARTS PLAN—A Model Based System for Use in Planning a Performing Arts Series." *Management Science*, February 1978.
28. Mushkin, Selma J., ed. *Consumer Incentives for Health Care*. New York: Prodist, 1974.
29. Somers, Anne R., ed. *Promoting Health: Consumer Education and National Policy*. Germantown, MD: Aspen Systems Corporation, 1976.
30. Zaltman, Gerald; Kotler, Philip, and Kaufman, Ira. *Creating Social Change*. New York: Holt, Rinehard & Winston, 1972.
31. Bucklin, Louis P., and Carman, James M. "Vertical Market Structure and the Health Care Delivery System," pp. 7–41. In *Marketing Analysis for Social Problems*, edited by Jagdish Sheth and Peter L. Wright, pp. 7–41. Urbana, IL: University of Illinois, 1974.
32. Richard, Lawrence; Becherer, Richard, and George, William R. "The Development of Marketing Management Technology in a Health Care Setting: The Health Maintenance Organization Experience." In *1976*

Educators' Proceedings, edited by Kenneth L. Bernhardt. Chicago: American Marketing Association, 1976.

33. Venkatesan, M. "Marketing of Health Maintenance Organizations: Consumer Behavior Perspectives," pp. 45–69. In *Broadening the Concept of Consumer Behavior,* edited by Gerald Zaltman and Brian Sternthal. The Association for Consumer Research, 1975.

34. Wind, Yoram and Spitz, Lawrence K. "Analytical Approach to Marketing Decisions in Health-Care Organizations;" and Parker, Bennett R., and Srinivasan, V. "A Consumer Preference Approach to the Planning of Rural Primary Health-Care Facilities." Both in *Operations Research* 24 (October–November 1976): 973–90, 991–1025.

35. Newman, Ian M., ed. *Consumer Behavior in the Health Marketplace: A Symposium Proceedings.* Lincoln, NE: Nebraska Center for Health Education, University of Nebraska, 1977.

36. Densmore, Max L., and Klippel, R. Eugene. "Marketing Management: A New Contributor to Health Care Management," pp. 135–38; and Henion, Karl E., and Batsell, Richard R., "Marketing of Blood Donorship, Helping Behavior, and Psychological Reactance," pp. 652–56. Both in *1976 Educators' Proceedings.* Edited by K. L. Bernhardt. Chicago: American Marketing Association, 1976.

37. Venkatesan, M. "Consumer Behavior and Nutrition: Preventive Health Perspectives," pp. 518–20; Wortzel, Lawrence H., and Clarke, Roberta N., "Environmental Protection for the Non-Smoker: Consumer Behavior Aspects of Encouraging Non-Smoking," pp. 521–24; Robertson, Thomas S., and Wortzel, Lawrence H., "Consumer Behavior and Health Care Change: The Role of Mass Media," pp. 525–27. All in *Advances in Consumer Research,* Vol. 5, Association for Consumer Research, 1978.

38. Ray, Michael L.; Ward, Scott, and Reed, Jerome B. "Pretesting of Anti-Drug Abuse Education and Information Campaigns." In *Communication Research and Drug Education,* edited by R. E. Ostman. Beverly Hills, CA: Sage Publications, 1975.

39. Moriarty, Mark M., and Venkatesan, M. "Adoption of an HMO as an Innovation." *Proceedings. American Institute for Decision Sciences:* 9th Annual Conference, 1977.

40. Rogers, Everett M., and Shoemaker, F. Floyd. *Communication of Innovations: A Cross-Cultural Approach,* pp. 138–39. New York: The Free Press, 1971.

41. Reizenstein, Richard C., and Barnaby, David J., "An Analysis of Selected Consumer Energy-Environment Trade-Off Segments," pp. 522–26; Becker, Helmut, and Fritzche, David J., "Energy Consumption and Marketing: A Comparison of German and American Lifestyles," pp. 527–32. Both in *1976 Educators' Proceedings,* American Marketing Association.

42. Craig, C. Samuel, and McCann, John M., "Communicating Energy Conservation Information to Consumers: A Field Experiment," pp. 432–36; Russo, J. Edward, "A Proposal to Increase Energy Conservation Through Provision of Consumer and Cost Information to Consumers," pp. 437–42. Both in *1977 Educators' Proceedings.* American Marketing Association.

43. Reizenstein, Richard C., and Barnaby, David J., "The Consumer and the Energy Shortage: A Post-Embargo Assessment," pp. 308–14; Milstein, Jeffrey S., "Attitudes, Knowledge and Behavior of American Consumers Regarding Energy Conservation with Some Implications for Governmental Action," pp. 315–21. Both in *Advances in Consumer Research;* Volume 4, Association for Consumer Research, 1977.

44. Milstein, Jeffrey S., "Energy Conservation and Travel Behavior," pp. 422–25; Cunningham, William H., and Joseph, Brondel, "Energy Conservation: Price Increases and Payback Periods," pp. 201–05. Both in *Advances in Consumer Research.* Volume 5, 1978.

45. Rothe, James T.; Oberg, Kenneth H., and Kerin, Roger A. "Synchromarketing of Electrical Energy: Consumer Receptivity and Marketing Tasks." *Proceedings.*pp. 238–40. American Institute for Decision Sciences: 8th Annual Conference, 1976.

46. Tankersley, Clint B. "Concern Over the Energy Crisis: Some Social Psychological Correlates." *Proceedings.* American Institute for Decision Sciences: 9th Annual Conference, 1977.

47. Montgomery, David B., and Leonard-Barton, Dorothy. "Toward Strategies for Marketing Home Energy Conservation." Stanford University, Graduate School of Business: Research Paper No. 372, June 1977.

48. Phillips, Nicolas, and Nelson, Elizabeth. "Energy Savings in Private Households—An Integrated Research Programme." *Journal of the Market Research Society* 18 (October 1976): 180–200.

49. Schneider, Lewis M. *Marketing Urban Mass Transit—A Comparative Study of Management Strategies.* Boston: Division of Research, Harvard Graduate School of Business Administration, 1965.

50. Lovelock, Christopher H. *Consumer Oriented Approaches to Marketing Urban Transit.* Ph.D. dissertation, Stanford University. Springfield, Virginia: National Technical Information Service, PB 220781, 1973.

51. U.S. Department of Transportation. *National Transit Marketing Conference Proceedings.* Washington, D.C.: Urban Mass Transportation Administration and American Public Transit Association, 1975.

52. U.S. Department of Transportation. *Transit Marketing Management Handbook,* "Marketing Plan," "Pricing," "Organization," "Transit Information Aids" Washington, D.C.: Office of Transit Management, Urban Mass Transportation Administration, 1976, 1977.

53. U.S. Department of Transportation. *The Transit Marketing Project: Summary of Consumer Research, Baltimore MTA and Nashville MTA.* Washington, D.C.: Office of Transit Management, Urban Mass Transportation Administration, June 1976.

54. Gilbert, Gorman, and Foerster, James. "The Importance of Attitudes in the Decision to Use Mass Transit." *Transportation* 6 (December 1977): 321–32.

55. Lovelock, Christopher H. "A Market Segmentation Approach to Transit Planning, Modeling and Management." *Proceedings.* The Transportation Research Forum: 16th Annual Meeting, 1975.

56. Kotler, Philip, and Dubois, Bernard. "Education Problems and Marketing," pp. 186–206. In *Marketing Analysis for Social Problems,* edited by Jagdish Sheth and Peter L. Wright. Urbana, IL: University of Illinois, 1974.

57. College Entrance Examination Board. *A Role for Marketing in College Admissions.* Princeton, NJ: 1976.

58. Kotler, Philip. "Applying Marketing Theory to College Admissions," pp. 54–72. In College Entrance Examination Board. *A Role for Marketing in College Admissions.* Princeton, NJ: 1976.

59. Lovelock, Christopher H. "Researching and Modeling Consumer Choice Behavior in Urban Transportation." In *Advances in Consumer Research,* Volume 2, edited by M. J. Schlinger. Association for Consumer Research, 1975.

60. Lovelock, Christopher H., "Department of the Treasury: Reissue of the $2 Bill." Boston: Intercollegiate Case Clearing House. 1975.

61. Zaltman, Gerald, and Jacobs, Pol. "Social Marketing and a Consumer-Based Theory of Marketing." In *Consumer and Industrial Buying Behavior,* pp. 399–408. Edited by Arch G. Woodside, Jagdish N. Sheth, and Peter D. Bennett. New York: North Holland, 1977.

62. Montgomery, David B. and Weinberg, Charles B. "Modeling Marketing Phenomena: A Managerial Perspective." *Journal of Contemporary Business,* Autumn 1973, pp. 17–43.

5

An International Perspective on Public Sector Marketing

Christopher H. Lovelock

As the use of marketing matures in the public sector, it makes increasing sense for managers of public agencies to study the approaches used by comparable organizations in other jurisdictions and to seek out answers to common problems. This chapter will focus on comparing analyses of marketing by three kinds of national public agencies—postal operations, passenger rail services, and energy conservation programs—thus raising the question, How comparable are similar agencies in other countries? To provide insights, programs in three countries—Canada, the United Kingdom, and the United States—will be analyzed and compared.

Britain, Canada, and the United States are all advanced Western industrial democracies. Nevertheless, significant differences in geography, population, economy, and governmental structure (see Exhibit 1) have led to differences in the political values, institutions, and traditions of each country. Any discussion of the marketing efforts of their post offices, passenger rail corporations, and energy departments must recognize the extent to which the factors discussed above shape the nature of the marketing task and either constrain or facilitate it.

POSTAL SERVICES

Postal service was among the first organized activities of government. It was essential to the effective management of

Christopher H. Lovelock is Asociate Professor of Business Administration, Harvard University.

Information for this chapter was obtained, in part, from interviews with managers in each of the nine organizations studied and from a wide range of public documents that they made available. The author is most grateful for this cooperation but assumes responsibility for the views expressed and conclusions reached. This paper has also benefited from helpful comments on earlier drafts by Professors Charles B. Weinberg of the University of British Columbia and Michael P. Mokwa of Arizona State University.

military campaigns and to continued contact with distantly located administrative centers. Only later did the mails assume major importance for commercial activity and personal correspondence. As a result, postal services in most developed countries are enveloped in a sense of tradition that influences management today.

The past decade has seen important changes in the management of postal services in all three countries. In 1969, the British Post Office became the first postal service to exchange its government department status for that of an independent public corporation, a change that was also proposed in the United States and Canada. The United States went part way in 1971, replacing the Post Office Department by the United States Postal Service, an independent agency of the executive branch of the federal government. Canada Post remains a government department at the time of this writing [but was transformed into an independent Crown Corporation in 1981]. Exhibit 2 summarizes key information concerning the three agencies.

Prior to the 1970s, marketing was virtually unheard of as a management function in postal services. Since then, the U.S., British, and Canadian postal services have made significant progress in some areas. Marketing organizations have been established, new services (products) have been

EXHIBIT 1
Comparative Background Information

Feature	United States	United Kingdom	Canada
Population in early 1979 (millions)	217	56	23
Land area (thousands of square miles)	3,615	94	3,852
Average population density (per square mile)	60	594	6
Percent of population in urban areas	74	78	76
GNP in 1978 (billions of U.S. dollars)	1,799	217	185
GNP per capita (U.S. dollars)	8,329	3,875	8,043
Government structure	Federal	Central	Federal
Government form	President and Congress	Parliament	Parliament

Source: Compiled by the author from government statistics and other sources.

developed and introduced based on analysis of customer needs, and programs for the various products have increasingly been subject to the rigor and discipline of formal marketing plans. But progress has been uneven, and the scope of marketing-related activities has not always extended across the full range of the marketing mix—product development, pricing, distribution systems, and communication efforts—as a look at each of these will show.

The Postal Product Line. The U.S. Postal Service is the largest of the three postal operations, reflecting not only the size of the U.S. population but also a higher number of items mailed annually per capita. This is accounted for in part by the widespread use of direct mail advertising in the United States. In recent years, Britain and Canada have aggressively sought to encourage development of the direct mail advertising industry as a means of building mail volume.

Britain's Post Office differs from its U.S. and Canadian counterparts in that it is responsible for providing a much more extensive range of services. In addition to its postal business, the Post Office also runs a large banking operation, the National Girobank, plus the nation's telecommunications services (although responsibility for these is soon to be transferred to a new public corporation). Even within the postal sphere, however, the Post Office offers a broader product line that USPS or Canada Post does. It has been aggressive in developing new types of services tailored to the needs of specific market segments (usually corporate mailers). These tend to be high-value-added products, such as different types of express package delivery services. Some of these are national in scope; others are limited to specific geographic areas.

The U.S. Postal Service and Canada Post have been slower to innovate. Nevertheless, both have introduced several new services. While most have been generated internally or developed in response to customer requests, some refinements have resulted from studying services developed elsewhere. For instance, USPS's Express Mail copied certain forms, policies, and procedures from Data Post, an express delivery service in Britain. But unlike Data Post, which is restricted to contracts with large mailers, Express Mail is available at selected major post offices to all mailers. The British Post Office has been monitoring the USPS experience and is now thinking of introducing an over-the-counter variant of Data Post.

Another successful USPS service, undertaken jointly with Western Union, has been Mailgram, whereby WU accepts and transmits a message electronically and USPS delivers a hard copy to the addressee. A new effort by the Postal Service to develop an electronic mail service, called E-COM, is being opposed vigorously by other communications companies but is expected to win limited government approval.

The scope of services offered by Canada Post is similar to that of USPS. A number of new products have been developed in recent years, including Telepost (a Canadian derivative of Mailgram) and various types of package services directed at the needs of large mailers. However, the agency's unsettled labor relations, which some observers blame on its government department status, have done serious damage to the quality of the postal product. This has made it hard for Canada Post to compete in the parcels and packages business, where it has no monopoly protection.

On the other hand, all three postal services have enjoyed considerable success expanding their philatelic services. These have proved popular with collectors and offer a high contribution.

Pricing Policy. First class mail rates in Britain are significantly higher than those in the United States or Canada, despite the lower level of personal incomes. Postal pricing policies in Britain are noteworthy on several counts. While subject to government review, pricing decisions are the responsibility of Marketing Department, which recognizes these decisions as a key element of marketing strategy. The Post Office is required by the government to set overall prices at levels that will ensure that total postal income meets total expenditure plus a target return of 2 percent on turnover. But the general approach adopted is to gear prices to individual services so that, while all services meet at least their direct costs, the contribution they make individually to overhead and profits varies in accordance with marketing and other considerations.

As a public corporation, the Post Office has far more control over its pricing decisions than does Canada Post or USPS. The flexibility that it enjoys has allowed it to relate prices to the realities of the market place and to compete vigorously for contract business from large corporate mailers. Other features of interest include the availability of both first and second class letter mail options (offering next working day and fourth working day delivery respectively) and the absence of discounts for nonprofit organizations.

At Canada Post, as in Britain, pricing studies and recommendations are the responsibility of the Marketing Unit. But the agency's status as a government department requires that the price be the same to all Canadians within each service category, despite very real differences in the cost of serving different markets. Rate changes for first and second class mail must be approved by Parliament.

At USPS, pricing decisions are the responsibility of the Finance Department, not Marketing, and are thus closely tied to cost considerations rather than marketing ones. USPS has been hampered in its ability to change prices because any such move must be approved by the Postal Rate Commission, an independent regulatory agency. When USPS wishes to change its rates it must submit an application to the PRC, which then hears testimony from interested parties, including both competitors and mail users. Rate hearings, from the date of first filing to a final decision, typically take ten months—a long time horizon for management, particularly in an era of rapid inflation. USPS is prohibited from cross-subsidizing services from one class of mail to another (although it may do so within a class). Hearings before the PRC have for the most part attempted to determine whether USPS has properly

EXHIBIT 2
Postal Service: Comparative Statistics

Item	U.S. Postal Service[a]	British Post Office[b]	Canada Post[c]
Base price of first-class letter (U.S. cents), January 1, 1980	15.0	20.0 (1st class) 16.0 (2nd class)	15.3
Number of items mailed annually (millions)	99,829	10,137	6,056
Items mailed annually per capita	460	181	275
Total employees	663,067	172,122	53,053
Number of items mailed per employee (thousands)	150,556	58,894	114,150
Total post offices and sub-offices	39,733	22,793	8,230
Post offices per 100,000 persons	18	41	36
Corporate structure	Independent government agency	Public corporation	Government department
Year of separation from government	1971	1969	N.A.
Mail service profit (loss) (millions of U.S. dollars)	1,423[d]	66	(437)
Mail service operating expenses (millions of U.S. dollars)	17,529	2,893	1,435
Paid media advertising expenditures (millions of U.S. dollars)	10.4	10.4	3.3
Other businesses operated by the agency	Money orders, retail service on passports, and U.S. Savings Bonds	Telecommunications, data processing, banking (GIRO), retailing of many government services, including National Savings	Money orders

[a]Year ending September 30,1979.
[b]Year ending March 31, 1979 (statistics are for postal business only).
[c]Year ending March 31, 1979.

[d]Operating revenues less operating expenses (excludes government-operating appropriations to compensate USPS for losses on specific low-priced services).

Note: All figures have been converted to U.S. dollars at the following rates: £1 = $2.00, $1 Cdn = $0.90.
Source: 1979 annual reports of each agency and personal communications.

attributed institutional costs among the different classes of mail. United Parcel Service, a major competitor, has been active in arguing that fourth class parcel mail should be assigned a higher share of institutional costs, thus driving up parcel mail prices and providing United Parcel Service with a price umbrella.

USPS offers substantially reduced bulk rates to non-profit organizations, a service for which it receives a government subsidy. The two-cents-per-item discount offered to large mailers as an inducement to presort their first class mail is a discount of a different nature. This is a relatively recent innovation, designed to reduce postal processing costs. It has been widely promoted through advertising and personal selling, and USPS claims it has been fairly successful.

Distribution. Britain and Canada have twice as many retail post offices per head of population as does the United States. In Britain, postal outlets serve as a virtual supermarket for government services. Counter clerks in large offices deal with more than 110 different kinds of transactions. In addition to postal business, they also handle such services as sale of licenses for vehicles, dogs, and other purposes; payment of pensions and family income supplements; provision of Girobank and National Savings Bank services; and sale of savings certificates and government securities. Nonpostal services are handled on a contractual basis for both central and local government departments; the Post Office receives a flat 4 percent commission, and such sales now account for some 60 percent of over-the-counter volume. New services and contracts are being actively sought, and post offices in certain large cities recently began selling transit passes. In 1979, the Post Office began an experiment whereby foreign exchange services were introduced in 14 large post offices. By contrast, the range of nonpostal services offered by U.S. and Canadian postal outlets is quite limited.

Both Britain and Canada have renovated numerous retail post offices with a view to providing a more attractive environment for customers and employees. USPS has started a trial refurbishment program, but most U.S. post offices, while sometimes impressive externally, remain drab and unattractive inside. Although USPS has placed a number of automatic post offices in freestanding locations such as shopping center parking lots, operating problems with the automatic vending machinery have discouraged expansion of this program.

In the United States, attempts to save money by closing rural post offices have, in general, been blocked by Congress. This raises the question of whether more extensive use, on the British model, could be made of retail post offices in the United States and Canada. But the USPS and Canada Post product lines are limited to mail and related services; their only nonmail service is postal money orders, and sales of these are declining steadily. Federal-citizen contacts for other services are relatively few. Whether state or provincial and local governments could sufficiently overcome their suspicions of federal government operations to let post office outlets distribute some of their services is an open question.

Communication Efforts. Given the size of each of the three agencies and the fact that they attempt to serve virtually the entire populations of their respective countries, the paid media advertising budgets employed by each are exceedingly modest. The ratio of advertising expenditures to operating revenues amounts to 0.06 percent for USPS, 0.36 percent for the British Post Officed, and 0.25 percent for Canada Post. A distinctive feature of Canadian communication efforts is that all messages must be prepared in both official languages, English and French.

USPS is able to take advantage of public service announcements for messages of a noncompetitive nature, such as encouraging mailers to mail early in the day or use zip codes. Prior to postal reorganization, this was the only type of advertising used. The use of paid media advertising by USPS is a controversial issue. Some congressmen apparently view such expenditures as an inappropriate use of "postal ratepayers' dollars."

All three agencies have developed sales forces to promote the use of postal services among corporate and institutional mailers, but the sales department at USPS headquarters does not have the line relationship to customer service representatives in the field that is enjoyed by their British and Canadian counterparts. The net result at USPS is relatively more emphasis on reactive customer service efforts as opposed to proactive new business development.

Appraisal. Britain's Post Office clearly handles a much broader range of responsibilities than does USPS or Canada Post. The Post Office is also noteworthy because it has made a profit on its postal business each year since 1976–77. Unlike USPS and Canada Post, it receives no government subsidies. High postal charges and a small, densely populated country are two factors in Britain's favor. On the other hand, mail volumes per capita and labor productivity are relatively low.

Applying the tools of marketing analysis and planning leads an organization to focus on the needs of its largest and potentially most profitable customers. But doing so may generate criticism for a public agency. For instance, in Britain a government review committee concluded that postal marketing efforts focused too closely on "very large customers" and argued that more attention needed to be devoted to smaller users and the general public (Carter 1977). Recent actions by the Post Office have displayed more concern for customer relations, including an informative corporate advertising campaign directed at the general public in 1978–79.

In all three countries, the postal service and the local post office are probably the most visible manifestation of the federal or central government in the community. Good service is taken for granted, but failures in the service are

EXHIBIT 3
Passenger Rail Services

Item	Amtrak (U.S.)	British Rail	VIA Rail Canada
Created	1971	1947	1977[a]
Number of premerger railroads	13	4	2
Passenger route mileage	26,000	8,497	15,000
Percent on-time performance[b]	62	91	N.A.
Total journeys made per year (millions)	19	724	6
Total passenger miles per year (millions)	4,029	19,100	1,700
Average journey length (miles)	212	26	310
Average number of journeys annually per capita	0.1	12.9	0.22
Average passenger miles annually per capita	19	341	68
Total passenger revenues (millions of U.S. dollars)	313	1,544	120
Average revenue per passenger mile (U.S. cents)	7.8	8.1	7.1
Annual government contract payment for pasenger services (millions of U.S. dollars)	0	955	239
Operating surplus (deficit) after contract payments (millions of U.S. dollars)	(582)	83[c]	N.A.
Paid advertising expenditures in 1979 (millions of U.S. dollars)	8.5	15	2.3
Other activities	Mail, package express	Freight, ferries, hovercraft, hotels, property engineering, consulting, advertising	None

[a]Originally formed as a subsidiary of the Canadian National Railway in 1977, VIA became a Crown Corporation in 1978. VIA figures exclude commuters.
[b]Defined by British Rail as not more than five minutes late; defined by ICC (for Amtrak) as within five minutes of schedule for each 100 miles traveled, subject to a maximum of 30 minutes for routes exceeding 600 miles.
[c]Includes freight business.

Source: Annual reports of each agency (FY 1978 for Amtrak and VIA, FY 1979 for British Rail) and personal communications.

readily seized upon as evidence of poor management and a bad product. A British study revealed the atmosphere in which postal executives work when it commented, "The Post Office record . . . deserves reponsible criticism, but not the exercise of our national habit of condemning all things British as though they were the worst in the world" (Carter 1977).

PASSENGER RAIL SERVICES

Like postal service, passenger rail service is sold to customers at a price. And like the mails, passenger rail travel is also shrouded in tradition and nostalgia. But the resemblance ends there. Governmental involvement in running and administering the mails goes back for centuries, along with the tradition of a jealously guarded letter mail monopoly. By contrast, passenger rail travel is a relative newcomer to the public sector, as a result of the de jure or de facto nationalization of privately owned services operated by independent railroad companies.

Exhibit 3 summarizes information concerning passenger rail services in the United States, Britain, and Canada. The combination of historical development patterns, government policies, and geographic dispersion of major population centers in the three countries has produced three very different rail passenger services. It should be noted that 55 percent of British Rail's annual passenger mileage is accounted for by commuter services, which tends to make the average trip distance appear relatively short as well as inflate the average number of journeys made per capita.

The Three Corporations. Great Britain's four private railway companies emerged from World War II in bad condition and were nationalized in 1947. The British Railways Board (BRB) is a holding company for a variety of different businesses and divisions. It includes the passenger and freight rail services of British Rail, a container-carrying company (Freightliner, Ltd), a shipping line (Sealink UK Ltd.), eleven harbors, British Rail Hovercraft Ltd., 29 major hotels, a station and on-train catering operation (Travellers-Fare), a locomotive and rolling stock construction company, an international consulting firm (Transmark), and a North American passenger sales operation (BritRail Travel International, Inc.). Rail passenger revenues, including contractual payments by government, accounted for approximately half the BRB's consolidated income of $5 billion in 1978–79.

By contrast, the National Railroad Passenger Corporation (better known by its trade name, Amtrak) and VIA

Rail Canada, Inc. (a name carefully chosen to be bilingual) are much younger and smaller organizations. Amtrak was formed in 1971 as a semi-public corporation to take over the intercity passenger rail services previously operated by 13 private railroad companies. (Other railroads have since transferred their passenger services to Amtrak). VIA became an independent Crown Corporation in 1978, charged with the responsibility of taking over intercity passenger rail services previously operated by the privately owned Canadian Pacific Railway (CP Rail) and the government-owned Canadian National Railway (CN Rail).

The Rail Product. British Rail, unlike Amtrak and VIA, has responsibility for almost all the variables that create or interfere with the passenger rail trip product. It owns the track in addition to the stations and the rolling stock; it is responsible for freight as well as passenger operations; and virtually all personnel whose behavior might have even a remote bearing on passenger service performance—from freight train crews to security officers—are its own employees. Amtrak and VIA lack this degree of control. Although Amtrak has acquired and is modernizing track in the Northeast Corridor (Boston-New York-Washington), elsewhere its trains operate over often poor-quality track owned by the railroads and may be subject to freight train interference. VIA runs over CN and CP tracks that are in fairly good condition and relies on these companies' operating personnel to run the trains.

British Rail operates three types of services—a national network of fast "Intercity" trains, commuter services into London and a few other major cities, and slower feeder and connector services. BR's commuter services are politically sensitive and of less consistent quality than the Intercity services; they tend to give the entire system a more negative image than it deserves. Amtrak and VIA have minimal involvement in short-distance commuter services and carry the bulk of their passengers on corridor services for distances of 100–500 miles. They also provide once-daily services over routes up to 3,000 miles long, during which trips most of the passenger complement turns over several times, although tourists may travel the entire distance as a form of scenic "land cruise."

Since the mid-1960s, British Rail has made major progress in upgrading its Intercity product. Mainline electrification and introduction of 125 mph diesel trains have greatly increased average train speeds and helped win an increased market share for rail, despite construction of parallel motorways (Keen 1979). On some routes, rail's market share exceeds 70 percent, but speed is not the only product attribute on which BR management has been working. The chairman, Sir Peter Parker, believes that "marketing a railway requires meticulous attention to detail . . . everything from the smile on the guard's [brakeman's] face to the cleanliness of the lavatories goes to make up the sales package" (Lester 1978). Parker is working to instill a

marketing consciousness throughout the system and formally credits marketing for the system's success in boosting passenger traffic (British Railways Board 1979).

Amtrak and VIA similarly are conscious of the need for internal marketing and are working toward this end, but they have somewhat less control at present. They are also working to upgrade their equipment and (in Amtrak's case) some of the roadbed.

When Amtrak first initiated service, it had minimal control over the equipment; so it focused attention on two product-related variables that it could control—cleanliness and on-board amenities, notably meal services. All three railways perceive the importance of meals as an adjunct to enjoyable rail travel and subsidize meal prices to stimulate ticket purchase.

Distribution. British Rail's route structure is dense, and there has been little change in the BR network since the early 1960s. VIA is in a period of consolidation as it seeks to rationalize the former CP and CN passenger services, several of which parallel each other across the lengthy transcontinental routes, although serving different cities en route. Amtrak inherited a sharply pruned passenger route system in 1971 and subsequently expanded it at Congressional urging. Critics charge that certain routes reflect political rather than market priorities; certainly some governors and congressmen have fought vigorously to retain or reintroduce rail service in their states.

In early 1979, the government proposed a 43 percent cut in the size of the Amtrak route network to eliminate many lightly used services. But in mid-year, when fuel shortages developed and the price of gasoline rose sharply, Amtrak enjoyed a big increase in patronage. The cuts actually made in fall 1979 were limited to about 20 percent—mostly on routes which Amtrak may not have been sorry to lose because of limited market potential and often poor-quality track.

Pricing. When Amtrak initiated service in 1971, it immediately revamped the inflexible pricing structure it had inherited and cut many fares. VIA's early moves centered on development of a new "Fare for All Plan," including many discount prices to replace the previous CN and CP fares. As these actions prove, passenger rail services freed of the regulation imposed on their private predecessors have more control over the pricing element of the marketing mix than over either product or distribution and can thus act faster in making changes (although in the case of the VIA all pricing changes require the approval of the Ministry of Transport, which is particularly concerned with the impact of rail pricing on bus competition).

Traditionally, the world's railways have adopted a conservative approach to pricing, computing standard rates according to distance traveled, with premiums for first class service and discounts for certain categories of passengers (principally children). Until 1968, British Rail had such a system accompanied by an inconsistent jumble of promotional fares that were hard to administer. That year the old system was abolished and replaced by a new approach that related base fares on each route to quality of product, strength of market demand, and nature of competitive activity (Ford 1977). A series of four different structures tailored to the demand curves of different market segments was built around these base rates. The intention was to discourage trading down by those able to pay the relatively costly standard fares, yet to maximize travel, especially during low-demand periods of the day or week, among more price-sensitive groups. A relatively recent pricing innovation at British Rail is the promotion of Railcards, available to senior citizens and students for $14 per year*; these entitle the owner to travel anywhere on the system for half the regular fare. Another version, the Family Railcard, costs $20, and requires one adult to pay the standard fare while allowing a second adult and up to four children to travel any distance for a flat fare of $1 each—a clear attempt to appeal to families who might otherwise travel by car. Subsequent BR research indicates a substantial increase in revenues as well as in the number of journeys made. It has also found that Railcards, especially the senior citizen's version, are often given as presents.

VIA's new pricing structure is also highly segmented, allowing discounts for off-season trips and travel by groups, elderly people, and children. All three rail services now accept credit cards for payment; although common practice in North America, this is an innovation at British Rail. Each of the three also offers system-wide passes, although BR only sells these overseas. BR also sells regional passes, which are available to domestic customers.

Advertising and Promotion.

British Rail's advertising budget in 1978–79 was about $15 million, and it has been running three separate campaigns—one to promote its Intercity services, a second to reach commuters and other rail users in London and Southeast England, and a third targeted at the general public and designed to influence opinion in favor of the railway system. A promotion with Kellogg's (allowing sharply discounted fares for accompanied children in return for cereal box tops) proved highly successful in 1977 and was copied by Amtrak the following year. The Amtrak promotion was promptly criticized by consumer groups for including sugar-coated cereals! BR has since moved on to joint promotion with soap powder manufacturers.

Annual advertising expenditures at Amtrak in 1979 were reduced by Congress from $10 million to about $5.8 million. Amtrak's marketing management sees advertising expenditures as highly cost-effective and would like to spend significantly more, having found that rail travel demand is highly responsive to advertising. This is not sur-

prising, given its very low market share and high potential for trial. But, in annual budget reviews, Congress has thus far limited Amtrak's advertising expenditures. In 1978–79, advertising used the slogan "We've been working on the Railroad" to dramatize the corporation's efforts to improve service. These ads featured Amtrak personnel who had been selected for outstanding performance, thus seeking to boost employee morale, too. With Amtrak's reservation lines swamped in the aftermath of the gasoline shortages of mid-1979, print advertising switched to factual information on services, fares, and travel times under the headline "These Days It's Easier to Ride Us Than to Reach Us."

VIA moved quickly after its formation to develop an aggressive advertising and promotional campaign ("Serious Marketing Gets VIA on Tracks" 1979). In addition to introducing the new corporation, advertising has successfully promoted connecting services and package tours by rail. The 1979 advertising budget was about $2.3 million. VIA is also developing a new reservations system called RESERVIA. In 1981, this system will be connected with Air Canada's RESERVEC II, making Canada the first country in the world with a nationwide intermodal reservations capability. Eventually it may be possible to use any RESERVIA terminal to make reservations for rail, air, rent-a-car, hotel, and (it is hoped) major ferry services.

Appraisal.

British Rail, Amtrak, and VIA are very different organizations in many respects. BR is a mature public corporation, operating a wide array of services in addition to intercity passenger rail transportation. It enjoys a contractual relationship with the government rather than begging for subsidies to cover its deficits. Amtrak, although displaying greater marketing expertise (which it has had to develop from scratch) is bedeviled by a poor product which it does not fully control. Its future—even the size of its advertising budget—is largely in the hands of politicians, many of whom remain deeply distrustful of the public corporation concept. VIA has some similarities to Amtrak but has learned from the latter's misfortunes (Roberts 1979). Like BR, it has a contractual relationship with government. It has inherited a better product from CN and CP than Amtrak did from most U.S. railroads and has the advantage of greater ridership; on a per capita basis, two and a half times more people in Canada ride trains than in the United States. Finally, VIA's marketing management team was built on the solid foundation of the passenger staff of CN Rail, which was probably the most marketing-oriented of all North American railroads during the 1960s and early 1970s.

ENERGY CONSERVATION

Unlike postal and rail services, energy conservation is a more abstract "product," and a difficult one to market. Individuals may perceive the costs of practicing conserving behavior as outweighing the resulting personal benefits. Yet

*Prices converted from pounds to dollars at current exchange rates.

the economic and political benefits of energy conservation for the larger society grow ever more apparent.

Yergin (1979) identifies three types of conservation. First is out-and-out *curtailment,* when supplies are interrupted and energy saving is forced upon people. Second is *overhaul,* representing truly dramatic changes in the way people live and work. The third is *adjustment,* entailing changes both in capital stock, such as purchase of home insulation and use of more energy-efficient appliances, and also in behavior, such as setting thermostats at more efficient levels, driving more slowly, and turning off unnecessary lights.

It is in this third category of conservation that marketing strategies by government agencies offer major leverage. As in postal marketing, energy conservation programs must be directed at almost the entire population, although some segments are more important than others. The marketing tools available to government agencies are basically *communication* (urging people to save energy and providing specific information and advice on how to do so) and *pricing* (using the mechanism of increased taxes to raise energy prices and thus discourage demand and offering economic incentives such as grants and tax legislation to encourage energy-saving capital investments).

Nonmarketing tools include *legislation* to change (1) product standards (ranging from buildings to autos to appliances) to make them more energy efficient; and (2) behavior (such as reducing highway speed limits and requiring operators of public buildings to adjust their thermostats). Even here, effective communications and financial penalties for noncompliance (a form of pricing) may be necessary program ingredients.

Before the crisis resulting from the Arab oil embargo of 1973–74, there had been limited recognition of the need for energy conservation; only minimal action had been undertaken at a national level in any of the three countries. The embargo and the subsequent quadrupling of oil prices by oil-exporting nations provided a major stimulus to governmental efforts to encourage conservation. But the actions taken in the three countries varied significantly. We'll look at each country seprately and then offer a brief comparative appraisal of conservation marketing efforts.

United Kingdom. The British government responded quickly to the energy crisis of 1973–74. It set up a Department of Energy in 1974 and instituted a 12-point energy conservation program the same year. Directed at both individual and industrial users, it included incentives, legal compulsion, economic pricing of energy, and a major communications campaign.

The communications campaign, firmly based on consumer research findings, began in January 1975 and has continued in modified form in subsequent years. Built around the slogan, "Save It," the program seeks to secure both immediate reductions in energy use and the longer-term changes in public attitudes and habits needed to secure continuing economies. The Department of Energy works closely with the Central Office of Information, a government agency that plays a coordinating role for all government advertising and publicity in Britain. The budget for 1978–79 was approximately $4.5 million.

Paid media advertising efforts have been supplemented by exhibitions, syndicated articles, booklets, and instructional films made available free by industry. There have also been publicity campaigns by the nationalized coal, gas, and electricity authorities and by the tightly regulated oil industry. Prices of all energy sources have been raised sharply. The increase in gasoline prices reflects not only rising costs but also sharp increases in excise taxes to discourage consumption.

The U.K. Department of Energy has worked closely with other government departments, the fuel supply industry, and manufacturers and distributors of insulation materials to ensure a coordinated policy and a coherent set of messages. In addition to consumer research, retail audits have been used to monitor movements of insulating materials through retail outlets as a measure of the effectiveness of communications efforts (Phillips and Nelson 1976).

As Britain moves toward complete energy self-sufficiency, reflecting its major coal deposits and North Sea oil and gas, the conservation marketing task is becoming harder. Communications messages now focus on the financial costs of energy waste, with advertising suggesting that waste is "disgusting" and conservation saves money. The slogan has been adapted to "Don't Waste It—Save It!"

Current policy emphasizes provision of information and promotion of specific advisory services and incentives. For instance, industrial advertising now promotes the availability of small government grants ($150) toward the cost of hiring energy consultants from an approved list to undertake one-day audits of plants and offices and identify opportunities for energy savings. The Department of Energy offers a quick, free advice service by telephone on any energy-related problem. Finally, the Department of Industry provides grants for energy-saving modernization programs in company plants.

Canada. Although Canada was not seriously affected by the 1973–74 oil embargo, the government moved promptly to reduce energy waste. Federal responsibility for energy conservation efforts has rested with the Conservation and Renewable Energy Branch of Energy, Mines, and Resources Canada.

In recent years, federal communication efforts have been budgeted at around $2.7 million (U.S.) annually. Virtually every element in the marketing communication mix has been used, including paid media advertising, publications, public relations, and various other promotional efforts involving third parties. The program is reviewed annually, with each year's campaign seeking to build on the base created by those of previous years (Hutton 1979).

As in the United Kingdom, efforts are directed at both industrial and domestic users, with major emphasis on self-help and practical advice. In an effort to prevent Canadians from developing the negative perceptions of energy conservation encountered among many Americans, who often view it as threatening to their comfort, independence, and economic security, communications attempt to create a positive image. The slogan, initially, "If You're Not Part of the Solution, You're Part of the Problem," has shifted to "Energy Conservation—Be Part of the Solution."

Innovative features of the Canadian program include the Energy Bus Program, which makes on-site energy audits for businesses, and an extremely popular 30-minute TV film, "The Hottest Show on Earth." This film uses a mixture of annimation, comedy, drama, and popular science to dramatize the importance of a potentially boring subject—home insulation—and to motivate people to take action on installing or reinstalling insulation. The government offers to pay the first $450 (U.S.) of insulation costs.

Publication of a series of short books on conservation is another Canadian innovation. One of these is "The Car Mileage Book," a free 106-page pocket book on how to buy, drive, and maintain a car to save energy and money. Within nine months of its first publication in September 1977, more than 2.4 million had been distributed through the mails, Gulf service stations, and provincial motor license bureaus. Two other major oil companies promoted availability of the book through bill stuffers to all credit card holders.

A distinctive characteristic of Canada's information efforts is their bilingual quality. All advertising is produced separately in both English and French, but one message is not necessarily a direct translation of the other. Consumer research by the Conservation Branch has shown that English-speaking Canadians respond better to rational appeals, whereas French-Canadians are more likely to respond to a relatively more emotional appeal. The key French slogan can be translated as "Energy Conservation—Let's All Do Our Part." A program known as "Ener$ave" in English becomes "Ener$age," literally "Energy-Wise" in French.

Reflecting the federal-provincial division of responsibilities, the Conservation Branch works closely with provincial energy departments and commissions. It delegates certain functions, such as operation of the Energy Buses, to the provinces. In general, the federal and provincial agencies seem to have succeeded in working together toward a common goal. There is also close coordination between the branch and selected citizen groups in disseminating communications and implementing conservation programs.

United States. In the view of some observers, the oil shortage of the winter of 1973–74 was seen by many Americans as *the* energy crisis, something that had happened rather than a portent of things to come. Politics delayed the formation of a cabinet-level Department of Energy (DOE) in the Federal Government until 1977. Prior to that time, responsi-

bility for conservation efforts was spread across many different offices. An agency known as the Federal Energy Administration (FEA) employed several people with titles such as "energy conservation marketing specialist," but political pressures confined its consumer marketing efforts to public service advertising involving such vague messages as "Don't Be Fuelish."

On the other hand, FEA was quick to initiate consumer research studies. A series of regularly conducted national surveys provided important insights into how American consumers felt about energy conservation, the extent to which they practiced it, and the reasons why they resisted it (Milstein 1977). But the agency showed little inclination to use these research findings to mount a forceful communication campaign.

Unfortunately, the situation did not improve significantly with the formation of the U.S. Department of Energy (which absorbed most of the FEA staff). Poor organization compounded by constant reorganization and jealously guarded empires within the federal bureaucracy led to a lack of coordination and clear direction. Conservation was seen as threatening by many regional interests, especially energy-rich states or those which felt economically and politically threatened by federally imposed changes. This situation served to intensify lobbying efforts to emasculate the DOE, and made it almost impossible for the department to develop and implement bold conservation programs.

Finally, in 1978, the Department's Consumer Motivation Branch (CBM) initiated a program with well-defined strategy and objectives. Consumer research played an integral part of both program formulation and evaluation. As reported by Hutton (1979):

> The overall objective of the CMB is to encourage private sector groups (e.g., financial institutions, retailers, etc.) to work voluntarily with the DOE to test and evaluate approaches which the private sector can later implement to motivate consumers to become most efficient users of energy. While the ultimate target of CMB activities is the consumer, it is the private sector which is the focus of CMB actions and the mechanism through which objectives will be achieved. (p. 13.)

Efforts by the CMB have centered on regional test marketing of programs to encourage customers to consider the energy costs of major appliances when purchasing them, and cooperative programs have been undertaken with local retailers. During 1979, a $2 million paid-advertising program, dubbed "Project Payback," was tested in six cities.

The Iranian crisis and oil price increases of 1979 gave new impetus to the need for a strong energy conservation program in the United States. Energy prices, especially gasoline, rose sharply but still remained far below those prevailing in most industrialized countries outside North America. Suggestions were made that a 50 cent per gallon tax be imposed to raise gasoline prices and discourage consumption, but the federal government appeared unwilling to adopt such a measure. Meanwhile, incentive programs to encourage conservation remained minimal.

In September 1979, it was reported that the DOE and several congressmen were urging development of a $50–95 million conservation advertising program similar to the Canadian effort. However, this proposal was reportedly stirring opposition within the government "from critics who contend that a costly ad campaign would waste taxpayer money" (Schmitt 1979). Subsequently, the DOE launched a month-long "Low Cost/No Cost" campaign in six New England states, designed to help households reduce home energy consumption by as much as 25 percent. A small booklet, which contained eleven inexpensive recommendations for saving energy in the home, was mailed to all households in the region. The mailing included a free plastic controller to reduce hot water flow from showers. Complementing the mailing was a month-long advertising campaign using TV, radio, and newspapers. The cost of the program, estimated at $3 million, was shared jointly by DOE and the private sector (U.S. Department of Energy, 1979).

Appraisal. The energy departments in Britain and Canada have made major efforts to market both the concept and the practice of energy conservation to their national populations, although it is difficult to assess precisely how much the communication programs have contributed to nationwide energy savings. Implementation strategies and message content in the two countries reflect their differing situations. But, in both cases, an aggressive ongoing program, modified over time in response to consumer research, is now institutionalized.

Energy conservation policy in the United Kingdom has relied to a large extent on the voluntary response of both corporate and domestic consumers to a combination of higher prices, practical advice, information, and exhortation. More recently, investment incentives have been introduced and publicized. The approach has been to persuade people of the *need* to save energy and to demonstrate specifically *how* to do so. Research findings have indicated that people were generally ignorant of such basic approaches as home insulation.

The Canadian strategy has been broadly similar. Its communication program is highly regarded among those responsible for conservation efforts in other countries and has been suggested by some as a model for U.S. efforts.

By contrast, U.S. efforts during the 1970s appear feeble, disorganized, and thwarted by politics. State and local agencies, utilities, and oil companies, have provided advice and exhortation on conservation. But there has been no federal leadership to coordinate these disparate efforts and build a strong, integrated program. Many legislators and federal officials still feel that governments should not spend public money on paid media advertising. As a result, DOE communications efforts have been confined at the national level to bland public service advertisements.

INSIGHTS AND IMPLICATIONS

What can be learned from these comparative profiles? What insights do they provide that might be useful to marketing managers in the public sector or to appointed and elected government officials concerned about obtaining effective performances from government agencies and public corporations? In the balance of this chapter, insights concerning public sector marketing are identified and key implications are discussed.

Marketing Expertise Is Transferable. There are many instances of international exchange of marketing concepts and practices between public agencies. For instance, a British Rail subsidiary, Transmark, has consulted to Amtrak; USPS adapted certain forms and procedures from the British Post Office when developing its Express Mail product; VIA Rail Canada executives monitor passenger rail marketing efforts in other countries and periodically exchange information with their counterparts in other national rail systems; the British Post Office has studied the private sector Bell System's marketing practices in the United States and also monitored marketing developments at USPS; and Britain, Canada, and the United States have shared insights from their energy conservation marketing and research programs at meetings of the 15-nation International Energy Agency. Marketing managers in public agencies have much to learn and little to lose from sharing insights and experiences with their counterparts in other countries. The "not invented here" syndrome should be avoided; there is no shame in borrowing. But it is essential that borrowed concepts be carefully evaluated in the context of the home country's market environment and then suitably adapted. It is also important to recognize that constraints may inhibit management's ability to develop a marketing program for an agency as effective as its foreign counterparts'.

Service Must Be Provided to Uneconomic Segments. Unlike most private firms, public sector marketers cannot ignore small, unprofitable, or geographically dispersed market segments. Thus national passenger rail corporations in all three countries are expected to maintain uneconomic routes for social reasons; and postal agencies must deliver to outlying rural areas and maintain retail post offices in thinly populated locations.

In most instances, it is unrealistic to set such market service requirements and then expect a public agency to operate in the black. However, a sense of market discipline is restored if (as happened with British Rail and VIA Rail Canada) the government enters into an annual contract with the agency to buy those services that are inherently uneconomic and that the agency cannot expect to operate at break-even or better. This provides more explicit focus on certain market segments or particular services in the agency's product line than a policy of subsidizing the agency to the extent of the annual deficit.

Public Agencies May Lack Control Over Their Product.
Many public agencies and corporations are not in full control of their product. Amtrak is still trying to modernize or replace the antiquated fleet of rolling stock it inherited, is still forced to operate over poorly maintained track owned by private railroads, and is subject to frequent interference with its schedules by other companies' freight trains. The implication for management, consumers, and legislators is that one shouldn't expect miracles from marketing. Funds may be needed for long-term capital improvement. It may be years before their benefits become apparent. Other problems requiring time for resolution include organizational restructuring, revisions of labor agreements, and changes in consumer habits and expectations.

Governments May Constrain Pricing Policies.
Governments have often tried to influence or even dictate public agencies' pricing policies (usually downwards) for social, economic, or purely political reasons. In the early 1970s the British government deliberately held down postal rates and rail fares in an attempt to restrain inflation. Eventually it found that financing the huge deficits incurred by these agencies was itself inflationary and allowed prices for these services to rise to more realistic levels. Many policy makers in Canada and the United States have urged that energy prices be raised sharply through the imposition of new federal taxes, as a means of discouraging consumption. But it has not proved politically possible to pass the necessary legislation.

Holding down prices results in a consumer surplus for those market segments that could and would pay more. One alternative is to develop pricing policies that increase revenues from less price-sensitive segments, while keeping prices within affordable bounds for those who are unable or unwilling to pay more. Doing this requires that management have good understanding of the demand curves of different segments. An alternative is to raise prices for all segments and offer direct subsidies to consumers with lower disposable incomes.

Politicians May Object to Paid Media Advertising.
Public agencies in the United States are more likely than those in Canada or the United Kingdom to find elected officials resisting the use of paid media advertising. The U.S. Department of Energy has been obliged to limit most of its communication efforts to public service announcements (PSAs) and public relations. Neither of these are as effective as paid media advertising because the marketer lacks control over the format, scheduling, and placement of the messages. The content of PSAs tends to be bland and inoffensive, since hardhitting, controversial messages that might offend another advertiser (or an editor's political sensibilities) are unlikely to be broadcast or published.

Moreover, the marketer has no guarantees that the content of publicity releases in the media will correspond to what was originally desired. Even where paid advertising is allowed, unrealistic constraints may be placed on the advertising budget, as has happened with Amtrak and USPS, thus blunting the effectiveness of communications efforts and making it difficult to use a segmentation strategy.

There is a clear need to educate both public managers and elected or appointed officials about the role that carefully developed and targeted communications campaigns play in helping public services and programs achieve their objectives. The limitations of PSAs and public relations efforts need to be made clear. Finally, it is essential to educate those who control financial appropriations to appreciate the concept of advertising as an investment and to recognize the importance of not usurping managerial prerogatives.

Political Involvement Harms Long-Range Planning.
Political involvement in the affairs of public agencies is often motivated by short-term political expediency, being exercised through such activities as budget reviews, public hearings, and attempts to change or delay the thrust of past legislation. This may make it very difficult for an agency to develop and adhere to a long-term strategic marketing plan.

Public agencies need to sell governments and individual legislators on the importance of developing and implementing long-range plans. In turn, governments must be prepared (1) to grant public agencies greater independence from the political arena, (2) to encourage and support long-range public planning (including marketing plans), and (3) to award multiple-year financing for market research and product development.

Sustained Government Commitment Is Needed.
National social change programs such as energy conservation are likely to entail unpopular departures from current practices. Both individuals and organizations may feel threatened. Popular antipathy, often born of ignorance or lack of perceived benefits, may lead legislative bodies to seek to delay or dilute carefully prepared programs. This may encourage consumers who oppose the changes, and even many fence-sitters, to refuse to comply with the behavior changes that are being advocated.

Public agencies cannot rely on communications alone to bring about voluntary change. Economic incentives, mandatory changes, or both (backed by enforcement in selected instances) may be necessary to obtain the desired cooperation. Sustained government commitment may be essential to maintaining the momentum of such social change programs.

Government Ambivalence May Reflect Political Realities.
Governments are likely to display ambivalence and lack of commitment to public agency programs in situations where the executive branch of government (the president) is in a weak position relative to the legislative branch (Congress);

or where there is a weak coalition or minority government in a parliamentary structure, lacking consensus on a specific policy issue.

Both situations strengthen the hand of dissident groups within the legislative body, thereby encouraging politically expedient compromises, especially where unpopular programs or agencies are concerned. The lack of progress in energy conservation programs in the United States is partly due to such problems. There was a general political consensus in Britain during the minority Labour government of Prime Minister Callaghan that energy conservation was highly desirable. But political expediency may have been behind the decision to return the speed limit to 70 mph. Canada's minority Conservative government fell in December 1979 as a result of a vote on the national budget which included a controversial proposal to increase the gasoline tax by 16 cents. The impact of these problems can be reduced, though not eliminated, by designing mechanisms that provide for less dependence by public agencies on short-term financing decisions by government and frequent use of facilitating legislation.

Public Sector Marketing Is More Complex in Federal Nations. The presence of both federal and state or provincial governments complicates the marketing of public programs by adding an extra layer of government within whose jurisdiction many program components may fall. To implement energy conservation programs may require changes in numerous state or provincial laws and affect local public agencies responsible for communicating changes to residents of the state or province in question.

There is a danger that, without carefully planned cooperation, agencies at the two levels of government may find themselves pulling in contrary directions and confusing their constituent markets in the process. On the other hand, the presence of this intermediary level of government offers federal agencies the opportunity to enhance their own marketing efforts through a policy of careful coordination. This can result in two sets of mutually reinforcing programs being directed at the market—one closely tailored to regional concerns and the other reflecting a national perspective.

U.S. Public Agencies Face More Outside Interference. Efforts by public agencies to develop new markets and introduce new products are more likely to meet resistance from special interest groups in the United States than in Britain or Canada. Amtrak, USPS, and energy conservation programs all have had their marketing efforts sharply criticized by lobbies and private firms, and sometimes they have been eviscerated or blocked altogether at the legislative level.

There is a clear need for U.S. agencies to adopt a more aggressive stance and fight for greater independence. Greater insulation between Congress and these agencies might reduce the incidence of such interference.

CONCLUSIONS

Comparisons of performance between agencies in different countries may be complicated by factors outside management's immediate control. Operating costs of public services reflect variations in population density, geography, climate, and wage rates. Direct price comparisons are distorted by shifting exchange rates and by differences in disposable incomes and relative purchasing power. Other financial comparisons may be obscured by different accounting procedures. Political and regulatory constraints, as well as labor agreements, not only affect costs but may also inhibit short-term efforts to improve the revenue base by adding or modifying services or making selective price changes.

Despite this caveat, an important conclusion remains: significant opportunities do exist for sharing marketing analyses, techniques, and strategies across national boundaries. A cross-national comparison of similar public agencies' performance in different countries may also provide valuable insights into the extent to which political structures and processes facilitate or impede effective marketing efforts by a particular agency.

In the aggregate, U.S. public agencies appear to be relatively less successful marketers than their British and Canadian counterparts. This is ironic given the long tradition of marketing expertise in the U.S. private sector, but it demonstrates that the political traditions and governmental structure of the United States are not particularly conducive to effective public management.

REFERENCES

British Railways Board (1979), *Annual Report and Accounts 1978*, London: British Railways Board.

Canada Post (1978), *Considerations Which Affect the Choice of Organization Structure for the Canada Post Office*, CB 32-34/1978, Hull, Que.: Supply and Services Canada.

——— (1979), *Annual Report 1979*, Hull, Que.: Supply and Services Canada.

Carter, C. F. (1977), *Report of the Post Office Review Committee*, Cmnd. 6850, London: Her Majesty's Stationary Office.

Ford, Roger (1977), "Pricing a Ticket to Ride," *Modern Railways* (August): 302-5.

Hutton, R. Bruce (1979), "Overview of 'The Energy Crisis and Consumer Conservation: Current Research and Action Programs' Workshop," in *Advances in Consumer Research*, ed. W. L. Wilkie, Vol. 6, pp. 12–14. Ann Arbor, Mich.: Association for Consumer Research.

Keen, P. A. (1979), "Inter-City Market Is a Moving Target," *Railway Gazette International* (May): 407–11.

Lester, Tom (1978), "Peter Parker Takes the Strain," *Marketing* (London) (December): 19–20.

Milstein, Jeffrey S. (1977), "Attitudes, Knowledge, and Behavior of American Consumers Regarding Energy Conservation with Some Implications for Governmental Action," in *Advances in Consumer Research*, ed. W. D. Perreault, Vol. 4, Atlanta, Ga.: Association for Consumer Research.

National Railroad Passenger Corporation (1979), *Amtrak 1978 Annual Report*, Washington, D.C.: Amtrak.

Phillips, Nicolas and Elizabeth Nelson (1976), "Energy Savings in Private Households: An Integrated Research Program," *Journal of the Market Research Society* (October): 180–200.

Roberts, Robert (1979), "VIA Gets a Better Start than Amtrak," *Modern Railroad* (October): 72–74.

Schmitt, Richard B. (1979), "An Advertising Blitz Urging Conservation of Energy is Mulled," *Wall Street Journal,* September 14.

"Serious Marketing Gets VIA on Tracks" (1979), *Marketing* (Toronto) (January 1): 4.

United Kingdom, Post Office (1979), *Report and Accounts 1978–79,* London: Her Majesty's Stationary Office.

U.S., Committee on Post Office and Civil Service (1975), *Report on Postal Service Sales of Postal Related Items,* Committee Print No. 93-26, Washington, D.C.: Government Printing Office.

U.S., Congress, House, Permanent Select Committee on Small Business (1974), *The Effects of the Postal Service's Policies on Small Busi-ness,* H. Rep. 93-1468, Washington, D.C.: Government Printing Office.

U.S., Department of Energy (1979), "Low-Cost/No-Cost Program Sponsored by Energy Department and New England Council" and "Fact Sheet: Low-Cost/No-Cost Program," News releases from Office of Public Affairs, Region 1, Boston, November 8.

United States Postal Service (1980), *Annual Report of the Postmaster-General, Fiscal 1979,* Washington, D.C.: United States Postal Service.

VIA Rail Canada Inc. (1979), *Annual Report 1978,* Montreal, Quebec: VIA Rail Canada Inc.

Yergin, Daniel (1979), "Conservation: The Key Energy Source," in *Energy Future: Report of the Energy Project at the Harvard Business School,* eds. R. Stobaugh and D. Yergin, pp. 136–82. New York: Random House.

6

Marketing Communications in Nonbusiness Situations

or Why It's so Hard to Sell Brotherhood Like Soap

Michael L. Rothschild

In order to effectively use marketing communications techniques for public and nonprofit sector problems, one must consider the extreme differences between these and private sector problems. Major differences may include the presence of very high or very low involvement, issues offering few perceivable benefits to individuals, and high monetary prices. A framework for considering very high and very low involvement cases is considered and options for marketers are presented.

The use of marketing techniques outside the private sector has increased dramatically in the past few years. Marketing is now utilized by government, education, health and social services, charity and many other types of nonbusiness (public and nonprofit) organizations desiring to communicate a point of view or elicit a particular behavior. One unfortunate similarity in both business and nonbusiness applications of marketing has been a high failure rate due to reasons ranging from poor needs assessment to poor delivery.

Problems more prevalent in nonbusiness cases include the intangibility of nonbusiness products, the nonmonetary price of purchase, the extreme lack of frequency of purchase, the lack of behavioral reinforcers, the need to market

to an entire but heterogeneous society/market, and the extreme levels of involvement varying from very low to very high. Because of these factors, the transference of marketing principles from the business to the nonbusiness sector is far more complex than originally had been thought.

The extreme divergence of nonbusiness situations must also be taken into account. One thinks of business as dealing primarily with products and nonbusiness as dealing primarily with services, yet the nonbusiness sector also markets products. One thinks of monetary prices in the private sector and nonmonetary prices in the nonbusiness sectors, yet businesses are very concerned with minimizing time and inconvenience costs for their customers while many nonbusiness organizations charge monetary prices (e.g., the Post Office, universities, charities). This paper deals with emerging tendencies in nonbusiness marketing communications and offers direction to those developing strategy or research. The cases discussed tend to be those which differ

Michael L. Rothschild is Associate Professor of Business, Graduate School of Business, University of Wisconsin, Madison, WI.
The author would like to thank Alan Andreasen, Christopher Lovelock, and A. J. Martin for their helpful comments on earlier drafts of this paper.

from private sector cases; those which are similar to private sector cases can avail themselves of existing work.

By not considering differences associated with nonbusiness products, marketers are neglecting the concept of a systematic situation analysis. This neglect often is coupled with the inexperience of the nonbusiness manager who may think of communications as the essence of marketing. As Weibe (1951) noted, the nonbusiness manager who sees the private sector's use of marketing communications tools asks, ''Why can't you sell brotherhood like soap?'' The answer, this paper suggests, is that it is very difficult for marketing communications to have an impact outside the private sector because of the key issues mentioned above. These issues, a framework to present the problems facing nonbusiness marketers, and some options for nonbusiness managers and researchers also are discussed.

COMMUNICATIONS EFFECTIVENESS:
ISSUES AND HYPOTHESES

Marketing communications is generally used in conjunction with product, price, and distribution; its potential can be most fully realized when its development follows the other marketing tools. In such a framework, one should consider noncommunications aspects to develop insights into communications issues. There are four major issues which impact on potential communications effectiveness outside of the private sector and lead to several hypotheses:

- Product differences.
- Pricing differences.
- Involvement differences.
- Segmentation differences.

Product and Price.

Product: The product must first be considered for its benefits so that appropriate behavior can be appropriately reinforced. In nonbusiness situations, traditional communications strategies may be inadequate due to difficulties in communicating a potential benefit to the consumer. Communicators seek out the Unique Selling Proposition to show consumer benefits of appropriate behavior. In the nonprofit area, often only weak personal benefits can be found which do not reinforce or maintain long-term behaviors. In order to establish or maintain a behavior, there must be a positive reinforcer (Rachlin 1970). In many nonbusiness cases, neither positive nor negative reinforcers are readily perceivable.

Secondly, one must consider the recipients of the product benefits. In the private sector, the purchaser of the product is generally also the consumer or a member of the consuming unit (e.g., the family). In nonbusiness cases, the product often provides little direct measurable benefit to the purchaser. For example, a person who considers purchasing the concept of driving more slowly pays (in time lost) for a product which primarily benefits society (with greater energy reserves). Since the purchaser may not immediately

perceive the personal benefit, it must be pointed out more clearly. Many social issue promoters and charities experience this difficulty.

Another product difference between profit and nonprofit markets is that most nonbusiness products, services, or issues are intangible and cannot be shown in advertising. It is considerably more difficult to describe this product to the public/market. Where an object can be shown, it is generally not the product itself, but rather the producer of the product (e.g., an orchestra or university) or some mechanism involved with the product (the potential purchaser of a military experience is shown, for example, a tank).

Finally, one must consider whether there is at least some minimal level of latent demand for the product or issue at hand. In the private sector, a large percentage of new products fail because they do not meet a need or fill a void. Often in nonbusiness cases, there is no latent demand or interest in the product, service, or issue. When there is no voluntarily sought after exchange, it is difficult to elicit behavior.

Price: The underlying theme of price has traditionally been related to monetary issues; price is generally a function of cost and profit or of elasticity of demand constraints. In nonbusiness cases, often there is no monetary cost. Since marketing deals with exchanges of value, one must consider the nonmonetary costs of the product.

One difficulty lies in the diverse nature of nonmonetary costs which include time cost (driving more slowly, joining the military), inconvenience cost (appropriately depositing litter), and psychic cost (the fear of giving blood). Each of these costs may be perceived as greater than monetary costs which dominate the price of consumer products.

The difficulties of nonmonetary pricing also are reflected in the potential perception of the nonmonetary issues as either cost or benefit. For example, the military experience product has attributes of potential danger and separation from family. For some these attributes are seen as costs; for others these are benefits. Monetary costs, in comparison, are rarely perceived as benefits.

While it is generally accepted in the private sector that communications strategies differ as a function of the cost of the product, there are few if any data which report success at overcoming some of the very high nonmonetary prices of nonbusiness products. When nonmonetary (and difficult to measure) prices are combined with intangible (and difficult to measure) product benefits the results may be a staggering communications problem which may not be solvable via traditional strategies. These points lead to the following hypotheses:

1. The lower the perceived personal value (positive reinforcement, quid pro quo) to the individual relative to the cost (monetary and/or nonmonetary), the more difficult the behavior change task, and the lower the likelihood of success of marketing communications.

2. The lower the latent or preexisting demand for the object, the

more difficult the behavior change task, and the lower the likelihood of success of marketing communications.

Involvement. In the past several years, involvement has emerged as a popular construct which is hypothesized as acting as a mediating variable in learning, information processing, attitude change, and behavior development. While most of the recent involvement work has examined private sector marketing, the major contribution of this construct may lie in its value in nonbusiness situations; here it seems that the range of involvement becomes more extreme in both the very high and very low ranges and therefore information processing, decision making and communications effects may differ dramatically.

In a recent explication (Houston and Rothschild 1978), involvement is felt to consist of three component parts:

- Situational Involvement [SI]: the level of concern generated by an object across a set of individuals at a particular point in time (Hupfer and Gardner 1971; Rhine and Severence 1970; Apsler and Sears 1968).
- Enduring Involvement [EI]: the preexisting relationship between an individual and the object of concern (Sherif, Sherif, and Nebergall 1965; Sherif and Sherif 1967; Rhine and Polowniak 1971).
- Response Involvement [RI]: the complexity of cognitive, affective, and conative development at several points along a sequence of information gathering and decision making activities (Bowen and Chaffee 1974; Rothschild and Houston 1977; Park 1976; Payne 1976).

SI and EI are felt to interact and impact upon RI so that SI determines the mean level of RI, and EI determines the variance about the mean. Most of the existing involvement research has considered the impact of communications

stimuli on response involvement (Krugman, 1965; Ray, et al. 1973; Johnson and Scileppi 1969).

In Rothschild (1978a), two models of affective development are proposed. In the high involvement case, attitude precedes behavior; the main impact of advertising is on the development of awareness and knowledge while additional personal selling is necessary to generate behavior. In the low involvement case, advertising directly affects behavior (at least in the short run) due to the absence of a well-formed attitude structure.

The construct of involvement is a key to understanding the differences, difficulties, and constraints encountered in using marketing communications techniques in the nonbusiness sectors; involvement gives insight into how individuals receive and use information in different situations. These differences need to be considered in developing a communications plan.

The product and price differences discussed above lead to varying levels of SI, and, therefore, ultimately to varying styles of information processing, learning, and decision making. In addition, one's past experience with the issue (EI) will also affect these dependent variables. One can speculate that levels of RI will be distributed as shown in Exhibit 1. That is, nonbusiness will, in many cases, generate more extreme levels of involvement than typically found in private sector cases. What has been thought of as high and low involvement in the private sector may only cover the mid-range of possible societal involvement levels. While private sector goods and services seem to be distributed over the middle of the continuum, nonbusiness issues may be slightly bimodal, favoring both extremes.

The marketing issues can be considered from the perspective of intuitively low or high involvement cases. In the

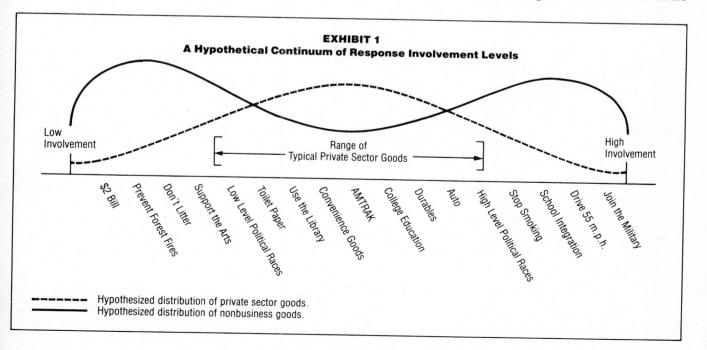

EXHIBIT 1
A Hypothetical Continuum of Response Involvement Levels

Low Involvement

Range of Typical Private Sector Goods

High Involvement

$2 Bill · Prevent Forest Fires · Don't Litter · Support the Arts · Low Level Political Races · Toilet Paper · Use the Library · Convenience Goods · AMTRAK · College Education · Durables · Auto · High Level Political Races · Stop Smoking · School Integration · Drive 55 m.p.h. · Join the Military

- - - - - - Hypothesized distribution of private sector goods.
———— Hypothesized distribution of nonbusiness goods.

low involvement case, the behavior has so little positive value to the individual that any price (in terms of the cost of inconvenience, information processing, or behavior change) will be too high for the value received. Because of the low value placed on any one form of behavior by the individual, only a short-run impact can be made. The change will be at best short-run because there is no reason to integrate the behavior into the belief structure; there is no positive reinforcing stimulus.

This scenario differs from the private sector case in that long-run behavior is established as a result of positive reinforcers. In a stimulus-response sense, one can envision the following:

$$S_1 \longrightarrow R_1 \longrightarrow S_2 \longrightarrow R_{2\ldots n}$$

where
S_1 = the communications stimulus,
R_1 = initial behavior,
S_2 = the reinforcer,
$R_{2\ldots n}$ = the repeat behavior.

In the typical business sector model, S_1 (advertising) leads to R (purchase) which in turn leads to S_2 (a product or service which is perceived to have a favorable or equitable cost/benefit relation). S_2 is necessary for long-run behavior; S_1 can only lead to short-run behavior.

In the nonbusiness case, issues of low individual involvement are often brought to the person's attention because there is some value to either society as a whole or some segment of society which is advocating a change in behavior. Often, there is cost to the individual and benefit to a larger group. In such a case, the individual would not consciously choose to be deflected from his/her inertial and apathetic path of least effort. There often is not a sufficiently strong S_2 to maintain behavior.

The issues discussed for low involvement will also hold in high involvement cases. In addition, present behavior may be so strongly related to the individual's central belief structure that most cost/benefit ratios will fall short of giving the individual a reasonable benefit in return for the cost associated with the desired behavior. Past individual behavior will overwhelm a current marketing communications effort.

For the very high involvement case, communications will fail if there is not a perceived benefit of high centrality. There must be a benefit which is both communicable and central to a large segment of the target market. Again, the discussion leads to these hypotheses:

3. The greater the involvement level of the object, situation, or issue (due primarily to complexity or price), the more difficult the behavior change task, and the lower the likelihood of success of marketing communications.

4. The greater the past involvement level of the individual (due primarily to past experience or the strength of social or cultural values), the more difficult the behavior change task, and the lower the likelihood of success of marketing communications.

Segmentation. Segmentation remains a cornerstone in applying the marketing concept to the practice of private sector marketing. In order to meet needs, one develops products to satisfy one or more distinct market segments and/or communicates the virtues of divergent benefits to divergent segments. Additionally, if a particular segment is felt to be unresponsive or unprofitable, it can be ignored.

In many nonbusiness cases, these options remain feasible and segmentation strategies will be called for, but in many others, all members of society must behave in a certain way and all must purchase the same product. Similarly, if the organization's mandate is to serve all of society, then unappealing segments must also be considered.

Furthermore, there are nonbusiness problems where all members of society must comply for the best interests of society (and themselves). An example occurred when Sweden shifted from driving on the left to driving on the right side of the street. All members of society needed to change behavior simultaneously. Other examples include the decimalization of currency in Great Britain and the metrification of measurement in the United States. All three cases allow segmentation in communications strategies, but do not allow for segmentation in the sense that some members of society can be neglected due to the difficulty in changing behavior.

It has been shown that cumulative response to messages occurs as a function similar to a modified exponential function and approaches an asymptote well below 100% of the potential audience (Kotler 1971). If nonbusiness communication is charged with gaining a response from all members of society, the cost of raising the asymptotic level of the response function may be quite high. A final hypothesis is offered.

5. The greater the level of participation needed within the society, the more difficult the behavior change, and the lower the likelihood of sucess of marketing communications.

SEVERAL EXEMPLARS

In the absence of a well-developed data set, several historical cases are examined to see the extent to which they fit the hypotheses. Each case should be considered not just for itself, but also as a representative of a class of objects or issues with similar values on the variables discussed above.

Military Enlistment. A review of situational involvement suggests the following difficulties. The product is a complex bundle of intangible attributes which combine as one family of brands in the generic product class of "multiyear experiences." The benefits are intangibles such as personal growth, education, skill training, excitement, adventure, travel, and opportunity to help one's country. The price is also complex, but predominantly is several years of one's life. Additionally, it includes giving up the right to make many independent decisions, changing life style, losing privacy, and the psychic cost related to the uncertainty of such a decision. The complexity of the product and its high cost make it intuitively very high in situational involvement.

Enduring involvement (the sum of past experiences) suggests further difficulties. For most individuals, there will be no prior usage experience from which to draw insights. There also will be limited experience in major issue decision making, since most prospective purchasers are 17- to 21-years of age. Finally, the decision concerning military enlistment has impact from peer, social class, and cultural values. Little prior experience plus great outside pressure suggest high enduring involvement.

On a more positive note, there seems to be a fair level of preexisting or latent demand, since some 400,000 units of product are purchased each year. In addition, the market for this product is highly segmentable; this also helps to ease the task of marketing communications.

Considering the above, response involvement would be extremely high and complex. Marketing theory would suggest here that the potential impact of advertising would be limited and that personal selling would be key to closing sales, as has been the case. The Army has found that advertising aids in attracting walk-in traffic, requests for information, and increasing knowledge, but has little to do with direct impact on behavior. While recruiters are more important than advertising, research has shown that without advertising, the efficiency of recruiters is diminished (Martin 1978). One should also note that numerous product changes since the inception of the all-volunteer military force have made the product more competitive in its class, thus enabling communications tools to be more effective in discussing potential reinforcers.

55 Mile-Per-Hour Speed Limit.
The generic issues of fuel consumption and speed of driving have generally had low situational involvement for most people. Even an "energy crisis" and several years of government messages have left many people apathetic regarding a behavior change in these areas. Therefore, the product being marketed can be seen as having little perceived value to many individuals although there is value to society in energy savings and a reduction in fatal accidents. Since most individuals cannot perceive a value, they will consider the costs of time and ego associated with driving at slower speeds.

Enduring involvement is much higher, though, for it is difficult to unlearn a lifetime of behavior, socialization (i.e., large cars with large engines are meant to be driven at high speeds), and values (i.e., time is a scarce commodity to be put to productive use) (Bem 1970; Rokeach 1968).

This shows the futility of marketing products with little preexisting or latent demand and no positively reinforcing attributes. There is little that marketing communications, per se, can do in such a case. The burden must fall on developing a more favorable cost/benefit relationship. The marketers of the 55-mile-per-hour speed limit have so far been unable to do this.

The 55-mile-per-hour speed limit case also highlights the difficulty of marketing to an entire society. In addition to the above problems, the behavior of those who comply with the limit is not reinforced when they see the energy conserved at the expense of their time wasted by fellow citizens. It is difficult to accomplish meaningful change when the majority has no incentive to comply.

Anti-Litter.
The issue of littering has low situational involvement for most people. Marketing theory would postulate that for low involvement, private sector products, advertising, and promotion could have a strong, short-run impact (Ray et al. 1973; Rothschild 1979). This paper makes a similar prediction for low involvement, public sector issues. That is, promotion can elicit short-run behavior with regard to nonbusiness issues as well.

Marketing has been successful in the long run for low involvement, consumer products when the products have a perceived advantage (or at least no disadvantage) for the consumer. In these cases, communications tools can lead to initial behavior and product benefits can lead to repeat behavior. Again, there is little perceived value to the individual in acceding to exhortations to stop littering. Only if one's behavior change led to some reinforcement would one continue with the new behavior. In most cases, an end to one's littering will lead to no perceivable diminution of overall levels of litter and, generally, one's past experiences will have led to such a prior belief. There probably is some latent demand for a clean environment, but without greater societal cooperation, unrewarded efforts will lapse back to old patterns. In isolated, unlittered areas the preserved clean environment does provide a reward.

A cessation of littering behavior offers benefits to society and costs to the individual because it is less convenient than the old behavior. In order for the new behavior to continue (assuming communications can have a short-run impact), there must be a benefit or reinforcement for the individual.

Voting: A Special Case of Short-Run Behavior.
This is an area which covers a wide range of involvement with offerings as diverse as presidential races, county clerk races, and referenda. A recent review of voting behavior shows a wide variety of involvement levels and a correspondingly wide range of potential communications impact (Rothschild 1978).

Over the past 30 years, political science data have consistently shown that political communications have very little impact on voting behavior (Lazarsfeld, Berelson, and Gaudet 1948; Campbell 1966; Campbell, Gurin, and Miller 1954; Key 1966; Blumler and McQuail 1969). In retrospect, one can see that virtually all reported cases have dealt with a race having high situational involvement (generally presidential). This strong pool of data supports the high involvement model.

EXHIBIT 2
Summary of the Four Cases

Case	Situation Involvement	Enduring Involvement	Benefits/ Reinforcers	Costs	Cost/ Benefit	Preexisting Demand	Segmentation	Conclusion
Military enlistment	Very complex High cost	Little past experience Cultural values	Personal intangibles	Several years of one's life Personal rights	Very good for some segments	Fairly high	Very specific and limited	Marketing communications can impact
55 mph speed limit	Low Little interest	Central beliefs	Few personal benefits Weak societal benefits	Time Ego/macho	Poor	Virtually none	All drivers	Low likelihood of of marketing communications impact
Antilitter	Low Little interest	Past non-reinforcing experiences	Few personal benefits Moderate societal benefits	Inconvenience	Poor	Low	All members of community	Short-run impact possible Long-run impact difficult
Voting	High to low—depends on race	Central beliefs Pressure to behave	Good citizenship	Time inconvenient Infrequent/low	Favorable for voting Less favorable for analyzing issues	Moderate	All citizens 18 years of age or older	Short-run impact likely Long-run impact not necessary

In the past few years, a new set of studies has shown a significant impact of communication on voting behavior (Palda 1975; Kline 1972; Patterson and McClure 1976; Rothschild and Ray 1974). These studies have concentrated on lower level, or low situational involvement, races, and the findings are consistent with the low involvement model. Since there are fewer strong beliefs that concerning issues in low level races, strong beliefs concerning issues in low level races, communications can more easily impact; since there is a strong belief that voting is a desirable behavior, it will take place; since the desired behavior is very short-run (one may vote on election day and then return to apathy), there is no need to develop the types of reinforcement which lead to long-run behavior. Indeed, the mere act of voting is reinforcing; one has been a good citizen, performed one's duty, and met society's expectations.

The impact of both marketing and societal variables in the voting cases can be seen. In all elections, there is a societal pressure to behave. In high level races, there are imputs from more credible news media and peers along with strong enduring involvement based on past voting behavior which outweigh the impact of marketing communications. In low level races, there is less enduring involvement, less interest, less news media, and less peer influence to dissipate the marketing communications influence. In this low involvement case, the above scenario, coupled with no need for long-run behavior, leads to the potential for a strong marketing communications impact.

A summary of the four cases is presented in Exhibit 2.

OPTIONS FOR THE MARKETER

Given a predominance of unfavorable communications situations in the nonbusiness sectors, what options are available to the marketer?

In a study of nonbusiness communications, the point has been made that nonadvertising promotional tools can be very valuable (Mendelsohn 1973). In the private sector, firms generally rely quite heavily on advertising; in the nonbusiness arena, there is much more likely to be a reliance on public relations, sales force, or other nonadvertising tools since:

- advertising is often frowned upon as an unethical and manipulative tool;
- the organizations often have very limited financial resources to use on communications; and
- when resources are available, they often are controlled by law or charter and cannot be used for advertising.

There are, though, communications tools which circumvent the above constraints and offer the potential of greater credibility and, as a result, more strength as an influencing agent. Mendelsohn (1973) has discussed several of his own studies where nontraditional (to marketing) tools were successfully used. These include:

A television program. "The CBS National Drivers Test" gave drivers a chance to test their knowledge and skills in their home. The program overcame driver indifference to hazards, made them cognizant of their driving problems, and directed them to a mechanism to remedy problems. The program overcame low involvement and generated appropriate behavior (35,000 drivers enrolled in driver education programs as a result).

A short film. "A Snort History," a cartoon about alcohol and traffic safety, was shown as a short subject in movie theatres. It served to overcome the apathy of low involvement and educate thousands of viewers on a subject of generally low interest.

A television series. "Cancion de la Raza," a soap opera series in Los Angeles, served to provide information to the Chicano community about a number of day-to-day legal and social problems encountered by members of the community. By presenting information in a familiar manner, reach was high and learning took place (although no data were presented to support this reported result).

The three examples are presented to suggest that in nonbusiness areas, marketers need to consider tools which go beyond those traditionally employed in the private sector. In many areas of extreme high and low involvement, the tools to be employed must be even more diverse than those suggested above. For many issues, behavior change or development can only occur as a result of an educational process conducted through the schools or the home. If brotherhood is an issue to be marketed, perhaps it must be done through the schools, the home, or legal channels.

If use of the product has no perceived positive reinforcement associated with it which would make long-run behavior desirable, then the product can be changed so that there is negative reinforcement associated with improper (or lack of) behavior. Bem (1970) discussed this issue in relation to self-perception theory and attitude behavior relationships. He felt that stateways (the law) can change folkways (norms and values). By being forced to behave, people will see that their behavior is not harmful or costly; their attitudes then change to become consistent with their new behavior and long-run behavior results.

Ray, *et al.* (1973) make a similar suggestion in presenting the dissonance-attribution hierarchy of effects model. They posit that a forced initial behavior may be necessary in order to get proper long-run attitudes and behavior in very high involvement cases. The present discussion suggests that the same strategy may be necessary in very low involvement cases where there is no individual incentive to behave in a certain way.

Enzensberger (1974) put this legal strategy in proper perspective by suggesting that behavior change acquired through communications is stronger than that which results from any manner of external force. Attribution theory would concur that if the individual could attribute his/her own behavior to an acquiescence to force, it would not be internalized as strongly as if the behavior were attributed to a voluntary judgment. Whenever possible, then, marketing communications would be preferable to legal sanction.

Finally, the role and purpose of marketing communications vis a vis the remainder of the marketing mix should be

kept in mind. A very high percentage of business sector products and services fail because they do not meet a need or offer a perceivable benefit to the consumer. This should be kept in mind in nonbusiness cases as well. Communications cannot carry a poor product offering; in too many nonbusiness cases, the offering has little appeal or little benefit to the individual. While this is certainly a *caveat* for marketing in any sector, it is especially noteworthy in the nonbusiness sectors, given the other obstacles to success which exist.

SUMMARY AND CONCLUSIONS

This paper has presented a number of issues which need to be considered in a situation analysis sense before objectives or strategies can be developed in a marketing communications campaign. The tools, techniques, and theories developed in the private sector can be valuable in the public and nonprofit sectors, but their limitations must be recognized.

Before developing a nonbusiness communications campaign, one must consider:

The involvedness of the situation and the relevant segments. Due to the potentially very high and very low levels, traditional promotion tools may be inadequate. Given the current state of the art of marketing communications, one must conclude that what can work reasonably well in private sector consumer goods cases may not work at all for nonbusiness cases. While most consumer goods exist within a broad range of middle level involvement, many nonbusiness issues exist in either very high or very low involvement environments. These environments may call for an enlarged set of communications tools and strategies.

The available positive and negative reinforcers. Since the benefits of nonbusiness issues may be less apparent to the message recipient, it is incumbent upon the sender to consider all possible behavior reinforcers. This especially would be the case where the more apparent benefits are societal rather than individual.

The nonmonetary costs. The costs associated with behavior towards nonbusiness issues may include several nonmonetary costs which raise the cost of behaving beyond the level of the perceived benefit. In such a case, communications tools will be hard pressed to present a convincing case for elicitation of the desired behavior.

The level of latent demand. Many nonbusiness marketing campaigns exist as a result of the efforts of a small group of individuals. When little latent demand exists, then little desired behavior will follow.

The relevant segments. For virtually all issues, there will be at least a small segment of society for whom the issue will have positive value, another segment for whom compliance with the law will be sufficient motivation, and another segment for whom engaging in the socially beneficial act will be sufficient motivation. For many issues, there will remain a large segment for whom a direct personal benefit must be shown if appropriate behavior is to result. This paper has considered issues relating to this last segment. The manager must, of course, consider the trade-offs of using segmentation strategies and whether or not segmentation is a permissible strategy.

The wide range of communications alternatives. Given the limitations of traditional marketing communications tools, one also must consider alternatives such as movies and television programs, or even broader alternatives such as in-school or in-home educational communications. It is generally felt that public service spots are not very effective. Perhaps the money spent on their production could be used more efficiently in one of the nontraditional media suggested above.

As has been noted several times in this paper, nonbusiness marketing problems are generally very different from and often more complex than traditional marketing issues. To improve managers' abilities to deal with these differences, several areas of research which deal with the major issues of the paper should be considered:

- Several researchers are currently considering the measurement of involvement as it pertains to private sector goods. This work should be extended to the nonbusiness arena where potential involvement differences are great.
- The work in behavioral learning theory has had very limited marketing application in both business and nonbusiness areas (Carey, et al. 1976; Deslauriers and Everett 1977; Everett, Hayward, and Meyers 1974; Kohlenberg and Phillips 1973; Powers, Osborne, and Anderson 1973). Research in the use of positive and negative reinforcers, reinforcement schedules, and shaping procedures could be insightful. Given the nature of nonbusiness issues, they may lend themselves to behavioral learning work; transferences could then be made to the private sector.
- Communications alternatives are needed. Testing to be done here could follow established private sector methods used on traditional media.

These areas of research can be further divided into two classes:

- Research to establish the relevant consumer perception with respect to the various dimensions of the model presented above.
- Research to generate and test the effectiveness of various marketing strategies aimed at overcoming some of the inherent characteristics which suggest low likelihood of success.

One benefit of examining nonbusiness issues is that the limits of existing private sector techniques are tested. This paper has examined the limits of marketing communications with respect to three variables: (1) extreme levels of involvement, (2) the absence of reinforcers, and (3) the need for highly centralized attributes. By determining limits for existing theories and techniques, the discipline of marketing communications will grow and the potential for strategic success will increase.

REFERENCES

Apsler, R., and D. Sears (1968), "Warning, Personal Involvement and Attitude Change," *Journal of Personality and Social Psychology*, 9 (June), 162–66.

Bem, D. J. (1970), *Beliefs, Attitudes and Human Affairs*. Belmont, CA: Brooks/Cole.

Blumler, J. G., and D. McQuail (1969), *Television and Politics: Its Uses and Influences*. Chicago: University of Chicago Press.

Bowen, L., and S. Chaffee (1974), "Product Involvement and Pertinent Advertising Appeals," *Journalism Quarterly*, 51 (Winter), 613–21.

Campbell, A. (1966), *Elections and the Political Order*. New York: John Wiley and Sons.

———, G. Gurin, and W. E. Miller (1954), *The Voters Decide*. Evanston, IL: Row, Peterson.

Carey, R. J., S. H. Clicque, B. A. Leighton, and F. Milton (1976), "A Test of Positive Reinforcement of Customers," *Journal of Marketing*, 40 (October), 98–100.

Deslauriers, B. C., and P. B. Everett (1977), "The Effects of Intermittent and Continuous Token Reinforcement on Bus Ridership," *Journal of Applied Psychology*. 62 (August), 369–75.

Enzensberger, A. M. (1974), *The Consciousness Industry: On Literature, Politics, and Media*. New York: Seabury.

Everett, P. B., S. C. Hayward, and A. W. Meyers (1974), "The Effects of a Token Reinforcement Procedure on Bus Ridership," *Journal of Applied Behavior Analyses*. 7 (Spring), 1–9.

Houston, M. J., and M. L. Rothschild (1978), "A Paradigm for Research on Consumer Involvement," working paper, 12-77-46. Madison: University of Wisconsin.

Hupfer, N., and D. Gardner (1971), "Differential Involvement with Products and Issues: An Exploratory Study," Proceedings of the Association for Consumer Research.

Johnson, H., and J. Scileppi (1969), "Effects of Ego-Involvement Conditions on Attitude Change to High and Low Credibility Communication," *Journal of Personality and Social Psychology*. 13 (September), 31–36.

Key, V. O. (1966), *The Responsible Electorate*. Cambridge, MA: Harvard University Press.

Kline, F. G. (1974), "Mass Media and the General Election Process: Evidence and Speculation," paper presented at the Syracuse University Conference on Mass Media and American Politics. Syracuse, New York.

Kohlenberg, R., and T. Phillips (1973), "Reinforcement and Rate of Litter Depositing," *Journal of Applied Behavior Analysis*. 6 (Fall), 391–96.

Kotler, P. (1971), *Marketing Decision Making: A Model Building Approach*. New York: Holt, Rinehart and Winston.

Krugman, H. (1965), "The Impact of Television Advertising: Learning Without Involvement," *Public Opinion Quarterly*. 29 (Fall), 349–56.

Larzarsteld, P. F., B. R. Berelson, and H. Gaudet (1948), *The People's Choice*. New York: Columbia University Press.

Martin, A. J. (1978), Personal Communications.

Mendelsohn, H. (1973), "Some Reasons Why Information Campaigns Can Succeed," *Public Opinion Quarterly*. 37 (Spring), 50–61.

Palda, K. S. (1975), "The Effect of Expenditure on Political Success," *Journal of Law and Economics*. 18 (December), 745–71.

Park, C. (1976), "The Effect of Individual and Situation-Related Factors on Consumer Selection of Judgment Models," *Journal of Marketing Research*. 13 (May), 144–51.

Patterson, T. W., and R. D. McClure (1976), "Television and the Less Interested Voter: The Costs of an Informed Electorate," *The Annals of the American Academy of Political and Social Science*. 425 (May), 88–97.

Payne, J. (1976), "Task Complexity and Contingent Processing in Decision Making: An Information Search and Protocol Analysis," *Organizational Behavior and Human Performance*. 16 (May), 366–87.

Powers, R. B., J. G. Osborne, and E. G. Anderson (1973), "Positive Reinforcement of Litter Removal in the Natural Environment," *Journal of Applied Behavior Analysis.* 6 (Winter), 579–86.

Rachlin, H. (1970), *Introduction to Modern Behaviorism.* San Francisco: W. H. Freeman.

Ray, M. L., A. G. Sawyer, M. L. Rothschild, R. M. Heeler, E. C. Strong, and J. B. Reed (1973), "Marketing Communications and the Hierarchy of Effects," in *New Models for Mass Communications Research, Volume II, Sage Annual Review of Communication Research,* ed. P. Clarke. Beverly Hills: Sage.

Rhine, R., and L. Severence (1970), "Ego Involvement, Discrepancy, Source Credibility and Attitude Change," *Journal of Personality and Social Psychology.* 16 (October), 175–90.

——— and W. Polowniak (1971), "Attitude Change, Commitment, and Ego Involvement," *Journal of Personality and Social Psychology.* 19 (February), 247–50.

Rokeach, M. (1968), *Beliefs, Attitudes and Values,* San Francisco: Jossey-Bass.

——— (1978), "Political Advertising: A Neglected Policy Issue in Marketing," *Journal of Marketing Research.* 15 (February), 58–71.

———, (1979), "Advertising Strategies for High and Low Involvement Situations," in *Attitude Research Plays for High Stakes,* ed. J. Maloney. Chicago: American Marketing Association.

———, and M. Houston (1977), "The Consumer Involvement Matrix: Some Preliminary Findings," in *Contemporary Marketing Thought,* eds. B. Greenberg and D. Bellenger. Chicago: American Marketing Association.

———, and M. L. Ray (1974), "Involvement and Political Advertising Effect: An Exploratory Experiment," *Communication Research.* 1 (July), 264–85.

Sherif, M. and C. Sherif (1967), *Attitude, Ego-Involvement and Change.* New York: John Wiley and Sons

———, and R. Nebergall (1965), *Attitude and Attitude Change.* Philadelphia: Saunders.

Wiebe, G. D. (1951), "Merchandising Commodities and Citizenship on Television," *Public Opinion Quarterly.* 15 (Winter), 679–91.

7

Advertising and Publicity Programs in the Executive Branch of the National Government: Hustling or Helping the People?

Dean L. Yarwood
Ben M. Enis

Publicity and advertising activities by federal agencies are of broad scope, wide diversity and deep significance. These activities began as the Republic was born, and have grown with it. And the rate of growth is accelerating. This phenomenon raises interest, and scholarly research. The administrative questions addressed in this paper focus on the effectiveness and efficiency with which publicity and advertising activities are conducted by the federal government. The public interest questions center upon the role that such activities should play in a democracy. By raising these questions, the authors hope to stimulate debate, provoke discussion, and inspire research among public administrators, elected officials, and scholars.

Congressional investigators looking into the extent of public-relations and advertising activity of the federal bureaucracy asked one agency for a sample of each of its publications. The answer: Bring an 18-wheel truck to haul them in.

U.S. News & World Report
October 6, 1980, p. 2.

A member of the Defense subcommittee of the House Appropriations Committee labels government advertising (except that for military recruiting) as "propaganda" and "puffery," and calls it disgraceful. He complains that he sees far too much self-serving agency publicity in his district [1]. In a different hearing, held about the same time, the chairman of a House Government Operations subcommittee com-

plains because the director of the Census Bureau decided to use public service announcements for the 1980 Census of Population. Fearing that an undercount of minorities will hurt his state in upcoming congressional reapportionment decisions and in competition for federal funds, the congressman wants the Census Bureau to use *paid* advertising [2]. These two instances illustrate the mixed attitudes Americans hold toward government advertising and publicity.

This paper briefly traces the development of the use of advertising and publicity in the executive branch of the national government and documents their current magnitude and scope. It then evaluates the efficiency and effectiveness of the administration of such programs. Because publicity and advertising programs are important aspects of the com-

Dean L. Yarwood is Professor of Political Science, University of Missouri–Columbia. Ben M. Enis is Professor of Marketing, University of Southern California. The authors gratefully acknowledge critiques of drafts of this paper by the following: Professor S. Watson Dunn, UM-C Department of Marketing; Professor Dale K. Spencer,

UM-C School of Journalism; Assistant Professor Richard Hardy and Professor Lloyd M. Wells, UM-C Department of Political Science; Jerry Giffen, information officer, Missouri Department of Social Services, and anonymous *PAR* reviewers. This research was funded by a grant from the Research Council of the Graduate School, UM-C.

munication function of modern government, it is essential that they be administered with sensitivity to the needs of democracy. The last section of this article highlights problems associated with government publicity programs in a democracy.

EVOLUTION OF GOVERNMENT ADVERTISING AND PUBLICITY PROGRAMS

Subject as they are to intermittent controversy, these programs often are mistakenly thought to be recent innovations in governance [3]. In fact, advertising activities that promote the proprietary functions of the federal bureaucracy date from the dawn of the Republic. As early as 1792, a statute required that openings for star mail routes be advertised in one or more newspapers for at least six weeks before contracts could be awarded [4]. Perhaps the true precursor of modern government advertising and publicity activities was the necessity for disseminating agricultural information to a largely rural population. This began as early as the 1830s when agricultural programs were physically located in the Patent Office. When Agriculture became a separate department in 1862 its enabling statute enjoined it to publicize ". . . information on subjects connected with agriculture in the most general and comprehensive sense of the word [5]." Its early public relations activities included news releases, bulletins, monthly reports, and annual reports; later, motion pictures, exhibits, and other forms of publicity were added.

Government publicity activities reached new heights during the New Deal period. Agencies that had extensive publicity programs included the Tennessee Valley Authority (TVA), Federal Housing Administration (FHA), Works Progress Administration (WPA), National Recovery Act (NRA), the Social Security Board, and the Departments of Agriculture and Interior. Among the symbols associated with the New Deal, the NRA's Blue Eagle logo was perhaps the most famous. Such activities continued apace during World War II, e.g., the "Rosie the Riveter" and "Loose Lips Sink Ships" campaigns. Today, the role of publicity and advertising in government operations is a most significant one.

CONTEMPORARY FEDERAL ADVERTISING AND PUBLICITY PROGRAMS

As a first approximation of the magnitude of advertising and publicity activities, an attempt was made to determine the total federal expenditure on such activities. There is, however, no single figure which reflects the total cost of all such programs. The various components of such a figure are scattered throughout the budget, sometimes under ambiguous and/or unlikely headings. Some insights into the cost of government publicity activities can be gained by looking into selected departments.

Over the years, Agriculture has been a leader in the use of such activities which are generally referred to as "public affairs" activities in GAO reports and congressional hearings. For example, Agriculture officials estimated that the department would spend over $22.3 million on such programs during fiscal year 1976 (the latest year for which figures are available). These activities would employ 650 persons in 21 offices which disseminate information to the public. DOA publishes over 3,000 different publications each year, of which perhaps the most famous is the *Agricultural Yearbook*. In 1976, approximately 233,450 copies of this volume were given *gratis* to members of Congress for distribution to their constituents. In addition, DOA distributed 9.3 million bulletins, 3.3 million of which were delivered by or sent out for members of Congress [6].

The public affairs activities of the former Department of Health, Education and Welfare are diverse. In fiscal year 1975, HEW estimated that it would spend $17 million for these activities, occupying the time of 347 persons in handling inquiries from the press, speech writing, preparing new releases, developing information booklets, and creating audio-visual materials. A HEW internal study found that, in 1976, the Office of Assistant Secretary for Public Affairs ". . . reviewed and approved approximately 65 film requests, 15 television productions, 15 exhibits, 8 audio proposals, and more than 30 other audio-visual proposals with a total cost of over $2 million [7]."

As might be expected, the public affairs bill of the Department of Defense exceeds that of all other departments. In fiscal year 1977, DOD had 1,322 persons employed in public affairs—more than four times the number of any other government agency [8]. In fiscal year 1980, expenditures for these activities came to just under $26 million; they were limited to no more than $25 million in the fiscal 1980 appropriations act [9]. This amount does not include money spent for advertising to recruit an all-volunteer force, an amount DOD estimated would top $112 million by fiscal year 1981 [10]. The General Accounting Office found that DOD's range of public affairs activities includes such things as traveling exhibits, weapons demonstrations, lecture tours, TV and radio programs, films lent to civic organizations, news releases for hometown newspapers, and so on. The military also gets invaluable publicity from its participation in motion pictures and TV programs. In 1976 and 1977, the services participated in one way or another in 58 such shootings, sometimes charging the film company a fee for use of equipment and personnel, but often making these available without charge. The services also make stock film footage available to commercial film companies to be copied at the companies' own expense [11].

Perhaps the most noteworthy development in government advertising and publicity programs in recent years is the increase in public service announcements (PSAs). Daytime and late night TV viewers, and magazine and newspaper readers, find themselves encouraged, enticed, admonished and scolded by these PSAs. There are two types of public service announcements. The first is produced by a government agency which pays the costs of production and distributes the ads to radio and TV stations which air them to satisfy public service obligations for license renewal. The other type of PSA is produced in cooperation with the National Advertising Council. The Ad Council selects a few campaigns from the hundreds of requests it receives each year from nonpartisan causes, both private and public. For each campaign, a volunteer agency is appointed from Ad Council members to produce and distribute the ads. The recipient organization is charged only for out-of-pocket production costs and costs resulting from field research.

The result of this practice is that government advertising receives a considerable amount of support from the private sector. For example, in 1979:

> Ad Council campaigns promoted export awareness for the Commerce Department, high blood pressure prevention for the National Heart & Lung Institute, car pooling and 55 mph speed limit for the Transportation Department, employer support of the National Guard and Reserve for the Defense Department, voluntary service for ACTION (Peace Corps, Vista, etc.), and education for technical careers for the Health, Education & Welfare Department. [12]

Moreover, the Ad Council and a volunteer agency, Ogilvy & Mather, created the campaign in support of the 1980 Census of Population. It cost the Census Bureau $750,000; its director estimated a campaign of paid advertising would have cost $40 million [13].

In addition to public service advertising, contract (paid) advertising has become a significant part of government public affairs activities in recent times. Indeed, Uncle Sam is one of the major advertisers in the country. In 1978, the U.S. government ranked 25th in total ad dollars spent [14]. This expenditure for paid advertising placed the federal government just behind such corporate giants as RCA, Coca-Cola, and McDonald's; it ranked just ahead of J. C. Penney, ITT and Colgate-Palmolive.

Other examples could be given. Perhaps those cited are sufficient to make the point that publicity and advertising activities in the executive branch have become a significant element of public administration. Under various names and conducted with varying degrees of skill, these programs in the federal government are of such magnitude that they should be examined closely by scholars, administrators and lawmakers. The next section discusses management issues involved in government publicity and advertising activities.

ADMINISTRATION OF PUBLICITY AND ADVERTISING PROGRAMS

The modern managerial view in private sector marketing is that both advertising and publicity, together with personal selling and sales promotion (e.g., trading stamps, coupons, contests) should be managed so as to maximize the persuasive impact of the organization upon its customers and other publics. Applied to the government bureaucracy, this maxim would mandate that policy and advertising activities be managed in a similar fashion.

Agency publicity activities consist of external communications involving the preparation and distribution of bulletins, pamplets, press handouts (except those dealing with current events), in-house periodicals, and annual reports intended for widespread public distribution. Advertising includes public service announcements produced with or without the cooperation of the Ad Council, as well as paid or contract advertising. A feature of modern government advertising and publicity programs is that they typically give agencies the capability of communicating directly with the public, bypassing the working press.

Given the magnitude of activities documented above, it is clear that a great many government employees are engaged in managing publicity and advertising activities. Though any estimate of the actual number of persons employed in such government positions is subject to debate, some estimates can be made. In 1977, the General Accounting Office surveyed the 20 largest government agencies and estimated that they employed 3,366 persons in public affairs positions. Moreover, the GAO reported that it had reason to suspect that the estimate was too low [15]. In 1979, *U.S. News & World Report* used the Freedom of Information Act to survey 47 government agencies and commissions; the magazine estimated that the agencies employed 4,926 information specialists [16]. The inference is clear: a great many managers in the federal bureaucracy are engaged in advertising and publicity activities and many higher administrators are charged with managing agencies and budgets that contain substantial publicity programs. These managers face a number of problems.

DEFINING THE TASKS TO BE ADMINISTERED

The initial problem is that the task to be administered is defined in different ways by different governmental agencies. Such words as "public information," "public affairs," "advertising" and "campaign" do not have common definitions. Consequently, government bureaucrats use the same term to mean different activities, and different terms to connote similar activities. For example, in the GAO survey cited above, the Department of Agriculture responded that it only employed eight persons in such positions. Since this response is clearly inconsistent with the magnitude of DOA's activities, the discrepancy can only be explained in terms of different definitions. Specifically, Agriculture insisted it merely distributed "public information." Thus, although the Agriculture Department had 21 different offices each employing from one to 123 persons engaged in public information activities, it had only eight persons directly engaged in "public affairs" [17].

The Department of Defense provides another example. As noted above, DOD has a statutory limit on how much it can spend on "public affairs"; however, it excludes from that limitation expenses for such promotional items as its special aerial teams, military ceremonial bands, service museums, and service related exhibits, among others [18]. These activities are not part of public affairs programs—as DOD defines the term.

In response to these sorts of practices, the GAO urged in a recent report that uniform government-wide definitions of public affairs activities be adopted. Said the GAO:

> Once government-wide definitions have been developed, definite lines of program responsibility can be drawn, coordination and oversight can be improved, and total costs can be assessed. It would also be easier to develop criteria for measuring public affairs effectiveness and would assist in measuring the productivity of the public affairs workforce. [19]

Nature of Public Administration of Advertising and Publicity. Even if government-wide definitions could be agreed upon, public administration of advertising and publicity programs would not be easy. There are two sets of difficulties; managerial and product-related. First, the management of advertising and publicity in any organization is a challenging task [20]. The *raison d'etre* of those activities is persuasive communication which involves dealing with the attitudes and behavior of people. The people-handling dimension of advertising, public relations, and other marketing-oriented activities contrasts sharply with the physical quantities handled by manufacturing or inventory managers, or the impersonal orderliness of monetary transactions faced by financial managers. Moreover, advertising and publicity are designed to occur outside the organization, i.e., to present the organization's positions and products to potential clients, congressmen, or voters. Such "boundary spanning" activities are always complex. Finally, a good case can be made that it is more difficult to manage in the public than the private sector. In addition to all of the pressures and complexities of the private sector, the public sector manager faces to a greater extent than his/her private counterpart such problems as conflicting objectives, diffuse authority, political pressures, frequent top management turnover, and so forth [21]. The total effect of these factors is that the administration of government publicity activities is exceedingly difficult.

A different set of difficulties results from the fact that the "products" that the public administrator has to market differ fundamentally from their private sector counterparts [22]. A recent article stresses three major differences: product intangibilities, involvement, and market segmentation [23]. First, government public affairs activities often involve intangible and abstract products. The volunteer army campaign, for example, promises "not just a job, but an adventure." But to lend an air of reality to the promises, the ads depict a tank or a jeep. Similarly, exhortations to "drive 55" are difficult to translate into tangible consumer benefits. The price paid for "consumption" of such products is often measured in nonmonetary terms. The military enlistee gives up time and the opportunity to do other things with that time. The driver

gives up the convenience of arriving sooner. In neither case is it possible for the "consumer" to weigh precisely the intangible benefits against the nonmonetary costs of consuming those products.

Second, government "products" tend to cluster at the extremes of the "involvement" continuum [24]. In general, the concept of involvement postulates that potential consumers tend to be interested in, committed to, concerned about—*involved with*—certain products more than others; e.g., an automobile more than a package of chewing gum. Some government programs, such as the Surgeon General's "stop smoking" campaign and the drive to build an all-volunteer military force are probably even higher on the involvement continuum than are durable goods like automobiles. That is, potential "consumers" are likely to hold very strong positive or negative feelings about these products. It is extremely difficult for advertising and publicity to change such feelings, and therefore to affect "consumption" behavior. At the other end of the involvement continuum, government products such as the Susan B. Anthony one-dollar coin and the campaign to prevent forest fires are very unlikely to involve many citizens to any great degree. Their indifference to these products makes it difficult to motivate them effectively to "consume" such products.

Finally, advertising campaigns in the private sector are often founded upon the concept of *market segmentation:* specific product benefits are targeted to homogeneous subgroups of the entire market. Many government programs, in contrast, must be marketed to the entire citizenry. While it is possible to target military advertisements to young men and women with specific characteristics, the "drive 55" campaign and the "read the label" programs must be addressed to all citizens. Marketing experts would predict a greater degree of success when segments can be specifically targeted.

The Government Publicity and Advertising Budget. In 1913, an advertisement announcing examinations for the position of "publicity expert" in Agriculture created a congressional storm which resulted in a law stipulating that "no money appropriated by this or any other act shall be used for the compensation of any publicity expert unless specifically appropriated for that purpose" [25]. Shortly thereafter, examinations were held for "information assistants" in Agriculture, thereby beginning a rich tradition of surrogate titles coined to circumvent the letter of the 1913 law [26].

Given the distrust of government advertising and publicity activities manifested in the 1913 legislation, and reaffirmed in legislation passed in 1966 [27], agencies often find it in their interest not to make the extent of their publicity and advertising activities readily identifiable. One way agencies obfuscate advertising and publicity budgets is by employing surrogate titles such as "public information officers," "public affairs specialists," and so on, to avoid the ban on "publicity experts."

Similarly, agencies distribute their publicity costs differently throughout their budgets. Thus, military recruitment advertising is budgeted under "Operations and Maintenance"; public information in the National Institute of Drug Abuse is budgeted under "Management and Information, Drug Abuse, Direct Program"; and the Energy Research and Development Administration budgeted public information under "Supporting Activities" [28]. In auditing military advertising accounts, the GAO comlained:

> Our analysis of the cost data provided [by the services] showed that what each service included as advertising costs varied widely. It seems that when the services are requested to submit advertising cost data to DOD or the Congress, each service uses its own discretion in selecting the format and determining what costs should or should not be included. [29]

As a consequence of both inconsistent budgeting of advertising and publicity activities, and the lack of government-wide definition of key terms, there is literally no way to ascertain the costs of such activities of government. These practices make it difficult for higher administrators who are charged with dealing with such costs to make effective decisions in allocating resources to various publicity programs.

A complicating factor is the decision to rely on public service ads (PSAs) vs. purchasing broadcast time on radio or television time or space in print media such as newspapers and magazines. The case for contract (paid) advertising is that it allows the administrator to control the time and/or placement of the advertisements, e.g., during evening primetime hours on television, or morning or afternoon drivetime for radio. Moreover, purchased advertising can be targeted to audiences for expected maximum impact. Public service ads, in contrast, are run by the media at times or in spaces that they choose. Since primetime in broadcast media, and choice space (e.g., the back cover or middle pages of a newspaper or magazine) are most valuable, PSAs generally are not placed in these positions. For example, the Army estimates that no more than four to eight percent of its PSAs are aired on primetime television [30]. In a recent hearing, the Army reported that public service activity had only a "minimal impact" on targeted audiences [31].

On the other hand, the case against paid government advertising is quite simple. First PSAs are free, except for production and distribution costs. Further, the more government pays for advertising, the less likely the Advertising Council and the media will be to donate effort, time and/or space. For instance, when the Army experimented with paid radio and TV advertising for two months in 1971, several stations announced that they would no longer air the Army's PSAs [32]. Finally, public service announcements probably seem more legitimate to the audience because the "commercial" motivation appears to be lacking.

Measuring the Effectiveness of Government Advertising and Publicity.
Prudent administration dictates that the effectiveness of advertising and publicity programs be monitored.

Though the results of studies are not entirely consistent, generally only marginal benefits are reported from them. For example, advertising costs for military recruiting increased from $6.7 million in fiscal 1970 to $96.1 million in fiscal 1974. Yet, analysis by the GAO of a number of studies showed that ". . . attitudes and images of the military, or the individual services in relation to each other, had changed very little over the five-year period" [33]. A study by Mullins et al. conducted for the Air Force Human Resources Laboratory compared the sources of influence and information of 1,967 Air Force enlistees in 1973 with those of 12,472 enlistees in 1974, each on the sixth day of their training. This study showed the effectiveness of Air Force advertising had remained about the same for males but had increased for females between the two periods [34].

The Center for Disease Control sponsored a study to encourage smokers to switch to cigarette with less tar. This campaign, conducted by John Adler et al. employed an experimental group exposed to the CDC's advertising while a control group was not. Diaries were kept for 2,000 families in both the experimental and control groups for six months before the campaign and for a year following it. Matched pre- and post-test records were also kept for 900 persons in each panel. Based on the diary data, it appeared that the CDC campaign had had some influence in reducing exposure to smoking of those in the experimental group. But the matched data, which should have been more sensitive to change, showed that the campaign had no significant effect [35].

The National Institute of Alcohol Abuse and Alcoholism commissioned Louis Harris and Associates, Inc., to assess the public's awareness of NIAAA's campaign against alcoholism. The study consisted of four surveys of a national cross section of the adult population taken between September 1972 and January 1974. Public awareness of the agency's works was found to be high; for example, 64 percent of the adult population recalled seeing at least one of the ads. When the actual storyboards of ten NIAAA advertisements were shown to participants, however, only one was recognized by as many as 30 percent of them [36].

A major problem in determining the effectiveness of public affairs campaigns is that they often are not planned with sufficient care. In its evaluation of public affairs activities at HEW, the GAO recommended that the department set criteria to enable managers to evaluate the soundness of such programs before funding them. Among the key recommendations of standards to be applied to public affairs programs are, "Does the campaign have clear and meaningful objectives?" "Has the intended audience been precisely targeted?" "What mix of information channels (media, community elements, professional organizations, etc.) are to be utilized?" "Specifically, how is the effectiveness of the campaign to be evaluated, i.e., behavior change, attitude change, dissemination of information?" [37] Without such standards, it is impossible to determine the impact a campaign has had or whether money spent in different ways might have had greater impact. *Advertising Age*, for example, stated editorially in 1975 that military advertising accounts were too large [38]. This comment is difficult to evaluate, since no criteria were set for such advertising.

Discussion of paid media advertising as opposed to public service announcements raises additional questions. First, there is no official way of ascertaining the value of government public service announcements because the Federal Communications Commission does not require the reporting to it of PSAs from logs of radio and TV stations. The only estimates of the value of PSA are based upon samples. For example, in recent years the military services have based their estimates of the value of their PSAs on reports of the Broadcast Advertisers Reports, Inc., a private firm. The Army, however, has no idea of the value of PSAs run prior to 1970 [39]. Moreover, when 31 federal agencies were asked by the GAO to provide estimates of the value of the PSAs, many were unable or unwilling to do so [40].

The GAO has been less than consistent on the matter of agency reliance on PSAs *vis-à*-vis paid advertising. When it conducted a study of military advertising in 1976, the GAO was not in favor of paid advertising. It cited advertising officials who estimated that utilizing paid advertising would cost the military 60 to 90 percent of its public service time; it quoted the media director of the Air Force's advertising agency who estimated that the Air Force would lose $12 million annually in PSA time. The GAO concluded that "... the clear possibility exists that a paid radio and television program stands a good chance of *reducing* the overall effectiveness of radio and television advertising [41]." But in 1977—the very next year—the GAO conducted a study of the campaign sponsored by the Environmental Protection Agency and the Federal Energy Administration to convince the public to buy more fuel-efficient automobiles. In this study, the GAO praised contract advertising and encouraged the agencies to embark upon paid advertising campaigns on a pilot basis. The FEA resisted, stating that such a program would reduce PSAs [42].

ADVERTISING, PUBLICITY AND THE AMERICAN DEMOCRACY

There is little doubt that modern government requires advertising and publicity programs. They are essential tools in the implementation of government policies. For example, modern U.S. agriculture, the envy of the free world, was given an important boost by DOA's public information program which reported the latest research and conveyed proper agricultural techniques to the nation's farmers. The work of Smokey the Bear, Woodsy Owl, and Johnny Horizon on behalf of the environment is the stuff of legends. One might as well attack Mickey Mouse as to speak ill of these creatures of the Ad Council.

In these times of technological complexity, publicity programs are necessary to report the activities of government in a form that is meaningful to the lay citizenry. Moreover, as the institutions which have traditionally facilitated voluntary law compliance diminish in influence, these programs are being used to inform citizens of their obligations under the law in such areas as customs, traffic control, and so on. In this way they reduce the personal costs of compliance with the law as well as the need for government to employ expensive legal procedures. In some areas such as tobacco and alcohol abuse, nutrition, and consumer affairs, government publicity programs, however modest, have been necessary to attempt to counteract the adverse effects of huge sums spent on advertising in the private sector. Rourke's statement that "... few if any executive agencies could discharge their governmental responsibilities if they were obliged to work under severe restrictions on the amount of information activity they could carry on [43]" has lost nothing in meaning over the years.

The necessity for such programs raises questions. While the previous section focused on how advertising and publicity programs *are* administered, this section shifts to the broader social context. The questions raised address the issues of how such programs *should* be administered given the needs of contemporary democracy. Five of the most important are considered.

Government as Propagandist. Government advertising and publicity inevitably involve propaganda, since they appeal to the masses as well as to individuals [44]. The federal government is the one source of legitimate system-wide political control, and as such occupies a preeminent position in the marketplace of symbol manipulators. Government advertising and publicity activities regularly use symbols that support social order and appeal to deeply held belief systems. Thus the Armed Services' television ad which urges individual youths to enlist also conveys the message that it is patriotic to do so and that national security is essential. Similarly, community values are regularly pressed into service to support campaigns to conserve on energy and to protect the environment.

The propaganda effects of such programs can cast unelected officials in the role of meddlers in the national value structure. Consider the PSA produced by the Public Health Service in cooperation with Planned Parenthood. It features celebrity Erik Estrada (star of the popular television program CHiPS), whom the producers think can communicate with youths from disadvantaged backgrounds. The message is "Don't have sex until you are ready." The ad implies that it is okay to have sex when the youth feels that he or she is ready. This message is intended undoubtedly for segments of the population in which illegitimacy is rampant and parental guidance is thought to be lax. PSAs are broadcast over mass media, however, and therefore cannot be targeted to specific audiences. Thus, Estrada's message goes as well to communities in which values and parental control are vastly different. One consequence of the advertisement may be to undermine parental authority and to contribute increasing teenage sexuality.

It can be argued that the propaganda consequences of government advertising and publicity programs project the image of government as a benevolent all-caring parent—a national nanny. It tells us to watch our diet, to get plenty of rest and exercise, to have our blood pressure checked regularly, not to be "fuelish," to drive safely, to buckle seatbelts, and to protect the environment. Citizens are told what to do in cases of consumer fraud, how to protect the unborn during the prenatal period, how to qualify for food stamps and medical care, and much more. With government cast in this role in much of its publicity, does this not risk blunting healthy skepticism toward government by the populace?

Government Credibility.

A second, but related, issue is the well-documented diminution of the credibility of government today. Contemporary advertising and publicity programs may have contributed to this problem. Throughout the Vietnam conflict, for example, DOD public relations personnel continually released overly optimistic assessments of the situation. Another example is the fuel efficiency ratings for automobiles published by the Environmental Protection Agency. An Energy Department study has shown that the figures overstate mileage by 21 percent, but EPA maintains that the ratings are useful for comparative purposes [45]. Many prospective automobile purchasers have not grasped this subtle distinction, and have used EPA's figures to rate cars rather than rank them. Another case of loss of government credibility involves advertisements for U.S. Savings Bonds. These bonds are widely recognized in financial circles as poor investments in time of high inflation. Some citizens knowingly make this trade-off in the name of patriotism, but others may have reason to feel that their government has duped them [46].

Sometimes credibility problems result because government embarks on publicity and advertising campaigns dealing with topics and/or circumstances for which such techniques are ill-suited. Even when experts do not agree among themselves about proper policies, public affairs officials have authorized TV and radio ads as though such consensus existed. In the case of the Swine Flu innoculations, for example, 46 million persons, queued up to get their shots, unnecessarily as it turned out. Moreover, a few suffered crippling reactions to the injections. In another case, a former chairman of the Advertising Council was very critical of the council's campaign (sponsored by Commerce Department funds) on behalf of the free enterprise system because, as he said, the economic system is too complex to be discussed intelligently in 30-second spot announcements [47].

Government credibility is most severely strained when publicity programs are focused on "products" that the public does not want. One recent instance involves the U.S. Treasury Department's Susan B. Anthony one-dollar coin. The public, fearing that it would too easily confuse the "Susie"

with the similarly sized quarter, rejected it. The U.S. Treasury was undaunted: it launched an advertising campaign and persauded the U.S. Postal Service to proffer the coin in change. Consequently, the public was charged twice. It first bore the costs of production, minting, and distribution of a coin it did not want. Then it paid for public affairs programs intended to induce acceptance of a coin it had already rejected. As former U.S. Senator J. William Fulbright noted when discussing the soaring public affairs budget of the Pentagon during the Vietnam era:

> There is something basically unwise and undemocratic about a system which taxes the public to finance a propaganda campaign aimed at persuading the same taxpayers they must spend more tax dollars to subvert their independent judgment. I am reminded of W. C. Field's admonition—'Never give a sucker an even break.' [48]

The final irony is that this effort too was unsuccessful.

Advertising and Publicity Programs and Executive Political Power.

A third issue is the strengthening of the power of bureaucratic agencies *via* advertising and publicity programs. Appropriations for such programs contribute in important ways to the agencies' ability to attract independent political support. Once attained, this support can be converted through the workings of the political process into increased budgets, more personnel and new program authorizations.

Advertising in the private sector is often part of a strategy of *product differentiation* as a way of reducing the effect of price competition. In the public sector, it can be regarded as a strategy to enhance name recognition so that the agency involved is not forced to rely solely on its record of service delivery as a source of support. Thus, Harris noted in his study of attitudes toward alcohol abuse that the ". . . NIAAA is making inroads into the public consciousness . . ." as the sponsor of many ads on the topic [49]. Greater agency recognition by the public at-large is undoubtedly a general consequence of such programs. With each showing of an ad or publication of a brochure, the agency and its functions are again brought to the public's attention. Sometimes an agency might advertise an auxiliary service and in this way broaden its clientele. It is difficult to imagine any other justification for the Postal Service spending over $3.3 million in fiscal year 1975 to launch a national stamp collecting campaign [50].

An agency's advertising and publicity budget also strengthens its political base by enhancing the agency's ability to serve its clientele. Often this results when a bureaucratic unit disseminates information of specific interest to its clientele. At times, public agencies may even pay the cost of publicity campaigns which enhance the programs of clienteles. Thus, officials of HEW told the GAO that they were urged by major health organizations such as the American Cancer Society and the American Medical Association to give "national leadership and coordination" to a campaign to educate the public about the effects of smoking [51]. And certainly the campaigns by the FEA and EPA to encourage more fuel-efficient automobiles have resulted in government assumption of part of the auto industry's promotion costs for weaning the public from "gas guzzlers" [52].

Perhaps the most controversial campaign by a government agency in recent years was the one undertaken by the Commerce Department to educate the public about the benefits of the free enterprise system. In 1974, that department took $239,000 from the budgets of two of its agencies to award a contract to the Ad Council for the first stage of such a campaign. It was alleged in some quarters that the idea for the campaign resulted from a speech given by the chairman of the board of Procter & Gamble to members of the Advertising Council. It did not help the credibility of the project with its critics that the volunteer company which promulgated the project for the Ad Council was Compton Advertising, Inc., a Procter & Gamble agency [53].

The Government/Media Relationship.

A fourth issue is the impact of paid advertising on the relationship between government and the media. The sizeable sums government spends on advertising give it considerable leverage, at least potentially, to influence media content and presentation. Congressman Collins (R-Tex), for one, has wondered if government could end up as senior partner in any business association with the media involving paid advertising [54]. Although there is no evidence that it has yet been done, prudent management practice would suggest, for example, that all government agencies should pool their media buying in order to avail themselves of applicable quantity discounts.

More fundamentally, questions were raised in House hearings held in April 1971 on paid government advertising as a threat to freedom of expression. In one case, a representative of N. W. Ayer & Son, Inc. (the advertising agency which had the Army account) revealed that in buying time during an experimental test of paid advertising in 1971, his company specified that such spots were not to be run in close proximity to newscasts in which Vietnam casualties were reported [55]. Another case involved Congressman F. Edward Hebert, then-chairman of the House Armed Services Committee. Hebert was so upset about the CBS program, "The Selling of the Pentagon," that he told *Advertising Age* that if DOD adopted a program of paid TV advertising, he did not want CBS on the schedule [56].

Writing after publication of *The Pentagon Papers,* Harry S. Ashmore, president of the Center for the Study of Democratic Institutions, attempted to assess the role of the news media in government deception about the American involvement in Vietnam. He wrote:

> The media as presently constituted could not function without the array of skills and resources provided them without cost in the name of public relations; and this consideration is compounded by their further reliance on advertising or political favors derived from the same sources. [57]

The inference is chilling. Quite obviously, government advertising and publicity have the capability of influencing the media, particularly if the government is a paying customer.

Who Guards the Guardians? Finally, there is the issue of control over government advertising and publicity activities, and the protection of the citizenry against its potential abuses. One agency that might be charged with such responsibility is the General Accounting Office. The GAO, however, functioning under congressional mandate, has, to date, been concerned with budgetary efficiency rather than overall program effectiveness. It has ignored, for example, the propaganda content of government advertising and the subtlety of the appeals employed.

Another possible source of oversight for government publicity programs might be the Federal Trade Commission. Indeed, former Chairman Michael Pertschuk said he would use the agency's personnel and procedures to monitor government advertising, but the FTC's statutory authority to regulate such activities is ambiguous at best. Moreover, in view of its recent troubles with Congress, it is doubtful that this agency would be eager to accept such responsibility. As Wilson and Rachal have persuasively shown, government agencies find it much easier to regulate business than other agencies of government [58].

CONCLUSION

This survey of government advertising and publicity programs has shown that they are not of recent origin; some have roots as old as the Republic itself. Contemporary publicity and advertising programs appear to be widespread and well supported. They reflect the profound influence of the professions of advertising and marketing which have grown so greatly in the private sector during this century. Perhaps the most significant recent development in government publicity programs is the amount and extensiveness of contract (paid) advertising.

Advertising and publicity programs are an important part of administration in the national executive branch. They are the screen upon which agencies project the images they want the public to see; they are also communication links from the agencies to their constituencies. There can be little doubt about the need for advertising and publicity programs in modern government. Government, for better or worse, is involved in most aspects of modern life and therefore requires much communication—for the good of both the individual and the system.

There are problems involving the administration of these programs, however. These range from critical definitional problems to ones dealing with the consistency of budgeting practices; they include questions about the effectiveness of such programs and how they can best be implemented in the public sector. It is clear that the management of an agency's advertising and publicity programs constitutes as important a challenge as most public administrators face. It is also clear that these programs require even more sensitivity and good judgment than do most administrative tasks.

The proliferation of government advertising and publicity also poses significant questions for a democracy. A number of these issues were discussed; the effect of these programs on the free press, on the political control of executive agencies, and on the waning credibility of governmental structures. The basic questions are how the citizenry can be protected from deceptive government advertising, and how these programs can be reconciled with the assumption that in a democracy, demands for public goods and services should originate with the people. It is clear that these programs can be, and have been, utilized both for communication and manipulation. Thus, the challenge for the public administrator is to use such programs effectively and efficiently while nurturing democratic political institutions and social values.

NOTES

1. House Committee on Appropriations, *Hearings on the Department of Defense Appropriations for 1981: Part 2*, 96th Congress, 2nd Session (Washington: U.S. Government Printing Office, 1980), pp. 798–99.
2. House Committee on Government Operations *Hearings on Problems with the 1980 Census*, 96th Congress, 2nd Session (Washington: U.S. Government Printing Office, 1980), pp. 56–60.
3. Early treatments of the general topic of government publicity include James L. McCamy, *Government Publicity* (Chicago: University of Chicago Press, 1939); Harold W. Stoke, "Executive Leadership and the Growth of Propaganda," *American Political Science Review*, Vol. 35 (June 1941), pp. 490–500; T. Swann Harding, "Genesis of 'One Government Propaganda Mill,'" *Public Opinion Quarterly*, Vol II (Summer 1947), pp. 227–35; Dick Fitzpatrick, "Public Information Activities of Government Agencies," *Public Opinion Quarterly*, Vol. II (Winter 1947–48), pp. 530–39; and J. A. R. Pimlott, *Public Relations and American Democracy*, (Princeton: Princeton University Press, 1951). More recent offerings dealing with publicity include Francis E. Rourke, *Secrecy and Publicity* (Baltimore: Johns Hopkins Press, 1966 [hardback ed., 1961]), esp. Chs. 8 and 9, and Herbert I. Schiller, *The Mind Managers* (Boston: Beacon Press, 1973), esp. Chs. 2 and 3. Rourke's discussion can be characterized as a balanced one whereas Schiller is highly critical of government publicity programs.
4. U.S. General Accounting Office, "Use of Formal Advertising for Government Procurement Can, and Should, Be Improved," August 14, 1973 (B-176418), p. 45. Another law, passed in 1809, stipulated that the Navy make ". . . all purchases and contracts for supplies and services . . . either by open purchases or by previously advertising for proposals. . . ." The requirement of advertising for supplies and services, with few exceptions, was applied to all government agencies, by 1860. See *idem*.
5. Cited in Harding, *op. cit.*, pp. 227, 228–29.
6. U.S. General Accounting Office, "Letter Report to Senator William Scott—Public Relations Personnel Costs in 20 Federal Agencies and Various Other Costs," June 10, 1977 (LCD-77-424), pp. 8–10; see also *ibid.*, "Letter Report to Congressman Matthew Rinaldo—Public Affairs Costs in the Department of Health, Education and Welfare, and the Department of Agriculture," September 30, 1975, (LCD-75-452), pp. 1–3.
7. U.S. General Accounting Office, "Difficulties in Evaluating Public Affairs Government-Wide and at the Department of Health, Education and Welfare," January 18, 1979 (LCD-79-405), p. 9.
8. GAO, "Letter Report to Senator William Scott," *op. cit.*, enclosure 1.
9. House Committee on Appropriations, *Hearings on the Department of Defense Appropriations for 1981; Part 2, op. cit.*, p. 797; 93 *Stat.* 1160, (1979).
10. House Committee on Appropriations, *Hearings on the Department of Defense Appropriations for 1981; Part 5*, 96th Congress, 2nd Session (Washington: U.S. Government Printing Office, 1980), p. 118, table.
11. Senate Committee on Appropriations, *Hearings on the Department of Defense Appropriations for Fiscal Year 1978; Part 3*, 95th Congress, 1st Session (Washington: U.S. Government Printing Office, 1977), pp. 672–78, 692–93.
12. "100 Leading Advertisers," *Advertising Age*, Vol. 50 (September 6, 1979), p. 156.
13. House Committee on Government Operations, *Hearings on Problems with the 1980 Census, op. cit.*, pp. 56, 60.
14. "100 Leading National Advertisers," *Advertising Age., op. cit.*, p. 1.
15. GAO, "Letter to Senator Scott," *op. cit.*, p.2.
16. John S. Lang, "The Great American Bureaucratic Propaganda Machine," *U.S. News and World Report*, Vol. 87 (August 27, 1979), p. 43.
17. GAO, "Letter Report to Senator Scott," *loc. cit.*
18. GAO, "Letter Report to Senator Scott," *ibid.*, pp. 2-3. The ceiling mentioned in the report is $24 million. This was subsequently increased to $25 million. Nonetheless it appears that DOD is no more successful in staying within its new limits. See note 9 above.
19. GAO, "Difficulties in Evaluating Public Affairs . . . ," *op. cit.*, p. 7.
20. See Ben M. Enis, "Governments as Marketers: Issues of Management and Public Policy," in *Government Marketing: Theory and Practice*, M. P. Mokwa and S. V. Permut, eds. (New York: Praeger, Inc.).
21. Joseph L. Bower, "Effective Public Management," Vol. 55, *Harvard Business Review* (March/April 1977), pp. 131–40.
22. See for example, Herbert H. Hyman and Paul B. Sheatsley, "Some Reasons Why Information Campaigns Fail," *Public Opinion Quarterly*, Vol 11 (Fall 1947), pp. 412–23; G. D. Wiebe, "Merchandising Commodities and Citizenship on Television," *Public Opinion Quarterly*, Vol 15 (Winter 1951), pp. 679–91; Harold H. Mendelsohn, "Some Reasons Why Information Campaigns Can Succeed," *Public Opinion Quarterly*, Vol. 37 (Spring 1973), pp. 50–61; and Paul N. Bloom and William D. Novelli, "Applying Conventional Marketing Wisdom to Social Marketing Problems," in Mokwa and Permut, *op. cit.*
23. Michael L. Rothschild, "Marketing Communications in Nonbusiness Situations or Why It's So Hard to Sell Brotherhood Like Soap," *Journal of Marketing*, Vol. 43 (Spring 1979), pp. 11–20.
24. *Ibid.*, pp. 13–15.
25. 39 *Stat.* 212 (1913).
26. Fitzpatrick, *op. cit.*, p. 531.
27. 5 *U.S.C.* 368, sec. 3107 (1976).
28. U.S. General Accounting Office, "Letter Report to Congressman Baucus—Government Expenditures for Public Affairs," July 12, 1977 (LCD-77-434), p. 2.
29. U.S. General Accounting Office, "Advertising for Military Recruiting: How Effective Is It?" March 29, 1976 (FPCD-76-168), p. 57.
30. The four percent figure is found in House Committee on Interstate and Foreign Commerce, *Expenditure of Public Funds for Broadcast Advertising*, 92nd Congress, 1st Session (Washington: Government Printing Office, 1971), p. 39; the eight percent figure is from GAO, "Advertising for Military Recruiting," *op. cit.*, p. 9, table.
31. Senate Committee on Appropriations, *Hearings on the Department of Defense Appropriations for Fiscal Year 1978; Part 2*, 95th Congress, 1st Session (Washington: U.S. Government Printing Office, 1977), p. 141.

32. GAO, "Advertising for Military Recruiting," *op. cit.*, p. 7. It should be noted that other stations declined the paid advertising but said they would continue to run Army PSAs. See House Committee on Interstate and Foreign Commerce, *Expenditure of Public Funds for Broadcast Advertising, op. cit.*, pp. 97–100.

33. GAO, "Advertising for Military Recruiting," *op. cit.*, p. 32.

34. Cecil J. Mullins *et al.*, "Effectiveness Evaluation of Air Force Advertising," September 1975, (National Technical Information Service #AD-A018 61016GA), p. 5.

35. John Adler *et al.*, "Effects of Anti-Smoking Campaigns Aimed at Less Hazardous Smoking," October 1972, (National Technical Information Service #PB-225 157/7), pp. 1–5, especially pp. 4–5.

36. Louis Harris and Associates, "Public Awareness of the NIAAA Advertising Campaign and Public Attitudes Toward Drinking and Alcohol Abuse: Phase IV," February 1974 (National Technical Information Service #PB 244 147), p. 142; p. 15, table.

37. GAO, "Difficulties in Evaluating Public Affairs . . . ," *op. cit.*, pp. 24–29.

38. "Editorial Viewpoint," *Advertising Age*, Vol. 46 (April 7, 1975), p. 14 as cited in GAO, "Advertising for Military Recruiting," *op. cit.*, p. 41.

39. GAO, "Advertising for Military Recruiting," *op. cit.*, p. 7; and House Committee on Interstate and Foreign Commerce, *Expenditure of Public Funds for Broadcast Advertising, op. cit.*, p. 47.

40. U.S. General Accounting Office, "Letter Report to Congressman Edwin D. Eshleman—Advertising Costs for 31 Federal Agencies," October 6, 1975 (LCD-76-415).

41. GAO, "Advertising for Military Recruiting," *op. cit.*, p. 12; 42, emphasis in original.

42. U.S. General Accounting Office, "Convincing the Public to Buy More Fuel-Efficient Cars: An Urgent Need," August 10, 1977 (CED-77-107), pp. 13–16; and 17, 32.

43. Rourke, *op. cit.*, p. 190.

44. This distinction between propaganda and advertising is offered by Stephenson and Nimmo in their discussions of symbols as components of systems of political control and as components of systems of convergent selectivity. In the former, symbols are used to manipulate groups of people and frequent appeals are made to established belief systems which reinforce the existing order (as with propaganda); in the latter, the appeal is to individuals to do something such as buy a product and there are competing sources of symbols from which individuals can make choices (as with advertising). See William Stephenson, *The Play Theory of Mass Communication* (Chicago: University of Chicago Press, 1967), pp. 33–35, 192–95; and Dan D. Nimmo, *Popular Images of Politics* (Englewood Cliffs: Prentice-Hall, 1974), pp. 143–47.

45. Associated Press, "EPA May Overhaul Its Mileage Ratings" (September 15, 1980). As of this time, the EPA is considering various formulas to adjust its laboratory figures to make them more reflective of expected model ratings. It does not plan to test mileage under actual road conditions, however.

46. Enis, "Governments as marketers . . . ," *op. cit.*

47. Philip H. Dougherty, "Campaign on Economy Weighed," *New York Times*, July 22, 1975, p. 45. This article is reproduced in House Committee on Government Operations, *GHT Hearing on Commerce Department Payment to the National Advertising Council for Promotion of the Free Enterprise System*, 94th Congress, 1st Session (Washington: U.S. Government Printing Office, 1975), pp. 37–38.

48. Cited by Nicholas Johnson in a dissenting opinion on the application of the Fairness Doctrine to Armed Forces recruitment announcements as reproduced in House Committee on Interstate and Foreign Commerce, *Expenditure of Public Funds for Broadcast Advertising, op. cit.*, p. 14.

49. Harris *et al.*, *op. cit.*, pp. 12–14.

50. GAO, "Letter Report to Senator Goldwater," *op. cit.*, p. 2.

51. GAO, "Difficulties in Evaluating Public Affairs . . . ," *op. cit.*, p. 15.

52. This campaign is discussed in GAO, "Convincing the Public to Buy More Fuel-Efficient Cars," *op. cit.*

53. House Committee on Government Operations, *GHT Hearing on Commerce Department Payment to the National Advertising Council for Promotion of the Free Enterprise System, op. cit.*, pp. 1–8.

54. House Committee on Interstate and Foreign Commerce, *Expenditure of Funds for Broadcast Advertising, op. cit.*, p. 170.

55. Ibid., pp. 99–100.

56. "Editorial Viewpoint," *Advertising Age*, Vol. 42 (March 15, 1971), p. 12 as cited in *ibid.*, pp. 150–51 (statement by Congressman Parren J. Mitchell, D., Md.)

57. Harry S. Ashmore, "Government by Public Relations," *The Center Magazine*, Vol. 4 (September/October 1971), p. 25.

58. James Q. Wilson and Patricia Rachal, "Can Government Regulate Itself?" *The Public Interest*, No. 46 (Winter 1977), pp. 3–14.

PART II

Developing A Consumer Perspective

Cases

8. City of Dallas   **79**

9. Water Conservation in Palo Alto   **91**

10. Seville Community College   **105**

11. The Golden Gate Corridor Busway   **107**

12. The Birds, the Bees, and the Bugs   **117**

Readings

13. Nonprofits: Check Your Attention to Customers   **131**

14. Diffusion of Innovations   **137**

15. Preventive Health Care and Consumer Behavior: **147**
    Towards a Broader Perspective

8
City of Dallas

Christopher H. Lovelock

George R. Schrader, city manager of Dallas, and members of his staff were debating how to improve citizen compliance with several important ordinances relating to the quality of life in the city. These ordinances concerned control of domestic animals (especially dogs), litter, cutting of high weeds, rat and mosquito control, and removal of junked cars. Dallas prided itself on being a well-run city, but the city manager felt that there was still room for improvement in each of these areas. Several approaches appeared possible in each instance. Stronger enforcement of city ordinances might be obtained by raising the fines for violations, by increasing the frequency of inspections by city employees, or through a communications program which sought to obtain voluntary compliance for citizens.

A detailed research study of these problem areas had been received the previous month, May 1977. Mr. Schrader believed it contained many valuable insights and was anxious to move forward on developing suitable programs.

Dallas, the seat of Dallas County and the second largest city in Texas, was first settled in 1841. Located on the Trinity River in northeastern Texas, about 75 miles south of the Oklahoma border, Dallas enjoyed a generally mild climate. The city had grown rapidly since the discovery of oil in eastern Texas during the 1930s. By 1977, it was the financial and commercial center of the Southwest, with an economy resting primarily on banking, insurance, electronics, aerospace, cotton, oil, and state and federal employment. The city of Dallas covered an area of 365 square miles and had a population of about 872,000. Approximately 30% of the population was Black, and another 10%, Mexican-American. The Dallas-Fort Worth "metroplex" had a population of over 2.5 million, making it the tenth largest standard metropolitan statistical area in the United States (ahead of Houston with 2.3 million).

Dallas was administered by a professional city manager, George R. Schrader, who was responsible to an elected city council and mayor. In contrast to many U.S. cities, the Dallas city government was generally considered to be apolitical and free of political appointees. Exhibit 1 shows the organizational structure of the city government. In 1976–77, the operating budget for the city was $307 million, up 9% from the previous year.

The basic unit of the city for control purposes was the statistical neighborhood, of which there were 33 in total. The size, population, and ethnic mix of these neighborhoods varied considerably. Exhibit 2 shows the number of households and median and mean incomes for each neighborhood

Christopher H. Lovelock is Associate Professor of Business Administration, Harvard University. The material in this case has been derived from public sources, primarily from a published document, *Marketing Municipal Services: A Study for the City of Dallas*, prepared in April 1977 by Daniel Bechtel, Linda Keene, William Griglock, Anish Mathai, and David Mixer (all members of the Harvard MBA class of 1977). Certain data have been simplified for the purposes of case analysis.

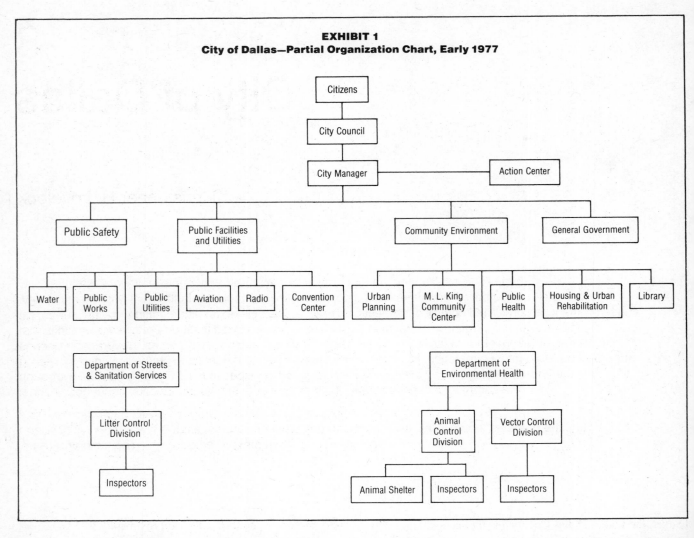

EXHIBIT 1
City of Dallas—Partial Organization Chart, Early 1977

at the time of the 1970 census. It also shows which neighborhoods had substantial minority group populations in 1977.

OBJECTIVES AND POLICY CONSIDERATIONS FOR CITY SERVICES

The City of Dallas had established clearly defined objectives for the seven functional areas which comprised its city services.*

1. *General Government:* Formulate city policy and assure its implementation through management and support activities.
2. *Culture and Recreation:* Provide year-round opportunities for constructive and pleasurable use of leisure time by supporting programs which permit a variety of recreational, cultural, and educational experiences.
3. *Public Safety:* Reduce the amount and effect of external harm to persons and property and maintain an atmosphere of personal security.
4. *Public Transportation:* Provide programs and systems for ground and air transportation to move people and goods safely, quickly, and economically.

*Source: City of Dallas 1975–1976 Program of Services.

5. *Housing and Urban Rehabilitation:* Create and implement viable housing policies to further residential development and rehabilitation and enforce housing and construction codes.
6. *Public Health and Community Service:* Provide programs and activities designed to achieve a healthful environment, and to provide social services for the disadvantaged.
7. *Public Works and Utilities:* Undertake design, construction, and repair of the street and thoroughfare system, and of the storm drainage and flood control system; provide for the sanitary disposal of refuse and trash; provide water and waste water services; and provide quality public communications.

Schrader believed that success in meeting the seven objectives would enable the city of Dallas to reach its goal of achieving and maintaining a high "quality of life." These objectives had evolved from policies designed to meet the needs of the Dallas community in the years ahead. Important policy considerations included: financial discipline to improve performance and control costs; conversion of service programs into commercially viable operations where feasible; rationalization of operations to eliminate parallel or duplicate service programs and staffing; and, development of new revenue sources to lower reliance on property taxes.

PERFORMANCE MEASUREMENT, SERVICE DELIVERY, AND CODE ENFORCEMENT

Teams of inspectors were responsible for enforcing city ordinances (Exhibit 1). The responsibilities of inspectors in the Litter Control Division of the Department of Streets and Sanitation Services included litter, weeds, and junked motor vehicles; inspectors in the Environmental Health Depart-

ment were responsible for stray animals and vectors (rats, mosquitos, and other disease-carrying pests).

These departments used two basic approaches in trying to meet the standards expected by the city administration. The first consisted of delivery of specific city services, such as litter removal, collection of stray animals, spraying of insecticides, cutting of high weeds, etc. The second represented efforts to enforce compliance with city ordinances through issuance of notices, citations, and legal action. The latter approach often generated an adversary relationship between city departments and citizens. In fact, some observers believed that overly zealous code enforcement actually

EXHIBIT 2
Dallas Demographics

Neighborhood	Population # Households	Income $ Median	Mean	Ethnic Mix* (1977 Estimate)
1. CBD	2,679	5,231	6,611	
2. Cockrell Hill	5,156	8,251	8,733	
3. East Dallas	22,017	5,176	6,029	50% Black
4. Elam	3,989	8,337	9,996	35% Black
5. Fair Park	2,650	9,096	9,872	40% Black
6. Ferguson	14,575	11,590	12,470	
7. Highlands Vicker	19,740	11,361	12,820	
8. Hillcrest	10,392	20,431	25,118	
9. Jefferson	26,638	6,837	8,062	
10. Jim Miller	11,156	9,096	9,872	
11. Keist	12,815	9,981	11,206	
12. Lakewood	14,933	7,980	9,727	
13. Lisbon	15,127	7,026	7,453	
14. Love Field	17,033	7,951	11,264	80% Black
15. Mountain Creek East	772	4,857	6,637	15% Black
16. Northwood	7,792	14,798	18,106	
17. Oak Lawn	14,897	5,771	7,547	
18. Park Forest	8,387	25,434	29,259	
19. Pleasant Grove (Bruton East)	5,015	9,765	10,134	
20. Polk South	7,048	13,984	15,836	
21. Red Bird	893	9,550	9,876	
22. Richland	25	6,625	15,434	
23. Simpson Stuart	5,165	7,651	8,667	
24. South Central Industrial	585	3,966	6,596	
25. South Dallas	8,574	3,108	3,871	85% Black
26. Stemmons North Industrial	1,186	5,373	6,809	
27. Stemmons South Industrial	1,350	4,829	5,808	
28. Trinity	11,644	5,421	6,223	80% Black
29. Walnut Hill	13,818	18,400	35,346	
30. West Dallas	10,010	4,439	5,018	80% Spanish-speaking
31. White Rock Creek Industrial	3,947	6,408	8,409	
32. White Rock East	9,340	10,539	12,567	
33. Woodland Springs	2,202	7,618	9,354	
Total	291,550			

Average household
Population = 2.9 persons

*City Totals:

White	60%
Black	30%
Spanish Speaking	10%**

**Note: Outside West Dallas, Spanish-speaking residents were widely dispersed throughout the city.

EXHIBIT 3
Map of Dallas Showing Highest Violation Neighborhoods for Specific Problems

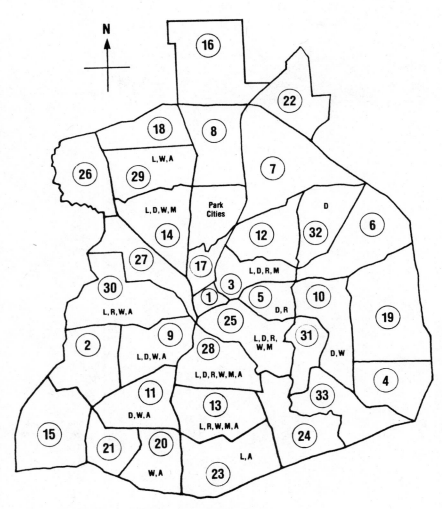

Numbers are keyed to neighborhood names in Exhibit 2.

Problems: L = Litter   R = Rats   A = Junk Autos
           D = Stray Dogs M = Mosquitos W = Weeds

reduced the effectiveness of service delivery programs. They also worried that employees of the departments in question might lose sight of broader city goals and see enforcement efforts as ends in themselves.

The Litter Control, Vector Control, and Animal Control divisions employed a total of about 80 inspectors. An inspector's salary averaged around $13,500; benefits and overheads brought the average annual cost to the city per inspector to around $19,000. Inspectors were responsible for patrolling neighborhoods and ensuring that standards were maintained. If a neighborhood had a section that was below par, the inspector issued a "notice" to the owners/tenants of the properties in question. However, there were no *explicit* standards for animal and vector control, so that "par" was left to the inspector's subjective assessment.

If the violation was not corrected within a prescribed period of time—usually ten days—a citation was issued to the violator, requiring him or her to appear in court. With a few minor exceptions, this procedure was followed by all departments. The fines levied for noncompliance varied at the discretion of the court, subject to a maximum of $200. A typical fine for a first offender was $5 to $10, but judges tended to be stern with repeat offenders. Since the city kept good records, repeated offenses by the same individual were readily identifiable.

The Litter Control Division had established a "clean ratio" as a performance measure. Inspectors were obliged to complete environmental survey reports for the areas they visited. The clean ratio was derived from inspectors' evaluations of five criteria: fills (illegal dumps), litter/trash, junk automobiles, weeds, and solid waste storage. Different weights were assigned to each of these violations in computing the overall performance measure. The city had set a clean ratio of 75% as the objective for the Litter Control Division. For the Vector and Animal Control divisions, however, performance measures were more subjective and therefore, less readily quantifiable.

Because objective evaluation criteria were lacking, it was hard to make comparisons between different areas of the city across the full range of problems. "Notices issued" and "complaints" were somewhat inadequate measures for identifying and isolating high-violation neighborhoods. In Vector Control, for example, inspectors concentrated on known mosquito breeding grounds, issuing hundreds of notices. Other parts of the city, where the problem was only marginally lighter, received relatively few notices. Furthermore, complaints about mosquitos tended to come from areas where the problem was less serious. Some observers believed that people in high-problem neighborhoods simply did not complain much to the city.

Despite these difficulties, it was still possible to isolate areas where the problems appeared to be severe. Based on a survey, Vector Control had identified six neighborhoods as being heavily rat infested; similarly, scientific measurement techniques had enabled the division to pinpoint those areas

where the *culex* mosquito was a serious problem. Animal Control had identified problem neighborhoods on the basis of the number of inspections, complaints, and citations. The Litter Control Division identified its high violation neighborhoods on the basis of the clean ratio and the number of notices issued.

High violation neighborhoods are pinpointed on a map of the city of Dallas in Exhibit 3. Exhibit 4 shows, for each neighborhood, the 1976 clean ratio, the number of notices issued by the Litter Control Division for litter, junked autos, and weeds, the number of inspections made by Animal Control, and the number of complaints received by Vector Control.

THE DALLAS CITY PROFILE

In 1974, the city government had initiated an annual survey of Dallas residents known as the City Profile. This surveyed the citizens of Dallas concerning their satisfaction with municipal services and measured attitudes toward certain key issues. A systematic random sampling of housing units was drawn from each of 20 communities which comprised the city of Dallas, utilizing updated census block records. At least 100 respondents were selected from each community.

The survey findings were used to identify service deficiencies and to establish program priorities. When broken down by statistical neighborhoods, the responses enabled city officials to pinpoint problem areas on a geographic basis (Exhibit 5). The responses to the 1976 *Profile* indicated that many residents perceived their neighborhood as having mosquito and/or rat problems (usually the former), as well as stray dog problems. Most considered litter service quality to be good or excellent and saw their neighborhoods as "usually clean" or "almost always clean." In none of the neighborhoods were junked cars or the condition of the alleyways cited as a problem by a significant proportion of respondents. Residents of all neighborhoods felt the litter control budget should remain at the same level. Although the quality of animal control services was rated as just "fair" in most neighborhoods, only East Dallas respondents wished to see the budget for this service increased.

THE LITTER CONTROL DIVISION

Most observers felt that Dallas was a relatively well-maintained city and suffered less from litter and garbage problems than other cities of comparable size. The Litter Control Division undertook inspection, notification, and citation of illegal dumping, littering, high weeds, and solid waste storage. It also enforced the removal of abandoned refrigerators and junked autos, provided alley-trimming service to reduce weed growth in alleyways used for storage and collection of solid waste, and issued waste-hauling permits. Finally, it provided removal service for dead animals.

EXHIBIT 4
Key Statistics for Litter, Vector and Animal Control Divisions

| Neighborhood | Clean Ratio 1976 | Litter Control Division Notices Issued 1975-76 | | | | | | Vector Control Division Complaints Received | | Animal Control Inspections Made |
| | | Litter | | Junked Autos | | Weeds | | Mosquitos | Rats | Animals |
		1975	1976	1975	1976	1975	1976	1976	1976	1976
CBD	75.6%	287	436	2	1	33	258	12	2	4,191
Cockrell Hill	55.6%	682	1,563	71	110	606	1,402	58	8	2,770
East Dallas	58.5%	2,227	2,695	99	108	988	1,085	88	91	5,938
Elam	47.9%	529	397	38	106	352	648	240	9	4,412
Fair Park	46.4%	1,908	1,225	99	111	927	695	18	35	5,048
Ferguson	69.4%	935	2,037	51	129	558	1,855	144	45	3,970
Highlands Vickery	77.4%	559	1,256	31	85	341	988	83	19	5,439
Hillcrest	87.8%	283	675	5	18	222	588	32	29	3,932
Jefferson	60.1%	2,184	3,862	198	184	1,226	1,916	110	106	7,037
Jim Miller	66.3%	1,376	1,075	37	104	1,114	1,243	121	18	5,275
Kiest	75.0%	1,006	1,517	38	106	777	1,545	51	28	4,583
Lakewood	74.2%	1,491	2,598	67	58	665	1,120	91	39	4,922
Lisbon	38.9%	5,180	4,288	318	150	3,353	2,239	32	69	5,746
Love Field	72.5%	2,233	2,955	91	92	1,127	1,959	30	56	8,046
Mountain Creek East	91.0%	13	62	2	19	17	58	16	0	2,194
Northwood	82.0%	257	505	12	29	226	555	14	40	3,618
Oak Lawn	64.5%	973	686	34	45	516	522	25	25	5,330
Park Forest	86.8%	659	1,440	32	31	704	1,467	16	31	3,345
Pleasant Grove	66.6%	396	740	13	46	436	686	93	6	4,915
Polk South	71.4%	494	1,221	40	84	658	1,267	27	12	3,261
Red Bird	58.4%	226	330	51	30	370	542	6	2	2,816
Richland	81.4%	4	5	2	0	10	29	5	0	2,324
Simpson Stuart	49.6%	1,295	1,880	64	76	1,026	1,721	15	9	3,087
South Central Industrial	59.9%	48	278	5	8	51	206	26	4	2,042
South Dallas	50.9%	2,484	2,820	80	61	1,597	1,628	24	62	7,962
Stemmons North Industrial	35.0%	159	202	17	27	181	238	34	5	4,660
Stemmons South Industrial	63.3%	628	335	48	36	402	647	33	12	5,750
Trinity	39.0%	2,918	3,143	188	120	1,785	1,595	32	32	4,968
Walnut Hill	79.8%	1,213	3,557	53	65	936	2,606	39	40	4,586
West Dallas	41.8%	6,969	5,496	300	137	4,490	3,313	74	9	10,451
White Rock Creek Industrial	39.4%	1,109	497	144	60	832	564	33	5	3,625
White Rock East	75.3%	541	937	48	63	276	603	92	37	3,788
Woodland Springs	60.7%	272	303	7	11	170	300	80	6	3,611
Totals	62.3%	41,494	39,303	2,285	2,312	26,052	29,441	1,794	891	153,342

Source: City Departmental Records

Exhibit 6 summarizes the division's performance for 1975 and 1976.

In the 1976 *Dallas City Profile*, 86% of respondents rated the city's garbage collection service favorably (Exhibit 7). The level of expenditure for this activity was felt to be "just right" by 76%. The condition of the alleys presented no problem to 78% of respondents, while 89% considered their neighborhoods "usually" or "almost always" clean. Only 13% of respondents cited garbage or litter in the alleys behind their homes as a neighborhood nuisance; the comparable figure for junked or abandoned cars was 12%.

The stated objective of the Litter Control Division was to raise the city's clean ratio to an acceptable 75% from the 1976 figure of 62.3%. The division had estimated that a total of 229,406 inspections annually would enable it to achieve the desired clean ratio. No basis was offered for this assumption, but it appeared to be an extrapolation based upon the experience of the past year, when 3,058 additional inspections had been conducted and a one percent increase in the clean ratio had been observed. At the present time, there were 24 inspectors in the division, each averaging 7,724 inspections during a year of 248 working days.

Apart from being unsightly, litter and improperly stored household garbage were also considered to be health and fire hazards. Although the city had laid down strict standards for storage of garbage, these were not always adhered to by

EXHIBIT 5
Neighborhood Views on Selected Topics

Neighborhood	Mosquito/Rat Problems?	Stray Animal Problems?	Neighborhood Cleanliness*	Litter Service Quality	Animal Service Quality
CBD	No	No	UC	Good	Fair
Cockrell Hill	No	Dogs	UC	Good	Fair
East Dallas	No	Dogs	UC	Good	Fair
Elam	Yes	Dogs	UC	Good	Fair
Fair Park	Yes	No	UC	Good	Fair
Ferguson	No	No	UC	Good	Fair
Highlands Vickery	No	No	UC	Good	Fair
Hillcrest	No	No	AAC	Good	Good
Jefferson	No	Dogs	UC	Good	Fair
Jim Miller	Yes	Dogs	UC	Good	Fair
Kiest	No	Dogs	AAC	Good	Fair
Lakewood	No	Dogs	AAC	Good	Fair
Lisbon	Yes	No	UC	Good	Good
Love Field	No	No	UC	Good	Fair
Mountain Creek East	Yes	Dogs	UC	Excellent	Fair
Northwood	No	No	AAC	Good	Fair
Oak Lawn	No	No	UC	Good	Fair
Park Forest	No	No	AAC	Good	Fair
Pleasant Grove	Yes	Dogs	UC	Good	Fair
Polk South	Yes	Dogs	UC	Excellent	Fair
Red Bird	Yes	Dogs	UC	Excellent	Fair
Richland	No	No	UC	Good	Fair
Simpson Stuart	No	Dogs	UC	Fair	Fair
South Central Industrial	Yes	Dogs	UC	Good	Fair
South Dallas	Yes	No	UC	Good	Fair
Stemmons North Industrial	Yes	Dogs	UC	Good	Poor
Stemmons South Industrial	Yes	Dogs	UC	Good	Poor
Trinity	Yes	Dogs	UC	Good	Fair
Walnut Hill	No	Dogs	UC	Good	Good
West Dallas	Yes	Dogs	UC	Good	Poor
White Rock Creek Industrial	Yes	Dogs	UC	Good	Fair
White Rock East	No	No	UC	Good	Fair
Woodland Springs	Yes	Dogs	UC	Good	Fair

*UC = Usually Clean, AAC = Almost Always Clean

Source: Dallas Profile Survey 1976

EXHIBIT 6
Litter Control Division Performance Summary, 1975–76

Activity	Litter		Junked Autos		High Weeds		Total	
	1975	1976	1975	1976	1975	1976	1975	1976
Complaints/Requests	10,715	10,547	1,639	1,376	8,106	7,790	20,460	19,713
Department Actions								
Notices	41,494	39,303	2,285	2,312	26,052	29,441	69,831	71,056
Citations	1,089	960	119*	87*	2,205**	2,078**	3,413	3,125
Compliance Rate (percent)	97.4	97.6	94.8	96.2	91.5	92.9	95.1	95.6
Average Correction Period (days)	19	15	22	20	21	16	20	16

* Junk autos removed.
** Includes weed locations mowed: 1,158 in 1975 and 935 in 1976.

EXHIBIT 7
Excerpts from Dallas City Profile 1976

(A) Rating of City Services[1]

Service	Percent Favorable (+1 to +3)		
	1976	1975	1974
Water Service	95	93	*
Fire Protection	94	91	96
Library Services	92	85	75
Park and Recreation Facilities	86	78	75
Garbage Collection	86	84	86
Police Protection	85	83	86
Control of Air Pollution	83	79	*
Beautification of Public Land	83	74	80
Street Cleaning	83	77	79
Traffic Signs, Signals	83	82	85
Bus Service	79	80	79
Consumer Protection, Education	76	72	*
Sidewalks	76	75	75
Street Maintenance and Repairs	73	70	74
Control/Elimination of Rundown and Abandoned Buildings	69	67	*
Control of Stray Animals	64	*	*
Regulation of Utility Companies	55	66	*

*Not surveyed.

(B) Neighborhood Nuisances Cited

Problem	Cited by Percentage of Respondents		
	1976	1975	1974
Stray Animals			
Dogs	30	28	31
Cats	18	18	16
Insects and Pests			
Mosquitos	21	24	29
Rats	14	12	10
Flies	5	8	9
Mice	5	5	4
Deceptive Practices by Merchants and Businesses	18	17	16
High Weeds on Vacant Lots	18	13	13
Abandoned, Poorly Maintained Buildings	17	18	18
Air Pollution	17	17	16
Traffic Noise	17	15	18
Garbage/Litter in Alley	13	12	12
Junked, Abandoned Cars	12	13	12

[1]Respondents were asked to rate each service from +3 to −3. A rating of +1, +2, or +3 was taken as favorable. Changes in ratings of less than 5 percentage points in successive years were not considered statistically significant.

---

citizens. The authors of the research study commissioned by the city manager noted that:

> Numerous cases of improperly stored garbage were observed. Examples included metal trash cans without lids and garbage stored in plastic bags. An overturned trash can or torn plastic bag often remained as evidence of a food hunting foray by some hungry animal.

Junked Motor Vehicles. The junked motor vehicle control program was administered by the Litter Control Division. Litter control inspectors enforced compliance with the junked motor vehicle ordinance as part of their regular duties. They responded to citizen complaints as well as conducting regular inspection tours. Owners could be cited for junked motor vehicles stored on their own property as well as for those left on the street.

In order to be classified as a junked motor vehicle by the city of Dallas, a vehicle had to meet *each* of the following criteria:

- The inspection sticker (if any) should have expired.
- The license plate (if any) should have expired.
- The vehicle must be inoperable (defined as missing a significant part required for operation, i.e., transmission, motor, tires, etc.)

Technically, if the vehicle failed to meet any *one* of these criteria, the owner could not be issued a junked motor vehicle violation. In practice, however, inspectors sometimes issued notices for vehicles in the "borderline" category (i.e., meeting two of the three criteria).

Once an inspector had classified a motor vehicle as "junked," a notice was issued informing the citizen that he or she was in violation of the law. The notice indicated the source of the violation and set a ten-day limit for correcting it. After ten days, the inspector checked to see if the citizen had complied with the notice; but if not, the inspector notified the city's towing service to pick up the vehicle, which was then taken to a contract crusher and shredded. However, inspectors exercised judgment before ordering this drastic step. In practice, several notices were usually issued before an order was given that the vehicle be impounded. When this action was taken, the citizen was not charged, but the city pocketed the proceeds from the sale of the scrapped vehicle.

There was a high rate of voluntary compliance. In 1976, only 87 out of the 2,312 notices issued for junked motor vehicle violations required further action by the city (i.e., seizing and crushing of the automobile). In the remaining cases, citizens took the necessary corrective action to remove their automobile from the junked motor vehicle classification, once they were told they were in violation of the law.

Owners of automobiles having little or no trade-in value had several options available to them. One was to sell the car to another individual. If the vehicle was in fairly good condition, a private buyer might be willing to pay slightly more than the trade-in value. A second option was to sell the car to an old-car dealer, auto parts dealer, or automobile salvage yard. A telephone survey of a sample of these outlets in the Dallas area indicated that they would pay between $25 and $75 for an automobile that was brought to them in operating condition (depending on the make and physical condition of the car). An inoperable car, which they would pick up, usually brought $15–$35. The owner's third option was to keep the car with a view to fixing it up again or using it as a source of spare parts for other cars they owned and operated. Other people held on to old, operable cars for purely sentimental reasons or because of inertia.

The control of junked motor vehicles was seen as a difficult and sensitive issue. In a memo, the superintendent of the Litter Control Division wrote:

> The junk motor vehicle program is the most touchy—causes the most citizen discontent—of all Litter Control programs because the vehicles so classified as junk do have a certain monetary value. Owners feel the vehicle is private property and the city—or any government for that matter—has no right to confiscate private property.

Tall Weeds. The city of Dallas' weed ordinance stated that weeds should be no more than twelve inches in height. Tall weeds were seen as a public health hazard in that they were havens for stray animals, rodents, and insects. They generated pollen which contributed to human respiratory diseases. They were also a public safety hazard in that they could conceal potentially dangerous traffic situations to drivers, bicyclists, and pedestrians. When an area was overgrown with weeds, it often became a dumping ground for garbage and solid wastes, which made the weeds even more difficult to cut—and so the problem compounded itself. Finally, high weeds represented a fire hazard and an eyesore.

Citizen concern over high weeds appeared to be increasing. In 1976, 18% of respondents to the *Dallas City Profile* had cited high weeds on vacant lots as a neighborhood nuisance, compared to only 13% the previous year (Exhibit 7).

Investigation of the problem showed that there were basically two types of high frequency violations. One involved weeds growing along alleyways between the maintained portion of the property and the vehicle passage lane (generally between the fence and the paved alley or wheel rut). The second concerned weeds growing on vacant improved or unimproved property, generally in development fringe areas.

Since weed violations occurred on property that somebody owned, a responsible party could usually be located. The city of Dallas *Code* defined the responsible party as "any owner or person in control of any occupied or unoccupied premises."

Unfortunately, location and notification of the responsible party was no guarantee of compliance. According to interviews with Litter Control inspectors, compliance was much higher among violators who were resident on the premises than among off-premise, absentee violators. Inspectors stated that many rental residents believed that landlords were responsible for all property maintenance, and that their own responsibility was limited to building interiors. Many residents also thought that the city was responsible for maintaining the cleanliness of alleys.

Weeds on vacant property represented yet another problem. Because of absentee ownership, notifying the responsible party was often difficult. According to inspectors, many landlords avoided all maintenance responsibility and simply allowed the city to cut their weeds. They paid the bill when it came—it was similar to what would be charged by a commercial firm—and continued to violate the ordinance time and time again.

DEPARTMENT OF ENVIRONMENTAL HEALTH

This department included the Animal Control and Vector Control divisions. The former had some 40 inspectors in early 1977 while Vector Control had 15. The Animal Control Division was responsible for operating the city's animal shelter, which was located on a major artery just south of the central business district, and close to the Dallas Zoo.

Animal Control. Domestic animals were a politically sensitive issue in Dallas. An organized group of citizens concerned with animal welfare had been instrumental in pressuring the city council to initiate changes at the animal shelter, including more humane methods of destroying unwanted animals. A veteran city council observer described this group as "very well connected, well organized, very articulate, and very emotional. But," he added, "they've pretty much worn out their welcome at City Hall. The city council just hates to see them coming now."

On the other hand, there was significant public discontent over stray animals. Control of strays had received the second worst rating of all city services in 1976, with only 64% of respondents expressing satisfaction with Dallas animal control services. Thirty percent cited stray dogs as a neighborhood nuisance and 18% cited stray cats (Exhibit 7). Among that group which had called City Hall in 1976 with a specific problem (22% of all households), more than one-fourth had done so to complain about stray animals and 4% had called about dead ones. The animal shelter was the most frequently called city office (Exhibit 8).

The annual cost to Dallas citizens for animal control totalled close to half a million dollars in 1976, up by 70% over 1971. It was expected to rise again in 1977. Inspectors had made over 150,000 animal inspections in 1976 and the problem appeared widely dispersed among all 33 statistical neighborhoods (Exhibits 4 and 5). When stray animals were caught, they were taken to the animal shelter. If not adopted by new owners within a certain number of days, they were humanely destroyed.

The city had recently adopted a plan for animal control which called for a 50% increase in the dog license fee (from $2 to $3) for spayed dogs and a 300% increase in the fee (from $2 to $8) for licensing unsterilized dogs. The city council hoped that this differentiation would encourage owners to take their dogs to spay-neuter clinics or to local veterinarians. But it was too soon to assess the impact of these

EXHIBIT 8
Citizen Contacts with City Hall

(A) Percentage of City Hall Callers Citing a Specific Problem[1]

Problem	1976	1975	1974
Stray Animals	28	25	30
Garbage, Trash Problems	13	12	13
Street Maintenance, Repairs	8	9	10
Water Problems	8	9	8
Traffic Problems	8	7	4
Crime, Vandalism	7	8	10
Neighborhood Appearance	5	7	5
Utility Problems (other than water)	5	4	3
Sewer Problems	5	2	3
Dead Animals	4	4	6
Consumer Problems	4	3	1
Alley Problems	2	4	3

(B) Percentage Contacting a Specific Office

Office	1976
Animal Shelter	28
Sanitation Services	14
Police/Nonemergency	12
Water	11
City Switchboard	10
Utilities other than water	9
Street Maintenance	7
Consumer Affairs	3
Health Department	2
Action Center	2
News Media	1
Mayor and Council	0.5
City Manager	0.5

(C) Overall Level of Satisfaction with Outcome of Contact

	1976	1975	1974
Satisfied	61	55	59
Not satisfied, did not correct problem	22	28	26
Not satisfied, no response	10	14	13
Not satisfied, too many referrals	3	—	—
Response not yet complete	4	3	2

[1]In 1976, 22% of the households surveyed indicated that they had contacted the city on a nonemergency basis at least once during the past year seeking information or assistance in solving a problem. Homeowners contacted the city more frequently than renters. The percentages in the tables above should be read as percentages of all City Hall callers; for example (28% × 22%) of all households called the city concerning stray animals in 1976.

Source: Dallas City Profile, 1976.

---

fee increases. About 25,000 dogs were licensed as of early 1977, representing only about one-sixth of the estimated dog population of Dallas. Many citizens failed to register their dogs, but nobody was sure what proportion of the unlicensed animals actually had owners.

Both owned and ownerless animals contributed to health and environmental problems and helped perpetuate the animal population explosion in the city. The potential magnitude of the dog population problem was emphasized by one author who calculated that:

> . . . any female [dog] . . . could produce 10,028 descendants in only eight years! This alarming statistic is based on the assumption that a female produces four puppies per litter. Half of these puppies are female, and they, in turn, bear one litter of four pups each year apiece. The offspring will number four the first year, sixteen the second year, 52 the third year, 160 the fourth year, 488 the fifth year, 1,468 the sixth year, 3,608 the seventh year, and 10,028 the eighth year!*

Experts concluded that a decrease in the animal population could only be achieved through control of random breeding. Recent emphasis had been placed on decreasing the number of free-ranging animals and on increasing the number of sterilized animals. Historically, sterilization services in Dallas had been expensive and available only at licensed veterinarians. But attempts were now being made to bring these services within the reach of the majority of pet owners through creation of municipally supported spay-neuter clinics. The City of Dallas was aware of current developments in animal control procedures. Its system followed the approaches recommended by various humane associations.

Unfortunately, gaining citizen cooperation with animal control efforts had proved difficult. Dogs and cats had long been an integral part of the human environment, and the attitudes of pet lovers towards these animals appeared very complex. The research report received by Mr. Schrader identified the following reasons why citizens might choose not to cooperate with animal control efforts in their neighborhoods:

1. Owners believe that it is unhealthy for an animal to be confined; that it must be able to get sufficient exercise to "stay in shape."
2. Owners endow pets with humanlike qualities. For example, an owner may believe his/her pet is intelligent, that it knows not to cross the streets against traffic, etc. Essentially, this is a belief that the pet can "take care of itself" in the outside environment.
3. Many owners think that they can train their pet not to exhibit undesirable behavior. They allow these pets to roam the neighborhood, believing that it is *other* dogs who don't know any better, who tip over garbage cans, bite people, etc.
4. Walking a pet on a leash can be a most undesirable job for a pet owner. It takes up time that could be spent on more important activities. It is so much easier to let the pet "walk itself" and come home when it gets tired or hungry.

---

*Nancy Flynn, "Every Litter Hurts a Bit," *Our Four-Footed Friends*. Boston, Massachusetts: Animal Rescue League, 1975, p. 9.

5. Owners believe that it is more humane to allow an unwanted pet to become a scavenger and "live by its wits" than to turn it over to an animal shelter where it may be put to sleep.

6. Many pet owners believe that spaying or neutering is tantamount to castrating a family member. The pet is perceived as having sexual needs similar to those of humans. Depriving it of such a basic need is thought to be cruel.

The report concluded that attempts to modify these attitudes and to change present behavior concerning pets must be an essential part of any program designed to help reduce this problem.

Some owners resorted to dumping unwanted pets. Sometimes a cute puppy or kitten turned into an unappealing adult dog or cat and the owner would lose interest. Other times, an owner might be stuck with a litter of puppies or kittens for which good homes could not be found. Faced with unwanted pets, owners had two basic choices. One was to turn the pets over to the animal shelter where they were likely to be destroyed if no home could be found. A second option, apparently adopted by many owners, was to abandon the animal in another part of the city, in the expectation that it would have a fighting chance on its own. Letting animals loose in this way was not directly associated with destroying them, thus lessening any guilt feelings their owners might have.

The problems caused by dogs and cats, both owned and ownerless, included: the noise they made; traffic hazards; threats to people, other animals, or property; and public health risks. Dogs were generally considered to be a much more significant problem than cats.

Free-roaming dogs rummaging through improperly stored garbage in search of food created a poor appearance for the neighborhood and lowered trash collection efficiency, as well as generating food for other pests. Studies of urban dogs showed them to be capable of maintaining their body weight from garbage and handouts. Death from starvation was quite rare.

Another significant problem was the tremendous quantities of feces and urine excreted by dogs. The New York City Bureau of Preventable Diseases had estimated that the average dog excreted 0.75 pounds of feces and 0.19 gallons of urine per day. Using these averages, the research study calculated that the estimated 150,000 dogs in Dallas collectively deposited over 20,000 tons of feces and ten million gallons of urine each year, much of it on city streets and sidewalks or in city parks. Commented the report:

> Unlike cats, dogs normally make no effort to bury their feces. In addition to the offensive odor and appearance of these deposits, there is mounting evidence that they play a major role in the spread of disease from dogs to humans.
>
> Dog feces contain worms and other parasites which contaminate the soil and are transmitted to humans frequenting these areas. Dog worms are more than a veterinary problem as the invasion of human beings by nematode larvae results in [several] diseases. . . . Symptoms and severity vary depending on where the larvae migrate. These larvae have been implicated in polio and epilepsy.

The implication of parasitism in strays should be obvious—fecal contamination may occur in unsuspected areas possibly used by children who are the most common victims of visceral larva migrants.

The disease leptospirosis is transmitted via the urine. Even dogs which have been vaccinated have been demonstrated to be carriers of this organism. Over the last five years, leptospirosis has gone from being an occupational disease of animal handlers to one occurring most frequently in young children and housewives. In each of these confirmed cases of leptospirosis in humans, the infected party had been in close contact with a dog.

One of the most disturbing things about the diseases connected with dogs is their high incidence among children. The disease organisms are most often transmitted through skin contact and ingestion. Studies have shown that pica (dirt-eating) is very common among young children, especially those from poorer neighborhoods. Play areas frequented by children and dogs are ideal sites for infection.

The report then went on to cite the findings of a 1974 conference on the subject of dog bite:

> Of all the problems related to uncontrolled dogs, none is as socially costly as dog bit injury. Better than one out of every 200 people are reportedly bitten yearly, and it is estimated that only a half to a quarter of all bites are reported.
>
> Complications of the bite may be trauma and pain or even long-term disfigurement. Perhaps the least obvious trauma caused by animal bites is psychological trauma. This is especially true when investigations as in Baltimore and Pittsburgh indicate that the most common victims of bites are youngsters.
>
> Rabies presents the most feared complication of an animal bite. First, and probably the most serious threat, is the concentration of this disease in spite of the great decline in the incidence of human rabies over the past 25 years. Secondly, and a significant threat, is the treatment prescribed to avoid disease. Post-exposure prophylaxis is painful, costly, and hazardous.*

The report warned that the large population of unvaccinated dogs in Dallas increased the likelihood of a disease outbreak, should the rabies virus be introduced into the area. Other complications of dog bite which were mentioned included bacterial infections and tetanus. The report continued:

> Dogs are also a major contributor to the fly problem. Accumulated fecal matter serves as a breeding site for flies which transmit enteric organisms from dog to man. In residential areas, dog feces rank next to garbage cans in fly production. A Savannah, Georgia, study showed that 60% of all garbage cans actively produce flies and that a single dog's fecal deposit produced from one to 588 (mean = 144) flies. In addition to salmonella, there are a number of other diseases which can be transmitted to humans by the fly, such as typhoid fever, paratyphoid fevers, parasite worms, tularemia, and anthrax.

Rodents. Rats (and to a lesser extent, other rodents) represented a public health menace to Dallas because of the many ways in which they could transmit disease—through their excreta, through the parasites which lived on them, and through their bites. Public health officials felt that the rat problem in Dallas was worse than suggested by reported

---

Proceedings, National Conference on the Ecology of the Surplus Dog and Cat Problem, Chicago, Illinois, 1974, p. 41.

statistics. They ascribed this both to the nocturnal habits of rats and to the social stigma associated with rat infestation. Rats were a largely invisible threat, and it took a trained eye to spot evidence of rodent activity.

In the heavily infested areas of the city—identified by experts as West Dallas, East Dallas, and South Dallas, Fair Park, Trinity, and Lisbon—only 25% of residents responding to the annual *City Profile* stated that rats were a problem in their neighborhood. This compared with findings that at least half of the residences in these areas were infested. Yet complaints of rat infestation to Vector Control from these areas in 1976 ranged from a low of nine in West Dallas to a high of 91 in East Dallas (Exhibit 4).

The research report went into some detail on the health hazards posed by rats:

> Humans living in close proximity with rats are exposed to a variety of health hazards. Rat bite is a frequent occurrence in many large urban areas. There are approximately 50,000 cases of rat bite reported annually in the United States, and it is believed that the number which go unreported is much higher. As in the case of dog bites, children are the most frequent victims of such attacks. The severity of these bites was demonstrated in a Florida study where "approximately 95% of the rat bite victims received medical assistance for injury associated with the bite."
>
> In addition to the injury of the rat bite, rat bite fever—which is caused by two bacteria, *Spirilium minus* and *Streptobacillus moniliformis*—was estimated to have occurred in 7% of the total cases of rat bites in some areas. Rats also contaminate food and water with excretions containing Salmonella bacteria, tapeworm eggs, and leptospirosis organisms. The oriental rat flea (*Xenopsylla Cheopis*) is the principal disease vector for plague and murine typhus.

The rat population was believed to feed mainly on human food garbage. A rat typically needed less than an ounce of food a day. In addition to eating garbage, rats were also known to obtain food from two other sources: dog feces and pet food dishes. In Baltimore, the city code required landlords to remove dog feces from their premises daily if they had been served with a rat violation notice. Rats had also been observed eating from petfood dishes while a dog snoozed in the same enclosure. Some authorities feared that where rats coexisted with household pets, they might infect the latter which, in turn, could transmit these diseases to their owners.

Mosquitos. Mosquitos were a seasonal problem in Dallas, occurring from mid-March to mid-October, with peaks in May and occasionally in August. Two types of mosquito were prevalent in the area: the so-called "pest" variety and the *culex* mosquito. The "pest" mosquito bred, for the most part, in large open bodies of water such as swampland; in general, it was thought to be more of a nuisance than a health hazard. The culex mosquito, by contrast, was known as a "container breeder," and was seen as a significant threat to health. It thrived on bacteria-laden, still water and its favorite spawning grounds were in small amounts of stagnant water, such as that which had collected in tin cans, old tires, birdbaths, discarded hub caps, and flower pots. The culex mosquito was the principal transmitter of St. Louis encephalitis (SLE) from contaminated fowl to human beings. Malaria was another human disease associated with this species of mosquito.

Because of the magnitude of the problem, Vector Control annually made major efforts to eliminate mosquito breeding grounds and reduce the insect population. These efforts included code enforcement, chemical treatment of breeding areas, and monitoring activities. The greatest success had come from treating larger bodies of water for "pest" mosquitos. However, because the culex mosquito bred in literally millions of containers, it was a much more difficult problem for Vector Control to handle. Officials felt that code enforcement could only accomplish a limited amount, and that citizen cooperation was needed to eliminate potential breeding grounds on private property. A representative of the Environmental Health Department estimated that citizen cooperation could reduce the magnitude of the culex mosquito problem by 50%–75%.

CONCLUSION

The city manager and his aides wondered what approaches would be best for dealing with each of the five problem areas. In addition to identifying the most appropriate strategy in each instance and preparing a tentative schedule, they also wanted to set priorities among these five areas.

9
Water Conservation in Palo Alto

Peter T. Hutchison
Don E. Parkinson
Charles B. Weinberg

Mr. Alan Jay, Chief Engineer of the Department of Water, Sewage and Gas (DWSG) in Palo Alto, California, did not know how to react to the first rain in weeks in drought-stricken California. It was the beginning of March 1977 and close to the end of what was normally considered the "wet" season in the region.

He wondered whether a few days of rain would result in a decrease in water conservation efforts. One thing the Chief Engineer knew for certain was that he could not continue to rely on the effect of the strong and extensive newspaper stories that had announced the launching of the initial water conservation campaign in January with headlines such as "Save Water or Else . . . Area Warned" and "Water Cut Target 10%".

THE DROUGHT OF 1977

For the second year in a row, Northern California had experienced record drought conditions, with rainfall less than 50% of normal and reservoirs levels at record lows.

Shortly after the start of 1977, most people, and particularly weather forecasters, realized that the unseasonable warm and dry weather that the Western portion of the United States was enjoying had the potential to change people's lifestyles, to cause industrial problems, and to threaten the existence of numerous farms and ranches that depended upon irrigated water.

In the early months of 1977, *Time, Newsweek,* and many other national magazines had reported extensively on the drought. The television networks had brought films and reports on the drought to Eastern viewers suffering from record cold and snow falls. People generally smiled at solutions such as the use of pipelines to send Eastern snow west and at slogans like "Save Water—Shower with a Friend," while trivia buffs prospered with such gems as "The toilet accounts for 40% of all indoor household water usage (up to seven gallons a flush)." However, the lack of rain had serious consequences for both the nation and the West.

Because 85% of the water used in California was consumed by farmers supplying 40% of the country's fresh vegetables and fruits, the reduced water supply was expected to result in shortages and higher prices for all. Utilities in the Pacific Northwest, which used hydroelectric energy as a major source of power, would have to turn to more expensive sources. Forest rangers were worried about fire hazards; outdoors enthusiasts, about the loss of fishing and boating opportunities; and homeowners, about keeping lawns and gardens green. Although long-term solutions such as weather modification, better irrigation techniques, and desalting water were being discussed, no amount of talk or money could change the fact that many reservoirs had gone

Peter T. Hutchison and Don E. Parkinson received M.S. degrees from Stanford University Graduate School of Business in 1977. Charles B. Weinberg is Professor of Marketing at the University of British Columbia.

dry, and there was no chance of any change in that condition until the end of 1977. No one had dared to consider the consequences of a third drought year.

Public Opinion in California. In March 1977, the California Poll conducted a representative statewide survey of 962 California residents and published the results in newspapers throughout the state. (The California Poll, which had operated since 1947, was an independent media-sponsored, public opinion news service which regularly carried out personal interview surveys on socially significant issues.) Eighty-five percent of those surveyed believed the drought was either "extremely serious" or "somewhat serious." When asked which user class should be cut the most if mandatory rationing became necessary, respondents replied as follows:

USER CLASS	% Saying Cut This Group Most
Business and Industry	50
Households	33
Health and Safety	3
Agriculture	3
No opinion	11

With regard to reduction of household water usage by 25%, only 10% of respondents said it would cause severe problems: however, 51% said a 50% cutback would cause severe problems. Finally, 93% claimed to be practicing some form of water conservation, such as using less water for bathing (70%), watering lawns less (67%), and less frequent car washing (58%). Twenty-four percent claimed to have installed devices in their toilet tanks to reduce the amount of water used to flush, and 16% said they had installed water flow restrictors to reduce the rate of water flow in showers.

PALO ALTO AND THE SAN FRANCISCO BAY AREA

The population of the City of San Francisco was 700,000, and that of the nine-county San Francisco Bay Area totalled some 4.5 million. The Bay Area's generally mild climate had an average temperature range of from 54°F to 77°F (in summer) and from 39°F to 58°F in winter. The average annual rainfall of 15.5 inches occurred mainly from October through March. It almost never rained in June, July, and August. In 1975–76 and 1976–77, the rainfall had been less than one half of normal.

Palo Alto, a city of 55,000 people located about 35 miles south of San Francisco and 15 miles north of San Jose, was one of a number of cities which formed an extensive urban corridor along the length of the San Francisco Penisula (Exhibit 1). The surrounding area offered a number of desirable features. Four hours' drive to the East, the Sierra Nevada mountains offered some of the best skiing, camping, and backpacking country in the United States. And 30 minutes to the West, across the foothills of the Peninsula, were the inviting but chilly beaches of the Pacific.

Palo Alto residents tended to be highly educated and had a median income level among the highest in the nation. They took an active interest in city affairs, and their city government was considered to be very well run. The *Palo Alto Times,* with a circulation of 50,000 in Palo Alto, Los Altos, Menlo Park, Mountain View, and the surrounding area, reported extensively on the actions of the local city governments. Palo Alto fell within the circulation area of the *San Francisco Chronicle,* the *San Francisco Examiner,* and the *San Jose Mercury-News.* City residents could receive broadcasts from six VHF television and 58 radio stations.

Adjacent to the city, but not within city limits, was Stanford University. The presence of Stanford, as well as other factors, had stimulated the development of a high technology emphasis in many companies located in Palo Alto. Firms such as Hewlett-Packard, Varian, and Syntex had headquarters offices, research centers, and manufacturing operations in the city. The business community of Palo Alto had in the past been supportive of most community projects and had also demonstrated an effective response to the initial water conservation program. Civic groups, such as the Chamber of Commerce, had also been supportive of community conservation projects.

THE WATER SYSTEM IN PALO ALTO

The Palo Alto Department of Water, Sewage and Gas (DWSG) was responsible for the planning, production, and marketing of the water supply service of the city.[1] This department was directly responsible to the Utilities Director, who in turn was responsible to the City Manager (See Exhibit 2).

Mr. Jay, the Chief Engineer, was in charge of the operations of the DWSG. He supervised an administrative assistant plus a planning and design team of six people. The customer service department of the city was divided into two parts: first, the clerical function, which

---

[1] The City of Palo Alto supplied electric, gas, and water to all residents and commercial or industrial customers in the city. One monthly bill for all three utility services was mailed to all customers by the city. Usage and billing rates for each utility were separately itemized. In addition, the City of Palo Alto also provided garbage collection, but this service was administered and billed separately from the other three services.

EXHIBIT 1
Map of San Francisco Bay Area Showing Pipelines and Reservoirs

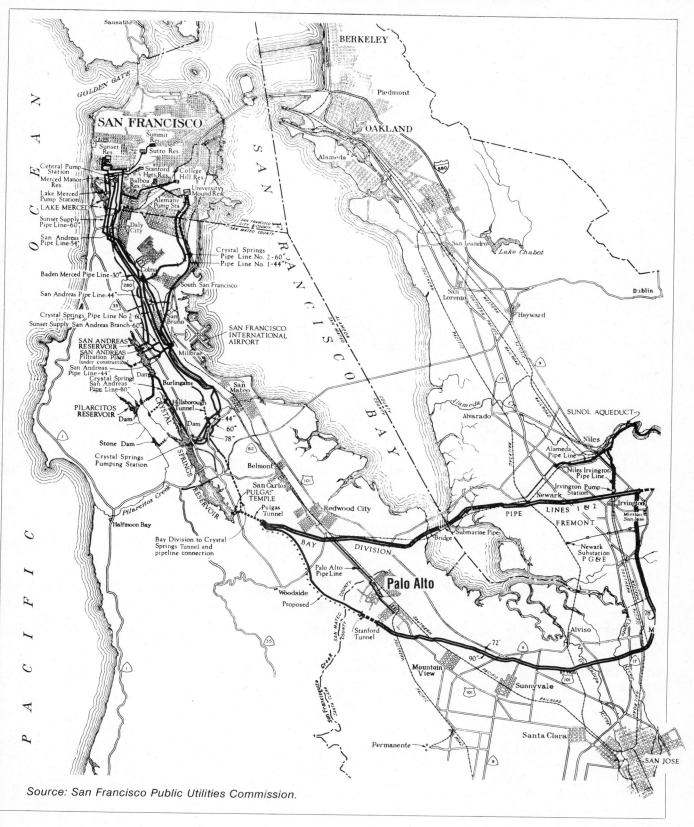

EXHIBIT 2
Palo Alto Utilities: Partial Organization Chart

```
                    ┌──────────────────┐
                    │   City Council   │
                    │    and Mayor     │
                    └──────────────────┘
                             │
                    ┌──────────────────┐
                    │      City        │
                    │     Manager      │
                    └──────────────────┘
                             │
        ┌────────────────────┼──────────────────────────────────┐
┌──────────────┐                                        ┌──────────────┐
│  Utilities   │                                        │     City     │
│  Director    │                                        │  Treasurer   │
└──────────────┘                                        └──────────────┘
        │                                                        │
┌───────┬────────────┬──────────────┬──────────────┐    ┌───────────────┐
```

Field Superintendent for Quality Control of Potable Water and Sewage Effluent	Field Superintendent for Distribution of Water, Gas, and Power	Chief Engineer of DWSG	Chief Engineer of Light and Power	Customer Service— Billings and Collection
25 Employees	37 Employees			

Under Chief Engineer of DWSG:
Administrative Assistant	6 Engineers

reported to the City Treasurer; and second, the technical function (complaints regarding quality or quantity of the water supply), which was administered by the field supervisors.

In connection with the water supply function, the DWSG had three goals:

1. To serve the populace with an adequate supply of drinking water for domestic, industrial, commercial, and public needs;

2. To provide this service at rates comparable to those charged by the utilities of neighboring cities and towns; and

3. To provide revenue to the general fund of Palo Alto by operating efficiently and earning a reasonable (5%–8%) return on investment. (Profit maximization was *not* a goal; nor was more than a prudent return on investment sought.)

These broad goals had been effectively translated into measurable operating goals. Examples stated by the DWSG were: (1) the DWSG strived to maintain water pressure within narrow tolerances. (Numerical standards were set and monitored.) (2) There was a constant monitoring of the quality of the potable water supplied, which was checked against a pre-set quality standard. (3) The customer service department had a goal of 15-minutes response time to a customer complaint. Currently a service crew arrived on the scene to investigate a complaint within 30 minutes of notification.

In addition, the DWSG provided such complementary services as technical advice on methods and new devices that could be employed by industrial and manufacturing customers to conserve water and consequently reduce costs. Mr. Jay and his staff had worked successfully with a number of local companies in developing efficient water usage programs well before the current crisis arose. In recent years, a number of local companies had achieved significant reductions in water consumption by recycling water used for cooling, by watering grounds at night when less evaporation took place, and by preventive maintenance programs.

Palo Alto's Water Supply. The source of supply for Palo Alto was the San Francisco Water Department (SFWD) System, which served the City of San Francisco and over 30 communities in the Bay Area. The primary source for the SFWD was the Hetch Hetchy, Lake Eleanor, and Lake Lloyd Reservoirs in Yosemite National Park, nearly 200 miles away. Rain and snow melt in the Yosemite area of the Sierra Nevada mountain range filled these reservoirs and the water was conveyed to the Bay Area through a series of tunnels and pipelines. The DWSG had a contract with the SFWD that expired in 1982. Although there were no specific provisions in the contract for renewal, there was no reason to believe that there would be any difficulties in doing so, as there had been none in the past. The

EXHIBIT 3
Water Supplied by SFWD to DWSG 1971–1976
(million cubic feet/month)

	1971	1972	1973	1974	1975	1976	Average
January	40	46	47	45	48	52	46
February	50	46	45	45	52	58	49
March	45	52	44	46	47	55	48
April	60	71	60	54	53	67[2]	61
May	66	83	79	74	67	82[2]	75
June	86	92	94	94	100[1]	98	94
July	93	95	104	89	99[1]	101	97
August	98	100	95	95	100[1]	97	98
September	92	90	89	100	89	82	90
October	73	71	71	72	73	67	71
November	65	49	54	63	58	66	59
December	48	44	45	48	56	50	49
Average	68	70	69	69	70	73	70

Source: DWSG records.

[1] Original data adjusted by summing three months supply and spreading equally to each month.

[2] Includes 5 and 7 million cu. ft. supplied from groundwater in April and May respectively.

contract did not specify any guaranteed supply to Palo Alto, but the city had been able to obtain as much water from SFWD as it had needed.[2] The total amount of water supplied by SFWD to Palo Alto was metered, and monthly dollar sales were determined at a pre-set rate. Monthly sales figures (volume of water) for the six year period 1971–76 are given in Exhibit 3.

As an alternative source of supply, the DWSG could draw on groundwater from its own well network. This source, which could supply about 40% of current demand, was used as a standby and had been used in 1976 when the supply from San Francisco was reduced because of a short strike by city workers. The quality of the groundwater was inferior to that supplied by the SFWD and required a considerable amount of softening. Prior to 1962, when Palo Alto began receiving its entire water supply from the SFWD, the DWSG had used the well system as its source of supply. At that time, the groundwater table was considerably drawn down, a condition that led to problems of subsidence and fears of salt water intrusions into the aquifers (water bearing ground). The latter was a very real and present threat, since some intrusion had already occurred on the eastern side of the San Francisco Bay. Prolonged use of the ground well system would threaten to "sink" neighboring cities.

The Demand for Water. Because the city's population was stable, the demand for water in Palo Alto had been

[2] If there was insufficient water in the SFWD, the contract provided to all users (including the City of San Francisco) would have the amount of water supplied cut back by a uniform percentage of the previous year's usage."

practically static for several years (Exhibit 3); no increase in demand was projected in the future.

The DWSG categorized its customers by usage into the following categories: domestic, commercial, industrial and public. The domestic consumers were further broken down into single family and multiple family (apartment and condominium type) units. In the later case, each family was not metered separately; instead the complex as a whole was metered. Customer data are shown in Exhibits 4 and 5.

Pricing Policy. The pricing policy for water in Palo Alto was based on the following criteria:

1. An equitable allocation of revenues and cost for the various classes of customers;

2. To provide a reasonable return on investment;

3. To provide the minimum basic requirement of a family for water at the lowest possible price (this was termed a lifeline rate);

4. To encourage conservation.

The level of prices was based primarily on the cost of the supply from SFWD (which accounted for approximately 63% of total revenue). Other costs such as distribution, administration, and general expenses accounted for approximately 19% of revenues.

The scale of charges was approved by the City Council, based on the DWSG's recommendation. The current scale of charges had been in effect since July 1, 1976. Until that date, the scale of charges had been such that the marginal cost decreased with increased consumption. The new structure made the unit price greater as consumption increased, so that a user of more than 1,000 CCF (1 CCF = hundred cubic feet) per month

EXHIBIT 4
Number of Customers and Annual Water Usage by User Class

Number of Customers Fiscal Year Ending June 30

	1971	1972	1973	1974	1975	1976
Single Family	14,083	14,150	14,178	14,146	14,251	14,268
Multifamily	1,235	1,261	1,281	1,240	1,252	1,253
Commercial	1,321	1,332	1,425	1,490	1,496	1,513
Industrial	227	228	265	271	272	271
Public Facility	198	200	218	213	208	203
City	121	124	71	207	259	260
Total	17,185	17,295	17,438	17,567	17,738	17,768

Annual CCF Per Customer

	1971	1972	1973	1974	1975	1976
Single Family	224	236	225	209	210	204*
Multifamily	435	415	398	410	431	413*
Commercial	709	768	744	662	890	855*
Industrial	7,886	7,835	7,410	7,734	8,211	8,229*
Public Facility	3,924	4,144	3,495	4,319	2,601	2,827*
City	2,571	2,608	3,426	1,497	1,212	991*
Total	436	452	444	443	448	455*

Source: DWSG.

* Estimated.

EXHIBIT 5
Water Demand in Palo Alto—Monthly and Quarterly Average for 1975–1976
(thousands of units—one unit = 1 CCF)

	Quarter I				Quarter II				Quarter III				Quarter IV			
	Jan.	Feb.	Mar.	Tot.	Apr.	May	June	Tot.	July	Aug.	Sept.	Tot.	Oct.	Nov.	Dec.	Tot.
Industrial	146	170	163	479	168	183	196	537	213	216	197	626	201	177	156	534
Public Facility	42	45	45	132	50	66	84	200	86	85	85	256	68	55	44	167
City Depts.	16	22	16	54	14	32	42	88	46	41	39	126	24	23	16	63
Domestic Single Family	180	163	167	510	190	273	379	842	406	363	361	1130	243	194	176	613
Domestic Multifamily	41	43	38	122	39	42	52	133	54	51	53	158	43	40	40	123
Commercial	77	88	83	248	75	90	110	275	123	120	110	353	93	79	71	243
Total	502	531	512	1545	536	686	863	2075	928	876	845	2649	672	568	503	1743

Source: Derived from DWSG—Monthly Sales Report.

would pay about 10% more per CCF above 1,000 than would a user of 50 CCF per month.[3] In addition, a general price increase of 8% was made. Careful analysis had shown that demand for water was not materially affected by this pricing strategy.

The extent to which the DWSG met its goal of maintaining its prices at levels comparable to those of neighboring utilities is shown in Exhibit 6. The average residential water bill was 4% above to 45% below adjacent cities, and average industrial bills were 6% above to 32% below adjacent cities.

---

[3] Water consumption is measured in terms of "units" of one hundred cubic feet. One unit = 1 CCF = 748 gallons.

THE WATER SHORTAGE PROBLEM

Despite the two years of record drought, on January 6, the general manager of the San Francisco Water Department (SFWD) informed Mr. Jay in Palo Alto that no curtailment of local water use would be necessary. Mr. Jay was somewhat surprised, therefore, when two weeks later, he heard on the radio that Bay Area suburban users would need to cut water consumption by 10%. The need for reduced water usage immediately received extensive coverage in the *Palo Alto Times* and the San Francisco newspapers.

Palo Alto's Water Conservation Program. Following the SFWD's request of a voluntary curtailment of 10%

EXHIBIT 6
Average Monthly Water Bill for Palo Alto and Other Bay Area Cities

	Usage* (CCF)	Palo Alto ($)	San Jose ($)	Mountain View ($)	Sunnyvale ($)	San Mateo ($)	San Francisco ($)
Residential	18	8.00	7.14	7.66	11.71	9.31	7.71
Commercial	60	22.78	25.84	24.05	34.41	31.52	24.61
Industrial	630	224.58	238.97	238.70	289.81	296.74	241.65
Industrial Large (1)	2,500	889.33	938.50	940.50	886.47	1,167.69	950.65
Industrial Large (2)	5,000	1,784.78	1,883.00	1,761.00	1,574.04	2,338.20	1,827.40
Industrial Large (3)	10,000	3,567.28	3,751.00	3,329.70	2,909.66	4,661.25	3,496.20

Source: DWSG Staff Report 3/18/76.

* Average usage in Palo Alto for different user classes.

in water consumption, the DWSG developed a conservation program aimed at all users, with special emphasis on domestic and industrial users. The thrust of the campaign was the conservation of water for the benefit of the community in general. After the Palo Alto City Council had adopted a resolution on water usage curtailment (see Exhibit 7A for supporting Staff Report), all Palo Alto residents were sent a message from the Mayor (Exhibit 7B), some informational materials (Exhibits 7C and 7D) and two water flow restrictors.[4] The industrial water conservation program is outlined in Exhibit 7E.

Mr. Jay felt that it was too early to assess the long run effect that DWSG's campaign would have. However, owing to the extraordinary publicity given to the water shortage problem by the press as well as radio and T.V., the community was well aware of the problem; it had reacted by reducing consumption 17% compared to 1976, since the emergence of the water shortage problem. The figures, in fact, were so satisfactory that there was a temptation to complacency. However, other resource crises (such as the fuel one of 1973) had shown the public's memory to be very short, and Mr. Jay feared that if the issues were no longer of interest to the media, the public would very rapidly return to its previous levels of consumption. The current shortage was clearly not just a short term problem. Because there was little expectation of significant amounts of additional rainfall before summer, the water shortage problem would probably last until the end of 1977 at least.

Mr. Jay knew that 70% more water usage occurred in the summer months when people tended their gardens and watered their lawns, and companies maintained the extensive landscaping around their factories, laboratories, and research centers (see Exhibit 5). He wondered whether those who conserved water when it was supposed to rain would also conserve when it was not supposed to rain. In addition, he felt that San

Francisco would soon raise the water reduction order to at least 25% less than the previous year's consumption.

The only comfort Mr. Jay had—which was not much—was that his colleagues in Menlo Park, Mountain View, and the other Bay Area cities served by the San Francisco Water Department and the City of San Francisco itself were faced with the same problem. Even worse off were some San Francisco communities that did not use the SFWD System; for example, Marin County, just north of San Francisco, faced a 57% reduction target. Because there were no Federal, State, or County conservation goals, each area user (or groups of users) had to set its own goals in accordance with its perception of its own demand and supply condition. Mr. Jay knew there were literally hundreds of officials who needed to design programs in response to the drought and, although he personally knew and had communicated with many of them, none had solutions to the problem.

The Need for Further Conservation Efforts. Though there was awareness of a water shortage problem in the community, Mr. Jay was concerned that the nature of the problem might not have been fully understood. Thus, he wanted to develop a plan that would ensure that the public had the correct perception of the long term nature of the problem and was provided with the information, motivation, and methodology they needed to help overcome the problem. Mr. Jay had a budget of $12,000 for a water conservation program. Nearly $7,000 had already been invested in the current campaign.

The Chief Engineer had to devise and implement a second water conservation plan that would reinforce the impact of the initial conservation campaign and encourage greater conservation in the immediate future. Although some had suggested a "mandatory" water conservation program, he was not sure that the City Council or the public would accept an extreme approach. Even in a mandatory program, allocations for different user classes would have to be made and decisions about how to treat unmetered apartment dwellers would be required.[5]

---

[4] A water flow restrictor, a disc installed on the pipe leading to the shower head, reduced the flow of water by as much as half when showers were taken. (See Exhibit 7D).

With regard to households, a mandatory limit on water consumption could be stated as a flat amount per person resident in the household or as a percentage reduction from usage in the same month of the previous year. The first approach was insensitive to variation in individual needs, the second approach would penalize those who had been efficient in previous years.

Past experience had suggested that a small price increase would have little effect, and even the doubling of the current water rates would only raise the average household bill to $16.00. It was very unlikely that the City Council would approve a policy banning the watering of lawns and, even if approved, the enforcement of such a ban would be exceedingly difficult.

As Mr. Jay sat pondering the problem and looking out of his window at the rain, his telephone rang with the news that the San Francisco Water Department had imposed a 25% mandatory reduction in water consumption throughout its service area. Mr. Jay realized he had a few weeks to prepare a water conservation plan for the City Council to discuss and, hopefully, adopt at its March 31, 1977, meeting. In presenting this plan, the Chief Engineer knew that not only would he need to defend it against alternative proposals, but he would also have to indicate why he believed that his plan would work.

---

[5] Typically, apartment buildings had one central water meter, so that it was not possible to determine how much water was being used by each separate unit.

EXHIBIT 7A
Staff Report

February 10, 1977

THE HONORABLE CITY COUNCIL
Palo Alto, California

San Francisco Water Curtailment

Members of the Council:

Since the request from the San Francisco Water Department to curtail water consumption was reported to you on January 24, 1977, staff has been working closely
with the City of San Francisco, members of the Bay Area Water Users Association,
and water agencies of Northern Santa Clara County to develop a uniform program
for water conservation. Resolutions similar to the attached one, which is submitted for your consideration, have been adopted by the Bay Area Water Users
Association representing contract users of San Francisco water. An almost
identical resolution has been approved by the treated water purveyors of Santa
Clara County and the Board of Directors of the Santa Clara County, and the Board
of Directors of the Santa Clara Valley Water District. The purpose of this report
is to request Council approval of the attached resolution, and to advise Council
of steps that are being taken to reduce water consumption in Palo Alto.

Background

Due to two successive years of record drought, the snow-melt inflow to the San
Francisco Hetch Hetchy system has dropped to 40 percent of normal. As a result,
storage in the Hetch Hetchy Reservoir is only 10 percent of capacity and water
production from the Tuolumne River watershed cannot meet the San Francisco
Water Department's goal of providing a minimum thirty-billion gallons (three-
months' supply) of local storage to serve the City of San Francisco and
Peninsula cities. (See Exhibit A). This water deficit has prompted the San
Francisco Public Utilities Commission to request all San Francisco water users
to reduce water consumption by at least 10 percent. Your Utilities Department
staff had developed such a program and the initial phases of it have already
been implemented.

Water Conservation Program - City Facilities

Initially, a memorandum was circulated to all City Department and Division
Heads requesting each to review their operation for opportunities to conserve
water. This memo evoked changes in operations in several departments that will
result in water savings. Notable efforts in conservation were the following:

> The annual water-main flushing program was canceled. Mains will be flushed
> selectively if required.

CMR:153:7

Exhibit 7A (Continued)

Page Two

. The hydrant-flow program has been curtailed to that required for ascertaining that no valves servicing fire hydrants are inadvertantly closed.

. Annual flower plantings in the City's parks will be eliminated.

. Flow restrictors will be installed on all City facilities where feasible.

. Use of the City Hall fountain has been curtailed.

. Engineering on facilities to deliver reclaimed wastewater to the Golf Course for irrigation needs have been expedited.

. Consideration is being given to the installation of tensiometer control on the Foothills Park irrigation system.

. Flow restrictors will be installed on all City showers and flushometer settings adjusted to reduce flow.

. The use of water for the cleaning of tennis courts and other paved areas has been discontinued.

. The level of irrigation required for the City's parks is being reviewed by maintenance personnel.

. A series of Wednesday night classes in water conservation have been offered by the Utilities Department staff members together with outside speakers.

Palo Alto Unified School District's Conservation Program

The Maintenance and Operations Coordinator of the Palo Alto Unified School District was contacted and responded promptly with an excellent program designed to substantially reduce the water consumption at School District's facilities.

Residential Conservation Program

It is proposed to send a mailing to all utility customers with the following material included:

. A letter from the Mayor requesting the participation of all citizens in the water conservation program (Exhibit B).

. A document showing areas where principal residential water uses occur and where savings may be achieved by the residential consumer (Exhibit C).

. An envelope containing two flow restrictors for showers.

. A sheet instructing the consumer how to install the flow restrictors and how to accomplish savings by installing plastic bottles in the flush tanks of toilets (Exhibit D).

CMR:153:7

EXHIBIT 7A (Continued)

Page Three

. Additionally, it is proposed to send a monthly reminder to all utility
  consumers that a continuation of the water conservation program is
  imperative. This program will be coordinated with other water purveying
  agencies in this area.

Industrial Water Conservation Program

The industrial water conservation program proposed by City staff is enclosed
herewith (Exhibit E). This program was presented to the Chamber of Commerce's
Utilities Task Force and many industrial facility managers on Thursday, February
3, 1977. This program appeared to be well received and stimulated a good exchange
of information between representatives of industry, the School District and the
City. Your staff is particularly encouraged by the fact that several industries
are studying the feasibility of using slightly degraded cooling water for irrigation purposes. This proposed reuse, in addition to saving water, will reduce
the hydraulic load on the Wastewater Treatment Plant.

Financial Impact

The total financial impact of the water conservation program will be reported
to Council at a later date. Direct expenses of approximately $10,000 are
anticipated over a period of one year for the purchasing and mailing of material
to the public. It is anticipated that this can be financed from the current
budget; thus a budget amendment will not be necessary. Less tangible impacts,
such as reduced water sales and purchases, and reduced sewer-use charges and
treatment costs, will require more time to properly evaluate.

Recommendation

It is staff's recommendation that Council adopt the attached resolution urging
the citizens of Palo Alto to observe the water conservation practices outlined
during the drought period.

Respectfully submitted,

Director of Utilities

Assistant City Manager

Attachments

CMR:153:7

EXHIBIT 7B
A Message From the Mayor

A MESSAGE TO THE RESIDENTS OF THE CITY OF PALO ALTO

FROM THE MAYOR

Two successive drought years have reduced the inflow to San Francisco's Hetch Hetchy water supply system by more than 60% and drawn accumulated reserves of water down to an undesirably low level. As a result, the San Francisco Public Utilities Commission, on January 25, 1977, requested all water purveying agencies served by Hetch Hetchy Water to effect a voluntary overall 10% reduction in consumption for at least the next 16 months. If this action fails to bring about the desired reduction in a short period of time, a mandatory program of water rationing will be imposed upon all users of San Francisco water.

As a contracting agency for San Francisco water, the City of Palo Alto is vitally affected by this request to conserve. It is essential that water savings are accomplished as soon as possible. I would therefore urge all Palo Altans to review their present water use practices, to discontinue all nonessential uses and to reduce essential uses wherever possible.

Palo Alto has long been known for its beautifully landscaped homes and parks, but here too we must curb our uses of water by refraining in our planting of water intensive annual flowers, and in the use of water hoses for the aesthetic wash down of cars, windows, houses and driveways, until the weather cycle again makes water more abundant.

Industrial processes that are wasteful of water should be reviewed and methods devised to recycle and conserve water wherever possible.

I am certain that with the cooperation of our citizens and industries, Palo Alto can achieve a saving in water consumption in excess of the 10 percent requested. Please look at the enclosed information which will help you reduce the consumption of water in your home.

Respectfully submitted,

STANLEY R. NORTON
Mayor

EXHIBIT 7C
Water Conservation Tips

YOUR PERSONALIZED WATER SAVING PLAN

Use the chart below to determine where the water is used in your house each day and where you want to cut back.

How many times a day do you use water??

Directions:

1. Locate in the "water use" column all the ways you use water.

2. On the row next to each water use write the number of times per day you use water in that way.

3. Multiply the number of gallons indicated for that water use by the number of times per day. Enter the answer in the "gallons per day" column.

4. After you finish filling in the "gallons per day" column, add up the total number of gallons in that column.

5. The total gallons per day can be used to devise your own water saving plan. If you wish to save 10% of the water you use, multiply the total by .10. (For example: a family of four found that they used 563 gallons per day. 563 x 0.10 = 56 gallons per day) The total for your water saving plan should be 10% less than your old total (in this example, 563 - 56 = 507).

6. Now go back to the chart and figure out how you can save that number of gallons. Put the ways you plan to use your water in the columns under "water saving plan". For example, the family of four took four showers per day. For their water saving plan they decided to insert a flow restrictor in their shower. The first line in the chart is what their entries for "shower" would look like.

WATER SAVING PLAN

Water Use		Typical Gallons per use	No. of times per day	Gals. per day	Water Saving Plan	
					# of times per day	Gallons per day
Example Shower	Normal, water running	25	4	100		
	Flow restrictor, water running	17				
	Wet down, soap up, rinse off	4			4	68
Shower	Normal, water running	25				
	Flow restrictor, water running	17				
	Wet down, soap up, rinse off	4				
Bath	Full	36				
	Minimal water level	11				
Brushing Teeth	Tap running	10				
	Wet brush, rinse briefly	½				
Shaving	Tap running	20				
	Fill basin	1				
Dishwashing	Tap running	30				
	Wash & rinse in dish pan or sink	5				
Automatic Dishwasher	Full cycle	16				
	Short cycle	7				
Washing Hands	Tap running	2				
	Fill basin	1				
Toilet Flushing	Normal	5				
	Water saving toilet	3				
	Toilet with displacement bottles	4				
Other						
			No. of times per week			
Washing Machine	Full cycle, top water level	8*				
	Short cycle, minimum water level	4*				
			No. of min. per week			
Outdoor Watering	Average hose (10 gallons per minute)	1*				

Note: To compare this with your utility bill, 748 gallons are equal to one unit.

Total gallons per day ____
10% saving (total gallons x .10) ____
Water saving goal ____

Water saving total ____

* The figures are the average per day for once a week use.

EXHIBIT 7D
Industrial Water Conservation Program

Industrial Water Conservation Program

. Flushometers - Set the rate of closing of these devices to use only that amount of water required for a proper flush of the apparatus served.

. Flow Restrictors - Install these devices wherever possible to limit flow to showers, lavatory basins, wash sinks, etc.

. Faucet Aerators - Install these devices on sinks, lavatory basins and where rinsing is commonly done.

. Area Wash Downs - The use of the wastewater stream to convey wastes to the Regional Water Quality Control Plant is still looked upon with favor, but the use of potable water to wash leaves and debris from lawns and parking lots is not. This job of cleanup can be achieved with more environmental favor by use of brooms or air blowers.

. Fountains - The use of ornamental fountains during periods of drought is a questionable use of water. If used at all, these facilities should utilize recycled water in a nonwasteful manner.

. Cooling Waters - If cooling waters are used in quantity then cooling tower should be utilized. If cooling tower wastewaters are seriously degraded, they should go to sanitary sewer after filing for industrial waste permit. Nondegraded water may pass to storm sewer or be used for irrigation.

. Rinse Baths - If possible, use the cascade rinse approach to minimize water waste. If water is not seriously degraded, consider storing it for irrigation of landscaping.

. Landscape Irrigation - Serious consideration should be given to converting shrubbery irrigation to the drip method. This method can cut use of water for this purpose by 20 to 50 percent. If this system is operated on a time clock, an overriding tensiometer may be installed to limit irrigation to times when soil moisture content is low.

. Turf Irrigation - Sprinklers

- Pressure at the heads should be proper (normally 35 psi). Excess pressure may cause atomization and hence waste due to evaporation and wind drift.

- Sprinkling in the rain is of no real value to either the turf, the storm sewer system, the water conservation program, or the pocket book, but is a regular activity engaged in by many of the industries on the hill. A good cure for this illness is the installation of a tensiometer, moisture sensory device to override the time-clock programming sprinkler irrigation. It is claimed that a savings of 25 percent or more may be achieved by irrigating when water is needed instead of when the clock says "go". These devices have been used successfully for many years to control irrigation of citrus groves in Southern California. Recent installations have been made in Palm Park in Redwood City, and four more are due to be installed in the Redwood Shores development.

10

Seville Community College

Christopher H. Lovelock

"I see a great potential here at Seville for new continuing education programs. The problem is how to get started."

The speaker was Dr. Eleanor Digrazia, President of Seville Community College, a two-year public institution that offered a number of courses leading to an Associate's degree in the liberal arts and various vocational fields. Founded in 1961, the college was located in Magraw, a growing city, with a population of about 250,000, in a southwestern state. In 1972, the college had completed the final phase of a planned expansion program and boasted modern, air-conditioned buildings on a small but attractive campus, easily accessible from most parts of the city. The college had good parking facilities and was served by two bus lines that operated on 30 minute headways until 11:30 p.m., Monday through Saturday.

Concerned about rising costs and an apparent reluctance, on the part of elected state and county officials, to increase community college budgets, Dr. Digrazia was evaluating other ways of increasing revenues. A study of existing course schedules and extra-curricular activities showed that the college facilities were underutilized in the evenings and on Saturdays. The campus was normally closed from 5:00 p.m. Saturday until 7:00 a.m. Monday, unless a special event (such as a concert or community meeting) was scheduled.

Christopher H. Lovelock is Associate Professor of Business Administration at the Graduate School of Business Administration, Harvard University.

Based on some preliminary inquiries, Dr. Digrazia believed that professional programs, in fields such as law and real estate, offered good potential for Seville. Real estate activity had always been significant in the region and was beginning to move into high gear again, as the economy recovered from the recession. She knew that many practicing and would-be realtors traveled over 30 miles to Fairfax, the state capital, to take extension courses in their subject at Fairfax State University. The Law School there offered a number of evening and week-end courses in special topics for lawyers and paralegal assistants. Continuing education programs in law and real estate were also sponsored by professional associations in both Fairfax (a city of 400,000 people) and Dos Rios, 45 miles in the opposite direction, which had a metropolitan population of over a million. President Digrazia had met several local lawyers and realtors who had expressed a desire to see such courses offered closer to home.

Getting part-time faculty would not be a problem, the President believed, since she knew a number of well-regarded professionals who had expressed an interest in teaching.

"I believe that there's a good market out there," said Dr. Digrazia. "We've got a nice facility here and a good location. Perhaps our main drawback is that many people see community colleges as just an extension of high school—13th or 14th grade, if you know what I mean."

11
The Golden Gate Corridor Busway

Charles B. Weinberg
Barton H. Weitz

In mid-February 1975 Amy Michaels, coordinator for the transportation section in a consumer action group, was reviewing a study of the Golden Gate Corridor Busway. Ever since the exclusive concurrent bus lanes were proposed, the consumer action group had received a number of complaints from motorists claiming the busway would increase commute time, underutilize the freeway, and cause accidents.

In response to these complaints, the consumer action group had commissioned a transportation consulting firm to collect information on the busway. To meet time and budgeting constraints, the study was performed in 30 days at a cost of $5,000.*

Based on this study, Ms. Michaels had to prepare a recommendation for the next meeting of the action group's Board of Directors, which was to meet on February 28, 1975. Although Ms. Michaels could, of course, report that the results were inconclusive, she hoped to be able to make a more definitive report. Her organization was well respected locally for its careful consideration of consumer issues. She was aware that her recommendations would be publicly available.

The Golden Gate Corridor was a fast growing residential suburban area in Marin and Sonoma counties, just north of San Francisco. Many of its residents commuted to and from San Francisco using the redwood Highway (U.S. 101), a six to eight lane freeway that provided the only continuous North-South route into the city. The land area encompassed by the corridor is shown in Exhibit 1.† Exhibit 2 provides some basic demographics relating the corridor to the total Bay Area population.

The major traffic flow occurred during the peak commuting periods in the morning and evening, when commuters overcrowded the highway, the buses, and the ferries.

Exhibit 3 shows the commute volume in terms of person trips by mode during the 6 a.m. to 10 a.m. morning peak period. The limited capacity of the six-lane Golden Gate Bridge restricted the overall traffic flow.

HISTORY OF THE GOLDEN GATE BUSWAY

The Golden Gate Bridge, Highway, and Transportation District operated both the Golden Gate Bridge and the Golden Gate Transit bus and ferry services between San Francisco and Marin County. The District had taken over responsibility for commute bus service from Greyhound on January 1,

Charles B. Weinberg is Professor, University of British Columbia, Faculty of Commerce & Business Administration, and Barton H. Weitz is Associate Professor, Wharton School, University of Pennsylvania. The assistance of Mr. John Crain, Bigelow-Crain Associates is gratefully acknowledged.

*The study was actually commissioned and paid for in December 1974. A small urban transportation research grant had been received late in 1974 and had to be spent in that calendar year.

†All exhibits in the case are taken from the report submitted by the consultant.

EXHIBIT 1
The Golden Gate Corridor

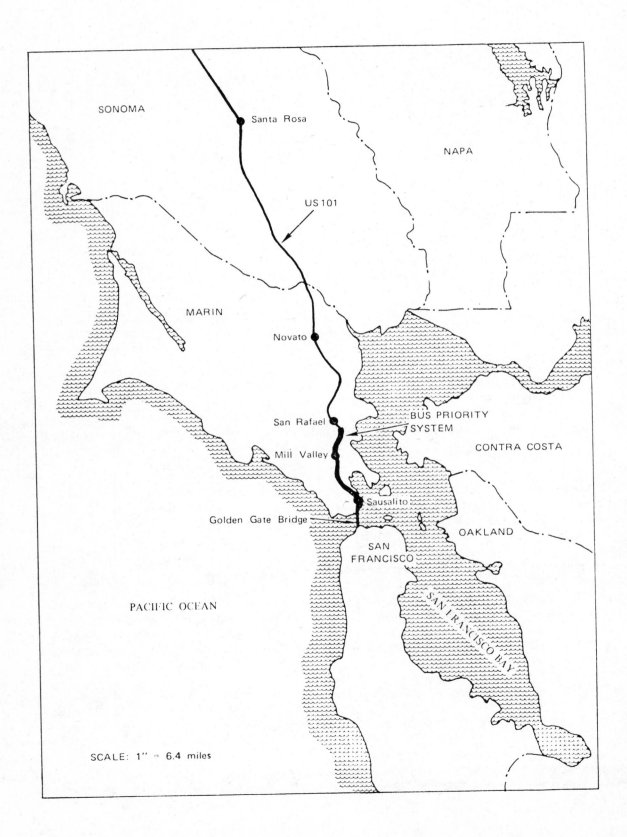

EXHIBIT 2
Demographic-Traffic Data

	Marin	Sonoma	Bay Area
Population (1970)	206,000	205,000	4,628,000
Employed (14 years and over)	85,000	70,000	1,899,000
Median Family Income	$14,000	$10,000	$12,000
Home-to-Work Mode	%	%	%
Auto driver	70.1	78.1	70.1
Auto passenger	10.7	6.7	9.0
Bus/Street Car	7.5	1.8	9.0
Other public transportation	0.8	0.1	0.9
Walk/work at home	7.3	9.5	8.3
Other	3.6	3.8	2.7

EXHIBIT 3
Corridor Commute Volumes

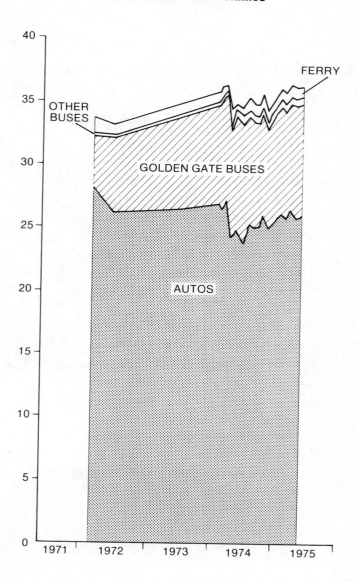

1972, and immediately began to improve bus service. Service levels were increased, new buses purchased, and local service introduced.

When the District added its own bus and ferry services, it moved from being a relatively passive supplier of bridge and highway service to becoming a multi-modal transportation system, cross subsidizing bus and ferry service in part from bridge tolls paid by cars. Short of an extraordinarily roundabout journey via Oakland, there is no road access from Sonoma/Marin to San Francisco other than over the Golden Gate Bridge.

In September 1972, a four-mile contraflow lane was established on U.S. 101 northbound from the Golden Gate Bridge to the Richardson Bay Bridge. During the evening rush hours, pylons and signs were used to convert a southbound lane into an additional northbound lane for exclusive bus usage. The contraflow lane, proposed by the District, was the result of an agreement between the District, the California Department of Transportation (Caltrans), the Metropolitan Transportation Commission (MTC), the Marin County Transit District, and the California Highway Patrol (CHP). Under this agreement, Caltrans was responsible for the design and construction of the contraflow facilities and paid for one-half of the costs. The District paid for the other half of the costs and was responsible for operating the lane reversal system. The CHP was responsible for enforcing traffic regulations.

In July 1974, the District requested that, once the two new lanes being built were completed, an exclusive, concurrent flow lane be provided for bus operations during morning and evening rush hour periods. No lanes were to be removed from motorist use; the proposal only concerned the new lane being added. The District argued that the exclusive lane would increase the attractiveness and, thus, the patronage of the bus service by improving schedule reliability and reducing the commute time. The availability of the lanes would reduce the effects of weather and traffic condition on the performance of the bus system. This request was supported by the Marin County Transit District and ten of the eleven Marin County cities. With the MIC acting

as chairman, a public forum on the exclusive bus lanes was held on October 10, 1974. Over 100 people attended. Sixteen of the 18 people who made statements supported the proposal, including representatives from two Federal agencies, the Urban Mass Transportation Administration (UMTA), and the Environmental Protection Agency (EPA). A reasonable time for written and oral responses to the forum was provided. Of the 610 respondents, about 440 supported the plan.

The U.S. Department of Transportation approved the project in November 1974, expressing great interest in the experiment. There had been a major national movement toward the use of busways as a possible quick method of providing rapid transit service to resolve congestion, pollution, and energy consumption problems in heavy traffic cor-

EXHIBIT 4
Illustration of Concurrent and Contraflow Bus Lanes

Southbound *Concurrent* Bus Flow Lane

Northbound *Contraflow* Bus Lane

EXHIBIT 5
Plan View Sketch of Bus Lanes

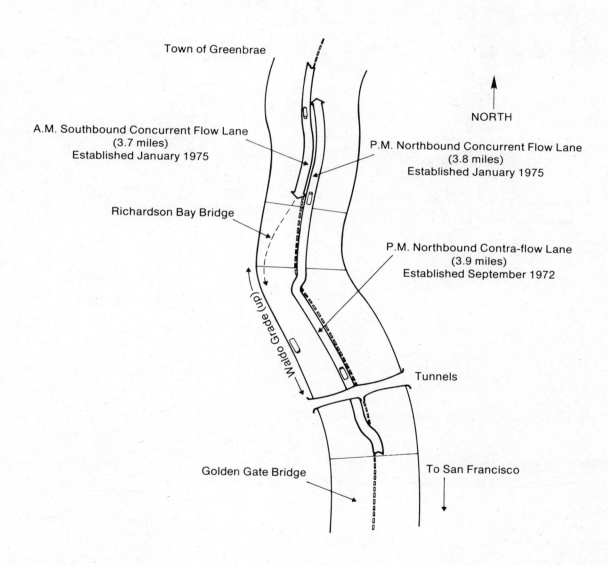

Town of Greenbrae

NORTH

A.M. Southbound Concurrent Flow Lane
(3.7 miles)
Established January 1975

P.M. Northbound Concurrent Flow Lane
(3.8 miles)
Established January 1975

Richardson Bay Bridge

P.M. Northbound Contra-flow Lane
(3.9 miles)
Established September 1972

Waldo Grade (up)

Tunnels

Golden Gate Bridge

To San Francisco

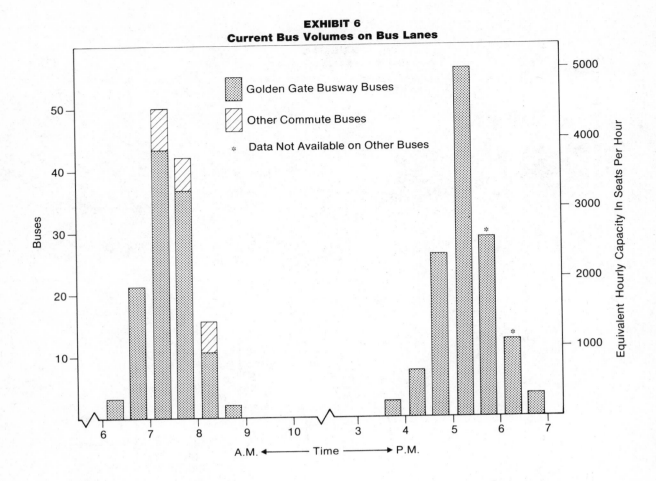

EXHIBIT 6
Current Bus Volumes on Bus Lanes

ridors. The Golden Gate Busway, could provide data of interest to various agencies developing busways around the country.

Bus service utilizing the concurrent flow lanes exclusively was initiated January 1, 1975. Some morning buses continued to stop at "passenger pads" along the freeway and, thus, did not use the busway. See Exhibit 4 for photographs of both concurrent flow and contraflow bus lanes.

Description of the Busway. In its present configuration the busway had a 3.7 mile exclusive, concurrent southbound lane for use during the morning rush period and a 7.7 mile (about half concurrent and half contraflow) exclusive lane for use during the evening rush hour. A simplified sketch indicating the basic flow is shown in Exhibit 5. During the morning rush period, the four miles from the Richardson Bay Bridge to the Golden Gate Bridge had no exclusive bus lane, since the last two miles of this stretch was an uphill grade that slowed a fully loaded bus to 25 mph, a speed that could be maintained in the morning congestion. In addition, during the morning, there was traffic congestion north of the Richardson Bay Bridge (where there were many freeway entry points), but little south of this Bridge.

BUSWAY SERVICE

The capacity of the busway was limited by the number of buses in service. Exhibit 6 shows the capacity as it varied over the two peak periods. These figures also included 16 other commute club buses using the exclusive lanes.

Each Golden Gate Transit bus had a capacity for 45 people. Between 7 and 9 a.m., 129 buses crossed the bridge after leaving the exclusive lanes. During the 7 to 7:30 period, when 50 buses crossed the bridge, the headway between buses dropped to 36 seconds, or about 2,900 feet at 55 mph. The fare structure for the commute service, shown in Exhibit 7, had not changed with the introduction of the exclusive concurrent lanes.

EXHIBIT 7
Fare Structure
(in dollars)

	S.F.	S.M.	N.M.	S.S.	N.S.
San Francisco (S.F.)	.50	.75	1.00	1.25	1.50
South Marin (S.M.)	—	.50	.75	1.00	1.25
North Marin (N.M.)	—	—	.50	.75	1.00
South Sonoma (S.S.)	—	—	—	.50	.75
North Sonoma (N.S.)	—	—	—	—	.50
Average miles from San Francisco		10	22	32	46

EXHIBIT 8
History of Capacity and Ridership of Services on Bus Lanes

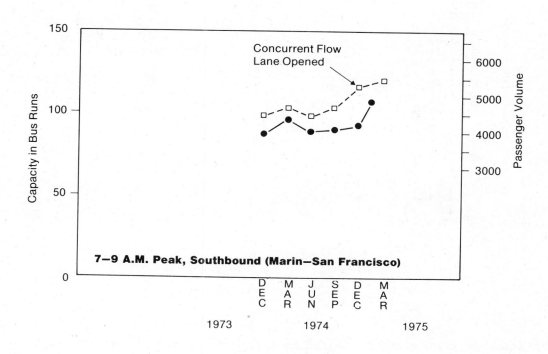

7–9 A.M. Peak, Southbound (Marin–San Francisco)

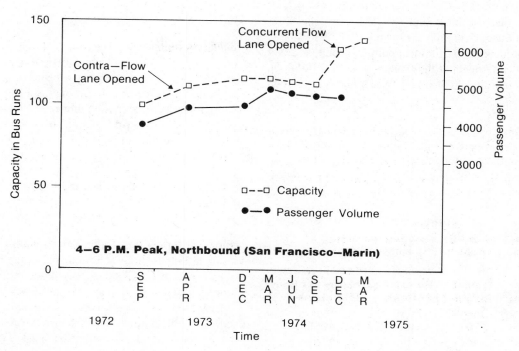

4–6 P.M. Peak, Northbound (San Francisco–Marin)

EXHIBIT 9
Current Busway Volumes

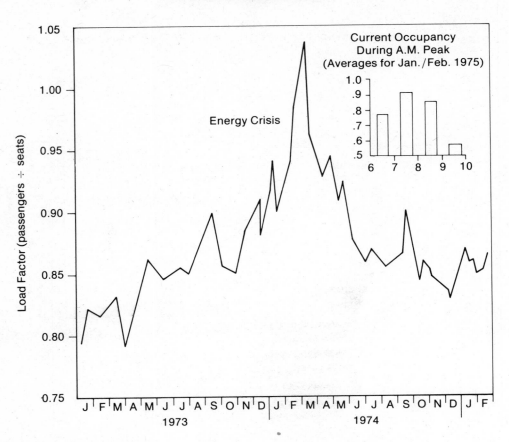

Busway Ridership. The trends in busway ridership are shown in Exhibit 8. These graphs depict trends in peak hour busway passenger volumes relative to capacity. The occupancy rate of buses over time is shown in Exhibit 9.

To examine periods of maximum ridership, a count was made of passengers at the Golden Gate Toll Booth on four Monday mornings. The results of this survey are shown in Exhibit 10.

Time Savings. The time savings attributed to the southbound, concurrent lane was determined by measuring trips on one "before-busway" day and two "after-busway" days. As a control group, trip time was also measured for a comparable number of nonbusway runs. The average savings in

minutes between December 16, 1974 (pre-busway) and January 8 and 13, 1975 (postbusway) is 7 minutes, as shown in Exhibit 11.

Schedule Reliability. The results of time studies performed on evening, northbound bus arrivals at a major loading/ unloading point in San Rafael are shown in Exhibit 12. An additional observation concerning schedule reliability concerned the decrease in the number of "relay runs." During the morning rush period, certain buses making an early commute run had time to return for a second run. When one of these "turnback" runs was late in returning to the suburbs, a substitute bus, called a "relay run," was sent instead. This was an added expense incurred to assure on-time service. Operating personnel noted a decrease in the number of relay runs since the advent of the exclusive concurrent lanes.

Highway Safety and Traffic Enforcement. There had been three accidents directly attributable to the reserved concurrent flow lanes. All three caused automotive damage, but none caused any human injuries. On January 20, 1975, during the evening peak period, a car suddenly veered from one lane into another, which in turn forced a truck to swerve to the left into the concurrent bus lane. The oncoming bus

EXHIBIT 10
History of Bus Occupancy Rates
(peak period, 6 to 10 a.m. at bridge)

Time Period	Transit Riders	Transit Riders per Hour	Auto Person Trips per Lane per Hour (Four Lanes)
6:15–7:30 a.m.	1380	1100	1525
7:30–8:30 a.m.	3160	3160	2125
8:30–9:15 a.m.	440	590	1875

EXHIBIT 11
Average Savings in Minutes in Arrival Time at the Golden Gate Bridge from 12/16/74 (re-Busway) to 1/8—13/75 (Post-Busway)

Buses Using Busway
(differential from 12/16)

A.M. Peak	Runs	1/8	1/13	Average
6:00–7:30	38	2.4	2.6	2.5
7:30–8:30	30	14.6	11.4	13.0
8:30–10:00	16	8.6	5.6	7.1
	84			7.1*

Buses Not Using Busway
(differential from 12/16)

Runs	1/8	1/13	Average	Busway Minus Non-Busway
19	−.4	.4	0	2.5
38	−.4	−.7	−.5	13.5
20	.1	1.6	.8	6.3
77			0.0*	7.1*

* Weighted averages.

could not brake quickly enough to avoid being side-swiped by the truck. On another occasion, a car moved into the exclusive bus lane and rear-ended a car when it moved back to the original lane again. The third occasion occurred when a car decided to enter the exclusive busway, swerved too quickly, and ran into the median strip across the bus lane.

Soon after the concurrent flow lanes were opened, there were a large number of violations; but the number had declined. The historical record of policy actions is shown in Exhibit 13. The police actions listed in Exhibit 13 represented only a fraction of the total violations that occurred.

EXHIBIT 12
Schedule Reliability of Evening Northbound Buses Arriving in San Rafael between 5:30 and 6:00 p.m.

Conditions	Arrival Time Compared to Schedule [1]	
	Mean	Standard Deviation
One day, clear weather pre-busway (3/13/74) [2]	2 min. late	8 min.
Four days, clear weather post-busway (1/13, 1/15, 1/17, 2/10)	4.2 min. early	7 min. [3]
Three days, rainy weather post-busway (1/31, 2/3, 2/7)	0.2 min. early	8 min.

Comments:
[1] Schedules were not changed post busway.
[2] Only one day's data available.
[3] Standard deviation high because many buses arrived early.

EXHIBIT 13
Police Actions on Bus Lane Violations

Week Ending	Tickets Issued	Warnings
20 December 1974	0	6
27 December	0	42
3 January 1975	35	37
10 January	39	18
17 January	51	15
24 January	66	12
31 January	27	3
7 February	17	10
14 February	11	8

On January 9 and 10, 1975, observations at a single point midway along the busway were made by the California Highway Patrol of all violators during the first and last hour of the exclusive busway periods. During these two hours, there were as many violators observed as were apprehended during the entire week.

Public Reaction. On one Saturday in January an all-day survey of public reactions was performed. Two hundred and thirty people were interviewed, about half at Northgate, a regional shopping center in San Rafael, and half at the smaller Town and Country Shopping Center in Corte Madera. (The latter location lay in South Marin County, and a commuter from that point could only use a part of the busway.)

The interviewers approached people at random at the shopping centers and asked the following five questions:

1. Do you commute to San Francisco from here?
2. What town do you live in? (If not Marin/Sonoma, interview terminated.)
3. How do you travel to work? (Car, Bus, Ferry)
4. Are you aware of the busway, the exclusive lanes for buses on 101?
5. What is your reaction to this use of the highway? Is it a good idea? Bad? What do you think?

The responses to the last question were graded on a five point scale with the result shown in Exhibit 14 (see also Exhibit 15).

EXHIBIT 14
Public Reaction to Busway

	Bus [1]	Non-Bus [2]	Sum		%
Very Positive	17	33	50		
Positive	16	86	102	152	66
Neutral	6	36	42	42	18
Negative	2	22	24		
Very Negative	2	10	12	36	16
Sum	43	187		230	100
%	19	81			

[1] Bus commuters (users of system).
[2] Non-bus commuters and non-commuters (non-users).

EXHIBIT 15
Public Reaction to Bus Lanes
(Specific Likes and Dislikes)

	Bus[1]	Non-Bus[2]	Sum	%
Convenience to Bus Users				
Saves time	18	46		
Saves gas/energy	3	5		
Should be extended	2	5	82	27
Convenient	1	1		
Saves money	0	1		
Sum	24	58		
Generally Good Idea				
Good idea for cars/buses (no explanation)	14	46		
Encourages bus use	8	27	116	38
Eases congestion	4	17		
Sum	26	90		
Neutral				
Indifferent/doesn't use/ unfamiliar with service	4	25		
No opinion	0	5	34	11
Sum	4	30		
Safety Questioned				
Wrong lane given to buses	1	8		
More separation needed between buses/cars	2	9	20	7
Sum	3	17		
Negative				
Bus lane wastes space	1	26		
Poor use of tax money, benefits select group	2	8		
Bad idea (no explanation)	1	7	53	17
No improvement on traffic congestion	1	7		
Sum	5	48		
Sum	62	243	305[3]	100
%	20	80		

[1] Users of system.
[2] Non-isers.
[3] Multiple answers allowed.

Costs and Savings. The total cost for construction of the 3.9 mile contraflow lane was $180,000. This included the socket holes for the pylons, the crossover road back to the northbound lanes, the signs, and about 50 yards of new connector lane that the buses used to move from the inside northbound lane to the contraflow lane. The construction cost for the 3.8 miles of northbound and 3.7 miles of southbound concurrent flow lanes was $3,200.000. This was the cost of constructing the additional shoulder lane. There was an additional cost of $30,000 for the traffic signing.

There were two components of the operating costs. Operation of the lane reversal system required $5,000 per month. The added cost for enforcement by the CHP was $4,200 per month. This cost represented the need for two extra patrolmen for six hours per day at $12.41 per hour plus 17 cents per mile.

The Golden Gate District believed that there would be significant cost reductions due to the exclusive lanes. Although it would be difficult to assess the costs savings until the system reached equilibrium and a new schedule was developed, it appeared that two elements of cost savings were the reduced number of relay runs and the reduction in working hours for the drivers. If the exclusive lanes permitted drivers to clock out 15 minutes earlier, a $20,000 yearly savings in salaries would be realized.

The following analysis attempted to express the cost savings in terms of a percentage saving in unit operating cost. The three components of the system's peak hour operating cost were:

1. Driver cost, busway related   36%
2. Driver cost, nonbusway related   12%
3. Nondriver and other costs (vehicle operation)   52%

The speed increases from 35 to 55 mph appeared to have had a 10% effect on most routes. For example, the 65 minutes required to go from Terra Linda to San Francisco, including the driver's break and pull-in/pull-out losses, was reduced by 6 or 7 minutes. This reduction would then have a potential 10% savings on busway driver costs, decreasing peak hour busway unit cost by about 3.6%.

There was no effect on the nonbusway driver costs, and only a negligible effect on the nondriver costs due to increased speed.

Paid down time costs would rise or fall according to how effectively the new mix of runs could be scheduled; however, the overall manpower efficiency factor of 65% was inherently tied to the Golden Gate Transit's work rules and, thus, probably would not change much.

ISSUES

Ms. Michaels' problem was to draw this information together and to develop a set of recommendations. Although she realized that the concurrent lanes had been used for less than two months and that more data might be useful, she hoped that she did have enough information to reach some conclusions about the impact of the busway. She recognized that some of her data could be challenged and wondered what response could be made.

12
The Birds, the Bees, and the Bugs

Robin B. Dow
Michael R. Pearce

When I came home, though, then came sorrow. Too, too plain was Signor Gonorrhea. I rose
very disconsolate, the poisonous infection raging in my veins and anxiety and vexation boiling in my breast.
What, thought I, can this beautiful, this sensible, and this agreeable woman be so sadly defiled?
Can corruption lodge beneath so fair a form? And yet these damn twinges, this scalding heat,
and that deep-tinged loathsome matter are the strongest proofs of infection.

*Boswell's London Journal
1762–1763*

In the spring of 1973, Mr. Tony Cosgrave presented a plan of action to alert the people of Saskatchewan to the dangers of and the treatment for venereal disease. Mr. Cosgrave had been asked to prepare a complete promotional program by Dr. W. G. Davidson, M.D., D.P.H., the provincial epidemiologist (epidemics) for Saskatchewan. Dr. Davidson considered venereal disease no longer just a medical problem, but a social problem as well, and believed a major effort was necessary to curb its increase in Saskatchewan. Mr. Cosgrave presented his plan to the Advisory Committee on the Venereal Disease Control Program (A.C.V.D.) and that committee was presently evaluating his proposals.

VENEREAL DISEASES*

Gonorrhea. Gonorrhea has been a frequent complication of lovemaking throughout the ages. The first record of gonor-

rhea was in the *Book of Leviticus* (about 1500 b.c.), where symptoms were described in detail. The Greek physician Hippocrates (400 b.c.) stated that gonorrhea resulted from "excessive indulgence in the pleasures of Venus," the goddess of love. In 1793 French general Carnot wrote that venereal disease, transmitted by the three thousand prostitutes serving his army, "killed ten times as many men as enemy fire." The problem of gonorrhea had apparently worsened since the Viet Nam conflict because many of the strains of the infection had become penicillin resistant.

The bacterium that causes gonorrhea, the *gonococcus,* is one of the most sensitive of all bacteria which cause human disease. Outside the human body the gonococcus dies within a few seconds because it does not survive sunshine, drying, or soap and water. Thus, doctors believe it

*Gonorrhea and syphilis are the most prevalent and dangerous venereal diseases, but there are other venereal diseass such as chancroid, grandloma and lymphogranuloma venerium. Only gonorrhea and syphilis will be discussed in detail in this case. The information provided here on these medical problems is not intended to be fully complete so it should not be relied upon for personal medical care.

Robin B. Dow was formerly an Instructor, and Michael R. Pearce is Associate Professor, both at the School of Business Administration, the University of Western Ontario.

is almost impossible to catch gonorrhea from toilet seats, cups, towels, etc., that have been used by an infected person. The only prevalent way the gonococcus can survive the transfer from one person to the other is through very close physical contact such as vaginal, anal or oral-genital sexual intercourse.

Most men with a gonorrhea infection of the penis first notice symptoms three to five days after becoming infected. Swelling of the meatus (the opening at the end of the penis), burning pain upon urination and a thick, yellowish green discharge from the meatus are common symptoms. Basically, when someone has been infected, they know it! Even without treatment, these symptoms might disappear on their own a few weeks after infection. Untreated, gonorrhea may result in sterility in both men and women, arthritis, meningitis or peritonitis (inflammation of the joints, brain, or membrane lining of the abdomen, respectively).

Fifty to 80 per cent of women infected with gonorrhea typically do not notice any discomfort or symptoms of their disease for the first few weeks or even months. Even then, the coloured discharge is difficult to detect. Other parasitic infections also tend to have the same type of discharge and make accurate diagnosis difficult. However, those who do experience symptoms have pain on walking or sitting, tenderness in the genitalia and heavy pus discharge.

Prevention of Gonorrhea.

Tuesday, 17 May. We went down a lane to a snug place, and I took out my armour, but she begged that I might not put it on, as the sport was much pleasanter without it, and as she was quite safe, I was so rash as to trust her, and had a very agreeable congress.

Wednesday, 18 May. Much concern was I in from the apprehension of being again reduced to misery, and in so silly a way too. My benevolence indeed suggested to me to put confidence in the poor girl, but then said cool reason, "What abandoned, deceitful wretches are these girls, and even supposing her honest, how could she know with any certainty that she was well?"

Boswell's London Journal 1762–1763

The use of the condom, the intestine of a sheep in Boswell's day, had been promoted for years as a means of preventing the transmission of social diseases, but this was not always 100 per cent effective as a preventive measure. United States Army experience had shown a 60 per cent reduction in the incidence of gonorrhea from 62.5 cases per 1000 to 35 per 1000 population through enforced use of the condom. There had been some experimentation with vaginal foams, but these had not been very satisfactory.

Many myths existed about prevention. Soap and water washing after contact might help somewhat, but birth control pills, contrary to opinions held by many people who visited clinics, did not prevent disease, only pregnancy. Therefore, part of the program had to deal with the promotion of a change in, or additions to, present contraceptive practices. Mr. Cosgrave thought this topic might well pro-

voke a much more unfavourable public reaction than contraceptive information campaigns mounted previously.

Treatment of Gonorrhea.

An individual could get treatment for gonorrhea or another venereal disease by visiting his or her regular doctor or by going to a VD treatment centre. Four of these centres, public health clinics specifically designated for VD, had been established in Saskatchewan to provide quick, simple, free medical treatment and advice for walk-in patients. Most visitors to these centres found their way there by word of mouth, referrals from doctors or by reading signs posted in washrooms in some public buildings, such as the Post Office. According to a clinic worker, many people preferred the treatment centres because they would be embarrassed to have their own doctor find out or they were worried the doctor would tell their parents or spouses about the situation. Dr. Davidson noted that as the incidence of venereal disease increased, the proportion of patients being treated by physicians decreased. "Many people are sensitive about venereal disease," he added. "Being middle class, they feel VD isn't a middle-class disease and shouldn't have happened to them."

Treatment at a VD clinic was relatively quick, on average about twenty minutes. Lab samples were taken, antibiotics administered if it seemed appropriate, and some vital statistics gathered (such as age, address, occupation and any known contacts). The situation was supposed to be strictly medical with no moralizing discussions. There was some disagreement over the success of these clinics, but most criticism centred on claims of inhospitability and poor locations.

There was also criticism of the way in which private physicians treated venereal disease. For example, Dr. J. D. Wallace, secretary-general of the Canadian Medical Association in 1973, claimed most Canadian doctors did not take venereal disease seriously enough, and that until they did the incidence of VD would remain at epidemic levels. According to Dr. Wallace, often doctors would not report VD cases to public health offices, would not check on possible contacts and did not engage in adequate follow-up treatment.

Dr. Davidson believed every case of VD had to be considered the source of a potential epidemic. Since no case existed in isolation, it was vitally important to locate and examine all relevant sexual contacts as soon as possible to prevent further spread of the infection in the community. There was a major problem in getting infected individuals to name their contacts, despite the fact that the name of the informant was never disclosed. Because the symptoms in males were much more obvious, most of the patients treated were men. In 1972, about 90 per cent of the patients at the VD centres were male. Dr. Davidson stressed to Mr. Cosgrave that something had to be done not only to convince women who had had relations with strangers or near-strangers to have a checkup but, more important, to convince the public that naming contacts was a thoughtful and considerate act.

Syphilis. Syphilis is a rare bacterium which has evolved successfully alongside man. Early syphilis in Africa was called yaws, and appeared as large, moist sores on the skin. As man moved from a moist environment into more northern, drier climates, the disease retreated to the moist areas of the human body (the mouth, nostrils, underarms, crotch and anus) and was known as endemic syphilis. The introduction of better sanitation began to make a significant impact on prevention of endemic syphilis, as the bacteria, which were passed by touch, were weak, fragile and often cured by simple cleanliness. In response to the challenge, syphilis has adapted, surviving in parts of the body which remain moist but which are rarely exposed to the outside world (the sexual organs and the anus).

The bacteria are transferred at any point where there is contact with an open sore, the most usual contact being intercourse. Wearing a condom does not prevent transfer, as the organisms can be transmitted to the area at the junction of the penis and the rest of the body, the part not covered by the prophylactic. The bacteria can then work their way right through the skin, and, within a few hours of entry, can reach the bloodstream and be carried to all parts of the body.

As early as three days or as long as three months after sexual intercourse with an infected person, the primary sore of syphilis, called the chancre, appears at the spot where the bacteria invaded the body. Generalized symptoms include enlarged and tender lymph nodes, headaches and nausea. Usually quite visible in men, the chancre of primary syphilis is often not visible in women, as it usually appears on the cervix or inner vaginal walls. If left untreated, the chancre heals within one to five weeks of its appearance.

Within two weeks to six months after the primary chancre disappears, a secondary syphilitic stage appears, a generalized skin rash with secondary lesions (sores). The appearance of this rash is extremely variable; the only factor common to most cases is that syhilitic rashes do not itch or hurt. Most commonly, the rash is seen as cherry-coloured, raised bumps of different sizes. In warm, moist areas of the body, the rash might form broad-based rounded growths. Dull red at first, they develop a greyish white surface that eventually breaks down to reveal a dull red surface oozing a clear liquid containing large numbers of syphilis bacteria, extremely contagious to other people. Without treatment, secondary stages might disappear two to six weeks after their appearance. Yet this stage may reappear at intervals up to two years after.

If secondary syphilis is not treated, it progresses to a stage called latent syphilis, in which there are no symptoms at all. About two-thirds of untreated people live the rest of their lives without any further disturbance from the disease. However, the remaining one-third may suffer from (a) *benign late syphilis,* a large destructive ulcer on the skin, muscles, digestive organs, liver, lungs, eyes or endocrine glands, which develops three to seven years after infection; or (b) *cardiovascular late syphilis,* which appears ten to forty years after infection, and affects the heart and major blood vessels and often leads to death; or (c) *neurosyphilis,* a fatal attack on the spinal cord and brain, which strikes ten to twenty years after the onset of the infection. Paralysis and insanity precede death. Syphilis can also be passed to a fetus if the mother has been infected but not treated, or to a breast-fed infant.

Prevention of Syphilis. Unfortunately, there was little that could be worn or used to prevent syphilis. Thorough washing before and after intercourse might have helped kill the fragile bacteria before they could enter the body. Like gonorrhea, the major prevention of the spread of the disease was ensuring that infected persons listed their contacts so that those infected could be treated.

Treatment of Syphilis. In order to combat syphilis, doctors used to administer weekly injections of arsenicals and other heavy metal drugs for a period of twelve to eighteen months, sometimes longer. In 1943, when penicillin was discovered, doctors found it an effective combatant against syphilis. Doses of penicillin were injected into the buttock of the patient (as for gonorrhea) for a period of one to three weeks depending on the stage of the disease. Dosage levels were a matter of controversy, but the cure for early syphilis was considered to be 80 per cent effective. There was some difficulty establishing the level of effectiveness because reinfection was possible and often common for many individuals who had suffered early infectious syphilis.

In Ontario, the law stated that females had to have three negative tests, while males had to have two negative tests. By regulation, anyone, once named as a contact and notified as such, who refused to come in for a test could be jailed. This was not the case in Saskatchewan.

EXTENT OF THE VD PROBLEM AND SOME ATTEMPTS TO SOLVE IT

Both syphilis and gonorrhea were increasing in frequency according to the number of notifications received by the Saskatchewan Department of Health from doctors and clinics. Between 1972 and 1973, syphilis (all stages) had increased from 164 to 189 cases (15 per cent increase) and gonorrhea from 3162 to 3637 cases (15 per cent increase). Exhibit 1 provides some statistics on the incidence of gonorrhea in Saskatchewan between 1968 and 1973.

The Advisory Committee on Venereal Disease (A.C.V.D.) noticed that the fifteen-to-thirty age group had the highest incidence of VD, was the fastest growing population segment, had experienced the fastest growth in VD infections over the past five years and had a high repeat

EXHIBIT 1
Incidence of Gonorrhea

	1968	1969	1970	1971	1972	1973	Percent Change 1968–1973
A. Total notifications of gonorrhea	2,094	2,373	2,267	2,797	3,162	3,637	+ 73.4
B. Number of notifications in 15–19 year age group	354	424	475	681	857	1,071	+202.5
C. Percentage of notifications in 15–19 year age group (B ÷ A = C)	16.9	17.8	20.9	24.3	27.1	29.4	
Population between 15–19 years	93,276	95,776	97,109	98,857	100,636	98,945	
Rate per 100,000*	379.2	442.7	489.2	688.8	851.9	1,082.3	

*For the total population of Saskatchewan. For further information about Saskatchewan, please see Exhibit 2.

treatment rate. Accordingly, they decided this group would be the main target of their new campaign.

Previous attempts to curb VD in Saskatchewan included some educational efforts in the high schools and a requirement for a syphilis test before receipt of a marriage license. The school programs had faltered apparently because the materials provided teachers were considered inadequate and because teachers felt uncomfortable discussing the topic. The school boards were receptive to outside help, but had received little. The Saskatchewan Marriage Act stipulated that all applicants for a marriage licence had to have passed a blood test for syphilis. Although gonorrhea was far more prevalent than syphilis, tests for gonorrhea infection were not required under the act.

EXHIBIT 2
Demographic Data: Province of Saskatchewan

Population	June 1, 1966 955,344	June 1, 1971 926,242		
Average annual change 1951–1971— 0.5%				
1971—53% urban, 22% rural non-farm, 25% farm				
1971—470,720 males 455,422 females			**Male**	**Female**
1971— 10–14 years			51,500	49,400
15–19 years			49,700	47,600
20–24 years			36,700	35,000
24–34 years			49,800	49,000
35–44 years			48,600	46,600
Cities Regina	140,000			
Saskatoon	125,000			
Moose Jaw	32,000			
Prince Albert	28,000			
Swift Curent	15,000			
North Battleford	13,000			
Yorkton	13,000			

Source: *Canada Year Book*, 1973

The Gonad Kit. In addition, a self-testing kit had been developed to enable women to check for gonorrhea infection t home. One thousand kits were being planned for production, and awaited only a decision from the A.C.V.D. on what budget would be available for them. They were to be distributed to university campus health centres, public health centres, doctors' offices, and by mail. The kits cost $.50 each (Exhibit 3 illustrates the instructions received with the kit), and advertising their availability would add to the cost. (See Exhibit 4 for sample newspaper ad.) In a pilot test, the kits proved to be an effective means of testing for disease, provided they were properly used.

THE ADVISORY COMMITTEE ON THE VENEREAL DISEASE CONTROL PROGRAM

The Saskatchewan Minister of Health, on recommendation by Dr. Davidson, established A.C.V.D. in 1973 to create a complete program to combat one of Saskatchewan's worst health problems. The A.C.V.D. comprised eight members of the Health Department and concerned citizens and met frequently to exchange statistics and ideas on what to do. Most A.C.V.D. members were concerned about the moral and political implications of trying to educate the public about VD preventive measures—they anticipated much more antagonism by some groups than the controversial sex education programs in the schools. Exhibit 5 contains a sampling of opinions of A.C.V.D. members and others on approaches to the VD problem in Saskatchewan.

The A.C.V.D. had a budget of approximately $100,000 to $150,000 per year for the next two years. There was considerable disagreement among committee members on how to spend that money. The doctors and the Health Department favoured putting most of the money into clinics, with more staff and drugs. Other members of the A.C.V.D. favoured upgrading physicians' education in areas where clinics did not exist and instigating a media campaign to educate the public about VD. Each new clinic would cost

EXHIBIT 3
The Gonax, a Self-Test Kit for Gonorrhea[1]

**A Kit Designed to Allow a Woman to Collect a Specimen in the Privacy of Her Own Bathroom
That Can Be Tested by the Laboratory for Gonorrhea**

Contents of Kit
- Small jar with brown jelly, plastic bag and twister.
- Tampax tampon.
- Instruction sheet with address label.
- Paper wad with chemicals (when wad is dampened with water, it slowly releases gases needed to help germs multiply so that the laboratory can find them).
- Metal mailing cylinder.

How to Collect the Specimen
- Read the instructions first. Locate the address label at the end of these instructions. Cut out the address label along the broken lines. Answer all the questions on the address label so that a report can be sent to you.
- Unwrap the tampon and adjust its length to expose about one-quarter inch of cotton.
- Insert the tampon as far as possible into the front passage. Leave it in for at least three minutes.
- Remove the tampon, and gently rub or dab the cotton end onto the chocolate jelly in the jar. Do not break the surface of the jelly.
- Throw away the tampon.
- Screw the top of the jar snugly. Then loosen the top about one-quarter turn so that the air can get in.
- Dampen the paper wad with water by passing it swiftly under a running tap. Do not soak. Put the water-dampened wad into the plastic bag.
- Drop the jar into the plastic bag on top of the paper wad. Press out the air from the plastic bag.
- Knot the plastic bag tightly to seal it or use the twister.
- Put the plastic bag with contents and your address label into the metal mailing container.
- Screw the lid onto the mailing container and put $.20 postage on the address label.
- Mail the container in an indoor mailbox (severe heat in summer or frost in winter may spoil your specimen). You may expect the report about a week after mailing your specimen.

What Is Gonorrhea and How Do You Get It?
Gonorrhea or clap is an infection of the vulva, vagina, urethra or penis which may develop a few days after sexual intercourse with an infected partner. The risk of infection increases with the number of sexual partners that either the man or the woman has had.

What Are the Symptoms in a Woman?
About one-third of women who become infected develop burning or itching upon urinating, tenderness, visible sores or a vaginal discharge. Any woman with any of these symptoms should visit her doctor or a public health clinic.
   About two-thirds of women who become infected do not develop any signs or symptoms of the infection, but their reproductive system and general health may be seriously damaged.

Who Should Take the Test?
A woman who has no symptoms, but fears that one of her sexual partners may have infected her, should take the test.

Will the Findings of This Test Be Kept Confidential?
Yes. The report will be mailed to your given address as shown on the address label. A copy of a positive report will be sent to the physician named to inform him that he might proceed immediately with the necessary treatment.

Does a Negative Report Mean That You Do Not Have Gonorrhea?
Only if you do not have any symptoms! A single negative test is only 80 per cent reliable. If you have symptoms, you should repeat the test—or better still—see your physician.

Ed Note: This kit is no longer available from the Sasketchewan Department of Health.

---

approximately $9000 to establish plus staffing costs of approximately $25,000 to $40,000 per year depending on circumstances. Existing VD clinics could be expanded with part-time staff at a cost of about $5000 per year for each additional public health nurse. Another related proposal was the expansion of the VD detection program at the provincial laboratory. Such expansion was thought by some to be necessary if the Gonax kit was successful. Preliminary estimates for this expansion were in the neighbourhood of $5000.

An information campaign directed at physicians and nurses had not been thought through. One suggestion was a series of information booths at medical conferences. A rough guess of $1000 per booth per conference was mentioned in the meeting.

A brochure had been prepared by the Saskatchewan Department of Health entitled "Bodyguards and Self-Defence: Your VD Protection Manual." These brochures cost $.10 each to print. Staff members of the department advocated a production run of one thousand copies to be distributed to schools, doctors' offices, libraries, clinics, hotels, motels, bars and occupational health centres. The following gives an idea of the contents of the brochure.

Bodyguards.

For the male:

- Applying a condom before sexual contact
- Urinating immediately after sexual intercourse
- Washing the genital area with soap and water immediately after sexual intercourse

For the female:

- Insisting that your male partner use a condom
- Gentle vaginal douching with a mild soapy solution after sexual contact
- Washing the genital area with soap and water immediately after sexual intercourse
- The use of some vaginal contraceptive gels and creams. These may kill venereal disease germs.

On the back of the brochure was the statement "Should you require any further information, telephone _____." The idea was to establish a telephone hot line to provide information on venereal diseases and to suggest a visit to the nearest VD clinic if the situation seemed to warrant it. One proposal involved counsellors answering the phones from 0800 to 2145 each day. Another proposal involved an "electronic secretary," a tape message receiver that would operate twenty-four hours a day. Each morning a clinic staff member would answer the messages of the previous day. Cost of the tape machine was $20.50 per month. Preliminary cost estimates for a telephone system, including INWAT long distance service adequate to handle calls from the entire province, were $300 connect costs and $750 per month equipment rental.

THE PROPOSED MEDIA CAMPAIGN

Dr. Davidson had not given Mr. Cosgrave a specific budget figure for an advertising campaign. As he examined various alternatives with the help of advertising agencies and the Department of Health staff, Mr. Cosgrave received several varying suggestions on how much to spend. He had not decided on an appropriate budget, but hoped the A.C.V.D. meeting would result in a consensus on the amount to be spent.

Mr. Cosgrave prepared a statement of objectives for the campaign, as shown in Exhibit 6. In addition, he laid before the A.C.V.D. a number of alternative media ideas for their evaluation. These ideas involved the use of print advertising, television advertising, radio and "shorts" as drive-in movies.

Print Advertising. There were four newspapers and about seventy weekly newspapers in the province. One agency suggested to Mr. Cosgrave that one-eighth page ads (two of which are shown as Exhibit 7) be produced at a cost of $882 and run ("placed") at a cost of $5184: $2020 to dailies, $2874 to weeklies, and $290 to other periodicals. Another group suggested one-quarter page ads at a production cost of $4000 (two of which are shown as Exhibits 8 and 9). They estimated that for "saturation provincial coverage" each insertion would cost $4800.

EXHIBIT 5
Sample Opinions Expressed About VD by Concerned Officials

1. "Schools cannot be expected to replace the social functions of the family, nor can the burden of transmitting a coherent and unitary value system properly be placed on a government."
2. "Can we treat those under eighteen without their parents' consent? Experience in Toronto shows that legislative constraints force those under eighteen to turn to black market drugs, most of which do not cure but simply suppress the symptoms."
3. "The problem with present pamphlets is the tone of moral condemnation which is inappropriate, and indeed counterproductive, in today's society. By implying that women who have VD are easy 'pick-ups,' they inhibit women from seeking treatment for fear of having themselves branded as such. By describing premarital relations illicit (i.e., unlawful) and suggesting physical exercise as an alternative to sexual relationships they 'turn off' young people who find this advice 'Victorian' and inane.
   "The new publications have, in my estimation, overcome these faults. The information transmitted is more accurate and rather than running counter to prevailing sexual behaviour patterns, they attempt to insert into those patterns a willingness to name sexual contacts out of respect for and responsibility to sexual partners."
4. Jack Migowski, ed., Maple Creek News Ltd.: ". . . . in many rural areas a very small percentage of the people actually receives daily newspapers and the only really effective way to get to those people is through the medium of the weekly press.
   "I am sure you realize that, also due to density of population, there is a larger problem in the cities than in the rural centres. However, we wonder what the percentage would be in the two situations. And because of the reluctance of the affected people to come forward that will always be an unknown factor.
   "However, I am sure that you also realize and appreciate the old saying of 'out behind the barn.' And where are the barns?????"
5. TO: Honorable A. E. Blakeney & Cabinet Ministers
   FROM: Minister of Public Health
   RE: VD Control Program 1973
   I would like the support of my cabinet colleagues to markedly step up our attempts to control the spread of syphilis and gonorrhea in the province. VD is now the most prevalent infectious disease in the province and Canada. My reasons for this request are:
   (a) The steadily mounting incidence of venereal disease, especially in the fifteen to nineteen year age group.
   (b) Some of the innovative and unorthodox steps suggested may provoke a public criticism; in particular, the necessity to detect a large part of affected but symptomless female carriers in the fifteen to nineteen year age group may create significant problems.
6. TO: Administrators of all Sask. Hospitals
   FROM: Dr. J. D. Berry, Director
   Regional Health Services Branch
   That some of the present VD clinics are inadequate is apparent to anyone visiting the premises of, for instance, the Saskatoon facility which is in no way conducive to the type of operation which the Committee believes desirable. It is desirable that all clinics induce a willingness to attend on the part of those at risk. Access and appearance are factors which affect attendance. Space, furnishings and equipment are necessary for successful operation by the nurse in charge.
7. Dr. J. T. Y. Chiao, Medical Health Officer: "My contention is that when teenagers who have contacted a venereal disease come into a clinic they require more than a therapeutic injection of a drug."
8. "Inserts should be placed in the 300,000 Saskatchewan Health Insurance Plan circulars which are distributed every year."
9. "A special pamphlet for the 'Gay Society' is available from B.C. at $.10 each, minimum order of 500. Strong interest has been expressed by the Gays for such a publication."
10. Community involvement is essential."
11. "How do we measure success of the new program? If we have a dramatic rise in the statistics because people are now coming in for treatment, and these statistics get into the press nationally, Saskatchewan will look like a hotbed of disease."
12. "Saskatchewan has been part of the 'Bible Belt' for years. How do you bring things like this to the people without having open hostility which will force the politicians to kill the project?"

EXHIBIT 6
The Proposed Campaign: Phases and Objectives

A Sure Cure for VD

We can't promote celibacy. We can't encourage condom use. And we aren't going to limit promiscuity.

Venereal disease is a disease. There is nothing "wrong" with it.

What is wrong is that some people who have contracted it are not getting treated.

Our ability to prevent VD depends upon our ability to:

1. Educate the public as to its nature and symptoms, and
2. Motivate people who have it to get treated.

Within these parameters we have created a three-phase campaign with a twofold objective.

Phase I Awareness

The initial phase of our campaign deals with awareness.

We want to advise people of the high levels of incidence and of the seriousness of untreated VD.

The stance we will adopt for this communication is reasonable and mature. We would like to encourage a thoughtful examination of personal attitudes towards VD and, hopefully, to create a more tolerant social environment.

VD is a by-product of the new sexual mores. And while the thought of sex and VD still makes many people uncomfortable, the thought of someone going untreated because of social inhibitions has to be worse.

Phase II Education

There's no point in hitting a hornet's nest with a baseball bat, unless you know what you're doing.

So if we don't have a good follow-up educational program there's no reason to create an awareness.

Consequently, we recommend the creation of a new VD booklet tailored to the Saskatchewan experience.

We propose to call it "Everything you wanted to know about VD but were afraid to ask."

In our opinion the booklet is the most important feature of the entire campaign.

If it's unfeasible, because of economics, to do a new one we would suggest using the book created in Ottawa. It's at least competent and contains the right tone and information.

The key to the education program is distribution. People, even when they're interested, will only commit so much energy to acquiring information. Therefore, the booklet should be effortlessly available.

We would like to investigate the possibilities of placing it in places like high school bathrooms, central government outlets, including liquor stores and drug stores. It's imperative that anyone who wants one can get one.

We should also advise people of the additional resources that are available. Like speakers for groups, clinic numbers, places for private consultation.

The booklet would carry the burden of communicating the physical symptoms of the disease. We really don't think this can be done effectively in an ad. And anyone who is motivated to get the booklet will read it and get a lot more out of it.

Phase III Motivation

Phase III is designed to get people who have or suspect they have VD to see a doctor.

The highest reported incidence of VD exists among people fifteen to thirty (71 per cent).

This also means that the highest unreported incidence exists here too.

Phase III consists of specific communications to people fifteen to nineteen and one to people twenty to thirty.

Besides being the statistically largest segment these people are also the easiest to reach and influence. (Anyway, what can you say to someone over thirty who refuses to be treated?)

The biggest problem perceived here is a social stigma and fear of parental reactions. Consequently, the discretion of the clinic personnel is stressed. We realize, of course, that this is an awkward and delicate line to walk. But our position is that it's better to be treated than not to be treated.

Through the use of our headings we create an immediate empathy with our market by stating, in their own words, the problem of VD as it exists in their surroundings. So, we achieve communication, but even more importantly, we form a basis for honest discussion of the problem between parent and child by pointing out their obvious barriers.

We would also like to stress this as an educational ground and explore ways to saturate the schools with the book and any additional resources we have.

Besides lowering the levels of incidence we will have given them a solid base and understanding for dealing with VD in the future when they have grown into other age segments.

How It Works Together

We see the various components of this campaign working together to fulfill an immediate and a future need.

By creating a more tolerant social environment and talking directly to the most sensitive area we'll reduce the present levels of incidence.

And by a massive educational program we will be able to control future levels.

You can get it

An information booklet on VD, its symptoms, treatment, and long-term effects if untreated, is available from libraries, doctors' offices, Metis Society offices, and hospitals, or the Saskatchewan Department of Public Health.

For more information, phone VD
Information Centre
Regina residents 523-9694
Out-of-Regina residents 800-667-0681

All information is kept confidential

Venereal Disease.
What You Don't Know *Can* Hurt You.

Saskatchewan Department of Public Health

The forgotten fact of life

A program has been set up by the Department of Public Health to make everyone aware of a high increase of VD throughout the province.

VD is Saskatchewan's fastest growing communicable disease; in the first half of this year there was a 20% increase in treated cases, which means an increase in untreated cases.

The most common venereal diseases are Gonorrhea and Syphilis. If left untreated they may lead to:

Gonorrhea: sterility and arthritic conditions. Women infected during pregnancy can transmit the disease to their unborn children.

Syphilis: untreated syphilis can cause blindness, insanity, sterility, and death.

Cure occurs only with proper medical treatment. All personal information is known only to your Public Health nurse or doctor.

Public Health Clinics

General Hospital
Regina, Sask.
Phone: 522-5467

Regional Health Care
1257-1st Avenue East
Prince Albert, Sask.
Phone: 763-7276

Wing "G" Ground Floor
University Hospital
Saskatoon, Sask.
Phone: 343-5323

53 Stadacona Street West
Moose Jaw, Sask.
Phone 692-4523

Venereal Disease.
What You Don't Know *Can* Hurt You.

For Further Information

Call (Direct and toll free)
V.D. Information Centre
Regina residents . . . 523-9694
Out of Regina residents . . . 800-667-0681

Saskatchewan Department of Public Health

EXHIBIT 8
Print Advertisement: It's Also a State of Mind

To a lot of people VD still carries a social stigma. That's a state of mind.

Venereal disease is transmitted through sex. So it's very often hard to talk about it.

But it is time to talk. Because VD has become the fastest-growing communicable disease in Saskatchewan. Greater than mumps, measles and chicken pox put together.

The first half of this year alone has brought a 20% increase in reported and treated cases.

And that means an increase in untreated cases. That a lot of people who have VD, or suspect they have it, aren't doing anything about it.

Because they're embarassed and worried about what people may say or think.

Which is tragic.

Because an untreated venereal disease, such as gonorrhea, can lead to sterility, arthritic complications and congenital defects in unborn children.

But cure is not possible without proper medical treatment. Symptoms are often hard or impossible to detect without a professional examination. And an untreated venereal disease spreads with further sexual contact.

And yet medically, VD is like any other infection. As such it can be quickly treated and cured. Properly and discreetly.

If it's diagnosed in time.

Protect yourself, your family and your friends. Find out the facts about VD. Now.

Because despite what anyone may say there's nothing worse than untreated VD.

VENEREAL DISEASE. WHAT YOU DON'T KNOW *CAN* HURT YOU.
FOR FURTHER INFORMATION CALL (Direct & Toll Free) VD Information Centre. Regina Residents 523-9694—Out of Regina Residents 800-667-0681
The Booklet "Everything You Always Wanted To Know About VD. But Were Afraid to Ask" is available "FREE" at ● Libraries ● Doctors' Offices ● Health Region Offices ● Hospitals

EXHIBIT 9
The Forgotten Fact of Life

If the facts about venereal disease came with the facts of life, VD wouldn't be quite the problem it is today.

But very often, they don't.

The facts are, that venereal disease is transmitted through sex. That symptoms are often hard or impossible to detect without a professional examination. That cure occurs only with proper medical treatment. And that an untreated venereal disease spreads with further sexual contact.

And today, venereal disease is Saskatchewan's fastest-growing communicable disease.

Greater than mumps, measles and chicken pox put together. The first half of this year alone has brought a 20% increase in reported cases. Which also means a significant increase in untreated cases.

That means a lot of people who have VD, or suspect they have it, aren't doing anything about it.

And that's tragic.

Because an untreated venereal disease, such as syphilis, can lead to blindness, insanity, sterility and even death.

And yet medically, VD is like any other infection. As such it can be quickly treated and cured. Properly and discreetly.

If it's diagnosed in time.

But the people who have VD, or may be susceptible, must have the facts. And a bit of understanding.

Because the final fact remains, there's nothing worse than untreated VD.

It's something no one can afford to forget.

VENEREAL DISEASE. WHAT YOU DON'T KNOW *CAN* HURT YOU.
FOR FURTHER INFORMATION CALL (Direct & Toll Free) VD Information Centre, Regina Residents 523-9694—Out of Regina Residents 800-667-0681
The Booklet "Everything You Always Wanted To Know About VD But Were Afraid To Ask" is available "FREE" at ● Libraries ● Doctors' Offices ● Health Region Offices ● Hospitals

EXHIBIT 10
Radio Audience Data

Teen Audience: 12–17 Years

Station	Peak Time Periods	Day	Average Audience	Adult Audience (18 +)
*CKCK Regina	8-8:30 A.M.	M-F	6 550	54 350
	10-11 P.M.	M-F	4 333	5 200
	3-4 P.M.	Sat.	3 000	8 500
	11 P.M.-mdnt.	Sat.	3 800	1 800
	9-11 P.M.	Sun.	3 750	40 500
	4-5 P.M.	Sun.	3 200	14 500
CKRM Regina	7:30-8 A.M.	M-F	1 500	12 350
	6-6:30 P.M.	M-F	650	5 100
	*10 A.M.-noon	Sat.	2 350	17 650
CFMC-FM Saskatoon	No appreciable teen audience			
*CFQC Saskatoon	7:45-8:15 A.M.	M-F	3 900	36 950
	9 A.M.-noon	Sat.	2 666	30 800
	5-6 P.M.	Sat.	2 400	6 900
	10-A.M.-noon	Sun.	4 950	49 900
CJUS-FM Saskatoon	Data not available			
*CKOM Saskatoon	7:30-8 A.M.	M-F	3 750	6 800
	10-11 P.M.	M-F	2 066	1 700
	7-8 P.M.	Sat.	1 900	2 100
	7-8 P.M.	Sun.	2 200	2.100
CHAB Moose Jaw	8-8:30 A.M.	M-F	600	6 200
	4:15-5 P.M.	M-F	400	2 050
	9-10 P.M.	M-F	300	650
	7-9 P.M.	Sat.	600	300
*CKBI Prince Albert	7:30-8:30 A.M.	M-F	2 125	26 525
	4:15-5:15 P.M.	M-F	875	3 925
	10-11:30 P.M.	M-F	700	1 425
	9-10 A.M.	Sat.	900	5 400
	8-9 A.M.	Sat.	800	2 200
	10-11 P.M.	Sat.	900	3 100
CBK Regina	8:15-9 A.M.	M-F	1 633	13 566
CFMQ-FM Regina	9-10 A.M.	Sun.	400	2 300
*CJME Regina	7:30-8:15 A.M.	M-F	5 200	10 366
	4-5 P.M.	M-F	3 350	2 675
	7-8 P.M.	M-F	2 400	2 300
	10-11 P.M.	M-F	3 200	2 267
	1-4 P.M.	Sat.	3 700	1 250
	1-5 P.M.	Sun.	3 500	3 442
	10-11 P.M.	Sun.	3 600	2 700
*CJGX Yorkton	7:30-8:15 A.M.	M-F	9 666	13 833
	10 P.M.-mdnt.	M-F	7 402	860
	9-11 A.M.	Sat.	1 250	10 850

Prepared by J. A. C. Struthers and Associates, 1960 Albert Street, Regina, Saskatchewan, 525-9566.

Television Advertising. There were eight television stations in the province. An animated thirty-second spot with voice-over was proposed. Production cost would be in the neighbourhood of $4000. One thirty-second commercial on the eight stations at prime time would cost a total of $718. Health Department staffers recommended twenty announcements for twenty days' exposure during August and September, one spot per day, for a total cost $14,360.

Radio Advertising. There were nineteen radio stations in the province. One thirty-second spot during prime time on the nineteen stations would cost a total of $250, a sixty-second spot would cost $306. Radio audience data are shown in Exhibit 10. One agency had prepared some sixty-second spots for VD in 1972 which Mr. Cosgrave felt might be appropriate. Production costs for four commercials were estimated at $300.

Drive-In Movie Shorts. A drive-in movie short was somewhat like a TV commercial and was shown before each movie at the drive-in. A 35 mm live action spot would cost approximately $2000 to produce. Placement costs varied greatly as shown in Exhibit 11.

As Mr. Cosgrave finished his presentation, he added his suggestion that $5000 be set aside to evaluate the effec-

tiveness of the campaign. Dr. Davidson then asked the members of the A.C.V.D., "What do you think we should do?"

EXHIBIT 11
Saskatchewan Drive-In Movie List

Regina	Cinema Queen City Starlite	For 3, $250
Saskatoon	Skyway Starlite Sundown Sutherland Park	For 4, $320
Prince Albert	Norlite Pines	For 2, $100
Moose Jaw	Golden West	$60
North Battleford	North Park	$40
Meadow Lake	Northland	$30
Nipawin	Skyview	$30
Yorkton	Crest	$50
Fort Qu'Appelle	Twilite	$25
Melfort	Sunset	$33.50
Lloydminster	C + H	$40
Kamsack	Sunset	$30
Unity	Twilite	$27

13

Nonprofits: Check Your Attention to Customers

Alan R. Andreasen

Nonprofit organizations chronically face financial difficulties. Now the situation has worsened because they are being squeezed between the uncertain economic climate and cutbacks in government support. While the managers of these institutions, may think that they have already tried everything possible, more than ever they must be innovative in developing additional funding sources. Most nonprofits have failed to exploit marketing techniques which can build support from users or customers that leads to improved cash flow. Managers of nonprofit organizations focus too closely on their products or services; they should give more attention to the needs and wants of their consumers.

The director of an urban art museum describes her marketing strategy as "an educational task." She says: "I assemble the best works available and then display them grouped by period and style so that the museum-goer can readily see the similarities and differences between, say, a Bracque and a Picasso or between a Brancusi and an Arp. Our catalogs and lecture programs are carefully coordinated with this approach to complete our marketing mix."

The public relations manager of a social service agency claims: "We are very marketing oriented. We research our target markets extensively and hire top-flight creative people with strong marketing backgrounds to prepare brochures. They tell our story with a sense of style and graphic innovation that has won us several awards."

A marketing vice president for a charitable foundation ascribes his success to careful, marketing-oriented planning: "Once a year we plan the entire year's series of messages, events, and door-to-door solicitation. We emphasize

Alan R. Andreasen is Professor of Marketing, University of Illinois.

the fine humanitarian work we do, showing and telling potential donors about the real people who have benefited from donations to us. Hardly a week goes by without some warm human-interest story appearing in the local press about our work. The donors just love it!"

These are the kinds of statements one hears from officials of successful nonprofit organizations that are highly respected for their supposedly innovative marketing approaches. The executives have attended courses and seminars on marketing, and their planning documents and speeches are laced with marketing jargon like "benefit segmentation," "product positioning," and "message strategies."

While they believe they are marketing oriented, these organizations actually have a product-oriented approach. They start with their own organizations and services, determine how they want to market them, and *then* turn to customer analysis to achieve their goals. Despite their protestations to the countrary, they do not begin the process with consumers. The distinction is subtle but important. Managers need to adopt a new view of marketing and its role in their organizations. The first step in this learning process is self-awareness—recognizing the underlying product or selling orientation in the approaches they and their institutions use.

Marketing has certainly achieved wide respectability in the nonprofit world. Hospital administrators, college presidents, and theater directors are often as familiar with the writings and speeches of marketing experts as they are with those of the traditional management sages. Yet all too many of these managers have adopted the trappings of marketing without grasping its essence. For this reason, marketing among nonprofit heads may go the way of such fads as motivation research and sensitivity training.

SELLING VS. MARKETING

While most readers probably well understand the distinction between a selling or product orientation and a marketing orientation, reconsideration of the terms ensures a common starting point for this article. A *product orientation* involves focusing on an organization's basic offering and a belief that the best marketing strategy for increasing sales is to improve this offering's quality. A *selling orientation* equates the marketing task with persuading target audiences that they ought to accept the offering—that it is superior to any alternatives.

The art museum director described at the outset of the article believes she knows what her audience should learn about art; she sees her principal marketing task as "educational." The public relations manager concentrates not just on what she has to say but on how to say it; effective persuasion is the key element in her marketing strategy. And the charitable foundation's director believes his story is one that donors will just love to hear (of course, he also loves to tell it).

These marketers start with what they wish others to know about their organizations and only later think about customers needs and wants. This is very different from a modern marketing orientation, which espouses the opposite approach. Institutions shouldn't ignore their own goals, preferences, strengths, and weaknesses; nevertheless, these concerns should not outweigh consumers' interests.

To illustrate, let's consider the typical art museum. As indicated in the opening quotation, most art museum directors see their marketing problem as one of assembling the best collections, displaying them well, and notifying the press and public of their availability. This product orientation manifests itself in the labels museums concoct for works of art, which museum directors see as a key marketing tool to get mass audiences to appreciate the artworks.

What information does a label usually include? First, facts about the artist: name, nationality, dates of birth and death. For whom is this information most important? Certainly for the museum director and his or her peers, since it ensures location of the artwork with others created by artists of the same nationality and period. Often labels also relate information about bequests, including donors' names. Of course, this information helps the director secure more donations (admittedly an important marketing task). On the other hand, given limited space, a donor's name is hardly a key piece of data for most museum-goers. Finally, there is usually a catalog (or inventory) number on the bottom of the label that helps the director keep track of the collection, prevent theft, and schedule repairs.

But what information would consumers like to see posted next to each work? If museum directors talked to consumers, as I have, they would discover that there is not one consumer market but three—each with different needs and wants but united against the typical labels. The three groups and their information needs can be defined as follows:

The Aesthetes. Some viewers are most interested in the aethestic-artistic properties of each work. They want to know about design, use of materials, color, and techniques. They want to know about anything unusual in the artist's style and about good or bad features of the work. The artwork itself is of key importance to this group.

The Biographers. These people are fascinated by artists, their lives, their choices of subject matter, and their models. They would like to know how a work fits into the artist's career and what special meaning it has for his or her growth and development. For this group, the key feature is not so much the work but the artist behind it.

The Cultural Historians. This group usually has had some formal or informal exposure to art or social history. Its members are interested in the work as an element in the sweep of cultural and artistic history. They want to know, for example, why this technique or this subject matter was chosen at this particular time and what the piece tells about the age, the country, and the broader artistic framework. Did the work influence other artists then or later? Does it reflect any of its predecessors? What was the society like that produced this artwork and this artist?

Clearly, three systems—not one—are needed. To some museum directors' surprise, such customer-oriented messages may not only broaden people's appreciation of the arts but also spur museum attendance or even donations. Directors might experience a leap in old-fashioned customer satisfaction, especially among those just beginning to explore museums and the arts.

KEY INDICATORS

How can nonprofit organizations determine whether they have a selling or product orientation rather than a marketing focus? Among the symptoms that I have found to suggest a product or selling mind set are the following:

1. Seeing the Offering as Inherently Desirable.

Nonprofit heads seldom entertain the possibility that potential consumers may not share their enthusiasm about their offerings. They cannot see why, given a clear description of their institution and what it provides, consumers would not want to respond enthusiastically.

Committed theater managers may find it hard to believe that right-thinking people wouldn't wish to attend a well-acted play; charitable organizations' directors sometimes cannot fathom an unwillingness to give; and those who head up nonprofit special-interest groups often can't see why people won't vote for, say, cleaner air or the ERA. Other nonprofits, including organizations designed to push such health-enhancing notions as wearing seatbelts and quitting smoking, also are surprised that they have difficulty generating a positive response.

One organization that overcame the notion that its offerings are inherently desirable is the National Cancer Institute. Most women, NCI discovered, agreed that practicing breast self-examination was a good thing to do, and many knew how to do it. Yet the majority were not practicing such examination or, at best, did so only rarely. What was the problem? If the examination yielded nothing, the woman would feel a sense of relief the first few times but eventually she would become bored at finding nothing and would stop the procedure. But the prospect of "success" was so frightening that most women never even tried the self-examination or, at any rate, didn't check themselves regularly. It was only when NCI understood these barriers—as perceived by the target audience—to an obviously good practice that it began to develop more user-oriented marketing programs. NCI's new stance, based on assurances that progress is being made against breast cancer (and thus one shouldn't fear discovering lumps), has resulted in increased self-detection.

2. The Notion of Consumer Ignorance.

Nonprofit managers tend to ascribe any lack of interest to the fact that consumers don't fully appreciate the nature of the offer. Or, if customers do understand, managers just haven't found the right incentives to motivate them.

Again the National Cancer Institute provides a good example of what a change to a marketing orientation can accomplish. For many years, the conventional wisdom among those charged with reducing cigarette consumption was that either smokers didn't believe smoking was bad for them or that they were not motivated enough to quit. But consumer surveys revealed that seven out of eight smokers did believe that smoking was a very bad habit and that many of them had in fact tried to stop. NCI concluded that what smokers needed as part of the marketing mix was a set of clear-cut techniques for quitting and a sense of hope that

they might succeed. Because of this new consumer perspective, NCI reoriented its program toward action rather than information.

3. Overemphasis on Promotion.

Many nonprofit organizations place too much stock in advertising and public relations. They are convinced that the director should concentrate on the message and its packaging. (Of course, the message directors usually have in mind is the story they want to tell.)

Many blood-collection agency heads believe that the best way to encourage donations is to tell consumers about the good things donors' blood can do or to stress that giving blood is a civic duty. They believe that people hold back from giving because they don't appreciate the gift's virtues or because they are afraid. Thus, agency heads reason, consumers need to be told about the benefits and assured that the costs are trivial—indeed, that giving can be fun.

While these messages work for some people, important segments respond to far different messages. For example, many men, especially blue-collar workers, can be motivated by challenges to their masculinity. The macho man who can tell his co-workers that he is a 20-gallon donor may feel well rewarded. (Indeed, some pain-and-suffering in the process might enhance the reward.) Thus, campaigns in factories focusing on individual giving records (bar charts or 10- and 20-gallon lapel pins) can be highly effective.

Many social, fraternal, and church group members can be motivated by the let's-all-participate aspects of a blood-mobile visit. They will respond to messages about camaraderie, about feeling left out if you don't join in, or about letting the group down if you don't go. All these messages have little to say about the occasion for the get-together or its value to society.

One blood bank director even uses sexual attraction as a marketing strategy. This director found a small segment of middle-aged men considered the attentions of the pretty nurses well worth the inconvenience of regular blood donations. This donor center has built a highly loyal following. The innovative marketer who listens to potential customers can gain surprising insights about what the target audience wants and what will get it to act.

4. The Secondary Role of Consumer Research.

If one "knows" that the problem lies with the consumer and that better promotion is the key to marketing success, the principal role for research is merely to confirm beliefs. Yet, as most profit-sector marketers will attest, research can challenge some managers' most fundamental assumptions about their customers. Take as an example officials of a small midwestern hospital who worried that patients were dissatisfied with some of its recently hired foreign-born doctors. Staff nurses reported frequent patient complaints about the doctors, sometimes because they "couldn't understand" what the doctors were saying. Moreover, different cultural backgrounds appeared to be seriously affecting doctor-patient rapport. The hospital turned to field research to find out how to cope with the problem.

The research indicated, however, that the foreign-doctor problem was not really serious in the eyes of patients or prospective patients. Few interviewees mentioned the issue voluntarily in the field study or scored it as a significant blot on the hospital's image. Doctors instead were rated just as easy to understand as doctors at rival institutions. Indeed many patients, far from complaining, perceived the foreign doctors as more serious and conscientious than their breezy, golf-loving U.S. counterparts. Needless to say, this research saved the hospital from spending many promotional dollars to correct a problem that didn't exist. What was really needed was a marketing program directed toward the hospital staff, especially the nurses and foreign doctors.

5. One Best Marketing Strategy. Since the nonprofit administrator is not often in close touch with the market, he or she may view it as monolithic or at least as having only a few crudely defined market segments. Subtle distinctions are played down. As a consequence, most nonprofits tend to develop only one or two marketing strategies, aim them at the most obvious market segments, and then run with them. This climate of managerial certainty precludes experimentation either with alternative strategies or with variations for market subsegments.

Also encouraging this approach is the fact that non-profit managers often come from nonbusiness backgrounds and may fear taking risks. Personal job survival and slow aggrandizement of the budget and staff are often their paramount objectives. And since such administrators are typically responsible only to a volunteer board—which meets irregularly and sometimes prefers to know little about day-to-day operations—they do their best to keep a low profile and avoid shaking up the board. Finally, since most non-profits are in fact deficit organizations that make up their losses with fund raising, aggressive marketing strategies are unnecessary. These forces, then, support the typical non-profit manager's natural inclination to be conventional, not adventuresome.

Yet the opportunities for careful experimentation abound. A case in point is Carleton College.* Since 1978, the Northfield, Minnesota school has systematically explored alternatives to the traditional single-brochure approach. A survey had shown that target high school students saw Minnesota as cold and isolated, Carleton itself as too "cerebral," and the library as too small. The standard brochure was updated to play down the cold weather, point out how

---

*"College Learns to Use Fine Art of Marketing," *Wall Street Journal*, February 23, 1981.

easy it is to get to the attractive Twin Cities, and feature a new picture of the library that shows it is really quite large.

More recently, Carleton discovered that regional differences affect perceptions of the college. So the school sends letters to Western students emphasizing outdoor activities and Carleton's informality and to Easterners stressing the school's academic prestige. And, finally, the school now informs those from Minnesota about its financial aid and the fact that Carleton enjoys a significant national, not just regional, reputation.

Since 1978, Carleton has seen its yearly applications increase from 1,470 to 1,875, while the response rate from mailings has jumped from 5.9% to more than 14%. It remains financially solvent and is protecting its reputation as academically selective.

6. Ignoring Generic Competition. While many nonprofit organizations consciously compete—the Heart Fund with the American Cancer Society, the Metropolitan Museum of Art with the Whitney or the Museum of Modern Art—many institutions don't have clear competitors because their services or so-called products are intangible or stress behavior changes. The competitors of those marketing, say, blood donations or forest-fire prevention are not immediately apparent. So it's not surprising that marketers ignore competition at either the product or generic level. But at the product level, blood banks, for example, compete with other charities for donors (who seek dollars, not blood). Even institutions with easily identifiable organizational competitors often face product competition from unlikely quarters. Thus, art museums compete with aquariums for family outings, with books and educational TV for art lovers, and with movies and restaurants as places to socialize.

Nonprofit organizations rarely plan strategies to compete at the product level because they lack a customer perspective. And this failure is even more serious at the nonproduct level. Before people will write their Congressman in support of ERA, for instance, they must give up their long-held ideas and divert their energies to the new cause. Inertia can be a powerful force, but enthusiastic non-profit marketers tend to ignore it. When they peddle change in behavior or new ideas, most nonprofits de-emphasize competition from the status quo.

7. A Marketing Staff Selected for Its Product Knowledge. In a modern marketing organization, staff members are selected on the basis of their knowledge of customer markets and of marketing research and management techniques. One can learn the key characteristics of a product in a few weeks, but market awareness and marketing expertise take years to master. Once gained, this expertise can be applied to many product or market contexts.

In many nonprofit organizations, knowledge of the product or service counts most. A preference for marketers with a product orientation prevails in nonprofit organizations because of three factors:

First, since marketing is unfamiliar to many nonprofit heads, they don't know how to evaluate marketing skills (while they can evaluate product know-how).

Second, many top nonprofit administrators accumulated most of their experience using product marketing and so are more comfortable working with people who have that orientation. Many business managers of arts organizations were once active performers or were formally trained in music, theater design, or museum curatorship. Most hospital administrators have either medical or public health backgrounds, and college presidents usually have Ph.D.s in academic disciplines. Seldom are these administrators selected purely for their management skills.

Finally, the world of nonprofits is a fairly clubby one where key people know other big names around the country; thus, a certain amount of favoritism prevails. A prospective staff member with the proper connections and the right vocabulary stands a much better chance of making it than a total outsider. The marketing professional, who probably doesn't know what "needs assessment" or "audience development" means, is at a disadvantage. This self-reinforcement means that the customer-oriented marketer who wants to come in and turn the organization around will be seen (whether consciously or not) as a threat.

A NEW WAY TO PASS THE HAT

How, then, can the marketing approaches in such organizations be changed? As noted previously, many nonprofit organizations' leaders are convinced they have already adopted the best marketing approaches. So the first step for concerned administrators is to assess the organization's managerial orientation.

It is also a good idea to start a customer research program. Customer research need not be expensive, and (as corporate marketers know) it is an essential precursor of each year's planning.

Furthermore, managers should rub shoulders with experienced marketers. Staff members can go outside regular channels for exposure to customer-oriented marketing. They might attend seminars, conferences, and courses by for-profit professionals or by academics who espouse customer-centered approaches. The institution can also bring a marketing consultant into the organization to evaluate problems and demonstrate how a modern marketer tries to solve them. And it can seek out one or more marketing professionals for the board of directors and observe how such professionals react to marketing problems.

Remember, the organizational atmosphere must change. Changing it is a straightforward process once nonprofit managers and staff become aware of what is at stake. And, since many not-for-profits are still exploring marketing's potential for helping them, the opportunities for adopting a constructive orientation are much greater than in fields where marketing has a longer history.

14

Diffusion of Innovations

Everett M. Rogers
F. Floyd Shoemaker

Much of the change which takes place in society nowadays is planned and directed.
Often a government agency or nonprofit organization is responsible for trying to encourage the development
and acceptance of new ideas and new behavior patterns. In planning and managing change programs,
it is important to understand how innovations affect (or fail to affect) existing social systems.

Although it is true that we live more than ever before in an era of change, prevailing social structures often serve to hamper the diffusion of innovations. Our activities in education, agriculture, medicine, industry, and the like are often without the benefit of the most current research knowledge. The gap between what is known and what is effectively put to use needs to be closed. To bridge this gap we must understand how new ideas spread from their source to potential receivers and understand the factors affecting the adoption of such innovations. We need to learn why, if 100 different innovations are conceived simultaneously, ten will spread while ninety will be forgotten.

WATER-BOILING IN A PERUVIAN VILLAGE: AN EXAMPLE OF INNOVATION THAT FAILED

The public health service in Peru attempts to introduce innovations to villagers to improve their health and lengthen their lives. The change agency enjoys a reputation

Everett M. Rogers is Professor of Communication, Stanford University.

F. Floyd Shoemaker is an official in the Michigan Department of Education.

throughout Latin America as efficient. It encourages people to install pit latrines, burn garbage daily, control house flies, report suspected cases of communicable disease, and boil drinking water. These innovations involve major changes in thinking and behavior for Peruvian villagers, who have little knowledge of the relationship between sanitation and illness.

A two-year water-boiling campaign conducted in Los Molinos, a peasant village of 200 families in the coastal region of Peru, persuaded only eleven housewives, who are the key decision makers in the family, to boil water. From the viewpoint of the health agency, the local hygiene worker, Nelida, had a simple task: To persuade the housewives of Los Molinos to add water-boiling to their pattern of existing behavior. Even with the aid of a medical doctor, who gave public talks on water-boiling, and fifteen village housewives who were already boiling water before the campaign, Nelida's program of directed change failed. To understand why, we need to take a closer look at the culture, the local environment, and the individuals.

Most residents of Los Molinos are peasants who work as field hands on local plantations. Water is carried directly from stream or well by can, pail, gourd, or cask. The three sources of water include a seasonal irrigation ditch close by the village, a spring more than a mile from the village, and a public well whose water the villagers dislike. All three are subject to pollution at all times and show contamination whenever tested.

Although it is not feasible for the village to install a sanitary water system, the incidence of typhoid and other water-borne diseases could be reduced by boiling the water before consumption. During her two-year residence in Los Molinos, Nelida paid several visits to every home in the village but devoted especially intensive efforts to twenty-one families. She visited each of these selected families between fifteen and twenty-five times; eleven of these families now boil their water regularly.

What kinds of persons do these numbers represent? By describing three village housewives—one who boils water to obey custom, one who was persuaded to boil water by the health worker, and one of the many who rejected the innovation—we may add further insight into the process of planned diffusion.

Mrs. A: Custom-Oriented. Mrs. A is about forty and suffers from sinus infection. She is labeled by the Los Molinos villagers as a "sickly one." Each morning, Mrs. A boils a potful of water and uses it throughout the day. She has no understanding of germ theory, as explained by Nelida; her motivation for water-boiling is a complex local custom of hot and cold distinctions. The basic principle of this belief system is that all foods, liquids, medicines, and other objects are inherently hot or cold, quite apart from their actual temperature. In essence hot—cold distinctions serve as a series of avoidances and approaches in such behavior as pregnancy and child rearing, food habits, and the entire health—illness system.

Boiled water and illness are closely linked in the folkways of Los Molinos; by custom, only the ill use cooked, or "hot" water. Once an individual becomes ill, it is unthinkable for him to eat pork (very cold) or to drink brandy (very hot). Extremes of hot and cold must be avoided by the sick; therefore, raw water, which is perceived to be very cold, must be boiled to overcome the extreme temperature.

Villagers learn from childhood to dislike boiled water. Most can tolerate cooked water only if flavoring, such as sugar, cinnamon, lemon, or herbs, is added. At no point in the village belief system is the notion of bacteriological contamination of water involved. Mrs. A drinks boiled water in obedience to local custom; she is ill.

Mrs. B: Persuaded. The B family came to Los Molinos a generation ago, but they are still strongly oriented toward their birthplace, located among the peaks of the high Andes. Mrs. B worries about lowland diseases which she feels infest the village. It is partly because of this anxiety that the change agent, Nelida, was able to convince Mrs. B to boil water.

Nelida is a friendly authority to Mrs. B (rather than a "dirt inspector," as she is seen by most housewives), who imparts knowledge and brings protection. Mrs. B not only boils water but also has installed a latrine and has sent her youngest child to the health center for an inspection.

Mrs. B is marked as an outsider in the community by her highland hairdo and stumbling Spanish. She will never achieve more than marginal social acceptance in the village. Because the community is not an important reference group to her, Mrs. B deviates from group norms on innovation. Having nothing to lose socially, Mrs. B gains in personal security by heeding Nelida's friendly advice. Mrs. B's practice of boiling water has no effect on her marginal status. She is grateful to Nelida for teaching her how to neutralize the danger of contaminated water, a lowland peril.

Mrs. C: Rejector. This housewife represents the majority of Los Molinos families who were not persuaded by the efforts of the change agent during the two-year health campaign. Mrs. C does not understand germ theory. How, she argues, can microbes survive in water which would drown people? Are they fish? If germs are so small that they cannot be seen or felt, how can they hurt a grown person? There are enough real threats in the world to worry about—poverty and hunger —without bothering with tiny animals one cannot see, hear, touch, or smell. Mrs. C's allegiance to traditional customs are at odds with the boiling of water. A firm believer in the hot—cold superstition, she feels that only the sick must drink boiled water.

Several housewives, particularly those of the lower social class, are rejectors because they have neither the time nor the means to boil water, even if they were convinced of its value. These women lack time to gather firewood and to boil water. The poor cannot afford the cost of fuel for water-boiling and the wives often work as field laborers beside their husbands, leaving them less time to boil water for their families.

Understanding Why Water-Boiling Failed. This intensive two-year campaign by a public health worker in a Peruvian village was largely unsuccessful. Nelida was able to encourage only about 5 percent of the population to adopt the innovation. In contrast, change agents in other Peruvian villages were able to convince 15 to 20 percent of the housewives. Reasons for the relative failure of the campaign in Los Molinos can be traced partly to the cultural beliefs of the villagers. Local tradition links hot foods with illness. Boiling water makes it less "cold," and hence, appropriate only for the sick. But if a person is not ill, he is prohibited by cultural norms from drinking boiled water. Only the least integrated individuals risk defying community norms on water-boiling. An important factor affecting the adoption rate of any innovation is its compatibility with the cultural beliefs of the social system.

Nelida worked with the wrong housewives if she wanted to launch a self-generating diffusion process in Los Molinos. She concentrated her efforts on village women like Mrs. A and Mrs. B. Unfortunately, they were perceived as a sickly one and a social outsider and were not respected as models of water-boiling behavior by the other women. The village opinion leaders, who could have been a handle to prime the pump of change, were ignored by Nelida.

The way that potential adopters view the change agent affects their willingness to adopt his ideas. In Los Molinos Nelida was seen differently by lower and middle status housewives. Most poor families saw the health worker as a "snooper" sent to Los Molinos to pry for dirt and to press already harassed housewives into keeping cleaner homes. Because the lower status housewives had less free time, they were not likely to initiate visits with Nelida about water-boiling. Their contacts outside the community were limited, and as a result, they saw the cosmopolite Nelida with eyes bound by the social horizons and cultural beliefs of Los Molinos. They distrusted this outsider, whom they perceived as a social stranger. Further, Nelida, who was middle class by Los Molinos standards, was able to secure more positive results from housewives whose socioeconomic level and cultural background were more similar to hers. This tendency for effective communication to occur with those who are more similar is a common experience of change agents in most diffusion campaigns.

In general Nelida was much more "innovation-oriented" than "client-oriented." Unable to put herself in the role of the village housewives, her attempts at persuasion failed to reach her clients because the message was not suited to their needs. Nelida did not begin where the villagers were; instead she talked to them about germ theory, which they could not, and did not need to, understand.

SOCIAL CHANGE

The theme to be developed throughout is: *Communication is essential for social change.* The process of social change consists of three sequential steps: (1) invention, (2) diffusion, and (3) consequences. *Invention* is the process by which new ideas are created or developed. *Diffusion* is the process by which these new ideas are communicated to the members of a social system. *Consequences* are the changes that occur within a social system as a result of the adoption or rejection of the innovation. Change occurs when a new idea's use or rejection has an effect. Social change is therefore an effect of communication.

What Is Social Change? *Social change* is the process by which alteration occurs in the structure and function of a social system. National revolution, invention of a new manufacturing technique, founding of a village improvement council, adoption of birth control methods by a family—all are examples of social change. Alteration in both the structure and function of a social system occurs as a result of such actions.

One of the more useful ways of viewing social change is to focus on the source of change.

1. *Immanent change* occurs when members of a social system with little or no external influence create and develop a new idea (that is,

invent it), which then spreads within the system. A farmer in the senior author's home community in Iowa invented a simple hand tool to clear cornpickers that were plugged with damp cornstalks. The invention was easy to make and a great time-saver. In a short time, most of the inventor's neighbors were using it. Immanent change, then, is a "within-system" phenomenon.

2. *Contact change*, the other type of social change, occurs when sources external to the social system introduce a new idea. Contact change is a "between-system" phenomenon. It may be either *selective* or *directed*, depending on whether the recognition of the need for change is internal or external.

Selective contact change results when members of a social system are exposed to external influences and adopt or reject a new idea from that source on the basis of their needs. The exposure to innovations is spontaneous or accidental; the receivers are left to choose, interpret, and adopt or reject the new ideas. An illustration of selective contact change occurs when school teachers visit a neighboring school that is especially innovative. They may return to their own classrooms with a new teaching method, but with no pressure from school administrators to seek and adopt such innovations.

Directed contact change, or planned change, is caused by outsiders who, on their own or as representatives of change agencies, intentionally seek to introduce new ideas in order to achieve goals they have defined. The water-boiling compaign in Peru is an example of directed contact change. The innovation, as well as the recognition of the need for change, originates outside the social system in the case of directed change. The many government-sponsored development programs designed to introduce technological innovations in agriculture, education, health, and industry are examples of contemporary directed change. Programs of planned change are largely the result of dissatisfaction with the rate of change that results from immanent and selective contact change.

The prevailing enthusiasm for planned change has not always been matched by overwhelming success. As communication research is conducted on the spread of new ideas and as the results are accumulated in a meaningful way, we shall be able to use these findings to design more effective programs of planned change.

Individual and Social System Change: Levels at Which Change Occurs. We have been looking at social change from the viewpoint of the innovation's origin. Another perspective is provided by the nature of the *unit* that adopts or rejects the new ideas.

1. Many changes occur at the *individual* level; that is, the individual is the adopter or rejector of the innovation. Change at this level has variously been referred to as diffusion, adoption, modernization, acculturation, learning, or socialization. We might term this the microanalytic approach to change analysis in that it focuses on an individual's change behavior.

2. Change also occurs at the *social system* level where it has been diversely termed development, specialization, integration, or adaptation. Here our attention is centered on the change process at the social system level and is thus macroanalytic in approach.

Of course, change at these two levels is closely interrelated. If we regard a school as a social system, then the school system's adoption of team teaching will lead to individual teachers' decisions to change their teaching methods.

Communication and Social Change. *Communication* is the process by which messages are transferred from a source to a receiver. We might think of the communication process in terms of the oversimplified but useful S–M–C–R model. A *source* (S) sends a *message* (M) via certain *channels* (C) to the *receiving* individual (R). One can easily see how communication factors are vitally involved in many aspects of the decision processes which together make up social change: A farmer's decision to move to the city or to participate in a government program, an industrialist's adoption of a new manufacturing technique, or the decision of a husband and wife to engage in family planning. In each of these instances, a message (M) is conveyed to individuals (R) via communication channels (C) from a source individual (S), which causes the receivers to change an existing behavior pattern.

Although communication and social change are not synonymous, communication is an important element throughout the social change process. Essentially, the concept of social change includes, in addition to the communication process, the societal and individual consequences that result from the adoption or rejection of an innovation. When examining social change, our concern is with alteration in the structure and function of a social system, as well as the process through which such alteration occurs. Thus to the S–M–R–C model, we might add (E) the effects of communication. (See Exhibit 1).

Communication and Diffusion. Diffusion is a special type of communication. *Diffusion* is the process by which innovations spread to the members of a social system. Diffusion studies are concerned with messages that are new ideas, whereas communication studies encompass all types of messages. As the messages are new in the case of diffusion, a degree of risk for the receivers is present. This leads to somewhat different behavior on their part in the case of innova-

tions than if they were receiving messages about routine ideas.

There is often a further difference between the nature of diffusion research versus other types of communication research. In the latter, we often focus on attempts to bring about changes in knowledge or attitudes by altering the makeup of the source, message, channels, or receivers in the communication process. But in diffusion research we usually focus on bringing about *overt behavior change,* that is, adoption or rejection of new ideas, rather than just changes in knowledge or attitudes. The knowledge and persuasion effects of diffusion campaigns are considered mainly as intermediate steps in an individual's decision-making process leading eventually to overt behavior change.

The focus on new ideas by diffusion researchers has led to a more thorough understanding of the communication process. The conception of the flow of communication as a multi-step process lacked clear conceptual development until it was probed by researchers studying the diffusion of innovations. They found that new ideas usually spread from a source to an audience of receivers via a series of sequential transmissions, rather than in the oversimplified two steps that had been originally postulated. By tracing communication patterns over time, diffusion researchers expanded the conceptual repertoire of communication researchers. Until students of diffusion began studying the flow of communication, consideration of the role of different communication channels at various stages in the innovation-decision process was masked. Specifically, it was learned that mass media channels are often more important at creating awareness-knowledge of a new idea, whereas interpersonal channels are more important in changing attitudes toward innovations.

Heterophily and Diffusion. One of the obvious principles of human communication is that the transfer of ideas occurs most frequently between a source and a receiver who are alike, similar, homophilous. *Homophily* is the degree to which pairs of individuals who interact are similar in certain

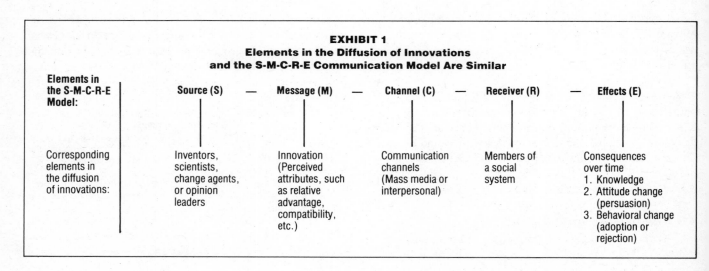

EXHIBIT 1
Elements in the Diffusion of Innovations
and the S-M-C-R-E Communication Model Are Similar

Elements in the S-M-C-R-E Model:	Source (S) —	Message (M) —	Channel (C) —	Receiver (R) —	Effects (E)
Corresponding elements in the diffusion of innovations:	Inventors, scientists, change agents, or opinion leaders	Innovation (Perceived attributes, such as relative advantage, compatibility, etc.)	Communication channels (Mass media or interpersonal)	Members of a social system	Consequences over time 1. Knowledge 2. Attitude change (persuasion) 3. Behavioral change (adoption or rejection)

attributes, such as beliefs, values, education, social status, and the like. In a free-choice situation, when a source can interact with any one of a number of receivers, there is a strong tendency for him to select a receiver who is most like himself. Similar individuals are likely to belong to the same groups, to live near each other, to be drawn by the same interests.

But in many situations, propinquity explains only a part of homophilous tendencies. *More effective communication occurs when source and receiver are homophilous.* When they share common meanings, a mutual subcultural language, and are alike in personal and social characteristics, the communication of ideas is likely to have greater effects in terms of knowledge gain, attitude formation and change, and overt behavior change.

Many examples could be cited to support the proposition about homophily and effective communication. In everyday life most of us interact with others who are quite similar in social status, education, and beliefs. And when we occasionally seek to communicate with those of a much lower social status, many problems of ineffective communication arise. Consider the middle class teacher who seeks to communicate with slum children, the social worker who tries to change the behavior of her lower class or foreign born clients, the technical assistance worker overseas who attempts to introduce innovations to peasants.

One of the most distinctive problems in the communication of innovations is that the source is usually quite heterophilous to the receiver. The extension agent, for instance, is much more technically competent than his peasant clients. This frequently leads to ineffective communication. The very nature of diffusion demands that at least some degree of heterophily be present between source and receiver. Ideally, they are homophilous on all other variables (education, social status, and the like) even though heterophilous regarding the innovation. In actuality, source and receiver are usually heterophilous on all of these variables because competence, education, social status, and so on are highly interrelated.

Time Lags in Diffusion. Evidence that diffusion is not a simple, easy process is the time that it requires. Change takes time, much time. Despite generally favorable attitudes toward change in nations like the United States, a considerable time lag exists from the introduction of a new idea to its widespread adoption. This is true even when the economic benefits of the innovation are obvious.

1. A forty-year time lag existed between the first success of the tunnel oven in the English pottery industry and its general use (Carter and Williams, 1957).
2. More than fourteen years were required for hybrid seed corn to reach complete adoption in Iowa (Ryan and Gross, 1943).
3. U.S. public schools required fifty years to adopt the idea of the kindergarten in the 1930s and 1940s (Ross, 1958), and more recently, about five or six years to adopt modern math in the 1960s (Carlson, 1965).

One of the goals of diffusion research is to shorten this time lag. It is clear that research alone is not enough to solve most problems; the results of the research must be diffused and utilized before their advantages can be realized. Even diffusion research findings must be diffused before their benefits can be derived.

In spite of the fact that the communication of most innovations involves a considerable time lag, there is a certain inevitability in their diffusion. Most attempts to prevent innovation diffusion over an extended period of time have failed. For instance, the Chinese were unsuccessful in their attempt to maintain sole knowledge of gunpowder. And today, a growing number of nations share the secret of the nuclear bomb with the United States. Similar are university administration and campus police attempts to prevent the widespread adoption of marijuana smoking among students.

Consequences of Innovations. The consequences of innovations are a third part of the social change process, following invention and diffusion. Consequences have an obvious interface with diffusion (for example, the selection of diffusion strategies affects the consequences that accrue).

Consequences are the changes that occur within a social system as a result of the adoption or rejection of an innovation. There are at least three classifications of consequences:

1. *Functional* versus *dysfunctional* consequences, depending on whether the effects of an innovation in a social system are desirable or undesirable.
2. *Direct* versus *indirect* consequences, depending on whether the changes in a social system occur in immediate response to an innovation or as a result of the direct consequences of an innovation.
3. *Manifest* versus *latent* consequences, depending on whether the changes are recognized and intended by the members of a social system or not.

Change agents usually introduce into a client system innovations that they expect will be functional, direct, and manifest. But often such innovations result in at least some latent consequences that are indirect and dysfunctional for the system's members. An illustration is the case of the steel ax introduced by missionaries to an Australian aborigine tribe. The change agents intended that the new tool should raise levels of living and material comfort for the tribe. But the new technology also led to breakdown of the family structure, the rise of prostitution, and ''misuse'' of the innovation itself. Change agents can often anticipate and predict the innovation's *form,* the directly observable physical appearance of the innovation, and perhaps its *function,* the contribution of the idea to the way of life of the system's members. But seldom are change agents able to predict another aspect of an innovation's consequences, its *meaning,* the subjective perception of the innovation by the clients.

ELEMENTS IN THE DIFFUSION OF INNOVATIONS

Crucial elements in the diffusion of new ideas are (1) the *innovation* (2) which is *communicated* through certain *channels* (3) over *time* (4) among the members of a *social system*. The four elements of diffusion differ only in nomenclature from the essential elements of most general communication models. For example, Aristotle proposed a very simple model of oral communication consisting of the speaker, the speech, and the listener. Laswell described all communication as dealing with *"who* says *what,* through *what channels* of communication, to *whom* with what . . . *results."*

The Innovation. An *innovation* is an idea, practice, or object perceived as new by an individual. It matters little, so far as human behavior is concerned, whether or not an idea is "objectively" new as measured by the lapse of time since its first use or discovery. It is the perceived or subjective newness of the idea for the individual that determines his reaction to it. If the idea seems new to the individual, it is an innovation.

"New" in an innovative idea need not be simply new knowledge. An innovation might be known by an individual for some time (that is, he is aware of the idea), but he has not yet developed a favorable or unfavorable attitude toward it, not has he adopted or rejected it. The "newness" aspect of an innovation may be expressed in knowledge, in attitude, or regarding a decision to use it.

Every idea has been an innovation sometime. Any list of innovations must change with the times. Black Panthers, computers, micro-teaching, birth control pills, chemical weed sprays, LSD, heart transplants, and laser beams might still be considered innovative ideas at this writing, but the reader in North America will probably find many of these items adopted or even discontinued at the time of reading.

The diffusion and adoption of all innovations is not necessarily desirable. In fact, some are harmful and uneconomical for either the individual or his social system.

It should not be assumed that all innovations are equivalent units of analysis. The several characteristics of innovations, as sensed by the receivers, contribute to their different rate of adoption.

1. *Relative advantage* is the degree to which an innovation is perceived as better than the idea it supersedes. The degree of relative advantage may be measured in economic terms, but often social prestige factors, convenience, and satisfaction are also important components. It matters little whether the innovation has a great deal of "objective" advantage. What does matter is whether the individual *perceives* the innovation as being advantageous. The greater the perceived relative advantage of an innovation, the more rapid its rate of adoption.
2. *Compatibility* is the degree to which an innovation is perceived as being consistent with the existing values, past experiences, and needs of the receivers. An idea that is not compatible with the prevalent values and norms of the social system will not be adopted as rapidly as an innovation that is compatible. The adoption of an incompatible innovation often requires the prior adoption of a new value system. An example of an incompatible innovation is the use of the IUCD (intra-uterine contraceptive device) in countries where religious beliefs discourage use of birth control techniques.
3. *Complexity* is the degree to which an innovation is perceived as difficult to understand and use. Some innovations are readily understood by most members of a social system; others are not and will be adopted more slowly. For example, the rhythm method of

family planning is relatively complex for most peasant housewives to comprehend because it requires understanding human reproduction and the monthly cycle of ovulation. For this reason, attempts to introduce the rhythm method in village India have been much less successful than campaigns to diffuse the loop, a type of IUCD, which is a much less complex idea in the eyes of the receiver. In general those new ideas requiring little additional learning investment on the part of the receiver will be adopted more rapidly than innovations requiring the adopter to develop new skills and understandings.
4. *Trialability* is the degree to which an innovation may be experimented with on a limited basis. New ideas which can be tried on the installment plan will generally be adopted more quickly than innovations which are not divisible. Ryan and Gross (1943) found that not one of their Iowa farmer respondents adopted hybrid seed corn without first trying it on a partial basis. If the new seed could not have been sampled experimentally, its rate of adoption would have been much slower. Essentially, an innovation that is trialable represents less risk to the individual who is considering it.
5. *Observability* is the degree to which the results of an innovation are visible to others. The easier it is for an individual to see the results of an innovation, the more likely he is to adopt. For example, a technical assistance agency in Bolivia introduced a new corn variety in one town. Within two years the local demand for the seed far exceeded the supply. The farmers were mostly illiterate, but they could easily observe the spectacular results achieved with the new corn and were thus persuaded to adopt. In the United States a rat poison that killed rats in their holes diffused very slowly among farmers because its results were not visible.

The five attributes just described are not a complete list, but they are the most important characteristics of innovations, past research indicates, in explaining rate of adoption.

Component elements in an innovation are often modified, adapted, and changed when the innovation is implemented by various adopters, as they fit the innovation to the distinctive conditions of their own situations.

Re-invention is the degree to which an innovation is changed by an adopter in the process of implementing its use. The amount of re-invention that occurs depends on the nature of the innovation, the similarity among the adopters' situations, and the policies of the change agency promoting the innovation.

When a high degree of re-invention occurs, it raises certain methodological questions about research on the diffusion of innovations. For example, how does one interpret a study of the rate of adoption if each adopter is selecting a slightly different innovation?

Given that an innovation exists and that it has certain attributes, communication between the source and the receivers must take place if the innovation is to spread beyond its inventor. Now we turn our attention to this second element in diffusion.

Communication Channels. *Communication* is the process by which messages are transmitted from a source to a receiver. In other words communication is the transfer of ideas from a source with a viewpoint of modifying the behavior of receivers. A communication *channel* is the means by which the message gets from the source to the receiver.

The essence of the diffusion process is the human interaction by which one person communicates a new idea to one or several other persons. At its most elementary level, the diffusion process consists of (1) a new idea, (2) individual A who has knowledge of the innovation, (3) individual B who is not yet aware of the new idea, and (4) some sort of communication channel connecting the two individuals. The nature of the social relationships between A and B determines the conditions under which A will or will not tell B about the innovation, and further, it influences the effect that the telling has on individual B.

The communication channel by which the new idea reached B is also important in determining B's decision to adopt or reject the innovation. Usually the choice of communication channel lies with A, the source, and should be made in light of (1) the purpose of the communication act, and (2) the audience to whom the message is being sent. If A wishes simply to inform B about the innovation, *mass media channels* are often the most rapid and efficient, especially if the number of Bs in the audience is large. On the other hand, if A's objective is to persuade B to form a favorable attitude toward the innovation, an *interpersonal channel,* involving face-to-face interchanges, is more effective.

Over Time. Time is an important consideration in the process of diffusion. The time dimension is involved (1) in the innovation-decision process by which an individual passes from first knowledge of the innovation through its adoption or rejection, (2) in the innovativeness of the individual, that is, the relative earliness-lateness with which an individual adopts an innovation when compared with other members of his social system, and (3) in the innovation's rate of adoption in a social system, usually measured as the number of members of the system that adopt the innovation in a given time period.

The Innovation-Decision Process. The *innovation-decision process* is the mental process through which an individual passes from first knowledge of an innovation to a decision to adopt or reject and to confirmation of this decision. Many diffusion researchers have conceptualized a cumulative series of five stages in the process: (1) from awareness (first knowledge of the new idea), (2) to interest (gaining further knowledge about the innovation), (3) to evaluation (gaining a favorable or unfavorable attitude toward the innovation), (4) to small-scale trial, (5) to an adoption or rejection decision. We prefer to conceptualize four main functions or steps in the process: (1) knowledge, (2) persuasion, (3) decision, and (4) confirmation. The *knowledge function* occurs when the individual is exposed to the innovation's existence and gains some understanding of how it functions. The *persuasion function* occurs when the individual forms a favorable or unfavorable attitude toward the innovation. The *decision function* occurs when the individual engages in activities which lead to a choice to adopt or reject the innovation. The *confirmation function* occurs when the individual seeks reinforcement for the innovation-decision he has made, but he may reverse his previous decision if exposed to conflicting messages about the innovation.

An example should clarify the meaning of the innovation-decision process and to show the importance of the time dimension. Mr. Skeptic, an Iowa farmer, first learned of hybrid seed corn from an agricultural extension agent in 1935 (the knowledge function). However, he was not convinced to plant hybrid corn on his own farm until 1937, after he had discussed the innovation with several neighbors (the persuasion function). Skeptic purchased a small sack of hybrid seed in 1937 and by 1939 was planting 100 percent of his corn acreage in hybrids. When did he adopt hybrid corn?

Skeptic adopted in 1939 when he decided to continue full scale use of the innovation (decision function). *Adoption* is a decision to make full use of a new idea as the best course of action available. The *innovation-decision period* is the length of time required to pass through the innovation-decision process; in the present instance it lasted four years. The innovation decision can also take a negative turn; that is, the final decision can be *rejection,* a decision not to adopt an innovation.

The last function in the innovation-decision process is confirmation, a stage at which the receiver seeks reinforcement for the adoption or rejection decision he has made. Occasionally, however, conflicting and contradictory messages reach the receiver about the innovation, and this may lead to discontinuance on one hand or later adoption (after rejection) on the other. In the case of Mr. Skeptic, a decision was made to *discontinue* use of the innovation after previously adopting it. Farmer Skeptic became dissatisfied with hybrid seed and discontinued its use in 1941, when he again planted all of his corn acreage in open-pollinated seed. Discontinuances occur for many other reasons, including replacement of the innovation with an improved idea. Discontinuances occur only after the individual has fully adopted the idea.

Innovativeness and Adopter Categories. If Skeptic adopted hybrid seed in 1939 and the average farmer in his community adopted in 1936, Skeptic is less innovative than the average member of his system. *Innovativeness* is the degree to which an individual is relatively earlier in adopting new ideas than the other members of his system. *Adopter categories* are the classifications of members of a social system on the basis of innovativeness. The five adopter categories used here are: (1) innovators, (2) early adopters, (3) early majority, (4) late majority, and (5) laggards. Mr. Skeptic is in the "late majority" adopter category. Diffusion research shows clearly that each of the adopter categories has a great deal in common. If Skeptic is like most others in the late majority category, he is below average in social status, makes little use of mass media channels, and secures most of his new ideas from peers via interpersonal channels.

Rate of Adoption. There is a third specific way in which the time dimension is involved in the diffusion of innovations. *Rate of adoption* is the relative speed with which an innovation is adopted by members of a social system. This rate of adoption is usually measured by the length of time required for a certain percentage of the members of a system to adopt an innovation. Therefore, we see that rate of adoption is measured using an innovation or a system, rather than an individual, as the unit of analysis. Innovations that are perceived by receivers as possessing greater relative advantage, compatibility, and the like have a more rapid rate of adoption (as we pointed out in a previous section of this chapter).

There are also differences in the rate of adoption for the same innovation in different social systems. Generally, diffusion research shows that systems typified by modern, rather than traditional, norms will have a faster rate of adoption.

Among Members of a Social System. A *social system* is defined as a collectivity of units which are functionally differentiated and engaged in joint problem solving with respect to a common goal. The members or units of a social system may be individuals, informal groups, complex organizations, or subsystems. The social system analyzed in a diffusion study may consists of all the peasants in a Latin American village, students at a university, high schools in Thailand, medical doctors in a large city, or members of an aborigine tribe. Each unit in a social system can be functionally differentiated from every other member. All members cooperate at least to the extent of seeking to solve a common problem or to reach a mutual goal. It is this sharing of a common objective that binds the system together.

In this section we shall deal with the following topics: How the social structure affects diffusion, the effect of traditional and modern norms on diffusion, the roles of opinion leaders and change agents, and types of innovation-decisions. All these issues involve interfaces between the social system and the diffusion process that occurs within it.

Social Structure and Diffusion. Both formal and informal social structures have an effect on human behavior and how it changes in response to communication stimuli.

Diffusion and social structure are complexly interrelated.

> 1. *The social structure acts to impede or facilitate the rate of diffusion and adoption of new ideas through what are called "system effects."*

The basic notion of system effects is that the norms, social statuses, hierarchy, and so on of a social system influence the behavior of individual members of that system. *System effects* are the influences of the system's social structure on the behavior of the individual members of the social system.

In the case of innovation diffusion, one can conceptualize an individual's innovation behavior as explained by two types of variables: (1) the *individual's* personality, communication behavior, attitudes, and so on, and (2) the nature of his *social system.*

Van den Ban (1960) studied the effects of traditional and modern norms (for a sample of Wisconsin townships) on the innovativeness of farmers. Although such individual characteristics as a farmer's education, size of farm, and net worth were positively related to his innovativeness, the township norms were even better predictors of farmer innovativeness. Van den Ban concluded that a farmer with a high level of education, on a large farm, and with a high net worth, but residing in a township with traditional norms, adopted fewer farm innovations than if he had a lower level of education and a smaller farm in a township where the norms were modern.

System effects (such as system norms, the composite educational level of one's peers, and the like) *may be as important in explaining individual innovativeness as such individual characteristics as education, cosmopoliteness, and so on.*

> 2. *Diffusion may also change the social structure of a system.*

Some new ideas are "restructuring" innovations in that they change the structure of the social system itself. The adoption of a village development council changes the village social structure by adding a new set of statuses. The initiation of a research and development unit within an industrial firm and the departmentalization of a public school are also restructuring innovations. In many instances the restructuring affects the rate of future innovation diffusion within the system.

System Norms and diffusion. We have just pointed out that a system's norms affect an individual's innovation-adoption behavior. *Norms* are the established behavior patterns for the members of a given social system. They define a range of tolerable behavior and serve as a guide or a standard for the members of a social system.

A system's norms can be a barrier to change, as was shown in our example of water-boiling in a Peruvian community. Such resistance to new ideas is often found in norms relating to food. In India, for example, sacred cows roam the countryside while millions of people are undernourished. Polished rice is eaten in most of Asia and the United States, even though whole rice is more nutritious.

We conceptualize system norms that are most relevant for innovation diffusion as either traditional or modern.

Individuals in social systems with modern norms view change favorably, predisposing them to adopt new ideas more rapidly than individuals in traditional systems. Traditional social systems can be characterized by:

1. Lack of favorable orientation to change.
2. A less developed or "simpler" technology.
3. A relatively low level of literacy, education, and understanding of the scientific method.
4. A social enforcement of the status quo in the social system, facilitated by affective personal relationships, such as friendliness and hospitality, which are highly valued as ends in themselves.
5. Little communication by members of the social system with outsiders. Lack of transportation facilities and communication with the larger society reinforces the tendency of individuals in a traditional system to remain relatively isolated.
6. Lack of ability to empathize or to see oneself in others' roles, particularly the roles of outsiders to the system. An individual member in a system with traditional norms is not likely to recognize or

learn new social relationships involving himself; he usually plays only one role and never learns others.

A social system with modern norms is more change oriented, technologically developed, scientific, rational, cosmopolite, and empathic.

There is one danger in attempting to fit our thinking into the framework of idea types: There is a tendency to overemphasize the extent of the differences. Traditional and modern ideal types are actually the end points of a continuum on which actual social system norms may range. We should not forget that the norms of most systems are distributed between the extremes that we have described.

One should not conclude that traditional norms are necessarily undesirable. In many cases, tradition lends stability to a social system that is undergoing rapid change and is in danger of disorganization. Modern systems have their own unique drawbacks, including slums, pollution of water and air, alienation, neuroses, and an almost endless list of social problems rooted in the consequences of "progress."

An individual may be a member of more than one social system. If the norms of the systems to which the individual belongs are widely divergent, he is likely to experience cross-pressures in making innovation decisions. For instance, a school teacher who is continuing his part-time graduate education in a university where new ideas are constantly discussed is likely to experience conflict when he attempts to introduce these innovations into the traditional school system where he teaches.

The *commitment* of the individual to the social system affects his conformity to its norms. An innovative teacher in a traditional school may be relatively unaffected by the norms because the local school is not important as a reference group to him. Thus, an individual's integration into a social system, as well as the nature of the system's norms, need to be studied in order to fully explain his adoption behavior.

Opinion Leaders and Change Agents. Now we turn to the different roles that individuals play in a social system and the effect of these roles on diffusion patterns. Specifically, we shall look at two roles: Opinion leaders and change agents.

Very often the most innovative member of a system is perceived as a deviant from the social system, and he is accorded a somewhat dubious status of low credibility by the average members of the system. His role in diffusion (especially in persuading others about the innovation) is therefore likely to be limited. On the other hand there are members of the system who function in the role of opinion leader. They provide information and advice about innovations to many others in the system.

Opinion leadership is the degree to which an individual is able to informally influence other individuals' attitudes or overt behavior in a desired way with relative frequency. It is a type of informal leadership, rather than being a function of the individual's formal position or status in the system. Opinion leadership is earned and maintained by the individ-

ual's technical competence, social accessibility, and conformity to the system's norms. Several researches indicate that when the social system is modern, the opinion leaders are quite innovative; but when the norms are traditional, the leaders also reflect this norm in their behavior.

In any system, naturally, there may be both innovative and also more traditional opinion leaders. These influential persons can lead in the promotion of new ideas, or they can head an active opposition. In general, when opinion leaders are compared with their followers, we find that they (1) are more exposed to all forms of external communication, (2) are more cosmopolite, (3) have higher social status, and (4) are more innovative (although the exact degree of innovativeness depends, in part, on the system's norms).

Opinion leaders are usually members of the social system in which they exert their influence. In some instances individuals with influence in the social system are professionals representing change agencies external to the system. A *change agent* is a professional who influences innovation-decisions in a direction deemed desirable by a change agency. He usually seeks to obtain the adoption of new ideas, but he may also attempt to slow down diffusion and prevent the adoption of what he believes are undesirable innovations. Change agents often use opinion leaders within a given social system as lieutenants in their campaigns of planned change. There is research evidence that opinion leaders can be "worn out" by change agents who overuse them. Opinion leaders may be perceived by their peers as too much like the change agents; thus, the opinion leaders lose their credibility with their former followers.

Types of Innovation-Decisions. The social system has yet another important kind of influence on the diffusion of new ideas. Innovations can be adopted or rejected by individual members of a system or by the entire social system. The relationship between the social system and the decision to adopt innovations may be described in the following manner:

1. *Optional decisions* are made by an individual regardless of the decisions of other members of the system. Even in this case, the individual's decision is undoubtedly influenced by the norms of his social system and his need to conform to group pressures. The decision of an individual to begin wearing contact lenses instead of glasses, an Iowa farmer's decision to adopt hybrid corn, and a housewife's adoption of birth control pills are examples of optional decisions.
2. *Collective decisions* are those which individuals in the social system agree to make by consensus. All must conform to the system's decision once it is made. An example is fluoridation of a city's drinking water. Once the community decision is made, the individual has little practical choice but to adopt fluoridated water.
3. *Authority decisions* are those forced upon an individual by someone in a superordinate power position, such as a supervisor in a bureaucratic organization. The individual's attitude toward the innovation is not the prime factor in his adoption or rejection; he is simply told of and expected to comply with the innovation-decision which was made by an authority. Few research studies have yet been conducted of this type of innovation-decision, which must be very common in an organizational society such as the U.S. today. In all authority decisions we must distinguish between (1) the decision maker, who is one (or more) individual(s), and (2) the

adopter or adopters, who carry out the decision. In the case of optional and collective decisions these two roles (of deciding and adopting) are performed by the same individual(s).

These three types of innovation-decisions range on a continuum from optional decisions (where the adopting individual has almost complete responsibility for the decision), through collective decisions (where the adopter has some influence in the decision), to authority decisions (where the adopting individual has no influence in the innovation decision). Collective and authority decisions are probably much more common than optional decisions in formal organizations, such as factories, public schools, or labor unions, in comparison with other fields like agriculture and medicine where innovation-decisions are usually optional.

Generally, the faster rate of adoption of innovations results from authority decisions (depending, of course, on whether the authorities are traditional or modern). In turn, optional decisions can be made more rapidly than the collective type. Although made most rapidly, authority decisions are more likely to be circumvented and may eventually lead to a high rate of discontinuance of the innovation. Where change depends upon compliance under public surveillance, it is not likely to continue once the surveillance is removed.

The type of innovation-decision for a given idea may change or be changed over time. Automobile seat belts, during the early years of their use, were installed in private autos largely as optional decisions. Then in the 1960s many states began to require by law installation of seat belts in all new cars. In 1968 a federal law was passed to this effect. An optional innovation-decision then became a collective decision.

There is yet a fourth type of innovation-decision which is essentially a sequential combination of two or more of the three types we have just discussed. *Contingent deci-*sions are a choice to adopt or reject which can be made only after a prior innovation-decision. An individual member of a social system is free to adopt or not to adopt a new idea only after his system's innovation-decision. A teacher cannot adopt or reject the use of an overhead projector in his classroom until the school system has decided to purchase one; at that point the teacher can decide to use or reject the overhead projector. In the Punjab State of India hybrid corn adoption is a contingent decision because hybrid corn requires a growing season two weeks longer than open-pollinated varieties, and villagers release their cattle to roam for forage across the unfenced fields once their corn is harvested. One can readily imagine the difficulty of making an optional decision to adopt hybrid corn in the Punjab without a prior collective decision by the entire village.

In recent years, several important studies have explored the innovation process in organizations, where the innovation decision is collective or authoritative in nature.

The innovation process begins with an individual, or a set of individuals, recognizing that their organization is facing a "performance gap" between expectations and reality. This problem recognition sets off a search for alternatives, one of which may be an innovation. The new idea usually comes from outside of the organization and often must be modified somewhat as it is implemented to fit the organization's conditions.

Thus, the innovation process in organizations consists of problem recognition, searching for alternative solutions, matching the innovation with the organization's problem, and implementation of the innovation. This leads eventually to its institutionalization, when it is no longer recognized as a separate element.

15
Preventive Health Care and Consumer Behavior: Towards a Broader Perspective

John A. Quelch
Stephen B. Ash

This reading examines the role of marketing in the design and implementation of effective preventive health care programs. While there have been successful marketing campaigns, more often the results have been mixed. The reasons for these results include an overreliance on mass media campaigns and lack of appreciation of the difficulty of the task undertaken. Short-term, immediate results may not always be possible. The design of the appropriate marketing campaign and the role of marketing itself depends upon the type of preventive intervention and the other resources and approaches available. A typology of preventive interventions is developed to assist in designing effective campaigns to secure adoption of preventive health care practices.

Preventive care aims to decrease mortality or the incidence, duration, or severity of disease. Increasing knowledge of the natural history of diseases, especially in the presymptomatic stages, has highlighted connections between consumer lifestyles and disease incidence. The more precise identification of risk factors associated with specific diseases has made the objective of effective prevention more realistic. The primary reason for increasing interest in preventive programs is, however, the rising cost of health care. Terris [1977], for example, has claimed that the application of known preventive approaches could save 400,000 lives and $20 billion. Although evidence regarding the effectiveness of preventive care programs is equivocal, they retain

an appeal based upon the prospect of substantial savings in diagnosis and therapy costs and the low capital investment which they require relative to therapeutic programs. In 1977, less than three percent of the $95 million spent in the U.S. on health care was channelled to prevention and health education [Kennedy, 1975]. Some proponents of preventive programs regard them as complementary to therapy, while others regard them as partial substitutes at lower cost. Either way, there appears to be increasing interest in the allocation of proportionately more health dollars to preventive programs.

This paper first examines the role of marketing to date in the area of preventive health care. Limitations on the effectiveness of marketing approaches as a result of both consumer attitudes and the nature of the marketing task are discussed. Other factors, independent of the marketing input, which also influence the success of and the resources

John A. Quelch is Assistant Professor of Business Administration, Harvard University. Stephen B. Ash is Assistant Professor, University of Western Ontario.

allocated to preventive interventions are next summarized. Finally, a typology of preventive interventions is developed to familiarize both policymakers and marketers with the broad range of alternative interventions available, and to emphasize that the role of marketing may vary in importance from one type of intervention to another.

MARKETING AND PREVENTIVE CARE

The role of marketing in preventive care is the subject of a recent American Marketing Association monograph [Cooper, Kehoe, and Murphy, 1978]. Proponents of preventive care have recently been turning to the marketing function to enhance the credibility and improve the effectiveness of preventive interventions [Fielding, 1977]. The marketing function includes four principal elements—product or service design, pricing policy, distribution policy, and communications policy. However, in recent health care applications of marketing, communications strategy has received particular emphasis [Schlinger, 1976]. The success of such programs appears to have been equivocal. Robertson and Wortzel [1978] reviewed the role of mass communications in preventive interventions directed at obesity, smoking, heart disease, and seatbelt usage, and concluded that the literature was replete with discouraging case studies. Even in those cases where significant results were achieved, the cost effectiveness of the programs may be questionable. Difficulties inherent in defining objectives, target markets, and media and message strategies for preventive interventions are highlighted. The implication is that the questionable success of mass media approaches is a result of inexperience and exaggerated expectations regarding their likely impact. Health educators have long been skeptical of the ability of mass media approaches to effect behavior change [Young, 1967]. Robertson and Wortzel emphasize that mass media are more effective in reinforcing existing attitudes and behavior than in changing lifestyles.

The explanation for poor success in securing both consumer trial and adoption of preventive health practices may lie in the ambitious nature of the communications task. The application to preventive health ideas of the following five criteria conditioning the rapidity of diffusion readily illustrates the challenge facing the health care marketer [Rogers, 1962].

Relative Advantage. The benefits of preventive care are usually neither immediate nor apparent to the consumer. The time and money which the consumer is prepared to invest in reducing the risks of future morbidity is likely to be conditioned by the consumer's future orientation and the perceived value of an uncertain investment. It is quite possible that some consumers may prefer one month in hospital to twenty years of self-sacrificing preventive care. In addition, when paying for services, consumers may perceive

more value in technologically-based diagnostic and therapeutic procedures than in good advice of a preventive nature.

Although connections between lifestyle and disease incidence are increasingly being identified, there are few diseases whose etiology is solely related to factors under the consumer's control. In addition, the consumer cannot influence the air he breathes, his work environment, or his previous behavior. Under these circumstances, the relative advantage of regular exercise, not smoking, and good nutrition may seem problematic since the benefits of behavior change may be outweighed by factors beyond the consumer's control.

Divisibility. It is quite feasible for the consumer to undertake a prevention-oriented behavior for a short period of time. The problem remains, however, that the results of such behavior change may not be immediately obvious or directly attributable to the change. One week of non-smoking is unlikely to eliminate smoker's cough, nor is one week of good nutrition practice likely to correct an obesity problem.

Compatibility. Preventive interventions are often aimed at changing lifestyle behaviors firmly rooted in the consumer's social environment, and in the case of food, alcohol, and tobacco consumption patterns, these behaviors may be frequently reinforced by commercial messages. As characterized by Hochbaum [1977], such changes characteristically involve giving up things we like, are unpleasant in themselves, and must last for a lifetime. Behavior modification is likely to be greatest among those in a state of readiness to change [Rosenstock, 1966] for whom the adjustment is least traumatic and for whom the incremental benefit is least substantial among those at risk. But as suggested by the Stanford study [Maccoby and Farquhar, 1975], if behavior modification occurs among the consumer's social reference groups or community, group reinforcement may enhance the effectiveness of the mass communications campaign.

Consumer attitudes towards the health care system are also of relevance. The traditional doctor-patient relationship has not encouraged consumers to believe that they can assume responsibility for their own care. Although increasing emphasis on preventive care enhances the consumer's role in health care, consumers are not used to outreach from the health care system or mass communications on health care issues.

Communicability. The benefits associated with preventive practices are not easy to explain since they are frequently couched in terms of probabilities and reduced risks rather than in terms of absolute guarantees. In addition, the benefits of preventive behavior are not usually visible to the consumer or readily attributed to the behavior, except through some vague (possible dissonance reducing) notion of "feeling better." The need to avoid being misleading detracts from the potential persuasive force of mass communications on preventive care.

Complexity. Different levels of perceived complexity are associated with different preventive interventions, partly as a function of each consumer's prior knowledge and experience. Some interventions, such as screening programs, involve the delivery of specific services. The consumer must be told the advantages of the source, eligibility requirements, appropriate triggering symptoms, where and when the service is available and how much it costs. The complexity of procedures and supporting products used in the delivery of the service may also require explanation.

In the case of other self-help prevention programs (such as good nutrition and exercise), the consumer is being persuaded to adopt an adjusted lifestyle rather than a specific service. Each individual's preventive care needs are different. Standardized mass communications may either be too general to be relevant to the individual consumer or err towards excessive complexity in an effort to cover all cases. In designing mass communications in the preventive care arena, a trade-off must often be made between accuracy and simplicity [Quelch, 1977]. In those cases where the specific behavioral actions required of the consumer are too complex to communicate through mass communications, the consumer can be advised where to obtain further "customized" information.

Thus, the nature of the communications task may help to explain why some preventive interventions do not appear successful. In addition, marketers and health care policy makers may differ in the standards and criteria which they use to define a successful intervention. A further explanation for poor performance may be an imperfect understanding of the marketing function among health care providers. When marketing is equated with advertising, inadequate attention is paid to the product, pricing and distribution elements of the marketing function. A good communications strategy alone cannot sell a poorly designed product or service which fails to address consumer interests and expectations.

The unfulfilled promise of health maintenance organizations (HMO's) may be partly a result of inadequate understanding of the marketing concept as much as a reflection of the unwillingness of consumers to invest in preventive care. HMO's were conceived to encourage preventive care at a time when fee for service was believed to be a disincentive to investment in preventive care. HMO enrollments have, however, been discouraging [Glasgow, 1972]. The advent of full national health insurance with first dollar coverage would remove financial barriers to obtaining preventive services. However, since diagnostic and therapeutic services would also be covered, there might be less incentive to invest in preventive care. Furthermore, Wortzel [1978] has indicated that demand for preventive services is more re-

lated to education and social class than to cost, such that full coverage may not increase demand among those consumers most in need.

PROSPECTS FOR PREVENTIVE CARE

The equivocal success of preventive programs to date is not solely a result of consumer attitudes or of deficiencies in the communications approaches used by preventive health care marketers. There are several other factors limiting the effectiveness of preventive communications directed at the consumer. The resources allocated to preventive programs in the future are likely to be a function of these factors as much, if not more than, the effectiveness of any marketing related activities. It is important that the preventive health care marketer understand these other constraining factors so that (s)he may better predict and explain the results of marketing programs.

Legislators of both parties have recently shown increasing interest in preventive health care. For example, the Subcommittee on Domestic Marketing, Consumer Relations, and Nutrition of the House of Representatives Agriculture Committee has recently completed major hearings on nutrition education. There are, however, problems with preventive programs which may dampen the current degree of interest in their implementation [Novelli, 1978]. Like consumers, policymakers and legislators have difficulty identifying the impact of investing time and money in preventive programs. Given the pressure to demonstrate effective usage of taxpayers' money in the short-term, there may be a temptation to invest funds in highly visible health care technology rather than in those comparatively mundane preventive programs which may have a broader reach, but the impact of which is less readily measurable and more long-term. Thus, preventive programs may raise health care costs in the short-term. Given that total health care costs appear to be a major public concern, it is unlikely that policymakers and reimbursers alike will be particularly enthusiastic about making somewhat speculative investments in preventive programs. These views are likely to be especially prevalent among those who believe that advances in medical science will facilitate the discovery of efficient and easily-delivered therapies, thereby diminishing the significance of preventive approaches.

The spiralling costs associated with the administration of existing nutrition-related programs, such as the school lunch and food stamp programs may make some legislators wary of funding preventive interventions. In fact, the burgeoning expense of these programs has perhaps been more a function of their social welfare objectives than of their nutrition-related objectives. Nevertheless, these expenses may suggest that preventive programs can readily assume a costly social welfare overlay—a factor which may limit the enthusiasm of some legislators and policymakers.

The fact that preventive programs sometimes incorporate diverse objectives related to other policy areas can complicate evaluation of program costs and benefits. Other problems in measuring the effectiveness of preventive programs have been reviewed by Lave and Lave [1977]. First, performance criteria and the time interval before which effectiveness can meaningfully be measured are difficult to establish. While effectiveness measurement problems also exist for therapies, segregating the impact of a preventive program from the influence of other intervening variables is particularly difficult. Whereas, in the case of therapies, one can count cures as a measure of success, in the case of preventive programs, success is measured in terms of nonevents [Morgan, 1977]. If no change in disease incidence is recorded in response to a preventive program, it may be unjustly deemed a failure because the rate of incidence might have increased had the program not been in operation. Only quasiexperimental designs are available to test such an hypothesis. Secondly, the problem of establishing realistic goals for preventive programs is enhanced by the lack of baseline data from previous efforts against which performance can at least be compared. Thirdly, evaluation is complicated by the fact that compliance with a preventive program may have negative side-effects. Consider, for example, the consumer who quits smoking but who experiences higher tension and puts on weight as a result. Finally, it is sometimes argued that the major preventive interventions have already been carried out, such that policymakers now face the task of choosing among more marginal programs.

Increased emphasis on preventive interventions requires an investment in the training of more specialists in preventive care. Any shift in emphasis in the direction of preventive care will not, therefore, occur overnight. In particular, the incorporation of preventive concepts (for example, nutrition and sex education) into the school curriculum and into continuing education programs is frequently advocated. However, at a time when the public school system is under criticism, it is unlikely that courses designed to cater to immediate problems such as finding a job will be readily incorporated.

Medical school curricula have also been criticized for including insufficient emphasis on preventive care, particularly nutrition. Dentistry and nursing schools have shown more progress in this regard. The medical profession is trained to measure its success in terms of cures rather than preventions. Whereas the dubious assumption is often made that cure is the result of therapy, a greater degree of skepticism is commonly associated with the assumption that prevention is the reason why a consumer does not become ill. The curative orientation of the medical profession, together with perceptions of lower professional skills requirements and financial rewards associated with preventive care, suggests that there may be some professional resistance towards any shift in emphasis. At the extreme, if preventive programs were wholly successful, there would be no need for therapeutic care. Prevention may not, therefore, be wholly attractive to the medical profession. However, any successful preventive program must secure the support if not involvement of physicians. Since patient-physician interactions present an opportunity to convey preventive information, raising the degree of physician commitment to prevention may, as a result of the physician's perceived source credibility, have a substantial impact on the consumer.

Whereas diagnosis and therapy require the active involvement of a health care professional, not all preventive action necessarily takes place within the health care system. Prevention can take place at work, at home, and in the environment independent of the intervention of health care professionals. Indeed, one rationale for preventive care is that responsibility for preventive care is largely assumed by the consumer at reduced cost to the system. In addition, other groups besides health care professionals are heavily involved in preventive programs. For example, the food industry heavily subsidizes nutrition education programs. While the involvement of many interest groups in the delivery of preventive care may be desirable, the result may be fragmentation of responsibility for the delivery of preventive care, a factor which may discourage the support of some health care professionals. In addition, there is the further danger of conflicting messages regarding preventive care being communicated to the consumer.

It is frequently argued that an ounce of prevention is worth a pound of cure, the implication being that investment in preventive programs will reduce demand for therapeutic services, and therefore overall health care costs. For several reasons, this may not be the case. Preventive programs may heighten consumer sensitivity to illness and may break down barriers which currently discourage some consumers in the frequency with which they seek care. Indeed, one frequent argument in favor of preventive outreach programs such as the Swine Flu immunization campaign is that they encourage the entry of those consumers not currently reached by the health care system. An alternative hypothesis might be that consumers who practice preventive care become self-assured to the extent of delaying seeking care when ill. The interrelationships of preventive, diagnostic, and therapeutic care-seeking behavior require further consumer research.

In addition, earlier identification of disease which may result from certain preventive (particularly screening) programs may result not in a more cost effective cure, but in the consumer receiving expensive treatment over a longer period of time. Some preventive programs such as mammography may, in certain cases, cause undesirable side effects which may require therapy. This is not to say that preventive programs which have such an effect should or should not be implemented. The purpose here is to suggest that such programs may not result in lower health care costs.

It has been pointed out that screening programs for diseases with low incidence rates may identify a high percentage of false positives who are then admitted to therapy.

Finally, the cost effectiveness of preventive programs depends, in part, upon the cost effectiveness of therapeutic programs since total health care resources must be allocated between them. While some believe that the limitations of therapeutic medicine are now being reached such that the time is right to increase efforts in the area of prevention, others believe attention should be directed towards the development of more cost effective therapies.

These several factors suggest that the resources allocated to preventive programs may not expand dramatically. As a result, the preventive health care area may not prove to be as strong a growth area for marketing applications as has sometimes been implied. Consequently, a more selective application of marketing concepts may be in order, based upon the premise that the relevance of these concepts may vary from one type of preventive intervention to another.

A TYPOLOGY OF PREVENTIVE INTERVENTIONS

Hitherto, this discussion has not differentiated among preventive interventions. The role of marketing has been treated in general although, as a reflection of reported applications, the emphasis has been on interventions requiring mass communication programs. The preventive health care marketer must, however, understand the broad range of preventive interventions available. The relative significance of the marketing input as a determinant of success is likely to vary from one intervention to another. It is possible that the most cost effective interventions may be those which require relatively low marketing input. Accordingly, the purpose of this section is to develop a preliminary typology of preventive interventions to provide the marketer with a broad perspective of the alternative interventions available and to suggest how the role of marketing may vary according to type of intervention.

Health care professionals use a typology which segments preventive intervention into three categories. Primary prevention includes actions designed to prevent the occurrence of disease or injury. Secondary prevention involves early diagnosis, and includes screening programs aimed at early detection of disease, risk factors, or disease complications. Tertiary prevention is an extension of treatment and would include actions prescribed to facilitate postsickness rehabilitation [Morgan, 1977].

Venkatesan [1978] has differentiated interventions aimed at public or private organizations in which the individual consumer is passive from those in which the consumer is active. Regulations of food product quality, for example, represent a preventive intervention which does not require active involvement of the consumer. The distinction

between interventions in which the consumer is active or passive mirrors the distinction between interventions aimed at risks which are self-imposed or environmentally induced. Interventions which do require that the consumer be active to be effective can be further segmented according to the degree of activity required. A pap smear test, for example, represents a one-time behavior; the annual check-up represents a repeated, but non-continuous behavior; good nutrition habits require continuous behavior to maintain effectiveness. The level of required behavioral commitment varies among preventive interventions. The challenge of the communications task and the degree of reinforcement required may be expected to be greatest for those interventions which require continuous behavior modification to be effective.

Morgan [1977] has noted that preventive interventions can focus on any of four areas—the environment, disease, the health care organization, and lifestyles. Etzioni [1972] has emphasized that lifestyles are a function of the environment. Consumer exercise patterns, for example, are shaped by urban and architectural designs and by transportation systems. If increasing consumer exercise received higher priority in the planning process, a greater impact might be achieved at lower cost than through a communications program urging consumers to exercise more. Etzioni states that efforts to change behavior through persuasion are often less effective than manipulation of the legislative and physical environment. Similarly, an Ontario Economic Council report [1971] emphasizes that environmental and technological approaches to improved prevention are too often overlooked. Hilbert [1977] also indicates that regulatory interventions have been more successful than persuasive interventions. In the absence of controlled studies comparing the effectiveness of these two types of intervention in preventive health care, such contentions must remain speculative. It should be noted from a historical perspective that persuasive approaches have only recently received much attention whereas regulatory approaches have been operational on an organized basis since the nineteenth century.

The typology of preventive interventions presented in Exhibit 1 is intended to formalize the observations of Etzioni and Hilbert in conjunction with the distinction drawn by Venkatesan. Three principal types of preventive interventions are identified: interventions which rely on legal leverage; interventions which rely on financial leverage, and interventions which depend for their success on the persuasive leverage associated with the communications message. Each of these three intervention approaches is next briefly reviewed.

Legal Leverage. Standards for product content and design, and regulations for product usage applicable to institutions and/or individuals can be established. Government agencies and legislation are commonly the source of such interventions.

EXHIBIT 1
Typology of Preventive Interventions

Types of Intervention	Individual Implementation Consumer Active	Organizational Implementation Consumer Passive
Legal Leverage	**Usage Restrictions** ■ Gun control ■ Speed limits ■ Compulsory seat belt usage ■ Ban on smoking in public places	**Product Quality Control** ■ Automobile design standards ■ Food product ingredient requirements ■ Lead content restrictions in paint **Workplace Control** ■ Occupational and industrial safety laws **Environment Control** ■ Pollution controls ■ Sanitation ■ Recreational facilities
Financial Leverage	**Incentives to Use Health Inducing Products/Services/Behaviors** ■ Subsidies to school lunch/food stamp programs ■ Extension of medicaid coverage to preventive care ■ Insurance company premium benefits ■ Restrictions on institutional access (nonimmunized children excluded from school) **Disincentives to Use Health Reducing Products/Services/Behaviors** ■ Taxes (alcohol, cigarettes) ■ Restrict product availability (liquor outlets)	**Incentives** ■ Government subsidies for fluoridation and sewage schemes ■ Allocation of research funds for technical development and research ■ Tax credits for exercise facilities at workplace ■ Market potential for new products (fortified foods, air bags) **Disincentives** ■ Product specific taxes or other marketing restrictions ■ Removal of production subsidies ■ Taxes on advertising "undesirable" products

Message Leverage	**Desired Behaviors Requiring Interaction with Health System**
	■ Primary Prevention
	  Vaccination
	  Immunization
	  Prenatal care
	■ Secondary Prevention
	  Check-ups
	  Screening
	  VD tracing
	■ Tertiary Prevention
	  Compliance with prescriptions
	Desired Behaviors Not Requiring Interaction with Health System
	■ Primary Prevention
	  Good nutrition
	  Exercise
	  Personal hygiene
	■ Secondary Prevention
	  Breast examination
		Voluntary Organizational Behaviors
		■ Product quality improvement
		■ Workplace improvement
		■ Environment improvement

The political ethics of such interventions have been discussed by Lalonde [1977]. They are most likely to be implemented when voluntary approaches have failed to achieve desired levels of compliance or in response to situations where the failure of an individual or organization to take actions of a preventive nature is likely to threaten the health or safety of others.

The principal problems associated with mandatory interventions are the costs of enforcement to insure compliance and consumer resistance to further lifestyle restrictions. Intervention results may be expected to occur more rapidly and be more readily measurable when legal leverage rather than either of the two other intervention approaches is used.

Financial Leverage. Taxes, subsidies and prices can be manipulated to offer incentives or disincentives to consumers and institutions to take prevention-oriented action. In addition to government agencies, insurance companies and other organizations may offer such incentives. In addition, potential market demand may act as a sufficient incentive in and of itself to stimulate the development and marketing of products with a preventive care function. Health care providers would classify most interventions involving financial or legal leverage as primary prevention.

Message Leverage. The motivation to respond to such interventions is principally the perceived relevance of the message. Neither legal sanction nor direct financial loss is likely to result from non-compliance with the recommended preventive behavior. The motivating message may originate from a myriad of government and non-government sources, formal and informal sources.

Of particular relevance to the typology is the distinction between persuasive interventions which require the consumer to interact with a health care professional, and those which do not. The former include screening programs and commonly involve the acquisition of a specific service at a specific point in time, frequently for a fee. As in the purchase of a product, there is closure to the task, and the presence of the health provider offers an assurance of quality control in the delivery of the service.

The second group of behaviors include exercise and nutrition programs and may be undertaken by the consumer on his or her initiative or at the suggestion of a health care provider. Whereas behaviors of the first type generally require a one-time or periodic consumer involvement, behaviors of the second type must ordinarily be adhered to consistently to be effective. Cessation of compliance may result in the attrition of benefits already gained. Since the beneficial results of behavior modification are not usually apparent in the short term, regular reinforcement is necessary to insure continued compliance. A further problem is that, in the absence of supervision by a health care professional, there is no assurance that the persuasive message will be correctly interpreted and that undesirable side-effects may not occur (for example, from over-exertion).

The second dimension of the typology presented in Exhibit 1 distinguishes between interventions targeted at individual consumers (consumer active) and interventions targeted at organizations (consumer passive). In the latter case, the success of the intervention depends in part upon the identification of key decision-makers within each target organization. In addition, it must be recognized that many interventions directed at organizations involve environmental changes which may facilitate or encourage prevention-oriented behaviors by individual consumers. Although the consumer assumes a passive role in the implementation of these changes, their success often depends upon the degree to which consumers actively respond to such changes in the desired manner. For example, the success of an intervention designed to encourage employers to provide exercise facilities at the workplace depends as much upon the number of workers who use such facilities as upon the number of new facilities which are established.

The typology attempts to organize the range of intervention options open to the health care policymaker. It must be emphasized that these options should not be regarded as mutually exclusive. In addressing a particular preventive health objective, it is possible that allocation of resources among a mix of intervention approaches relying on a combination of legal, financial, and message leverage might prove more cost effective than allocation of all available resources to the single best intervention approach. For example, the objective of controlling per capita alcohol consumption may be facilitated by mandatory restrictions on bar opening hours (legal leverage), taxes on alcoholic beverages (financial leverage), and a consumer information campaign highlighting the dangers of excessive alcohol consumption (message leverage).

The typology is not intended to imply that the marketing function either will or should necessarily play a greater role in the development of preventive health programs.

Rather, the purpose is to indicate that the role assigned to marketing should be adapted to each type of intervention. In addition, the effective application of marketing concepts to preventive health care intervention programs requires a balanced consideration of all four elements of the marketing function rather than an over-reliance on communications policy.

REFERENCES

Cooper, Philip D., William J. Kehoe, and Patrick E. Murphy, *Marketing and Preventive Health Care: Interdisciplinary and Inter-Organizational Perspectives,* Chicago: American Marketing Association, 1978.

Etzioni, A., "Human Beings Are Not Very Easy to Change After All," *Saturday Review,* 55 (June 3, 1972), 45–47.

Fielding, J. E., "Health Promotion: Some Notions in Search of a Constituency," *American Journal of Public Health,* 67:11 (November, 1977), 1082–1086.

Glasgow, John M., "Prepaid Group Practice as a National Health Policy: Problems and Perspectives," *Inquiry,* 9 (1972), 3–15.

Hilbert, Morton S., "Prevention," *American Journal of Public Health,* 67:4 (April 1977), 353–356.

Hochbaum, Godfrey M., "A Critical Assessment of Marketing's Place in Preventive Health Care," in Philip D. Cooper, William J. Kehoe and Patrick E. Murphy, *Marketing and Preventive Health Care: Inter-disciplinary and Interorganizational Perspectives,* Chicago: American Marketing Association, 1978, 3–11.

Kennedy, Edward, *National Disease Control and Consumer Health Education and Promotion Act of 1975.* Report, 93rd Congress, 1st Session, 1466 (1975), 24.

Lalonde, Marc, "Beyond a New Perspective," *American Journal of Public Health,* 67:4 (April 1977), 357–360.

Lave, Judith R., and Lester B. Lave, "Measuring the Effectiveness of Prevention I," *Millbank Memorial Fund Quarterly/Health and Society,* 55:2 (1977), 273–290.

Maccoby, Nathan and John W. Farquhar, "Communication for Health: Unselling Heart Disease," *Journal of Communication,* 25 (1975), 114–126.

Morgan, Robert W., *Prospects for Preventive Medicine,* Occasional Paper 2, Toronto: Ontario Economic Council, 1977.

Novelli, William D., "Insurmountable Opportunities and the Marketing of Preventive Care," in Philip D. Cooper, William J. Kehoe and Patrick E. Murphy, *Marketing and Preventive Health Care: Interdisciplinary and Interorganizational Perspectives,* Chicago: American Marketing Association, 1978, 99–103.

Ontario Economic Council, *Issues and Alternatives 1976: Health,* Toronto: Ontario Economic Council, 1976.

Quelch, John A., "The Role of Nutrition Information in National Nutrition Policy," *Nutrition Reviews,* 35:11 (November 1977), 289–293.

Robertson, Thomas S., and Lawrence H. Wortzel, "Consumer Behavior and Health Care Change: The Role of Mass Media," in H. Keith Hunt, ed., *Advances in Consumer Research Vol. 5,* Association for Consumer Research, 1978, 525–527.

Rogers, E. M., *Diffusion of Innovations,* New York: The Free Press, 1962.

Rosenstock, I. M., "Why People Use Health Services," *Millbank Memorial Fund Quarterly,* 44 (1966), 94–127.

Schlinger, Mary Jane, "The Role of Mass Communications in Promoting Public Health," in Beverlee B. Anderson, ed., *Advances in Consumer Research Vol. 3,* Association for Consumer Research, 1976, 302–304.

Terris, M., "Strategy for Prevention," *American Journal of Public Health,* 6:11 (November 1977), 1026–1027.

Venkatesan, M., "Consumer Behavior and Nutrition: Preventive Health Perspectives," in H. Keith Hunt, ed., *Advances in Consumer Research Vol. 5*, Association for Consumer Research, 1978, 518–520.

Wortzel, Lawrence H., "Summary Contents: Perceptions of Problems and Limitations of Preventive Health Care and Marketing," in Philip D. Copper, William J. Kehoe and Patrick E. Murphy, *Marketing and Preventive Health Care: Interdisciplinary and Interorganizational Perspectives*, Chicago: American Marketing Association, 1978, 116–118.

Young, Marjorie A. C., *Review of Research and Studies Related to Health Education and Communication: Methods and Materials*, Health Education Monographs No. 25, New York: Society of Public Health Educators, 1967.

PART III

Strategic
Issues

Cases

16. Beth Israel Hospital, Boston **157**

17. Amtrak **169**

18. The Richardson Center for the Blind **185**

Readings

19. Consumer Energy Conservation Policy in Canada: **197**
Behavioural and Institutional Obstacles

20. Competing for Scarce Resources **207**

Beth Israel Hospital, Boston

Terrie Bloom
Christopher H. Lovelock
Penny Pittman Merliss

In spring 1978, David Steinberg,* a trustee of Beth Israel Hospital, was reviewing the status of the hospital's maternity service. He was faced with a complex problem. On one hand, obstetrics was losing money. On the other, Beth Israel's maternity unit provided a major service to the Greater Boston community, and constituted an important part of the teaching program of Harvard Medical School. Finally, obstetrics and gynecology were so closely related clinically that any major change in the status of obstetrics would have significant repercussions in gynecology.†

The finance committee of the board of trustees had requested that Steinberg, chairman of the special projects subcommittee, come up with specific recommendations for the future. He was considering various options. The hospital could replace all or some of its maternity beds with medical/surgical beds. Or it could try to reduce the deficit in obstetrics by attracting more obstetrical patients, by improving the income realized on each patient, or both. No matter which course he proposed, Steinberg would have to devise a strategic plan presenting his recommendations to the finance committee and ultimately to the board of trustees.

The Beth Israel Hospital of Boston was a 432-bed major teaching hospital of Harvard Medical School. In addition to its role as a tertiary care center,‡ it served as the community hospital for the adjoining town of Brookline (Exhibit 1). Finally, as a constituent agency of the combined Jewish Philanthropies, Beth Israel provided leadership in the planning and delivery of health care to the Jewish community, in addition to serving the needy of every faith, race, and nationality.

Institutional Philosophy. Since its opening in 1916, Beth Israel had developed a close relationship with Harvard Medical School as well as a growing reputation for excellence in medical teaching and research. The hospital participated in the training of about 1200 physicians and other health care professionals each year, including medical students; new physicians (known as interns, residents, and fellows) who were doing postgraduate work; and various types of occupational and physical therapists.

At the same time, Beth Israel had become known as an institution that sought to address the emotional as well as the physical needs of patients. Its mission was stated as the

---

Terrie Bloom is a member of the Harvard MBA Class of 1981; Christopher H. Lovelock is Associate Professor of Business Administration, Harvard University; and Penny Pittman Merliss was formerly a Research Associate at Harvard University. Certain data in the case have been disguised.

*Disguised name.

†Obstetrics concerns the medical management of pregnancy, labor and delivery; gynecology is that branch of medicine dealing with the female genital tract.

---

‡Tertiary care is the most sophisticated level of health care, delivered by specialists, usually located in academic medical centers, to patients with relatively serious or unusual medical problems. Primary care is the treatment of ambulator ("walk-in") patients with more routine problems.

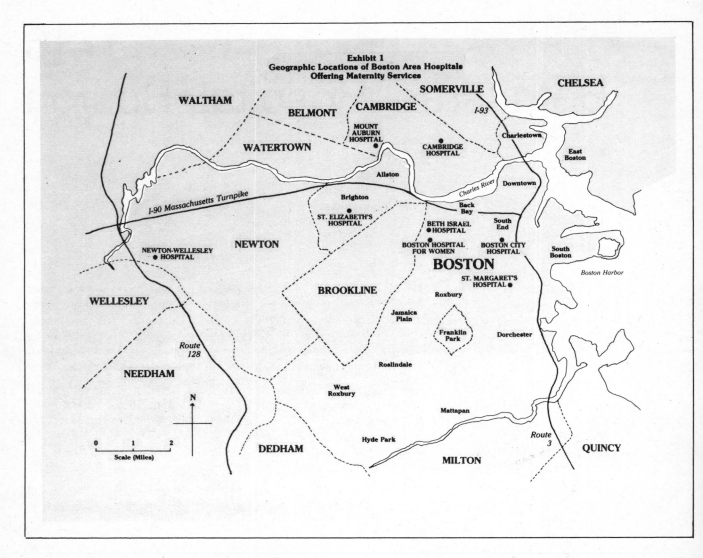

Exhibit 1
Geographic Locations of Boston Area Hospitals
Offering Maternity Services

delivery of "patient care of the highest quality, in both scientific and human terms"; Beth Israel had been the first hospital in the U.S. to issue a statement on the rights of patients. Both inpatient and outpatient services were focused on patient care, with teaching designed to strengthen the quality of that care as well as to educate physicians and nurses.

Organization. The hospital's board of trustees was its governing body. The board delegated certain powers and duties to a number of standing committes, including the medical conference committee, which reviewed patient care, and the finance committee. The finance committee, in turn, designated subcommittees to monitor the hospital's financial operations. Among these was the special projects subcommittee, chaired by David Steinberg, which reviewed clinical services. The board delegated responsibility for ongoing operations to the hospital's director, Mitchell T. Rabkin, M.D.

Dr. Rabkin, who had been general director for eleven years, believed strongly in the importance of good care throughout all phases of the hospital environment:

Most patients judge the quality of their hospital experience not so much on the basis of clinical excellence as on the basis of the personalization of care and the caliber of the "hotel" services. We seek to maintain the highest standard in all areas. We also recognize that the institution is people, and that in order for the staff to sustain the level of warmth and personalization that we strive for, we have to maintain a working environment conducive to their happiness as well.

Facilities. In 1978, Beth Israel's facilities comprised 12 buildings. Eight of these were dedicated to patient care, and four were sites for research or administration. Within these buildings the hospital annually provided care to 18,000 inpatients, received 200,000 outpatient visits, and maintained about $5 million of research.

Beth Israel had experienced more growth during the early 1970s than in any other period. The construction of the $28 million Feldberg Building added 78 beds in 1976, bringing maximum capacity to 452 beds. Of the 432 beds available in spring 1978, 329 were medical/surgical, 89 were

EXHIBIT 2
Beth Israel Hospital: Projected Occupancy Rates
Average Daily Census and Payor Mix (Inpatients) for Fiscal Year Ending 9/30/78

	Number of Beds	Occupancy Rate	Census (Average No. of Patients per Day)	Payor Mix by Financial Class*				
				Blue Cross/ Blue Shield	Medicare	Medicaid	Private Insurance	Other
Medicine	150	97%	145.0	24%	50%	7%	9%	10%
Surgery	155	88%	136.8	34%	36%	6%	13%	11%
Gynecology	44	61%	26.8	43%	3%	28%	18%	8%
Psychiatry	14	94%	13.2	35%	13%	29%	11%	12%
Obstetrics	45	65%	29.2**	42%	0%	29%	18%	11%
Other Adult Units (Intensive Care; Clinical Research Center)	24	70%	18.3	29%	44%	8%	10%	9%
Total Adult	432	85%	369.3	32%	33%	12%	13%	10%

*Blue Cross/Blue Shield and Medicare reimbursed hospitals the reasonable cost of providing services to their beneficiary groups; Medicaid paid a "per diem" rate for inpatient care regardless of actual services rendered (which in the aggregate, represented most, but not all, of the costs); and private insurance paid the hospitals' charges or a fixed dollar amount for covered services.

**Obstetrical census is made up of women who deliver as well as those who are in the hospital for obstetrical problems. As many as 20–25% of the patients on the obstetrical service may be in for reasons other than to deliver a baby.

Source: Beth Israel Hospital (disguised data).

ob/gyn, and 14 were psychiatric. The hospital also maintained 52 bassinets for newborn babies.

Despite the increased number of beds, occupancy rates on the medical and surgical floors and in the psychiatric unit had remained uniformly high. Occupancy in obstetrics and gynecology, however, was lower. With rare exceptions, obstetrical beds could not legally be used to accommodate overflow demand from other services. Gynecology beds could be used for surgical patients, but this practice was avoided, since the two services were located on different floors of the hospital. The psychiatry inpatient unit had a long waiting list at all times; a policy of allowing short leaves of absence accounted for the less than 100% occupancy level. Exhibit 2 summarizes Beth Israel's projected occupancy rates, average daily patient census, and payor mix for 1977–78.

THE BOSTON HEALTH CARE ENVIRONMENT

The health care industry in Boston was large and complex. There was a general consensus that the city was "overbedded" (had more inpatient beds than were needed to accommodate demand) and suffered from costly duplication of services, although the extent of these phenomena was disputed. The net result was keen competition for patients.

The problem of duplication and high costs could be traced to three major causes. First, the health care delivery system was centered around Boston's three medical schools —those of Harvard University, Tufts University and Boston University—each of which maintained academic and clinical relationships with a number of teaching and community hospitals (Exhibit 3). Since each medical school required a full spectrum of teaching services in order to educate its students, there was considerable duplication of services in hospitals affiliated with these schools.

In addition to the expenses resulting from duplication of services, the cost-reimbursement system of financing much hospital care also contributed to rising costs. Most health insurers (so-called third-party payors) followed the practice of reimbursing hospitals for "reasonable costs" incurred in the process of delivering care. This system was claimed not to give hospitals any incentive to choose the most cost-effective way to provide care, since any costs under a certain limit would be reimbursed.

The third factor was the advent of the Medicare and Medicaid health insurance programs, developed in the mid-1960s to assure access to care for two previously under-served populations, the elderly and the poor. The demand for health care services generated by the introduction of Medicare and Medicaid had exceeded expectations and reinforced the trend toward increased bed capacity and greater expense during the late sixties and early seventies.

Planning and Regulatory Efforts. Inflation in health care had been running at almost twice the overall rate. As the percentage of GNP devoted to health continued to climb through the late sixties and early seventies, the federal government adopted two tactics to control costs: planning and regulation. The goal was to consolidate duplicate services wherever possible, and to discourage unnecessary capital expansion.

In 1972, the Certificate of Need (CON) program was initiated. This required that any major capital expenditure or major change in service proposed by a hospital be reviewed

EXHIBIT 3
Boston, Cambridge and Newton Teaching Hospitals*

Hospital	Medical School Affiliations	Control	Total Number of Beds	Number of Maternity Beds	Occupancy Rate for Maternity Unit in 1975
Beth Israel	Harvard	Nonprofit	432	45	74.8%
Boston City	Boston University	City	500	72	57.6%
Boston Hospital for Women	Harvard	Nonprofit	222	116	80.4%
Boston State	Boston University, Tufts	State	230	—	—
Boston VA	Boston University, Tufts	Veteran's Administration	815	—	—
Carney	Boston University	Church	376	—	—
Children's	Harvard	Nonprofit	343	—	—
Faulkner	Tufts	Nonprofit	248	—	—
Kennedy Memorial	Boston University	Church	88	—	—
Lemuel Shattuck	Tufts	State	200	—	—
Massachusetts Eye & Ear	Harvard	Nonprofit	174	—	—
Massachusetts General	Harvard	Nonprofit	1084	—	—
Massachusetts Mental Health Center	Harvard	State	106	—	—
N.E. Deaconess	Harvard	Nonprofit	472	—	—
N.E. Medical Center	Tufts	Nonprofit	452	—	—
Peter Bent Brigham	Harvard	Nonprofit	332	—	—
Robert Breck Brigham	Harvard	Nonprofit	96	—	—
St. Elizabeth's	Tufts	Church	417	24	62.6%
St. Margaret's	Tufts	Church	117	68	65.6%
University	Boston University	Nonprofit	383	—	—
West Roxbury VA	Harvard	Veteran's Administration	279	—	—
Cambridge Hospital	Harvard	City	187	30	39.6%
Mount Auburn	Harvard	Nonprofit	300	20	48.1%
Newton-Wellesley	Tufts	Nonprofit	339	33	54.4%

*Excerpted largely from the *Directory of Accredited Residences 1977–1978*, Laison Committee on Graduate Medical Education (American Medical Association, Chicago, 1977, pp. 58–89). Maternity Unit data are taken from *The Health Systems Plan for Massachusetts*, Vol. 2A (HPCGB, Inc., September 1977), and from Massachusetts Department of Public Health Annual Hospital Statistical Report, Fiscal Year 1975.

by a state agency to determine (1) the need for the project, and (2) whether the proposal represented the most cost-effective means of achieving the desired result. In Massachusetts, any capital expenditure in excess of $150,000 was considered major, as was a transfer of more than four beds from one service to another. Any hospital that made a major capital expenditure or change in service without CON approval risked loss of reimbursement.

Approval of new construction could be made contingent upon the elimination of some other, underutilized service currently provided by the hospital. One of the most common compromises made by a hospital seeking a CON was elimination of either its obstetrical or its pediatric unit.* These services had proliferated historically as a result of strong community preference for local care, but they became underutilized as the birth rate dropped. With the negotiating

power afforded by CON, planners were able to eliminate some of the duplication and to work toward regionalization of obstetrical and pediatric services.

The effectiveness of CON as a planning tool was somewhat limited, since it could only be applied reactively, in response to a hospital's request for approval of a major capital expenditure or change in service. Moreover, a hospital that was dissatisfied with a CON decision could file a bill with the state legislature requesting permission to proceed with its plans anyway.

Pressures on Maternity Units. The federal government continued to strive for a more systematic approach to health planning and published the National Health Planning Guidelines in 1978. These guidelines set minimum standards for obstetrical units of 75% occupancy and 1,500 births per year. A considerable number of maternity units in Massachusetts and throughout the country did not meet these standards; each was liable to lose its obstetrical service unless it

*Pediatrics is that branch of medicine concerned with the diseases of children and their treatment.

succeeded in increasing its total. Additionally, the draft of the new Massachusetts State Health Plan recommended a 25% reduction in the number of maternity beds in Boston, from 325 to 244.

The state's move to reduce maternity beds was prompted by the recognition that underused obstetrical services were relatively expensive to maintain. Medical/surgical procedures were often elective rather than emergency, and therefore were scheduled as beds became available. In contrast, obstetrical admissions were predominantly random events (Exhibit 4). Thus, a maternity unit had to be staffed to accommodate an above-average census (occupancy rate) to ensure that this fluctuating demand could be met.

In addition to increased regulation, hospitals were also experiencing a variety of pressures from their patient population. The women's movement was having a major impact on women's attitudes toward birth. Not only were women tending to have fewer children (Exhibit 5), and spending less time in the hospital per delivery (in 1978 the average stay for a normal delivery was four days), but they collectively voiced the opinion that the bearing of children was a healthy process over which they should have some measure of control. As noted by *Boston* magazine:

> There is a reevaluation of what used to be routine clinical practices for all women giving birth and a growing tendency among doctors now to apply those practices only when needed. . . . More attention is being paid to the emotional needs of the entire family—mother, father, newborn and siblings.*

A growing number of women were also interested in out-of-hospital delivery. In the Boston area, groups such as Home Birth and Birth Day were encouraging births at home. A newspaper report estimated that between 1957 and 1977 the annual number of home births in Boston had risen from about 70 to some 500. Also becoming popular were "birthing centers," where women with normal pregnancies could be delivered by midwives and return home after a short stay, incurring costs far below those of most deliveries. Since home births and birthing centers provided little sophisticated, on-site, technological backup, physicians disagreed as to their safety for mother and baby. Because Massachusetts law required that midwives work under a doctor's supervision, no birthing centers had opened in the Boston area.

IDENTIFYING TARGET MARKETS

A hospital attracted maternity patients principally through its obstetrician/gynecologists, particularly those in private practice. Most women, especially those from the suburbs, tended to place a higher priority on choice of obstetrician than choice of hospital; the physician's reputation and the convenience of his or her private office were the most compelling factors in

*Gail Kelley, "Special Delivery: A Consumer Guide to Giving Birth in Boston," *Boston*, April 1978, p. 74.

choosing a doctor. Since obstetricians in private practice tended to restrict their practices to no more than one or two hospitals, in order to minimize their travel time, a woman's choice of hospital would be dictated by her obstetrician's affiliation. Hence, a key to a hospital's success in filling its beds was to attract private physicians to the active staff and maintain their loyalty.

The obstetrician/gynecologist's choice of hospital might stem from any of several considerations, ranging from academic to social. Some preferred a major academic hospital, with its many opportunities for teaching and continuing education. Graduates of obstetrical residency programs fre-

---

EXHIBIT 4
Daily Number of Patients in the Obstetrics Ward: Frequency Distribution, Nov. 1, 1977 to May 1, 1978

Number of Patients	Frequency (Days)	Percent of Days
13	2	1.1
14	2	1.1
17	5	2.7
18	3	1.6
19	1	0.5
20	5	2.7
21	7	3.8
22	6	3.3
23	8	4.4
24	4	2.2
25	9	4.9
26	12	6.6
27	12	6.6
28	15	8.2
29	10	5.2
30	11	6.0
31	7	3.8
32	10	5.2
33	11	6.0
34	9	4.9
35	5	2.7
36	5	2.7
37	1	0.5
38	6	3.3
39	5	2.7
40	3	1.6
41	2	1.1
42	3	1.6
43	2	1.1
45	1	0.5
	179	100.0%

Note: Interpret this chart as reading: on two days during this six-month period (1.1% of the time) there were 13 patients in the Obstetrical Unit; on 11 days (6.0%) there were 30 patients.

Source: Beth Israel Hospital Daily Census

EXHIBIT 5
Total Births in Boston and Massachusetts
Fiscal Years 1970–1977

Hospitals	1970		1971		1972		1973		1974		1975		1976		1977	
Beth Israel	3,096	16.0%	2,859	16.2%	2,766	17.4%	2,517	16.8%	2,335	16.7%	2,152	15.5%	2,016	14.9%	2,010	14.5%
Boston Hospital for Women	7,023	36.3%	6,380	36.1%	5,924	37.2%	6,001	40.0%	5,946	42.6%	6,028	43.4%	6,168	45.4%	6,283	45.2%
Boston City	2,343	12.1%	2,085	11.8%	1,826	11.5%	1,665	11.1%	1,296	9.3%	1,598	11.5%	1,601	11.8%	1,679	12.1%
St. Elizabeth's	1,610	8.3%	1,534	8.7%	1,230	7.7%	1,141	7.6%	1,057	7.6%	1,121	8.1%	984	.7.3%	1,024	7.4%
St. Margaret's	5,299	27.4%	4,819	27.3%	4,161	26.2%	3,697	24.6%	3,318	23.8%	3,007	21.6%	2,808	20.7%	2,900	20.0%
Total Boston Hospitals	19,371	100.0%	17,677	100.0%	15,907	100.0%	15,021	100.0%	13,952	100.0%	13,906	100.0%	13,577	100.0%	13,896	100.0%
Cambridge	939		969		923		849		762		752		743		N/A	
Mt. Auburn	1,369		1,236		1,066		893		680		693		696		N/A	
Newton-Wellesley	1,220		1,162		1,114		1,021		1,039		1,036		1,158		N/A	
Total All Massachusetts Hospitals	96,290		83,337		79,063		74,110		71,777		69,574		67,555		N/A	

quently became loyal staff members after their training was completed, if they could be set up in a practice. Others might be influenced by the quality and scope of services offered by a given hospital: for this reason, some might choose a general hospital with specialty backup in internal medicine and general surgery over a hospital that restricted its practice to obstetrics and gynecology. Likewise, a hospital that included an obstetrical service but lacked gynecology would have a lower appeal than one with both services. Finally, an obstetrician might join the staff of a hospital with a religious affiliation out of personal preference or to accommodate patients' wishes.

A second major target market consisted of women who placed their first priority on choosing the hospital. This group of women then had the option of selecting a private obstetrician on the hospital's staff or of using the hospital's outpatient obstetrical services (where available). In contrast to her suburban counterparts, the urban woman was more likely to choose a hospital directly, either because she perceived the hospital as offering more comprehensive services, or because financial circumstances virtually excluded her from the private physician's office. Boston women, who had a number of maternity services to choose from, might weigh a variety of factors, including recommendations of friends or relatives, cost of services, convenience, and a hospital's religious affiliation. However, there was no market research available to indicate the relative importance of these factors in a woman's decision.

A third market consisted of groups, such as health maintenance organizations (HMOs) and neighborhood health centers, that provided walk-in obstetrical care but turned to

hospitals for inpatient services.* Groups selected hospitals for their members on the basis of price, quality, and practice arrangements (e.g., opportunities for neighborhood health center staff to follow their patients in the hospital).

Competitive Strategies. Facing a declining birth rate as well as constant pressure from government, hospitals began to develop strategies for attracting maternity patients. Virtually all Boston-area hospitals were aware of the importance of favorable publicity in generating demand for their obstetrical services. Most relied on publicity from stories in the local media; some used other communication strategies, too. St. Margaret's Hospital, for instance, had published an eight-page, full-sized, paid supplement in the *Boston Sunday Globe* on June 19, 1977, promoting its "Center for Life" concept in obstetrical care. Other hospitals developed newspaper advertisements or brochures for general distribution discussing their obstetrical services.

Since many health insurance policies did not provide comprehensive coverage for maternity services, pricing was often an important competitive strategy. Even such well-known thirty-party payors as Blue Cross/Blue Shield did not always provide maternity coverage as extensive as that which covered other medical and surgical costs. Because the extent of coverage depended on the policy negotiated within each insured organization, some women with Blue Cross insurance were covered for all prenatal visits, plus delivery; others found that only in-hospital labor and delivery charges would be paid. Most Blue Cross plans also required that members be enrolled at least ten months before delivery in order for coverage to apply. Coverage offered by for-profit commercial insurers was even more variable. Some paid 100% of prenatal and delivery costs; others paid as little as $500 per pregnancy. Patients holding these policies, according to the hospital's financial office, were often "employees of smaller companies that can't afford good Blue Cross coverage." Indigent patients covered by Medicaid in Massachusetts enjoyed the highest state Medicaid

---

*A health maintenance organization (HMO) was a prepaid health plan through which, for one annual premium, a person became eligible for comprehensive medical care. HMOs provided ambulatory care on site, but arranged for inpatient care to be provided in one or two selected hospitals. HMOs generally reimbursed hospitals the "reasonable cost" of whatever inpatient services their patients used.

benefits in the U.S. Medicaid generally paid 80–85% of their prenatal and delivery costs; the rest were absorbed by the hospital.

Some women would telephone each of the local obstetrical units to determine the cost of a delivery, and base their choice partly or wholly on this factor. Most of Boston's hospitals responded to this price-sensitive market by instituting a so-called "package price." This covered prenatal clinic visits in the hospital's outpatient department, delivery, and postpartum care. Women delivered by private obstetricians were not eligible for the package price; on the other hand, they tended to be better insured for maternity services. The package price ranged from $500–850 at different hospitals; individual charges for comparable services totalled from $1,200–1,600. Although the package fee did not cover the hospital's entire cost (including overhead) of providing the services, it did cover direct costs. Some patients who initially entered the hospital as self-pay patients turned out to be eligible for Medicaid, which was a better source of reimbursement.

Hospitals recognized that the physical appearance of their maternity units was important in attracting patients. Since the prevalent mode of delivery was to have the mother awake and the father (or another companion) present, the physical appearance of the labor and delivery area was now even more important than in the past; most hospitals provided tours for couples who were "shopping around" for an obstetrical service. The Boston Hospital for Women (BHW), the Peter Bent Brigham, and the Robert Breck Brigham hospitals had recently merged and would be moving in 1980–81 to a new $118 million facility, in the same neighborhood as the present BHW buildings. Both physicians and hospital administrators felt that the new facility could offer BHW a competitive edge in attracting obstetrical patients.

One of the biggest sources of patients for any of the Boston hospitals was the Harvard Community Health Plan (HCHP), a fast-growing HMO with branches in Kenmore Square, and in nearby Cambridge. Prior to January 1, 1975, the Kenmore branch of HCHP had divided its 400 deliveries between BHW and Beth Israel, but it proved infeasible for one obstetrician to cover two separate units during evenings and nights. Observers believed that the decision to consolidate the entire operation at BHW rather than Beth Israel was probably based on the allegiance of HCHP obstetricians toward the hospital at which most of them had trained. As a result of the transfer of these 200 deliveries, Beth Israel experienced a slight drop in market share (from 16% to 15% of all deliveries in Boston hospitals). But in the spring of 1978, the Cambridge branch of HCHP was considering a transfer of its now more than 700 annual deliveries away from the Boston Hospital for Women, and possibly back to Beth Israel. HCHP's decision would have a major impact on the balance of obstetrical services in Boston.

Beyond these considerations lay the problem of planning the management of maternity services so as to conform, as far as practicable, to the expectations of the women who were giving birth. The philosophies of the obstetrical staffs of each Boston hospital were considerably different, as were their interpretations of current trends and their willingness to innovate in an effort to cultivate new markets.

St. Elizabeth's, Boston City, and Beth Israel exemplified three different approaches to obstetrical care, as summarized by local media:

> *St. Elizabeth's:* "We're traditionalists." That's how Dr. James Whelton, director of ob/gyn services at St. Elizabeth's Hospital in Brighton, characterizes his hospital. "A number of hospitals have alternative birth centers. We don't. We've concentrated our efforts in renovating the postpartum area." Which is indeed festive, with its magenta, orange, green, and yellow color scheme.
> The hospital hasn't had much incentive to explore alternatives; according to Whelton, only 7 or 8 percent of the women who gave birth there last year requested natural childbirth.*
> *Boston City:* Boston City Hospital offers a contractual setup that allows patients of private physicians to use the hospital. The woman writes a list of requests that is signed by her doctor and evaluated by the staff. As long as the attending physicians goes along with the woman's wishes and she has had extensive childbirth preparation, the requests are usually approved. At the time this story was being researched, one woman who was planning to have her baby at Boston City asked that her four-year-old daughter be allowed to witness the birth. A child and an adult psychiatrist were going to interview the family before any decision was reached. "But we're considering it," said staff pediatrician Jeffrey Gould, "which is more than we would have done a year ago."
> *Beth Israel:* "Have It Your Way," the fast-food advertising pitch is serving a loftier purpose in the maternity ward at Boston's Beth Israel Hospital. A framed version of the slogan hangs on the wall to inform mothers—and fathers—that they have a choice in the way their child will be delivered.†

Exhibit 6 summarizes obstetrical procedures and other policies at four Boston hospitals, as reported in the *Boston Globe*.

Some obstetricians, even in the most patient-oriented maternity units, were reluctant to change their traditional modes of practice to accommodate what they perceived as transient fads. Others feared the potentially adverse financial consequences of patient-supported practices such as midwife delivery. Thus, even though all institutions were interested in determining patient preferences, the actual implementation of change in obstetrical practice—indeed the perception of a need to change—varied considerably from hospital to hospital and even from one practitioner to another.

THE BETH ISRAEL MATERNITY SERVICE

In 1978, the medical staff of Beth Israel's obstetrical service consisted of 12 full-time obstetrician/gynecologists, whose

---

*Kelly, "Special Delivery," pp. 135–7.
†Herbert Black, "The Revolution in Childbirth," *New England Magazine (Boston Sunday Globe)*, May 14, 1978, p. 22.

EXHIBIT 6
Profiles of Obstetrical Policies at Four Major Boston Hospitals

Question	St. Elizabeth's (1000 babies/year)	St. Margaret's (3000 babies/year)	Beth Israel (2061 babies/year)	Boston Hospital for Women* (6000 babies/year)
1. How much can the father participate?	Through delivery, including nonemergency C-sections.	Through delivery. Still considering C-sections.	Through delivery, including nonemergency C-sections.	Through delivery, including nonemergency C-sections.
2. How much can the family's other children participate?	Visits Wed. & Sun. in family room; can only see baby through window.	Visits in family room and cafeteria, not allowed in mother's room. See baby through window.	Visits in mother's room if baby not there. Can see baby through window.	Special visiting hours if accompanied by other parent; every morning 7:30—8:30 in mother's room. See baby through window.
3. How much medical intervention is routine?	Episiotomies & fetal monitors almost always; drugs—doctor's option. Enemas optional.	Fetal monitors routine. All other up to doctor.	Fetal monitors almost always. Episiotomies, drugs, use of stirrups no longer routine, up to doctor.	Everything up to doctor; trying for fewer episiotomies.
4. What are minimum costs?	$550 package plan for out-patient. $1300 for private patients.	$105/day.	$850 package plan for out-patients, private patients $150/day for mother, $93 for baby, plus $321 delivery room.	$1600 approximately for average stay.
5. Are certified nurse-midwives available for delivery?	No.	No, but childbirth teachers can accompany mother through birth.	Yes.	Yes, but still working out rules and regulations for deliveries.
6. Can baby "room-in" with mother?	Yes, except when other children present.	Yes, at mother's choice, except when other children present.	Yes, baby also 'given' to parents at delivery. Not if children also in room.	Yes, except when other children present.
7. Are alternate methods of childbirth (Lamaze, Leboyer) accepted?	Yes, modified.	Yes, modified.	Yes, modified.	Yes, modified.
8. Are homelike "birth rooms" available?	No.	Soon. Room being built.	Soon. Establishing ABC (Alternate Birth Center) in fall.	Looking into it.
9. What emergency infant care is available?	Special care (level 2) nursery.	Intensive care (level 3).	Special care (level 2) but Joint Program in Neonatology with BHW and Children's Hospital provides intensive care for infants.	Same as Beth Israel.

*Formerly known as the Boston Lying In Hospital.

Source: *The Boston Globe*, July 21, 1977.

practices were located within the hospital, and 38 "attending" physicians in private practice who admitted patients to the hospital. The service's chief of staff, Emanuel A. Friedman, M.D., was somewhat concerned about the fact that the attending obstetrician/gynecologists were getting older, for older practitioners tended to concentrate their practices in gynecology rather than obstetrics.

Newborn babies were cared for either by private pediatricians or by the Joint Program in Neonatology* (JPM)—a joint venture between Children's Hospital, the Boston Hospital for Women, and Beth Israel. The JPN began its operation in 1974, subsequent to Beth Israel's decision to give up its 14-bed pediatrics unit as a condition for getting a Certificate of Need to construct the Feldberg Building. Conceived as "one nursery in three locations," the JPN provided care at all three hospitals, yet the most sophisticated technologies were available in only one site. Thus, infants born at BHW or

*Neonatology was a subspeciality of pediatrics concerned with the care of newborn babies.

Beth Israel who required surgical treatment were transferrd to Children's Hospital; and Beth Israel babies requiring medical intensive care were transferred to BHW. Although the number of transfers was minimal (1–2% of babies born at Beth Israel and BHW), the system made it possible for each baby to receive the best possible care.

Beth Israel's obstetrical unit consisted of 45 beds distributed over two floors. During the early 1970s, in response to the declining birth rate, the hospital had considered converting its maternity beds to medical/surgical beds. However, because the hospital would have lost some of its obstetrician/gynecologists as a result, it could have been forced to eliminate the gynecology service as well. The net result would have been a much narrower clinical and teaching program, and the idea was abandoned

The unit had been built in 1952, and had not undergone any major renovations (with the exception of air conditioning) since. The majority of patient rooms were semi-private, containing two beds, although there were some private rooms as well as some triples. The physical appearance of the

EXHIBIT 7
Beth Israel Hospital: Cost Analysis of Obstetric Service and Related Activity Cost Analysis
Fiscal Year (FY) 1978 (Projected Actual)*

(All Figures in Thousands of Dollars)

	Obstetrics Floors	Delivery Room	Nursery	Fetal Monitoring	Outpatient (Prenatal & Postpartum)	Total
Gross Revenue	$1,478	$ 815	$ 987	$ 126	$ 196	$3,602
Adjustments	(182)	(100)	(10)	(15)	(90)	(400)
Net Revenue	1,295	714	976	111	105	3,201
Direct Costs						
Salaries & Wages						
Nursing Service	447	393	320			1,151
OBS-GYN Administrative Office	44	179	—	55	—	280
Neonatology Service	—	—	9	—	—	9
Outpatient Clinics	—	—	—	—	92	92
Total Salaries & Wages	492	563	330	55	92	1,534
Fringe Benefits	98	112	66	11	18	306
Total Compensation	591	675	396	67	111	1,841
Supplies**	68	115	62	21	5	273
Total Direct Cost	659	791	458	88	116	2,114
Allocated Costs	728	336	206	18	87	1,378
Total Direct & Indirect Costs	1,388	1,128	665	107	204	3,493
Fixed Depreciation & Interest	48	29	13	—	5	97
Total Cost	1,436	1,157	678	107	210	3,590
Margin—Gain (Loss)	$ (141)	$ (443)	$ 297	$ 3	$ (104)	$ (388)

* Disguised Data.

** Approximately 30% of supplies costs were variable, the balance were treated as fixed costs.

Source: Beth Israel Hospital.

obstetrical unit was adequate, but it paled by comparsion to the colorful, spacious Feldberg Building opened in 1976.

The hospital's administrators were considering the possibility of renovating the labor and delivery area. Changes in the character of obstetrical practice at Beth Israel had rendered the size and layout of the existing facility inadequate. The teaching program had increased in both quality and size since Dr. Friedman's appointment in 1969. Accordingly, as more high-risk obstetrical cases came into the hospital, there was a need for more space for resuscitation equipment for babies and for additional personnel in each delivery room. The inclusion of fathers in the labor and delivery process also required more space; and if the Cambridge branch of HCHP were to bring its deliveries to Beth Israel, one or more additional delivery rooms might also be needed.

Proposals ranged from renovating the existing labor and delivery area ($1.5 million), to renovating another, larger area within the hospital ($2.5 million), to adding another floor to the Feldberg Building ($3 million or more).

The first option would improve the appearance of the labor and delivery suite, but would not provide any additional space. The second option, which included renovation and conversion of the old operating room suite, would provide additional delivery rooms, each larger than the current ones. On the other hand, the location of this space was not ideal; it was several floors away from the rest of the maternity unit and did not provide all of the support space considered desirable. The third option, the addition of a ninth floor to the Feldberg Building, would free the space in the old operating rooms for other needs. Given the constraints on the hospital's capital resources, and pressure from the state's Determination of Need office to keep capital expenditures as low as possible, the hospital administration felt it imperative to choose the proposal that fulfilled current and future requirements at least cost.

Complicating the issue was the problematic financial position of Beth Israel's obstetrical unit. Its loss for FY 1978 was projected to run close to $400,000 (Exhibit 7).* A major contributing factor was the inadequacy of third-party reimbursement (health insurance) for obstetrical services. Twenty-nine percent of the obstetrical patients at Beth Israel

---

*The magnitude of the unit's total contribution, including related admissions of OB patients to other services (notably gynecology), could not be ascertained.

during FY 1977 were either holders of commercial insurance policies or self-pay patients (without coverage). Commercial insurance generally contributed a fixed dollar amount toward the cost of maternity stay, but the maximum rarely came close to the $1,600 average charge for a normal delivery. And even though self-pay patients were charged only the $850 package price, many could not pay even this amount. Thus, adjustments to revenue for bad debts and free care were high.

Service Changes. Historically, Beth Israel's obstetrical services had followed the same narrowly prescribed policies as many other academic maternity units. Indeed, as Carmel Brochu, R.N., clinical (nursing) director of obstetrics and gynecology, recalled:

> When I came to Beth Israel, it had very rigid rules and regulations. There were nurses that dealt with the babies, and nurses that dealt with the mothers, and there was little interaction between them. The mother was heavily sedated and the baby was given to her at set times in the same way she would be given a meal tray. The nurses had particular ways of wrapping the infant, and the mother was not allowed to undress the baby; consumers had not reached the point of making demands. My background as a nurse-midwife in England had taught me to view the family as a whole; it was difficult for me to adapt to practices I saw here.

Brochu felt that the turning point at Beth Israel had occurred with the introduction of family-centered maternity care, around 1970. From that point on, the father could attend the birth in the delivery room, and remain with mother and baby for as much time as the couple desired; the mother could keep the baby in her room as long as she wished; and family visits to the mother's room were encouraged.

As the women's movement gained momentum, Beth Israel attempted to respond to demands by women for medical services that met their needs in a sensitive manner. There were several female obstetrician/gynecologists on the staff, and half of the hospital's ob/gyn residents were women. Staff members stated that the hospital was committed to the idea that women should control the birth process to the greatest extent possible. Beth Israel made optional many of the medical interventions—including drugs, anesthesia, and surgical incisions—that had formerly been considered routine. In Dr. Friedman's view:

> Flexibility is the byword for obstetrics. Within the bounds of safety for both mother and baby, we allow the patient virtually to formulate her own delivery process.

As an example of the unit's desire to provide services that accommodated the individual mother's needs, a staff member cited its dealings with neighborhood health centers. The nursing staff had "gone out of their way" to learn Chinese customs relating to the birth process, as well as Chinese dietary prescriptions, as part of the relationship the hospital maintained with the South Cove Community Health Center in Boston's Chinatown.

A major innovation in Beth Israel's maternity service occurred in July 1977 when the hospital responded to a change in Massachusetts law allowing nurse midwives to deliver babies. Previously, Massachusetts had prohibited this practice, and limited the activities of midwives to pre- and postdelivery care. Although Beth Israel had hired two nurse midwives some years earlier, their activities had been limited in accordance with law. Once the restrictions were lifted, however, Beth Israel became one of the first institutions to implement midwife delivery.

Patient satisfaction with the midwives was said to be high. Women felt that the midwives paid a great deal of attention to them during prenatal visits, and were sensitive to their concerns. The midwives expressed a desire to help women choose the type of birth experience that they would feel most comfortable with. In the words of one woman,

> The delivery was as close to a home birth as possible. I was awake and participating in everything and needed no drugs, but all the technical backup was ready in case anything went wrong.

A second major innovation was the construction of an Alternative Birth Center (ABC) early in 1978. The ABC was a further response to women who wanted to deliver their babies with a minimum of medical intervention, while knowing that help was close at hand should it be required. Accordingly, the ABC was made available to low-risk mothers who had a high probability of normal delivery and who wished to deliver by "natural" childbirth (without anesthesia or surgical intervention).

The ABC differed from traditional labor and delivery suites in several ways. Each of the two "birthing rooms" within the ABC was furnished to look like a bedroom. The sophisticated instruments that were kept in the room for use in emergencies were hidden from view. The process of delivery differed markedly as well. In traditional suites, a woman was wheeled from labor room to delivery room and had to shift from a bed to a delivery table during the most active phase of labor. By contrast, a woman in the ABC labored and delivered in one room and one bed. In both instances, the mother returned after delivery to a standard hospital room for her postpartum care.

Due to the tremendous extra cost involved, and the fact that the long-term popularity of the ABC concept was not known, the ABC did not provide anesthesia; thus, some women who favored the concept might still choose to deliver in the labor and delivery suite, where anesthesia was available. If a major renovation of the main suite were undertaken, it was reasonable to assume that the concept of combined labor and delivery could be expanded to rooms where anesthesia could be administered.

Pricing, Communications, and Outreach. The hospital had instituted an $850 package price for obstetrical services, which included prenatal and postpartum care in the Beth Israel outpatient clinic in addition to a routine delivery. A deposit was required at the time of the initial prenatal visit, and the remaining balance was divided by the number of

EXHIBIT 8
Distribution of Maternity Admissions for Boston, Cambridge, and Newton
by Patient's Home Location, 1974–75

Boston	Beth Israel Hospital Medical-Surgical*	Maternity	Boston City Hospital	Boston Hospital for Women	St. Margaret's (Boston)	St. Elizabeth's (Boston)	Mt. Auburn (Cambridge)	Newton-Wellesley (Newton)
Allston/Brighton	5.9%	2.9%	0.9%	3.2%	0.3%	18.0%	1.9%	1.3%
Charlestown/East Boston	0.3	0.3	4.8	2.2	0.9	4.3	—	—
Back Bay/South End/Downtown	6.4	6.0	8.1	6.5	0	3.3	0.5	—
South Boston	0.5	0.8	2.7	0.7	12.6	0.6	0.1	—
Dorchester	5.3	10.5	37.4	7.2	26.1	2.2	0.3	0.2
Roxbury	6.2	12.9	30.0	8.1	2.3	0.6	0.4	—
Mattapan/Hyde Park	4.3	6.9	5.7	3.5	6.7	3.0	1.0	0.7
Jamaica Plain/Roslindale/W. Roxbury	7.8	7.9	5.5	7.5	10.1	9.3	—	1.7
Other Boston	1.4	1.4	1.3	0.2	0.3	0.1	0.1	0.2
Total Boston	38.1	49.5	95.7	39.0	59.3	41.3	4.3	4.1
Belmont	0.7	1.0	—	—	—	1.5	6.5	0.7
Brookline	15.1	4.9	—	2.5	—	2.6	0.3	0.6
Cambridge	2.4	4.2	0.2	4.5	0.2	3.1	18.5	0.2
Chelsea	2.4	0.9	0.1	1.3	—	4.2	—	—
Dedham	0.3	0.4	—	0.9	1.6	1.3	0.4	2.6
Milton	1.1	0.4	—	1.1	2.7	0.9	—	0.2
Needham	0.7	0.9	—	0.7	0.1	1.1	—	5.2
Newton	4.7	2.9	—	4.4	0.3	4.6	—	23.4
Quincy	1.2	1.3	—	1.5	7.7	1.0	1.5	0.3
Somerville	1.3	1.5	0.1	2.8	0.6	2.2	10.3	0.5
Waltham	0.7	1.4	—	1.1	0.2	3.0	3.5	9.0
Watertown	0.7	1.2	—	1.4	0.2	5.4	11.5	4.6
Wellesley	0.2	0.5	—	1.0	—	0.6	0.1	7.3
Other locations	30.6	29.1	2.5	37.7	27.0	27.1	42.6	42.2
Total	100.0%	100.0%	100.0%	100.0%	100.0%	100.0%	100.0%	100.0%

*Medical-surgical admissions at Beth Israel shown for comparison.

Source: Massachusetts Hospital Association

months remaining until the expected date of delivery. In total, about 10% of births at Beth Israel were paid for on this basis.

The hospital's direct cost for providing a delivery in the ABC was slightly less than the direct cost of a delivery in the traditional labor and delivery suite. However, Beth Israel offered only one package price lest some women be encouraged to deliver in the ABC (without anesthesia) not by choice but by financial necessity.

Beth Israel pursued several strategies in publicizing its patient and family-centered maternity services. Dr. Friedman stated that he favored the concept of advertising within ethical boundaries, but that the medical profession "is limited by custom to minimal advertising." There were specific professional guidelines as to what was and what was not appropriate. Although a few advertising programs had been initiated by Beth Israel, Dr. Friedman believed these to be less extensive than those carried out by obstetrical units at other hospitals.

J. Anthony Lloyd, who had been the hospital's director of public relations since November 1977, believed that publicity should emphasize the human side of care at Beth Israel:

> The care and attention that our patients receive go far beyond that required for competent delivery of services, and we try to convey that idea. For example, when I was working on a press release on the Alternative Birth Center, I applied this principle by focusing on one family's relationship with the Beth Israel from prenatal visits through postpartum care. The story unfolded from the family's point of view, and illustrated the warm, personalized care for which we strive.

Lloyd listed print, broadcast, direct mail, and professional staff as media through which the public relations office had informed the community about the hospital's maternity services.

Beth Israel also participated in educational programs, both within the hospital and outside in the community. These included a women's health series, headed by a group of Beth Israel obstetricians and nurses and advertised through local newspapers; parent education courses held at the hospital for expectant parents; and film festivals to which the general public was invited.

Finally, the hospital sought to facilitate patient access to its services. Through contracts with several health centers scattered throughout the city, Beth Israel staff provided prenatal care in a convenient, local setting to a variety of distinct patient groups. The easy availability of Beth Israel's prenatal care for these clinics greatly enhanced the appeal of the hospital's delivery services. Moreover, because the offices of Beth Israel obstetricians in private practice were widely dispersed (located up to 20 miles west of Boston), the hospital had succeeded in making its services available throughout a wide geographic area (Exhibit 8).

REVIEWING THE SITUATION

As he tried to evaluate Beth Israel's obstetrical service, Steinberg asked himself how it contributed to teaching and community service. Should the hospital continue to offer obstetrical care, or could a good argument be made for closing or shrinking the size of the OB unit? If so, should these beds be transferred to another service, or eliminated?

On the other hand, if the hospital's board decided to continue offering obstetrical services at Beth Israel, then it would have to find ways of improving the unit's financial performance. Steinberg believed that the obstetrical package price merited some study. The $850 fee had not been increased for several years, and he wondered if it might be possible to raise it—perhaps to $1,000—without sacrificing its value as a marketing tool or negating its philanthropic purpose.

Also, he needed to evaluate the possibility of promoting the obstetrical service to a patient population with better insurance coverage, and determine the strategies that might best achieve this goal. Although the hospital was committed to providing its services to all patients regardless of their ability to pay, a well-rounded payor mix was needed to keep the deficit in obstetrics at a minimum.

Lastly, Steinberg knew he must address the issue of renovating the labor and delivery area. Confronted with the prospect of the BHW's forthcoming move to new quarters, he was acutely aware that Beth Israel's obstetrical facilities had not had a facelift in more than 25 years.

17
Amtrak

Christopher H. Lovelock

Executives of the National Railroad Passenger Corporation, better known as Amtrak, faced both good news and bad news in summer 1974. The good news was that system-wide patronage for the first half of 1974 was up by 32% over the same period of the previous year, with trains on some of the more popular routes sold out weeks and even months in advance. The bad news was that the corporation faced a critical shortage of passenger cars, with many more than projected having to be withdrawn from service for repairs. Also causing concern to some was the bad publicity engendered by Amtrak's continuing poor punctuality record; in June 1974, only 60% of long-distance trains and 83% of short-haul trains had arrived on time.

It was expected that some of these problems would be alleviated in due course by purchase of new equipment due for delivery from 1975 onwards, and by Amtrak's insistence on tougher performance standards by railroads under contract to the corporation. However, the outlook for significant improvements during the balance of the summer peak season was not particularly encouraging.

An important issue facing Amtrak executives at this time was how to handle the summer situation from a marketing standpoint, within the context of developing a consistent long-term strategy.

PASSENGER RAIL TRAVEL IN THE UNITED STATES

The nation's railroads played a key role in the development of the young United States, and the completion of the last link in the transcontinental railroad in 1869 signified the beginning of an era in which the passenger train reigned supreme as the leading form of intercity transportation in the United States. This era reached its peak in 1929, which saw the greatest number of passenger trains ever operated in the nation.

The Decline of Rail. From this peak, intercity rail passenger service entered a decline which was inter-rupted by World War II but continued briskly thereafter. In large measure, the financial picture paralleled the decrease in ridership. Rail service operated at a profit in only four years during the period 1930 to 1970. From 1962 to 1970, the annual intercity rail passenger deficit increased from $394 million to $476 million.

The most significant reason for the decline of rail passenger transportation was the development of three major competing modes: air, bus and private car. All three were spurred by very large Federal investments. The airlines were heavily supported by operating and airport construction subsidies, while equipment development benefited greatly from commercial application of much military R&D.

Christopher H. Lovelock is Associate Professor of Business Administration, Harvard University.

The bus and auto modes, meantime, were aided by the widespread construction of public roads, most notably under the Interstate Highway Act of 1956 which, by 1971, had brought into being close to 40,000 miles of new high-speed, limited access highways. Exhibit 1 charts the rise of intercity auto, bus and air travel and the decline of passenger rail.

The Railroads' Response. According to many observers, once the shift to air, bus and car had begun, it was accelerated by the managements of many railroads, in the belief that there was no way to make passenger rail service profitable again (a view shared by many economists). The declining sales situation was aggravated by steadily rising costs.

Although a few railroads, such as the Atcheson, Topeka & Santa Fe, made efforts to reverse the downwards trend of ridership, it was alleged that some lines deliberately encouraged this trend with poor service and inferior equipment. When patronage on a given route had declined sufficiently, the railroad would then petition the Interstate Commerce Commission (or state regulatory body in the case of intrastate services) for permission to reduce service or even eliminate it altogether.

The pressure for discontinuance was further intensified in 1967 when the Post Office Department decided to discontinue attaching Post Office cars to passenger trains, thus depriving the railroads of substantial passenger-related revenues.

From nearly 1500 intercity trains in the late 1950s, the total had shrunk to a little over one-third that number by mid-1969. During the 12 months ending July 1, 1969, the rate of abandonments continued briskly, with a further 67 intercity passenger trains being withdrawn from service. Railroad executives insisted that they were not deliberately trying to drive passengers away from rail travel and that the decline simply reflected the greater attraction of air, bus and car travel.

Passengers and even the ICC argued otherwise. In April 1968, an ICC examiner recommended that the Commission should take an activist role and order the Southern Pacific to improve its daily "Sunset Limited" service on the lengthy Los Angeles–New Orleans route by such measures as running the train on time (it was often many hours late) and providing dining cars.

Targeted for some of the strongest complaints was the Penn Central, which was accused, amongst other shortcomings, of "filthy" cars, "disgusting odors" in the rest rooms, and malfunctioning lights and air-conditioning. An article in the *Wall Street Journal* told the saga of a rat that terrorized passengers on the "Spirit of St. Louis." The rat was ignored by the conductor for 100 miles and finally trapped in a passenger's handkerchief and thrown off the train. On another occasion, reported the *Journal,* 35 passengers on the "Spirit" became so incensed by the lack of lights, water and air-conditioning that they climbed off and lay down in front of the locomotive for an hour and a half until a broken generator belt was replaced.[1]

The Formation of Amtrak. By 1970 half the nation's passenger trains were subject to discontinuance proceedings before the ICC, and fears were being expressed that intercity rail passenger service was nearing extinction. As a result of pressure from legislators, state regulatory agencies, and consumer groups such as the National Association of Railroad Passengers, Congress enacted the Rail Passenger Service Act (Public Law 91-518). This was signed into law in October 1970.

The purpose of the Act was stated as follows:

> The Congress finds that modern, efficient, intercity railroad passenger service is a necessary part of a balanced transportation system; that public convenience and necessity require the continuance and improvement of such service to provide fast and comfortable transportation between crowded urban areas and in other areas of the country; that rail passenger service can help to end the congestion on our highways and the airports; that the traveler in America should to the maximum extent feasible have freedom to choose the mode of travel most convenient to his needs; that to achieve these goals requires the designation of a basic national rail passenger system and the establishment of a rail passenger corporation for the purpose of providing modern, efficient, intercity rail passenger service; that Federal financial assistance as well as investment capital from the private sector of the economy is needed for this purpose; and that interim emergency Federal financial assistance to certain railroads may be necessary to permit the orderly transfer of railroad passenger service to a railroad passenger corporation.

Major provisions of the Act were as follows:

1. The designation of a "basic system" of passenger routes by the Secretary of Transportation, to be operational until at least July 1973.

2. The formation of the National Railroad Passenger Corporation, as an independent, for-profit corporation, to manage most of the national intercity rail passenger routes by contracting for services with existing railroads.

3. The participation of railroads in the Corporation upon payment of one year's avoidable passenger losses or equivalent. In return, the subscribing railroads received either common stock or a tax reduction. Railroads that did not join were required to continue all passenger service without change until 1975.

---

[1] "Passenger Plight: Officials, Train Riders Claim Some Railroads Try for Lousy Service." *Wall Street Journal,* September 5, 1969.

4. An initial grant of $40 million to the Corporation and loan guarantee authority of up to $100 million.

5. Formation of a board of directors, consisting of eight public members appointed by the President (one to be the Secretary of Transportation and one a consumer representative), three elected by the common stockholders (the railroads) and four elected by the preferred stockholders.[2]

6. Exemption of the company from ICC regulation of fares and service.[3]

7. Requirement to service any route that a state, regional or local agency requested, provided the agency agreed to pay at least two thirds of the losses incurred thereby.

In late October 1970, a proposed "basic system" was announced by the Secretary of Transportation. This deprived many cities of rail service, eliminated connections to Canada and Mexico, and left out some important links within the U.S., notably West Coast service from Seattle to San Diego. As a result of protests by the general public—more than 3,000 letters were received by the White House—and lobbying by local and national legislators, the initial proposal was revised to include many of the deleted routes. A promise was also made to consider restoration of Canadian and Mexican links at a later date.

Three railroads—the Southern, the Rio Grande and the Rock Island—elected not to join the new corporation, but to continue operating their own passenger services. Also excluded were the services of Auto-Train, a private company which had a contractual agreement with Seaboard Coast Lines for ferrying passengers and their automobiles from Washington to Florida on Auto-Train owned equipment.

Appointed as president of the National Railroad Passenger Corporation in early 1971 was Roger Lewis, formerly chief executive of General Dynamics. Lewis, 59, had also served as Assistant Secretary of the Air Force and executive vice president of Pan American World Airways.

Prior to the NRPC's takeover of rail passenger service on May 1, 1971, the trade name Amtrak was introduced. The consulting firm which invented the new name (and also designed an eyecatching corporate symbol in red, white and blue) had recommended avoidance of any name using the word "rail" because of its unfavorable connotations for travelers.

Initial funding for Amtrak came in the form of a $40 million grant from the Federal Government, plus loan guarantees of another $100 million. The 20 par-

ticipating railroads then paid the Corporation $197 million, an amount equal to their 1969 losses on those passenger trains which Amtrak proposed to continue operating. Over the next year or so, Amtrak used $87 million of these funds to buy from the railroads 1,585 used cars and 274 old locomotives. Additionally, agreements were reached whereby Amtrak contracted with the railroads for operating its trains and for the use of tracks, terminals and additional locomotives. The cars represented the best of the more than 3,000 owned by the railroads, but many were still in sorry condition.

AMTRAK INITIATES SERVICE

Amtrak's initiation was not a particularly auspicious one, with Mr. Lewis resisting last-minute lobbying by union leaders for extension of protective labor agreements and attempts by key legislators to add or restore service to their home districts. The Corporation began service on May 1 by lopping off about half the nation's remaining passenger trains. Overnight, the total dropped from 547 to 243. The theory was that a severely pruned system would yield significant cost savings, while attracting enough new passengers to make the operation ultimately profitable.

The trains operated by Amtrak included prestigious, high quality services such as the Santa Fe's "Super Chief" from Chicago to Los Angeles, and the glamorous, high speed Turbotrains and Metroliners in the Boston–Washington corridor. The latter were operated by Penn-Central (over track which was often so poor that it restricted their speeds to a fraction of their potential) but the high technology equipment had been sponsored by the U.S. Department of Transportation. Many of the other services inherited by Amtrak, however, were sad shadows of their former glory, such as Southern Pacific's "Coast Daylight" and Penn Central's "Broadway Limited." Others consisted of short distance corridor services of varying quality.

One of Mr. Lewis's first concerns was to build an executive staff. Most of the initial staff of 33 were clerks; the corporation was being run by consulting personnel and a small group of financial and scheduling experts on loan from other agencies. The majority of train and station personnel were railroad employees who retained the low morale generated by years of indifference towards passengers on the part of their employers.

Marketing Activities. An early executive appointment was that of Harold L. Graham as marketing vice-president. Graham, 53, was formerly vice president-worldwide service for Pan American and moved quickly to develop an advertising program for Amtrak. Among the possible advertising themes proposed by the corporation's advertising agency, Ted Bates & Company, were:

---

[2] Since no preferred stock was actually issued by Amtrak, there were only 11 directors in 1974.

[3] Nevertheless, the Corporation had to seek ICC approval for permission to discontinue any "basic system" service after July 1973.

EXHIBIT 1
Intercity Travel by Automobile, Bus, Air and Rail, 1940–1971
(Billions of Passenger Miles, semi-log)

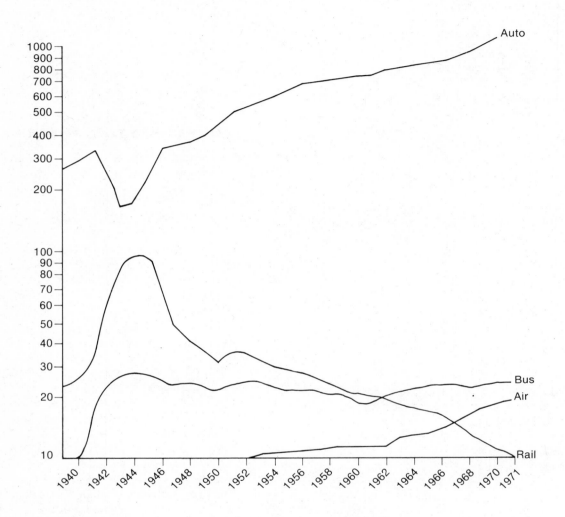

Source: Interstate Commerce Commission.

"Amtrak: we aim to put you back on the track";
"The beginning of the revolution in train travel";
"Train with us into tomorrow";
"Trains will never be the same again";
"It's about time somebody did something about train travel"; and
"We're making the trains worth traveling again."

The last-mentioned theme was selected and a $900,000 advertising and promotion campaign subsequently initiated from the period July 1971 to January 1972, using newspapers, magazines and radio.[4] The ad-

vertisement shown in Exhibit 2 appeared widely in the print media. Amtrak also initiated market research to find out more about what people thought of trains and why they rode—or did not ride—them.

Mr. Graham stated that almost everything happening in Amtrak came within marketing's province: "every point at which we contact the public is involved."[5] This was seen as starting with the equipment improvement program and continuing through quality of train operation, maintenance and cleanliness. Market-

---

[4] "Amtrak budget so far is only 'pat on the back,' Benham says." *Advertising Age*, June 28, 1971.

[5] "Amtrak sets $2,800,000 drive; hopes to find role in transportation." *Advertising Age*, Nov. 15, 1971.

EXHIBIT 2
Preliminary Amtrak Advertising in Print Media, 1971

AMTRAK. WE'RE MAKING THE TRAINS WORTH TRAVELING AGAIN

(All we ask from you is a little patience)

Amtrak Passenger Representative with a model of a modern Amtrak car now in service.

What is Amtrak? We're America's first nationwide passenger rail system.

When President Nixon signed the Rail Passenger Service Act, it gave us the responsibility for managing the country's intercity rail network starting May 1, 1971.

That meant merging the services and solving the obstacles of what had been 22 different passenger railroads, each with its own built-in problems. While at the same time running 1300 trains a week over 20,000 miles of track to 340 cities in the U.S.A.

It may not be the country's biggest headache. But it's close. That's why when we took over we made only one simple promise. To make the trains worth traveling again. It's going to take time, and work. But we're going to do it. Just be patient, please.

You're going to ride the best 1200 cars in the country. You can't run a good railroad without good railroad cars. So our first order of business was to take stock of our rolling stock. We examined all 3000 passenger cars formerly in service. And we're keeping only the 1200 best, most of them stainless steel.

You talk—we listen. For the first time there are passenger representatives riding our trains just to get your ideas about rail service. You've already made it clear that you want your trains a lot cleaner than in the past. And they will be.

Eat a little better. Right now we're concerned with making sure that you get a real good dinner every time you enter our dining cars. And that even a snack in an Amtrak coach is always fresh and tasty.

We want to save you time, money and aggravation. Some of the most annoying problems of going by train take place before you even step aboard. And we know it. That's why we're putting such a high priority on faster and simpler reservation and ticketing procedures. We don't like red tape any better than you do.

People who care are caring about you. If you've been aboard an Amtrak train lately, perhaps you've noticed how attentive our personnel are. Nobody has a greater stake in the success of Amtrak than the people on our trains. After all, their future is riding on it.

All this, of course, is only a very small start on a very big job. But we are making progress—and we're proud of it. Come aboard an Amtrak train this fall and see for yourself.

We're making the trains worth traveling again.

ing-related activities also included a "personal service" training program for Amtrak employees.

The marketing program proposed by Mr. Graham also included new red, white and blue uniforms for all employees dealing directly with the public; a single, easily identifiable Amtrak ticket design; airline tie-in tours for foreign visitors; two- and three-week family package tours; a uniform pricing formula for fares; and sharply revised routing schedules for smoother passenger connections. Graham also looked forward to a computerized, nationwide reservations system and a tie-in with major credit card companies. A $2.8 million advertising campaign was announced for 1972.

By the beginning of 1972, some of the changes which Amtrak had initiated were becoming more apparent. For the first time, national railroad schedules and route maps in easy-to-read format were provided in a single, pocketable brochure. Train crews included a growing number of Amtrak's own employees, known as passenger representatives. Dressed in smartly cut red and blue uniforms, these young men and women had received training from Continental Airlines and contrasted sharply with the generally aging, male, railroad employees who served as porters, conductors and dining car attendants under contract to Amtrak. Morale, too, seemed to be improving among many of the latter, although complaints were still being received from the public about railroad personnel. Meantime, improved and inexpensive meals were being served on board the trains, many of which had lacked meal service altogether in recent years.

A growing number of the cars which Amtrak had purchased from the railroads had been refurbished with colorful new interiors and carried Amtrak's distinctive red, white and blue motif on the outside. A number of cars purchased from western railroads, which tended to be newer (that is, dating from the late 40s and early 50s) were introduced into service on eastern routes which had previously had to suffer broken-down, pre-war equipment.

AMTRAK'S OPERATIONS IN 1972

Although Amtrak's top management professed to take an optimistic view of the future of intercity rail passenger transportation, the corporation's critics were becoming increasingly vocal.

Criticism of Amtrak. Typical of the views of many railroad executives were those of Benjamin F. Biaggini, president of Southern Pacific. In an interview with *U.S. News and World Report*, Mr. Biaggini expressed little confidence in Amtrak's future:

There is no market for long distance, intercity passenger transportation by rail. People won't ride it and they won't pay what they should to support the service. I don't think the taxpayers of this country should put up 300 or 400 million dollars a year to support such a service if the demand is not there. . . .

The real bread and butter of passenger transportation is business travel, and the businessman simply cannot afford the time it takes to go by train. . . .

Biaggini pointed out that the railroads had lost their passenger business "at a time when we were providing the finest service in the world." In support of this contention, he cited beautiful, streamlined trains equipped with "barber shops, valet service, maids, couriers, nurses and dining cars where you could get the thickest steaks."

Mr. Biaggini concluded:

I think Amtrak's function should be to preside over an orderly shrinkage of rail passenger service.[6]

There was criticism, too, from both friends and opponents of Amtrak in Congress, especially when it became clear that the corporation was going to need substantial additional funding. Some argued that Amtrak should have been more daring and innovative with new types of service, new fare packages and bold new advertising. Criticism of another sort came from airlines and bus companies, which complained about the expenditure of government money to advertise against them.

Management's Strategy. While optimistic about Amtrak's future, Roger Lewis took a cautious view of the best way to proceed:

I think we've got to get far surer about what sort of passenger service is needed than we are.[7]

Without a great deal of resources, Lewis placed most emphasis on obtaining better use of Amtrak's existing assets. He noted that there were few ideas which had not been tried by some railroad at some time in the past but questioned the value of "luxury cruise" approaches to marketing rail travel, especially for short and over-night trips.

I'm very strong for offering better basic service, such as running on time and good clean equipment. I'm very strong for bold marketing approaches—family fares, group packages, combinations with airlines, buses, hired automobiles, and the like. . . .

I think we can do a lot to produce better service at a lower cost, and that will attract more passengers than some of these more glamorous things—although we're going to try some of them.

Lewis stressed that improvements such as these, instilling greater courtesy in personnel and improving the

---

[6] "Future of Passenger Trains. Interview with B. F. Biaggini, President, Southern Pacific Company." *U.S. News and World Report*, January 3, 1972, pp. 44–45.

[7] "Amtrak: A noble experiment in trouble." *Business Week*, Arpil 15, 1972, pp. 74–75.

communications and reservation system, were not unduly expensive. He expressed the hope that they would result in a reversal of the previous declining trend in passenger rail travel and provide Congress with a rationale for funding new cars and locomotives. If, in turn, the combination of improved service and better equipment succeeded in attracting more passengers, then Amtrak should be able to obtain public support for investments in track upgrading to enable trains to run at the high speeds for which they were designed. However, he cautioned that "the problems of creating a nationwide system over the property of 13 previously separate railroads are pretty formidable." [8]

Harold Graham also appeared to take a fairly sanguine view of bad publicity:

I am not discouraged by bad publicity, because I think there is an American failing that we expect the application of an idea to have instantaneous results. I think there was a general public expectation that when you put together a new corporation and it started on May 1, that automatically made everything all right. [9]

During the 12 month period ending June 30, 1972, Amtrak reported operating revenues of $152.5 million and total expenses of $306.3 million. For fiscal year 1972–73, management projected similar costs but an increase in revenues to $179.4 million.

During the first half of 1972 the corporation had begun selective modification of routes, service frequencies and fares. Reducing the one-way fare between Boston and New York from $12.75 to $9.90 yielded a 30% increase in traffic in the first four months, and systemwide passenger statistics showed that the downward trend had been reversed. New Metroliners were introduced on the New York–Washington route in response to growing demand, while some unsuccessful experimental routes, such as New York–Cleveland–Chicago, were dropped.

The Louis Harris Opinion Poll. In October 1972, Amtrak released the results of a $200,000 opinion poll conducted for the corporation by Louis Harris and Associates. Three thousand people nationwide had been surveyed the previous May on their opinions about the future of intercity train travel. Only 4% of them had taken an intercity trip by train in the previous 12 months. [10]

Some of the major findings of the poll were that:

1. 64% favored continuing intercity passenger train service "even if it means Federal subsidies."

2. 82% felt they must have the option of passenger rail travel.

3. 90% believed "trains are vital for the country."

4. 75% held the view that "long distance passenger train travel is essential in a national emergency."

5. 54% thought that it was "a very important priority for the nation to improve the quality and availability of rail-passenger travel" more than bus travel, faster air travel or new airports.

6. 56% felt that it was "very important to develop fast, comfortable intercity passenger trains."

The survey results also provided insights into what factors people considered important in travel and how trains were rated on these. Rail travel received particularly good ratings on safety, "Look out and see interesting things en route," "Arrive rested and relaxed," and "Be able to get up and walk around," but was poorly rated on a number of other characteristics, including speed, flexibility, and quality food at reasonable prices (Exhibit 3).

Shortly after release of this poll, Amtrak initiated a five-month, $600,000 advertising campaign, using both print and broadcast media. The themes of this campaign—comfort, convenience and safety—were based on the results of the Harris poll, and it was targeted at cities along the six main rail corridors in the country. Many of the advertisements also provided schedule and fare information. An example appears in Exhibit 4.

PROGRESS IN 1973

As Amtrak neared the end of its second year of operation, Roger Lewis commented:

We've had a whale of a problem getting geared up. [But] the first step is being taken to rebuild passenger service in this country...
We've got a long way to go. It's going to take time and money... [However] not only has the decline in ridership been reversed, but after only modest physical improvement, the public has shown support for Amtrak. [11]

While Lewis could point to some solid gains, the corporation's performance left no room for complacency. A TV news documentary on CBS cast Amtrak in the role of a squanderer of public money. It included comments critical of top management by Senator Vance Hartke of Indiana and a statement by Louis W. Menk, Chairman of the Board of the Burlington-Northern railroad and also an Amtrak director, that the long-haul train should be allowed to die.

On the other hand, criticism of the railroads was

[8] "Is there really a future for passenger trains?" *U.S. News and World Report,* February 28, 1972, p. 52.

[9] "A Smoother Track Ahead for Amtrak?" *Railway Age,* January 10, 1972, p. 26.

[10] "Harris Poll projects big future for Amtrak," *Railway Age,* October 9, 1972, p. 39.

[11] "A trimmer Amtrak is given a chance." *Business Week,* March 17, 1973, pp. 24–25.

EXHIBIT 3
Findings of Survey on Travel Motivators and Train Ratings

% of Respondents Rating "Very Important"	13 Top Motivators for Travel	Train Rating Positive (%)	Negative (%)	% of Respondents Saying: "Train is the Best Way to Go" Total Public	18 to 29	College	$15,000 and over
	Items on which Train Travel is Rated Positively						
63	Cost of trip	36	28	13	10	12	11
46	Personal comfort	45	31	19	11	16	13
41	Safety	67	11	36	29	33	31
31	Look out and see interesting things en route	63	18	38	31	43	43
13	Arrive rested and relaxed	50	26	18	14	15	13
13	Be able to get up and walk around	61	18	62	61	65	63
9	Arrive on time	42	31	16	12	17	13
8	Friendly, helpful employees	40	27	11	6	8	6
	Items on which Train Travel is Rated Negatively						
19	Reach destination quickly	35	41	5	3	3	2
15	Flexible when can leave	25	42	8	6	6	6
18	Quality food available	32	39	15	9	13	11
17	Good food at reasonable prices	23	36	13	11	12	9
9	Modern washroom facilities	33	33	16	11	14	13
	Percent of respondents taking intercity trip by train in last twelve months			4	6	7	6

Source: Louis Harris Poll for Amtrak (reworked from data published in Railway Age*).*

also growing, not only on account of the continued sniping at Amtrak by many of their executives, but also because of sentiment that the roads were partly responsible for Amtrak's poor on-time record, due to badly maintained tracks and failure to give passenger trains priority over freight. In 1972, 47% of Amtrak's long-distance passenger trains ran late.

Despite expectations that significant cuts might be made in Amtrak's route structure in July 1973, the date set for such a possibility, these fears proved unfounded and additional funding was provided by Congress (Exhibit 5 shows the 23,500 mile national route structure in Fall 1973).

Taking a forward view, Amtrak continued with an increasingly vigorous promotional policy emphasizing car rental tie-ins (Exhibit 6), inclusive tours and family fare plans (Exhibit 7). It also took delivery of 40 new diesel-electric locomotives and ordered a significant number of additional new locomotives and new passenger cars. These purchases were made possible by a passage of a bill granting the corporation another $500 million in Congressional loan guarantees. A major innovation, which yielded significant press coverage, was the introduction of two new turbine powered trains leased from France.

Another area in which the corporation was progressing was in assuming more direct control over its workforce instead of employing railroad personnel. Many existing train, station and reservations personnel were hired directly from the railroads, while others were recruited from the outside. In a sharp reversal of railroad tradition, 60% of the service attendants on the newly initiated "Montrealer" from Washington to Montreal were young women. Flexible working agreements allowed the on-board service director to move these train personnel to various jobs en route as service needs dictated. By the end of 1973 Amtrak had more than 5,300 employees on its payroll, compared with 1,522 a year earlier.

Amtrak's efforts to improve the quality of service provided by its employees seemed to be paying off. During the last five months of 1973, more compliments than complaints were received concerning personnel (Exhibit 8).

EXHIBIT 4
Amtrak Newspaper Advertising, Winter 1972—1973
(Version Used in San Jose Area Newspapers)

SEE A LITTLE MORE ALONG THE WAY

Amtrak to Los Angeles $15.50. To Seattle $34
You won't miss a thing all the way. The big picture windows in our coach give you the kind of easy viewing you can't get on a plane, a bus or jockeying your own car. It's all part of the tension-free travel that only Amtrak offers. So are the deep, comfortable two-abreast coach seats. The bedroom accommodations. The aisles wide enough to stretch your arms as well as your legs. The meals that let you enjoy what you eat without fretting over what you pay. And the money-saving Family Fares available to most destinations. Next trip go the safe and scenic way. Take it easy. Take the train.

Northbound — Read Down		Southbound — Read Up
(Daily)		(Daily)
Lv. 10:05 a.m.	Los Angeles	Arr. 6:55 p.m.
Arr. 10:21 a.m.	Glendale	Arr. 6:32 p.m.
Arr. 11:25 a.m.	Oxnard	Arr. 5:25 p.m.
Arr. 12:18 p.m.	Santa Barbara	Arr. 4:38 p.m.
Arr. 2:45 p.m.	San Luis Obispo	Arr. 2:15 p.m.
Arr. 5:29 p.m.	Salinas	Arr. 11:28 a.m.
Lv. 6:58 p.m.	**San Jose**	Lv. 10:05 a.m.
Arr. 8:20 p.m.	Oakland	Lv. 8:45 a.m.
Arr. 8:50 p.m.	San Francisco (via bus)	Lv. 8:15 a.m.
(Mon. Thu. Sat.)		(Mon. Thu. Sat.)
Arr. 1:05 p.m.	Portland	Arr. 3:50 p.m.
Arr. 5:20 p.m.	Seattle	Lv. 11:50 a.m.

Other Low One-Way Coach Fares:
To Santa Barbara $11.50. To Portland $28.50.

Car Rentals: Amtrak ticket holders get special rates from Airways Rent-A-Car. Call toll free 800-336-0336 before leaving or call the local Airways Office when you arrive.

Los Angeles Bus Connections: Special connecting bus service from Los Angeles Union Terminal to Lakewood, Long Beach, Anaheim-Disneyland and Orange.

We're making the trains worth traveling again.

For reservations, call your Amtrak-authorized Travel Agent or call (408) 287-7453 in San Jose, (415) 327-6452 in Palo Alto.

EXHIBIT 5
Amtrak System Map 1973–1974

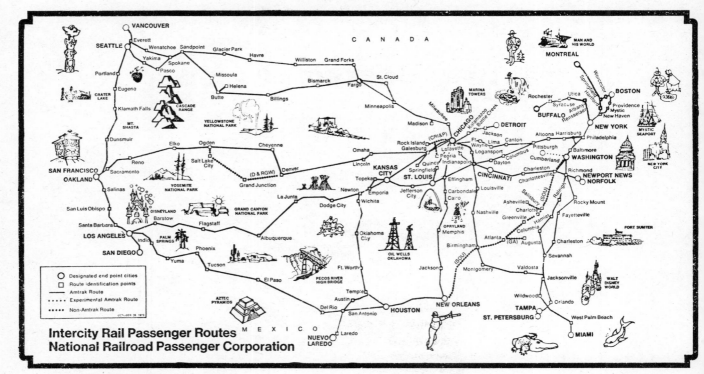

Source: Amtrak National Schedules.

Sales through travel agencies doubled in 1973 to $16 million. By year's end, Amtrak had more than 6,600 agencies, 800 of them outside the U.S. and Canada. Considerable advances were also made in expanding the corporation's field sales force, which covered both passengers and package express service.

As the year moved to its close, the existing upward trend in Amtrak patronage was given a sharp boost by the onset of the energy crisis. Amtrak responded quickly with a new advertising campaign, supplementing its existing third-year advertising and promotional budget of close to $5 million. It also sought additional old cars from the railroads to handle the increased loads. Daily calls to Amtrak reservations centers climbed to 60,000, almost double those of the 1973 peak summer months.

Amtrak was thus able to end the year on an upward note. However, despite a 24% increase in revenues over 1972 to $202 million, expenses rose sharply too, and the net deficit for the year increased by 8% to $159 million (Exhibit 9). During 1973, it carried 18 million passengers while operating at an average 50% load factor.

PROBLEMS AND OPPORTUNITIES IN 1974

1974 began with a continued sharp increase in patronage. During the first three months, normally a period of relatively low travel demand, ridership was up by 41% over the same period in the previous year. This compared with pre-energy crisis forecasts of only 15% gain. As a result, Amtrak found itself faced with demand levels which it had not expected to reach until 1977.

At weekends, trains were packed and thousands were forced to stand for journeys undertaken during the long Washington's Birthday weekend. Whereas Mr. Lewis was previously concerned with getting the public to "think rail," he now observed:

> Our constraint is not going to be so much rider attitudes as it's going to be our ability to handle the increase in traffic.[12]

In attempting to improve train reliability, Amtrak was in the process of renegotiating operating contracts with the railroads with defined performance standards being written into the contracts. The objective was to impose penalties for failure to meet these on-time standards, while paying bonuses when they were exceeded.

However, equipment failures were still causing significant problems, reflecting both the age of the passenger cars Amtrak had purchased from the railroads and the fact that maintenance yards were expected to handle a wide range of cars built for numerous different railroads.

---

[12] "Look What's Happening to Amtrak." *Railway Age*, May 13, 1974, pp. 18–24.

HOW YOU CAN GET A CAR FOR A WEEK WHEN YOU AMTRAK TO FLORIDA ON OUR BARGAIN "WEEK OF WHEELS" PLAN.

Here's how it works:

4 round-trip WOW* fares qualify for an intermediate-sized car.

3 round-trip WOW fares qualify for a compact car.

2 round-trip WOW fares, plus $21.00, also qualify for a compact car.

2 round-trip WOW fares, plus a half fare (child age 5-11) and $10.50, also qualify for a compact car. From New York, $111.00 round-trip coach. From Chicago, $116.00 round-trip coach.

Amtrak's round-trip Week of Wheels fares are good from New York or Chicago to the following Florida cities: Orlando, Winter Haven, Tampa, St. Petersburg, West Palm Beach, Ft. Lauderdale, Hollywood and Miami. To determine Week of Wheels fares from connecting points to New York or Chicago, simply add on the regular coach fare. Family Plan discounts

* Week of Wheels

also apply to Week of Wheels fares. If you would like to keep this car an additional week or two, Amtrak has special discount rates.

For our Week of Wheels brochure with all the details, call your Travel Agent. Or write: Amtrak Fulfillment Dept., P.O. Box 4733, Chicago, Illinois 60680, or Amtrak Fulfillment Dept., P.O. Box 3000, Bellmore, N.Y. 11710.

We're making the trains worth traveling again.

Amtrak

EXHIBIT 7
Amtrak "Family Plan" Advertising, 1973

AMTRAK'S FAMILY PLAN. HOW MUCH MONEY WILL IT SAVE <u>YOU</u>?

A lot of people still don't realize how much money they can save traveling together on Amtrak's Family Plan.* Here's how it works:

Head of the family pays full coach fare. (Nobody else does.) The spouse and children twelve through twenty-one pay two thirds. Children five through eleven travel for one third. Children under five usually go free. (One child under five may travel for free for each passenger in your group eighteen or over.)

And train travel gives you so much more to enjoy. Comfortable reclining two-abreast seats, perfect for sightseeing or sleeping. Big picture windows. Plenty of space to move around. (You know how important *that* is when you travel with children.) Delicious meals at modest prices. Even a children's menu on most trains.

Train travel has become the fun way to go. And Amtrak's Family Plan lets you share it together. To find out exactly how much you can save from your city, call Amtrak or your Travel Agent and plan a vacation our way.

All fares shown are one-way coach. Good on trips originating Mondays thru Thursdays only.

Typical Savings on Amtrak's Family Plan	New York to Miami	Chicago to Denver	Los Angeles to Seattle
Father—full fare	$ 55.50	$ 48.50	$ 50.50
Mother—⅔ fare	37.00	32.50	34.00
Children twelve thru twenty-one—⅔ fare	37.00	32.50	34.00
Children five thru eleven—⅓ fare	18.50	16.50	17.00
TOTAL	$148.00	$130.00	$135.50

*Amtrak's Family Plan applies whenever the one-way coach fare is $7 or more, and applies on all Amtrak trains except Metroliners. Family Plan savings also apply to first class travel.

Amtrak

We're making the trains worth traveling again.

EXHIBIT 8
Consumer Comments Received by Amtrak, August—December 1973

	Number of Comments Received	
Categories	**Criticism**	**Praise**
Air Conditioning/Heating	717	29
Equipment Condition	712	313
On-Time Performance	692	90
Personnel	525	746
Reservations	486	35
Schedules	437	159
Food and Beverage	296	404
Consist [1]	266	37
Standees	254	0
Station Services	230	65
Fares & Ticketing	182	44
Other Marketing	173	34
On-Board Services	167	406
Roadbed	132	16
Checked Baggage	103	15
Other General	95	21
Smoking	73	11

Source: Annual Report.

[1] The term "consist" means the number and types of passenger cars used on a train.

In an effort to overcome this, Amtrak planned to introduce standardized parts on its next round of heavy overhauls.

The Summer Capacity Problem. At any given time, Amtrak usually expected to have at least 1,500 cars in operation, out of a total fleet of some 1,900. The balance of the fleet were undergoing scheduled overhauls or were "bad orders"—out of service for maintenance and/or repairs.

Management anticipated that capacity was going to be stretched to the limit during the peak summer months. Some trains were fully booked months in advance, while others were filling fast. Assignment of cars had been carefully planned to make the most efficient use of the limited equipment available.

This expectation of capacity problems was reinforced in early July, when passenger statistics for June became available. These showed that ridership for the first half of 1974 was up by 32% over the previous year (Exhibit 10) although the gain for the month of June was up only 16% over 1973. Accompanying the ridership figures were on-time statistics which showed that although punctuality had improved for short-haul trains, with 82.7% of these arriving on time, only 60.4% of long-haul trains had arrived on time in June, versus 65.1% in the previous month (Exhibit 11).

Hard on the heels of this information came the news that the number of "bad orders" was increasing. It became apparent to management that instead of the 1,500 cars anticipated, they should not count on having more than 1,400 passenger cars in service during the balance of the summer. The issue was raised as to how the corporation should respond to this problem and what action, if any, the Marketing Department should take.

EXHIBIT 9
Statement of Operations for the Years Ended December 31, 1973 and 1972

	1973*	1972*
Operating revenues	$202,093	$162,576
Operating expenses:		
Maintenance of way and structures	4,495	4,958
Maintenance of equipment	65,515	60,001
Traffic	26,517	20,142
Transportation	158,244	129,403
Dining and buffet service	33,285	28,030
General	30,456	37,038
Taxes on payroll and property	21,604	15,727
Equipment rents	5,194	5,798
Total operating expenses	345,310	301,097
Operating deficit	143,217	138,521
General and administrative expense	10,759	7,462
Interest expense	4,651	1,528
Net deficit	158,627	147,511
Accumulated deficit, beginning of year	239,089	91,578
Accumulated deficit, end of year	$397,716	$239,089

Source: Annual Report.

* Thousands of Dollars.

EXHIBIT 10
Amtrak Origin and Destination Count by Route
January—June 1973 vs. January—June 1974

	Daily Frequency (Both Directions Combined)		Total Passengers Carried (000)		
	1973	**1974**	**1973**	**1974**	**% Change**
LONG HAUL SERVICES					
New York City—Florida	6	6	314	497	58
NYC/Washington—Chicago	2	2	110	162	48
NYC/Washington—Kansas City	2	2	105	120	15
Chicago—Florida	2	2	50	84	70
Chicago—New Orleans	2	2	77	111	44
Chicago—Los Angeles	2	2	131	164	25
Chicago—Oakland	2	2	105	163	55
Chicago—Seattle	4	4	256	340	33
Chicago—Houston	1	2	117	152	30
New Orleans—Los Angeles	1	1	45	58	33
Washington—Chicago	2	2	56	63	13
Washington—Montreal	2	2	59	88	49
Los Angeles—Seattle	2	2	123	190	54
St. Louis—Laredo	—	1	—	240	NA
SHORT HAUL SERVICE					
New York City—Washington	69/52/56*	78/58/71*	3,418	4.000	17
New York City—Boston	22/19/19*	22/20/23*	580	884	52
New York City—Buffalo	10	10	215	370	72
Philadelphia—Harrisburg	20/10/10*	24/13/13*	314	433	38
Springfield—New Haven	12/8/10*	14/6/10*	78	113	46
Chicago—St. Louis	4	6/5/5*	111	148	33
Chicago—Milwaukee	10	10	117	129	10
Chicago—Detroit	4	4	73	120	65
Los Angeles—San Diego	6	6	161	214	33
Seattle—Portland	4	4	72	89	24
SYSTEM TOTALS					
First class			203	256	26
Coach			6,722	8,865	32
Grand Total			6,925	9,121	32

Source: Condensed from Amtrak press release.

* Weekdays, Saturday, Sunday.

EXHIBIT 11
Amtrak's On-Time Performance on Key Routes, June 1974*

	Trains Operated	Percent On-Time	
SHORT HAUL	June '74	June '74	May '74
New York–Washington			
Conventional	588	91	84
Metroliners	840	81	67
Boston–Washington	555	92	82
New York–Boston			
Shore Route	142	92	87
Inland Route	470	75	70
Turbotrains	110	53	62
New York–Buffalo	300	77	72
Philadelphia–Harrisburg	500	86	82
Chicago–Detroit	120	78	75
Chicago–St. Louis			
Conventional	69	47	79
Turboliners	110	47	76
Chicago–Milwaukee	303	84	87
Seattle–Portland	180	89	82
Los Angeles–San Diego	180	87	93
Total Short Haul	3,992	83	81
LONG DISTANCE ROUTES			
New York–Chicago	60	7	40
New York–Florida	240	79	82
New York–Kansas City	60	0	5
Seattle–Los Angeles	60	60	81
Chicago–Cincinnati–Washington	60	0	0
Chicago–Florida	120	60	62
Chicago–New Orleans	60	32	18
Chicago–Houston	60	62	71
Chicago–Los Angeles	60	63	74
Chicago–Oakland	60	78	89
Chicago–Seattle	120	75	95
New Orleans–Los Angeles	26	77	52
Washington–Montreal	60	78	82
Total Long Distance	1,191	60	65
Total Amtrak	6,159	77	75

Source: Condensed from Amtrak press release.

---

   * The ICC method of computing on-time performance counted a train as on time if it arrived within five minutes of schedule for each 100 miles traveled, subject to a maximum of 30 minutes for routes exceeding 600 miles.

18
The Richardson Center For The Blind

Roberta N. Clarke
Benson P. Shapiro

In the early spring of 1972, Mr. Ronald Saibot, director of the Richardson Center for the Blind, was reviewing the position and policies of the organization. He thought about a wide range of general policy issues: "Are we doing what we ought to be doing? Are we, in fact, providing the rehabilitation and adjustment for blinded people we think we are providing? Are we serving the people we should be serving?"

There were few other agencies located in the broad area served by the Richardson Center, which provided educational, rehabilitative, and therapeutic services for the blind. One was a school for blind children between the ages of 6 and 18; only children of normal intelligence with no other major handicaps were accepted into this school. In addition, a local state institution for the retarded had a large blind unit which provided limited mobility training and education for the mildly retarded blind. Also, special education departments in the various school systems throughout the state sometimes provided specialized education for blind children capable of maintaining the academic pace of their non-blind classmates.

Beyond these few services of an educational or rehabilitative nature, there were many agencies in the state that provided for the social, emotional, medical, and daily living needs of the blind. They offered such services as social blind get-togethers, shopping and transportation help, reading services (particularly oriented to the elderly and blind college students), and two braille libraries.

BACKGROUND OF THE CENTER

The Richardson Center, of Golden Valley, Minnesota,[1] a nonprofit agency which provided services to the adventitiously blind,[2] began in the 1930s as a custodial home for nonsighted elderly women. Over the years, the Center had changed its orientation from custodial care to rehabilitation. After having started new programs aimed at self-sufficiency and rehabilitation, it discontinued the elderly women's program in 1965. Four major programs were offered by the Center to blind persons in 1972: (1) East House, which offered rehabilitation to the newly blinded who were between the ages of approximately 18 to 60, (2) West House, which accepted people aged 55 and above who had

Roberta N. Clarke is Assistant Professor, School of Management, Boston University. Benson P. Shapiro is Professor of Business Administration, Harvard University.

[1] Golden Valley was a suburb of Minneapolis. The greater Minneapolis metropolitan area had a population of just under 2 million people; this was approximately half of the population of the state of Minnesota.

[2] Blindness can be divided into two broad categories: (1) congenital blindness, which is blindness from birth, and (2) adventitious blindness, in which a sighted person loses his sight through accident, illness or disease.

recently become or were becoming blind, (3) Community Rehabilitation Services, which sent mobility trainers and social workers into the community to work with blind people in their own environment, and (4) the College Introductory Program, which prepared young blind adults to enter college. Other services provided by the Center which did not directly fit into one of their rehabilitation programs were a newsletter, a reader service, and a driving and shopping aid service. There was also a modest research program which included a study on the role of the psychiatrist in the rehabilitation process for the blind.

Philosophy of the Center. During the 1950's and 1960's, the Center was directed by Dr. Pennypacker, a dynamic and charismatic man, around whose philosophy the Center's programs were shaped. Although Dr. Pennypacker had died in August 1970, his philosophy about blindness and how to treat it still inspired the whole agency. He believed blindness to be the greatest physical disability caused by loss of one of the senses, and felt that the human psyche was uniquely affected by the trauma of loss of sight. In order to deal with this trauma, it was felt that a full-time psychiatrist was needed on the staff as an integral part of the rehabilitative process. This thinking was in addition to the previous practice of concentrating on training in working, eating, etc.

Dr. Pennypacker also believed that mobility training was an important but previously unappreciated part of the rehabilitative process, and he instituted into the Center's programs the teaching of the Hoover cane technique. The Hoover cane was longer than a usual cane and was used as a kind of antenna or wand, designed to act as an extension of the blind person's touch senses, to permit him to gain mobility within his community.

The clientele to which the Center chose to address itself was also a function of Dr. Pennypacker's philosophy. Having worked with blinded veterans from World War II, Dr. Pennypacker had perceived the need for rehabilitation for the newly blinded and for older blinded people, but it was apparent that very few services of this nature existed (see Appendix). Therefore, thae Center was changed by Dr. Pennypacker to serve these types of people.

Because of the orientation toward psychiatric treatment and mobility training as part of the rehabilitation and adjustment process, and because of the specific segments of the blind population which they served, the Center management believed that it was unique among organizations dealing with the blind. "We have an idea," said Mr. Saibot. "It is novel and different." This sentiment was echoed by an administrator from the Minnesota State Commission for the Blind, who stated that the Center's programs were offered by no other agencies in the region.

THE REFERRAL PROCESS

The referral process through which blind people were brought to the attention of the center was long and complex. It was relatively easy for a blind person to be dropped or "mislaid" during the process.

The first step in the referral process was that of the blind individual being reported to the Minnesota State Commission so that he or she could be entered into the state register for the blind.[3] This initial contact was made by friends or family, by the individual personally, or by hospitals, clinics or doctors dealing with the individual. Diabetes clinics often reported a number of people for whom the prognosis was poor, since diabetes was the second highest cause of blindness.

In almost all cases, the individual was first diagnosed as being legally blind[4] by an ophthalmologist, who was required by law to report to the state all persons diagnosed as blind. However, the state did not prosecute ophthalmologists who failed to report findings of blindness, and it was estimated by the state agency that fully 20% of the state's legally blind citizens were not reported. The reasons for failure to report were numerous. Ophthalmologists were thought to be unaware of the services available to the blind and saw no advantage to blind people in reporting them. This was particularly true of the elderly blind, for whom it was felt by many physicians that there was no possible or worthwhile rehabilitation. This feeling of futility was also felt by many newly blinded persons, who hoped to avoid some of the "stigma" associated with blindness by not being officially registered as blind. A number of individuals who were legally blind but still had partial sight feared that being entered into the state register would cause them to lose their jobs, and others equated benefits for the blind with welfare or charity.

Once a person had been reported to the state as being legally blind, this blindness would be confirmed by an ophthalmologist (or under certain conditions, an optometrist[5]), and he or she would be entered into the

---

[3] The state register for the blind was a list of all reported blind state citizens, kept for statistical purposes and for the State Commission for the Blind as a list of present and potential clients.

[4] Legal blindness was defined as having visual acuity of 20/200; that is, what a person with excellent vision can see at 200 feet, a person who is legally blind can see at no farther than a distance of 20 feet (with corrected vision, such as glasses).

[5] Optometrists are trained to scientifically examine the eye to detect disease or defects. They may only prescribe correctional lenses or eye exercises. Ophthalmologists are licensed physicians specializing in the study and treatment of defects and diseases of the eye. They are allowed not only to prescribe correctional lenses and exercises, but also to perform surgery and to prescribe drugs.

Minnesota state register within 2 weeks. A social worker from the Minnesota State Commission for the Blind would visit the home of every newly registered person to explain the range of services available to blind people, such as vocational rehabilitation, financial and medical assistance, sheltered workshops[6] and lending libraries. During the visit, the social worker would also ascertain the needs and eligibility of the person and, based on these findings, would make recommendations to the state commission as to what services would most appropriately fulfill the person's needs.

If, at this point, the social worker did not perceive in the client a need or potential for vocational rehabilitation, the client would be offered other services such as the medical and financial assistance mentioned above which the social worker deemed more appropriate. In this case, the client would not be exposed to the availability of vocational rehabilitation services, such as those offered by the Center.

If, on the other hand, it was perceived that the client would benefit from vocational rehabilitation, a vocational rehabilitation counselor from the Minnesota State Commission would be assigned the case, to perform diagnosis and data collection, and to provide an evaluation. If the counselor's evaluation was that the client would not profit from any of the available rehabilitation services, none would be recommended, although all the other non-vocational state services were still available. Otherwise, the counselor would develop a rehabilitation plan for the client, usually with a specific mix of agencies serving the blind to deliver the services. It was then the job of a caseworker from the Minnesota State Commission to contact the agency designated by the vocational rehabilitation counselor to inform it of its potential client. If the client were accepted by the agency, the state commission paid the cost of client services to the agency and the client entered the agency's program. Progress within the program was then monitored by a commission social worker to insure that it was, in fact, matching the client's need.

Difficulties at the State Commission Level. The referral process was fraught with difficulties at the state level. One administrator at the Minnesota State Commission for the Blind stated: "After a rehabilitation counselor has recommended the services of the Center for a newly blind person, people here at the commission may procrastinate about calling the Center about potential clients. Each caseworker here has a workload of 60 to 70 people and is kept very busy just trying to get

the general physical exam and eye reports necessary to complete incomplete files, so that their clients can become eligible for services. With such a heavy workload, routine jobs such as phone call referrals can be overlooked. People from the Center could come here more often to recruit, but they don't—so a client may never make contact with the Center, although he could have been served by the Center."

In a more critical look at his own staff, he stated that the field workers from the Center frequently reminded workers at the state commission of the Center's needs for clients. He estimated that the field worker from East House visited the Minnesota State Commission once every two months and called once a month, and that West House's field worker visited the state agency once every two weeks. In spite of the visits from the two Center field workers, he said that, although recently they had become better informed, many of the commission's social workers knew very little about the Center, and might never recommend that their clients, particularly the aged, see a rehabilitation counselor in order to learn more about the Center.

According to the administrator, approximately two-thirds of the Center's clients came from the Minnesota State Commission for the Blind. "Although their rates are a little higher than we would like, we've always had sufficient funds to cover the cost of sending a client there. Other nearby states, however, have sometimes found their rates prohibitively high, and won't pay the expenses asked by the Center. Of course, we realize that the Center costs more than a training program because it provides room and board and has more trained staff. In addition, East House's and West House's services are both quite unique because there are very few services catering to the adventitiously newly blind adult (East House) and none in this or neighboring states other than West House that serve the geriatric blind. Furthermore, we purchase all of our community mobility training services from the Center, which last year accounted for 137 of the total 286 people receiving any rehabilitation services at all."

DESCRIPTION OF THE CENTER SERVICE PROGRAMS

The Center was composed of four parts directly serving the blind: East House, West House, the College Introductory Program and Community Rehabilitation Services. The first three programs were live-in programs (with a few exceptions) whose facilities were two buildings on the Golden Valley grounds of the Center.

East House. The program at East House, which began in 1954, was a fifteen week course, held three times a year for 17 to 18 newly blinded adults, with ages rang-

---

[6] Sheltered workshops provide steady employment for people with a variety of handicaps who, because of their handicaps, might not be able to find a job in a regular employment situation. These were typically operated on a not-for-profit basis by welfare and charitable organizations.

ing from post-high school to, but not including, old age. The average age of a trainee (client)[7] at East House was forty-two. The program provided adjustment-type rehabilitation training with the twofold purpose of (1) helping the person understand what has happened to him because of the blindness and how to be comfortable with it, and (2) helping the person to acquire the skills to live with blindness. Personal pyschological adjustment to blindness was considered the first step on the way to vocational rehabilitation.

John Hector, who had been the chief administrator of East House since 1968, and who had started working at the Center in 1953, described his job as being "to see that the house (the building housing East House's program) stays full, and to take the necessary steps to fill the house; to keep the staff abreast of what's going on; to be sure that the building meets basic safety standards; to be certain that medical attention is kept up to date; to execute the program (rehabilitation and adjustment training), and to hire and maintain staff and to tell them of our policies and goals."

Another aspect of his job which Hector talked about was "making budget. I submit a budget, but the Board *really* sets my budget. It would be nice if I could pay my staff more money, but I can't because we don't have it. Sometime, soon, we will have to look at our pay scales objectively and bring them up to scale. Another problem is that the facilities for East House are monastic. They barely meet the minimal standards of acceptable living. Our trainees have little or no privacy. There are days when we couldn't take one person extra. We must get better living quarters for these people.

"We also may have a problem because our program is extremely rigid in terms of scheduling. All the trainees come and leave at once; they leave at the end of fifteen weeks even if they could benefit from staying longer. We need more flexibility to meet each person's needs. We're working with a lot of people with personality problems, some of which were brought on by the blindness. We have only seventeen staff members at East House. A number of the staff are part-time people who are experienced, but we have problems in scheduling them because they're often not here when we need them, and we have trouble compiling what we need to do in short spans of time. Maybe what we need is a reorganizing of duties. If we had an interchangeable staff between East House and West House, it would allow for a broadening of experience and skills among the total staff and would probably lessen the inflexibility we presently have.

---

[7] Although the state commission called them clients, the Center called all the people to whom they delivered services "trainees," on the basis that they trained them. The name "trainee" was applied to any person in any of the four programs offered by the Center.

"Referral is not a big problem here, although it is a problem at West House. I met the estimates in trainee numbers here last year, and I don't expect trouble in meeting them in the near—or far—future. There is a problem of logistics in terms of interagency communication. We've had more contact between the Center and the Minnesota State Commission for the Blind lately. Here at East House, we have a good relationship with the Minnesota State Commission because of long established contacts with them, and because I have a lot of personal contact with them. I personally field complaints from them. We're more like a team working together; it's a very comfortable feeling.

"Mr. Saibot has been to visit the commission. He needs to go there once in a while. And our field representative visits them 10 to 12 times a year. The field representative also visits state blindness agencies in neighboring states about six times a year. We've encouraged the counselors at the Minnesota State Commission to visit and they have felt free to come here not necessarily on business. The commission is hiring new counselors and we want to set up a relationship in which the staff and the counselors deal with each other when the counselors come on business rather than dealing only with me."

West House. West House's Geriatric Adjustment Program served the geriatric population of the adventitiously blind. The program it offered was of no specific period of time in length, inasmuch as the length of an individual's stay was dependent on his personal needs. The average length of stay of a trainee was two to two and a half months although the stays ranged from one to five months. Trainees at West House were 55 years old or more. Many of them had other disabilities, in addition to blindness, due to their age.

The program taught the trainees spatial mobility, braille, and personal care while helping them to adjust psychologically to the recent loss of their sight. The program was centered around adjustment to blindness, but, unlike East House, was not vocationally oriented; the age of many of the trainees precluded them from entering the workforce. Some were, however, below retirement age. Others were peripherally related to the workforce. For example, a newly blinded 56 year old woman might learn how to get around the house and kitchen herself so that her husband would not have to quit his job to take care of her, thus helping to keep them both off welfare or social security. Or a blind aged man in a rest home could be taught how to care for his own personal needs and how to use a cane so that he could walk around without help, thus preventing him from being sent to a more expensive, more labor-intensive nursing home.

[handwritten: max 19 avg 10]

The physical capacity of the building housing West House was 18 to 19 beds. However, rarely had there been more than ten trainees in the program at one time. According to a caseworker at the Minnesota State Commission for the Blind, West House could not be financially viable unless it had at least ten beds filled, although he did not believe that West House presently had the staff to serve more than twelve trainees. During most of January 1971, West House had only one trainee. An administrator at the Minnesota State Commission felt that West House's undercapacity was due in part to the fact that aged people tended to be somewhat inflexible and did not change their habits easily. They therefore hesitated to uproot themselves for one to five months to live at the Center. In response to this, West House had recently set up a small, day program in which the trainees went home to sleep every night. However, the number of patients who could benefit from this program was limited by geographical considerations.

West House was opened in 1965, when East House had already been in existence for eleven years. According to Mark Cohen, chief administrator of West House, who had originally worked for East House, the attitude of the staff at West House was "we're second best" because East House was more established and more successful economically. Mr. Cohen continued: "We've always had trouble recruiting trainees to the program and it's been very bad for the morale of the staff. Because of our chronic undercapacity, we have been beset with financial trouble; last year, money was so tight that no one received a raise in the whole Center. Now, we have fifteen trainees, more than ever before. We're now at the point where we're not talking about survival anymore. We're gearing up by adding more staff slowly, as more trainees come in. We're now turning our attention toward the program itself: What are we doing with old blind people? Before, it was assumed that West House's program was taken from East House, but maybe this should not be so."

In spite of the fact that enrollment in the program had recently taken a turn for the better, Mr. Cohen reported that he still felt overwhelmed by the necessity of handling organizational details. He was frequently meeting with other parts of the Center about the kitchen, the dining room and the switchboard, all of which were housed in his building. He recognized that his biggest problem was still the referral process: "When a social worker from the Minnesota State Commission doesn't refer a client to a vocational rehabilitation counselor, as happens particularly often with aged clients, that's it. We never get a chance at that client. We have met with social workers, supervisors, and vocational rehabilitation counselors. We've had to educate virtually everyone at the commission as to what

we were, whom we served, our capabilities, limitations and potential. We call them. We invite them to our staff meetings. We've really worked at communication and have seen, I believe, a great improvement in the past year."

John Hector, of East House, offered his view of West House: "West House has affected the whole Center; they have cost us a tremendous amount, when they had very few trainees. Maybe they ought to be cut off when they cannot support themselves, but I'm not advocating the closing of West House. I don't have any wounded feelings about them, because they have had only an indirect effect upon us. Besides, I don't know what else they could have done. I've never seen people who have tried harder."

Dr. John Kelley, director of research at the Center, felt more strongly that West House should not exist in its present form. Dr. Kelley had held a number of positions over the course of his twenty-three years at the Center. He had been medical director, director of research, part-time administrator of West House and director of rehabilitation services. Presently, he was still serving as medical, research and rehabilitation services director, but research was his prime interest.

"When West House was opened in 1965, it cost a lot of money to get it going. Some of that money was withdrawn from research funds so that almost no money was left for research. Research is still being suppressed because West House has been draining so much of the available funds. Cost effectiveness has been ignored at West House. They began with the idea of providing rehabilitation services to old blind people, but the price they charge for providing these services is too small. They should be asking the Minnesota State Commission for more money per trainee. They're not charging enough for what they deliver, which is a Cadillac package of services.

"Someone on the Board of Directors of the Center will see the light soon and will practice economy. The needs of the elderly blind exist, but what services do you offer them? You can't generalize about the needs of all elderly blind people. The more you offer the same thing to everybody, the more they don't need it. For instance, not all the trainees want to learn braille, yet they all are given classes in braille at West House. They should look into restaffing West House with more generalists and fewer specialists. It would cost less and alleviate staff scheduling problems. But West House really hasn't changed over the past few years."

The College Introductory Program. The College Introductory Program was a six week summer program given to blind young adults about to enter college, as an introduction to college life. The trainees in the program

[handwritten right margin: other say kill West House]

[handwritten right margin: Needs vs Svcs]

[handwritten bottom: MGMNT Problems   Referral]

were not necessarily newly blinded. The trainees, during the six weeks, lived at East House, which was unused at this period each year. There had never been a problem of filling this program to its capacity of 28 people.

Community Rehabilitation Services. Community Rehabilitation Services, which had been in existence since 1952, served clients of all ages in the community who were legally blind or partially sighted. Its staff of ten mobility teachers, one psychiatric social worker and one community social worker served all of Minnesota and parts of neighboring states. They worked at school with blind children, with workers at their jobs, and with patients at nursing homes, among other places. They often educated not only the client himself, but also those around the client, as to how to deal with blindness. Although it varied from client to client, depending upon individual needs, four basic skills were taught: mobility (teaching people how to get around with the use of a cane), handwriting, money distinction and eating (social graces). The number of lessons a client had varied according to his individual needs.

A majority of the referrals came through the Minnesota State Commission for the Blind, a small number came from the Minnesota Department of Special Education,[8] and a small percentage of the clients, who had heard of the Center through word of mouth, or from the mass mailing for fund-raising purposes, called directly without previously having gone through any agency. Priorities as to whom to train first were based on needs, motivations, goals and job of the client. Age was not a priority in either direction.

Community Rehabilitation Services' busiest season was from April to November, because during the winter months, snow made mobility training hazardous. Said Russell Platt, director of Community Rehabilitation Services, "During the busy season, we get more calls than we can respond to." Over the past year, his staff had served 235 people, and Mr. Platt anticipated that the next year would find them with over 400 clients. Some of these clients were adults who were unwilling to be in residence at East House or West House but who still needed the training. Others were legally blind people who were partially sighted, for whom neither East House nor West House had a program.

According to Mr. Platt, one of his major priorities was to hire more mobility instructors, because the demand for them was so great. Only a very few schools, however, had Master's degree programs in this field. Nevertheless, Platt's staff had almost doubled in the past year, and Platt thought that the growth might continue

---

[8] The Department of Special Education handled any child or teenager in the state educational system who, because of a physical, mental or emotional handicap, needed special attention.

for a while because more people could be worked with in the community than in the Center and the potential of his program was just beginning to be recognized.

DISCUSSION OF THE CENTER'S GOALS AND PROBLEMS

Within the Center, there were varying degrees of concern about whom they should be serving and how best to serve whomever their clients might be.

John Hector, of East House, looked at it this way: "There are four different populations with which we can concern ourselves: (1) the geriatric blind who have lived just long enough to develop visual problems, like the clients at West House, (2) the adventitiously blind, non-geriatric population, similar to the population at East House, (3) the congenitally blind, those blind from birth, who tend to be served by academic schools for the young blind, or who are multiply handicapped, and (4) the partially sighted. This fourth group are people who have enough vision so that they are uncomfortable with people who are really blind, but who don't have enough vision to function as a totally sighted person. We sometimes take them at East House, but our program is totally unsuited for them. A new program is needed for them but it would require a different orientation of the staff in order to understand the human makeup of these people. We *don't know* how much they can see and they have difficulty telling what they can see because pride gets in their way. A program for these people would require a different time frame too. It might require more in the way of medical care also, because we would probably be dealing with quite a few diabetics.

"The question to consider is: do we try to create a new program for these people, or try to fit them into our present programs or not serve them at all? The executives' group (the people at the Center in top management positions) stated at one of their meetings in the past year that they would not start anything new that would cost the Center money. Dr. Pennypacker, while he was here, was a great one for starting programs on a prayer. He started new programs so frequently that we could hardly get our heads above water. But people couldn't say no to him because he had a certain charisma, a mystique, about him. Mr. Saibot, who took Dr. Pennypacker's place, has stepped into a tough job.

"In my opinion, the future looks brighter. We know which direction to go in from here. We can't afford any new costly programs now, because our present programs require costly projects. We're doing continued work on referral; we know what populations we're not taking care of and we're looking into what programs we might develop for them. We are hoping to be able to raise salaries and improve the facilities soon."

Mark Cohen, of West House, addressed himself to what he considered to be the general problems of the Center: "Our major problem is money. We can't afford adequate staffing; we need more physical and occupational therapists. The Center is licensed as a rest home, but we need to de-emphasize the nursing qualities. There are, of course, nursing requirements for rest homes and the medical needs of our trainees, but we must lessen the distinction between medical and non-medical personnel. A staff member has to be willing to act in a nursing capacity at one time, and in a teaching capacity at another. It is necessary to mold ourselves to fit our clients, instead of fitting our clients into slots. But the staff hasn't made these adjustments yet. We must also be willing to make changes. Dr. Pennypacker's philosophy had been treated like the Gospel, and no one has yet dared to make any real changes since he left."

The concern of Mr. Saibot, director of the Center, was with questions affecting the total Center, such as referral, flexibility and delivery of services as promised, to both the state agencies and to the trainees. He expressed doubt about the Center's ability to measure how well they were attaining their stated goals. He blamed this inability to measure partially on the lack of followup of former trainees. Because they had no measure of how successful they were, the Center—and the agencies and individuals with whom they dealt—could only take it on faith that they were doing wha they said they were doing, that is, providing rehabilitation and adjustment for blinded people.

The subject of aged blindness particularly interested Mr. Saibot, and much of his discussion centered on it: "We claim to be a leader in aged blindness, but what are we doing to maintain that claim? Is our research (study in the areas of physical rehabilitation, and the role of the psychiatrist in the rehabilitation process for the blind) helping us to substantiate that claim? And is it worthwhile to us in terms of cost effectiveness? And in terms of getting money for our programs, we don't know who to go to. Under current federal legislation, the definition of vocational rehabilitation is very unclear and often does not apply to the aged. Although there is money available for vocational rehabilitation of the blind, it does not often go to programs for the elderly blind because they are seen as not able to be rehabilitated and/or the remainder of their lives may not be spent in what is normally termed a vocation. There is a strong attitude against spending money on the rehabilitation of the elderly. However, the White House Conference on Aging, which I attended in November–December 1971, indicated that the federal administration was becoming aware of 'senior power,' and was willing to consider benefits for the aged.

"We have tried to tailor our program at West House to the elderly. This is unlike the process which most institutions follow. They tend to build a program and then find the people to fit it. They produce a product for which they can receive funds and then they look for their clientele. On the other hand, we saw a need for a program for the aged blind, and tried to build the program around them. Because the elderly present a more complex set of needs, such as medical, psychological and physical, we have had to be more flexible in our thinking about them. We have too many rules, which we must overcome, in order to better cater to their needs."

FINANCING

Most of the trainees at the Center came from Minnesota (over half) or neighboring states, although there were some from quite distant states and a few from foreign countries. The trainees were generally referred to the Center by their state agencies, who bore much of the cost of rehabilitation. The Federal Government reimbursed a percent of each state's rehabilitation cost, but the decision of allocation of funds was left up to the individual state agency. The price per trainee which was asked of the state agencies by the Center covered approximately 60% of the Center's total costs. There were a few states which refused to pay the full price (60%), asked by the Center.

EXHIBIT 1
Comparative Statement of Revenue and Expense
For the Periods Ending 7/3/1971 and 6/27/1970

	53 Weeks Ending 7/3/1971	52 Weeks Ending 6/27/1970
Operating Revenue	$982,937	$804,069
Operating Expenses		
East House Rehabilitation Center	$169,945	$153,085
West House Geriatric Adjustment Center	189,953	169,993
Community Rehabilitation Services	87,417	79,144
Brook Research Program	48,102	28,763
Public Education and Fund Raising	177,961	133,493
Community Services	29,141	65,043
Dietary	66,327	53,667
General and Administrative	222,423	175,831
Total Operating Expenses	$991,269	$859,019
Net Operating Revenue (Loss)	($ 8,332)	($ 54,950)
Other Revenue		
Endowment Fund	$ 3,639	$ 3,655
Crystal Fund	5,251	4,565
Other	3,631	2,359
Total Other Revenue	$ 12,521	$ 10,579
Net Revenue (Loss)	$ 4,189	($ 44,371)

In this case, the Center bore the remainder of the unpaid cost. According to its business manager, the Center had never turned a client away for lack of money.

The other sources of funds which covered the remaining 40% of costs came from unsolicited gifts, bequests, and a demonstration grant from HEW to (1) establish West House as a regional geriatric center, and (2) determine the effectiveness of psychiatric training as part of the rehabilitative effort. The Center had a fund-raising program of general solicitation. They sent out a mass mailing to 350,000 people within the state in an effort to solicit donations and to inform people of the Center's activities. In 1971, the Center held its first Annual Spring Appeal, which was directed at businessmen. (See Exhibits 1 and 2 for financial statements.)

Mr. Wolbarsht, business manager of the Center,

spoke briefly about finances and their effect upon the Center: "The Center is a little stretched for funds; we have occasionally found it necessary to ask the Minnesota State Commission to raise the rates paid us, but our prices are not unreasonable. If we were more affluent, we could be doing some things better. Our physical facilities are lacking, particularly East House, to which we would like to add an addition, but the costs are prohibitive. However, except for the facilities, no trainee has ever been short-changed because of the lack of funds here. We've always given the trainees as much as we have had to give. We're in the process of changing our fund-raising techniques, and have hired a new person whose total job is to raise funds. We think that we can do better in fund raising than we have in the past."

EXHIBIT 2
Comparative Schedule of Operating Revenue
For the Periods Ending 7/3/1971 and 6/27/1970

	53 Weeks Ending 7/3/1971	52 Weeks Ending 6/27/1970
Contract Services Revenue		
East House Rehabilitation Center	$237,960	$231,800
College Introductory Program	18,000	15,000
Total East House Revenue	$255,960	$246,800
West House Geriatric Adjustment Center	142,880	120,035
Community Rehabilitation Services	80,440	68,375
Total Contract Services Revenue	$479,280	$435,210
Fund-Raising Revenue		
Annual Spring Appeal	$28,953	$ 0
Christopher Fund	3,055 $ 32,008	5,027
Mail Program	271,118	236,292
General Gifts	26,701	12,549
Foundation Gifts	3,000	2,000
Special Gifts	13,346	16,502
Memorial Gifts	29,762	29,279
Total Fund-Raising Revenue	$375,935	$301,649
Government and Other Specific Purpose		
Fund Transfers		
Federal Grants	$ 72,770	$ 66,220
Less: Center's Matching Share	34,066	26,468
Net	$ 38,704	$ 39,752
Research Revenue	21,102	489
Net Transfers	$ 59,806	$ 40,241
Bequests	$ 67,916	$ 26,969
Total Operating Revenue	$982,937	$804,069

APPENDIX
Excerpts from "The Blindness System"

Donald Schon

Agencies specifically concerned with the blind exist at the federal, state, and local levels. They fall into two parallel systems, one public and the other private—although the clarity of this distinction has been eroded in recent years as private agencies have sought and received greater amounts of public funds. *There are, in all, approximately 800 agencies for the blind,* both public and private. These differ with respect to the services they provide and the basis on which they are organized. Some are specialized in individual functions, such as Aid to the Needy Blind or residential schools for the blind. Others are large, multifunctional agencies. Still others are consulting agencies or producers and distributors of materials for the blind. In addition to the providers of services, there are special organizations concerned with blindness-related research, both medical and nonmedical, and with manpower training. All these constitute what I will call the *official* blindness system, which provides services specifically to the blind.

The problem of data. The available data concerning blindness in the United States are exceedingly poor—so poor, in fact, that no significant quantitative statement about the system can be made with any high degree of certainty. Consider, for example, the central question of how many blind people there are. At the present time, there are three principal estimates:

Source	Rate per 1000	Total U.S.
MRA Projection to Total (1965)	1.5	290,000
NSPB Fact Book (1965)	2.1	416,000
National Health Survey	5.6	1,090,000

Of the three estimates, the highest is more than 3 times the lowest. These wide variations exist because different agencies use different definitions of blindness, different test methods, and different sampling procedures.

The Model Reporting Areas (MRA) are 14 associated states which maintain registers of persons with severe vision impairment. They define blindness as "visual acuity of 20/200, if the widest diameter of the field of vision subtends an angle no greater than 20°." This is a variant of the standard accepted definition of "legal blindness." The MRA reporting system requires that persons be listed as blind by an ophthalmologist using the standard Snellen charts. There is reason to believe, however, that ophthalmologists underreport blindness: first, by failing to report as blind persons (often relatively well-to-do) those who wish to avoid the stigma of blindness; and second, because many poor and black persons who are legally blind never go to an ophthalmologist.

Nevertheless, the data concerning the numbers of the blind are actually rather better than those concerning the effect or cost of services provided to the blind, or the number of blind persons receiving benefits from agencies not considered blindness agencies.

The mismatch of services and clients. There has been, since the turn of the century, a significant change in the makeup of those people identified as blind. In the period between 1900 and the 1930s, the blind were identified primarily as children and adults of working age. The dominant causes of blindness were war, industrial accident, and disease, and the blind were likely to have only the single handicap of blindness. During the 1930s, federal and state aid to the blind came into being on a significant scale, carried along on the wave of New Deal social legislation. This period of change saw the establishment of certain major programs for the blind. *The sheltered workshop,* publicly or privately supported, trained blind adults for occupations thought to be particularly appropriate to the blind—piano tuner, for example, or broom maker, or vending stand operator. *The school for the blind* provided separate track, physically segregated education for the blind child. And in the early 1940s, state *vocational legislation* promoted rehabilitation for adults of working age. All such programs treated fitness for work and economic indepen-

EXHIBIT 1
National Resource Flows Related to Blindness
(thousands of dollars)

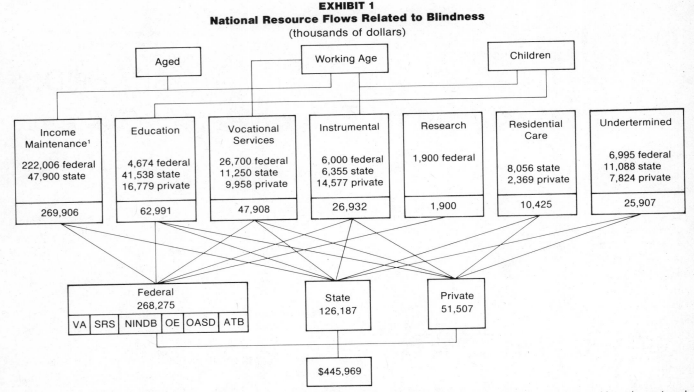

[1] This figure includes $118,130 of Veterans Administration funds which are allocated on the basis of visual impairment and are not limited to legal blindness.

dence through employment as the central tests of rehabilitation.

Today, the makeup of the blind has changed. The population of the severely visually impaired in the United States is now heavily weighted toward (1) the aged blind; (2) the multiple-handicapped, especially among children; (3) the poor ethnic minorities, especially the low-skilled; (4) those with significant residual vision. All sources indicate that a high percentage of the blind are persons over 65, although the estimates vary from 40 percent (MRA) to 65 percent (NHS, which uses a broader, functional definition of blindness). The dominant causes of blindness today are senile degeneration, diabetes, and other multiple etiologies characteristic of old age and, among children, genetic and prenatal influences which tend to be associated with other disabilities in addition to blindness. The over-all pattern, both for the aged and for children, is one of multiple disability. Projections of the prevalence of blindness and the makeup of the blind to 1970 and 1985 suggest that, with the increase in the numbers of persons over 65, these trends will continue.

These developments mean that, for an increasing majority of the blind, economic employment is an unrealistic goal. *Nevertheless, agencies for the blind continue to behave as though this shift in the blind population had not taken place.* In the selection of clients and

the provision of services, their programs are oriented to work or to education leading to work. They measure the success of their services in terms of their clients' achievement of some measure of economic independence. Only a small number of significant exceptions to this general pattern exist within the blindness system.

At the time of its inception, each of these work-oriented programs represented a significant innovation in what was considered humane treatment for the blind. Yet each has tended to become established and frozen in place as an aspect of the way services to the blind "must" operate. Thus, the blindness system today is an array of agencies and services dating from different periods, based on different assumptions concerning the character of the blind population, pursuing different goals, and using different technologies. The effect is rather like complex geological strata in which substances of widely varying origins and characters exist side by side.

The result is that the official blindness system provides services to only a relatively small fraction of those who are actually blind and eligible for assistance. Since the services offered are largely education, rehabilitation, and care, *only about 20 percent of the total blind population are actually being served today.* In general, these 20 percent are either children with the single handicap of blindness or adults of working age and potential for employment. The 80 percent who receive no services tend to be those without apparent potential for employment or educational advancement: the aged, the multiple-handicapped, the poor, and the low-skilled. Such persons are shunted off to other systems which provide minimal income-maintenance or custodial care, or are ignored. A substantial portion of the 80 percent may receive some form of support from the informal system of family, friends, and community.[1]

Why have the design and mix of official services been so unresponsive to changes in the needs and capacities of the blind? The answer is that, for good bureaucratic reasons, agencies tend to behave as if they believed that the blind need, or should have, *the services which happen to be offered by the agencies* rather than that agencies should modify services in response to changing characteristics of the blind population. This is true both of the kinds of services offered and of the methods or techniques by which such services are delivered. To be sure, there are exceptions. But in the case of services designed specifically for the "newer" categories of the blind, the exceptions do not exceed three agencies in each category. And even in the case of services designed for more traditional categories of the blind—mobility training, comprehensive rehabilitation, or training in the use of low vision aids—only a few agencies have shown themselves to be innovative in any significant degree. Taken together, these exceptional, change-oriented agencies constitute only a tiny fraction of the entire official blindness system. The overwhelming pattern remains firmly based on the assumption that "the blind" are employable adults, children with the single handicap of blindness, and the totally blind. The shifting population of the blind has falsified that assumption, yet the pattern of programs remains.

Strategies, constraints. Why does this blindness system behave in such a fashion? One important factor is to be found in the purposes of the organizations and individuals who serve the blind. Now, because the system is in reality a *non*system, there is no group or institution capable of setting a common objective for all elements of the blindness system. Nevertheless, it is clear from the statements of participants and observers that there are three main objectives which enjoy widespread currency, in practice or in rhetoric, within the blindness system:

(1) Minimize the cost to the blindness system of providing services to the blind. This is the principle of "least cost to the system itself."

(2) Minimize the cost to the nation of providing services.

(3) Optimize human functioning for the blind. This objective, frequently voiced by professionals within the system, focuses on what services may enable the blind to *do* or *become*, rather than the economic criteria of performance.

Each of these objectives implies a different strategy for allocating resources and defining configurations of service and coverage.

Least cost to the blindness system. If it were to operate under this principle alone, the blindness system would provide services only to those blind people who are likely to be able to enter the labor force. This way, the system encounters only those who can be trained to leave the blindness system quickly, thereby maximizing turnover rates and minimizing the cost to the blindness system. Hence, the system would select children with the single handicap of blindness and adults of working age and would provide them with education and instrumental and vocational services. The others—multiple handicapped children, adults over 44, etc.—it would either shunt off to other systems or provide with minimal care or maintenance.

Least cost to the nation. Under this principle, the system would operate much as it does under the first principle. The main difference is that, under this second objective, it would be far less selective in providing educational, instrumental, or vocational services. The cumulative costs of income maintenance or custodial care are so great that it is cost-effective to give job-oriented services to all individuals for whom there is *any* finite chance that they will be able to leave the system. The first objective, which does not require the blindness system to bear the costs of long-term maintenance or support of those blind who are unable to work, provides the system with no incentive to behave this way.

Here, the analysis touches on a peculiar and interesting feature of the blindness system. *Those who must decide whether or not to provide services to an individual are institutionally separated from those who stand the cost and trouble of long-term maintenance and care.* The current system's fragmentation removes the incentive to provide services so as to avoid later maintenance and care.

Optimize human functioning. This objective implies that, even if there is no possibility of his gaining economic independence, it is worth devoting resources to a blind person in order to make him function somewhat more independently. This means, in other words, that an additional benefit—personal independence—counts in off-setting costs incurred in the system. The consequence of such an objective, of course, is to increase the cost of operating the system. In 1966, for example, an additional $1 billion (on a base of about $446 million) would have

---

[1] See the study conducted by the Bureau of Labor Statistics for the American Foundation for the Blind, "National Survey of Personnel Standards and Personnel Practices and Services for the Blind—1955."

been needed for a blindness system which attempted to maximize human functioning. A very large portion of that increase would have gone for services to the aged.[2]

In terms of these three models, the current blindness system is a hybrid. With respect to the way in which it determines what categories of the blind shall receive services, it functions according to the principle of the least cost to the system itself. Those blind without high potential for gainful employment are either ignored or shunted off to other systems (such as welfare, veterans' care, etc.). But with respect to those whom it *does* select for training or care, the blindness system tends to behave as if its purpose were to optimize their human functioning. Its expenditures on the blind it chooses to encounter are high.

The sources of innovation. During the past 25 or 30 years, there have been a few significant innovations in serving the blind. Because new technologies and methods must play a large role in any improvement in service to the blind, it seems worthwhile to consider two of the more interesting cases of innovation.

The only important technical innovation in travel for the blind in this century has been the "long cane" method, which is the invention of Dr. Richard Hoover. It consists in replacing the old orthopedic cane with a light, long cane, the purpose of which is to sense the environment rather than to serve as a support. The long cane precedes the training foot in an oscillating motion and permits the skillful user to move rather

rapidly over varied terrain. Hoover, a former physical education instructor, developed the cane while serving in a U.S. Army group set up to provide rehabilitation for blinded World War II veterans. At the time, accepted practice in the blindness system was to assume that the blind have little capability for travel and that what little such capability could be developed required instruction from a teacher who was himself blind. (This approach is still in currency in many sectors of the blindness system.) The group of blind veterans were for the most part vigorous and healthy. They found that little or no rehabilitation had been prepared for them, and they besieged the commanding general, pounding with their canes on his desk, demanding the program they had been promised. It was in this context that Hoover was given an opportunity to develop and teach his method. That method was revolutionary in its assumptions that the blind could travel independently, that a long antenna-like cane could help them, and that a sighted instructor could teach them.

The introduction of the long cane technique was an unusual event which was quite out of keeping with the traditional behavior of the blindness system. Seen against the backdrop of such traditional behavior, three special circumstances characterize its introduction. First, the champion of the invention was an "outsider." Hoover had previously worked in blindness agencies, but merely as a physical education instructor. It was only later that he became an ophthalmologist. Second, the invention was precipitated by a dislocating, crisis-like event for which the system had no prepared response. And third, there was a strong and active group of blind clients who were in a position to make demands and to enforce them.

[2] Although the money costs of this third system are important, the problem of manpower resources constitutes an even more powerful constraint.

19

Consumer Energy Conservation Policy in Canada: Behavioural and Institutional Obstacles

Gordon H. G. McDougall
Randolph B. Mank

If consumer energy conservation policy is to succeed in Canada, both behavioural and institutional obstacles must be identified and overcome. The behavioural barriers, identified through a national household survey, include consumer resistance to policies that affect their lifestyles. The institutional barriers, obtained from a series of interviews with government officials, include weak federal-provincial relations. Viewed from a federal perspective, these obstacles are discussed and then linked to policy types. A prior understanding of the obstacles which a particular programme type is likely to face should allow more effective execution of the programme and enhance the probability of success.

At the heart of Canada's energy strategy is the realization that residential energy consumption must decline in order that the goal of energy self-sufficiency may be reached [1]. Indeed, Canada holds the dubious distinction of having the highest per capita energy consumption in the world. While geography and climate accounts to some extent for this position, there can be little doubt that consumer behaviour is also responsible. The task of altering these behaviours has broad implictions. It is a task which is inseparable from Canada's stated goal of self-sufficiency, which itself has

Gordon McDougall is a Professor in the School of Business and Economics, Wilfrid Laurier University; Randolph Mank is a doctoral candidate in the Department of Government, London School of Economics. The authors would like to acknowledge the support of Consumer and Corporate Affairs, Canada. The consumer data discussed in this article was collected by the first author and John D. Claxton, University of British Columbia, and J. R. Brent Ritchie, The University of Calgary.

grown from a wariness of dependence on foreign oil and a worsening balance of payments problem.

If energy conservation policy is to succeed in Canada, two groups of obstacles will have to be overcome. They can be described generally as behavioural/attitudinal and institutional obstacles. The behavioural/attitudinal obstacles are manifested in consumer resistance to energy conservation. There are deeply entrenched ways of thinking and behaving with respect to energy use which can be attributed to an era of inexpensive energy.

The institutional obstacles are visible in the inability of traditional government mechanisms to cope effectively with the energy problem as it relates to the consumer. From the federal perspective, the institutional obstacles in Canada include intra- and inter-departmental organization, the federal political structure, and a lack of government-industry cooperation. If the federal government is to achieve its stated aims it will need to address and to some extent eradicate these obstacles.

In this paper, the behavioural/attitudinal and the institutional obstacles are delineated in such a way as to reveal their complementarity. That is, in order to encourage energy conservation, it is necessary for the federal government to proceed on both fronts. The argument is developed in two parts. The first part uses primary data from over 2,000 Canadian households to describe and explain consumers' attitudes and behaviours, and the second uses the results of a series of interviews with officials from industry and federal and provincial governments to identify the major structural obstacles to energy policy formulation and implementation at the federal level in Canada. The broad objective is to link policy types with the obstacles which they are most likely to encounter, and thus to underline the need for programme implementation strategies which anticipate specific obstacles.

BEHAVIOURAL OBSTACLES

To achieve the energy goals set for Canada it is necessary to reduce demand in the consumer sector. A number of policies are available, ranging from appeals for voluntary consumer reductions to mandatory regulations. Past research has indicated that energy conservation programmes fall within the typological framework depicted in Exhibit 1 [2]. That is, a programme can be one of four types:

- a voluntary/non-financial programme which provides information and advice on how to conserve energy;
- a voluntary/financial programme with offers tax and price incentives to encourage particular conservation measures;
- a mandatory/non-financial programme which restricts the availability of energy or energy-inefficient products; and
- a mandatory/financial programme which imposes financial penlties on all consumers who refuse to conform to regulations or laws governing energy use.

Often it is difficult to separate voluntary from mandatory policies. For example, a policy of increased energy prices might at first glance appear to be mandatory/financial. Clearly such a policy would make it mandatory for suppliers to charge higher prices. But to the consumer the policy is voluntary/financial. That is, the consumer's decision to reduce energy consumption would be based on how much he could afford or would be willing to pay, and his perception of the value of energy relative to the value of those things he must give up to maintain his level of energy consumption. Though the consumer is pressured to conserve, it is by no means mandatory that he do so.

But pricing policy is a special case. Other policies providing home insulation grants and home audits are truly voluntary. They in no way restrict the consumer's market choices.

Clearly, from a political and a philosophical viewpoint voluntary policies are preferable. However, the success of these types of policies is dependent upon the support and participation of the majority of the population. To determine the support, or lack thereof, for a variety of energy policies a national Canadian consumer survey was undertaken. The objectives were:

- to determine current energy consumption and conservation patterns including attitudes towards the energy issue;
- to identify major groupings of households based on actual energy consumption;
- to relate these major groupings to situational, demographic and attitudinal factors; and
- to initiate a comparative analysis of consumer receptivity to alternative energy conservation policy proposals.

The research objectives led to a database that included information on:

- Annual household energy consumption in terms of home heating energy, electricity and petrol.
- Dwelling, electrical appliance, and car characteristics.
- Home heating, electrical appliance and car use habits.
- Family demographics.
- Female and male head of household:

  > general and energy-specific conservation attitudes;
  > household energy conservation knowledge;
  > household energy conservation activities; and
  > household preferences for different government
  conservation actions.

THE SAMPLE

The data were collected from three main sources [3]. An initial survey of 2366 Canadian households (a total of 3000 consumer panel members of a marketing research firm were initially contacted) was made from which information was obtained on energy consumption, situational and demographic factors and the energy views of the male and female head of the household. A further survey of 1587 of the same households (1952 home owners who responded to the initial survey were contacted) was carried out to obtain information on detailed household characteristics using the questionnaire designed for the ENER$AVE programme (a Canadian home audit information programme). In addition, degree-day data (the number of degrees that the daily average temperature is below 65°F, summed over a year) were obtained for each household surveyed.

EXHIBIT 1
Energy Conservation Programme Types

	Non-financial	Financial
Voluntary	Home audits	Home insulation grants and loans
Mandatory	Rationing	Licensing fees

EXHIBIT 2
Perceived Seriousness of Selected Issues in Canada (1975–81)

Issue[a]	Mean Rating by Year[b]								
	1975	1976	1977	Spring 1978	Fall 1978		1979	1980	1981
					Male	Female			
Inflation	3.63	3.55	3.58	3.60	3.64	3.77	3.55	3.62	3.56
Unemployment	3.11	3.19	3.53	3.78	3.26	3.42	3.45	3.30	3.20
Energy shortage	2.32	2.88	2.92	2.84	2.50	2.90	2.78	2.93	2.69
Cost of energy	n/a	n/a	n/a	n/a	3.35	3.52	3.24	3.28	3.24
Number	1422	1436	1413	1409	1833	2212	1654	1637	1606

[a]Question: I would like you to think about the following issues and tell me how seriously you feel each one is affecting us in Canada today. Would you say it is very seriously affecting Canada, somewhat seriously, not too seriously, or not seriously at all?

[b]Data for Fall 1978 is from the survey described in this paper. Data for all other time periods is from a longitudinal telephone survey conducted in seven major Canadian cities and sponsored by Energy, Mines and Resources, Canada and Consumer and Corporate Affairs, Canada. Rating was done on a scale of 1 to 4 where 1 was 'not serious' and 4 was 'very serious.'

Because the households surveyed were part of a consumer panel of a professional research firm, some biases were expected relative to the total Canadian population. The major difference between the sample and the overall population was home ownership. Approximately 4 out of 5 households (84%) in the sample owned or mortgaged their homes whereas only about 3 out of 5 (62%) Canadians own their homes. The major implication of this difference is that household energy consumption for the sample will be higher than the national average (i.e., homeowners tend to consume more energy than flat dwellers).

It was considered desirable to have this bias in the survey because there is a greater potential for energy saving among home owners, who naturally have more control over their energy use. Policies such as financial incentives to insulate homes are more relevant for those who pay energy costs directly and, for this reason, homeowners are the target audience for most domestic conservation policies.

It is difficult to establish policies for the 38% of the population who rent their accommodation. They are unlikely to invest in insulation, even with financial incentives, because it is not their property and hence they cannot recoup their investment. Further, the landlord is unlikely to re-insulate the dwelling because the tenant normally pays the heating bill in individual dwelling units and in multiple dwelling units (i.e., apartment buildings), there are considerable technical problems in re-insulating.

Comparisons with a number of other socio-demographic characteristics indicate that, other than home ownership differences, the sample reflects the Canadian population [4].

Consumer Perception of the Energy Issue.

As shown in Exhibit 2, the perceived seriousness of the energy shortage issue reached a peak in 1980 and, like the other issues listed, declined in 1981. Relative to other issues, energy scarcity was ranked lowest in each year. Although consumers see energy scarcity as an important issue they do not see it as *the* most important or even the second most important issue in Canada. This evaluation, whether right or wrong, provides the policy maker with a rough guide to consumer priorities. Clearly the cost of energy is seen as a more important issue than scarcity, which suggests that consumers may look with incredulity upon any attempt to increase prices on the basis of energy scarcity.

On the whole, Canadians are more concerned with inflation and unemployment than with the energy issue. This finding indicates that radical policies such as petrol rationing, penalizing excessive energy use, or raising the price of energy by a substantial amount are not politically feasible. Indeed, such a cure would surely be seen to be worse than the ailment. To justify such severe measures, the government would need to convince the public that links exist among these issues. A public convinced of the interconnections among inflation, unemployment, and energy scarcity would be more likely to believe that tough action on one could lead to correction of the others.

Attitudes Towards the Energy Issue.

Through factor analysis, four scores indicating attitudes towards the energy situation were developed. For the sake of brevity, only the attitudes for the male head of household are reported in Exhibit 3. The results illustrate the somewhat incongruous attitudes held.

While respondents agree most strongly with the notion that individual efforts are important in energy conservation, they also agree that the cause of the energy problem is business and government. Further, while they agree that energy conservation is important for the future, they are not willing to accept restrictions on energy consuming activities. There appears to be an underlying 'I'm alright Jack' syndrome. People agree that it is important to conserve energy, and that individual efforts can help but they are

EXHIBIT 3
Attitudes Towards the Energy Situation—Four Dimensions

Attitude	Number of Questions	Alpha	Mean Rating[a]	Standard Deviation
Importance of energy conservation, now for the future	5	0.80	3.94	1.15
Impact of individual efforts important in energy conservation	6	0.69	4.30	0.98
Willingness to accept restrictions on energy consuming activities	5	0.59	2.35	1.00
The cause of the energy problems is business and government	4	0.62	4.03	1.05

$N = 1858$

[a]Rating was done on a scale of 1 to 6 where 1 was 'definitely disagree' and 6 was 'definitely agree.'

unwilling to support activities which may affect their current behaviour or lifestyle.

From a policy maker's viewpoint, these consumer attitudes are somewhat discouraging. Canadians appear to be paying little more than lip service to the energy conservation issue. Any effort to increase their concern is likely to have little impact, judging from the very limited success of the publicity and advertising programmes of the past few years. Further, the negative response to any notion of curtailing energy consumption clearly limits the policy options available to the decision maker.

Self-Reported Energy Conserving Activities. Energy conserving activities were measured in three areas: general, in-home, and travel. In each of the areas there was a wide range of responses which reflected the degree of difficulty of the effort or monetary investment required. In the areas of in-home and travel related consumption, relatively easy activities were performed by over 50% of the sample (e.g., car tuning), whereas more difficult tasks, such as furnace modification or tasks which affect personal lifestyles such as the use of public transport, were performed by only about 10% of the respondents.

For policy makers the implications are that people seem to be willing to engage in simple conserving behaviours that do not change their lifestyles to any significant degree. Unfortunately, major energy savings require fairly major changes by the consumer (e.g., furnace retrofit, insulation). Attempts to increase the percentage of people engaging in the major energy saving activities would probably require either financial incentives or mandatory regulations. The impact of advertising alone (either of a persuasive or informative nature) is likely to be minimal.

Policy Preferences. Respondent preferences for five conservation actions which might be imposed by governments were examined for home heating, electricity, and petrol consumption (Exhibit 4). In all three areas, the order of preference for the five potential actions is such that it seems individuals attempt to minimize the direct impact of the regulation on themselves. In all cases doubling the price of

the energy type was the least preferred option. The general implications of these results are:

- that policies and programmes which are based on voluntary participation will meet with the least consumer resistance, but will also have limited conservation impact;
- that policies which result in substantial price increases or restrictions of energy supply will meet with serious consumer resistance; and
- that policies which address standards for product energy consumption and insulation will meet with limited consumer resistance and will offer reasonable conservation gains because of the mandatory aspect of the policy and the relative size of the energy savings [5].

Energy Consumption Profiles. Based on actual energy consumed for one year, households were classified within an energy taxonomy and then profiled on the basis of socio-economic characteristics. Households were placed in one of nine categories (a 3 × 3 matrix) depending on whether their petrol consumption level was low; medium or high (as determined by the distribution of consumption over the sample) and whether their consumption level for in-home energy was low, medium or high. The four extreme categories and the average category within the taxonomy were then labelled. The labels and corresponding descriptions are:

- Churchmouse—low user of energy for both home and car;
- Bear—low user of energy for the car but high in-home user;
- Roadrunner—low user of in-home energy but high car user;
- Hippo—largest energy user, high in-home and car; and
- Beaver—average energy user for both in-home and car.

The rubric 'poor as a churchmouse' aptly fits those classified as low energy users in the home and the car (Exhibit 5). On every characteristic indicating economic well-being, the 'churchmice' are considerably below any other energy type and the sample average. They annually consume approximately 20% of the BTUs (expressed as 10^6) that 'hippos' consume (97.8 versus 507.2) and approximately 33% that of the sample average. The 'churchmice' have the lowest incomes, number of appliances, number of finished rooms, and number of vehicles. 'Churchmice' appear to be low

EXHIBIT 4
Preference for Government Policy Actions[a]

Sector	Possible Action[b]	Rank Order of Preference
Home heating	Double price of heating fuel	5
	Heavy surcharge for fuel over minimum (65°F)	4
	Compulsory annual furnace inspection/maintenance	1
	Required home insulation standards in 5 years	2
	Upgrading of furnace standards every 3 years	3
Electricity	Double price of electricity	5
	Two price system 'surcharge for peak periods'	3
	Tax on energy inefficient products	2
	Heavy surcharge on electricity over household allowance	1
	Rotating blackouts during peak periods	4
Petrol	Double price of petrol	5
	Limit of 10 gallons/week—heavy surcharge on additional amounts	4
	High license for large cars	3
	Speed limits at 50 mph with loss of license for violators	1-2[c]
	Allow only cars giving 50 mpg by 1981	1-2

[a]Question: The government could take steps to reduce energy consumption by consumers of gasoline, home heating fuel and electricity. Read each of the five actions, and, assuming the government was considering implementing them, decide which one you feel is most acceptable; write in "First" beside that action. Decide the one you feel is least acceptable, and write in "Fifth" beside it. Then decide the order of the other three, writing "Second," "Third," and "Fourth" beside them.

[b]Expressions describing possible actions have been abridged.

[c]Two actions tied for first and second place.

energy users because of economic circumstances, not because of a 'conserver' lifestyle.

The contrast between 'bears' and 'roadrunners' reveals the impact of different lifestyles on energy consumption. While both have similar incomes (around the sample average), 'bears' have used their incomes to buy larger homes (but surprisingly not more appliances) and 'roadrunners' have used their incomes to buy cars. The result is that 'bears' have about 33% more furnished rooms and one less car than do 'roadrunners.' The difference in lifestyles is due, in part, to differences in ages ('roadrunner' males are 19 years younger than 'bears') and in locales ('bears' tend to live in colder climates).

'Hippos' are virtual opposites to 'churchmice.' On all measures of economic well-being they lead the way, often by a considerable margin (e.g., their average income is $7000 *more* than the sample average, and they own one car *more* than the sample average). The consequence is an annual energy consumption rate that is more than double the sample average.

The 'beavers,' those using average or medium amounts of in-home energy and petrol, represent the average Canadian. Comparing the 'beavers' characteristics to the sample average reveals no differences between the two. In all respects, from income to appliances, 'beavers' are close to or on the median. They exhibit a lifestyle that is relatively energy intensive.

An attempt was also made to profile the groups in terms of their attitudes towards the energy situation. No

significant differences were found between the groups on the basis of the four attitudinal measures (both male and female attitudes were analysed) discussed earlier. This finding is consistent with other studies which have concluded that variations in energy consumption could not be explained by attitudes towards conservation [6]. The results offer further support for the notion that household energy consumption levels are determined primarily by economic circumstances, rather than attitudes held.

The profiling of households by level and source of energy use provides the policy maker with the necessary information for selecting target markets for programmes and for estimating the possible effects of those programmes on the targets. For example, increases in energy prices will impact primarily on the non-discretionary income of the 'churchmice' and the discretionary income of the 'hippos,' Similarly, programmes directed at in-home energy consumption are likely to have little spill-over effect on petrol consumption (the correlation between in-home and petrol consumption was surprisingly low, $r = 0.23$). Finally, the profiles can be used as baseline data for evaluating the effectiveness of conservation programmes implemented in the short-term.

INSTITUTIONAL OBSTACLES

If energy consumption patterns are to be changed, the first step must be to overcome the institutional or structural obstacles which hinder concerted action. To discover the

EXHIBIT 5
Energy Types by Selected Characteristics

Characteristics	Churchmouse	Bear	Roadrunner	Hippo	Beaver	Total Sample
Annual BTU consumption ($\times 10^6$)	97.8	260.9	304.6	507.2	254.3	275.1
Socio-economic characteristics:						
household income ($)	13600	20270	19530	27210	19910	19910
age (male head of household)	55	58	39	46	48	48
number in household	2.9	3.1	3.9	4.6	3.6	3.7
appliance index	21	23	26	33	28	27
Dwelling characteristics:						
number of finished rooms	6.5	8.2	6.9	8.5	7.3	7.4
Vehicle characteristics:						
number of vehicles	0.6	0.8	1.9	2.5	1.5	1.5
Regional characteristics:						
degree days	8100	8828	8291	8753	8453	8428

nature of these obstacles a series of 25 personal and 20 telephone interviews were conducted. The interviews were semi-structured and a series of questions was used to stimulate discussion within certain areas. The areas included the following:

- current energy conservation programmes;
- evaluation studies of current energy conservation programmes;
- energy conservation programmes under consideration; and
- institutional obstacles to energy policy formulation and implementation.

Additional issues were dealt with as they arose and respondents commented freely on other aspects of the energy problem.

Officials were selected on the basis of their involvement in the energy policy process. Within Canada this involvement was at various levels including the federal and provincial governments, industry, and research institutes. Thirty-four of the interviews were conducted in Canada, the remaining 11 with individuals in the USA and Europe. The interviews outside Canada were conducted for the purpose of other research objectives but also served to put the Canadian experience in an international context.

The first objective of the interview process was to identify the major obstacles to energy conservation policy formulation and implementation in Canada. The second objective was to determine the degree to which the obstacles impacted on the four major policy types (referred to earlier in Exhibit 1).

One implication of determining the impact of various obstacles on the policy types is that it provides a prescription for the path of least resistance. But, more important, such an analysis provides the decision maker with an understanding of the obstacles to be overcome in formulating and implementing any *type* of energy conservation programme.

The need for such an understanding is great. Conservation programmes which are clearly cost-beneficial are not always implemented if they are faced with a host of political/structural obstacles. Using price as a mechanism for conservation is a case in point. In financial terms, it costs the federal government nothing to increase the price of energy; and certainly a substantial increase would deter many consumers from wasting energy. But the political obstacles to such a measure are enormous. In fact the 1980 Canadian federal election was lost by the Progressive Conservatives partly because they proposed to increase the price of oil to Canadian consumers.

A prior understanding of the obstacles which a particular programme type is likely to face would facilitate a more effective 'selling' of the programme. Indeed, programme design by itself is inadequate in the Canadian context. It must be coupled with a strategy for overcoming anticipated obstacles to implementation.

Four major obstacles to energy conservation policy formulation and implementation were identified in the research. They are federal-provincial relations, intra-departmental organization, inter-departmental overlap, and lack of government-industry cooperation. What follows is a general discussion of these obstacles with one or two examples of each. Respondents have been promised the usual confidentiality and will therefore not be identified by name.

Federal-Provincial Relations. The most common response is that federal-provincial relations need to be improved to allow for the effective implementation of conservation programmes. At the federal level, one senior official in the Department of Energy, Mines and Resources expressed the view that the central and provincial governments were 'at war' over the issue of energy policy jurisdictions. On the other side, a provincial official in the Ontario Ministry of Energy, indicated a resentment of the federal government's tendency to institute conservation measures without first consulting the provinces [7]. A similar sentiment was expressed at the provincial level in Alberta.

One major point of contention was the federal government's handling of the Canadian Home Insulation Programme (CHIP). The programme was designed to encourage home insulation through financial incentives in the form of taxable grants. It was to be administered by the Central Mortgage and Housing Corporation (CMHC), a branch of the federal government. Unfortunately, the provinces were not informed of the programme until a few hours before it was announced to the press in 1976.

To exacerbate the problem, the federal government decided, on the basis of consultations only with Quebec, that the responsibility for administering CHIP would be transferred early in 1980 from the CMHC to the appropriate housing ministries of the provinces. Though each province has some form of housing administration, few have the administrative machinery to handle a home insulation programme. The transfer will result in considerable expense in terms of both financial resources and man-years for each province.

The reason for the jurisdiction problem can be traced as far back as the British North America (BNA) Act which in 1867 laid down the operating principles for the then new country. While the provinces were given jurisdiction in the area of property and civil rights (BNA, S91, ss13), the dominion was allowed to legislate in matters of interprovincial and international trade (BNA, S91, ss2). The federal government was also given the power to legislate in all matters affecting the 'peace, order, and good government' of the country (BNA, Preamble). Constitutionally, then, the potential for jurisdictional dispute on matters of energy supply and demand has been great from the very beginning.

While the federal government can control the sale of a province's energy resources to other provinces or countries, a province can determine the way in which the energy will be used within its borders [8]. There is no dispute over the ownership of resources. The BNA Act stipulates that all lands, mines, minerals and royalties shall belong to the provinces (BNA, s.109). On the other hand, if the energy problem becomes serious to the extent that it affects the peace, order and good government of Canada, presumably the federal government could legislate in matters relating to energy use as well. At present, however, each provincial government has an energy department which in turn has a conservation policy branch. The result is that 11 separate government departments are legislating in the same area, with little coordination among them. Consumers often receive mixed signals from the provincial and federal governments and from industry.

The problem is made worse by the fact that the relationship beteen the 'have' and the 'have-not' provinces is based on supply and demand. That is, the new 'have' provinces, Alberta, Saskatchewan and soon Newfoundland, supply the new 'have-not' provinces, Ontario and Quebec, with energy resources. Because Ontario and Quebec are centres for manufacturing in Canada, their economic base is totally reliant on the supply of energy from provinces which in the past resented the economic and political dominance of the east.

The shifting of wealth from east to west has been sudden and drastic. Ontario, once considered the most resource-rich province, received revenues of about $14 per capita from resource development in 1978. During the same year, Alberta received revenues from resources amounting to round $1900 per capita. It is estimated that Alberta's revenues will at least double by the end of this decade, making the transfer of wealth irreversible [9]. One can assume that federal-provincial and interprovincial relations will be strained even further as economic power continues to grow out of proportion to political power.

Intra-Departmental Organization. The second most often mentioned obstacle to effective energy conservation policy formulation and implementation is intra-departmental organization at the federal level. For example, the 'Ener$ave' programme, which offers free home audits for Canadian homeowners, has been left virtually leaderless as a result of a dispute within Energy, Mines and Resources over promotions. While one would expect to find a certain amount of rivalry within any large organization the extent to which bruised egos can deter the effective formulation and implementation of conservation programmes should not be understated.

In addition, communication within the departments is often not conducive to well integrated policy output. Again, within Energy, Mines and Resources, the junior and intermediate level staff have very little contact with the senior level officials. This problem may be a result of the frequent shifting of the senior actors which in turn is a result of relatively frequent elections and cabinet shuffles.

But the communication problem at Energy, Mines and Resources goes much deeper. Up to October 1966, it was called the Department of Mines and Technical Surveys, an indication of the highly scientific matters dealt with at that time. When the responsibility for energy matters was given to the department late in 1966, a new administrative arm was grafted onto the existing organizational body. A tripartite structure still exists. The Mineral Policy and the Science and Technology Branches continue to be highly technical, while the Energy Policy Branch is less so.

The result is that there is somewhat of a language barrier between the scientific and the nonscientific professionals. The Conservation & Renewable Energy Branch (CREB), which promotes the 'soft-path' solutions to the energy problem, is even less technical in nature. CREB's difficulty lies in convincing technically oriented people that the solution to the energy problem is not necessarily a technological one.

Inter-Departmental Overlap. Rivalry among the departments involved in the energy policy process is common at the federal level in Canada. Indeed, besides Energy, Mines,

---

EXHIBIT 6
Federal Department Involvement in Energy Policy

National Research Council	Increase energy efficiency in commercial buildings and residences; energy conservation and storage
Transport Canada	Increase energy efficiency in the transport system
Agriculture Canada	Improve energy efficiency in the food supply system
Energy, Mines and Resources	Thermal energy waste management; increase energy efficiency in the burning of coal, oil and gas
Fisheries and Environment	Municipal and industrial waste energy
Industry, Trade and Commerce	Increase energy efficiency in industrial processes
Urban Affairs Canada	Location and urban form
Consumer and Corporate Affairs	Consumer products and behavior
Public Works	Improve energy efficiency in government buildings

Source: Energy, Mines and Resources, *Energy Conservation in Canada: Programs and Perspectives*, Report EP-77-7, Canada, 1977.

---

and Resources, the Departments of Industry, Trade and Commerce, Consumer and Corporate Affairs, Transport, Environment, and Public Works, to name a few, all have significant input into energy policy. Exhibit 6 provides some details of departmental involvement in this area. In one sense, the table shows the pervasiveness of the energy problem in Canadian government today. But in another sense it suggests a certain amount of overlap.

The competition between Energy, Mines and Resources and Consumer and Corporate Affairs is particularly enlightening. The mandate of the CREB is to advise, formulate, and implement on all matters relating to wise energy use. Consumer and Corporate Affairs has within its organizational structure a Consumer Research Sector which is involved in documenting the consumer side of the energy problem. In practice, overlap clearly exists. Energy conservation studies conducted by Consumer and Corporate Affairs are funded by the Interdepartmental Panel on Energy Research and Development which is a part of Energy, Mines and Resources.

The result is that research activities within a branch of one federal department are being funded by another federal department. Moreover, the funding department has within its organization a branch (CREB) which presumably is mandated to conduct just such research. For Consumer and Corporate Affairs the problem is one of bureaucratic control. Indeed, this department can have no meaningful input into energy policy unless it funds and makes use of its own energy research. Most officials agreed that the energy policy efforts of the two departments should be merged, or at least more effectively coordinated.

LACK OF GOVERNMENT-INDUSTRY COOPERATION

The fourth most often mentioned obstacle is the lack of government-industry cooperation. The most illustrative example of this is Consumer and Corporate Affairs' efforts to implement an energy labelling programme. 'Energuide' is aimed at the manufacturers of large household appliances. Through the programme, energy efficiency labels are placed on the appliances and a booklet containing the energy efficiency ratings of the products is distributed to the consumer. Because of strong pressure from the Canadian Manufacturers Association (CMA) and the Canadian Appliance Manufacturers Association (CAMA), it was decided that the approach adopted in the USA, whereby a large number of appliances would be targeted, an efficiency rating for each appliance would be given, and dollar cost of the appliance's likely energy consumption would be displayed, could not be used in Canada. Instead, it was decided to focus on one appliance at a time.

The first target was the refrigerator. Consumer and Corporate Affairs wanted a label placed on the outside of all new refrigerators stating the energy rating of the unit. The ratings were done in conjunction with the Canadian Standards Association, Ontario Hydro, and the Canadian Electrical Association. In the end the label was placed on the inside of the refrigerator where it was not readily visible to purchasers. In the case of other appliances such as electric ranges, dishwashers, and clothes washers, the label has been placed on the outside and only after time-consuming negotiations. The current target is the clothes dryer. Even the seemingly minor energy conservation measures, then, often meet with great resistance. Of course to industry the measures are far from minor. For example, since the publication of the first Energuide booklet, 30% of the refrigerators have been re-designed. The result has been an average 20% reduction of energy use for re-designed appliances [10]. Such improvements in other major appliances would result in significant reductions of household energy consumption.

Though the federal political structure [11], intra-departmental organization, inter-departmental overlap, and the lack of government-industry cooperation are the most commonly mentioned obstacles, they are by no means the only ones. Fiscal restraint, for example, means that the government is unwilling to begin expensive new projects. The priority position of supply issues means that the bulk of federal money is being channelled into the development of new energy resources. The most expensive of these is the nuclear power programme, which of course has yet to meet with public approval.

Finally, the energy intensive infra-structure which was developed during the years of cheap energy now constitutes a drain on available energy resources. To change the infra-structure is both expensive and time-consuming. Consider, for example, the cost of altering transport modes and meth-

EXHIBIT 7
Barriers to Conservation Programmes

	Non-financial	Financial
Voluntary	Behavioural barriers: high Institutional barriers: low Example: Advertising programmes may have minimal effect on population but offer few institutional problems	Behavioural barriers: low Institutional barriers: high Example: Grants for retrofitting have been marginally successful. Institutional concerns include: control, payment and management
Mandatory	Behavioural barriers: low Institutional barriers: high Example: Car efficiency standards have met with minimal consumer resistance, considerable resistance (in early stages) from industry	Behavioural barriers: low Institutional barriers: high Example: Tax incentives accompanying mandatory programmes would face similar institutional obstacles to the above category

ods or re-arranging the placement of industries *vis-a-vis* city cores to conserve energy. The ramifications would be both socio-economic and political. Hence, it is necessary to assess the merits of each energy conservation programme in the light of the institutional obstacles it is likely to encounter.

A METHOD TO ASSESS BARRIERS TO CONSERVATION PROGRAMMES

The preceding discussion indicates that residential energy conservation policies face two types of barriers in Canada, behavioural and institutional. Decision makers must consider both barriers in the design and implementation of conservation programmes. These considerations are not intuitively obvious. In Exhibit 7 an attempt has been made to assess the severity of the obstacles which various types of conservation policy are likely to face in Canada. The attempt is presented here as an illustration of the stage of the policy process that is being advocated, rather than as the final word on which policies will work and which policies will not work. The table brings together the obstacles discussed above and the traditional policy types to assess the likely impact of the former on the latter.

The first cell in Exhibit 7 indicates that, based on the preceding analysis, consumer response in terms of engaging in meaningful, significant conservation behaviours to a voluntary non-financial policy such as an advertising programme will be low and consequently, the behavioural barrier is high. On balance, we conclude that the behavioural obstacle between an advertising programme (the policy) and energy conservation (the goal) is a major one. The empirical evidence shows that conservation is more a matter of economics

than one of choice. The institutional obstacle would be minor because promoting energy conservation disturbs almost no one. The other cells should be read in the same way, remembering that it is the technique rather than the substance of the table which is likely to be of value to the policy maker.

CONCLUSIONS

The assignment for policy makers can be divided into three parts: identification, selection, and implementation of programmes. Identification of possible energy conservation programmes is a straightforward task. A relatively large number of conservation programmes are known, some have been tried, few have been evaluated. The selection stage can be viewed as an iterative process. Programmes can initially be selected for consideration by using a number of criteria including the size and nature of the energy savings, the impact on consumers, and the enforceability of the policy.

Having selected programmes for consideration, a further step is to assess the obstacles to implementation presented by behavioural and institutional realities. It is here that the experience and knowledge of the policy maker must be used to determine whether, through design and implementation, the behavioural and institutional problems can be overcome. For example, housing insulation standards, a mandatory non-financial programme, may meet with relatively little consumer resistance but the institutional barriers, particularly the lack of government-business interface, are considerable.

The policy makers need to devise strategies for implementation and assess their probability of success *before* the programme begins. Considerable effort must be focused on identifying programmes where the non-obvious barriers—behavioural and institutional—have a reasonable chance of being overcome. In brief, the argument here is that any given energy conservation programme is only as good as the strategy used to implement it. In this sense policy makers will need to possess both political expertize and marketing skills if Canada is to move closer to the goal of energy self-sufficiency.

NOTES

1. *The National Energy Program,* Canada, 1980.
2. John L. Evans, J. R. Brent Ritchie and Gordon H. G. McDougall, "Energy use and consumer behavior: a framework for analysis and policy formulation," *Journal of Business Administration,* Vol. 10, No. 2, 1979, pp. 165–81.
3. For more details on the methodology see: G. H. G. McDougall, J. R. B. Ritchie and J. D. Claxton, *Energy Consumption and Conservation Patterns in Canadian Households,* Vol. I, Unpublished Report, Consumer and Corporate Affairs Canada, Ottawa, Canada, 1979; and G. H. G. McDougall, J. R. B. Ritchie, J. D. Claxton and R. B. Mank, *Energy Consumption and Conservation Patterns in Canadian Households,* Vol. II, Unpublished Report, Consumer and Corporate Affairs Canada, Ottawa, Canada, 1979.
4. In summary, the sample had the following characteristics: (a) 93% owned one or more vehicles, and on average owned 1.5 vehicles; (b) the fuel used to heat the home was oil in 46% of households (primarily in Eastern Canada), natural gas in 36% (Ontario and Western Canada), electricity in 14%, and other (e.g., wood) in 4%; (c) the average age of homemakers was approximately 44 years; (d) average family income was $19,000; (e) an average of 3.45 people lived in the household; and (f) the median education level was high school graduate.
5. Paul C. Stern and Gerald T. Gardner, "Psychological research and energy policy," *American Psychologist,* Vol. 36, No. 4, April 1981, pp. 329–42.
6. J. R. Brent Ritchie, Gordon H. G. McDougall, and John D. Claxton, "Complexities of household energy consumption and conservation," *Journal of Consumer Research,* Vol. 8, No. 3, December 1981, pp. 233–42.
7. Before any Ontario energy officials were allowed to speak to the interviewer, a senior official of the Ontario Conservation and Renewable Energy Group insisted upon consulting with his federal counterpart. In a letter, the provincial official asked whether the research was to be 'the basis of the Federal policy planning along the lines that we have seen previously where federal programs are designed in isolation and subsequently force fed to the provinces?'
8. British North America Act, S91 ss2. The Citizens Insurance Co. *vs* Parsons, and the Queen Insurance Co. *vs* Parsons cases of 1881 were the first to distinguish between intraprovincial and inter-provincial and international trade.
9. Marc Lalonde, Minister of Energy, Mines and Resources, *Energy Pricing and National Unity: The Federal Dilemma,* an address to the Seventh Annual Financial Conference of the Conference Board of Canada, Toronto, 6 May 1980.
10. This estimate was provided by the Chief of the Energuide Program, Consumer and Corporate Affairs, Canada, January 1980.
11. The countries which according to the IEA have the most comprehensive and effective conservation programmes are the Netherlands, Sweden, and Denmark. All are non-federal states.

20
Competing for Scarce Resources

Ellen Greenberg

Competition is a fact of life for almost all organizations. Nonprofit organizations face both direct and indirect competition for funding, for personnel, for users, and for influence and prestige. As resources in all these areas become scarce and the environment turbulent, a requirement for success is the development of effective competitive strategies.

The term "competition" conjures up many images—hockey games at Madison Square Garden, price wars among gas stations or supermarkets, brand competition between consumer firms, and comparison testing of colas on television. The nonprofit organization would appear to be the last place where the adjective "competitive" would seem to apply. These organizations, sometimes called the "Third Sector," include public hospitals and state universities, religious organizations, child-care agencies and mental institutions, charities, and performing and visual arts organizations.

Many of these organizations, including some of the very largest, fail to analyze their competitive position vis-a-vis funds, staff, other resources, and even clients or users, because they do not utilize basic concepts of strategic management. Often they are unable to plan strategically because they lack a clear definition of the organization's mission and goals.

THE GROWTH OF THE THIRD SECTOR

The nonprofit organization—or Third Sector—has grown both in numbers and importance over the past two decades.

Ellen Greenberg is a Doctoral Candidate, Columbia University Graduate School of Business.

These institutions evolved to supplement the private and public sectors—either when the organization's purpose or goal is considered of crucial importance to the public and the potential profitability is low, or to avoid increasing reliance on the growing governmental bureaucracy [1]. It is this key characteristic of nonprofit organizations—the ability to take on tasks and provide services without the financial and legal constraints of the private and public sectors—that has resulted in their increasing prominence.

Other characteristics that frequently appear in nonprofit organizations include the intangibility of service and the possible existence of multiple service objectives. The consumer or user may have little influence on the agency, often because the organization may be a local monopoly and user payments are not a primary source of funds. The contributors of resources—including foundations and government agencies—may interfere with internal management and restrain the use of rewards and punishments. Lastly, the presence of a charismatic leader or the mystique of the agency may be an important factor in the management of the organization and the determination of its goal [2].

By the early 1970s, nonprofit organizations began implementing the techniques practiced by businesses and taught in business schools, including advertising, public relations, financial planning, and accounting. Each discipline has modified its approach for nonprofit organizations. The latest of these functional areas to be applied to the third sector has been strategic management. Despite the lack of hard research illustrating the effectiveness of planning in these organizations, many academicians and executives are becoming increasingly convinced of its value. Columbia University's Institute for Not-for-Profit Management has as its main thrust the development of a strategic plan for each participating agency. The response of both the not-for-profit executives and faculty has been extremely positive.

Despite the enthusiasm for strategic planning, there is no single or simple paradigm for the process. Many nonprofit agencies are not capable of using a sophisticated process like that of General Electric or IBM. Because of their small size and limited resources, the nonprofit organization faces barriers to long-range planning. The executive is usually pressed for time and has most of the problems of an executive in a medium-sized corporation without the luxury of additional personnel that the larger organization could hire.

For small organizations, like the majority of nonprofit agencies, a simple system for strategic management, perhaps augmented by the use of outside consultants, should be instituted [3]. The types of strategies a small business could utilize are share-increasing; growth; profit- or income-maximization; market concentration and asset reduction; turn-around strategies; or liquidation and divestiture strategies. Substituting survival or break-even strategies for profit-maximization, the nonprofit organization may pursue any of these strategies.

Much of the strategic planning literature is general enough to be applied to the nonprofit sector. However, these organizations also need more specific guidelines. Some of these can be derived from the characteristics of the organization. For example, the fact that many of these organizations are less dependent on technological innovation than on human resources suggests that they do not need to plan on a long-time horizon. The advances in the organization's "technology"—such as improved drug treatments or changes in psychological therapy—are likely to be available in the public domain. Retraining staff or new hiring may take a shorter time than retooling an assembly line.

In addition to these considerations, the nonprofit organization must deal with goal conflicts because of multiple service objectives and criteria that may cause conflict in planning. This is complicated by reduced consumer influence and the fact that users often have little or no influence on the acquisition of resources. Perhaps the most crucial implication of the nonprofit organization's characteristics for strategic planning is the recognition of the separation of clients or users from resource contributors.

WHAT IS COMPETITION?

Competition may be defined as a form of interaction between organizations where one organization can achieve its

---

EXHIBIT 1
Areas of Competition for Nonprofit Organizations

Internal to the Organization	External to the Organization
Resources:	Users:
Funding and other economic factors	Clients, customers, or audience
Physical resources and facilities	Competing organizations:
Personnel	Enterprise competitors
Expertise and experience	Product-form competitors
Influence and prestige	Generic competitors

---

goals only at the expense of another. In the complicated and turbulent economic and political environment of the 1980s, competition includes scrambling for resources as well as rivalry for clients or users and potential members and their loyalties. These concepts lead to the conclusion that nonprofit organizations, even those with the most worthy of missions, must compete with many other organizations, especially those which require similar or identical resources and clientele. Exhibit 1 is a listing of Areas of Competition for Nonprofit Organizations.

Kotler suggested a general model for examining competition. Organizations face competition on three levels; generic, product-form, and enterprise. All organizations are aware of their enterprise competitors: those specific organizations that are producers of the same product or service. The two other types are less obvious and for this reason deserve special attention. Product-form competitors are those organizations whose output is another version of the product or service, which may be competitive with the focal organization. Generic competitors include other broad product or service categories that might satisfy the same needs as the focal organization. All business organizations have come to recognize the value of broadly defining their products, emphasizing the basic customer need(s) that may be served. Nonprofit organizations must begin to do the same.

In a munificent, placid environment, resources and users are in abundance and little attention need be paid to competitors, even of the enterprise form. As the environment becomes more scarce, moving toward the turbulent field [4], any organization interested in survival must acknowledge not only its direct competitors, but also indirect competitors for both resources and users—it must account for both product-form and generic competitors.

Consider as an example a drug halfway house in a large city. At first glance, its competition appears to be other halfway treatment centers in the neighborhood. Using Kotler's model, the halfway house also competes with other types of drug treatment programs—methadone maintenance clinics, hospital outpatient centers, in-hospital facilities, and private physicians. At the generic level, particularly in a scarce and turbulent environment, the halfway house and other drug treatment programs compete with alternative activities, including use of the drug itself, which may entail crimes such as robbery and prostitution; prison; or other underworld activities. This may seem an extreme example, but it does point out some directions the focal drug halfway house might check in determining its competitive strategy. It could direct its publicity campaigns at emphasizing its distinctive competence in both treating drug problems and improving one's standard of living, developing work habits, providing companionship and a supportive environment—factors other treatment programs may not provide. This type of campaign could be used in both obtaining resources and attracting users.

Similarly, hospitals, despite the fact that they generally do not advertise and are not usually considered as competitive organizations, do compete with midwives, faith healers, quacks, manufacturers of patent medicine, and even neighboring hospitals for both patients and staff [5].

AREAS OF COMPETITION

Competition for Funding. This is the most obvious form of competition, and most organizations do consider this, no matter how little strategic planning is done. However, there is more involved in competing for funds than trying to write proposals and plan more attractive programs than other organizations offering similar services or products. Applicants for foundation funding may compete with many other types of organizations, and even individuals. Health and welfare organizations compete with military and public-service organizations when applying for government funding; this becomes more true in the long term. Organizations in the private and public sectors are also lobbying for funding and/or cutting grants to nonprofit agencies.

One pitfall organizations face when seeking financial resources is the failure to consider the potential influence of funding agencies on the overall strategy of the agency. For example, religious organizations that receive public funds may be forced to become nonsectarian, which may alienate many of their traditional supporters, clients, and staff. Catholic Charities of Brooklyn [6] currently faces a problem of this nature. Because of its large size and the scope and number of programs operating throughout Brooklyn and Queens, Catholic Charities must address itself to multiple publics, including the populations it services, the government agencies and other funding sources, and Catholic and non-Catholic communities. As a consequence of the large number of nonsectarian programs, Catholic Charities' image is not as good at the neighborhood or parish level as it is with government agencies and political leaders. Private financial support, as well as volunteered time, goods, and services from Catholic families, has decreased. Since promotion is poor even within the church, most of the parishion-

ers recognize neither the values and missions motivating the agency nor the need for additional support.

A second danger in searching for funding may be called "backing into funding." Some causes are considered "popular" or "sexy" at a given time, and funding is made available to catchment areas, or prescribed geographical regions. Readily available funds are tempting. The executive director of a large settlement house in New York confided: "Some settlement houses think it would be immoral to refuse funding that would increase gross income. This year there is a lot of money available for programs for pregnant teen-agers. But the most pressing problem in my neighborhood is senior citizens, which is not considered a hot program this year. My board of directors would be pleased if we received any grant, but I have other considerations. If we took on a teen-age pregnancy program, it would take up some of our facilities, staff time, and administrative resources, all of which can be put to better use in trying to find money for senior citizens' programs. Our agency is now in a position of strength and can refuse to back into funding that would deplete our other resources. Not all the settlement houses do the same."

This example shows the importance for each organization to define its mission and identify its distinctive competences in terms of the real needs of its constituency. Money available for new programs, without adequate facilities to back up the services and money to pay for administrative overload, will put undue pressure on the organization. Even worse, it may decrease the energy and resources available for seeking funds for programs really needed and for taking on such programs should support be forthcoming. Agencies must be aware of the creeping commitment that ensues when they take on projects because funding is available for their catchment area. Once an agency has taken on a program to aid, for example, the handicapped, it cannot simply drop the program when it realizes that it has overcommitted itself. The agency has some obligation to follow through with the affected population, and divestiture of programs must be considered as carefully as the planning of new projects.

Competition for funding occurs in other arenas besides government agencies and large foundations. Many nonprofit institutions, particularly charitable and arts organizations, depend to a large extent on private and corporate donations. These institutions would do well to follow the advice of fund raisers who stress the importance of identifying the motives of donors as a basis for planning fund-raising drives. Most people contribute because they get something in return—a feeling of pride, relief of guilt feelings because of their elevated status, alleviation of fear of getting a particular disease, association with a prestigious organization [7].

Evidence of such fund-raising strategies are all around us. Donors to public broadcasting stations carry prestigious totebags and umbrellas as public evidence of their good taste in supporting high-quality television programming. Major supporters of the arts see their names in programs.

Many organizations sell T-shirts and other souvenirs to raise money, at the same time giving the buyer a sense of membership; the organization simultaneously receives free "advertising" on these donors' chests. Hospitals send fund-raising requests to former patients, hoping for generosity from those no longer ill. Neighborhood agencies often rely on local pride to boost their fund-raising efforts. And, of course, all nonprofit agencies, regardless of purpose and scope, stress the attraction of tax-deductible donations—a benefit all taxpayers can appreciate.

In the competition for funding, an agency competes not only with other institutions offering similar, related, or substitutable services, but with organizations using the same form of fund-raising appeal. Thus, the American Lung Association competes not only with other health- and research-oriented organizations, but with all organizations that use direct mailings to potential contributors. Other competitors, of course, include cigarette companies and all industries whose processes pollute the environment. The American Lung Association is a good example of an organization whose goal and mission are not well-defined for the public. Since tuberculosis is no longer a severe threat, the agency has shifted its focus to informing the public about emphysema, the dangers of smoking, and other environmental hazards. But the image of healthy pink lungs—or even gray, damaged lungs—is neither attractive nor shocking enough to convey the drama of the earlier campaign against T.B. Since polio has been virtually eradicated, the March of Dimes faces a similar problem of mission definition.

Thus, competition for funding encompasses two essential, though seemingly contradictory, phases: analysis of all the competitive organizations and forms of fund raising; and clear definition of the specific mission or competitive niche for the focal organization, so that it may best concentrate its efforts in obtaining resources.

Competition for Personnel. Unlike many organizations in the private sector, including all manufacturing firms, most nonprofit agencies are labor-intensive. As mentioned above, the "technology" that is needed for nonprofit organizations to function at their most efficient levels often appears as public knowledge—e.g., new medications or changing governmental regulation—and requires trained personnel with dedication to their job and willingness to update their skills.

Nonprofit organizations have long relied on a cadre of social workers, clergy, volunteers, artists, and professionals whose commitment to their careers and causes supersedes desire for fame, wealth, and promotion. Yet as nonprofit agencies become more sophisticated and differentiated, and as they continue to adopt business management techniques, these organizations must increasingly consider the competition for personnel. Staff in these organizations typically receive low salaries; have low status in the community; have little room for advancement because of the absence of career ladders; and suffer from peer deprivation when agencies are so small that a professional may have no colleagues within the immediate environment. A cosmopolitan attitude among professional staff—characterized by loyalty to the profession rather than the employing organization—is likely to develop. In addition, worker burnout—exhaustion and depression due to overwork in unpleasant working situations—is a frequent complaint, especially in social service agencies. These factors contribute to high turnover among nonprofit agency staff, as well as the inability of some organizations to attract high-caliber staff in original hires.

Unless nonprofit agencies experience huge increases in funds and growth, many of these problems are inevitable, at least in the short run. However, the severity of these factors may be lessened by awareness on the part of the executive staff and directors. Participation by larger segments of the staff in the definition of organizational mission and the planning process may result in increased loyalty to the organization. Sharing of problems and soliciting ideas may also help. Most important, perhaps, is the explicit recognition of the importance of human resources to the nonprofit organization. Again, the clear statement of the organization's mission and goals may be the single most important factor in attracting and retaining personnel.

Competion for Users. Unlike competition for funding, many agencies are unaware of the competition for users. The term "users" comprises customers, clients, and audience, and includes both current users and potential users who are either unaware of the product or services offered or who need to be persuaded to use these outputs of the organization.

Competition for users appears in several forms. For some organizations—for example, nonprofit theater companies—the issues are similar to competitive strategies in the private sector and require using effective advertising and public relations. In many theater and dance companies, the search for audience is twofold: there is a need to inform the public of the existence and quality of the organizations' products, as well as obtain audiences for individual organizations. Consequently, many of these groups have formed cooperative alliances, such as the League of Regional Theatres and Theatre Communications Group nationwise, and in New York City, the Dance Alliance, the Black Theatre Alliance, and the Off-Off Broadway Alliance. The individual organizations use the collective organization to publicize their aims and activities; at the same time, they compete for their separate audiences. These types of organizations have an advantage over hospitals or welfare agencies: consumers may attend one company repeatedly without excluding others; they may patronize half a dozen off-off Broadway theaters during the course of a season.

The types of competition other kinds of agencies face have been discussed above in the drug treatment facility and hospital examples. Since this type of analysis defines a very wide market, because of limited resources it is necessary for the focal organization to clearly define its target group within the market and limit its product offering to appeal to these groups. Some organizations are limited in their product-market scope by fiat, such as religious charters and catchment areas defined by the funding agency. Yet even with these situations, an agency can take actions to increase its clientele and improve awareness of its services. For example, the Brooklyn Society for the Prevention of Cruelty to Children receives notice of all reported cases of child abuse in the borough of Brooklyn. However, it could increase the number of users by publicizing its resources and services, emphasizing the caring and confidential nature of its work. The agency wishes to encourage use of its services when alternative means, such as professional treatment by private therapists, are not available to the children. The BSPCC fears that there are abused children whose cases are not reported because of fear of publicity or lack of awareness.

Other agencies face more overt competition for users. Because of the growing use of contraceptive devices, availability of legal abortion, and the trend for unmarried women to keep their children, there is competition among child-care agencies for healthy white infants. These organizations are slowly changing their orientation toward placing mixed race, handicapped, and older children; this movement is accompanied by a small but growing public awareness campaign, as well as a trend for adoption by single parents.

Competition for Influence and Prestige.

Implicit in the discussion of competition among nonprofit organizations is the desire for influence and prestige. Some organizations are so large and powerful, and so well-known, that they receive an adequate share of resources and clients regardless of the state of the environment and the efforts of competing organizations. For example, "the American Cancer Society knows that in any open competition with other agencies, it will receive more funds than most other organizations because of the public's tremendous concern with, and awareness of, the injurious effects of cancer [8]." The International and American Red Cross are in analogous positions. Similarly, in strong Catholic communities, Catholic agencies have a fixed market and are more financially independent than similar organizations because of diocesan support. Despite its image problem with traditional supporters, discussed above, Catholic Charities of Brooklyn has considerable clout in its environment because it has taken over many caretaking activities that otherwise would have had to be performed by city, state, and federal agencies. As the former Executive Director of Brooklyn's Catholic Charities, Auxiliary Bishop Joseph M. Sullivan, said: "We are constantly being asked to take on new projects that no one else will handle—and we've had to learn to refuse some of them. However, when we do take on a new project, we do so on the condition that we receive 100 percent funding from the governmental agency concerned [9]."

Unfortunately, few organizations have the influence of the Red Cross or the Cancer Society. Most organizations have not only a task to perform in producing their service or product, but may also produce information about the organization and its mission, such as information about drug abuse or the availability of rape counseling. Dissemination of such information increases the visibility and prominence of the organization. This in turn will help in the development of commitment to the organization by its members. As the influence of an organization grows, so will its ability to obtain other resources, including technical and financial know-how.

Nonprofit organizations wishing to increase their visibility can use traditional public relations methods—to recruit clients, become known to local newspapers, and appear on public-service spots. Staff, clients, and directors should be utilized as much as possible in these processes.

THE BOARD OF DIRECTORS

The board of directors can be an important competitive factor. Many boards are formed solely on the basis of their interest in the organization's mission, and this can be useful if the board members participate in the task of the organization. The board should be both a source of contacts and influence for the agency. A carefully selected board, comprised of bankers, lawyers, business and political leaders, including women and minorities, will meet both constituency and management requirements. The board might aid in the tasks of strategic planning and defining the organization's mission and may also serve to aid in fund raising, provide an outlet for publicity into the community, use their skills as consultants, and lend their prestige to the organization.

Many agencies find themselves stuck with "society" boards who act as figureheads or, even worse, take no interest at all in the organizations [10]. The nonprofit organization would find it useful to build in a system requiring evaluation for tenure or periodic reelections to remove the deadwood.

CONCLUSION

Once the organization has considered the various areas in which it competes for resources and users and identified its competitors, it must decide on its strategy. In the most general terms, the organization must look for its competitive advantages, play up its strengths, and begin to drop its weakest programs. This may require some tough decisions, as discussed earlier, since most nonprofit agencies are humanistically oriented and could not simply terminate a commitment. While strengthening its own position—perhaps consolidating programs to reduce fixed costs—the agency must also look for the weaknesses of competing organizations and try to eliminate the weaker competitors through aggressive advertising, fund raising, and publicity campaigns. Despite the apparent success of the United Fund, collaboration is seldom an effective strategy, causing a drain on all the organizations involved. When resources are scarce, the organizations with the most effective competitive strategies will survive.

REFERENCES

1. Amitai Etzioni, "The Third Sector and Domestic Missions," in *Emerging Concepts in Management,* Max S. Wortam, Jr. and Fred Luthans, eds. (2d ed., New York: Macmillan, 1975).
2. William H. Newman and Harvey N. Wallender III, "Managing Not-for-Profit Enterprises," *Academy of Management Review,* Jan. 1978, p. 26.
3. Charles W. Hofer and Dan Schendel, *Strategy Formulation: Analytical Concepts* (St. Paul: West Publishing, 1978), pp. 58–59.
4. F. E. Emery and E. L. Trist, "The Casual Texture of Organizational Environments," *Human Relations,* Feb. 18, 1965.
5. James D. Thompson and William J. McEwen, "Organizational Goals and Environment," *American Sociological Review,* 1958.
6. Ellen Greenberg, *Catholic Charities of Brooklyn* (Case) (New York: Institute for Not-for-Profit Management, Columbia University, 1981), forthcoming.
7. Philip Kotler and Sidney J. Levy, "Broadening the Concept of Marketing," *Journal of Marketing,* Jan. 1969.
8. Eugene Litwak and Lydia F. Hylton, "Interorganizational Analysis: A Hypothesis on Coordinating Agencies," *Administrative Science Quarterly,* 1962, p. 347.
9. Greenberg, note 6 *supra.*
10. See, e.g., Ellen Greenberg, *Dorchester House Board of Directors* (Case) (New York: Institute for Not-for-Profit Management, Columbia University, 1978).

BIBLIOGRAPHY

Emery, F. E., and Trist, E. L., "The Causal Texture of Organizational Environments," *Human Relations,* Feb. 18, 1965.

Etzioni, Amitai, "The Third Sector and Domestic Missions," in *Emerging Concepts in Management,* Wortman, Max S., Jr., and Luthans, Fred, eds. (2d ed., New York: Macmillan, 1975).

Greenberg, Ellen, *Dorchester House Board of Directors* (Case) (New York: Institute for Not-for-Profit Management, Columbia University, 1978).

Greenberg, Ellen, *Catholic Charities of Brooklyn* (Case) (New York: Institute for Not-for-Profit Management, Columbia University, 1981), forthcoming.

Hofer, Charles W., "Research on Strategic Planning: A Survey of Past Studies and Suggestions for Future Efforts," *Journal of Economics and Business,* 1976.

Hofer, Charles W., and Schendel, Dan, *Strategy Formulation: Analytical Concepts* (St. Paul: West Publishing, 1978).

Kotler, Philip, *Marketing for Nonprofit Organizations* (Englewood Cliffs, N.J.: Prentice-Hall, 1975).

Kotler, Philip, and Levy, Sidney J., "Broadening the Concept of Marketing," *Journal of Marketing,* Jan. 1969.

Litwak, Eugene, and Hylton, Lydia F., "Interorganizational Analysis: A Hypothesis on Co-ordinating Agencies," *Administrative Science Quarterly,* 1962.

Newman, William H., and Wallender III, Harvey W., "Managing Not-for-Profit Enterprises," *Academy of Management Review,* Jan. 1978.

Pfeffer, Jeffrey, and Salancik, Gerald R., *The External Control of Organizations: A Resource Dependence Perspective* (New York: Harper & Row, 1978).

Schendel, Dan E., and Hofer, Charles W., eds., *Strategic Management: A New View of Business Policy and Planning* (Boston: Little. Brown and Company, 1979).

Thompson, James D., and McEwen, William J., "Organizational Goals and Environment," *American Sociological Review,* 1958.

PART IV

The Marketing Mix

Cases

21. Museum Wharf **215**

22. Wessex College **231**

23. Montecito State College: Division of Extension Studies **233**

24. American Repertory Theatre **243**

Readings

25. Marketing Mix Decisions for Nonprofit Organizations: **261**
An Analytical Approach

26. The Mass Media Family Planning Campaign **271**

27. The Baptists Want You! **277**

28. Evaluating Social Persuasion Advertising Campaigns: **287**
An Overview of Recent C.O.I. Experience

21
Museum Wharf

Roger Davis
Christopher H. Lovelock

Four yellow school buses were lined up, nose to tail, on the Congress Street bridge next to Museum Wharf. Outside the long, six-story brick structure, flags were flying briskly in the chill March wind blowing off the harbor. In the lobby, a group of school children was pressing eagerly towards the large exterior elevator that would take them up to the Museum of Transportation. Another group of smaller children was clattering up the wide stairs leading to The Children's Museum. Several accompanying teachers were doing their best to maintain some semblance of order. It was a typical Monday morning during the school year at Museum Wharf.

In the third floor conference room, administrators of the two museums were reviewing the eight-month period since July 1979, when they had inaugurated their new joint home. Of particular concern was what relationship the museums should have in the future with respect to promotional activities. Michael Spock, director of The Children's Museum, glanced out the window towards the nearby office towers of downtown Boston. "We both have good relations with the schools," he said gesturing towards the buses below. "I think the task now is to build up attendance among tourists and local residents." Duncan Smith, his counterpart at the Museum of Transportation, nodded agreement. "There's so much competition in this city," he remarked. "Both of us need to toot this place. But the question is, do we do it jointly or separately? Frankly, I'm worried about the fuzzy image of the two museums and the way we seem to blur together in people's minds."

Roger Davis is Lecturer in Marketing, Baylor University, and Christopher H. Lovelock is Associate Professor of Business Administration, Harvard University.

A TALE OF TWO MUSEUMS

Boston was well known for its museums and other visitor attractions. These included: the paintings and art treasures of the Museum of Fine Arts (MFA) and the Gardner Museum; the eighteenth century frigate, USS Constitution (better known as "Old Ironsides"); the Museum of Science with its slogan, "It's fun to find out"; the artistic and scientific exhibits of the several Harvard University museums; and the dramatic marine exhibits of the New England Aquarium. Other local attractions included the Franklin Park Zoo, and the archives and museum of the John F. Kennedy Memorial Library, opened in late 1979. Two smaller, but growing, museums had relocated in 1979 from separate locations in the inner suburbs to a new, shared facility on the edge of downtown. These were The Children's Museum and the Museum of Transportation. Exhibit 1 shows the location of each of these attractions on a map of the Boston area.

The Children's Museum. In 1913, a group of university and public school science teachers in Boston founded The Chil-

EXHIBIT 1
Major Museums and Attractions in the Boston Area

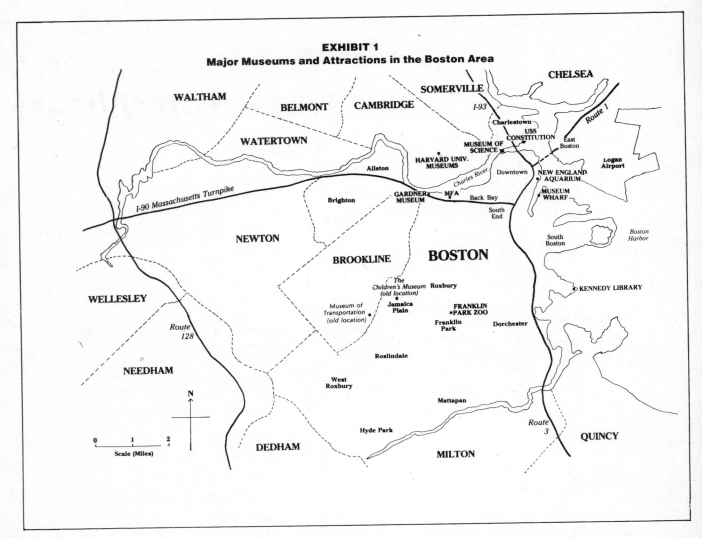

dren's Museum (TCM) to supplement natural science programs in local schools. Its initial location was in the Jamaica Plain area of Boston, about four miles from the city center. In 1936, the museum moved to a larger facility in the same area.

Michael Spock, whose graduate training was in education, was appointed director of TCM in 1962. He introduced innovative ways of extending the reach of the museum, as well as an aggressive approach to grant seeking. TCM's offerings included participative exhibits, community-based activities, and training programs for teachers and community workers. Spock described the museum's distinctive mission as follows:

> What makes TCM different is the commitment we have to helping everyone learn from an increasingly tough and demanding world through direct experiences with real materials. We believe in learning by doing.

The museum's Resource Center conducted workshops, developed and published educational materials, and lent or rented exhibit-related materials to students, teachers, museum members, and community workers. One offering, called "Recycle," involved objects donated by manufacturing plants (which would otherwise have discarded them). The items in question ranged from defective camera lenses to washers to pieces of shaped wood or styrofoam. They were sold by weight or measure as raw materials for children to use in arts, crafts, science, and other learning projects.

The Exhibit Center accounted for most of the museum's direct contact with the public. It consisted of "hands-on" exhibits for families, designed primarily for children from preschool age through early teens. Overall administration of the museum and its programs was the responsibility of the Support Services group.

The success of these innovations soon taxed the capacity of the Jamaica Plain facilities. Space problems placed a ceiling on attendance. Since more than half of TCM's operations budget came from admissions, the museum was rapidly becoming restricted in its ability to develop new programs and exhibits. Another cause for concern was the relative inaccessibility of the Jamaica Plain location (Exhibit 1). It was not served by Boston's extensive rapid transit system, and the directors felt that it was hard for out-of-town visitors to find. By the early '70s, feasibility studies were being conducted to help determine requirements for a new building in central Boston.

Museum of Transportation.

Until it moved to Museum Wharf, the Museum of Transportation (MOT) was located in an old carriage house in Brookline, a suburb of Boston (Exhibit 1). From its beginning in 1947 as the Antique Auto Museum, it had developed into a museum of different types of transportation.

Duncan Smith, who became director of MOT in 1970, had previously been an exhibits designer for the Museum of Fine Arts. His arrival at MOT marked the beginning of a decade of change for the museum. First he added other transportation antiques, such as bicycles, to the collection. Special meets were held featuring different types of transportation. The name of the museum was changed in 1971 to reflect its new emphasis. Then in 1978, the entire museum was renovated and a hands-on activity center added. Special efforts were made to reach out to the schools and new educational programs were developed. Gradually, the museum evolved into a "museum of transportation archaeology," as Smith described it. He elaborated:

> By this I mean that the museum not only shows antique cars and bicycles, trains and ships, but also explains them in terms of their social context so visitors can see just how transportation has affected their lives. . . . It's full of folklore and myth. Someone was always mad because his horse kicked him, his bicycle had a flat tire, his car ran out of gas on the freeway, or the airline lost his luggage. We're building a museum that looks at transportation through these many perspectives.

Soon after Smith's arrival at MOT it became apparent that the Brookline location was not adequate. It did not have the space necessary to house many of the proposed exhibits. It, too, had an out-of-the-way location, which limited its attendance. Smith began to look around for a new location that would allow the museum to expand its offerings and attract more visitors. One site considered was the old Watertown Arsenal, about five miles from downtown Boston. But the sharp rise in oil prices in 1973 convinced Smith that heating costs would be prohibitive and that a central location, close to public transportation, was essential.

A New Home for Both Museums.

Smith and Spock were neighbors in private life; they often discussed with each other the problems involved in finding suitable locations for their respective museums. Though the directors had not decided that shared facilities were the solution to their relocation decisions, they had noted that sharing would be beneficial for both museums, offering some economies of scale and the opportunity to pool resources in areas such as admissions, a retail shop, parking, and security.

In early 1975, Spock learned that the Atlas Terminal Warehouse, overlooking Fort Point Channel on Boston's waterfront, was for sale. Though the building was too large for TCM, its location and structural qualities were very desirable. Spock felt that this might be the opportunity to join forces which he and Smith had been thinking about. The two men saw that with renovation, the 19th Century brick and timber warehouse would meet the existing space requirement of both museums and still leave room for future expansion. In December 1975, MOT and TCM jointly signed a purchase contract. Prior to its opening in July 1979, the building was renamed "Museum Wharf."

REDEVELOPMENT IN BOSTON

During the 1960s and 1970s, the City of Boston witnessed a dramatic rebirth of its historic central area, spurred by a series of major redevelopment and restoration efforts. Particularly noteworthy was the revival of the badly deteriorated wholesaling and warehousing sections along the waterfront, long a victim of Boston's decline in importance as a seaport.

Beginning with construction of the New England Aquarium (opened in 1969) and the Harbor Towers apartments, the waterfront started to take on a new life. Old warehouses, only a few minutes' walk from the new Government Center administrative complex and the office towers of the booming financial district, were converted into expensive apartments and condominiums. The Bicentennial saw the opening of the Faneuil Hall Marketplace. Housed in restored, historic buildings, this cluster of restaurants, small stores, and professional offices quickly became immensely popular with residents and visitors alike. The Museum of Fine Arts, located two miles away, opened a "branch" in one of these buildings. In 1978–79, the nearby Washington Street retail area, containing two major department stores, was converted into a pedestrian mall and promoted by the Mayor's Office of Cultural Affairs as the "Downtown Crossing." (In 1980, responsibility for joint promotional efforts was transferred to an organization of local merchants.)

The Fort Point Channel Area.

The directors of MOT and TCM felt that Museum Wharf was in the path of redevelopment in Boston. It was located in a several-block cluster of tall, solidly constructed brick commercial buildings just across the Fort Point Channel (an extension of Boston harbor) from South Station and the new Federal Reserve Bank tower (Exhibit 2). Three bridges spanned the channel.

The Wharf was about seven minutes' walk from South Station, which was served by commuter rail, Amtrak, and subway. Plans were in hand to renovate the station and construct a new transportation center there that would serve as a terminal for intercity buses. The Central Artery, a major expressway, passed in front of South Station and had on and off ramps within two blocks of the station. The most direct access by car to the Museum Wharf parking area was across the Northern Avenue swing bridge, an old-fashioned structure built of a latticework of steel girders, which had railroad tracks running down the median of the bridge deck.

EXHIBIT 2
Museum Wharf and Downtown Boston

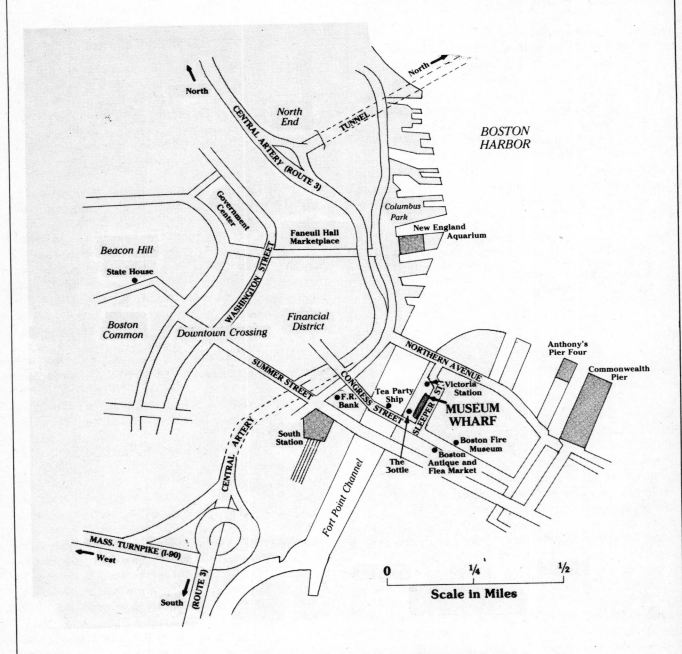

Note: The street network has been simplified for clarity

EXHIBIT 3
Comparative Price Schedule for Six Boston Museums, March 1980[a]

	MOT	TCM[b]	Museum of Fine Arts[c]	Museum of Science[d]	New England Aquarium	Tea Party Ship
Adult	$3.00	$3.00	$1.75	$3.50	$4.00	$1.75
Children	2.00	2.00	Free	2.25	2.50	1.00
Senior Citizens	2.00	2.00	—	2.25	3.00	—
College ID	2.00	—	—	2.25	3.00	—
School Group	1.80	Free	—	Free	2.00	—
Friday night	1.00	1.00	—	1.00	2.00	—
Wednesday afternoon	—	—	—	Free	—	—
Sunday	—	—	1.25	—	—	—
Tuesday (after 5:00)	—	—	Free	—	—	—
Civic Groups	—	Free	—	—	—	—
Adult	—	—	—	—	2.00	—
Children	—	—	—	—	3.00	—
College and Senior	—	—	—	—	2.50	—
Special Needs	—	—	—	—	2.00	—
Adult Group	—	—	—	3.00	—	—

[a]MOT and TCM planned to increase admissions prices to $3.50 for adults and $2.50 for children, effective April 15, 1980.
[b]All nonprofit Massachusetts community and school groups admitted free through a special state appropriation.
[c]Admission to the MFA branch in Faneuil Hall Marketplace was free.
[d]The Museum of Science, located about two miles from Museum Wharf, contained several transportation-related exhibits.

Most of the buildings on the museum side of the channel were occupied by commercial and industrial firms, including wholesale suppliers of office equipment, linoleum, and wall coverings, as well as printing firms and a manufacturer of custom furniture. Signs of a change in this mix included renovation of the second floor of one building for an art gallery, and conversion of street level space in another into an elegant law firm office.

There were a number of other attractions nearby which the museums' directors felt would contribute to attendance at Museum Wharf. New England Aquarium, a marine life museum, was 15 minutes' walk from Museum Wharf. The Tea Party Ship, a for-profit museum and gift shop reached from the Congress Street bridge, was moored in the Fort Point Channel directly across from Museum Wharf. The Boston Fire Museum, managed by MOT, was scheduled to open in fall 1980 in a late nineteenth century firehouse, one block away. The Boston Antique and Flea Market, another newcomer to the area, was open every Sunday just across the street from the Fire Museum site. A little further away, on the edge of the harbor, were Anthony's Pier Four (a well-known seafood restaurant) and Commonwealth Pier, site of the annual New England Flower Show and other exhibitions.

MOT and TCM administrators felt that the redevelopment taking place along Boston's extensive waterfront, combined with increased accessibility, was likely to lead to further investment in the area. Private developers had recently announced plans to "recycle" one of the commercial buildings near the Wharf and convert it into condominiums.

However, in March 1980, the general tone of the immediate vicinity of the Wharf remained that of a slightly rundown commercial area.

MUSEUM WHARF

Originally constructed as a wool warehouse in 1889, the museums' new home was six stories. high, 370 feet long, and 70 feet deep; it contained 144,000 square feet of space. A broad apron, suitable for development into a small urban park and display area, separated the full length of the building from the waters of the 200-yard-wide channel.

The museums shared the $5.2 million purchase, renovation and financing costs. Additional sums of $400,000 and $1 million were spent by MOT and TCM, respectively, for final preparation and installation of their exhibits. Although private donations supplied most of the funds for the project, substantial credit was provided by Boston-area banks and tax-exempt bonds. Even after major renovation, the cost per square foot was estimated at less than half that of a brand new building.

The first floor consisted of joint lobby and retail space. TCM was located in 39,000 square feet on the second, third, and fourth floors, and MOT in 30,000 square feet on the fourth, fifth, and sixth floors. Space was reserved for retail tenants on the ground floor; 51,000 square feet on the upper floors were set aside for future expansion of the museums.

Inside the lobby were an admission desk and entrances to both museums. Though the museums shared the desk, they charged separate admissions (see Exhibit 3 for price schedule). The cash registers printed slips specifying the museum to be visited, the number and type of admissions (adults, children, discounts) and—through a link with the computer owned by TCM—stored this admissions data for later retrieval.

Visitors entered TCM by climbing a wide stairway which led from the lobby to the second floor. Smaller stairways provided access from the second floor to the third and fourth floors. Handicapped visitors could reach the exhibit areas by elevator. TCM's exhibits included the "Giant's Desktop," where everything from a pencil to a coffee cup to a telephone was twelve times the normal size; "Living Things," a natural history corner with small urban animals from mice to cockroaches; "City Slice," a three-story cross-section of a city street and Victorian house; "Grandparents' House," including working kitchen and attic with trunks of old clothes and Victorian memorabilia; "What If You Couldn't?" an exhibit about handicaps; "We're Still Here," an exhibit showing how American Indians lived then and now; and "WKID-TV," a news studio with closed circuit television.

Visitors to MOT rode a large glassed-in external elevator to the sixth floor, enjoying a fine view of downtown Boston and part of the harbor. The fifth and fourth floors were reached either by connecting stairs or by the elevator. MOT's main exhibit was called "Boston—A City in Transit." Visitors progressed through nine time periods, from 1630 to the present day, seeing and hearing the development of transportation in and around Boston. In the process, they experienced a colonial shipyard, a nineteenth century railroad station, an early subway stop, and a mid-twentieth century automobile showroom. Other exhibits included: audiovisual presentations of the history of the shipping trade and immigration into Boston; "Crossroads," a hands-on section where both adults and children could ride a model hovercraft, slide down a fire pole, pedal a high wheeler, or climb on board an early trolley; a film about the development of flight; and a selection of MOT's extensive antique carriage and auto collection (the balance remained in the museum's old site in Brookline).

Besides the two museums, the Wharf included two restaurants. There were also a small park and a dairy bar on the apron overlooking the channel. Antique vehicles provided outdoor rides during the warmer months.

Impact of Museum Wharf.   The two commercial establishments most affected by the opening of the museums were the Victoria Station restaurant and the Boston Tea Party Ship and Museum.

Victoria Station, a unit of the national restaurant chain, was located next to Museum Wharf at Northern Avenue and Sleeper Street. Like others in the chain, the restaurant had a British railway theme. Part of the structure was housed in converted railroad boxcars. Victoria Station had been in business at that location for over six years when Museum

Wharf opened. The manager thought that the overall impact of her new neighbors had been beneficial. She commented:

> It's easier now for us to identify our location. People know where Museum Wharf is. They don't know where Sleeper Street is. We've also increased our meal counts since the opening. The only real problem stemming from the museum is parking.

The manager had noticed that the customers at Victoria Station were younger and more likely to bring children than previously. She also felt that the general atmosphere of the area had changed and become more attractive. She believed that her customers felt more comfortable and secure now that there were more people visiting the immediate area.

The site for the Tea Party Ship had been designated by the City of Boston in 1972. An old wooden Danish sailing vessel was purchased, modified to resemble an eighteenth century brig like the *Beaver,* and sailed across the Atlantic to Boston. It was moored in the Fort Point Channel next to a wooden bridge tender's house containing a gift shop. This exhibit, which commemorated the famous Boston Tea Party protest of 1773, opened in 1974. Visitors could not only learn about the incident and see what the original ship, the *Beaver,* must have looked like, but could themselves hurl tea chests (connected to the ship by lines) into the harbor.

Barbara Attianese, the director, felt that the opening of Museum Wharf had been beneficial to the area. She commented:

> When we opened, we felt a little like pioneers in this part of Boston. There were few other attractions nearby, so we had to bear the burden of attracting people to this area. With the opening of Museum Wharf, we expect that the area will get more attention, from improved parking, lighting, and security to more interest among business and civic leaders.

Attianese did not feel that Museum Wharf was in competition with the Tea Party Ship, but instead saw them as complementary attractions:

> Our price is lower—$1.75 for adults and $1.00 for children—and the average time spent in our museum is 30 minutes. We are a different type of attraction from MOT and TCM. We benefit from their location here because of increased exposure resulting from more traffic over the bridge.

As further evidence of the good feelings generated between the Tea Party Ship and Museum Wharf, Attianese pointed to an arrangement between her museum and MOT, whereby a discount was given to school groups who booked visits to both MOT and the Tea Party Ship. She envisioned an even more cooperative future.

Other Food Service Operations.   The retail businesses located in the Museum Wharf building were a McDonald's fast-food restaurant, a medium-priced seafood restaurant called "Trawlers," and the Museums' Shop. Outside the building stood "The Bottle," a dairy bar within a 40-foot-high wooden replica of a milk bottle.

In 1978, the McDonald's Corporation had agreed to operate a company-owned restaurant—as opposed to a franchise—at Museum Wharf. The site appeared well suited to McDonald's strategy of appealing to families and children. Opening in December 1978, McDonald's was the first occupant of the Wharf to begin continuous operations.

Business at McDonald's for the seven months prior to the opening of the museums was described as slow. Some of the customers came from the Federal Reserve Bank across the bridge and other commercial buildings in the area, but mostly when the weather was mild. Following the grand opening of the museum, sales rose dramatically through August and then fell as museum business dropped at the beginning of the school year.

John Betts, manager of the McDonald's outlet, said that though museum-related trade was a substantial part of his business, a core of customers unrelated to the museums had developed. He estimated that 60% of weekday sales were not associated with the museums. On weekends, he felt that up to 85% of sales were museum related. Even with the museum, Betts reported that this McDonald's was a low-volume store. He attributed much of that to the early closing time of the museum (6:00 p.m. during summer months and 5:00 p.m. in winter), observing:

> Because there is little or no traffic here after the museums close, we close at 7:00 p.m., except on Fridays when the museums are open until 9:00 and we remain open until 10:00.

Betts, however, was not discouraged. He felt that as the area continued to develop and become established, the restaurant would become very successful.

Trawlers restaurant had closed in November, allegedly for renovations. Business had reportedly been good during the day, but evening traffic had apparently been poor. In early March 1980, Museum Wharf administrators learned that Trawlers had closed permanently, and began a search for a new restaurant tenant with better financing.

"The Bottle," which sold a variety of cold dairy products and salads, was closed during the winter months. An eye-catching landmark, the Bottle was featured prominently in the museums' pre-opening publicity and was adopted as the symbol of Museum Wharf, appearing on maps and directional signs. Once a distinctive ice-cream stand located in Taunton, Massachusetts, it had been donated by Hood Dairy Company to Museum Wharf and shipped there by barge.

Museums' Shop. The Museums' Shop was located on the ground floor of Museum Wharf between McDonald's and the museum lobby. It was a joint operation of the two museums, which had agreed to share the profits (or losses). At their previous locations, the two museums had operated shops in cramped quarters that were out of the normal flow of visitor traffic. It was felt that these out-of-the-way locations, combined with budgeting constraints, had prevented the shops

from increasing sales. With the move to Museum Wharf, serious consideration was given to franchising the shop to an outside operator. After careful study, it was concluded that the profit potential of the shop was great enough that it should be operated by the museums themselves. Further discussions led to an agreement that TCM would run the shop.

Judy Flam, manager of the Museums' Shop, felt that prior to the move to Museum Wharf neither museum had taken its shop seriously. However, she believed the new shop would prove profitable. Flam predicted sales of $300,000 for the fiscal year ending June 1980. This was five times sales of TCM's Jamaica Plain shop and over three times the combined sales of the two separate shops. By the end of December 1979, sales of the shop had exceeded $185,000 and the $300,000 goal seemed easily reachable.

The merchandise in the shop reflected the themes of both museums. It included books, models, electric trains, T-shirts with museum logos, and a wide variety of relatively inexpensive items aimed at children. Numerically, there were many more items with a children theme than with a transportation theme. However, many of the transportation-related items were higher priced, so that the disproportion was reduced when inventory values were used as the basis of comparison. Flam estimated that the volume of traffic in the shop generated by TCM was four or five times that generated by MOT. She cited the "kid's shop" was evidence of this. "Two-thirds of our dollar sales," she said, "come from one-third of our floor space. In that section of the shop—we call it the 'kid's shop'—all items are priced under $5.00."

The high percentage of low-priced items sold led Flam to conclude that many of the higher priced items displayed with MOT visitors in mind would not sell in sufficient volume in the shop to merit stocking in the future.

PROMOTIONAL ACTIVITIES

Recalling the questions faced by the museum administrators prior to the opening of Museum Wharf, Duncan Smith commented:

> We actually faced two decisions. First, what should our short-term promotional strategy be and second, what should our long-term promotional strategy be? We felt that there were essentially three alternatives available. We could promote the pieces, the building, or the area.

"Pieces" were the individual units which composed Museum Wharf; this strategy would have resulted in separate promotion of each unit in Museum Wharf. The "building" was Museum Wharf; a "building" strategy would require promotion of Museum Wharf and tenants. Area promotion would involve Museum Wharf, its tenants, and (at a minimum) Victoria Station and the Tea Party Ship.

The Opening Campaign. No long-term promotion strategy decisions were made prior to the opening, but directors of the

---

EXHIBIT 4
Initial Joint Advertising Expenditure Breakdown, June–August 1979

Insertion Orders/Budget

The following insertion orders were executed:

Where Magazine	⅓ page, eight weekly insertions, 7/7 through 8/25	$ 1,193.20
Panorama Magazine	¼ page, eight weekly insertions, 7/9 through 8/27	408.00
Metro Transit	250 car cards on main rapid transit lines, July and August	3,000.00
	75 bus rears, Massachusetts Pike and Downtown, July and August	6,000.00
	Additional 200 car cards on main rapid transit lines and 250 cards inside buses, July and August	no charge
	Additional 25 bus rears in surrounding towns, July and August	no charge
Boston Globe	3 columns × 115 lines opening ads—6/22, 6/29, 7/2, 7/5	3,648.38
	2 columns × 60 lines individual exhibit ads in rotation, two per week for 7 weeks, 7/9 through 8/20	4,662.00
Metroguide	6″ × 3 columns, one insertion, 6/21 Boston issue	477.70
Production Costs:	Bus rears and car cards, Wisewell	1,128.00
	Type, illustration, production, HH	not known
	Total Committed to Date	$20,517.28

Discounts Obtained: *Where*, 5%; *Boston Globe*, standard 25% nonprofit; *Metroguide*, standard 15% nonprofit plus 15 insertion frequency discount; Metro Transit, $900 off car cards plus additional car cards and bus rears as noted above; *Panorama*, standard 15% nonprofit.

Source: Museum Wharf.

---

two museums agreed that short-term objectives would best be accomplished through the use of a "building" strategy.

By the time the opening date arrived, Museum Wharf had received heavy publicity throughout New England, reinforced by extensive advertising. The initial campaign was designed to publicize the relocation of the museums to Museum Wharf and to emphasize both museums' individual exhibits and programs. Advertising, budgeted at about $20,000, consisted of ads in newspapers and special interest magazines, and display cards on buses and subway cars. (See Exhibits 4 and 5 for expenditure breakdowns and representative print ads.) Though some media expenditures were planned and budgeted through August, most ended in July.

Administrators of both museums expressed dissatisfaction with the initial advertising campaign. They believed that it did not reflect the reality of Museum Wharf and had confused the images and exhibits of the two museums. Duncan Smith said bluntly that the advertising had simply "created the image of a children's amusement park," adding:

> My previous assumption was that any news is good news. Now I know that transmitting the wrong image can be damaging. We've all learned a lot about the client's responsibility to ensure that the agency develops effective advertising. In the future, we've got to face up to the issue of whether we're selling individual museums or a site with a bag of things in it.

Publicity was handled jointly for the museums by Jonathan Hyde. Prior to joining TCM as public relations director in 1977, he had had five years' experience as senior editor and writer for a university publications office. Hyde admitted that he had not been comfortable with the initial joint promotion effort:

> At the time of the opening, the two institutions had different amounts of public visibility. It's fair to say that public knowledge of MOT was much less, their admissions base was much less, and they had recently gone through fairly dramatic changes in what that institution saw as its mission. From my perspective the public had not caught up with those changes when we opened. Those issues, plus the fact that it was the "International Year of the Child," resulted in TCM's getting the lion's share of the publicity. I was faced with trying to turn opportunities for TCM into joint pieces.

The grand opening of Museum Wharf on July 1, 1979, was the beginning of two successive record-breaking months for both museums. Though attendance was expected to drop in September, neither museum had thought that attendance would fall back as much as it actually did. Exhibit 6 compares monthly attendance figures at MOT and TCM with those for the Museum of Fine Arts, Museum of Science, and Aquarium. TCM's attendance was only slightly below budget for September, but MOT's was almost 50% below the budgeted level. Budgeted attendance for each museum reflected financial needs as well as market analysis.*

Subsequent MOT Promotional Efforts. As October progressed, it became apparent to MOT administrators that

---

*1979–80 fiscal year budgeted attendance for MOT was 280,000, accounting for 41% of total budgeted expenses of $1.3 million; but projected attendance was 216,000. At TCM, both budgeted and projected attendance were 500,000, representing 45% of total budgeted expenses of $1.6 million.

EXHIBIT 5
Representative Joint Advertisements for Grand Opening

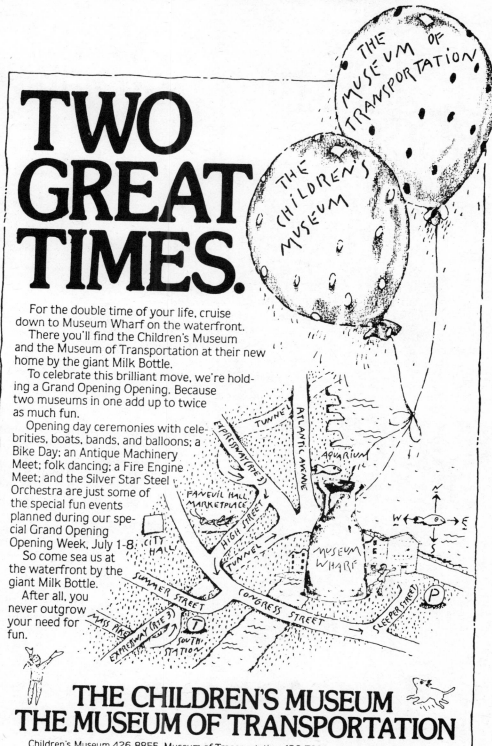

EXHIBIT 5
(continued)

DRIVE YOURSELF BUGGY

You can really get carriaged away at the Museum of Transportation. Assembling and sitting on an 1880's carriage is only one of the fun ways to transport yourself on the new Museum Wharf. Call 426-7999 for all the fun details.

THE CHILDREN'S MUSEUM
THE MUSEUM OF TRANSPORTATION
Open daily behind the giant milk bottle at 300 Congress Street, Boston.
Take the Red Line to South Station.

WKID AROUND.

Appearing on WKID, the Children's Museum TV station, is just one of the entertaining things children can do at the Children's Museum on the new Museum Wharf.
Call 426-8855 for all the fun details.

THE CHILDREN'S MUSEUM
THE MUSEUM OF TRANSPORTATION
Open daily behind the giant milk bottle at 300 Congress Street, Boston
Take the Red Line to South Station.

MODEL T HEE, HEE, HEE.

Climbing in, on and under a Model T can be a moving experience at the Transportation Museum on the new Museum Wharf in Boston. It can also be a lot of fun. Call 426-7999 for all the fun details.

THE CHILDREN'S MUSEUM
THE MUSEUM OF TRANSPORTATION
Open daily behind the giant milk bottle at 300 Congress Street, Boston.
Take the Red Line to South Station.

FEE FI FO FUN.

The fun is twelve times bigger than life on The Giant's Desktop at the Children's Museum. You can wander among a ruler as tall as a tree and a coffee cup you could swim in. In fact, there's big fun for small fry (and big people, too) throughout the entire Children's Museum at Museum Wharf. Call 426-8855 for all the fun details.

THE CHILDREN'S MUSEUM
THE MUSEUM OF TRANSPORTATION
Open daily behind the giant milk bottle at 300 Congress Street, Boston
Take the Red Line to South Station.

EXHIBIT 6
Monthly Attendance Figures for
Five Boston Museums[a]

1978	MOT[b]	TCM[c]	Museum of Fine Arts	Museum of Science	New England Aquarium
July	3,699	17,847	125,636	91,801	128,149
August	4,288	26,879	38,096	103,818	131,881
September	1,550	closed c	36,059	36,689	57,334
October	2,612	20,650	55,039	64,355	59,880
November	2,082	13,095	79,945	75,740	59,464
December	1,466	12,273	68,897	73,741	42,815
1979					
January	1,767	11,911	75,459	75,957	40,757
February	3,588	21,889	39,929	96,267	62,471
March	3,509	18,009	47,877	93,557	68,639
April	4,255	18,003	59,686	90,820	86,249
May	6,678	closed	64,986	108,670	94,085
June	4,027	closed	134,615	83,439	86,537
July	15,803	70,398	31,657	71,397	112,234
August	18,454	83,201	41,810	97,548	128,690
September	7,289	26,676	46,856	24,144	46,831
October	6,906	30,630	85,313	55,473	51,046
November	7,972	36,595	75,449	65,834	55,794
December	8,299	31,684	36,211	65,644	48,201
1980					
January	8,167	32,012	38,371	68,676	53,740

[a] Data for Boston Tea Party Ship & Museum not available.
[b] School groups accounted for 35% of MOT attendance and 10% of TCM attendance in fiscal 1979–1980.
[c] Prior to the move to Museum Wharf, TCM had customarily been closed during the month of September.

Source: Museum Wharf.

actual attendance would remain well below target. A series of discussions at MOT led to the planning and development of an advertising campaign to begin in late November.

MOT administrators felt that a big part of the attendance problem was related to the public's expectations of MOT. They felt that though the initial advertising and publicity had successfully communicated Museum Wharf to the public, it had not been effective in communicating the breadth of MOT's exhibits. They were also concerned about a "fuzzing" effect which they believed contributed to confusion about what Museum Wharf really was. This concern was expressed by Joan Fowler, head of marketing and development for MOT, whose previous background had been in arts administration and conference management. Said Fowler:

> I've noticed that when people refer to this place they call it "The Children's and Transportation Museum." I'm wondering if the joint expenditures were a good use of our money. I feel the site name is still up in the air, still fuzzing in people's minds. What we have to do is to let people know that we are separate in our products. We may both be museums, but the products are different.

Fowler believed that the best way to do this was through separate advertising to correct the misconceptions of the public about MOT and Museum Wharf. So a new advertising campaign was developed, budgeted for $18,000 and designed to run from late November 1979 through February 1980. It consisted of an initial advertisement in *The Boston Globe Calendar** and a series of smaller ads in subsequent *Calendars* emphasizing the different exhibit themes which were introduced in the initial ad. The recurring theme of these ads was, "We're not just a bunch of old cars" (see Exhibit 7).

In late December, MOT took another step to eliminate misconceptions about the relationship between the two museums. MOT administrators felt that the original layout of the lobby was dominated by the large stairway that led to The Children's Museum. They felt that the prominence of this stairway, coupled with the greater public visibility of TCM, left many visitors with the impression that MOT was a tenant of TCM or a less-than-equal partner. In an attempt to overcome this perception the lobby was renovated so that, as visitors entered the area by the elevator leading to MOT, their eyes would be caught by wall panels and small exhibits with a transportation theme. An information desk staffed by a MOT employee was placed in the same area. Some MOT administrators wondered whether their museum should go further and institute a separate admission counter.

MOT gained further publicity (and income) by conducting "Gas Guzzler" auctions of large, high-gasoline-consumption automobiles. Since these cars had been donated to the museum and were transportation related, donors could deduct for tax purposes the *Blue Book* value of the vehicles.* MOT had also been making an aggressive effort to expand membership. Through a series of special events, notably at weekends and during vacations, administrators sought to ensure that something new was taking place when people visited the museum. They also seized opportunities for major media coverage, including the use of MOT for functions and press conferences.

Although MOT administrators felt that their promotional efforts had helped, they concluded that initial projections of 216,000 visitors for the 12 months ending June 1980 would not be reached. So, in late February 1980, they reduced the first-year attendance projection to 180,000.

Promotional Efforts by the Children's Museum. Though TCN's attendance had fallen below budget for September and October, cumulative attendance remained above budget

The Boston Globe, the larger of Boston's two daily newspapers, had the highest circulation of any New England newspaper in 1980. The *Calendar* was a weekly supplement in the Thursday edition, containing detailed entertainment listings and articles about current attractions in Boston and New England.

*The *Blue Book* was a guide to second-hand prices for different models of automobiles. However, reflecting recent sharp increases in gasoline prices, cars that gave poor gas mileage were selling at well below *Blue Book* prices.

EXHIBIT 7
Museum of Transportation Advertisements

This car was built for backseat drivers.

The driver of the 1917 Ohio Electric sat in the back seat, facing forward. The passengers sat up front, facing the driver. . . an arrangement that was fine for conversations, but disastrous for pedestrians!

The Ohio Electric is just one of the strange and wonderful vehicles you'll see at the Museum of Transportation. We have boats and sleds and bikes and buggies and trucks and trolleys and trains and skates. Come visit us, and enjoy all those things that have been moving people since America began.

Museum Wharf, 300 Congress Street, Boston, near South Station. 426-7999.

THE MUSEUM OF TRANSPORTATION ⟹

How Boston got where it is.

EXHIBIT 7
(continued)

The Museum of Transportation isn't just a bunch of old cars.

There's more. Like boats and sleds and bikes and buggies and trucks and trolleys and trains and trikes and roller skates and a big glass outdoor drive-in elevator.

This museum isn't just a bunch of old things to look at. It's a whole bunch of new things to do. You'll attend the opening of America's first subway system. Or watch your ancestors arrive on the boat. Or get on the boat yourself—in an exact reproduction of the cramped passenger quarters of the 17th century ship *Arbella.* You can stand at the open-air controls of an old Boston trolley, ride a hovercraft, slide down a fire pole, or take the wheel of a Model T firetruck.

At the Museum of Transportation, you'll learn why the auto was hailed as the end of urban pollution, find out how railroads started America's watch industry, and discover how at least one Bostonian made a fortune on ice. Come visit us, and see what the Museum is all about—things that have been moving people since America began.

Museum Wharf, 300 Congress Street, Boston, near South Station. 426-7999.

THE MUSEUM OF TRANSPORTATION ⟶
How Boston got where it is.

Thank you to Texaco, Robert Stanley, John Dodge Prints, Railway & Locomotive Historical Society, S.P.N.E.A., Bostonian Society, Boston Globe.

EXHIBIT 8
Children's Museum Advertisement

Don't leave home for the Children's Museum without it.

CHILDREN'S MUSEUM EXPRESS CARD

3714 6950?? 6100?

Brad V. White

"Do you know me? Most people don't, but when I carry this card, people at the Children's Museum know me."

Children who come to learn and play at the Children's Museum get an extra charge out of the Children's Museum Express Card.

It's expressly for kids.

And carrying it means you've got fun at your fingertips.

Museum-wide computer recognition.

The Children's Museum Express Card gives kids museum-wide recognition.

When you send in the application for a card, the information you supply is stored in our computer. This information, whether it's a date of birth, how many children at the Museum have the same first name or same color hair, or the date of your last visit — is ready to surprise and please the card holder.

It's a great opportunity to kid around with a computer and learn at the same time.

Here's what express card holders get.

- Lifetime, personally coded Children's Museum Express Card.
- Lifetime access to personal history stored in the Children's Museum Computer.
- One year membership in the new Children's Museum providing:
  Unlimited free admission.
  10% discount in the Museum's store, recycle shop, kit rentals, workshops and courses.
  Children's Museum Newsletter.
  Invitation to special events.
  Gumball machine window sticker.

Our new home is even more exciting than the old Jamaica Plain Museum, and we think kids will agree. So fill out the Children's Museum Express Application below and return it with a check for $10 to Children's Museum, 300 Congress Street, Boston, MA 02210.

It's a handful of fun and information.

That's why we say, "Children's Museum Express. Don't leave home for the Children's Museum without it."

Children's Museum Express Card Application.

To get your Children's Museum Express Card, just fill out this application, enclose check and mail.

DONOR'S PERSONAL DATA:

Name _____
Address _____
City _____ State _____ Zip _____
Signed _____
$10 per card.

CHILD'S PERSONAL DATA: ☐F ☐M

Name _____ Date of birth _____
Address _____
City _____ State _____ Zip _____
Optional Information:
School _____
Age _____ Color eyes _____ Color hair _____
Parents' names _____
Grandparents' names _____
☐ Please check here if you request additional applications.

for the year. In late February 1980, projected attendance for the first year was revised downwards from a target of 500,000 to 485,000.

Since the conclusion of the opening advertising, TCM had relied, with one exception, on publicity-generated media coverage to maintain visibility. The exception was a membership campaign that began in December. Directed at children, it consisted of public service spots and one-page flyers (Exhibit 8) distributed through retail outlets in suburban neighborhoods. The campaign was built on a spoof of a current American Express card advertising campaign ("Don't leave home without it"). There had been some internal opposition at TCM to this campaign because of its apparent upper-income theme and the possibility that there might be an adverse reaction from some segments of the population.

THE PLANNING MEETING

In mid-March 1980, administrators of the two museums met to discuss planning for the spring and summer seasons. Both groups expected to increase their promotional efforts in the coming months, but there had been much debate on whether to proceed individually or to join forces as they had the previous summer. Each group was anxious to be cooperative but felt their first responsibility was to select that approach which would most benefit their own museum.

22
Wessex College

Christopher H. Lovelock

"Ferdie, I've got this terrific idea for a new program that could be a real money spinner!"

R. Ferdinand Haleck, Director of Alumni Relations at Wessex College, smiled quietly to himself. He was used to these sudden, enthusiastic intrusions into his office by Jeremy Jones, his young assistant. Most of the latter's ideas were somewhat harebrained, but he did have an occasional good idea. "Let's hear it, Jerry!" he said.

"Well," said Jones, "you know how quiet it is on campus in the summer, even though this is supposed to be a popular vacation area. There are zillions of empty rooms on campus, unused classrooms galore, empty labs, the library's a morgue and—apart from the outdoor pool—precious little use is made of the athletic facilities . . ."

Haleck broke in. "I hope you're not going to suggest that we have another crack at re-opening the summer school," he said, a trifle sharply. "We've tried that twice in the past 10 years and lost a fortune both times. There's no way we can expect more than a handful of day students in this location, and our reputation simply isn't strong enough to compete with the biggies in the summer school stakes. The Wessex area may be lovely, but, unless you're a nature freak, it's dullsville for most kids—they want to be in Boston or California."

Christopher H. Lovelock is Associate Professor of Business Administration at the Graduate School of Business Administration, Harvard University.

Wessex College, founded in 1833, was a private, coeducational four-year college with 2,300 students, located in northern New England. It had a good regional reputation in the liberal arts and certain of the sciences. A significant proportion of its graduates went on to undertake graduate degrees, many in professional fields.

"No, no!" responded Jones. "What I'm thinking of is an Alumni College. A lot of places offer them during the summer now. You bring alums back for a week or two, select some sort of intellectual theme to legitimize it, lay on some classes with a few of your better professors, and throw in social events and a couple of outings. They live in the dorms, eat in the dining halls —although you have to provide some decent food—and, generally, relive their student days. Some bring their wives or husbands, and most of them just love it. You can get away with charging them quite a hefty price because it's still cheaper than going for a holiday to a resort hotel. If things work out well, it's usually good for increased annual giving in later years, too. I don't see how it could miss!"

Haleck winced momentarily, remembering that the former President of Wessex had used that identical phrase in promoting the concept of the summer session. However, he had to admit that the idea sounded intriguing. "Why don't you go and take a good look at it," he suggested, "and see what it would take to make the Alumni College idea successful at Wessex?"

Copyright © 1977 by the President and Fellows of Harvard College. No part of this case may be reproduced in any form without prior written permission from the publisher.

23

Montecito State College: Division of Extension Studies

Christopher H. Lovelock

"We need to take a hard look at how we're going to promote our extension programs and courses next year." Dr. Rosemary Shannon, Dean of Extension Studies at Montecito State College, was meeting in March 1983 with her assistant, Harry Fourman, to discuss plans for advertising and other communications for the 1983–84 school year.

Montecito State College (MSC) was located in Montecito, a suburb of the large western city of Sherman, JF. The City of Sherman had a population of 755,000, while the metro area had a population of 1.8 million. On average, there were 2.6 persons per household.

The College, one of several in the Jefferson State College System, was comprised of the undergraduate day division, the graduate school, and the Division of Extension Studies. MSC had been created in 1952 from the merger of Montecito Polytechnic College and Sherman Teachers' College. The facilities of the two institutions were finally combined in 1958 with the completion of a major expansion program at the 90-acre campus of the old "Poly."

In 1982–83, MSC enrolled a total of 6,200 students in the day division, 2,950 in extension studies, and 1,100 in the graduate school. Its undergraduate courses emphasized

This case was prepared by Associate Professor Christopher H. Lovelock as a basis for class discussion rather than to illustrate either effective or ineffective handling of an administrative situation. It is a revision of an earlier version developed for the Institute for Educational Management.

a variety of technical and business-related subjects, education, and the liberal arts. The graduate school offered MA, MS, and M.Ed. degrees in a number of fields, and had a good regional reputation for its programs in education, management, hotel administration, and psychology.

EXTENSION STUDIES

The Division of Extension Studies was responsible for a wide range of undergraduate and graduate courses offered during the late afternoon, weekday evenings, and Saturday morning hours, as well as for day and evening courses during two intensive summer sessions. Although these offerings were directed primarily at people holding jobs or other responsibilities that made it difficult to attend on a full-time basis during the day, about 15% of the enrollees in extension courses were full-time undergraduates.

In addition, the division also sponsored a range of continuing education programs—short, noncredit workshops, courses and seminars. Certificates were awarded upon satisfactory completion of selected courses. The structure and format of these ranged from one- to two-day workshops

EXHIBIT 1
Course Registrations in Division of Extension Studies, 1978–79 to 1982–83

Course Registrations in Division of Extension Studies, 1978–79 to 1982–83

Campus	1978–79	1979–80	1980–81	1981–82	1982–83
Montecito	3,775	3,829	4,006	4,218	4,163
Sherman City	615	603	545	421	481
North Sherman	—	110	213	246	232
Weston	68	96	—	—	—
Puget	—	—	—	113	98
Arvin	118	—	—	—	—
San Lucas	—	165	198	214	209
Total Academic Course Registration[a]	4,576	4,803	4,962	5,312	5,203
Total Continuing Education Enrollments[b]	628	714	773	820	903

[a]About 80% of these registrants sought academic credit; the balance enrolled as auditors.
[b]Not broken out separately by campus since almost all continuing education courses were held at MSC's main campus in Montecito.

Source: Division of Extension Studies, Montecito State College.

and seminars, to courses of five two-hour sessions given at weekly intervals, to twelve three-hour sessions offered twice weekly over a six-week period.

The tuition for degree courses in the Extension Division was $45.00 per credit hour for state residents and $75.00 for nonresidents and foreign students; auditors (noncredit) paid $35.00. Tuition fees were set by the Regents of the Jefferson State College System and had to be approved by the State Legislature. These fees were the same for all seven colleges in the system. Although degree courses ranged in length from 2 to 5 credits, the great majority carried 3 credits. After excluding cancellations, a total of 185 extension degree courses was offered at MSC in 1982–83. Fees for the continuing education programs ranged from $45–$200—depending on the nature and length of the offering—and were at the discretion of the dean, subject to the approval of the president of the College.

The division had substantial automony with the College. It was required to be self-supporting, but was not assessed for many institutional costs, such as classroom space. Courses were taught by both full-time and adjunct faculty who, in most instances, were paid a fixed stipend per course. Part-time faculty were paid a flat rate of $1,500 to $1,800 per semester for a 3-credit course, depending on rank. Typically, courses met once a week for 2 1/2 hours, although a few had two 75-minute classes each week.

The 1982–83 brochure listed 109 different extension courses for credit, many of them offered in both semesters. But, with a few exceptions, courses were automatically cancelled if student registrations failed to reach a pre-defined minimum. Some 900 of the students in Extension Studies in 1982–83 were participants in continuing education programs. (This figure excluded participants in one- and two-day seminars or company-sponsored programs.) The balance

of 2,050 accounted for a total of some 5,200 course registrations during fall and spring semesters. Not all students were enrolled both semesters.

Dr. Shannon, a tenured associate professor of political science, was appointed dean of extension studies in July 1982 and had essentially inherited her predecessor's strategy for the current school year (including the two summer sessions). She expressed the view that MSC needed to devote greater commitment to its extension program, whose quality she regarded as uneven.

Satellite Campuses. In addition to the permanent campus in Montecito, where all day undergraduate and graduate courses were offered, MSC also operated four "satellite" campuses in the evenings for its degree courses. These consisted of high school facilities, made available to MSC free of charge, in Sherman City, and the suburban towns of North Sherman, San Lucas and Puget. Course registrations in these four satellite campuses accounted for 20% of the total; enrollments per course were lower than at the main Montecito campus and there was a much higher rate of course cancellations. Exhibit 1 summarizes enrollments in extension studies at MSC over the past five years, while Exhibit 2 shows the geographic breakdown of students' home locations in 1982–83.

Continuing education programs were generally held at the Montecito campus, although a few had been held at one or other of the satellites. Periodically, CE courses would be commissioned from MSC by a large employer or other organization. In this case the employer's offices or a nearby hotel would be used.

MSC had operated a satellite campus in Sherman City ever since the full-time operations of "Teachers" had been consolidated in Montecito. For many years, this had been the only satellite operation, but from 1979 onwards the College began to experiment with different locations, some of which had subsequently been closed due to lack of success in attracting students. Past experience had shown that satellite campuses tended to draw from a much smaller radius than did the main campus. In selecting specific facilities, the division now looked for easily accessible sites situated near major highways. Availability of adequate parking was essential, while access to public transportation services was a strong plus.

After careful appraisal of the performance of the different satellite campuses in fall semester 1982, Dean Shannon had decided to close the existing Puget campus and to look for a new location in northwest Sherman County. She believed she had identified a promising site in Pine Creek.

One of the objectives of the satellite campuses was to attract students who might begin their studies at a satellite and then later go on to complete their degrees by taking more advanced courses at Montecito. However, few appeared to be doing this. On the other hand, students who lived near a satellite would sometimes travel all the way into Montecito to take courses there which were available at the satellite. Dean Shannon was not entirely sure why this happened (but surmised that it might reflect the greater use of part-time, adjunct faculty at the satellites). She noted that this practice indirectly led to cancellation of courses at satellites, because course registrations there had often been only one or two students short of the minimum (typically 15 students).

Competition. Dean Shannon described the market for evening credit courses in the Greater Sherman area as "highly competitive," with strong competition coming from the University of Sherman and Wallace College (both private institutions), Sherman State College, Lakeview Junior College, and Valley Junior College. Additional competition came

from the University of Jefferson and two county-financed community colleges in the metropolitan area. The dean did not consider the two proprietary schools in Sherman City to be direct competitors, since they were oriented primarily towards vocational education in fields such as computer programming and dental hygiene.*

Like Montecito State, a growing number of both public and private institutions operated satellite campuses in the suburbs and in outlying towns. Typically, the facilities used were local high schools whose classrooms were available for evening use. Exhibit 3 shows the location of all main and satellite campuses in the Greater Sherman area.

Tuition at private institutions was sometimes twice as high per credit hour as MSC's. Wallace College, which emphasized business and the social sciences, had been very aggressive in promoting its offerings, making extensive use of radio and newspaper advertising. Although enrollments had risen steadily at their main campus in Santa Rosa, Dean Shannon had heard that their three satellite campuses were not doing especially well.

The two proprietary schools, one owned by a major industrial conglomerate, advertised widely on TV. The *Sherman Monitor* had recently published an expose of one of these schools charging that its advertising deliberately misled prospective students. It was rumored that the state attorney general's office would soon undertake an investigation.

Communications. The principal approaches used to promote the Extension Division had been to undertake advertising in the *Monitor* and selected suburban papers, and to publish a catalog. Some 20,000 copies of the catalog were prepared and printed each summer at a total cost of $10,800. About 4,000 were mailed out to a variety of organizations and agencies, including public libraries, and company personnel departments. Others were sent out in response to requests or distributed at various locations on campus. The unit cost of printing an extra copy was 16.3 cents, and bulk rate mailing costs were 5.2 cents per copy. The catalog was printed in black and white on medium quality stock.

For its 1982–83 advertising, the division had used the *Sherman Monitor* and selected local newspapers. Although some competitors took full-page newspaper advertisements, and used these to list each and every course offered, MSC's strategy had been to take smaller format advertisements (between one-eighth and one-fourth of a page) which promoted the Montecito State name, listed the locations of the main campus and the various satellite campuses, highlighted the fields in which extension courses were offered, and provided a clip-out coupon and a telephone number which could be used to obtain further information.

EXHIBIT 2
Home Location of Extension Registrants, 1982–83[a]

Location[b]	Students Enrolled for Credit in Extension Courses	Participants in Continuing Education Seminars
City of Sherman	29%	17%
Balance of Sherman County	7	8
North Sherman	9	11
Balance of Orezona County	30	23
Santa Rosa County	9	22
Wendell County	14	16
Other	2	3

[a]This included students taking courses at the satellite campuses.
[b]See Exhibit 3.

Source: Division of Extension Studies, Montecito State College.

---

*Proprietary schools are run as profit-making business offering vocationally oriented courses. Typically, they do not offer courses for academic credit (although certificates are awarded on completion of a course) and are not accredited.

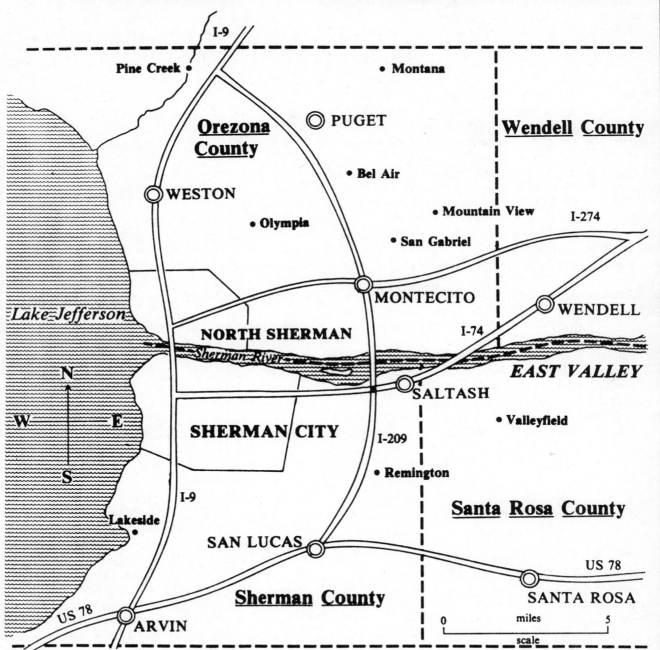

EXHIBIT 3

MAP OF GREATER SHERMAN AREA SHOWING CITIES IN WHICH ACADEMIC EXTENSION COURSES WERE OFFERED

NOTE: The Greater Sherman Metropolitan Area includes all Sherman and Orezona Counties, plus SW Wendell County and NW Santa Rosa County. There are over 40 separate towns and municipalities in the Metro area (which is heavily urbanized), but only selected town names are shown on the map, which also shows the major freeways serving the Metro area. The largest suburban centers outside Sherman City and North Sherman are marked with a double circle.

EXHIBIT 4
Responses to Mail Survey of Fall 1982 Extension Division Students (All Campuses)
Who Did Not Re-Register in Spring 1983

Note: Survey was conducted February 1983. 206 completed questionnaires were received, giving a response rate of 32%. Selected questions only are listed below and non-responses are not shown.

Total Number of Courses for Which You Registered in Fall 1982?

One	126
Two	45
Three	3
Four	2

Your Primary Purpose in Registering Last Semester?

Degree credit	105
Professional advancement	44
Desire for knowledge	21
General interest	15
Self improvement	11
Meet new people	5

Your Primary Source of Learning About the Course(s)?

A friend or relative	45
Employer/employment agency or education/training office	20
Advertisement in *Sherman Monitor*	16
Advertisement in local suburban newspaper	16
A student enrolled in the program	11
Receipt of unsolicited pamphlet, bulletin, brochure	10
Solicited pamphlet	10
Instructor/counselor at another institution	8
Official pamphlet, bulletin, brochure seen at work	7
Advertisements/information on radio/TV	7
Close to home	5
Other	9

Did All the Courses You Took Last Fall Measure Up to the Description in College Material Received by You? (4 point scale)

1. Completely	96
2. Reasonably so	57
3. To some degree	17
4. Not at all	12

Did You Feel That All the Courses You Took Last Fall Were Effectively Taught? (5 point scale)

1. Very effective	84
2. Fairly effective	43
3. Average	25
4. Rather ineffective	12
5. Very ineffective	10

Principal Reason for Not Attending Spring 1984?

Job responsibilities conflicted	36
Financial difficulties	30
Moved too far to travel	21
Program required more time than am prepared to invest right now	17
Couldn't find any course of interest	14
Family problems or conflicts	13
Health problems (mine or in family)	12
Veterans benefits discontinued	9
Wanted more advanced course	8
Completed all degree requirements	5
Did not fit schedule	5
Course not offered	4
Other	20

Planning to Register Again in Evening Division?

Next summer	24
Next fall	44
No—attending a private institution	8
No—attending another public institution	19
No—planning to attend a private institution	9
No—planning to attend another public institution	13
No	21
Uncertain	38

Your Sex?

Male	97	Female	109

Your Present Age?

17–19	4	35–39	22
20–24	51	40–44	10
25–29	48	45–49	6
30–34	36	50–54	5
		55 or over	2

Highest Level of Educational Achievement?

Master's degree or higher	13
Bachelor's degree	48
More than two years of college	35
Associate degree	25
Some college but less than two years	56
High school graduate/equivalency	9

Source: Division of Extension Studies, Montecito State College.

In early December 1981, the Extension Division had joined forces with other divisions of the College to develop a four-page newsprint brochure, mailed to 100,000 homes in Montecito and surrounding towns. This included a listing of all spring semester extension courses. The total costs of this mailing (of which Extension Studies paid one-third), were $3,900 for production and printing, plus $5,700 for preparation and mailing. A certain amount of radio advertising had been used by the division of extension studies; 1982–83 costs amounted to about $5,000. However, Dean Shannon expressed doubts about the value of radio advertising. Few registrants could be traced to radio advertising in a recent survey (Exhibit 4), nor was radio often mentioned when telephone enquirers were asked by extension staff how they had learned of Montecito State.

In February 1983, the division had conducted a mail survey of evening degree students registered in fall 1982 who did not graduate at the end of that semester and had not reregistered in January for the spring semester. Among other things, this asked respondents their primary source of learning about the courses they took. Of the 638 questionnaires mailed, 206 had been completed and returned. Selected responses are shown in Exhibit 4. Friends and relatives were given as the primary source of information about courses, followed by professional referrals, *Monitor* advertising, and advertisements in local suburban newspapers.

In addition to being listed in the catalog, most of the 70 continuing education courses offered in 1982–83 were also promoted by direct mail. The division had developed or purchased several mailing lists, enabling it to target brochures promoting specific courses or seminars at groups likely to be interested in the programs in question. These lists included: members of professional organizations (e.g., accountants, lawyers); employers (divided into several categories, according to the size, location and activities or product of the organization); school superintendents, chambers of commerce, public libraries throughout the state, and past participants.

Mailings were running at the level of 200,000 a year. The unit cost of producing and printing a brochure ranged from one cent to six or seven cents, depending on length and format, paper stock, and use of color in printing. Bulk mailing costs were 5.2 cents per unit. No mass media advertising had been used to promote continuing education (CE) courses, although press releases promoting specific courses were sometimes picked up by the newsletters and other periodicals published by state and local professional associations. CE mailing expenditures in 1982–83 were budgeted at $18,100.

Several changes were planned for 1983–84. Dean Shannon had assigned primary responsibility for advertising decisions to her assistant, Harry Fourman, and had also placed him in charge of the satellite campus program. Fourman, who held an MBA from the University of Jefferson, combined his appointment as assistant dean of Extension Studies with a half-time appointment as instructor in management at MSC. As a start, Fourman had compiled some information on the nature of the extension programs offered at MSC and each of its competitors (Exhibit 5).

ADVERTISING AND PUBLICITY AT MSC

The responsibility for advertising and publicity at Montecito State was in the hands of Roberta Jensen, director of public information. The public information office served every department on campus, including alumni activities. It handled all news items for the College and developed publicity to promote major events. Jensen headed up a group of four people, including a publications editor and a news bureau coordinator. Her own background included a degree in communications, work for the *Chicago Tribune* and a Sherman advertising agency, and three years as assistant director of public relations for a major hospital in Sherman. She had joined MSC in fall 1981.

Total expenditures on publications at MSC amounted to some $100,00 a year. The Division of Extension Studies accounted for about 30% of this. Although large pieces, such as catalogs and the annual report, were sent to outside printers, Jensen noted that more work was being done in-house than before, with small flyers being designed, pasted up and typeset on campus. The public information office did not know the total costs incurred by the College for mailing publications, since mailings were handled on a departmental or division basis. Certain items were bulk-mailed by third class mail, and the College also had two second class mailing permits enabling it, as a nonprofit organization, to mail items such as catalogs more cheaply but supposedly faster. However, various constraints and restrictions had to be observed to qualify for this reduced rate.

MSC did not use a public relations agency for publicity and news releases, preferring to handle such activities in-house. For media advertising, though, the College used a local advertising agency. The total advertising budget was relatively small compared to that of some of the private junior colleges and proprietary schools in the area. Including both media purchases and production costs, MSC's advertising expenditures in 1982–83 were projected to total just over $90,000. The Division of Extension Studies accounted for over 50% of this total.

Rather than working on a commission basis with the advertising agency (whereby the latter's remuneration came from a 15% commission received from the media with whom the advertising was placed), MSC had put the agency on a retainer of $1,300 per month and had arranged for it to rebate the commissions directly to the college. This retainer covered consulting services and development of media campaigns, including design of copy and artwork. The advantage of the retainer from the agency's standpoint was that it provided a guaranteed income which would not be affected by fluctuations in the college advertising expenditures. From MSC's standpoint, it meant that there was no incentive for the agency to recommend additional advertising outlays with a view to boosting its commission income.

In an effort to maximize exposure for Montecito State, the public information office used public service announcements (PSAs) on radio and TV to promote college events and programs, as well as seeking newspaper listings in the "Calendar" sections. However, Ms. Jensen felt that the media were generally reluctant to accept PSAs to promote academic courses. Commenting on the different media in the Greater Sherman area, she observed:

> Sherman has one major, metropolitan daily paper, the *Sherman Monitor*. There used to be both morning and evening editions, but now it's only published mornings. Frankly, it's not one of the great newspapers of America, but it is quite widely read, and gives us an opportunity to hit a wide variety of people.
>
> We have a half-dozen varying quality suburban dailies, and a terrific number of weekly papers, both independent and chain. Most of the suburban dailies are published in the evening. Some households subscribe to both the *Monitor* and a suburban daily. The further you get from Sherman City, the more likely people are to buy a local daily rather than the *Monitor*.
>
> The problem with advertising in suburban papers is that the costs really mount up—collectively, they nickle and dime you to death. The advertising agencies all tell me that the *Monitor* is more effective, though sometimes I have my doubts. But the agencies tell you to use those suburban papers for publicity. They'll nearly always run your news stories, since they need "filler." The *Monitor* doesn't.

EXTENSION 5
Extension Programs at Degree-Granting Institutions in the Sherman Metro Area

Institution	Type	Main Campus Location	1982–83 Satellite Campus Locations	Extension Course Registrations (1982–83)	Fee Per Credit Unit	Academic Calendar	1983 Fall Classes Begin	Principal Communications Efforts (1982–83)
Montecito State College	Public Four-Year Some Grad Programs	Montecito	North Sherman Puget San Lucas Sherman City	5,312	$45	Semester (finishes before Xmas)	Sept.19	Direct Mail *Sherman Monitor* Local Newspapers Radio (some)
Arvin Community College	Public Two-Year	Arvin	—	2,102	$35	Quarter	Oct. 3	Direct Mail Local Newspapers
Lakeview Junior College	Private Two-Year	Weston	Bel Air Puget Olympia North Sherman	5,100	$80	Semester (finishes before Xmas)	Sept. 7	*Sherman Monitor* Local Newspapers OCT Buses Radio
Orezona Community College	Public Two-Year	Mountain View	Montana	2,311	$35	Quarter	Oct. 3	Local Newspapers Radio
St. Anne's College	Private Four-Year	Bel Air	—	484	$85	Semester (finishes after Xmas)	Sept. 21	Local Newspapers
Sherman State College	Public Four-Year	Sherman City	—	2,950	$45	Semester (finishes before Xmas)	Sept.19	*Sherman Monitor*
University of Jefferson	Public Four-Year Many Grad Programs	Lakeside	Arvin Sherman City Puget	6,442	$55	Quarter	Sept. 12	Direct Mail *Sherman Monitor* Local Newspapers Radio
University of Sherman	Private 4-Year Many Grad Programs	Sherman City	North Sherman Olympia Puget Valleyfield Weston	7,106	$75	Quarter	Sept. 26	Direct Mail *Sherman Monitor* Local Newspapers Radio, TV, Buses
Valley Junior	Private Two-Year	Saltash	Mountain View Remington San Gabriel San Lucas	6,421	$70	Semester	Sept. 19	Radio *Sherman Monitor* TV Billboards *San Lucas Post*
Wallace College	Private Four-Year Some Masters Programs	Santa Rosa	Saltash San Lucas Wendell	500	$95	Semester (finishes before Xmas)	Sept. 12	Direct Mail Radio *Sherman Monitor* *San Lucas Post*
Wendell College	Private Four-Year	Wendell	—	1,244	$90	4-1-4	Sept. 7	Local Newspapers

We've not purchased TV time at all. We wouldn't settle for anything less than first-rate commercials. Just to produce two different 30-second TV spots and two different 10-second spots could run anywhere from ten to fifteen thousand dollars. The cost of running the ads would be relatively inexpensive by contrast, depending on what station and time slot you use. My question is whether any return we might generate would justify the cost.

We've used radio for extension studies, but always in conjunction with other media, such as newspapers, and direct mail. The theory behind this is that one medium reinforces another. We tend to use radio towards the end of a campaign—for instance during the last two weeks of a six-week campaign. We believe that it provides a good reminder, a final "push" to make your prospects act. Our extension students are mostly employed, working people, so we often go after "drive time," which is expensive.* There are a large number of different radio stations in this area and most of them tailor their programs to fairly specific market segments.

We haven't been able to trace many enquiries to those radio ads. However, advertising agencies will tell you that people don't always remember accurately where they learned about a specific product. We've surveyed people on where they first heard about our programs, and often they'll list a newspaper in which we *didn't* advertise!

Two things we haven't used are car cards on the buses and billboards. I've noticed that Lakeview advertises quite heavily on the buses—their ads have little brochures you can tear off and mail in for further information. Nobody around here except the proprietary schools and Valley Junior seem to use billboards, although I know colleges in other cities do.

DEVELOPING A COMMUNICATIONS PROGRAM

In early March 1983, the extension studies staff were evaluating alternative communications strategies for 1983–84.

---

*"Drive Time" is time during the morning and evening commute periods when large numbers of people are listening to the radio in their cars as they drive to or from work.

EXHIBIT 6
Sample Advertising Rates for Newspapers Circulating in Greater Sherman Area

Newspaper	Rate Per Line[a]	Lines Per Page[b]	Total Circulation (thousands of copies)
(A) Major Dailies			
Wall Street Journal (Western Edition)	7.80	1,776	2,003[c]
Sherman Monitor	5.45	2,400	511
(B) Suburban/Local Dailies[d]			
Arvin Independent	.38	2,400	9
East Valley Star Advocate	.50	2,400	40
Montecito Sun	.79	2,400	55
Pine Creek Enquirer	.29	2,352	11
San Lucas Post	.91	2,464	73
Weston Journal	.30	2,352	14
(C) Suburban/Local Weeklies			

Thirty-one of the towns and cities within or near Greater Sherman had their own weekly newspaper. Advertising rates were typically in the range of 27–55¢ per line.

[a] The agate line is the basic advertising cost unit for newspapers. (There are 14 agate lines per column inch in classified advertising.) Although rates tend to vary according to location in the paper and discounts may be given for large format ads or multiple insertions, for the purposes of case analysis, please work from these line rates and assume no discounts.
[b] This provides some sense of the format and size of the paper's pages. The *Sherman Monitor* page format of 2,400 lines represents approximately 13½″ × 21″ (284 sq. ins.) of space within the printed margins. In making rough calculations for case analysis, take 12 lines as equivalent to 1″ × 1″ of display advertising space.
[c] Estimated circulation in Sherman Metro area: 69,000.
[d] Most of these suburban dailies also circulated in adjoining towns and cities.

Source: *Newspaper Rates and Data,* Standard Rate and Data Service, Inc., January 1983.

Although the start of the fall semester was still over six months away, a long lead time was required. Meetings were also being held with the director of public information, Roberta Jensen, and would be held later with MSC's advertising agency.

At their first meeting together, Roberta Jensen told Harry Fourman:

> One of the things MSC hasn't done as well as it might is to figure out the effectiveness of different advertising approaches. I suspect that habit and intuition have played a significant role in making advertising decisions. Candidly, it looks as though the advertising agency has played a very passive role in media selection in recent years.

Harry Fourman looked thoughtful. "The trouble," he said, "is that we don't have one single funnel through which all our responses flow." He paused, then continued:

> We do know that the phone starts to ring as soon as advertising begins. We've also found that while we get good response rates from return of newspaper coupons and self-mailer cards asking for information, the ultimate registration rates resulting from these enquiries have been relatively low.

In 1982–83, the division's budget for promoting degree and continuing education programs offered during the fall and spring semesters had been set at $88,800 (the budget for the summer sessions was set separately). Expenditures were broken down as follows:

Printing of catalogs, brochures, etc.	$20,800
Postage costs	12,600
Radio advertising	5,000
Labor (mailroom, labeling, etc.)	7,000
Newspaper advertising:	
Sherman Monitor	33,700
Selected suburban dailies	6,800
Advertising production costs	2,900
Total Budget	$88,800

Despite rising costs, the vice president–finance had indicated that this budget figure would have to remain unchanged in 1983–84.* The question was how to allocate these expenditures among the different alternative media. Of particular interest to the dean and assistant dean of Extension Studies was the relative emphasis that should be given to promoting the satellite campuses and the many continuing education programs. To help him in analyzing the situation, Harry Fourman had compiled a table highlighting the home locations of extension students for 1982–83 (Exhibit 2). At his request, Roberta Jensen had provided some basic cost data on advertising in Sherman area newspapers (Exhibit 6),

---

*Although bulk rate mailing costs were expected to remain at 5.2 cents per unit for the current year, it was estimated that printing and production costs in 1983–84 would be 5% higher than during the 1982–83 academic year and that labor costs at MSC would be 6% higher. The newspaper and radio advertising costs shown in Exhibits 6 and 7 were about 7% above the rates paid by MSC in 1982–83.

EXHIBIT 7
Memo on Radio, TV, Billboard, and Transit Advertising Costs

To: Harry Fourman
From: Roberta Jensen

March 3, 1983

It's easier said than done to give you "representative" advertising rates for radio and TV stations in the Greater Sherman area, since these rates are subject to so many variations, but I'll try to give you some feel at least for the numbers involved.

Television

There are five commercial TV stations which can be received in the Sherman metro area. Four have their transmitters in or near Sherman City, while the fifth broadcasts from Wendell and its signal can be picked up in most parts of the metro area, but the quality of reception varies. These stations are:

KZBA-RV	Channel 3	CBS Affiliate
KCCL-TV	Channel 4	NBC Affiliate
KFFO-TV	Channel 8	ABC Affiliate
KSSM-TV	Channel 12	NBC (Wendell)
KIRM-TV	Channel 23	Independent

Rates for each of these stations vary substantially by time of day and nature of program, reflecting both type and size of audience reached. The table below should give you some feel for the range of rates charged for different stations at different times of day. All rates are for a single 30-second spot, based upon the purchase of 10–12 such spots. Exact times for running the spots cannot be specified but are at the discretion of the station. Smaller purchases would cost more on a per-unit basis.

TV Channel	Early AM	Local Daytime	Evening Prime Time	Late Evening	Late Night
3, 4, 8	$80–150	$200–500	$1,300–3,200	$350–500	$100–250
12	50–120	150–210	700–1,500	300–450	65–90
23	40–70	50–150	300–600	150–250	40–70

Radio

We certainly have a lot of radio stations in the metro area. There are 15 AM stations and 9 FMs. Some of these, such as KQFD and KRPC-FM, are National Public Radio affiliates, and accept no advertising. Below, I've listed some sample advertising rates for a 30-second radio spot (assuming, again a purchase of 10–12 such spots). I've confined the list to AM stations—FMs are usually cheaper, but tend to reach a smaller audience; among other things, not that many people have FM car radios, and FM transmissions, being UHF and usually lower power, tend to reach a smaller geographic area than AM.

Station	Programming	Principal Target Audience	Drive Time (AM)	Drive Time (PM)	Mid-Day/ Evening	Late Night
KEFJ	Music, easy listening	Adults 35–49	$45	$35	$32	$27
KHHD	Talk, sports, news, music	Adults 18–65	$125	$95	$50–$80	$50
KMPC	Top 40s, rock	Teens, adults 18–65	$40	$30	$22	$12
KROQ	Rock, etc.	Teens, young adults	$110	$75	$55–$125	$45–$65
KJIM	Talk shows, popular music for adults	Adults 35 +	$110	$85	$60–$100	$30
KHRP	Classical music	Adults 18 +	$60	$55	$53	$50
KCSB[a]	Black Oriented	Black adults	$30	$25	$22	—
KMNC	Continuous news and information, traffic reports	Adults 18–49	$190	$130	$55–$115	$30–$55
KCHX	Spanish language (talk and music)	Spanish-speaking adults 18 +	$35	$25	$25	$15

[a]Goes off air at sundown.

Outdoor Advertising

It's a bit easier to give an answer on billboards. (I'm assuming you're not interested in the fancy painted variety, just the type you stick paper on.) Billboard rentals vary somewhat according to location and whether or not they're illuminated. A typical cost in the Sherman area would be $315 per month. To this, you've got to add design and production costs of 15–40%, plus the cost of putting them up. At a very rough guess, I'd say that a three-month campaign involving ten billboards would cost you a total of about $11,500; for one month, the cost would be around $5,400.

Transit Advertising

As you probably know, there are two transit districts in the metropolitan area—the Sherman Santa Rosa Transit Authority, which operates south of the river, Orezona County Transit which serves all Orezona County and has commuter services into Sherman City. The SSRTA has 500 buses and a daily ridership of 220,000 passengers; OCT has 300 buses and 100,000 riders. OCT is generally regarded as the better run of the two. Most of their buses are fairly new, they attract a lot of commuters, and there's relatively little vandalism (I know all this because my husband Jack takes OCT to work every day!) Both sell 11″ × 28″ car cards for interior display in the vehicles. They usually charge $10 per card per month and you've got to specify at the outset how many months you want; I should be able to get us a 25% discount because we're a public operation. Each transit district has a minimum placement of 50 cards, and you have to take pot-luck on which routes they appear on. But they won't put in more than one car card per bus unless you request it. To print up a three-color card averages $4.30 per card on a print run of 200 cards. After that, the incremental cost is about $1.45 per card.

and also sent him a short memo concerning advertising costs for radio, TV, billboard, and transit advertising (Exhibit 7).

Enrollment figures had dropped slightly for extension courses over the past year, but risen for continuing education (CE) programs. The goal that Shannon and Fourman had agreed on for 1983–84 was to increase CE enrollments from 900 to 1,000 and to increase the number of extension course registrations from 5,200 to 5,500.

A New Development. As Fourman sat working at the desk in his rather cramped little office with the door ajar, he heard his name called. It was Dean Shannon. "Hi, Rosemary!" he said. "What's up?"

Shannon pulled over a chair and sat down.

> I just got out of a meeting with the president. He agreed to increase our communications budget for next year when he heard that we had signed up Pine Creek High for our new satellite campus. He lives up that way himself and agrees with me that the north county area has real growth potential. The problem with our Puget campus was that access was difficult, whereas Pine Creek is just two blocks from a freeway exit and also has very good bus service.

But he's not happy with MSC's satellite program and told me that next year may be our last chance. Unless we can get course registrations up to a total of 1,200 at the four satellites, he says he'll be forced to consider eliminating them, except the Sherman one, which he has to keep for political reasons.

Fourman leaned forward, anxiously. "So how much money is he willing to let us have next year?"

> Ninety-five thousand, but it's not exactly carte blanche. On the one hand, he said that we should try to be innovative, that he thinks the division has been in a rut as far as its communications are concerned. Then in the next breath he said that he feels our advertising should be "dignified"—whatever *that* may mean—and shouldn't make us look like one of those proprietary schools. He also had to overrule Harvey Stimson, the VP–Finance, who was furious about our increased budget—he feels advertising is a waste of money.

She pulled a face, then continued:

> The main thing is, he wants to go over the division's marketing plan for fall and spring semesters with us personally next month. He says it's high time he educated himself as to what marketing is all about!

24
American Repertory Theatre

Penny Pittman Merliss
Christopher H. Lovelock

It was 9:15 in the morning, and already the phone was ringing in the office of Sam Guckenheimer, comptroller of the American Repertory Theatre (A.R.T.) in Cambridge, Massachusetts. Guckenheimer grabbed the receiver from across a pile of computer printouts and strained to listen as voices and typewriters chattered behind him. "Could you speak up, please?" he asked his caller. "I'm in the middle of four conversations, one of them with a machine."

Depending on the time of day, Guckenheimer could be found wearing any one of several hats. After finishing college he had attended the Yale School of Drama for two years and, as A.R.T.'s comptroller, was in charge of budgeting and finance. He had also majored in Slavic languages and literature as an undergraduate and was presently at work on a new translation of Gogol's *The Inspector General,* the fourth play of A.R.T.'s spring 1980 repertory. But at the moment, his most pressing task was designing A.R.T.'s first direct-mail subscription offer, to be mailed to a test group of 25,000 potential subscribers within 30 days.

HISTORY OF A.R.T.

The seeds of the American Repertory Theatre were sown in 1966 when Robert Brustein was invited to create a professional resident repertory theatre at the Yale School of Drama

in New Haven, Connecticut. Brustein, an actor and theatre scholar who was also one of America's leading drama critics, was named dean of the school. His resident company, the Yale Repertory Theatre, became renowned for the quality and originality of its productions; drama critic Clive Barnes described the Yale Rep in 1978 as "one of the finest theatre companies in the English-speaking world." The company's repertory was eclectic, ranging from new interpretations of foreign and American classics to premieres of works by relatively unknown playwrights.

From the outset, the theatre was conceived as a not-for-profit, subsidized operation. As Brustein commented:

> The profit motive requires an appeal to the lowest common denominator for the widest possible audience . . . the more serious artist does not always make his or her appeal known immediately. It takes some time before the audience catches up in some cases. In other cases, the audience is ahead. But what do we do about our James Joyces and our Stravinskys and our Picassos and our Ibsens and our Brechts until they've become absorbed into the culture and become more popular? We have to serve them, we have to subsidize them, we have to support them. And that's why some institutions exist.

Penny Pittman Merliss was formerly a Research Associate at Harvard University and Christopher H. Lovelock is Associate Professor of Business Administration, Harvard University.

Brustein's emphasis on professional performance and production standards aroused some opposition on campus, particularly among undergraduates seeking more stage time for amateur productions. In 1978 A. Bartlett Giamatti was appointed president of Yale. After months of conflict, Giamatti, a supporter of undergraduate theatre, informed Brustein that he would be replaced as dean of the drama school. Following intense negotiation, Brustein and his company—renamed the American Repertory Theatre—announced their intention to move to the Loeb Drama Center in Cambridge, Massachusetts, under the sponsorship of Harvard University.

The Loeb Drama Center. Harvard had long encouraged undergraduate extracurricular theatricals, a tradition which culminated in the development of the Loeb Drama Center. The $1.8 million building, funded by a $1.5 million gift from John L. Loeb, an investment banker, was opened in 1960.

Located on the edge of an upper-income residential area, the Loeb was a five-minute walk from Harvard Square, a busy retail area next to the University. The Harvard Square neighborhood contained many specialty stores, including more bookstores within a half-mile radius than any other area of its size in the world; some remained open till almost midnight. A newsstand adjoining the Square subway stop boasted that it offered the world's most extensive stock of international newspapers and periodicals. Local restaurants were equally cosmopolitan, offering visitors a choice of Chinese, Italian, French, Arabic, Spanish, Mexican, Swiss, Cuban, German, Indian, Brazilian, and Vietnamese cuisine, in addition to fast food and vegetarian cooking. Three movie theatres were within easy walking distance of the Square, and several bars and coffeehouses in the area scheduled regular performances of jazz and folk music.

The Loeb had no parking lot for patrons, and on-street parking was limited. The nearest public parking lots, four blocks away, charged a flat rate of $2 for evening parking. Public transportation service to the area, however, was extensive. Harvard Square was the terminus of the MBTA subway system's Red Line and a major subway-bus transfer point. Downtown Boston could be reached by train in 10 minutes.

Praised by one Boston theatre critic as a "magnificent facility," The Loeb's main auditorium contained a fixed bank of 402 comfortable seats, rising in the rear of the house. The remaining 154 seats were mounted on two motorized platforms, resting on hydraulic lifts, which could be banked to produce a traditional proscenium stage, an arena, or an Elizabethan apron. Sightlines were excellent.

Yet with the exception of a summer theatre and occasional special attractions (often one-person shows or small dance troupes), the Loeb's main stage was dark for much of the year. In 1978–79, student productions occupied the main stage for a total of only 14 weeks (56 performances), leading one observer to refer to the Loeb as a "Rolls Royce without a chauffeur."

THE BOSTON THEATRE ENVIRONMENT

Their expectations aroused by Boston's reputation as "the Athens of America," many newcomers to the city were surprised to discover how rarely Boston was exposed to theatre and dance of the first rank. Only four legitimate theatres survived downtown in 1979, all of them located only a block from the notorious "Combat Zone."* Boston contained only one auditorium large enough to accommodate first-class ballet troupes; this was also the city's major convention facility, and the acoustics were so bad that no ballet company comparable to the New York City Ballet or the Bolshoi had visited the city in years. The internationally respected Boston Symphony Orchestra (BSO), founded in 1881, enjoyed the highest earned income of any orchestra in the U.S., but was the only professional performing arts institution in the city with a permanent home until Sarah Caldwell's Opera Company of Boston finally managed to purchase a theatre in 1978.

Financial Problems. Some observers felt that a general lack of funds was the real reason why Boston had failed to establish itself nationally as a center for the performing arts. Although Massachusetts ranked third among the 50 states in number of artists and arts organizations (after New York and California), it ranked fifteenth in per capita state spending on the arts.

Unlike New Yorkers, Bostonians could look to only a few large local businesses for corporate support. The problem was exacerbated, according to some observers, by the fact that large donors to the arts did not always achieve the immediate social prominence they found in other cities. As *Time* magazine once put it: "Boston has class that is bred on Beacon Hill, not bought with hefty contributions to the arts."

Response to Repertory. Failure to develop a permanent, professional resident theatre company was not a problem unique to Boston, however. Philadelphia, Atlanta, Houston, and even New York City lacked a company comparable to A.R.T. Several explanations for this deficiency had been advanced. Although repertory companies offered performers regular employment and a chance to perform against "type," the physical and emotional demands of repertory acting could be severe. Since plays ran in rotation, actors might find themselves performing three or four major parts in different plays within the same week—or rehearsing one play while they took leading roles in another. Salaries, though they conformed to union standards for a theatre of the Loeb's size ($239 per week minimum through June 1980), did not approach the pay offered by motion pictures, television, or major Broadway work, and repertory theatres were rarely

---

*An eight-block area (referred to by city officials as the "adult entertainment district") that contained most of the city's pornographic bookstores, cinemas, and stage shows.

able to use stars to attract the public. Even more important to many actors than salary was the loss of national exposure which they might suffer by working outside New York or Hollywood.

In addition to a relatively long-term commitment from performers, successful repertory theatre, it was generally agreed, also required the presence of a loyal audience willing to support a variety of plays ranging from traditional to experimental. Carolyn Clay, arts critic for *The Boston Phoenix,* distinguished two disparate theatre audiences in the Boston community. The first was a group located primarily in the suburbs who would come downtown to large commercial theatres like the Shubert, the Wilbur, and the Colonial for proven hits and big stars. Boston had once been well known as a tryout town for Broadway-bound plays, and, according to the press agents questioned by Clay, was still considered a better barometer of New York taste than Washington, D.C. Nevertheless, Clay noted:

> Most of the people I spoke with agreed that Boston, which used to be more adventuresome in its capacity for Broadway-bound hopefuls, would rather see a show that had already made it in New York.

The prices charged by downtown theatres (up to $22.50 for a top seat at a musical in 1979) were seen by some as motivating this customer preference for guaranteed appeal.

The other major school of taste in Boston, Clay felt, was represented by more intellectual theatregoers, many residing in Cambridge. This audience patronized improvisational revues like those offered by the Next Move Theatre in Boston and was relatively more likely to support college or experimental productions. Shows like British actor Alex McCowen's reading of St. Mark's Gospel, performed at the Loeb in 1978 following a successful run in London, also appealed to this group. Even McCowen's show, however, was far from obscure; it had received rave reviews in British publications and *The New Yorker* before reaching the Loeb.

The most successful plays in Boston were those that managed to bring these two audiences together. The consensus among the professional theatre people interviewed by Clay was that "recognizability" was essential in selling theatre to Bostonians; even the managing director at the Loeb admitted that the audience for truly avant-garde theatre was "wildly limited" in Boston. Moreover, the college student population, which helped to support a number of repertory and art cinemas in the area, was rarely visible at legitimate theatre productions.

Anticipating A.R.T.'s arrival, Clay concluded:

> There *is* an audience here for weighty and adventuresome, if not for radical, theatre. Perhaps, if we acquire such a company for ourselves, and it feeds us a reasonably steady diet of quality laced with controversy, we'll learn to take pot luck.*

*Carolyn Clay, "Beyond the Theatre Fringe," *The Boston Phoenix,* December 5, 1978, p. 12.

A.R.T. management had discovered some preliminary statistics which appeared to support this view. Previous national research sponsored by The Ford Foundation had indicated that people with at least some college education were more than three times as likely to attend the theatre as people with high school education or less; the Boston Standard Metropolitan Statistical Area (population 2.7 million) had a proportion of college graduates and professionals over 50% above the national mean.

On the other hand, despite the widely held opinion that Boston would welcome a company of A.R.T.'s standing, no theatre in the city had developed a consistent, loyal audience. Two previous attempts to develop a lasting audience for repertory theatre in Boston had both failed eventually. The Charles Street Playhouse disbanded its repertory company in 1968 after five years; the Boston Repertory Theatre had disbanded in 1978 after ten years. Many people had ideas about what Boston audiences liked, but no one really knew—and no one in any of the city's arts organizations had carried out detailed market research studies over an extended period.

PLANNING THE FIRST SEASON

Brustein and his company came to Boston knowing they would need to undertake a major fund-raising effort. It had been estimated that an initial 14-week season of four plays (112 performances) would cost roughly $1 million.* Harvard would contribute $163,000 of this sum in cash, as a grant from the Faculty of Arts and Sciences. (It would also provide maintenance and utilities and allow A.R.T. the use of the University's accounting, billing, and other miscellaneous services totalling about $175,000 in value.) In return for this contribution, A.R.T. planned to offer full-season student pass subscriptions to Harvard/Radcliffe undergraduates at $10 per pass. Students would be asked to pick up their tickets at the box office beginning two weeks before each production opened, after full-price subscription sales had concluded; subject to box office discretion, they could be seated anywhere in the house. No other special offers were planned for the Harvard community, which A.R.T. management considered a captive audience. A.R.T. had raised $214,000 for 1979–1980 from government agencies and national foundation grants; over 60% of the first season's budget would have to come from community contributions and ticket sales.

Management stated that, as was customary for the company, the repertory for the first Cambridge season had been chosen without regard to commercial appeal (although the first play, Shakespeare's *A Midsummer Night's Dream,* had been a hit at Yale in 1975). The original New Haven produc-

*Performances were scheduled for six evenings (Tuesday-Sunday) and two afternoons (Saturday-Sunday) weekly. It was estimated that extending the initial season would cost roughly $30,000 per week. Costs for the following six-play season, running from September to June 1980–81, were estimated at $1.7 million.

tion of this tale of magic, romance, and slapstick was being revived for A.R.T.'s Cambridge premiere, with designers, director, and several actors recreating their original work. Music would be provided by Boston's "Banchetto Musicale," a group of early music specialists whose instruments were copies or restorations of 17th–18th century models. According to Brustein, beginning the season with a revival would give a sense of continuity to the work of the transplanted company and show new audiences what A.R.T. had done in the past. *A Midsummer Night's Dream* was scheduled to open on March 21, 1980.

The second play of the season was *Terry by Terry,* written by Mark Leib, a student at the Yale Drama School. It had been performed in workshop in New Haven and would receive its professional premiere on April 4. *Terry by Terry* was a two-part play within a play. The first act presented a Kafkaesque parable of a young boy who refused to talk; the second depicted the anger, alienation, and comic protest of the young playwright who wrote the parable.

Happy End, a comic musical melodrama with book and lyrics by Bertolt Brecht and music by Kurt Weill, was the company's third offering, opening April 25. Set in Chicago in 1919, the play combined bumbling gangsters with "Salvation Army lasses" and was more overtly humorous than Brecht and Weill's famous *Three-Penny Opera. Happy End* had been presented at Yale in 1972 and 1975, but would be performed in Cambridge as a totally new production.

The last play of the season, Gogol's *The Inspector General,* was scheduled to open May 22. This satire of petty bureaucracy had attracted a good deal of attention when Brustein announced that it would be directed by a Harvard senior, many of whose controversial undergraduate productions had received excellent critical reviews in Boston. *The Inspector General* had been presented at Yale in 1970 to a relatively unfavorable critical and public reception. It too would receive a completely new production—as well as a new translation—for the first Cambridge season.

Reviewing the upcoming repertory, Guckenheimer commented:

> As you can see, it's far from a line-up of greatest hits. We did have to come in and sell very well as soon as possible—that's one reason we chose *A Midsummer Night's Dream.* Yet, from a broader perspective, we tried to assemble a season that is very characteristic of the range of plays we have done and continue to do—one premiere, one Shakespeare, one neglected modern play, one translated European classic.

The company's need for strong subscriber-contributor support was exacerbated by the very nature of repertory theatre. Because plays ran in rotation for fixed periods of time, a repertory company could not "milk" a successful production indefinitely, as a Broadway theatre might. Nor could a flop be closed before its appointed time. On the other hand, successful repertory productions like *A Midsummer Night's Dream* could be packaged, stored, and re-presented. A.R.T. had over 80 plays in its repertory, and planned to draw on these for at least two of its six productions during 1980–1981.

In Search of an Audience. Sam Guckenheimer had begun to explore the notion of building a subscriber/contributor base with the aid of market research during the spring of 1979, when he was a student in theatre administration at the Yale School of Drama and the company was preparing for its move to Cambridge. Convinced from his experience as an undergraduate at Harvard that the city would welcome an organization of A.R.T.'s caliber, Guckenheimer began to assemble studies produced by other arts groups in an effort to develop his own audience survey for Boston. Robert Orchard, A.R.T. managing director, listened to Guckenheimer's ideas with interest and hired him shortly thereafter, charging him with the task of defining A.R.T.'s new audience.

From the beginning, everyone involved in the project shared the conviction that A.R.T. should not use the results of market research to shape the company's offerings. As Guckenheimer phrased it:

> We were going to do a certain kind of theatre no matter what people wanted. Our task was to find people who wanted our kind of theatre.

Evaluating Previous Research. One of the difficulties of the project was the lack of reliable existing research; only one significant national survey of theatre audiences had ever been conducted. In 1974 the Ford Foundation had sponsored an extensive study designed to measure the size and characteristics of audiences for all the performing arts. Five hundred telephone interviews were conducted on a random sample of the population in each of 12 cities; all cities were regionally dispersed locations in which the performing arts were especially active.* Selected results are reproduced in Exhibits 1 and 2.

The previous studies undertaken by individual arts organizations varied widely in complexity, ranging from nonspecific one-page questionnaires to intricate lists of essay questions probing likes and dislikes. In none of the 10 examples which Guckenheimer examined had respondents been contacted by name (one theatre began its cover letter: "Dear Washington-Area Friend to the Performing Arts"). Many questionnaires were simply handed out to audiences after performances, rather than mailed to any particular area or group. After reviewing these previous efforts, Guckenheimer felt more strongly than ever the need for a detailed, methodologically rigorous survey on which to build A.R.T.'s market strategy:

> There have been very few situations in the arts where a calculated expectation of return has determined the design of a marketing campaign, where the regional audience has been clearly segmented

---

*Cities surveyed included Boston, New York, Philadelphia, Chicago, Cincinnati, Minneapolis, Atlanta, Washington, Houston, Seattle, San Francisco, and Los Angeles.

EXHIBIT 1
Exposure to Professional Performance of the Arts During the Past Year [a]

Art Form	Location of Respondents	Exposed Once Only	Exposed Two or More Times Per:			Total Exposed	Total Not Exposed
			Year	Month	Week		
Movies on television	Boston	3%	16%	34%	37%	90%	10%
	12 U.S. Cities	4	17	30	41	93	7
Movies in movie theatre	Boston	6	44	15	1	66	34
	12 U.S. Cities	6	45	16	2	69	31
Live professional play	Boston	6	7	0	0	13	87
	12 U.S. Cities	5	10	*	0	16	84
Live professional Broadway musical	Boston	9	8	*	0	17	83
	12 U.S. Cities	8	9	*	0	18	82
Live professional jazz, rock, or folk music	Boston	6	13	2	1	22	78
	12 U.S. Cities	8	15	2	1	25	75
Live professional symphony	Boston	3	5	*	0	8	92
	12 U.S. Cities	4	5	*	0	10	90
Live professional opera	Boston	1	*	0	0	1	99
	12 U.S. Cities	2	2	0	0	4	96
Live professional ballet	Boston	1	1	0	0	2	98
	12 U.S. Cities	3	2	0	0	4	96

[a]All numbers are rounded to the nearest percent. If literally none of the respondents was exposed, "0" is used. If a marginal number of respondents (fewer than one-half of one percent) was exposed, an asterisk (*) is used.

Source: *The Finances of the Performing Arts,* a report to The Ford Foundation, 1974.

and analyzed in advance, or where a new theatre has been able to scale its house and schedule its season according to a prior knowledge of the local market.*

Although A.R.T. management had had some experience with subscription mailings in New Haven, the Yale Rep had not undertaken research or testing of subscription offers prior to sending them out. In its most recent Yale season, the company had sent out three mailings. The first went to 1,200 households, accounting for 2,500 existing subscriptions, and resulted in 1,500 subscription renewals. The second, sent to a mailing list of 17,000 names which management had compiled, yielded 400 subscriptions. The third mailing, which went out to a large number of purchased lists totalling 150,000 names, yielded a mere 600 new subscribers.

In committing themselves to the survey, Guckenheimer and Orchard faced some opposition. A Ford Foundation consultant who specialized in arts marketing urged that the money be used for direct mail advertising instead. But Guckenheimer's support for the survey never wavered:

> How else would we have the information necessary to design the test mailing, except by going by the seat of our pants—or following the advice of the local publicists, each of whom disagrees with everybody else?

He also supported extensive use of direct mail as opposed to newspaper or other media advertising, noting:

*"Scaling the house" consists of setting varying ticket prices according to time of performance and location of seats.

You cannot, in a newspaper ad, in a cogent way, convey enough information to sell someone a subscription. You can sell a pair of tickets for a single night, but not a series of plays, or a range of prices, or a whole institution, unless you want to take out a full-page ad.

Moreover, if you look at the kinds of things that are sold in newspaper ads—or the kinds of behavior that are encouraged—the promoters try to get you into a store for a sale, or get you to go to a movie, or get you to watch TV. Few can convey a message the way we want to—with color, glossy paper, and sophisticated graphics. We want to tell people that there will be a new life for the theatre in Boston, beginning on the first day of spring, 1980. How do you do that in a newspaper ad?

"Newspapers are not cheap, either," Guckenheimer commented, pointing out that though they might offer a good way to reach huge numbers of people and convey a small amount of information ("this product will be available next week in your grocer's freezer"), "they are not a good medium through which to communicate a large amount of information to a small number of people." A full-page ad in the Sunday *New York Times,* widely read by A.R.T.'s target audience, Guckenheimer observed, would cost $19,000 and reach every Sunday *Times* reader in the U.S. By contrast, a four-page, four-color 8 1/2-by-11 flyer stuffed into the Boston editions of the Sunday *Times* would reach 50,000 readers for a total printing and stuffing cost of $5,000.

Designing the Survey. Guckenheimer's objectives for the survey were twofold. First, in the absence of concrete experience, he wanted to predict how many people would come to A.R.T., how much to charge them, and how best to

EXHIBIT 2
Findings from 1974 Ford Foundation Study

Exposure to Live Professional Performance of Four Arts, 1974

Among Those Who Attended	Percent Who Also Attended:				Attended No Other Arts
	Theater	Symphony	Opera	Ballet	
Theater	—	31	13	19	63
Symphony	45	—	27	27	36
Opera	50	75	—	25	25
Ballet	60	60	20	—	20

Total Percent Exposed During Past Year by Income, 1974

	Movie	Theater	Musical	Jazz	Symphony	Opera	Ballet
Up to $7,500	47	7	8	17	4	2	3
$7,500 to $15,000	72	14	15	24	8	3	3
$15,000 to $25,000	83	25	28	32	16	6	6
$25,000 and over	83	38	44	36	28	13	13

Total Percent Exposed During Past Year by Education, 1974

	Movie	Theater	Musical	Jazz	Symphony	Opera	Ballet
Some high school	57	7	9	20	5	2	2
High school graduate	71	12	15	22	5	2	2
Some college	81	23	25	35	14	6	7
College graduate	81	39	39	31	26	11	13

Total Percent Exposed During Past Year by Occupation, 1974

	Movie	Theater	Musical	Jazz	Symphony	Opera	Ballet
Executive-Managerial	75	24	27	26	14	6	4
Professional	83	28	25	33	18	5	9
Teaching	84	35	36	28	27	10	11
Student	93	17	19	49	15	6	6
Housewife	59	13	15	14	7	3	3
White collar	75	19	23	28	11	4	5
Blue collar	63	10	11	20	4	1	2
Retired	37	9	11	8	7	4	4

Income Composition of Audiences of Four Performing Arts, 1974

	Theater	Symphony	Opera	Ballet
Up to $7,500	13%	12%	15%	20%
$7,500 to $15,000	40	37	34	32
$15,000 to $25,000	33	34	32	30
$25,000 and over	14	17	19	18
	100%	100%	100%	100%

Educational Composition of Audiences of Four Performing Arts, 1974

	Theater	Symphony	Opera	Ballet
Some high school	18%	21%	20%	18%
High school graduate	26	18	18	16
Some college	23	24	24	26
College graduate	33	37	38	40
	100%	100%	100%	100%

Source: *The Finances of the Performing Arts,* a report to the Ford Foundation, 1974.

attract them. Second, he wanted to establish an information system to monitor A.R.T.'s audience over time. By examining data on the changing size and characteristics of this audience, he hoped to be able to predict its responsiveness to new programs and promotional campaigns.

Work began on the survey in New Haven during April 1979. Sponsored by a grant from Theatre Communications Group, Inc., Jan Geidt, A.R.T.'s Director of Press and Public Relations, was sent on a tour of four well-known regional theatres across the country to examine their marketing efforts. She returned with several observations:

> We were strongly urged to identify our potential audience in terms of demographics—i.e., geography, age, profession, education. Efforts to reach this audience, I was told, should include everything from social activities to paid and nonpaid advertising, billboards along travel routes, handout information, bus displays, and anything else to saturate these specific locales.
>
> As the director of marketing at the American Conservatory Theatre in San Francisco expressed it: "Establish as a base those natural pockets of the population where support is most likely to come from, and keep gearing your efforts to those supporters."
>
> The staff of the Seattle Rep, which is 92% subscribed this year, told me that there is still room, and need, for the single ticket buyer; one of their concerns is dispelling the idea that their performances are always sold out. On the other hand, Seattle's managing director pointed out that careful control of seats is the key to early success. He believes we should plan only so many performances (or subscription series) as we realistically believe can be filled. This ensures a look of success—and from this solid base we can expand.
>
> All these theatres share one of our constant problems: how to keep productions that remain in a repertory for several months "newsworthy" over a period of time.

Technical advice for the project was given by a Cambridge management consultant, who warned that the survey should contain only those questions whose answers would affect actual decisions: "It's very easy to fall into the game of 'it would be nice to know,'" he said. Accordingly, questions were designed with three criteria in mind: maximum information yield for management decisions; maximum intelligibility for respondents; and ease of conversion into numerical data for processing and statistical analysis. Originally a telephone survey had been planned, but it was discarded because of the relatively low incidence of regular theatregoers (estimated at 3%–5%) in the population; constructing a sample from the phone book and completing interviews by telephone with 400 theatregoers would have cost approximately $15,000. In contrast, the entire cost of the mail survey, including consulting fees ($8,000) and the expenses associated with coding, keypunching, programming, and computer time ($4,000) came to approximately $20,000.

The questionnaire was pretested three times on friends, relatives, and business associates of the A.R.T. staff (but not on a sample of the mailing group). Several questions posed initially were radically changed or rejected as too complicated; for example, one question, which asked how much respondents would pay to see each of six different kinds of productions, offered a choice of 13 responses in each category.

Guckenheimer had identified four key variables to examine: price sensitivity, attendance patterns, exposure to different media, and voluntary contribution patterns. Questions on these categories, plus others on subscription preferences, artistic preferences, location, and personal background of respondents, composed the final version of the questionnaire.

By the beginning of June 1979, Guckenheimer had completed the questionnaire design and was planning a cover letter. A.R.T. asked Kitty Dukakis, who was well known both for her interest in the arts and as the wife of the previous Massachusetts governor, to sponsor this letter. The final versions of the letter and the questionnaire (reproduced with percentage response distributions) are shown in the Appendix.

Developing the Sample. The mailing list for the survey was drawn from two sources. A group of 2,023 names was drawn from 7 of the 12 Boston-area census tracts which had the highest median educational level and the highest incidence of professional and managerial workers in the labor force. Of these 12 original tracts, seven were located in Cambridge. Guckenheimer had chosen Cambridge and all five tracts outside Cambridge. These names were supplied by a broker. Another 2,235 names were obtained from the mailing lists of ten arts-related organizations in Boston, each of which had been asked to supply a random sample of up to 300 names.

In describing A.R.T.'s potential audience, Robert Brustein had stated: "Our audience is anybody who can enjoy our work, and I think that means it can come from any class, any sex, any race, any part of town." Neither Orchard nor Guckenheimer saw any contradiction between this definition of audience and the survey sample. Orchard pointed out:

> The goal of the mailing was to identify people who would respond and subscribe without ever having seen an A.R.T. production. This group was almost by definition high education and high income, up on the theatre scene, aware of Brustein's reputation, or generally supportive of the arts.

Guckenheimer added:

> The theatre's goal in its first year is to bring income to a dependable level as quickly as possible; then we can go after less responsive groups. Any other policy would be like building the computers before reaping the grain.

Included in the final mailing package (addressed to respondents by name) were the cover letter; the questionnaire; and a prepaid reply envelope, to be returned by first class mail.

The survey was mailed as scheduled on July 5. Over 1,200 responses had been received by August 3, when keypunching began; 1,343 were ultimately tabulated. Approximately 300 of the pieces directed to census tract addresses were returned to Guckenheimer as undeliverable. Although there were variations in the response rates for the census

---

EXHIBIT 3
Breakdown of Returns from Organizations Contributing Names to the Survey Mailing List

Source	Percentage of Total Returns	Net Response[a]
Geographic[b]	30.3%	22%
Ideas Associates[c]		
Individuals	4.6	48
Groups	3.7	25
Schubert Subscribers	7.9	39
Opera Company Subscribers	8.4	50
Friends of The Loeb	5.2	56
Boston Ballet Subscribers	4.9	30
Boston Shakespeare Company Subscribers	4.9	30
Friends of The Fogg (Art Museum)	8.6	45
Loeb Subscribers	13.6	64
Boston University Celebrity Series Subscribers	9.3	40
	100.0%	

[a]Net Response = Returns expressed as a percentage of questionnaires mailed less undeliverable pieces.
[b]Represents individuals targeted through census tracts.
[c]An organization serving as a ticket broker to both groups and individuals within the Boston area.

Source: A.R.T. records.

---

tracts mailing list and those for the arts-organization lists (Exhibit 3), subsequent analysis showed no significant differences in the nature of the responses given by census tract versus arts-organization respondents.

ANALYZING THE RESULTS

After the survey results were tabulated (see Appendix), Guckenheimer's consultant suggested that he undertake a further analysis of the data in order to look for characteristics that might identify A.R.T.'s target audience. In particular, Guckenheimer was interested in segmenting survey respondents in terms of the subscription benefits they desired. He did not expect the survey results to produce concrete answers, but hoped to be able to use the data to uncover "possibilities" which he could convert to concrete sales.

Guckenheimer's most immediate need was to determine what sources he should use to compile A.R.T.'s first subscription solicitation mailing list. Potential lists of addresses that he had identified included five possible sources: (1) Individuals residing in targeted census tracts (information available at a cost of about $20 per thousand names). If mailings were restricted to census tracts having a median education level of at least 16 years—four or more years of college—then the list for Greater Boston would total 17,000 names; if the median were lowered to 14 years and up, the

total would amount to 63,000 names. (2) Members of, or subscribers to, other local arts organizations (cost about $35 per thousand)*; this could generate a total of up to 25,000 names if all available sources were used, but an estimated 8,000 of these would be multiple listings. (3) Subscribers to specialized publications such as *Massachusetts Lawyers Weekly* (17,000 names in the Greater Boston area, available at a cost of $60 per thousand) or to *Bon Appetit*, a gourmet cooking magazine with 22,000 subscribers in Greater Boston (cost about $35–$40 per thousand). (4) Up to 70,000 charge account customers from expensive retail stores in the Boston area (about $55–$60 per thousand). (5) Five thousand buyers of expensive small appliances, notably food processors (available from a corporation which processed warranty cards for the appliances and searched out income data; cost, about $80 per thousand).

Eventually A.R.T. management hoped to send enough subscription solicitations—at an average unit cost for printing, stuffing, and mailing of about 28¢ each—to sell out the season. General experience suggested that A.R.T. could expect to sell an average of 2.0–2.5 per seats per subscriber. The entire subscription campaign, including advertising, was budgeted at $70,000, including the $20,000 already spent on the survey. Because both Guckenheimer and Orchard wanted the theatre to be sold out for all subscription performances, the length of each play's run would not be determined until a significant number of subscription orders had come in. A.R.T. planned to offer 10–16 weeks of subscription performances, followed by approximately four weeks of nonsubscribed performances whose seats would be easier to promote than an equivalent number of seats spaced out over the full 16 weeks.

Ticket prices presented another problem. A.R.T.'s goal was to maximize box office income while simultaneously maximizing attendance. According to Guckenheimer:

> Our prices should be high enough so that anyone who can will pay a lot to attend will do so. At the same time, anyone who really wants to come should be able to.

There were other constraints on pricing. A.R.T. management felt it important to have a top ticket price "high enough to distinguish us from the church basement productions," as Guckenheimer put it; "but on the other hand, we do depend on outside funding, and for that reason we can't be out for blood like the commercial theatres." At Yale, the company's top ticket price (for the most desirable seats on Friday and Saturday nights) had been $8; bottom price (for the least desirable seats for matinees, Monday nights, and previews) had been $3.50. Guckenheimer expected to raise these prices at the Loeb, following interpretation of the survey results and a review of the ticket prices and

---

*In the future, these names might also be obtained by trading A.R.T.'s list for that of other local arts organizations.

EXHIBIT 4
Representative Subscription Plans Offered by Performing Arts Organizations in the Boston Area[a]

Organization	Status	Hall	Seating Capacity	Type of Offering	Individual Ticket Prices High/Low	Subscription Plans	Percentage of Occupied Seats Sold by Subscription
Boston Ballet	Non-profit	Music Hall	4200	Classical ballet.	$17.00 $4.00	Two plans. First offers entire season's of four productions at 33% savings. Second, mailed in December, offers subscriptions to last two productions of year, at 33% savings.	45%
		John Hancock Hall	1200	"Choreographers' Showcase"; premieres of new works (once a year).			
Boston Pops	Non-profit	Symphony Hall	2625	Three-part program featuring light classical music, soloists, and popular music. For Pops performances (May–July), orchestra seats of Symphony Hall removed and replaced by tables seating five people; light meals and alcoholic beverages sold during performance. 85–90% sold to groups.	$11.00 $3.50	None. Most seats sold in blocks of 50–2000 to corporations, universities, charitable organizations, and other large groups.	0%
Boston Symphony Orchestra	Non-profit	Symphony Hall	2625	Classical and modern music.	$16.00 $5.00 Rush: $3.50 (½ hour before performance Fri-Sat)	Fourteen plans, ranging from full season of 22 concerts to shorter series and open rehearsals. Also covers concerts given in Providence, R.I., and New York City. Discount: 5%.	85–90%
Boston Shakespeare Company	Non-profit	BSC Theatre	320	Shakespeare; occasional revivals.	$8.50 $4.00 Student rush: $4.00 (½ hour before performance)	Eight plans, each offering a selection of plays from a play season. Discounts range	50–60%
Boston University Celebrity Series	Non-profit ("Profits sent to B.U. scholarship fund)	Symphony Hall	2625	Wide variety of classical music, dance, No rock or popular music.	Only subscriptions available: $66.50 $45.50	Thirty-five to forty plans. Patrons choose seven productions from a list of about 50, at discounts of up to 33%.	Varies, has reached 100%
		Jordan Hall	1019				
		John Hancock Hall	1200				
		Music Hall	4200				
		Berklee Performance Center	1226				
Charles Street Playhouse	For profit	main stage	525	Primarily Broadway hits reaching Boston for the first time—always cast in New York. Infrequently hosts Broadway-bound tryouts. A "four-wall rental" theater; each production brings in its own management staff.	$12.95 $8.00 (varies)	None. Theatre hopes to acquire non-profit status, develop a repertory company, and offer subscriptions by January 1981.	0
		cabaret	175–200				
Chateau de Ville	For profit	Three locations in suburbs adjoining Boston	Not available	Well-known light comedies, musicals, often revivals; revues, including burlesque; occasional solo performers. Dinner available before the show at extra charge (varies).	$22.95[b] $7.95	None	0
Colonial Theatre	For profit		1658	Broadway (or Broadway-bound) plays and musicals.	Musical $20/$10 Drama $20/9	None. Through Show-of-the-Month Club, mails notices of coming attractions to 30,000 people. Show-of-the-Month discounts range from 0–15%.	20–80% sold through Show-of-the-Month, depending on New York reputation of the show.
Shubert Theatre	For profit		1968	Broadway (or Broadway-bound) plays and musicals.	Musical $22.50/$10 Drama $20/$9	One plan. Requires subscribers to attend entire season and offers no discounts. Benefits: preferred seating, prior notification of productions.	Varies widely; subscribers compose about 33% of house for first two weeks of play's run.
Wilbur Theatre	For profit		1200	Broadway (or Broadway-bound) plays and musicals; occasional dance troupes.	Musical $18.50/14.50 Drama $16/$9	None. Uses Show-of-the-Month (see above).	Less than 50% sold sold through Show-of-the-Month
Harvard/Radcliffe Dramatic Club	Student	Loeb Drama Center	556	Wide variety of dramas, comedies, musicals; both classic and modern plays.	$4.50 $3.50 Rush: $2 (½ hour before performance) $1 discount to Harvard students	One plan, offers season of three plays for 30% discount.	25%
Next Move Theater	Non-profit	Next Move Theater	186	Premieres and plays new to Boston, ranging from musical adaptations of classical comedies to satirical revues to new productions of 20th century classics.	$9.50 $7.50 Student rush: $4.50 (20 minutes before performance)	Three plans, first offered in 1979–80. Subscribers choosing Wed/Thurs/Sun nights receive 33% discount; those choosing Fri/Sat pay full price. Subscription covers season of four shows, plus free admission to one additional revue.	18%
Opera Company of Boston	Non-profit	Savoy Theatre	2700	Primarily well-known classical operas with major stars; some modern works, occasional premieres.	$27.00 $8.00	One plan, offers season of four operas for discounts of 8–22%.	80%

[a] Excludes most college productions and smaller groups like the Boston Camerata or Boston Repertory Ballet.
[b] The top price shown here was obtained when big name soloists were performing.

EXHIBIT 5
American Repertory Theatre Survey and Questionnaire
Cross Tabulations of Price Sensitivity Against Other Variables[a]

	Q10: Price Willing to Pay Per Play at Repertory Theatre: (for a series of eight plays)				Number of Positive Responses
	$6.00 or Less	**$8.00**	**$10.00**	**$12.00 or More**[b]	
Q6: Factors encouraging subscription:					
Discount ticket prices[c]	73%	45%	32%	24%	629
Guaranteed priority seating	30	38	45	57	407
Guaranteed ticket availability	13	21	21	27	192
Q12: Media used to find out about plays:					
Radio commercials	5	2	1	6	43
Shubert Theatre subscription series	4	9	21	21	97
TV review	8	10	3	15	92
Q13: Newspaper read more than half the time:					
Weekday *Boston Globe*	56	64	72	72	677
Sunday *Herald American*	7	12	20	21	104
Weekday *New York Times*	18	23	23	37	200
Boston Phoenix	14	10	14	13	123
Real Paper	16	9	13	7	123
Q20d/e: Activities before/after show:					
Go to cafe/bar/restaurant *after*	41	48	57	55	533
Shop/browse in Harvard Square	41	35	31	28	428

[a]Shown here are those items in Questions 6, 12, 13, and 20 d-e where a statistically significant difference ($p < 0.05$) existed between the responses given in each of the four price categories. (Appendix for exact wording of questions.)
[b]Combines $12.00, $14.00. $16.00, and more than $16.00 categories; "No Sure" responses have been excluded.
[c]Interpret the data as follows: 73% of those saying they would be willing to pay $6.00 or less (in Question 10) checked discount ticket prices as one of the factors (in Question 6) that would most encourage them to subscribe, whereas only 45% of those saying $8.00 checked this factor, 32% of those saying $10.00, and 24% saying $12.00 or more.

---

subscription plans offered by other Boston arts organizations (Exhibit 4).

The final task Guckenheimer faced was designing a subscription offering for potential A.R.T. subscribers, based on the information furnished by the survey. Freelance designers would produce the brochure describing the season's repertory; it was Guckenheimer's job to draw up a subscription coupon. How many different kinds of subscription packages should A.R.T. offer, he wondered, and how should they be distinguished from each other? What benefits might a subscription include, and how could they best be communicated on the coupon? To whom should he mail the different types of offers? What prices should be charged for the various subscriptions? And would it be possible to ask subscribers for a contribution to A.R.T. at the same time? At Yale, contributions had never been solicited from individuals in or outside of the subscription campaign. However, the technique of adding a contribution line had been used successfully for

subscription renewals by several opera and ballet companies. Guckenheimer had heard that this approach could add 5% –10% in contributions over the total dollar value of all renewals.

With a mixture of anticipation and apprehension, he began to leaf through the pile of computer printouts on his desk. He had run a series of cross-tabulations (Exhibit 5) on the survey data, relating willingness to pay certain ticket prices (survey question 10) to a variety of other variables (questions 6, 7, 11, 12, 13, 14, 15, 20 d-e). These results, Guckenheimer hoped, would clarify the relationship between each of the various factors that would encourage people to subscribe and the activities they might combine with a visit to the theatre. Once the subscription offering had been mailed, he would also use the survey results to develop a strategy for promoting sales of individual seats for approximately 35 nonsubscription performances in midsummer.

Appendix
Survey of Prospective Audience

Cover Letter

Kitty Dukakis

J M Johnson
55 Willard St.
Cambridge MA 02138

July 5, 1979

Dear J M Johnson,

I am writing to you on behalf of the American Repertory Theatre Company (A.R.T.C.)--a non-profit, professional resident theatre scheduled to open in Boston next spring--to ask for your opinions. For this purpose we have enclosed a brief questionnaire on cultural activities in the Boston area.

This study will assist the A.R.T.C. in serving the interests and needs of the metropolitan area's residents, and the results will be shared with many arts organizations around Boston. We have sent the questionnaire to a limited number of people, some selected randomly, others by their involvement with the various cultural institutions in the area.

Please show your interest by filling out the questionnaire and returning it in the postage-paid envelope provided no later than Wednesday, July 18. In order for the A.R.T.C. to obtain an accurate cross-section of views on the cultural activities of Boston, it is very important that we receive your responses.

Your answers will, of course, be anonymous. However, if you would like to request further information about the cultural organizations that have helped us prepare this study, we have enclosed a separate postcard which offers you this option.

We hope that you will find these questions interesting and that they might further stimulate your thinking about cultural activities in the Boston area. Thank you very much for your assistance.

Sincerely yours,

Kitty Dukakis

KD:sg
encls

Survey Questionnaire and Response Distributions*

This survey is being sponsored by the American Repertory Theatre Company (A.R.T.C.) to understand the interests and opinions of the residents of Greater Boston on the region's cultural activities. Your answers to this questionnaire will help the A.R.T.C. and other local arts organizations better serve the needs of the metropolitan area's residents.

The questionnaire should take you about 15 minutes to complete. Of course, your responses will be anonymous. Please answer all of the questions to the best of your ability. There are no right or wrong answers, but for statistical purposes, it is important that we receive complete responses.

When you have finished the questionnaire, please return it in the postage-paid envelope provided, no later than **July 18.**

Thank you very much.

*As reproduced here, the questionnaire includes the percentage distributions for responses to each question.

A. ATTENDANCE

1. Have you ever attended a live theatre performance? *(Check one.)*

	Yes	No	Not sure
	99.6 ☐	0.4 ☐	☐

2. In the past year, have you attended any live performances of:
(For each category, check the box next to the appropriate answer.)

	Yes	No	Not sure
a symphony orchestra?	77.6 ☐	21.9 ☐	0.6 ☐
chamber music?	58.1 ☐	40.9 ☐	1.0 ☐
an opera?	46.5 ☐	52.9 ☐	0.6 ☐
a ballet?	60.7 ☐	38.4 ☐	0.9 ☐
modern dance?	43.8 ☐	54.5 ☐	1.7 ☐
musical on a Broadway tour?	61.3 ☐	37.9 ☐	0.8 ☐
drama on a Broadway tour?	60.9 ☐	37.5 ☐	1.6 ☐
production at a professional regional theatre?	64.4 ☐	33.9 ☐	1.7 ☐
university theatre production?	57.5 ☐	41.4 ☐	1.0 ☐

3. During the past two or three years, how often have you been to performances at the following places:
(For each performance hall, check the box next to the appropriate answer.)

	Not at all	Once or twice	Three or four times	Five or more times	Not sure
Symphony Hall?	16.1 ☐	28.5 ☐	16.1 ☐	39.2 ☐	0.2 ☐
Boston Shakespeare Company?	75.8 ☐	13.9 ☐	4.4 ☐	5.8 ☐	0.1 ☐
Loeb Drama Center?	43.6 ☐	25.7 ☐	10.9 ☐	19.2 ☐	0.5 ☐
The Shubert Theatre?	24.5 ☐	42.0 ☐	15.4 ☐	16.3 ☐	1.8 ☐
The Colonial Theatre?	28.3 ☐	40.9 ☐	14.8 ☐	13.9 ☐	2.1 ☐
The Wilbur Theatre?	30.1 ☐	40.5 ☐	15.0 ☐	11.4 ☐	3.1 ☐
The Music Hall?	32.7 ☐	40.1 ☐	13.9 ☐	10.7 ☐	2.5 ☐
The Next Move?	75.6 ☐	18.8 ☐	4.5 ☐	0.6 ☐	0.5 ☐
Trinity Square Repertory Company? (Providence)	93.0 ☐	4.5 ☐	0.4 ☐	1.9 ☐	0.2 ☐
Charles Street Playhouse?	51.0 ☐	36.3 ☐	9.1 ☐	2.8 ☐	0.7 ☐
Savoy Theatre?	70.0 ☐	11.7 ☐	7.7 ☐	7.2 ☐	3.4 ☐

B. SUBSCRIPTIONS

4. A list of performing arts institutions is shown below. Please check the name(s) of those to which you have subscribed for a full season or series of performances. *(Check as many as apply.)*

32.4 ☐ Boston Symphony Orchestra   23.2 ☐ Opera Company of Boston   12.5 ☐ Shubert Subscription Series

26.0 ☐ Boston University Celebrity Series   12.6 ☐ Theatre Guild   27.7 ☐ None of these

21.0 ☐ Loeb Special Series   17.8 ☐ Boston Ballet   0.8 ☐ Not sure

5. Many cities now have professional resident repertory theatres, where a permanent acting ensemble produces a season of several plays from the broad range of dramatic literature. The productions alternate performances in repertory, and one actor may appear in two or three plays in a given week. If such a repertory theatre were established in Boston, is it likely that you would: *(Check one.)*

5.8 ☐ Not attend at all?

13.4 ☐ Probably attend just one performance?

21.4 ☐ Probably subscribe to a four-play half season?

8.4 ☐ Probably subscribe to a full eight-play season?

51.0 ☐ Probably attend more than one performance, but not subscribe?

6. What two or three factors would **encourage** you most to subscribe to a theatre season or series of performances? *(Check up to **three** items which you consider to be most important.)*

55.0 ☐ Discount ticket prices   9.7 ☐ Membership newsletters/calendars

10.8 ☐ Restaurant or parking discounts   19.8 ☐ Greater likelihood of attending regularly

35.7 ☐ Guaranteed priority seating   16.1 ☐ Desire to support the institution

17.4 ☐ Guaranteed ticket availability   8.5 ☐ Ability to attend with friends more easily

28.2 ☐ Ease of ordering tickets   3.4 ☐ Desire to attend many performances by one particular group

17.3 ☐ Special ticket exchange privileges   52.9 ☐ Interest in a particular selection of performances

☐ Other: *(Please specify.)* _____

7. What two or three factors would **discourage** you most from subscribing to a theatre season or series of performances? *(Check up to **two** items which you consider to be most important.)*

34.2 ☐ Too much money to commit at once   31.4 ☐ Unfamiliarity with performance group

32.4 ☐ Too much advance planning required   16.6 ☐ Limited interest in attending so many performances of one ensemble

52.6 ☐ Limited interest in the particular selection of performances

☐ Too inconvenient *(live too far away, takes too long to get there, difficulty leaving the house at night, etc.)*

☐ Other: *(Please specify.)* _____

8. When is it most convenient for you to attend a live theatre performance? *(Check your two most preferred times.)*

8.9 ☐ Weekday matinees   53.7 ☐ Weekday evenings   1.1 ☐ Not sure/Don't attend

13.6 ☐ Saturday matinees   62.0 ☐ Friday - Saturday evenings

23.4 ☐ Sunday matinees   18.1 ☐ Sunday evenings

C. PRICING

9. If you were going to one production at **a resident repertory theatre,** what would you be willing to pay? *(Check one.)*

22.2 ☐ $6.00 or less 31.2 ☐ $8.00 22.5 ☐ $10.00 10.3 ☐ $12.00 3.5 ☐ $14.00 1.2 ☐ $16.00 1.1 ☐ More than $16.00 8.0 ☐ Not sure

10. If you were going to a series of eight plays at a resident repertory theatre, what would you be willing to pay **per play**? *(Check one.)*

45.8 ☐ $6.00 or less 26.5 ☐ $8.00 11.4 ☐ $10.00 3.9 ☐ $12.00 1.0 ☐ $14.00 1.1 ☐ $16.00 0.5 ☐ More than $16.00 9.7 ☐ Not sure

D. CONTRIBUTIONS

11. Have you ever contributed to any of the following institutions: *(For each institution, check the appropriate answer.)*

	Yes	No	Not sure
Boston Symphony Orchestra?	40.2 ☐	57.8 ☐	1.9 ☐
Opera Company of Boston?	23.2 ☐	74.7 ☐	2.1 ☐
Boston Ballet?	20.4 ☐	78.7 ☐	0.9 ☐
Boston Shakespeare Company?	8.3 ☐	90.4 ☐	1.3 ☐
Museum of Fine Arts?	50.1 ☐	47.4 ☐	2.5 ☐
Loeb Drama Center?	17.7 ☐	80.8 ☐	1.5 ☐
Fogg Art Museum?	16.6 ☐	81.7 ☐	1.7 ☐
WGBH (Channel 2)?	77.3 ☐	21.4 ☐	1.3 ☐

E. MEDIA

12. How do you usually find out about the plays which you attend? *(Check the two most frequent sources you use.)*

4.3 ☐ TV Commercial
3.9 ☐ Radio Commercial
50.8 ☐ Newspaper Ad
33.4 ☐ Mail Brochure
0.9 ☐ Poster in MBTA
2.0 ☐ Poster elsewhere
35.4 ☐ Recommendation from a friend
9.2 ☐ Shubert Subscription Series
8.1 ☐ Theatre Guild Membership

8.8 ☐ TV Review
3.7 ☐ Radio Review
50.9 ☐ Newspaper Review
Which critics: 27.0 % completed this

9.5 ☐ Newspaper Story
0.9 ☐ Not sure

☐ Other motivating factors: *(Please specify.)* 7.9 % completed this

13. The names of several newspapers and magazines available in the Boston area are listed below. How frequently do you read each of these journals? *(For each publication, check the appropriate box to indicate frequency of reading.)*

	Never	Less than half the issues	More than half the issues	Almost every issue	Not sure
Weekday Boston Globe?	10.3 ☐	27.0 ☐	8.4 ☐	53.3 ☐	0.9 ☐
Sunday Boston Globe?	11.4 ☐	18.9 ☐	7.9 ☐	61.1 ☐	0.7 ☐
Weekday Herald American?	71.8 ☐	14.8 ☐	1.4 ☐	11.4 ☐	0.6 ☐
Sunday Herald American?	78.6 ☐	9.2 ☐	1.3 ☐	10.2 ☐	0.7 ☐
Weekday New York Times?	45.1 ☐	33.0 ☐	6.1 ☐	14.4 ☐	1.4 ☐
Sunday New York Times?	32.6 ☐	30.1 ☐	6.5 ☐	29.7 ☐	1.1 ☐
Christian Science Monitor?	79.1 ☐	13.5 ☐	1.5 ☐	4.5 ☐	1.3 ☐
The Boston Phoenix?	52.0 ☐	34.1 ☐	6.1 ☐	6.3 ☐	1.5 ☐
The Real Paper?	52.2 ☐	33.8 ☐	6.9 ☐	5.6 ☐	1.5 ☐
Boston Magazine?	48.1 ☐	26.5 ☐	6.2 ☐	17.9 ☐	1.3 ☐
Time?	34.6 ☐	28.2 ☐	7.7 ☐	28.0 ☐	1.5 ☐
Newsweek?	42.7 ☐	28.3 ☐	5.7 ☐	21.1 ☐	2.2 ☐

14. What are the local radio stations to which you listen regularly? *(Please list up to three by name [call letters] or dial numbers.)*

Name_____ Dial Number_____ AM _____ FM _____

Name_____ Dial Number_____ AM _____ FM _____

Name_____ Dial Number_____ AM _____ FM _____

15. How much television do you usually watch? *(Check one.)*

68.1 ☐ Less than 10 hours per week   26.7 ☐ 10 - 20 hours per week   5.0 ☐ More than 20 hours per week

F. ARTISTIC PREFERENCES

16. The names of some artistic leaders and their respective institutions are listed below. Would artistic direction by any of these people make you more inclined to attend the performances of a particular organization: *(For each person listed, please check the appropriate answer.)*

	Yes	No	Not sure
Seiji Ozawa? *(Boston Symphony Orchestra)*	63.1 ☐	26.5 ☐	10.4 ☐
Sarah Caldwell? *(Opera Company of Boston)*	55.9 ☐	29.3 ☐	14.8 ☐
Arthur Fiedler? *(Boston Pops)*	49.1 ☐	41.9 ☐	9.0 ☐
Robert Brustein? *(Yale Repertory Theatre)*	34.6 ☐	31.7 ☐	33.7 ☐
Adrian Hall? *(Trinity Square Repertory Co.)*	15.2 ☐	41.8 ☐	43.1 ☐
E. Virginia Williams? *(Boston Ballet)*	22.1 ☐	45.4 ☐	32.4 ☐

17. How interested are you in seeing any of the following kinds of plays: *(Check one answer for each category.)*

	Very interested	Somewhat interested	Not very interested	Not at all interested	Not sure
Musical comedies	40.6 ☐	34.7 ☐	17.3 ☐	7.2 ☐	0.2 ☐
Comedies	43.6 ☐	45.9 ☐	8.6 ☐	1.3 ☐	0.6 ☐
Dramas	64.3 ☐	30.7 ☐	3.5 ☐	0.8 ☐	0.8 ☐
American classics	43.0 ☐	44.1 ☐	10.3 ☐	1.4 ☐	1.1 ☐
Shakespeare or other English classics	43.0 ☐	38.1 ☐	15.0 ☐	3.3 ☐	0.6 ☐
Translated European classics	30.9 ☐	38.8 ☐	20.8 ☐	6.8 ☐	2.6 ☐
New plays	38.3 ☐	45.7 ☐	11.3 ☐	2.1 ☐	2.7 ☐
Light operas	21.0 ☐	34.7 ☐	23.9 ☐	19.1 ☐	1.3 ☐

G. LOCATION

18. The Loeb Drama Center is a 550-seat theatre on Brattle Street off Harvard Square. Are you familiar with it?

79.8 ☐ Yes   18.6 ☐ No   1.6 ☐ Not sure

19. Have you ever attended a performance at the Loeb?

67.4 ☐ Yes   31.2 ☐ No   1.4 ☐ Not sure

20a. If you heard about an interesting professional theatre production at the Loeb, would you be likely to attend?

88.1 ☐ Probably
(Please continue to questions b-f.)

11.9 ☐ Probably not
(If you have checked this box, then please skip ahead to question 21.)

b. What means of transportation might you use to go to the Loeb?

19.2 ☐ MBTA   62.8 ☐ Car

1.6 ☐ Taxi   15.1 ☐ Foot or Bicycle   1.2 ☐ Not sure

c. Would you be likely to go out to eat **before** the performance?

53.0 ☐ Probably   47.0 ☐ Probably not

d. Would you be likely to go out to a cafe/bar/restaurant **after** the performance?

42.3 ☐ Probably   57.7 ☐ Probably not

e. Would you spend part of the evening shopping or browsing around Harvard Square?

39.2 ☐ Probably   60.8 ☐ Probably not

f. What would be the most convenient evening performance time for theatre at the Loeb? *(Check one time on each of the two lines.)*

	7:00 or earlier	7:30	8:00	8:30	9:00 or later	Not sure
Sunday-Thursday	10.8 ☐	30.6 ☐	45.7 ☐	10.5 ☐	1.0 ☐	1.5 ☐
Friday-Saturday	5.7 ☐	16.4 ☐	51.0 ☐	21.7 ☐	3.9 ☐	1.2 ☐

21.   What factors might keep you from attending the Loeb?

_____

_____

H.   BACKGROUND

22.   What is your age?

1.3 ☐ 18 or under *6.9* ☐ 19-25 *30.0* ☐ 26-35 *20.6* ☐ 36-45 *19.1* ☐ 46-55 *13.2* ☐ 56-65 *8.9* ☐ 66 or over

23.   Are you: *55.8* ☐ Female?   *44.2* ☐ Male?

24.   Are you: *42.7* ☐ Single?   *57.3* ☐ Married?

25.   What is the last grade in school or college that you completed?

0.4 ☐ Grade *3.5* ☐ High *1.4* ☐ Technical or *11.7* ☐ Some *18.2* ☐ College *15.1* ☐ Some *49.7* ☐ Graduate
School   School   Vocational   College   Degree   Graduate   Degree
                        Training   School

26.   What is your zipcode at home? _____

27.   What is the zipcode of your place of employment? _____

28.   What is your occupation? _____

29.   What is the occupation of the head of your household *(if different)?*

_____

30.   And for statistical purposes only, which of the following broad categories represents your household's annual income?

7.3 ☐ Under   *21.1* ☐ $10,000   *21.0* ☐ $20,000   *27.6* ☐ $30,000   *23.0* ☐ $50,000
$10,000   -19,999   -29,999   -49,999   or over

Thank you very much for your time and interest. If you would like to receive more information about the arts organizations that have helped the American Repertory Theatre Company prepare this study, please return the prepaid reply postcard when you return this questionnaire.

25

Marketing Mix Decisions for Nonprofit Organizations: An Analytical Approach

Charles B. Weinberg

What price should a nonprofit organization charge users and how much effort should the organization devote to developing, delivering, and communicating its services to users and to attracting contributions from donors? A review of current practice in these areas illustrates some of the problems that arise from currently employed decision rules. A formal structuring of the nonprofit organization's marketing mix problem leads to the determination of optimal decision rules. In many cases, these rules suggest that a nonprofit organization should charge lower prices and devote more of its resources to marketing than a similarly situated business should.

This article examines and models the marketing mix decision for nonprofit organizations (NPOs) and contrasts the results obtained to those for businesses.

Three differences between businesses and NPOs seem particularly salient for modeling the marketing mix decision. First, the objective function is not (even theoretically) profit maximization. This obviously complicates any optimum seeking algorithm. Second, few NPOs meet all their costs from user fees alone which means that they must design marketing programs which appeal and provide benefits to both users and funding sources, be they donors, taxpayers, or government agencies. Third, NPOs predominantly deal in intangibles; while many businesses also provide services, the bulk of the theoretical and practical work in analytical marketing has been concerned with the marketing of goods.

Some particular problems that arise when dealing with services are (1) that limited inventorying of services can take place (an unused theater seat on a Monday night is empty forever and cannot be used, for example, on the following Saturday night) and (2) that substantially more of the total cost often varies with the capacity of the system rather than with the number of users. This suggests a need for coordination among service operations and marketing management and, presumably, management science approaches to support this coordination. In this article, we focus on the first two distinctions between NPOs and businesses and leave the third point of services for future research.

COMPARISON OF OBJECTIVE FUNCTIONS

A critical difference between nonprofit organizations and businesses is that many nonprofits incur substantial deficits and thus require either government grants or private benefac-

Charles B. Weinberg is Alumni Professor of Marketing, University of British Columbia.

tions. Some nonprofits, such as performing arts groups and hospitals, charge a price for their services so that users bear some of the costs of the provided services. Other organizations, such as libraries and religious groups, often make no direct charge for their services.

The marketing task of the nonprofit is more complex than that of a business, which generally prospers if it can satisfy consumer needs better than the competition. The NPO must not only provide goods and/or services (generally referred to as "products") which meet user needs, but it also must satisfy the donors from whom it attracts resources. NPOs thus face a dual market problem. For some nonprofits, this often means that the products offered to users must appeal to the donors' intuitive appraisals of client needs and may limit the range of services provided [Collins 1982]. An example of this is the limitations that some donors place on the counseling and educational services that family planning agencies can offer to their clientele.

In many cases, an organization's success in serving clients will lead to success in raising funds from benefactors. For example, a manager of one performing arts series explained that he turned to an aggressive marketing policy to build an audience for several reasons—one being that it is easier to raise money for a performing arts series that is sold out at half price than one which is half empty at full price.

Specification of the objective function for making marketing mix decisions is, of course, crucial. In the business sector, the objective function for determining the optimal marketing mix is usually based on profit maximization. Although the definition of profit in an actual organizational setting is never as straightforward as theoretical treatments would suggest and few would suggest that a firm makes *every* decision based on profit maximization, most will agree that profit is a goal of nearly every business enterprise—probably the predominant one. Few business executives deliberately pursue policies which they think will in the long run yield profits far below what otherwise could be earned. Among the alternatives to profit maximization are satisficing behavior, sales maximization, market share maximization, cost minimization, long run survival, personal goals of managers, and growth.

By definition, nonprofit organizations are not profit maximizers. In order to achieve insights into the nature of the marketing mix decision for nonprofits and to be able to compare their decisions to those of businesses, we need to specify an objective function that captures the distinctiveness of the nonprofit sector and is broad enough to cover a range of nonprofit organizations as well. Consequently, in this article we assume that the objective function for a nonprofit organization, when making marketing mix decisions, is *maximization of the amount of its products or services which are consumed or utilized*, subject to the amount of *revenues and donations* being at least equal to the cost of providing the service. For example, one symphony orchestra stated the following among its objectives (selected from a larger set):

- To expand the local market for the services of the orchestra up to its capacity to serve it well. Such an expansion will seek to reach an increasingly broad spectrum of the population, thus broadening the base of support for the orchestra.
- To provide the funds required to achieve the orchestra's objectives and to break even financially on a cumulative basis at least every three years.

Of course, this objective function is subject to a number of qualifications. For example, an NPO is concerned with maximizing usage among targeted segments with products compatible to its basic orientation—few symphony orchestras would perform rock concerts, even if they could. Different weights may be placed on usage by different market segments and/or on different components of the product line. "Ancillary" services may be managed with more of a profit than an usage orientation. For example, gift shops in museums are often justified on the basis of net revenue contribution. One transit authority, whose general goal is rider maximization, plans to provide express services to race tracks on a profit maximization basis and deluxe commuter services to certain suburbs on a break even basis. Future research will be directed towards examining the range and prevalence of objective functions used by NPOs. However, as noted, it appears appropriate to focus on usage maximization to distinguish NPOs from profit maximizing businesses.

SOME APPROACHES TO DETERMINING THE MARKETING MIX

In this section, we review and critique different approaches to the problem of determining the marketing mix for nonprofit organizations. We begin by briefly reviewing the public sector economics literature, which focuses primarily on price and pays little attention to other elements of the marketing mix. The public sector model is not directly applicable to nonprofit organizations. However, many managers are familiar with the basic result: set price equal to marginal cost. Consequently, it is useful to discuss this literature here.

Next, we examine the notion of producer self-satisfaction as the dominant motive when a nonprofit organization determines its marketing mix. Although self-satisfaction is an important component in an organization's choice of product-market to serve and can influence marketing mix decisions, we show it is limited as an overall model. The final and major portion of this section classifies and analyzes the major rules of thumb that nonprofit managers appear to be using in making marketing mix decisions.

Public Sector Economics. A portion of the economics literature focuses on price setting in government agencies for which user charges can be assessed. The decision rule that this literature generally presents is for the agency to set price equal to marginal cost per unit. In most cases, this rule will leave some fixed costs not covered by user fees. The usual prescriptions for meeting the fixed expenses are either to cover the fixed cost by revenues from the general taxing authority of the government or to levy a charge which varies per user as opposed to per unit. The per user charge does not affect the number of units consumed by a user, but it can influence the number of users.

The major argument offered for the price equal to marginal cost rule is one of economic efficiency. It can be shown that if all other markets are efficient, then setting price equal to marginal cost is optimal from a global viewpoint. The price equal to marginal cost rule is also attractive because if the government, as a monopoly supplier, were to be replaced by a set of perfectly competitive suppliers, then price would be equal to marginal cost. Although the perfect competition and complete external efficiency conditions are seldom observed, the notion of charging the user only marginal cost is an intuitively appealing one.* It is consonant with the belief that those who benefit from public services should pay for them. Presumably, only if there are social benefits (positive externalities) that would not otherwise be available to society at large should a government agency be willing to price below marginal costs.

When the effects of marketing variables such as advertising are also included, the public sector economics model has some difficulty in specifying an optimal course of action. In particular, the model does not allow for advertising to affect ''taste'' (preferences) and even viewing advertising purely as information also causes difficulty. In brief, if the relationship between demand and price can be affected by advertising and other marketing variables, then the rule of setting price equal to marginal cost does not uniquely determine the quantity marketed. For example, if the marginal cost of production is constant per unit, and the effect of increasing expenditures by 20% is to increase demand by 10% above the current level, then setting price equal to marginal cost does not determine whether utilization will be at its current level or at 10% above its current level. If marginal cost is not constant, then the advertising level partially, albeit indirectly, determines the marginal cost to which price is set equal. Furthermore, the marginal cost is influenced by whether advertising is treated conceptually as a fixed or variable cost.†

Finally, the public sector economics model views fund raising as exogenous. Presumably, no valuable resources are used in raising funds to cover operating deficits, and the public sector manager cannot take actions to market his or her

organization and alter the amount of funding it receives. Yet, at least some of the time that officials of state and local governments and even of federal agencies spend testifying before the U.S. Congress and its committees and meeting formally and informally with Congressional staff assistants must be classified as fund raising.

Self-Satisfaction (Producer Satisfaction).

Etgar and Ratchford [1974] propose a dual market structure similar to the one discussed earlier. The perspective is that of the management of a nonprofit organization which controls three variables—price, advertising to users, and advertising to benefactors. However, an additional variable, producer satisfaction, is also introduced. The authors claim that the primary objective of most nonprofit organizations is producer satisfaction: that is, the

> product is created mainly for the satisfaction or producers themselves. . . . The organization will modify its product away from the one which gives its own members the most satisfaction only insofar as is necessary to obtain enough revenue from these customer groups to survive financially. [Etgar and Ratchford, 1974, p. 259].

A philharmonic orchestra which plays classical music rather than rock music is used to exemplify this argument. Although it is certainly true that in most professional organizations the members derive personal satisfaction, the focus on maximization of personal interests seems limited as a general model. Furthermore, in the operationalization of the model, Etgar and Ratchford define satisfaction as a variable independent of the quantity of the product consumed. Thus, orchestra members would be indifferent between a one-performance and twenty-performance season at the same satisfaction level and between one person in the audience and an auditorium filled to capacity.

However, this criticism is not meant to suggest that producer satisfaction can be neglected, especially in the case of artistic organizations. For example, Adizes [1975] argues that:

> The purpose of the not-for-profit artistic institution is to enable artists to create and communicate their output to the society at large according to their artistic consciences. The organization should develop the needs of the audience so that the audience will be able to absorb its product, rather than developing a product that is dictated by the needs of the existing market. The purpose of the artistic organization is to expose an artist and his message to the widest possible audience, rather than to produce the artist and the message which the largest audience demands [Adizes, 1975, p. 80].

An artistic organization which neglects the needs of its artists in order to meet current market needs will often find that its artistic vitality declines. Yet, on the other hand, audience needs cannot be neglected if the artist is to have an audience. There is obviously no simple solution for this dilemma. However, as Adizes implies, attempts at solutions should not be static but rather concerned about the dynamics of audience development over time. [See, for example, Ryans and Weinberg, 1978.]

---

*Many public utilities (e.g., electric, gas, and water) have a price structure of fixed fee plus a charge per unit consumed. The per unit charges, however, are often above the marginal costs. This was demonstrated by California water agencies which found themselves unable to meet costs as users reduced water consumption in response to the drought of 1977.

†Furthermore, in some cases advertising can increase price sensitivity. Thus Eskin [1975] found that for a new consumer food product, the company should choose between a higher advertising, low price strategy and a low advertising, high price strategy.

We have focused here on the relationship between self-satisfaction and the organization's product. However, self-satisfaction can also affect other aspects of the organization's marketing program. For example, with regard to distribution, a number of welfare agencies locate their offices at a distance from the low income areas in which their clients live in order to meet the desires of their own employees. As another example, in the area of communications, some advertisements appear to be more concerned with the (ego gratifying) needs of the sponsors than the needs of the clients.

Rules of Thumb. Many nonprofit managers, faced with a lack of formal analytic decision rules and difficult problems in measurement of response functions, have generated rules of thumb for making marketing mix decisions. These rules tend to treat each of the elements of the marketing mix as independent decisions. In this section, we review some of these rules and illustrate them with examples. No formal surveys of the decision rules employed have been taken, so the results are suggestive and impressionistic. In addition, the rules are chosen to illustrate points on a spectrum and many managers may use blends of these rules in practice. Some of these rules are as follows:

1. Professional (or Production) Approach. The organization provides the best possible services as it sees them and believes enough people will make use of those services to justify their existence. This approach is known as "minimal" or "no-sell" marketing.

> Organizations practicing minimal marketing do not consciously perform a marketing function and assume that demand will grow for their product simply because they are offering it, or offering it well. Many hospitals assume that there will be an adequate number of patients for their beds simply because of the growing population and the availability of their services. Many universities assume that there will be an adequate number of student applicants for the same reasons. They think "Why should one have to sell a worthwhile service?" [Kotler, 1975, p. 8]

Often organizations taking this approach face markets characterized by increasing demand and limited competition and are thus able to adopt a product policy and marketing approach which is not based on responsiveness to market needs. During the 1970s, as many colleges encountered problems in student recruitment and hospitals faced financial difficulties due to underutilization and other factors, administrators at these institutions, often belatedly, turned to marketing approaches to help understand problems and develop comprehensive marketing-oriented solutions.

2. Price Rules.

2.1. Cost plus or minus pricing. Price is related primarily to cost with relatively little attention paid to demand effects. The cost base varies by organization and may include only marginal costs or may include all fixed overhead costs. Demand effects are sometimes considered in the sense that the organization wants to break even on its cost base.

The Red Cross Blood Bank program provides an example of this approach. As discussed below, the program has recently been converted into one for which there are no donor credits and all users pay only a processing fee. The processing fee, or price, varies by region of the country, but, according to a Red Cross brochure, is based on the "irreducible cost of recruiting, processing, collecting, and distributing the blood to the hospitals."

2.2. Minimal and free pricing. The organization believes that price should not be an obstacle to usage and consequently tries to offer its services free or at a token price which bears little relation to cost. The organization implicitly is assuming that benefactors will cover costs.

Ginsberg puts this type of pricing strategy into historical perspective as follows:

> Since the aim of philanthropy is to make useful goods and services available to the poor who could not otherwise secure them, many nonprofit organizations long followed the practice of offering their services free of charge or at a price far below cost. As a consequence, their pricing policy was frequently so haphazard that it did not even justify the term "policy." Recently, however, several forces have been operating to alter the situation and to force many nonprofit organizations to rationalize their pricing structure. Many middle- and even high-income groups increasingly desire to obtain the services of nonprofit organizations, such as universities, hospitals, symphony orchestras. However, philanthropy has not been able to provide subsidized services for all. Moreover, there is no reason why wealthy persons should give large sums away so that others in the middle-income brackets can obtain services free of charge or substantially below cost. . . .
>
> Many hospitals, colleges, and other nonprofit institutions continue to price their services at or below cost, and some continue to provide services to certain groups without charge. Nonprofit agencies have a personal approach and a welfare orientation which is lacking in profit-seeking enterprises. They are often overtly discriminatory, such as when they make special efforts to attract those who cannot pay their regular rates. This is true of colleges which offer scholarships to deserving students.
>
> The process of costing is not the same in profit-seeking and nonprofit enterprises. The latter are only slowly coming to consider cost accounting systems, which charge interest on invested capital and depreciation on plant and equipment. Because these expenses are so often neglected in computing costs, tuition at nonprofit colleges and the charges made by many hospitals bear even less relation to true costs than the public generally assumes to be the case [Ginsberg, Hiestand, and Reubens, 1965, p. 77–8].

2.3 Fair pricing. The organization sets what it believes to be a fair price for its services based either on an intuitive feeling of what "fair" means or on a review of what other organizations offering similar services are charging. Fair pricing rules often include segmentation factors. Many nonprofit organizations offer discounts if an individual is a member of an appropriate age or occupational group.

For example, a student report summarized one zoo's pricing policy as follows:

> Admission is $2.00 for adults and does not include parking. Discounts are given to children, groups, members, and college students. No real research has been done on pricing, although questionnaires and suggestion cards have revealed some complaints

about the price and parking. The guideline in setting prices is what comparable recreational and educational institutions charge.

Of course, what is "fair" is often difficult to determine. Historically, British Rail, like most railways charged passengers in proportion to the distance traveled. However, in 1968, British Rail converted to a selective pricing system in which route fares were based on quality of product, strength of market, and degree of competition, an approach which reflected much more of a marketing orientation than the previous one. One objection to the new system was that "the concept of a 'fair fare' would disappear—no longer would the cost per mile for each ticket type be the same for everyone" [Ford, 1977, p. 302].

2.4. Ability to pay. Some nonprofits base their prices on the individual user's ability to pay. As noted above, these pricing policies are often overtly discriminatory, such as when a college offers a scholarship to a deserving, needy student, but reflects the welfare orientation of these organizations.

Several museums have adopted an ability to pay approach to admissions pricing. Faced with the dilemma of needing to increase revenues from visitors but wanting to broaden the socio-economic mix of their audience, museums have turned to a policy of "pay-what-you-like-but-pay-something" as a compromise solution. Under this system, an admission charge is "suggested," and a nominal minimum of $.25 or so may also be established.

An ability to pay approach is a pricing system which is segmented on an individual basis. When this approach is used for expensive items like a college education, the school should ideally develop a very careful system for setting the price. When the item is relatively low in cost, such as with museum admissions, the organization needs to develop a pricing system that will motivate people to pay what they can, in fact, afford to pay. In the case of museums, the suggested price can be a very critical component in determining total revenue.

3. Marketing Communication Rules.

3.1. Use available free goods. Nonprofit organizations generally have access to free advertising and free volunteer (personal selling) help and some organizations, rather than budget for a specific quantity of communication effort, employ whatever is available. There are dangers in this approach because free advertising cannot always be directed specifically at chosen target segments; moreover, the management of a volunteer organization can be expensive and time consuming.

Many of the problems with the use of volunteer help relate to the issue of *control* of the amount, duration, and quality of the volunteer's effort. Volunteers in fund raising programs often are embarrassed to ask friends to increase their monetary donations from previous levels and will not aggressively pursue recalcitrant donors. Also, volunteers may not find it convenient to adjust their time schedules to the needs of the organization. Perhaps even more important than

control of the amount of effort are the problems involved in directing the volunteers' efforts into the areas that the organization wishes to pursue. One social service agency found it difficult to develop an outreach program for alienated, "antisocial" senior citizens because the volunteers mainly wanted to work with well-adjusted seniors similar to those whom the agency was already serving.

The problems of control are often compounded because many nonprofits do not realize the difficulty of managing a part-time, unpaid volunteer organization. In contrast, many businesses devote considerable time and attention to the management of their paid, full-time field sales force consisting primarily of career employees. The nonprofit's management often naively assumes that since the "volunteers are here because they want to be here," the volunteers will all be highly motivated towards achieving a common goal.

Many of the problems relating to the use of public service advertising also are based on the loss of control. An organization committed to not paying for advertising must restrict its choice of advertising agencies to those willing to work for free or for out-of-pocket expenses only. In addition, it cannot specify the scheduling of its advertisements. If, for example, the advertisement is to be broadcast on television, the organization has no control over the time of day when it will be broadcast, the TV stations on which it will be shown, and what the time interval between commercials will be. Another problem with public service campaigns is that they often must be non-controversial in order to satisfy the sensitivities of the multiple parties involved in providing a free campaign. Of course, there have been some very successful public service campaigns, but many organizations have been disappointed by the results achieved.

The Red Cross Blood Bank program in the United States illustrates the difficulty of working under a no paid advertising stricture. Until 1977, donors and their families received free blood in case of need while non-donors had to pay a replacement fee for blood utilized and sometimes had to replace the blood as well. In 1977, the Red Cross switched to a volunteer no credit system in which any person in a Red Cross supplied hospital receives all the blood needed with only a processing fee and not a replacement fee being charged. The Red Cross's ban on paid advertising has prevented Red Cross Blood Banks from informing people about this new system, its overall benefits, and, in particular, from communicating with potential donors who may feel that they have lost something because they no longer receive replacement credits. The result of the advertising prohibition is that other elements of the marketing mix, for example, paid donor recruitment personnel, have to bear a disproportionate share of the overall marketing communication task with consequent inefficiencies for the total system.

3.2. Announcement only. Marketing communication is used primarily to announce the availability of services and other functional attributes of the service. Little effort is made to describe comprehensively the services offered, to provide persuasive information about the service, and to motivate trial and repeat usage of the service.

The difficulty encountered by Health Maintenance Organizations (HMO) which offer prepaid medical care by a group of doctors illustrates the effects of being confined to the announcement only type of advertising. Because many Americans are accustomed to a fee-for-service individual practitioner medical service, becoming a member of an HMO often involves substantial changes in people's attitudes and behaviors. Although some individuals may convert based on only a limited marketing campaign, quite often a substantial membership base is required for the HMO to be financially viable. As with other consumer goods and services, an effective way to help develop a substantial market in a short period of time is often a marketing program which includes extensive advertising to persuade the potential consumer to become informed about or try the service and to remind triers to become regular users or, in this case, members. Yet, one of the reasons that "Prepaid Health Plans Run into Difficulties as Enrollment Falters [Lublin, 1975]—as a 1975 *Wall Street Journal* headline summarized the situation—is that many have confined themselves to very limited types of advertising.

3.3. Demand Oriented. Some public sector organizations appear to have carefully analyzed the relationship between marketing communication and demand and are using what might be classified as an "objective and task approach." For example, the Baptist General Convention of Texas conducted a major campaign based on market research results and assessments of the possible accomplishments of mass media and personal communications to motivate more people to attend church [Martin, 1977].

4. Fund Raising as a Separate Activity. Most public sector organizations seem to view fund raising as a distinct and separate activity, although it often requires the time of key organizational members. In some organizations, fund raising budgets are based on the results of a careful study of the response of donations to fund raising effort [see, for example, "Stanford University: The Annual Fund," 1977]; in other organizations, the budget setting process is more intuitive. There appears to be a general notion of setting marginal revenue equal to marginal cost, especially when individual elements of a fund raising program are being evaluated. A constraint on employing the marginality rule is that some donors—especially foundations—expect fund raising costs to be a small fraction of funds raised. However, many nonprofit organizations, especially smaller ones, have fund raising costs which exceed 20% of funds raised [Gross, 1976]. These, of course, are averages and the marginal cost of the last dollar raised is almost surely higher. Even large organizations may find that particular components of their overall fund raising are costly. For example, the Stanford University Annual Fund ["Stanford University: The Annual Fund," 1984], which seeks yearly contributions primarily from alumni, has a cost to funds raised ratio of 12%. This ratio,

which is generally regarded by professional fundraisers as low, is higher than the cost to funds raised ratio for other Stanford University giving programs. For some organizations, the critical question is how to allocate a given fund raising budget, while, for others, the critical question is specification of the budget size.

DETERMINATION OF THE OPTIMAL MARKETING MIX

In the previous section, we classified and discussed a number of the approaches that nonprofit managers have used to make marketing mix decisions. As can be seen, many of these approaches are casual and fail to take full account of the complexity involved in developing a marketing program. The approaches employed tend to focus on one element at a time rather than looking at the interactions among marketing mix elements. Even within an element, the approaches do little to examine the relationship between different levels of that variable and results. Yet, the notion that there is a causal link between marketing effort and demand is fundamental for a manager who wishes to develop effective and efficient marketing programs. This relationship between effort and demand, often termed a "response function" and used to develop a "conditional sales forecast," can help provide the basis for deciding such questions as the price to charge, the amount of money to spend for advertising, and the intensity of the distribution system to design.

The advantages of viewing the marketing mix problem from the perspective of a conditional sales forecast are both conceptual and practical. From a conceptual viewpoint, this approach forces a manager to state explicitly what the major determinants of demand are and, to the extent possible, what the nature of the relationship between demand and these determinants is. This helps the manager to understand what the impact of different marketing plans will be. When the manager can actually provide numerical estimates of the response relationship between the marketing mix variables and demand, then he or she has the basis for a practical tool to help make decisions. The most sophisticated use of response functions occurs when they are formally included in a marketing model [Aaker and Weinberg, 1975].

Framework and Model Specification.* In order to specify the marketing mix model mathematically, the following notation is needed:

p price per unit of consumption
x marketing expenditures to users
y marketing expenditures to donors
$q = f(p,x)$ quantity of services used by clients
$s = g(q,y)$ subsidies raised
$c = h(q)$ cost of producing q units (total cost)

---

*The reader not interested in the mathematical development of the optimal solution may wish to go directly to Exhibit 2 and the section "Illustrative Example."

The functions of f, g, and h are assumed to have all necessary derivatives. The symbols x and y represent variables, but the model can be extended to include x and y as vectors. The model formulated here does not explicitly account for multiperiod effects, such as the carry-over of advertising, but this is to be a subject of future research.

It should be noted that the subsidies or donations function, $s = g(q,y)$ is dependent on the quantity q. This is included to capture two effects. First, donors may perceive organizations which have larger user bases as being more worthy of support. Foundations often require that organizations indicate the level of community support they have as part of the grant application. An organization which pro-

vides food and shelter for the needy, for example, might expect that the more needy people it serves, the likelier it is to attract donations. The second reason for including q is that it affects the size of the target market for many organizations. For example, the results of a fund raising campaign for a university should be dependent on the number of graduates of the school. Or, as a second example, a performing or visual arts institution may find its audience to be a primary target for fund raising efforts.

The marketing mix problem for an NPO can be stated as follows:

$$\text{Max } q = f(p,x) \tag{1}$$

subject to

$$pf(p,x) - h(q) - x + g(q,y) - y = 0 \tag{2}$$

The non-negativity constraints on p, x, and y will not be stated and will be assumed to be met throughout. The optimal solution to this problem will be denoted p^*, x^*, and y^*.

If the nonprofit organization cannot raise donations, then (2) can be modified so that the term $g(q,y) - y$ is omitted. If the nonprofit organization has a fixed subsidy, independent of q and y, then the term $g(q,y) - y$ can be replaced by the amount of that subsidy.

A profit-maximizing business's objective can be stated as

$$\text{Max } \Pi = qp - h(q) - x \tag{3}$$

Weinberg [1980] examines extensively the comparative solutions of (1) and (2) and of (3). However, for present purposes, it is sufficient to confine our discussion to the case in which the response functions $f(p,x)$ and $g(q,y)$ are represented by power functions and costs by a linear function. These functional forms are frequently used in empirical work and the main comparative results will hold if other functional forms are used. Thus, we have the following demand, subsidy, and cost functions:

$$f(p,x) = \alpha_0 p^{-\alpha_1} x^{\alpha_2} \quad (\alpha_0, \alpha_1, \alpha_2 > 0) \tag{4}$$

$$g(q,y) = \beta_0 q^{\beta_1} y^{\beta_2} \quad (\beta_0, \beta_1, \beta_2 > 0) \tag{5}$$

and

$$h(q) = c_f + c_v q \quad (c_f, c_v \geqq 0) \tag{6}$$

Although the optimal solution to this marketing mix problem can be stated in general form, in order to provide a more compact representation, it is convenient to assume that $\alpha_1 + \alpha_2 = 2$ and $2\beta_1 + \beta_2 = 1$. For this case, the optimal price strategies (p^*) for the profit maximizing firm and for usage maximizing organizations which can and cannot obtain contributions are given in Exhibit 1.

The optimal marketing effort to users, x^*, can be stated in terms of p^* in all three cases to be the following:

$$x^* = \left[\frac{\alpha_0 \alpha_2}{\alpha_1}\right]^{1/(1-\alpha_2)} [p^*]^{-1} \tag{7}$$

EXHIBIT 1
Optimal Price Strategies

(Assuming $\alpha_1 + \alpha_2 = 2$ and $2\beta_1 + \beta_2 = 1$)

Profit Maximizing Firm

$$p^* = \frac{c_v \alpha_1}{\alpha_1 - 1}$$

Nonprofit Firm Without Donations

A. Fixed Costs $= c_f$

$$p^* = \frac{(k_2 - k_1) - \sqrt{(k_2 - k_1)^2 - 4c_f c_v k_2}}{2c_f}$$

B. No Fixed Costs ($c_f = 0$)

$$p^* = \frac{c_v k_2}{k_2 - k_1}$$

Nonprofit Firm with Donations

A. Fixed Costs $= c_f$

$$p^* = \frac{(k_2 - k_1 + k_3) - \sqrt{(k_2 - k_1 + k_3)^2 - 4c_f c_v k_2}}{2c_f}$$

B. No Fixed Costs ($c_f = 0$)

$$p^* = \frac{c_v k_2}{k_2 - k_1 + k_3}$$

Notation:

$$k_1 = \left[\frac{\alpha_0 \alpha_2}{\alpha_1}\right]^{1/(1-\alpha_2)}$$

$$k_2 = \frac{\alpha_1}{\alpha_2} k_1$$

$$k_3 = \frac{2\beta_1}{\beta_2}(\beta_0 \beta_2)^{1/2\beta_1} k_2^{1/2}$$

EXHIBIT 2
Numerical Example of Optimal Decisions

	p^*	x^*	y^*	Gross User Revenue	Profit From Users
Profit Maximizing					
No fixed costs	$2.67	$3,720	—	$14,882	$5,581
Fixed costs = $5,000	$2.67	$3,720	—	$14,882	$ 581
Usage Maximizing, No Donations					
No fixed costs	$1.33	$7,441	—	$29,764	0
Fixed costs = $5,000	$2.02	$4,921	—	$19,682	0
Usage Maximizing Donations					
No fixed costs					
$\beta_0 = 10$	$1.25	$7,915	$378	$31,659	− $1,512
$\beta_0 = 50$	$0.90	$10,984	$3,922	$43,954	− $15,687
Fixed costs = $5,000					
$\beta_0 = 10$	$1.72	$5,763	$275	$23,051	− $1,101
$\beta_0 = 50$	$1.02	$9,705	$3,466	$38,823	− $13,862

Constants for Numerical Example:

$$\alpha_0 = 1{,}000, \, \alpha_1 = 1.6, \, \alpha_2 = 0.4 \qquad \beta_1 = 0.4, \, \beta_2 = 0.2 \qquad c_v = \$1.00$$

Further, for nonprofit organizations which can obtain donations, the optimal marketing expenditures directed to the contributor market are given by

$$y^* = \left[\frac{\alpha_1}{\alpha_2} \left(\frac{\alpha_0 \alpha_2}{\alpha_1} \right)^{1/(1-\alpha_2)} (\beta_0 \beta_2)^{1/\beta_1} \right]^{1/2} [p^*]^{-1} \qquad (8)$$

If there are fixed costs ($c_f > 0$), then both the profit and nonprofit organizations would not operate if those costs could not be met from revenues and contributions. However, once the decision to operate is made, the presence of fixed costs increases the optimal price and decreases the optimal marketing expenditures to be made by an NPO; there is no effect for a business.

Illustrative Example. In order to illustrate the implications of the marketing mix decision rules, a numerical example is developed in this section. The parameter values chosen are hypothetical, although they would appear to be representative of at least some nonprofit organizations. The numerical examples are summarized in Exhibit 2.

In particular, demand for service is given by

$$q = \alpha_0 p^{-\alpha_1} x^{\alpha_2} = 1000 p^{-1.6} x^{0.4} \qquad (9)$$

and contribution responsiveness is described by

$$s = \beta_0 q^{\beta_1} y^{\beta_2} = 50 q^{0.4} y^{0.2} \qquad (10)$$

The coefficients of price ($\alpha_1 = 1.6$) and marketing effort ($\alpha_2 = 0.4$) represent a moderate degree of sensitivity of demand to the price and and marketing variables. Similarly, contributions are moderately sensitive to total usage

of the services ($\beta_1 = 0.4$), but somewhat less sensitive to effort devoted to the benefaction market ($\beta_2 = 0.2$). In other words, a 50% increase in usage would increase donations by 20% ($1.5^{0.4} = 1.2$); increasing marketing effort by 50% would increase donations by 10% ($1.5^{0.2} = 1.1$). The α_0 and β_0 are scale values; Exhibit 2 provides an alternative value of β_0 (10) which provides 80% less contribution dollars at any value of q and y.

In order to show the effect of fixed costs on the optimal solution, Exhibit 2 shows the optimal values of the decision variables for the cases of zero fixed costs and for $c_f = 5000$. Variable cost, c_v, is $1.

The usage maximizing organization not only charges a lower price than the profit maximizing firm, but also spends more money on marketing ($10,984 vs. $3720). For the nonprofit organization, the loss from users is exactly equal to the amount by which donations (e.g., $19,509) exceed the marketing expenditures to the donor market (e.g., $3922). Both the price and the marketing expenditures for the nonprofit organization which cannot raise donations are intermediate between the other two organizations. By definition, the nonprofits show no deficit. When the potential of the benefaction market is reduced ($\beta_0 = 0.10$), the optimal price is increased from $0.90 (below variable cost) to $1.25 in the case of no fixed costs.

The effect of fixed costs on the level of service offered differs for the profit and nonprofit firms. For the profit maximizer, assuming that fixed costs are covered by revenues so that the firm remains in business, there is no effect on the optimal values of p^* and x^*. The nonprofit firm, however, because it cannot incur a deficit, must increase p^* (from $0.90 to $1.02) and decrease x^* (from $10,984 to $9,705) as compared to the case of no fixed costs. Nevertheless, output is still higher than for the profit-maximizing firm.

In summary, the numerical examples illustrate the degree to which a nonprofit organization should optimally charge lower prices and spend more on marketing than a profit maximizing firm facing identical demand and cost functions.

CONCLUSION

This article has reviewed approaches to determining the marketing mix, developed a formal structure of a nonprofit organization's marketing mix problem, and derived optimal decision rules. For the situation discussed, the NPO should charge lower prices and devote more of its resources to marketing than a similarly situated profit-maximizing business should. The latter was unexpected. Furthermore, because of the availability of contributions, in some cases an optimally behaving NPO should charge below marginal cost.

REFERENCES

Aaker, D. A., and Weinberg, C. B., "Interactive Marketing Models," *Journal of Marketing* (October 1975).

Adizes, I., "The Cost of Being an Artist," *California Management Review* (Summer 1975).

Collins, L., "Three Million Served Last Year," *The Financial Post Magazine* (May 1982), pp. 48–56.

Eskin, G., "A Case for Test Market Experiments," *Journal of Advertising Research* (April 1975).

Etgar, M., and Ratchford, B. T., "Marketing Management and Marketing Concept: Their Conflict in Non-Profit Organizations," *1974 Proceedings*, American Marketing Association.

Ford, R., "Pricing a Ticket to Ride," *Modern Railways* (August 1977).

Ginsberg, E., Hiestand, D. L. and Reubens, B. G., *The Pluralistic Economy*. New York: McGraw-Hill, 1965.

Gross, M., "A New Study of the Cost of Fund Raising in New York," *The Philanthropy Monthly* (April 1976).

Kotler, P., *Marketing for Nonprofit Organizations*. Englewood Cliffs: Prentice Hall, 1975.

Lublin, J. S., "Prepaid Health Plans Run into Difficulties as Enrollment Falters," *Wall Street Journal* (February 11, 1975).

Martin, W., "The Baptists Want You!" *Texas Monthly* (February 1977).

Ryans, A. B., and Weinberg, C. B., "Consumer Dynamics in Nonprofit Organizations," *Journal of Consumer Research* (September 1978).

"Stanford University: The Annual Fund," in Lovelock, C. H., and Weinberg, C. B., *Public and Nonprofit Marketing: Cases and Readings*. New York: John Wiley & Sons, 1984.

Weinberg, C. B., "Marketing Mix Decision Rules for Nonprofit Organizations," in J. Sheth, ed., *Research in Marketing*, Vol. 3. Greenwich, Connecticut: J.A.I. Press, Inc., 1980.

Weinberg, C. B., "Modeling the Marketing Mix Decision for Nonprofit Organizations," in R. Leone, ed., *Proceedings, Market Measurement and Analysis Conference* (March 1980). Providence, R.I.: The Institute of Management Science, 1981, pp. 218–222.

26
The Mass Media Family Planning Campaign for the United States

Richard K. Manoff

Family planning is a major societal issue throughout the world. This article summarizes the Planned Parenthood mass media campaign in the United States in the early 1970's. In particular it discusses the interactions with the Advertising Council, which coordinates much of the public service advertising in the United States.

We were asked by the Advertising Council to appraise the Planned Parenthood Federation project in two steps, the first of which was to explore the practicability of such a campaign. Several members of the board of the Advertising Council did not believe that the problem could be handled through advertising. This may have been a euphemistic way of indicating some of the latent opposition to the idea. In the second step, if we concluded that the campaign was practicable, we were asked to indicate how it could be dealt with in advertising.

Our eventual report was that first, yes, the campaign was practicable and, second, it could be handled by dealing with the problem in terms of the quality of life in America; that is, conditions in our country are such —the high cost of raising children, the crowded conditions of our cities, etc.—

as to make childbearing and childrearing far more difficult than before. Our campaign would sensitize people to think and carefully plan the having of children in the context of these conditions. While the conditions are not themselves the direct result of a rising population, the presence of more people in our society does have an exacerbating effect on them.

There are other justifications for a family planning campaign in the United States, in our opinion. The U.S. is the world's biggest consumer of raw materials. Our concern with the pollution of the world's atmosphere and the depletion of its natural resources must lead us to the conclusion that the prevention of the birth of an American child is more significant than of a Chinese child whose per capita consumption of the world's materials will be one-twentieth as much.

In terms of motivation to action, we knew that self-interest would have to be the primary incentive; that there was not much to be derived from appeals to social respon-

Richard K. Manoff is President, Manoff International, Inc., and Chairman, Richard K. Manoff Inc.

Reprinted by permission of the author, from *Using Commercial Resources In Family Planning Programs: The International Experience* (Honolulu: East-West Center, 1973):113–18. No part of this article may be reproduced in any form without prior written permission from the publisher.

sibility or benefit. Our experience instructs us that broad, socially abstract appeals of this kind usually invite the individual to defer to his neighbor: "Let the other fellow do it, not me." In all my years in communications I have known few efforts and no successes that were persuasively themed in this fashion. On the other hand, I know of many efforts that owe their success to a demonstration of how social benefit and self-interest are interdependent.

We presented our case to the Ad Council. It was persuaded that it could be carried out, and so gave us the task. Had I known in advance what we were in for, I would have had a less sanguine attitude toward our assignment. But the effort has been most stimulating and instructive. I have learned much about human nature and political maneuvering and about my ignorance in both areas.

It took two years to get our campaign approved. Whenever our campaign was presented to a reviewing committee (and we had more reviewing committees than I could possibly remember), some surgical action was always inevitable. We went through amputations, transplants, and radical organ excisions. In our final presentation I was constrained to remind the group that it had taken us two years to obtain their approval and in that period some eight million American children were born. I also ventured the guess that this campaign would go down in history as the one with the longest gestation period.

You will assume from this account that our campaign falls a good deal short of the objectives that Planned Parenthood had hoped for and that I, as a communications man, knew we should have strived for. But compromise is a fact of life, and it is also essential because it makes eventual action possible. Without compromise our campaign would never have been approved.

We had three target populations. The first was made up of opinion leaders. In the United States we have specific magazines whose readership generally is made up of those whose positions in society give their opinions a measure of influence over their fellow men. Such magazines as Harper's and Atlantic are cases in point.

Our second target is made up of young couples entering into the period of family formation. Actually, they are difficult to distinguish from the general populace in terms of media selection. So, in effect, in seeking to reach them we had to reach out for everyone.

Also, since all Ad Council campaigns depend on the beneficence of the media, we did not have the control of media selection to begin with.

Our third target was the young adult population.

These three target groups are not particularly clearly discerned in the print advertisements, although they are in the radio and television messages. Radio in the United States, for the most part, is a young adult medium. It is extensively programmed for music and we use it primarily to reach young adults.

Our creative strategy was, as I have indicated, to motivate self-interest: *family planning is good for you*. Our media strategy was to depend on the generosity of the media. This has never been a wise strategy and it hasn't turned out differently this time. But we had no choice.

The audience attitudes we had to deal with involved differences in religious views about conception, contraception, and birth control in general; political philosophies, such as the feeling on the part of some militant blacks that population control is basically genocidal; and the social philosophy of the population "hawks," who hold that the total answer to pollution and environmental degradation is birth control and almost ignore the central role of modern industrial technology in causing these problems.

We had to deal with all these points of view because at one time or another those who held them asked for special emphases in our messages. We protected our copy, by keeping our ultimate consumers in mind and convincing our review committees that the only important consideration was the proper incentive to motivate them. Our position was that the campaign would be severely reduced in impact if social appeals were allowed to overwhelm the appeals to self-interest.

However, we were forced to accept a very limited objective: To raise the question of family planning and to increase awareness of it. We were not allowed to use such terms as "birth control" or "contraceptives."

Our injunction was limited to an offer of literature. We could not say: "Come to a family planning clinic," or "Visit a family planning clinic to get advice." All we could say was, simply, "Planned Parenthood. Write for Information."

Not even our offered booklets were permitted to be specific in describing birth control devices and services.

Despite all the restrictions, however, I do believe our campaign has had its effect on the attitude of Americans toward family planning. I must refer once again to my philosophy of incremental improvement. What really matters is improvement, no matter how little may take place. In time, that effort accumulates increasing impact both from the multiplier effect of its exposure and from the growing liberalization of attitudes.

The issue of family planning gives rise to many fascinating contradictions. One of the more colorful has to do with the radically different attitudes expressed among media. For example, the April 2, 1971 issue of Life Magazine devoted its cover and major article to the problem of high school pregnancy in the United States. According to Life Magazine, the question of high school pregnancy and the pregnant bride is morally and socially acceptable for public discussion. It is also socially acceptable in Seventeen, a teenage magazine, which ran an article on "Questions you ask most about birth control." But unfortunately, when you get to television and radio, you enter a somewhat different world. For when we proposed a message for television on the same subject we were summarily turned down. As a matter of fact, the Columbia Broadcasting System at first rejected all our television messages, although the National Broadcasting Company and the American Broadcasting Company accepted them.

This kind of contradiction among our media did not simplify our task. We had to make further accommodations in an already over-accommodated campaign in order to get it to the public.

A sample of our advertisements directed at opinion leaders is shown in Exhibit 1. At the bottom of the advertisement is a description of Planned Parenthood. The need for this was revealed in our research: Planned Parenthood was not well known nor was its name obvious enough.

We developed advertisements such as those shown in Exhibits 2 and 3 for the general public. The objective of these ads is to legitimize the concept of family planning and to add it to the social and ethical vocabulary of the United States.

For our young adult audience, we had to employ a different sensibility. In dealing with young people, we knew that we could treat our message with a bit of humor and whimsy in order to achieve the right *tonality*. By tonality we mean the emotional environment of the message. Proper tonality is achieved through the use of terms and expressions

that are engaging for our target audience. Some of our advertisements for young people are shown in Exhibits 4 and 5.

It might be of interest for you to see the headlines used in two proposed advertisements that did not run.

> "One thing about the population problem,
> you don't have to get out of bed to fight it."

> "Darien, Connecticut, is doing its best
> to contribute to our population growth."

The latter was a deliberate effort to point out that the major increase in population in the United States is coming from middle and upper income families, which is contrary to popular understanding. Lower socio-economic groups do tend to have more children per family, but since they are outnumbered by middle and upper income families, the latter are producing more children in the aggregate. We thought that this was an important piece of attitude education for the

---

EXHIBIT 1

What a pity that having children is often more important than wanting them.

The pressures for having children are great.
Some are social.
Like a mother-in-law asking for the hundredth time when she's going to see grandchildren.
Or an aunt wondering out loud whether the couple is selfish.
Other pressures are personal.
Like the self-doubt in many men and women over whether they actually can "make" a baby.
Other pressures are less obvious.
Like not enough family planning services available for everyone who desires and needs them.
As we said, the pressures are great.
But as far as we're concerned, there's only one, repeat one,

reason for a couple to have a child: because they really want it.
And are ready for it: emotionally, not just financially.
And there's only one time to have that child: *when* they want it. When it can be a welcome addition rather than an accidental burden.
Unfortunately, research has

consistently shown that not enough Americans (from every walk of life) are aware of the benefits of family planning or how to go about it.
That's what we're all about. And frankly, we can use all the help we can get.
Especially from thoughtful people who understand how unplanned pregnancies can intensify the already severe problems society has still to solve.
People who will, at the very least, help others understand that there's a difference between having children—and wanting them.

Planned Parenthood
Children by choice. Not chance.

For further information, write Planned Parenthood, Box 581, Radio City Station, N.Y., N.Y. 10019

Planned Parenthood is a national, non-profit organization dedicated to providing information and effective means of family planning to all who want and need it. advertising contributed for the public good

---

EXHIBIT 2

An unexpected child can really rock the cradle.

Don't get us wrong.
We think children are priceless, too.
But if a child happens to be unplanned, it *could* mean financial pressures.
You see, a child is not just an extra mouth to feed. It's a whole other life to be provided for.
And that takes money.
Fact is, the cost to raise a child to age 18 ran around $25,000 (more for some, less for others, dependent on family income) in the mid-60's. And what inflation will do to the cost in the future is anybody's guess!
But no matter what the amount is, it's easy to see that the cost of rearing children is an economic reality one can't ignore. That is, if each child is to get what he or she deserves.
Which is why we advise every couple to plan how many children they want. And when they want them: when they can be a welcome addition rather than an accidental burden.
Because, as we all know, it's awfully hard to give with a full heart when one's pockets are empty. **Planned Parenthood**

For further information, write Planned Parenthood, Box 431, Radio City Station, New York, N.Y. 10019.   Children by choice. Not chance.

Planned Parenthood is a national, non-profit organization dedicated to providing information and effective means of family planning to all who want and need it. advertising contributed for the public good

EXHIBIT 3

EXHIBIT 4

EXHIBIT 5

American people, who labor under the misguided opinion that only the poor people are breeding us into disaster.

For television, we produced two messages which are shown in storyboard form in Exhibits 6 and 7. We had both sixty- and thirty-second versions of each message.

We also prepared one other television message, referred to earlier, which was not produced because the networks would not approve it.

This message has a lovely church setting where a wedding is about to start. Everybody eagerly awaits the bride. Our camera moves close in on the people in the pews who fidget and stare at the rear of the church waiting for the bride to appear.

Then our camera cuts to the minister who finally signals by a slight nod of the head that the ceremony is ready to begin.

EXHIBIT 6

EXHIBIT 7

We cut to the nervous groom who runs his finger under his collar, and to the best man, who is trying to look relaxed. They too face the rear of the chapel.

Finally the organ sounds and then our camera shifts to the rear of the chapel to pick up the bride as she steps through the double door on the arm of her father. She is beautiful. She is radiant. She is also quite pregnant.

Then for the first time we hear the words of the announcer who says, as the bride and her father glide slowly down the aisle:

"The purpose of this message is not to shock you. It's just to point out one out of five brides in this country is pregnant before the ceremony. We think there is only one time to have a child: when you really want one."

We close on: "Planned Parenthood. Children by Choice. Not by Chance."

That message never saw the light of day. Nobody would approve it. But its time will come.

Materials for radio included recorded messages (and scripts for live presentation) of ten-, thirty-, and sixty-second spot announcements. Here are two of the sixty-second recorded announcements:

"GET TO KNOW THE TWO OF YOU"

OPEN WITH PP THEME MUSIC, THEN UNDER.

Girl: What sign were you born under?
Boy: Do you really think rock has had it?
Girl: How do you like your coffee in the morning?
Boy: Do you like to sleep late on weekends?
Girl: Can a wife work and be a mother at the same time?
Boy: Should a husband help with the housework?
Girl: Where would you like to live—city or country?
Boy: Should we spend a couple of years in Europe?
Girl: How often should we have relatives over?
Boy: Do we take our parents in when they get old?
Girl: How many children do you want?
Boy: How many children do **you** want?

MUSIC UP, THEN UNDER.

Announcer: Before a couple can decide how many children they want, there are a lot of questions that have to be answered: what you're both really like . . . what you both really want out of life. Only time can give you the answers. But an unexpected pregnancy can rob you of that time. And the fact is that more than half of all the pregnancies each year **are** unexpected. (BEAT) Get to know the two of you before you become the three of you.

For more information, write Planned Parenthood, Box 898, Radio City Station, New York 10019. That's Box 898, Radio City Station, New York 10019. Planned Parenthood. Children by choice. Not chance.

Girl: How well do you think you **know** me?
Boy: How well do you think you know **me?**

"THE FUTURE"

OPEN WITH DOCUMENTARY-TYPE SOUND MONTAGE OF STUDENTS TALKING ABOUT THEIR HOPES AND THEIR DREAMS OF THE FUTURE.

Boy 1: Tomorrow? Wow. Like, well . . . I want to be doing something positive . . . like maybe, uh . . . social work . . .
Boy 2: . . . medical research. That's where it's going for me . . . such things can be done . . .
Girl 1: . . . probably wind up in the suburbs with my husband . . . doing the things everybody does . . . but they can't take my education away!
Boy 3: . . . figure, then, with an M.A. from Harvard Business, my wife and I can take my old man's car franchise and really break the bank!
Girl 2: . . . not to be a great actress! But if I can teach the feeling to children . . .
Girl 3: . . . a different lawyer than my father-in-law. Get it down to the people.
Boy 4: . . . know the film business is rough . . . but if you don't make it, well, you can always do commercials!
Announcer: No matter what your plans for the future—an unexpected pregnancy can change them. And the fact is—more than half the pregnancies each year **are** unexpected. So if you want your future to be what you planned—don't take a chance with it. For more information, write Planned Parenthood, Box 898, Radio City Station, New York 10019, That's Box 898, Radio City Station, New York 10019. Planned Parenthood. Children by choice. Not chance.

From these examples, it will be seen how easily the same material transfers from print to television to radio. We always strive for this consistency of language and tonality from medium to medium. It is not always possible, but it should always be an objective.

27

The Baptists Want You!

William Martin

In 1976–1977, the Baptist General Convention of Texas developed an extensive marketing program to increase the membership in their church. This program included consumer research to help determine the creative strategy for the advertising campaign, a marketing budget of more than $1.5 million dollars, and coordination of the efforts of 4,200 Baptist churches, their ministers, and members.

God, as is His custom, has once again confounded the wise. After listening to a generation of theologians speak bravely of His death, the Almighty has established Himself as the odds-on choice for Comeback of the Decade. Conservative churches are growing, evangelical Christianity has been declared mainstream American religion, and a Southern Baptist Sunday school teacher has become Leader of the Free World. And now, as if that were not enough, the Baptist General Convention of Texas is about to launch a media blitz designed to share the good news of God's love with every man, woman, and child in the state an average of forty times apiece during a four-week period in February and March. The $1.5 million campaign, to be called Good News Texas, will feature commercials for Christ on television and radio, ads in newspapers and other print media, booster spots on billboards, pins on lapels, and an extensive personal visitation program to be run by the local churches. It is going to be pure Baptist. Well, almost pure. To help them do it right, the Baptists have hired one of the largest and most successful advertising firms in the country, the Bloom Advertising Agency of Dallas. Neither Sam nor Bob Bloom has roots in the Christian branch of the Judeo-Christian tradition.

I have mixed feelings about all this. Some of my best friends are Baptists, always have been. Still, I have never been able to shake completely the conviction that Baptists are the Aggies of religion. That in itself is not enough to damn them, but it does sort of set them apart. Part of my problem with Baptists stems from the fact that I grew up in the Church of Christ (Romans 16:16). As you may know, Church of Christ people believe the circle of the saved is rather small, and not many of them would care to sound too certain about their place in it. Baptists, on the other hand, never seem to tire of telling how sure they are they are saved and how good this blessed assurance feels. I thought their "once saved, always saved" doctrine of salvation was unsound—too easy; cheap grace; why, that would mean you could do anything you wanted to—but at least they had some doctrine, which was more than you could say for the Methodists, and at least we all agreed that nothing could send you to Hell faster than kissing the Pope's toe. No, the main problem wasn't doctrine. It was style. No matter what I believed, I could no more have been a Baptist when I was growing up than I could spend every Thursday night at the bowling alley or wear a seafoam-green leisure suit today.

William Martin is Associate Professor of Sociology, Rice University.

For one thing, Baptists were so *organized* about inviting people to church. Once I was in the barbershop getting my weekly haircut when Mr. Joy Tilley, who was a big Baptist—I think it says something that the counterpart of "staunch Presbyterian," "devout Catholic," and "pillar in the Methodist Church" is "big Baptist"—stuck his head in and invited the barber to come sit in his pew at a revival then in progress. That astonished me. We had a few elderly members who sort of had squatter's rights to pews they had occupied for years, but we would never have dreamed of assigning somebody a particular pew and then sending them out to drum up people to pack it.

The contrast carried over to the revivals themselves. The mark of a successful Church of Christ revivalist was his ability to drive the nail of terror into slumbering souls. Though some Baptist revivalists made use of hellfire and brimstone, I always felt that the mark of a successful Baptist preacher was his ability to make you laugh and feel good. That didn't seem much like religion to me.

This difference was further reflected in the Sunday schools, where we gave our classes sensible, functional names—"Preschool," "Elementary," "Junior High," and "Young People"—and encouraged attendance by quoting scriptures, especially Hebrews 10:25 ("Forsake not the assembling of yourselves together"), and threatening slackers with hellfire. Baptists called their classes things like "Sunbeams" and "Pioneers" and "Aviators" and drew crowds by having the youth minister bounce over the church bus from a trampoline.

I used to marvel at what they would do to appeal to young people. Our high school assembly programs fell into two primary categories: magicians, myna birds, and trick-shot artists sent out from the Southern School Assemblies organization and—this was before Ms. O'Hair took God out of the schools—preachers holding revivals over at the Baptist church. They would juggle and tell a few jokes and then talk to us earnestly about taking care of our bodies, which are temples of the Holy Spirit (I Corinthians 6:19). Once a revival team from Baylor entertained us with several hymns and gospel tunes arranged for trumpet trio. Then the leader, a young man with the unforgettable name of Horace Oliver Bilderback, placed a trombone mouthpiece in his trumpet and played "Let the Lower Lights Be Burning," while one of his fellow clerics moved an imaginary trombone slide out in front. That, to me, was the pure essence of the Southern Baptist Church.

At times, to be sure, I envied my Baptist friends and made some effort to be one of them. I went to the Baptist Vacation Bible School several years and made bookends and potholders and whatnot shelves, and did right well at a Bible game called Sword Drill—"Attention! Draw swords! (No thumbs over the edges, now.) John 3:16! Charge!"—and I thought it was keen that their pastor, Brother Rose, illustrated his devotional lessons with magic tricks and showed us slides of his trip to the Holy Land. Once, I joined the Royal Ambassadors (and got elected Ambassador-in-Chief) just to have a chance to go to the summer encampment at Alta Frio, but I lost my nerve before the bus left and stayed home. Later, I longed to go on hayrides and swimming parties with the Training Union and even wished I could go into San Antonio and hear Angel Martinez preach in a white suit. But it was just no use. I was like a lonely traveler watching a group of Shriners cutting up in a hotel lobby: it might be fun for a day or two to wear a fez and ride a little motor scooter down Main Street, but you wouldn't want to go home and still have to be one.

Before all the Baptists walk out on me, I have a confession to make. About four or five years ago, I became sort of a Baptist myself. After spending the better part of the sixties studying religion at Harvard, I grew a bit weak on matters of doctrine and decided I would do more harm than good by sticking with the Church of Christ. When I came back to Texas, I cast around a bit and finally wound up at a church that I suppose could be described as liberal and ecumenical, though even now I find it difficult to identify myself as a theological liberal, so strongly was I taught to believe that few states of being are more pernicious. Still, at least half the people in this church grew up as Baptists, a good handful of them are former Baptist preachers, and even though the Union Baptist Association of Houston threw them out for accepting members from other denominations without rebaptizing them, they still persist in calling themselves Baptists. I have had some trouble with it. I am embarrassed when they look at me in amazement because I have never heard of Lottie Moon, and I get a little squirmy when they sing "Do Lord" at the annual retreat up in the woods, and I admit it doesn't make a dime's worth of difference to me whether Baylor wins or loses a football game. Still, we don't have revivals and if we did we wouldn't have trumpets or trombones or jugglers, and nobody checks to see why you haven't been coming to Sunday school and, as far as I can tell, nobody much cares about the details of your belief, so long as you are kind and try to help folk when they need it. It doesn't have anything like the zip of a straight-out evangelical church, but ex-Fundamentalists are some of the best people you'll find anywhere, so I expect I'll keep my letter in a while longer. Besides, if Good News Texas works, we may all be Baptists by summer.

Baptists, of course, have always been aggressive. They sought "A Million More in Fifty-four" and they have sponsored Billy Graham Crusades and hold "Win Clinics" to instruct people in the techniques of personal evangelism. But this is bigger, better, grander than anything they have ever done before.

My immersion in the project came in Dallas at a regional meeting of the Baptist General Convention of Texas (BGCT). The Good News Texas portion of the program was co-chaired by Drs. L. L. Morriss and Lloyd Elder. Morriss, with his smooth gray hair, metal glasses, and high-quality fall woolens, could easily pass for a corporation executive. His speech and manner befit his appearance—one senses he does little by accident. Lloyd Elder's obvious intelligence, warmth, and gentle wit are engaging, but his slightly more rumpled look and apparent unconcern for slickness make it easier to believe he is a seminary professor or church executive.

Morriss declared he was as excited as "an auctioneer at an auction of used furniture," a metaphor I thought fell somewhat short of the mark. He was excited, he said, about what God had done for Texas in the past and about what He is doing now. He introduced Elder, who was also excited. Good News Texas, Elder said, would have three major targets: (1) the 4.7 million Texans—one third of the state's population—who do not belong to any Christian group, persons "who are completely uninvolved in the things of Christ," (2) inactive and apathetic church members, including 700,000 Baptists, and (3) the active membership of local Baptist churches. He summarized what the Bloom Agency had done so far and sketched out the main lines the media campaign would follow. Then he reminded the assembly that Good News Texas "is not a goodwill campaign for the convention. It is not church advertising. It is going with the best product we have, and that is the gospel of Jesus Christ."

Elder then called on Dr. Jimmy Allen, the pastor of San Antonio's First Baptist Church. Allen is a big man who wears his graying hair rather long for a Baptist preacher and gives off an unmistakable impression of high energy. Working from a few notes scribbled on the back of an envelope, he spoke of "the rhythm in the way God moves in His world, in the tide, in our heartbeat, in the very energy levels of our lives." "There are times," he said, "when God moves in great force and power in our lives, and then there are times of wandering in the wilderness when we begin to appreciate the fact that we cannot live in ecstasy all the time. There must be a hunger before there is filling. There must be thirst before there can be a slaking of thirst. I am convinced we are at the edge of a spiritual awakening in our nation and that some of us are in places where we can already sense the tide of God coming in."

Allen noted that *Newsweek* had carried Charles Colson's testimonial, that the *Fort Worth Star-Telegram* had printed an editorial that told how to be saved, and that CBS had interviewed members of his church for an hour-long documentary on the meaning of salvation. He went on for about twenty minutes, talking about how much we needed revival and how much he hoped God might choose Baptists to be part of the central apparatus by which He moved. Then, in a hushed voice that visibly moved the audience with its intensity, he concluded: "I find myself saying, 'God, could this be the time? Lord, could you be ready now? Is it something that will take our breath away?' I find myself saying, 'O Lord, let it be good news, not just for Texas, not just for Texas Baptists, but for a nation and a world that desperately needs to find out that, indeed, there is good news.'"

Later that afternoon, I sat down with Morriss, Elder, and BGCT executive director Dr. James Landes. Though he was quick to note he is a chemical engineer by training, Dr. Landes' beneficent countenance and rather sermonic manner make it clear he has been around a lot of preachers.

"The rationale of Good News Texas," Landes said, "is the commandment 'Go ye into all the world.' I have seen the heartbreaking conditions so many people are experiencing throughout this state. I had no alternative but to study how to spread the message that there are people in the world who *care,* who are interested in persons just because they are human beings, regardless of race or color or creed, and that the reason these people care is because they believe God *is,* and Christ *is,* and the Scriptures are a mirror of Christ's mind. I realized also that many of our leaders were reaching out for some undergirding arm that could strengthen and help them in their ministry in the local church. So, as I thought and prayed and did a bit of meditating in between fly fishing on the riverbanks of Colorado, I said, 'Lord, if this great big denomination with two million people and forty-two hundred churches and missions will make up its mind to do one thing across a period of a couple of years, there is no telling what good could come of that.' And I thought if we could just plant a seed, maybe it could grow, maybe it could bless a whole state and the nation. I shared that dream with my associates here on the administrative staff and they asked me to share it with the executive board. I came away somewhat shocked but deeply gratified, because men who do not normally react enthusiastically to another evangelistic thrust got to their feet and said, 'This sounds different, get with it!'"

As we talked, Landes and his colleagues echoed what Jimmy Allen had said about the soon-coming revival. Exciting things are happening among our laymen, they said. Signs of awakening are blowing across our nation. But if revival was coming with or without their help, as they seemed to be saying, why didn't Baptists take their $1.5 million and spend it some other way? "Somebody has to be the agent," Landes replied. "God always works through an Abraham, a Moses, an Isaac, a Joseph, a John the Baptist. He doesn't work without working through people. If Texas Baptists have the favorable image the research for this project shows we have, then we've got a *responsibility* commensurate with it. If God wants to use us, we have a responsibility to be available."

I brought up something that had struck me from the moment I saw the first piece of promotional literature about Good News Texas. The logo for the campaign is the Christian fish symbol, with the state of Texas stuffed inside it like Jonah. To accommodate both Amarillo and Laredo, the fish is drawn a bit fat, so that it looks something like a football with a tail or perhaps a Gospel Blimp. Several years ago a mild satire, widely circulated in evangelical circles, described the misadventures of a Christian group that hired a blimp to broadcast sermons and drop leaflets on the hapless community below. Though it attracted great attention, the townspeople were irritated and offended, and the initial spirit and purpose of the enterprise were lost and perverted. I was curious about whether these men had considered the possibility that Good News Texas might be a Baptist version of the Gospel Blimp.

Elder was aware of the perils. "If we just saturated the media with the gospel message," he said, "and expected something to happen automatically, that would be the Gospel Blimp approach. Just pay your money and send up the blimp. But we are making a real effort to keep that from happening. We are trying to equip ministers and lay people in the local churches to be *witnesses,* so that they don't just let the blimp fly over, but can knock on doors and present the gospel to people as caring, sharing neighbors."

Jimmy Allen had said Baptists would need to remember that "when God comes to town, He doesn't always stay in our house. He moves where He chooses to move and leaps over all kinds of barriers." How would they feel if the Methodists or Presbyterians or Church of Christ picked up some new members on Baptist nickels? The prospect did not seem to dismay them. They were, in fact, informing other denominations in the state about their plans so that if the awakening comes, they can also be ready for it. There is, of course, some confidence that their 4,200 outlets will give Baptists a healthy share of whatever market develops.

This ecumenical talk emboldened me to raise a point I regarded as of at least mild interest. Why had they chosen the Bloom Agency? Granted, it was recognized as one of the best agencies in the country and its Dallas location provided the advantage of close and frequent contact, but was there no sense of incongruity in hiring a Jewish-owned agency to conceive and produce an evangelistic campaign for Southern Baptists? Apparently not. The Baptists chose their agency the same way Procter and Gamble or Exxon might, with a steering committee of seventeen people and a much larger consultation group from across the state that heard presentations by a number of respected firms.

"Bob Bloom is a good salesman," said James Landes. "When he was through, I heard a Baptist preacher from East Texas say, 'I don't need to hear anybody else. The man knows where he is going.' When that group voted, they did so with a great feeling of confidence in the ability and desire of the Bloom Agency to help us do what we wanted to do. It was almost unanimous. It was an overwhelming decision." Landes admitted to some early personal reservations but insisted things had worked out "more beautifully and fantastically than we had expected." Then he suggested I check out the backgrounds of the men at the agency with primary responsibility for the account.

The Bloom Agency occupies several floors of the Zale Building, which sits alongside Stemmons Freeway like a giant homemaker's misplaced toaster. Instead of the customary rooms and hallways, the agency uses "action offices," work spaces defined by movable partitions about five and a half feet high, which can be shaped to fit needs that change with each new client or campaign. Flexible white hoses bring electrical and telephonic nourishment to each of the modules, so that one can tote up the number of offices currently in use by counting the accordion-pleated umbilici. The occupants of these spaces decorate them as if they are planning to stay for years, so I presume one has a fair chance of hanging onto one's own partitions, but I was told reshuffling is not uncommon.

The furnishings run heavily to chrome, glass, and plastic, with plenty of plants and bright colors. Most of the offices are densely decorated in pop-artifactual chic, with tapestries and macrame hangings and inspirational posters framed in Lucite and fire-alarm boxes and street signs and—everywhere—reminders and remnants of past campaigns. Shelves in the reception area hold symbols of the agency's various clients: Bekins, Southwest Airlines, Owens Sausage, Amalie Motor Oil, Rainbo Bread, Lubriderm Cream, Whataburger, and a score of others. I looked in vain for a New Testament or a Broadman Hymnal, but I guess the display had not yet been brought that far up to date.

Bob Bloom showed me around and talked about the Baptist account. "We are in the consumer advertising business," he explained. "Our job is to communicate with the general public and get a response from them. That is what we do best. We try to generate retail purchases, to get people to buy motor oil, or a home, or seats on an airplane. We have never been involved in anything like this before, but the thing that stimulated us was the feeling that the BGCT could give us what we want in a partnership role, a sharing of responsibilities as opposed simply to doing what we tell them. They know how to listen, how to guide, how to tell us when we are off base, and they know how to stroke, so we are pleased to have the association from that standpoint. I was impressed that they could not only accept but embrace aspects of our craft that we have difficulty getting business people, including some Harvard MBAs, to accept."

How did he account for this? "I'm not really sure," Bloom said. "I guess they are just smart. I had expected a sharp drop-off in intelligence between the leaders of the organization and the men in lower positions. In a business organization like a bank, for example, once you get past the president and a few directors to some of the department heads, you find some terrible prejudices about certain things, a lack of understanding about advertising and research, and an unwillingness to bend. I expected that with the Baptists, but frankly, I found a lot of sharp men at all levels. And they are very flexible. When we got out with the pastors, I expected to confront some prejudice, both from my being Jewish and in their willingness to marry our craft with their pulpit responsibilities. I just didn't find any of that. I found a high degree of comprehension when we went through the various alternatives with them. I kind of expected someone to get up and make an appeal to 'throw all that stuff away and just give people the simple gospel.' It didn't happen. They had smart, agile minds and they really embraced what we were trying to do. If I could get forty rabbis together to do that, I would be terribly surprised. They are also very sincere about the undertaking. It is great to have a client who believes in what he is doing, as opposed to someone who is just grinding out a product.''

Did he have any misgivings about mounting a campaign whose basic premise he, as a Jew, did not believe? ''I never felt any real sensitivity on that issue, except in regard to the terminology, which was very alien to me. Once I became confident they were willing to accept me as a spokesman for the agency and as a craftsman with some expertise, I became very comfortable with it. My role has been much the same as with any client. I feel I am particularly good at organizational work and strategic thinking. I am not concerned with the technological aspects of a motor oil—what it will or won't do for an engine—and I can't comment on the religious aspects of this project. What I am interested in is how we can communicate the selling points to the customer.''

Bob introduced me to his father, Sam Bloom, the agency's founder, who professed an interest in the project that went beyond craftsmanship. He was concerned ''about both the standards and ethics which appear to be declining in politics and business.'' The Baptists, he thought, were on the right track on these matters. Their willingness to lay $1.5 million on the line to bolster the ethics and morality of the state was a courageous act and he was ''terribly enthused'' to have a part in it.

I visited with most of the key personnel working on the account in the agency's new think tank, a tiered and carpeted room with no furniture except for ashtrays and huge pillows covered in plaid, madras, batik, and Marimekko. A tray on one of the lower tiers held coffee, Styrofoam cups, little packets of Cremora, Imperial Sugar, Sweet 'n' Low, and a box of those red-and-white plastic sticks that are too skinny to stir anything. On the assumption, I presume, that ideas generated in the room would be too dramatic to jot down on 3 × 5 cards with a ball-point pen, jumbo pads of paper and Magic Markers lay within easy reach. While a person in Faded Glory jeans with stars on the pockets went out to get Frescas and Tabs and Cokes for the non-coffee drinkers, we took our positions, shifted around a bit to look properly relaxed, and began to talk.

Dick Yob, research director for the project, explained that ''the days of doing what we *think* will work are becoming extinct because of the amount of money that is involved. We have to go out and find what really does communicate. Our approach has been to come at this like we would any package goods account, since that is basically what we know how to do.'' The first step had been to see what problems were bothering Texans these days. To accomplish this, Yob hired the Dallas marketing research firm of Louis, Bowles and Grove, Inc., to show a list of problems to approximately 300 Dallas and Austin citizens—divided evenly between active Baptists, inactive Christians, and non-Christians—

and ask which most accurately mirrored their own feelings and which were the problems they heard other people discuss. On both counts, all three groups ranked hypocrisy as the number one problem, by agreeing with such statements as ''It's getting harder to trust anybody or anything'' and ''People are not what they pretend to be. They say one thing and do another.''

Survey participants were then offered three possible solutions: (1) reading the Bible, (2) joining a group of active Christians, and (3) entering into a personal relationship with Jesus Christ and following his teachings. All three groups agreed that of the three answers, Christ was the best—though only 27 percent of the inactive Christians and 14 percent of the non-Christians actually felt it was an appropriate solution for them. More than two-thirds of the non-Christians chose none of the three options. In short, despite evidence of considerable spiritual and emotional malaise among backslidden and secular Texans, the field appeared to be something less than white unto harvest. Still, the Baptists and the agency agreed that a personal relation with Jesus was the most commercial of the products they had to offer. The next step was to decide how to package it for wholesale distribution.

At this point, the burden shifted to Bill Hill, the agency's creative director. He did not find the yoke an easy one. What could they say that would communicate effectively to all three target groups? And what vehicle would they use to say it: testimonial? dramatizations? slice-of-life vignettes? cartoons? jingles? During our first conversation, Hill had a discernible case of advertiser's anxiety. ''We are trying to avoid coming across as too churchy,'' he said, ''and we want to avoid clichés. The men working with us from BGCT are theologians. When they say 'Christ died for you,' there is a lifetime of knowledge behind it and all sorts of subtleties ripple out of it, but to the people they have singled out as the primary audience—non-Christians—that is a cliché and it may be a turnoff. We want to save the Jesus message to the very end of the TV spots, so we can get people nodding and saying, 'Yes, that is a problem. Yes, I would like to have a solution to that problem.' Then, at the end, we want to say, 'That solution is available to you through Jesus Christ.' We are trying to say, in the simplest form possible, that 'something that happened two thousand years ago is a real force that is relevant to your own individual problems right here and right now. If you are really concerned about your own problems and about what is going on in the world, and you have tried everything else, what have you got to lose?' We are not really trying to say *how* Christ is the answer, but simply *that* he is. We may go into *how* a little more in the other media.'' The problem of doing justice to the gospel in a brief commercial is tough, Hill admitted: ''I keep writing forty-two-second commercials because I just can't boil it all down into thirty seconds. In a thirty-second-spot, about all we can say is, 'This aspirin contains more pain relievers than all the others combined.' ''

Guy Marble outlined the key public relations aspects of the campaign. His main task would be to bombard local churches throughout the state with newsletters, articles, speechs, posters, lapel buttons, and other communiqués to allow them to take full advantage of the media campaign when it hit their area. The agency people and Baptists both agreed that the word would be barren, like seed on stony ground, unless the local churches were ready not only to urge personal evangelism, but also to accept and nurture those who might be converted. As Jim Goodnight, who has overall responsibility for the account, put it, "We are going to give people the opportunity to respond, but when a guy walks in the back door of a Baptist church some Sunday morning to find what he has been looking for—what happens then will be up to the members of that church. If they are not ready for people who may not share any of their values, then it won't work. If they are ready to accept people 'just as I am,' I believe there will be a tremendous awakening of visible growth in both numbers and spirit." Another promotion task will be to make sure the local churches understand the strategy that will govern the campaign. "When we buy time for these commercials," Goodnight explained, "we are not going to be buying the Sunday Morning Revival Hour. We are going to be buying *Mary Hartman, Mary Hartman* and *All in the Family* and *Sonny and Cher.* You can anticipate the kinds of reactions thousands and thousands of Texas Baptists are going to have —'What are we doing supporting that kind of program?' Of course, our purpose is not to support the program. It's where we have to go to reach the people we want to reach."

Despite the frequent comparison of selling the gospel to selling aspirin or motor oil, it seemed clear these men were taking the matter more seriously than that. I recalled what Dr. Landes had said about checking their backgrounds, so I asked each of them to characterize his religious position. The agency didn't exactly turn out to be a collection of Madison Avenue cynics. Dick Yob is a graduate of Catholic University at Marquette, sends his oldest son to parochial school, and is active in the Church. Bill Hill is the son of a Baptist preacher in Amarillo but became so disillusioned with evangelical Christianity by the time he reached high school that for several years he dabbled in Zen, studied Rosicrucian literature, and considered going to live with the Dalai Lama in Tibet. Instead, he got married and became an Episcopalian. For the past seven years, he has participated in a Bible class taught by conservative Biblicist Mal Couch, a graduate of fundamentalist Dallas Theological Seminary who specializes in the interpretation of Biblical prophecy. Public relations advisor Guy Marble describes himself as "a lapsed Methodist," but his colleague Frank Demarest is a member of the Northwest Bible Church in Dallas (also aligned with the Dallas Theological Seminary) and admits he stands a bit to the right of Southern Baptists in his theology. Jim Goodnight grew up in the Park Cities Baptist Church in Dallas but switched to the Church of Christ after he married the granddaughter of G. H. P. Showalter, a Church of Christ patriarch

and former editor of one of its most conservative papers, the *Firm Foundation.* Though he locates himself in "the liberal, ecumenical wing of the Church of Christ" (a figure of speech like "virile impotence"), he is still active in the Preston Crest congregation in Dallas and has taught classes in C. S. Lewis' *Mere Christianity,* hardly a radical treatise.

These men, it turns out, are not the only Christians in the Bloom Agency. "You would be amazed," Goodnight said, "at the number of people within the agency who wanted to work on this account. Not only have a number of these closet Christians surfaced, but about twenty-five of us now meet each Wednesday at noon to pray and share our concerns and testimonials." "It's really neat," Demarest said. "All our working lives we have had this separation between our Christian faith and what we do on our jobs. For me, this is the first time to bring the two together."

"There is a terrible intensity among the people on the team," Hill said. "This is not just another piece of package goods. This is something that is going to affect people's lives. I really feel what I am doing. I keep thinking, 'We are going to save Texas!' and that gets to be a bit of a hang-up and causes a mental block." Another problem, Goodnight observed, is that "each of us gets his own theology and beliefs, his own personal slant woven into it. One of the hardest thing to do in any advertising is to wash yourself out of it and consider only the people you are trying to write for and what their needs are."

"With most products," Yob pointed out, "you are selling to people who are already users. It is a matter of getting them to switch brands or buy more of your product. But in this campaign, non-users are the number one target."

That afternoon I attended a meeting between members of the Bloom team and key staff members at the Baptist Building. Mainly, they were catching each other up on how things were going in their sections of the ball park. Jim Goodnight read the strategy statement that had emerged from their research. "What we are trying to do," he said, "is communicate to people that the frustrations they experience with the hypocrisy and lack of integrity in today's world is the result of misplaced priorities, and that the solution is to place their trust in Jesus Christ who will never fail them, rather than on the imperfect things of the world." The Baptists liked that a lot.

Demarest, Marble, and Mary Colias Carter reviewed PR plans. A steady stream of articles would appear in the *Baptist Standard* to "soften up the terrain," and a piece would appear in the next issue of the *Helper,* BGCT's women's magazine. Pastors would be supplied with information they could use to raise money for the program. Every church would receive material explaining the nature and scope of the project. Marble reported that he and his associates had done "much agonizing posterwise," but promised the first in a series of posters would be ready in "six weeks max."

They also talked a bit about honorary chairmen. Billy Graham had agreed to serve as national honorary chairman, but both the Baptists and the Bloom representatives wanted to make sure the campaign did not become a Graham affair. "We are not going to be able to use him much in a public way," Marble said. "If he is flying from coast to coast, we may be able to get him to stop off at DFW airport for a press conference and say how great Good News Texas is. We can do little things like that without much financial or time commitment, but that will be about the extent of it. Right now, we just want to get half a day with him at his place in North Carolina to produce several short items that could be used to stir up enthusiasm in the local churches." In addition to Graham, two state chairmen would be chosen—people who could generate prestige and interest in Jesus just by their association with the campaign. After all, one Baptist executive observed, "Public relations is the name of the game."

Over the next several weeks, Bill Hill and his associates developed four proto-commercials in "animatic" form —a series of still drawings with voice-overs rather than the live action or true animation that would be used in the final product. Each of the four took a different slant and would be tested to see which, if any, might appeal most to the Texas contingent of a lost and dying world. If none clicked, it would be, quite literally, back to the drawing board. If one seemed clearly better than the others, it would become the model for the actual spots to be used in the campaign. On three successive evenings in early October, representatives of Louis, Bowles and Grove showed the spots to "focus groups" drawn from the three target populations. Active Baptists met the first night in three churches scattered around Dallas.

I am not supposed to identify either the church or the people I observed, so I won't, but I promise you it was a real Baptist church, with a poster thermometer in the foyer that showed how the fund drive was going.

Judy Briggs, a market researcher for Louis, Bowles and Grove, told the group they were to give their reactions to some commercials being prepared for television. She did not say they were Baptist commercials or mention Good News Texas. She then showed the commercials on a videotape machine and asked the group to fill out a questionnaire after they viewed each one.

The first commercial, identified as "Promises," offered shots of politicians, automobile dealers, and various businessmen making familiar promises—"You've got my word on it." "It's a sure thing." "You can depend on it." It ended with a note to the effect that Jesus is the only one whose promises can be trusted and "Isn't it time we listened?" The positive responses to "Promises" indicated the Christians held a disillusioned view of humanity: "Everybody is trying to put something over on us." "People will let you down, but if you trust in God, He won't let you down." "You have to put your faith in the Lord and not in other people." I got the message, but I felt sad, and the stark ceiling light illuminated other, almost forgotten rooms in my soul, rooms not fur-

nished with warm and reassuring memories, rooms abandoned because the heat had been shut off and the broken panes let in too much damp and cold.

The next example showed a man arising to the sound of a strident alarm and struggling to meet the day as he listened to the depressing litany of the morning news. Then a voice-over announcer asked, "Wouldn't it be a change to wake up on morning without anxiety over what the day might bring? To know that whatever the world throws at you, you'll make it? If that kind of change would be welcome, then get with the one person who can do the changing—Jesus Christ. For a change." This, too, seemed to confirm the experience of the group: "We can't depend on the news being good," they said, "but if we have Jesus Christ with us, it makes no difference. You have to have Him because what problems can you face without Christ?"

The third effort did not lend itself so easily to clichéd response. In this one, a black man told of how he had been a revolutionary, seeking social change by whatever means seemed expedient. But not long ago, he said, he had run across another revolutionary and it had changed his life completely. He can change yours, too, the man promised. Then he said, "My name is Eldridge Cleaver. I'm Living Proof."

Bill Hill had told me one of the commercials would be a testimonial, and I would not have been surprised to have seen Charles Colson or Johnny Cash telling about what God had wrought in their lives. I try to keep up with the box scores on notable conversions, but I had somehow missed the news that the icy soul of Eldridge Cleaver had been warmed with fire from above. I was impressed that Texas Baptists would consider pumping hundreds of thousands of dollars into publicizing the testimony of a man who might still be regarded with skepticism and caution by some of the new white brothers. And I was especially curious about how the members of this largely working-class church might react.

I studied the lone black member of the group, a man about 45. Was he an Uncle Tom who would fear that the sight and sound of this panther in lamb's clothing might stir resentment left over from the sixties and jeopardize his perhaps lately won and still tenuous place in a predominantly white congregation? Would he say of Cleaver, as Peter had said of Christ, "I never knew him"? No, he wouldn't. "This is very beautiful," he said. "It comes from a controversial person a lot of us can identify with. We know Eldridge Cleaver was searching for something he could not find in the world, but only in Jesus Christ. I had much the same problems in my life at one time. It was very hard for me to accept certain things, but now I am able to face these things and accept them." That is not exactly revolution, but it isn't "white folks always been nice to me" either.

A middle-aged woman who had taken much longer than anyone else to fill out her questionnaire spoke next. I sensed she was about to vent a little of the racist spleen we often associate with working-class fundamentalists. "This was also my favorite," she said. "It shows that Christ is a

Man for all men. He is not a white man's savior or a black man's savior or a Jew's savior. He is for everyone. I think every minority feels pressures and I think there are times in everybody's life when they feel like they are a minority, even though nobody else may look upon them that way. When you are low man on the totem pole in your office and everybody says, 'You do this' and 'You do that,' and it seems like you do everything for everybody, then you can identify with the feeling of being a little bit left out.''

The final commercial depicted a child learning to ice skate with the loving help of a parent-figure in a unisex outfit like the Olympic speed skaters wear. The narrator told how important it is to have someone you can depend on when the going gets a bit hazardous and concluded with the slogan, ''Learn to live with Jesus Christ.'' I liked it best of the four. Its symbolism was aesthetically appealing and I liked the way it avoided both the negative connotations about human nature (though I am not especially sanguine about the natural goodness of our kind) and the spurious overgeneralization implicit in any case based on a single testimony. The nine focus groups agreed more strongly than on any other point that ''Ice Rink'' was clearly the poorest of the four commercials. ''It was boring,'' they said. ''It just beat around the bush and didn't really say anything.'' ''I can't ice skate, so I don't identify with that one at all.'' ''A waste of film.'' I decided not to become a consultant on mass evangelism.

Ms. Briggs asked who they thought might sponsor commercials like these. Oh, the Catholics or SMU or maybe the Dallas Council of Churches. Not one named the Baptists. Baptists have W. A. Criswell; they don't need Eldridge Cleaver.

The meetings with the Baptist groups were designed to see if any of the commercials were likely to run into the kind of opposition that might make funding or other forms of cooperation difficult. But the real test, everyone agreed, would be with those who described themselves as nominal or inactive Christians and those who openly acknowledged they were not religious in any conventional sense. A pool of such people had been obtained by distributing questionnaires in Dallas office buildings; groups representing both sexes and a broad range of ages had been selected from this pool. In keeping with the piety of the groups, we met at a neutral site, the Marriott Inn. Curtiss Grove, a partner in Louis, Bowles and Grove, was moderator for the evening. As we waited for people to assemble, he lamented having to pass up a cocktail party down the hall.

The group looked pretty representative of backsliders I have known: a workingman in his thirties; an overweight balding man who talked knowledgeably about the video equipment; a tall, thin older man who wore a tie with a leisure suit and looked as though he smoked a lot and was perhaps familiar with the taste of liquor; a woman who was pretty in the way that Southwest Airlines stewardesses are pretty, and a thin, serious man who appeared to be with her; a young woman about twenty who wore blue eye shadow and orthodontic braces; a neat woman in her thirties who looked

like she was probably in charge of several people where she worked and had a reputation for getting things done on time; one of those ubiquitous, interchangeable young men with a moustache and styled hair and a preference for shiny shirts with sailboats or jockeys on them; a foxy brunette in a suede jacket and lots of bracelets and rings and dark fingernail polish who seemed a poor conversion prospect; and several others I knew then I wouldn't be able to remember. For the most part, they represented a bit higher socioeconomic status than the Baptists I had visited the night before.

Grove is good at his job and easily elicited comments from the group. Interestingly, their reactions were not remarkably different from those of the active Baptists, except that none of them rated the Cleaver commercial highest and four of the twelve designated it their least favorite. (As it turned out, this response was something of an anomaly; the other two groups meeting at the same time felt strongly that the Cleaver spot was the best.) When asked what the commercial sought to accomplish, one man guessed it was trying to stir up pity for Cleaver. Another thought it too controversial even for minority-group people and felt its appeal would be limited to revolutionaries or people ''with awful problems.''

Each of the other spots got three or four votes as the best of the lot, but what one felt was pungent, another would judge pedantic. The 28-year-old in the shiny shirt said he didn't think any was much better than the others, since they were all about God and the church. A young man about nineteen seemed rather bemused by the whole business, as though he thought his sainted mother had somehow arranged to get him invited to a subtle soulwinning campaign, maybe even paid his way. But all things considered, I think this group uttered more pious clichés than the dedicated Baptists. Since they did not know they had been chosen because of their shared lukewarmness, they seemed to feel some need to let their colleagues know they were believers. In spite of what may have been a bit of overcompensation, however, I sensed almost none of the assurance I had seen and heard the night before. Several people got sad looks on their faces and lit up cigarettes. I believe they were pretty serious about it all. I had agreed not to ask any questions and I may have misread their reaction, but I had not expected what I sensed and it seemed unmistakable. I wouldn't be surprised to learn that the older man in the leisure suit had started going back to church with his wife.

As before, almost no one perceived the commercials as Baptist in origin. The President's Council on Physical Fitness, the Cerebral Palsy Association, an ice rink, the Department of Health, Education, and Welfare, Channel 39, and Sominex all seemed as likely as the Southern Baptists to sponsor such spots.

On the third night, self-designated unbelievers viewed the spots. This was the crucial test, the people at whom the main thrust of the campaign was aimed, but their preferences turned out to differ little from their more pious predecessors. Neither ''Morning News'' nor ''Promises'' struck a responsive chord. One man who at first thought "Morning News" was touting CBS news was irritated when it proved to have a religious theme. Another picked up the religious slant earlier but just thought, "Here we go again." A woman complained that "it doesn't tell me what to do with my problems, except give them to someone else. A little information about how Jesus is going to handle my problems would be helpful."

"Promises" caused even stronger negative reactions—one woman characterized it as "hateful" and said, "It made me want to lock myself in a room and shoot anybody that makes promises"—and "Ice Rink" once again came in as the unanimous last choice. One woman described it as "childish the way they wanted you to put yourself in Jesus' hands with no mention of adult choices." Another took issue with the whole ice-skating metaphor; she didn't feel at all like an ice skater, but rather "a yo-yo, every day I feel like a yo-yo." A man about thirty said he felt a better metaphor would be someone playing poker, or perhaps even solitaire. I doubt seriously the Southern Baptists will pick up on that.

Once again the Cleaver commercial was picked as the best—unanimously by one caucus. A man who freely called himself an agnostic said, "I know what Cleaver's life has been, and if this guy says he can pull it out with Christ, well, I may think there is something to it." He admitted to some doubts whether Cleaver might just be trying to escape a prison sentence by publicly embracing religion, but rejected them: "I have not agreed with Cleaver in the past, but I have respected his integrity." Others did question Cleaver's sincerity, but what carried the day was the feeling that "it gave me a choice. It told me what his opinion was, but it didn't say, 'You take my opinion, buddy, because it is good for you too.' "

The success of the Cleaver spot naturally raised the question of whose testimonials people could accept. The subject shouldn't be an ordinary person, someone from the viewer's own neighborhood ("I would figure someone was just trying to get on television and get some publicity"); it certainly shouldn't be Richard Nixon or Patty Hearst ("It is still to close. With Cleaver you can almost feel the guy has paid his debt and now has a whole new slant on life"). The ideal person, one man thought, would be a noncriminal figure who still had room for notable repentance—the two names mentioned were Billy Graham and Earl Scheib, the $29.95 auto paint job man.

Interestingly, the non-Christians had no difficulty accepting the idea that Southern Baptists might be behind the commercials. The us of testimonials seemed "more Baptist" than any of the other approaches, even though Eldridge Cleaver seemed like an unlikely star. One woman suggested that if Baptists were indeed the sponsors, they would do well to hide the fact, since "many people are turned off by their extremist actions."

If the consultants were looking for useful criticism, the non-Christians gave them plenty of that, but if they were looking for some signs that Good News Texas was going to send unbelievers flocking to church, the meeting provided little basis for hope. One man quickly deduced that his group contained no practicing Christians and said, "I think people like us tend to rely on ourselves rather than look outside for some kind of placebo. I don't care whether people believe in Jesus or Muhammad or Darrell Royal; just because they believe it and get out and preach it doesn't mean it's true. I just don't buy the idea that you can blindly put your faith and trust in any person, including Jesus."

The bad news for Good News Texas was that the non-Christians didn't like the whole idea of religious commercials. "I am turned off by commercials of this sort," said one. "It cheapens religion to sell it like toothpaste." "There is nothing in these commercials that appeals to me in any way or makes me feel I should investigate Christianity," another said. They make it sound like Jesus is going to open up a used-car lot." But one man who also had a negative reaction to selling Jesus on TV conceded that "television is such a powerful communications medium that if they use it right, it can help. There are some people whose only way of touching anything outside their home is television."

It is Bloom's job, then, to see that TV is used right. The hope that any single commercial might provide Baptists with an offer lost Texans could not refuse seemed pretty well dashed. Still, the response to news that the sins of the apostle of Black Power had been washed away had proven sufficiently promising to convince Bloom and the BGCT that testimonials were the route to take. At the state convention in San Antonio two weeks later, L. L. Morriss proclaimed that the theme of Good News Texas would be "Living Proof" and would concentrate on "presenting the testimony of people who have experienced the saving grace of our Lord." Dr. Landes announced that Baylor football coach Grant Teaff and actress Jeannette Clift George had agreed to serve as honorary co-chairmen and played a tape from Billy Graham, who said the world was hungry for good news and he was pleased to have a part in the boldest evangelistic venture in the history of Texas Baptists.

By the first of December, some of the top converts in the country had been lined up to add their testimony to Cleaver's. There had been minor problems. Some Christian entertainers had been discouraged from participating by their agents, who feared it might hurt their image with the public. Others had been screened out when their faith was adjudged not yet solid enough to guarantee against an embarrassing relapse during the campaign; no one, for example, would want to take a chance on Jerry Lee Lewis if he were suddenly to go into one of his periodic conversion phases. The final list included country singers Jeannie C. Riley and Connie Smith, Mexican musician Paulino Bernal, Consul-General of Honduras Rosargentina Pinel-Cordova, Houston Oiler Billy "White Shoes" Johnson, and Allan Mayer of Oscar Mayer and Company. A couple of big ones had gotten away. For some reason, Charles Colson had backed out and had to be replaced by Dean Jones, and a former Hell's Angel who conducts a bike ministry on the West Coast didn't leave a forwarding address when he set out on his latest missionary journey. But all the others were ready to go and film crews were heading for Nashville and L.A. to record their stories. We'll see the results soon.

As I wait, I am aware of poignant feelings. I have watched and listened as good, sincere, intelligent men and women groped for a way of making that which stands at the center of their lives plausible and attractive to those who live outside the sacred canopy. Perhaps it will work. I think I could accept that in good grace. I generally feel pretty comfortable around people who take their religion seriously, especially if it is one of the leading brands. But I confess I do not believe historians will remember 1977 as the year the Great Awakening came to Texas. I expect Baptist churches may be stirred up considerably and some wayward Christians may return home like the prodigal. These are the groups that

have always responded best to the call of revival. The main work of evangelism in American history—with, it should be noted, some exceptions—has been to keep believers plugged into their systems. That in itself is a significant accomplishment and may well justify the cost and effort involved. Of course, here and there a real scoundrel or a true skeptic may be turned around and set on the Glory Road, but I expect Good News Texas will come and go without making a great deal of difference in the lives of the 4,700,000 sinners at whom it is primarily aimed. That will no doubt discourage a lot of folks, but maybe it shouldn't. After all, even though He knew how to use a bit of dash and sparkle to draw a crowd, Jesus never got anything like a majority, and if the Word of God is anything to go by, He never expected to (Matthew 7:13–14).

APPENDIX

Dignity in Church Advertising [1916]

O. C. Harn

The church has discovered in advertising, a new force which it believes it can use in furthering its work. There is danger that, in its enthusiasm over its discovery, mistakes may be made. . . .

Dignity is an attribute which should be possessed by all advertising which advertises dignified things. Some advertising men believe that dignity is a handicap to forceful, resultful publicity; but that is because they do not know what dignity is. They confound it with dryness, dullness— old-fogyness.

This is a wrong conception. A dignified man may be the most intensely interesting man in your circle. He may be the best business-getter. He may be the man above all others to whom to look to get things done.

Contrast the dignified methods of . . . advertising success with this sickly attempt found in a collection of church advertisements.

"Don't be a lemon! Tie on to the happy Sunday-nighters."

O. C. Harn was Advertising Manager, National Lead Co., at the time this article was written.

Excerpt from *Advertising and Selling*, Nov. 1916, p. 15.

Or this: A paper wrapper was folded about a piece of pasteboard to imitate chewing gum and the label was printed thus:

Chew this over!	Dr. White's Compound for human ills	The Flavor lasts.

This, if you will believe it, was used to advertise the service a church has to offer for the benefit of men!

But, you say, flippant and even vulgar preachers seem to have success in getting serious results. Why will not advertising work similarly?

I would say first that, as it is the exception in the commercial world for trivial advertising to bring the results desired, so is it the exception in the pulpit. . . .

A final caution, do not get the idea that dignity precludes warmth, earnestness, appeal to the emotions, startling effects, and force (or punch, if you like the overworked word—I don't).

The great orator knows well how to use all these means of moving his audience—knows it better than does the clown.

Evaluating Social Persuasion Advertising Campaigns: An Overview of Recent C.O.I. Experience

John Samuels

This article concentrates on the evaluation of the effectiveness of social persuasion advertising campaigns, where the aim is a behavioral change on the part of the target audience. Theoretically, such an evaluation centers on three principal elements: clearly stated objectives for the campaign, a valid and reliable measurement technique, and a satisfactory research design. An example is given of the classic situation at work, but the main body of the paper is concerned with the problems which confront researchers when they are unable to fulfill the requirements of the classic situation. Deviations from the ideal are discussed in detail with examples from the Central Office of Information, a service agency of the British government. The discussion provides a generalized framework for planning evaluation studies of this kind.

The Central Office of Information is a common service agency which prepares publicity for Government Departments. The Research Unit at the COI was set up in 1973 with the objective of helping management in its decision taking. The work of the Unit, which has been fully described elsewhere [1], can be broadly divided into three groupings: target market studies, the pre-testing of communications, and the evaluation of the effectiveness of our communications. This paper is concerned with the third area of our activity, within the general theme set by the Seminar Committee "How can social research help to evaluate the efficiency of non-profit organisational activities?"

Although some of the techniques that will be referred to are novel and of interest in their own right, the principal purpose of the paper is to present details of COI's recent experience in a number of areas of social persuasion within a *systematic framework*. Having such a framework enables the researcher to focus his attention when confronted with new areas of investigation and to arrive at the optimum solution more swiftly.

GENERAL SCOPE OF THE PROBLEM

The COI has over recent years been asked to conduct a number of advertising campaigns the aim of which is to achieve socially desirable ends by persuading people to modify their behaviour in some way. Such campaigns are commonly characterised by *the absence of any direct measure* of the thing that the advertising is trying to influence (i.e., there is no equivalent of "sales data'). Typically the genesis of these campaigns is that there is a concern about some 'primary' aspect of the country's life (X) and it is believed that some other 'secondary' aspect of life (Y) is related to X

John Samuels was formerly with the Central Office of Information, London, England.

EXHIBIT 1
Recent Examples of X's and Y's

X Primary aspects of life that have been the objectives of social advertising campaigns	**Y** Secondary aspects believed to be related to X and which have formed the specific subject matter of campaigns
Prevention of Accidents and Their Social and Economic Costs	• Wearing seat belts • Maintaining safe following distances • Reducing drinking before driving • Correct pedestrian behaviour
Energy Conservation	• Promoting energy consciousness • Installation of energy saving devices (loft insulation, etc.
Crime Prevention	• Locking car doors and keeping valuables out of sight
Fire Prevention	• Keeping matches out of children's reach • Education in how to cope with chip-pan fires

In most of the examples given, the Y one wants to influence is a behaviour. Often a campaign will have a principal aim of influencing behaviour and subsidiary aims of influencing attitudes. However in almost all cases our major interest has been in behaviour, and in most instances the X is usually measurable (accident statistics, urine statistics, etc.) and the researcher's problem is that there is no readily available measure of Y.

---

in such a way that an improvement in Y will automatically lead to an improvement in X. The general problem which faces the researcher is that as no direct measure of Y is available, a special piece of research is required to measure it if any assessment is to be made of the effectiveness of the campaign.

Some examples of X's and Y's from our recent advertising activity will perhaps help clarify this point and are set out above.

THE CHARACTERISTICS OF THE CLASSIC SITUATION

In attempting to produce a systematic framework for approaching this problem area, a useful starting point would seem to be to define the ''classic situation'' (in the way that the economists start with a description of 'perfect competition'). There appear to be three requirements of the classic social persuasion campaign effectiveness study (and almost all of our work falls short of the classic in some way!). The three requirements are:

1. *Clearly stated objectives for the advertising campaign.* It is axiomatic that unless the objectives of the campaign are clearly stated, it is impossible to design research to assess whether they have been achieved. Unless one knows what achievement one is attempting to measure, one cannot even set the sample size for the research. The decision in this area does not usually of course belong to the researcher and his problem centers around trying to extract objectives from the decision-makers in such a way as to be able to devise satisfactory research. This problem of 'action standards' is of course a general one and not restricted to campaigns of social persuasion!
2. *A valid and reliable measurement technique.* It is a second essential requirement that, having decided on the objectives of the campaign, it is necessary to devise a valid and reliable technique for measuring whatever it is you are trying to change. This is in a sense easier if the objective is something

like awareness or knowledge—most researchers would agree that we can devise relatively valid and reliable questions to measure these (e.g., little tests of knowledge or 'Which makes have you heard of?' type questions). It is not really much more difficult conceptually to devise valid and reliable measures of behavior, but is more difficult *operationally* and approaches to this problem are discussed at length later. Attitude measures are a separate problem and discussion of this second requirement of the classic situation will be restricted to behavioral measures.

3. *A satisfactory research design.* The third requirement of the classic situation, having defined one's objectives and devised a valid and reliable way of measuring them, is to set up a satisfactory research design that will lead one to be able to say with some confidence what the effect of the advertising has been. This is the old problem of being able to rule out the effect of other variables that may have contributed to change. In the classic situation we would attempt to achieve this by having *before* and *after* measurements in *matched test and control* areas where the only difference between the two areas is the injection of the advertising. Thus we crudely define the effect of the advertising as

$$\frac{(T_2 - T_1) - (C_2 - C_1)}{T_1} \times 100$$

where T = test, C = control, 1 = before, 2 = after.

It is worth noting at this point that one variable which can upset such a simple approach in normal market research is potentially (but only potentially—see later) absent in COI's work, namely competitive activity.

Having elaborated the requirements of the classic situation, we can look at some of COI's work on evaluating social persuasion advertising, firstly at our best example of the classic situation and then at further examples of deviations from the classic to see how we attempt to deal with less than perfect situations.

THE (NEAR) CLASSIC SITUATION—
SEAT BELT ADVERTISING

The nearest the COI Research Unit has come to the classic situation is the campaign to persuade people to wear seat belts which has already been fully described in an ESOMAR paper [2]. For the present purpose consideration can be restricted to examining how far the research project measures up to the three basic requirements.

1. *Clearly stated objectives.* The objectives of the seat-belt wearing campaign have been stated in terms of increasing the proportion of drivers and front-seat passengers who wear a seat belt. In a perfectly classic situation, such an objective would be further refined by adding some indication of the *amount* of change aimed at. This is not normally provided for the researchers, but in effect in setting a sample size for observations to which all parties agree, a *minimum* objective is set in terms of the increase in wearing levels which is statistically significant. The current research design is such that the 95% confidence limits are 2.6% at 30% and below this level of change we cannot conclude that the campaign has had any measurable effect.

3. *A valid and reliable measurement technique.* The question of measurement technique has been resolved in the case of seat belts by a method which involves stopping a representative sample of cars and *observing* whether the drivers and front-seat passengers are wearing their belts. Initially other approaches (questioning people about their behavior, observation of passing cars, etc.) were tried because of their cost and other potential advantages, but the method finally adopted was found to be the only valid and reliable one: *valid* in the sense that we are observing the specific behavior we are trying to influence with the campaign, *reliable* in the sense that independent assessments of the same situation by different observers produce the same results (i.e., it is fairly easy to tell whether or not a belt is being worn).

3. *A satisfactory research design.* In the initial seat-belt surveys we were able to use the classic design of before and after surveys using test and control areas. Indeed in the early work described by Lévens and Rodnight [2] a large number of surveys were conducted at various points in time before, during and after the campaign. Considerable care was of course needed in matching test and control in terms of location of observations and so forth and some of the questions that had to be resolved were: whether observation sites should be representative of the test or control or whether both should be national microcosms, extent of possible contamination between test and control, hours of day and days of week for observation, etc. These are all discussed in the original paper.

Thus, in the seat-belts campaign we have had a near-classic case with the three essential requirements adequately met such that a fairly firm evaluation can be made of the effectiveness of the advertising campaign. Indeed in this case it is possible for the client to then make a formalised assessment of whether the actual level of expenditure has been justified. This can be done via a cost benefit analysis based on (i) assumptions about the number of lives saved and injuries

that are less severe as a result of increased wearing levels and (ii) the 'cost' of lives and injuries in economic and social terms [3].

In some ways the 'success' of seat-belts in research terms has brought problems in that it set a classic model which we have not subsequently been able to repeat. It has raised expectations both among the researchers themselves and among their clients, which we have recently come to realise are too idealistic and we are having to come to terms with the fact that research can rarely provide so clear-cut an assessment of the effectiveness of a campaign. On the other hand it represents an ideal towards which we can strive and the next section of the paper deals with deviations from the classic situation and how we have tried to cope in less than ideal circumstances.

DEVIATIONS FROM THE CLASSIC SITUATION

Clearly Defined Objectives. It is in the area of the lack of absolutely specifically defined objectives that the seat-belts campaign falls short of the completely classic ideal. This characterises much of our other work too. Ideally, it is essential to obtain before hand agreement to objectives, stated in more specific terms than "to improve *Y* behavior." This is something of a chicken and egg situation—until social persuasion publicity has been attempted in any specific area it is somewhat difficult to know what advertising can realistically be expected to achieve or the time-scale over which any achievement can be expected. However once some general parameters are known it should be possible to set more specific targets—and in the long run, unless this is done, research will be less useful in its 'objective' role as a check on the wise spending of public money.

Valid and Reliable Techniques. It is in the area of devising valid and reliable techniques to measure the behavior we are trying to influence with social persuasion advertising that the researcher is presented with his greatest challenges. In seat belts we were able to succeed in this completely. We have other successes too: for instance in assessing the penetration of different thickness of loft insulation, because we suspected that this might not be accurately reported for various reasons, we send be-trousered interviewers climbing into lofts of houses armed with torches and rulers. Similarly for the campaign attempting to persuade people to lock car doors and windows, interviewers during the day and policemen at night actually physically checked windows and doors to see if they were locked or not. In both cases we are making a direct observation of the thing we are trying to measure. However in many instances, for various reasons, we are unable to observe directly the precise behavior we are trying to influence and we fall back on some "next best" measurement. Such measurements fall into three broad categories:

(i) A simplification or selection of the behavior we are interested in

(ii) A simulation of the behavior

(iii) Reporting of the behavior.

Some examples of each of these categories will show the sort of situations where we have to deviate from the ideal and some indication of the degree of success we've achieved.

(i) *Simplification or Selection*. Perhaps the simplest example of "Simplification" was the campaign to persuade people to keep matches out of the reach of children. In the evaluation of this campaign interviewers inspected the home and noted the places where they could see matches and then coded the home as "definitely safe," "definitely unsafe," or "unsure" in accordance with certain specified rules. This was not of course the only measure of the campaign's effectiveness, but it did not seem to work as a behavioral measure in that the proportion coded as "definitely safe" actually went down in the post-campaign measurement. This was at odds with most other findings in the survey and we were forced to conclude that the observation itself was not a valid and reliable measurement device. It was postulated that the observers themselves were influencing the result in that they had (a) become more efficient observers with greater acquaintance with the task and (b) had had their perception of danger heightened by working on the survey and the campaign itself.

Another example is vehicle separation distances where the objective of the campaign was to persuade motorists to drive a safe distance behind the vehicle in front. The observation technique used was an elaborate system of filming which has been fully described in another ESOMAR paper [4]. Basically this involves filming cars passing a point at a given film speed, and with the camera a given distance from the road; counting, in analysis, the number of frames between cars enables one to assess the distance between them. Elaborate though the methodology is, it in fact is only a simplification or selection of the behavior we are interested in because we can only see what is in the camera's view and not what happens just after or just before the split second of filming. Thus many of the cars may appear to be following too close but have in reality just been overtaken or are about to be overtaken (one can in fact make assumptions which enable one to discard some observations in analysis by calculating the respective speeds of the two cars in each following situation and discarding those situations where there is a small separation gap and large difference in speed as being in an 'overtaking' situation). The use of a static camera too means that one must restrict oneself to simple situations such that the film data is as unambiguous as possible (e.g., the open road with no turnings in the road or junctions with other roads in the vicinity)—so one is dealing with only a selection of road situations. A final reason why this represents simplification is that the cost of the filming means that observations must be restricted to a very small number of sites.

The results of this research showed no changes in driving behavior as measured by these observations, though in interview surveys conducted in parallel people did claim to have changed their behavior. Because the observation measurement represented only a simplification of the situation, it was not possible to say categorically that the campaign had had no effect (motorists might have changed their behavior but only in driving circumstances which we had not investigated on film, e.g., in more complex road situations, and in non open-road situations). In fact the objectives of the campaign had been stated specifically in terms of driving under the conditions we were filming (i.e., drivers driving at 40+ mph)—so we were able to conclude that the campaign had not been *successful* set against this criterion (though it may have been *effective* judged by other criteria).

This project prompts another general point that can be made about observation of behavior. Just as we felt Children and Matches was an example of bias introduced by the research process affecting behavior of the *observers*, so this project was potentially an example of bias arising from the research process affecting the behavior of the *observed*. There was a very real danger that the presence of a camera by the roadside would influence drivers to change their behavior (by driving more slowly because they thought it might be a police observation for example). For this reason very great care was taken to hide or camouflage the cameras.

In both of these cases where we have taken observations of a simplification or selection of the behavior we are trying to influence, the observation results were at odds with the results of parallel information on reported behavior (though in the case of separation distances this did not prove a problem because of the way the campaign objectives had been defined). The lesson for the researcher would seem to be that, while the reported behavior *may* be less reliable or valid than observed behavior, great caution is needed in interpreting any data which are a simplification or selection as, by definition, they may not tell the whole story.

(ii) *Simulated Behavior*. A second type of approach that we have tried when we have been unable to observe the specific behavior we are trying to influence has been to attempt to get respondents to simulate their behavior.

A good example of simulation is our work on Chip ("Frying") Pan Fires. The aim of this campaign was to teach people the correct procedure to follow if a chip pan were to catch light. What basically happened was that interviewers actually asked respondents to go into their kitchen and act out a situation where their chip pan had caught fire. This worked remarkably well. Respondents were very willing to play the game and interviewers found the coding of the information a relatively easy task. Here there were considerable differences between test and control areas which suggested that the campaign had been very successful and the 'simulated behavior' data was very consistent with other data collected in the interview.

A further example of simulated behavior is our work on child pedestrian safety. The aim of the campaign is to promote the Green Cross Code and inculcate safe road crossing behavior. Much consideration has been given over the years to the possibility of mounting observational studies of children crossing the road. However to date the sampling problems have seemed too great: the basic problem is that the places where children cross the road in consistently large numbers and with sufficient frequency to make observation economically viable are almost always 'policed' by crossing guards, etc. We have therefore fallen back on techniques involving a simulation of behavior. The technique we are currently using involves presenting the child with pictures of a number of road crossing situations. The pictures are covered with a sheet of acetate and the child is asked to draw on this the route he would take across the road. With other photographs the child is asked to describe in detail how he would cross the road, and where he would stand, and there is a final series of photographs featuring right and wrong situations. The techniques seem to work well in practice and in particular those involving drawing do elicit responses from children as young as 5 years old—some of whom do not answer more conventional questions. The results of these sorts of data collection do demonstrate the extent to which the message has been understood and internalised and whether the child is able to apply the general principles to specific situations.

In both of these cases we have found simulated behavior techniques to be of considerable use in assessing the effectiveness of an advertising campaign. We do not know of course whether the drama and shock of a very unusual situation would actually inhibit correct behavior in the case of chip pan fires; nor do we know whether safe procedures will be adopted in every road crossing situation a child encounters. However we believe that knowledge of the 'correct' behavior and being able to apply it in a simulated situation takes us some way along the road and is a reasonably valid measure of a campaign's effectiveness, in the sense that it is a necessary condition for the individual to be able to behave in the desired way in the real life situation.

(iii) *Reported Behavior*. A third approach when it is not possible to observe actual behavior is to ask people to report their behavior. Now there are many reasons why this is generally a less desirable alternative and one to which we would not immediately be attracted when we are evaluating social persuasion campaigns. Firstly people may be *unwilling* to report their behavior correctly because some answers may be socially less acceptable than others; secondly some people may be *unable* to report their behavior accurately because it is too trivial or alternatively too intricate for them to remember accurately. However on occasion one may be forced back on reported behavior as the only alternative available, in which case the researcher's effort must be directed towards promoting an environment in the interview as conducive as possible to accurate and true reporting.

A current example of a campaign where we are using reported behavior in our evaluation is Drink and Drive. This campaign aims to reduce the numbers of people who drive after having had an alcoholic drink and in fact *theoretically* it has in it the seeds of another classic case—in that a valid and reliable measure for assessing whether a person has had alcohol exists and this could theoretically be applied to a representative sample of drivers. There are at present insurmountable practical difficulties involved however because the behavior involved is illegal, and we have therefore opted for reported behavior. The results of our research are not yet available, so I can not say how successful or otherwise our techniques have been. However we have attempted to minimise the possible misreporting that might arise from respondents giving socially acceptable answers by positioning the survey as a drinks survey. We obtain data on drinking occasions away from the home and for each occasion besides the quantity drunk we ask a lot of other questions (whether food taken, who was in the party, etc.) including mode of transport to next destination. Where this is "car" we then ask whether the respondent was driver or passenger. Later in the questionnaire it becomes clear to the respondent that the survey is about drinking and driving. However our pilot work is encouraging and suggests that few people anticipate the full nature of the survey until after the behavioral information has been obtained. We are undertaking extensive work in order to examine the validity of our methodology and we would hope to report on this at greater length on another occasion.

Satisfactory Research Design. The researchers task in selecting a satisfactory research design is perhaps slightly easier than that of devising a valid and reliable measurement instrument. The classic situation is to select one area of the country as a test for the campaign and then to select a matched control area. There was no problem with seat belts because the campaign was a test campaign and it was in television where exposure can easily be controlled in Britain. Similarly on the Separation Distances and Drink and Drive projects referred to above any problems that did arise were satisfactorily resolved. On other occasions where the campaign is intended to be national and not a test campaign there may be a willingness to "go national except for one TV area"—this is how the evaluation of the television licence campaign has been tackled.

However two possible problem areas do exist:

1. Where for policy reasons the campaign must be national and it is not possible to leave a control area unexposed;
2. Where the campaign is to be a *national press* campaign and it is not so easy to leave a control area unexposed.

In each of these sets of circumstances, one is left with taking measurements before and after a campaign and trying to deduce whether changes have been brought about by the advertising or some other variable. An example of the first set of circumstances would be Domestic Energy Saving which has already been discussed in one ESOMAR paper [5] and is the subject of another at this Seminar [6] where the urgent subject matter of the campaign was such that it would not have been possible to exclude any one TV area. The approach we have adopted has been to cover a wide range of possible indicators of changes in people's awareness, attitudes, and behavior and, from the pattern of answers to this range of questions over several surveys, attempt an assessment of the effectiveness of advertising. It is not of course at all easy because some of the other variables involved are very strong.

The Crime Prevention campaign which aimed to persuade people to lock car doors and windows is an example of a campaign where it was not possible to have a control area because the medium used was the *national press*. In this case we conducted before and after studies with, as explained above, the principal measure being the physical checking by interviewers and police of the windows and doors of parked cars. The pre-campaign study was conducted during the particularly hot summer of 1976 and the post-campaign study in the winter of 1977. As might be expected there was a significant increase in the observed percentage of cars with all windows closed which could largely be explained as a seasonal effect. Season should not have affected car *door* locking and here no statistically significant difference was found. A fair conclusion was therefore that there was no behavioral evidence of a campaign effect since the rise in car security after the campaign could be attributed to a seasonal element in car usage and the non-seasonal aspect of security behavior had not been effected. Admittedly we would have been on less sure ground in presuming a positive advertising effect if car door locking had changed than we were in assuming no advertising effect when it did not change. In this particular case another aim of the campaign was to increase knowledge of the fact that cars over five years old are at greater risk than newer cars. An increase in knowledge was in fact observed and since seasonality would not be expected to be an influence it seemed fair to assume an advertising effect even in the absence of a control area.

SOME FURTHER POINTS

The main purpose of the paper has been to present a range of COI's recent experience within a systematic framework for considering the problems posed in attempting to evaluate social persuasion advertising. As has been pointed out a distinguishing characteristic of most publicity campaigns in this area as opposed to those for branded goods is the absence of 'sales' data and so the emphasis in our work is on obtaining such data. This has tended to lead us to emphasise behavioral measurement and observation techniques in a carefully controlled experimental situation as our ideal solution. We have consequently amassed considerable experience in this area in a very short space of time. In gaining this experience we have

learned some other lessons. They are not necessarily new lessons but they have been graphically illustrated to us because they have arisen in the course of empirical work. For that reason it is perhaps worth re-iterating a few of them.

Some Aspects of Observation as a Research Technique. We have learned at first hand some of the "text-book truths" about observation as a research technique:

- It can be very expensive.
- You need to be very careful that you are sure what exactly it is you are sampling—is it people or time or what?
- The training of "observers" and the precise definition of what to observe and how it is to be recorded are of paramount importance.
- There is a need to be aware of the effect of the observation both on the observer and the observed and the potential biases these may introduce.

Our advice in this area would be "expect problems, and allow for extensive piloting."

Media Weight Experiments. We have had the opportunity with some of our campaigns (e.g., seat belts, and chip pan fires) to conduct media weight tests. These have been of considerable interest in that on seat belts a heavier weight of advertising was found to produce a greater overall effect, whereas on chip pan fires a lower weight was found to be equally effective. The lesson we have learned though is the quite simple one that a weight test only tells you about the weights you have tested for the subject matter under review! Thus for Campaign A one knows whether weight 1 or weight 2 is better, but not whether either is optimum; and one knows nothing from such a test about whether weight 1 or weight 2 will be better for Campaign B. It is a prohibitively expensive way of going about deciding on the optimum weight and this must at present still be a question of judgement guided by research findings.

Timing of Evaluation Studies. In all campaign evaluations one has to decide on when to make one's observation and this of itself implicitly assumes a model of when advertising effects are likely to be observable. In the case of seat belts and domestic energy saving we have been fortunate in that we have been able to take readings at a number of different points in time. Thus we know for seat-belt advertising a fair amount about the timing of reaction in behavioral terms to the advertising and the decay curve when advertising ceases. However for most campaigns cost forces us to have only a before and after (and occasionally a mid-campaign) reading.

We have tended to adopt a procedure whereby we make the pre-campaign reading as near to the start date of the campaign and the post-campaign reading as soon after the campaign as possible. In this way we are able to minimise any interference from other variables but we are also of course left with a static picture of what is a dynamic situation and we know very little about such things as how quickly particular effects are achieved, how long they last after the campaign, etc.

Measures Other Than Behavior Ones. It will be clear that in most cases the emphasis in our work is on trying to find the best measure of the particular behavior we are interested in. On occasion it will be an objective of the campaign to induce changes in awareness, knowledge, or attitudes and here of course we would include measurement of these aspects in our evaluation. However for many cases the objectives will be principally or solely behavioral and the question arises of whether we should attempt to measure anything other than behavior in our evaluation, particularly if this adds greatly to the cost of the project (which it may do if a separate survey is required). It is our view that on occasion we do need to go beyond the immediate behavioral aims and measure attitudes and knowledge. This will be most true at the beginning of any particular subject's history as a topic for publicity. For example at the beginning of the seat-belts campaign attitudes and knowledge were measured as well as behavior in order to be able to understand and interpret results; similarly on Separation Distances in order to understand whether the change or lack of it (as it transpired) was due to people, *not being aware of the message, not understanding it, not believing it* or simply *not putting it into practice.* However when a subject has been researched a number of times, we feel it should be possible, if the objectives are purely behavioral, to dispense with most of the other measures. Thus with seat belts once it was established that people's knowledge of the value of belts was at a fairly high level and that attitudes were reasonably favorable, it became possible to dispense with these measures and only obtain a behavioral one—though of course an occasional look at the complete picture is advisable if major changes are contemplated or impasses seem to have been reached.

Competitive Activity. A final small point concerns competitive activity. Since in most instances with social persuasion campaigns there is no competitive advertising to take into account in assessing effectiveness, it is tempting to discount this general variable. However there are ways in which it may be influential, and the point here is that one must be vigilant and monitor the market-place in exactly the same way as with commercial advertising. Firstly there is our own

activity (e.g., films shown freely on television) which may be influential and be responsible for some part of a favorable shift. Secondly there is the possibility that commercial advertisers may be advertising at the same time in related subject areas (e.g., as with Domestic Energy Saving). Thirdly there is the problem of editorial coverage contaminating results.

These points matter less if one has a classic design of before and after in test vs. control areas, but one has to be vigilant to ensure that something extraneous has not intervened to contaminate the control. A good example of the potential for this happening was in the Drink and Drive campaign when there was a fair amount of local and regional press coverage in the *control* area lamenting the fact that people in the area were to be "left out" of an important campaign of social persuasion!

CONCLUDING REMARKS

The paper has not set out to say anything that is particularly new, but rather to systematise our own experience. The social persuasion campaigns mounted by COI are subject to an *annual* Parliamentary vote, so that it is impossible, with any degree of certainty, to plan ahead over a number of financial years for any *one* campaign. This tends to mean that the opportunity for development of techniques and approaches within a given area of social persuasion is limited. Thus a premium is placed on learning lessons *across* campaigns. This paper is intended to demonstrate that that is exactly what we are beginning to do.

REFERENCES

1. Phillips, N. H., "The Work of the Central Office of Information Research Unit," *Statistical News,* No. 31, November 1975.
2. Levens, G. E., and Rodnight, E., "The Application of Research in the Planning and Evaluation of Road Safety Publicity," ESOMAR Congress 1973.
3. Dept. of Transport., *Road Accidents Great Britain 1975*. This volume estimates that 4,500 fatal or serious casualties were avoided as a result of seat belt wearing in 1975 (p. xvii) and also gives 'costs' of fatalities (£36,000 each) and other types of casualties (p. xviii).
4. Waters, L., and MacAfee, K., "A Study of Vehicle Speed Measurement Using Film Techniques," ESOMAR Congress 1976.
5. Phillips, N. H., and Nelson, E. H., "Energy Saving in Private Households—an Integrated Research Programme," ESOMAR Congress 1976.
6. Mills, P., and Nelson, E. H., "Panelisation in Attitude Surveys: An Experimental Study." ESOMAR Congress 1977.

PART V

Implementation

Cases

29. United States Postal Service   **297**

30. Stanford University: The Annual Fund   **307**

31. Ethical Problems in Marketing Research   **321**

32. London Goodwill Industries Association: Used Bookstore   **325**

33. Rapid Transit in Los Angeles   **335**

Readings

34. Strategies for Introducing Marketing into   **353**
    Nonprofit Organizations

35. Should Not-for-Profits Go into Business?   **361**

34. Marketing National Change: Decimalization in Britain   **367**

29
United States Postal Service

L. Frank Demmler
Christopher H. Lovelock

"The Post Office has always been operated as if it were an ordinary Government agency. In what it *does,* however, the Post Office is a business: its customers purchase its services directly, its employees work in a service-industry environment, it is a major communications network, it is a means by which much of the nation's business is conducted." [1]

When the President's Commission on Postal Organization submitted its Report, *Towards Postal Excellence,* in June 1968, it emphasized the need for a full-time marketing function. "Only a Post Office quick to identify and meet market needs," it said, "can successfully serve a changing economy." By 1974, many postal executives believed that significant progress had been made in introducing marketing to an organization with no previous experience of this function.

The Post Office Department was established as an agency of the federal government in 1789. This agency was part of the Executive Branch, and from 1829 to 1971 the position of Postmaster General was at the cabinet level. In the years shortly before 1971, Congress had control over postal rates and the salaries of postal workers. Although the Post Office was one of the nation's largest businesses, it was not run as a business, but as a cabinet agency of the U.S. Government.

Discussing the special nature of the Post Office Department and its successor agency, a senior USPS executive commented:

L. Frank Demmler is a former Research Assistant and Christopher H. Lovelock is Associate Professor, both at the Graduate School of Business Administration, Harvard University.

[1] *Towards Postal Excellence,* Report of the President's Commission on Postal Organization, June 1968, page 1.

The Post Office was, historically, a political play child of both the executive and legislative branch. The Postmaster General was the chairman of the winning national party; Larry O'Brien being the most recent example; James Farley probably being the most famous. Local postmasters were appointed based on party affiliation.

In the past the Post Office had offered new services or expanded existing ones by just adding them on to the structure which existed at the time. With no overall planning or coordination at the highest levels, the Post Office Department had become a conglomerate of parts by the mid-1960s and operational problems continued to mount as new parts were tacked on.

The role of Congress further accentuated these problems. Pay scales and fringe benefits were set by Congress. The interplay of Congressional politics determined postal rates, and it was alleged that, due to lobbying efforts, rates reflected the views of some sectors of business rather than the interests of the general public. Revenues went directly to the Treasury, and the Post Office Department was dependent upon annual appropriations which, while covering the rising deficit, provided decreasing amounts for capital investments. (The Post Office Department operated at a deficit in 48 of its last 52 years.) Finally, Post Office Department jobs were a primary source for repaying political favors. This sometimes resulted in selection of managers without regard to their training or experience relative to the jobs involved. This factor and the relatively rapid turnover of personnel (reflecting, in part, changes in Administrations) were a major obstacle to any long-range planning or programs.

The Reform Movement. These conditions created a movement for postal reform in both the public and private sectors. Although growing in strength, the catalyst which mobilized the forces was the total breakdown of the Chicago Post Office in October 1966. Ten million pieces of mail sat immobile for almost three weeks until a special task force appointed by the Postmaster General, vested with special authority, could gradually restore order.

Investigation into what had occurred revealed that the breakdown was caused by a lack of management authority, personnel problems, extremely low productivity, a poorly designed physical plant, and breakdowns in this plant.

Political pressure was exerted and in April 1967 President Lyndon B. Johnson established the President's Commission on Postal Organization (Kappel Commission). The Commission submitted its findings in June 1968, with its primary recommendation the creation of the United States Postal Service as a federal government corporation. The report stated that the infusion of professional management and a move to more "business-like" operations could reduce costs by at least 20% while improving service.

Not long after submission of the report there was a change of Administration. The new Administration lent its support to the effort to draft and pass enabling legislation quite similar to that recommended in the report. In addition, the new Administration made the difficult decision to forego using the patronage system to fill postal positions. The Postmaster General at the time, Winston M. Blount, also took the first step in reorganization on June 5, 1969, by establishing the Bureau of Marketing and Planning. This bureau was comprised of three formerly independent divisions of the Post Office Department and allowed for a more coordinated management effort, while also providing a vehicle for long-range planning.

FORMATION OF THE UNITED STATES POSTAL SERVICE

On August 12, 1970, President Richard M. Nixon signed the Postal Reorganization Act, which became effective on July 1, 1971. The fact that the original Presidential Commission had been formed by the Johnson Administration, and the legislation signed by the Nixon Administration, served to underscore the bi-partisan recognition that reform was needed. The subject at issue was, on one hand, an American tradition and, on the other, a giant public utility affecting the daily commercial life of the nation.

The Postal Reorganization Act clearly reinforced the special public service responsibilities of the new organization. The Act stipulated, for example, that the Postal Service had "the obligation to provide postal services to bind the nation together through personal, educational, literary, and business correspondence of the people." In addition, "the costs of establishing and maintaining the Postal Service shall not be apportioned to impair the over-all value of such service to the people."

Two very basic changes took place, however, as a result of the Act. One change dealt with the financing of the Postal Service. The cost of services was to be borne by users, not taxpayers, and a series of fiscal objectives culminating with a breakeven position in 1984 was established. These financial changes made the Postal Service more like a business than a government agency.

The second basic change was that the Law really made the Postal Service responsible for the planning, development, promotion, and provision of adequate and efficient postal and other services at fair and reasonable rates. In order to carry out this responsibility intelligently, it was necessary for the Postal Service to establish an internal marketing organization, which heretofore had not been considered necessary. The law also required, in part, that it provide types of service responsive to customer needs. Historically, decisions had been made largely on the basis of operational or legislative considerations.

The Act also contained other features aimed at ensuring the Postal Service's independence. First, a rational rate-making procedure was dictated. The keystone of this procedure was the creation of a Postal Rate Commission, composed of five technically qualified persons appointed by the President to serve staggered six-year terms. The Postal Service would propose rate changes to the Rate Commission. The Commission would hold public hearings, then develop a recommendation for submission to the Governors for final decision. Rates previously had been set by Congress.

The Board of Governors was an 11-person body including the Postmaster General and the Deputy

EXHIBIT 1
Headquarters Organization Structure of United States Postal Service, 1973

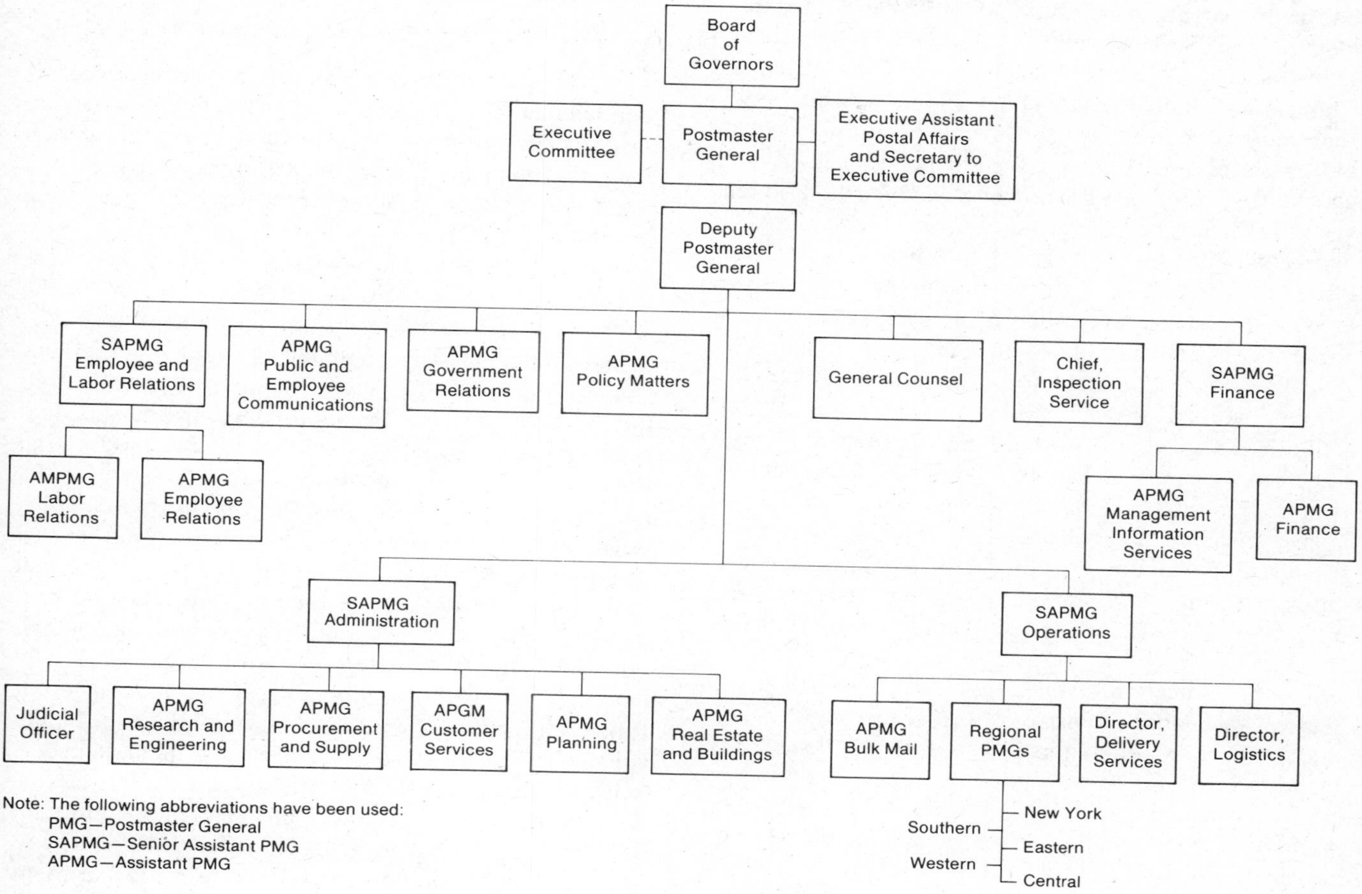

Note: The following abbreviations have been used:
    PMG—Postmaster General
    SAPMG—Senior Assistant PMG
    APMG—Assistant PMG

Source: U.S. Postal Service.

Postmaster General. The remaining nine members were appointed by the President and approved by the Senate for staggered nine-year terms. These nine selected the Postmaster General in addition to making important decisions. The eleven-person Board had final authority in all the Postal Service's other decision-making areas, and the nine Governors were not legally bound to accept the recommendations of the Postal Rate Commission.

The Act empowered the Postal Service to raise capital funds through bond issues. The limit to such funding was $10 billion, with a maximum of $2 billion in any one fiscal year.

The Postal Service and the four postal unions were directed to initiate collective bargaining with each other. Additionally, promotion and appointment on merit was specified for full-time postal employees, replacing the former procedure under which major postmasterships and top management positions had been political appointments. By October 1974, over 10,000

postmasters (out of a total of over 33,000) had been appointed on merit.

In order to carry out the mandates of the Postal Reorganization Act, Postmaster General Blount announced a reorganization of the Post Office Department on May 12, 1971. The new organization had three goals:

1. Operating responsibilities were to be decentralized to the regional and district levels.

2. The organization was to be such that it was possible to focus on the major businesses of the Postal Service.

3. The organization was to acknowledge the special postal management requirements of large metropolitan areas.

The organization in late 1974 was as shown in Exhibit 1. The Executive Committee operated as an internal policy level review body. Virtually all major financial or marketing proposals were presented to this group for approval prior to discussion with the Postal Service Board of Governors. Each Region had an organization which was basically similar to that in headquarters, with the exception of such functions as Government Relations, Planning, etc.

Basic Statistics. As of June 30, 1974, the magnitude of the Postal Service could be reflected in a series of numbers. The Postal Service employed 710,433 people. The annual budget was $11.3 billion, of which 85% represented labor expenses. During the fiscal year, 90 billion pieces of mail were moved, which translated into an average 297 million pieces per day. Over the past ten years this figure had increased at a rate averaging 2.5% annually. The Postal Service operated 31,000 post offices, ranging in size from one corner of Seward's General Store in Menemsha on the island of Martha's Vineyard in Massachusetts to Chicago's main post office, the biggest in the world. The latter's 21,000 employees worked on nine floors of a 13-story, 60-acre building, and received, sorted, and dispatched 15 million pieces of mail a day. The Postal Service's fleet of almost 100 thousand vehicles made it the country's largest consumer of fuel outside the military. As a result, each one-cent increase in the price of gasoline and diesel fuel increased annual operating costs by $3.5 million. Exhibit 2 summarizes key financial statistics from 1970–74.

An indication of the degree to which the Postal Service was labor-intensive was provided in a 1968 study. The ratio of net fixed assets to employee was found to be $1,145. This could be compared to $35,630 in the leading companies of the telephone and telegraph industry, $7,170 in manufacturing, and $2,836 in merchandising.

The actual transportation of the mail between post offices cost over $707 million in 1972. This included a complex network of 15,000 contract truck routes, 8,000 commercial air flights, 169 air-taxi routes, and 154 passenger and freight trains.

The handling of mail was also complex. It was comprised of six steps: collection, culling, canceling, sorting, transportation, and delivery. Although there had been a movement toward mechanization, a study showed that one letter might be handled by up to 43 different individuals. Thus the chance for error was very great.

Prior to postal reorganization, no service standards had ever been defined. Standards were therefore issued in 1972. These were set by top management and subsequently validated by market research. The most desired quality for mail delivery was found to be consistency of service, with consumer expectations being highest for local mail. In the case of first-class mail, objectives were delivery of local mail in one day, non-local but within 600 miles in two days, and beyond 600 miles in three days. The goal of the Postal Service was to meet these objectives for 95% of all pieces.

However, meeting that goal would have still meant that almost 2.5 billion first-class letters (5% of total) arrived late in 1974.

THE CUSTOMER SERVICES DEPARTMENT

The Kappel Commission report strongly recommended that the new organization be firmly based on the concept of meeting customers' needs through a marketing approach. The Postal Reform Act provided the means for the establishment of a true marketing function.

Marketing activities within the USPS were centered in the Customer Services Department, under the direction of the Assistant Postmaster General (APMG) for Customer Services, William D. Dunlap. Mr. Dunlap, 36, had joined the Postal Service in May 1969 from the Procter & Gamble Company, where he had previously held the position of New Products Marketing Manager. After assignments as Special Assistant to the Postmaster General responsible for press relations, development of new philatelic programs, and special assignments, he was appointed as APMG for Product Management in 1971 and named to his present position in June 1973. He reported directly to the Senior Assistant Postmaster-General for Administration.

Partly at Mr. Dunlap's urging, several other Procter & Gamble "graduates" had joined him in the Customer Services Department, among them James L. Schorr, 32, Director of Advertising, and Robert F. Jordan, 33, Director of Product Management. Mr. Jordan, who held an MBA from the University of Connecticut, had previously worked in the Advertising Department of the Packaged Soaps and Detergents Division at P & G, where he had held product management responsibility for several nationally distributed, branded products. He had joined the USPS in April 1972.

The mandate provided by the 1970 Act, Mr. Dunlap said, gave the USPS the flexibility to make major changes in the structure of the system.

> In our particular area, our job is to develop and market new products and services while doing a better job of making our current services more customer oriented.

However, Mr. Jordan presented a warning concerning the overall impact of the Act:

> Just because there is a law written, it does not change the inertia of operating in a certain way and the value systems that are present in any large, established organization.
>
> I think that people coming from the outside, like I did, really didn't appreciate that. I think there was some confusion between a legislative act and a divine miracle. There's a great gap between the two. The only thing, I think, that can be said is that because it has the strength of law, the Postal Service has an advantage over organizations that don't have that catalyst.

EXHIBIT 2
1970—1974 Financial History Summary
(June 30 Fiscal Year)

	1974	**1973**	**1972**	**1971***	**1970**
Statement of Operations			(In Thousands)		
Operating revenues	$ 9,008,314	$8,338,945	$7,884,188	$6,664,988	$6,346,655
Government appropriations	1,750,445	1,485,595	1,424,191	2,086,496	1,355,040
Total Income	10,758,759	9,824,540	9,308,379	8,751,484	7,701,695
Salaries and benefits	9,641,557	8,450,914	8,145,538	7,467,036	6,524,819
Other expenses	1,653,782	1,475,527	1,439,831	1,488,228	1,342,450
Total Operating Expenses	11,295,339	9,926,441	9,585,369	8,955,264	7,867,269
Operating Loss	536,580	101,901	276,990	203,780	165,574
Other income, net	98,221	88,937	101,555	—	—
Net Loss	$ 438,359	$ 12,964	$ 175,435	$ 203,780	$ 165,574
Balance Sheet					
Assets					
Current assets	$ 1,718,458	$1,950,676	$2,059,829	$1,989,212	$1,501,827
Property, plant, & equip., & other assets	5,115,850	3,674,005	2,676,796	1,415,466	1,259,405
Total Assets	$ 6,834,308	$5,624,681	$4,736,625	$3,404,678	$2,761,232
Liabilities					
Current liabilities	$ 2,167,925	$1,483,665	$1,437,929	$1,346,165	$ 890,314
Reserves	3,254,618	2,325,464	1,500,390	372,796	333,368
Long-term debt—USPS Bonds & Mortgages	264,983	250,000	250,000	—	—
Equity	1,146,782	1,565,552	1,548,306	1,685,717	1,537,550
Total Liabilities and Equity	$ 6,834,308	$5,624,681	$4,736,625	$3,404,678	$2,761,232
Analysis of Changes in Equity					
Beginning balance	$ 1,565,552	$1,548,306	$1,685,717	$1,537,550	$1,149,834
Deduct:					
Retroactive adjustments recorded at 7/1/71	—	—	—	(243,678)	—
Balance July 1	1,565,552	1,548,306	1,685,717	1,293,872	1,149,834
Net loss	438,359	12,964	175,435	203,780	165,574
	1,127,193	1,535,342	1,510,282	1,090,092	981,260
Add:					
Capital Contributions	21,235	27,403	32,539	—	—
Government appropriations—Capital**	—	—	—	486,825	380,000
Buildings and other transfers to/from government agencies	(1,646)	2,807	5,485	108,800	173,290
Ending balance	$ 1,146,782	$1,565,552	$1,548,306	$1,685,717	$1,537,550

Source: Annual Report of the Postmaster General, 1973–74.

* The United States Postal Service was established July 1, 1971. Financial statements prior to that date are those of the Post Office Department. Such statements for 1970 and 1971 have been restated above to be in a format generally consistent with 1972–74.

The Act also had specific marketing implications. For example, it stated that "In determining all policies for postal services, the Postal Service shall give the highest consideration to the requirement for the most expeditious collection, transportation, and delivery of important letter mail." Mr. Jordan reflected:

> That doesn't make much sense from a marketing point of view. It incorrectly equates speed of delivery with service. It also suggests that the cost of providing faster and faster service would have to be borne by all users when only a small fraction really need expedited delivery.

The Structure of the Marketing Organization. With the mandate of the Postal Reform Act, a marketing organization was developed within the Customer Services Department which evolved over time to the structure in Exhibit 3, comprised of two Divisions and six Offices.

EXHIBIT 3
Organization of Customer Services Department, United States Postal Service

```
                          ┌─────────────────────┐
                          │ Customer            │
                          │ Services            │
                          │ Department          │
                          ├─────────────────────┤
                          │ APMG W. Dunlap      │
                          └─────────────────────┘
        ┌─────────────────────┐          ┌─────────────────────┐
        │ Special             │          │ Planning and        │
        │ Events              │          │ Management          │
        │ Division            │          │ Division            │
        ├─────────────────────┤          ├─────────────────────┤
        │ G. Mgr. E. Horgan   │          │ G. Mgr. R. J. Strasser │
        └─────────────────────┘          └─────────────────────┘
```

Office of Stamps	Office of International Postal Affairs	Office of Advertising	Office of Product Management	Office of Customer Marketing	Office of Consumer Advocate
Director G. Morison	Director E. Stock	Director J. Schorr	Director R. Jordan	(Vacant)	Director T. Chadwick

The Special Events Division had several responsibilities. Postal Forum, Inc., a wholly-owned, separate corporation, ran a national convention. A primary objective of the Division was to operate the Postal Forum, a national meeting of some 3,000 postal customers, conducted annually. Additionally, the Division was responsible for all industrial conference relationships, such as tradeshow activities.

The Planning & Management Division acted in a service relationship between Dunlap and the Offices, in terms of the planning and implementation of the management-by-objectives system which had been instituted in the Customer Services Department.

The Office of Stamps was responsible for both the regular stamps and the entire philately operation. It had both product and marketing responsibility for its own products.

The Office of International Postal Affairs represented the U.S. Postal Service in the Universal Postal Union. Established in 1874, the UPU consisted of 152 member countries dedicated to the basic goal of creating one "international postal community." Even when nations were at war, the UPU saw to it that mail was delivered between them. This office also negotiated bi-lateral agreements with other countries on postal matters such as the recently concluded agreements on International Express Mail. Within the U.S. Postal Service, the Office served as a focal point for contacts with foreign administrations and interpreted the Universal Postal Union regulations for operating officials.

The Office of Advertising had functional responsibility for all measured media advertising. This included three areas of advertising. Public service advertising, such as for ZIP codes, was designed and then broadcast at no charge. Corporate advertising consisted of paid advertising messages responsible for attitude shifts and image building, not dollar volume, and included such campaigns as "There is No Such Thing as Junk Mail." Product advertising—promotion of special postal products and services—was the functional responsibility of this office, but had to have the concurrence of the managing office or Product Manager.

The Office of Product Management (discussed in greater depth later in the case) was responsible for the overall management of all elements and activities related to USPS products.[2] Additionally, this Office had market research responsibility for the entire Postal Service.

The Office of Customer Marketing was formed to consolidate the "field marketing" functions into one office. This office had the responsibility for sales training, sales planning, and evaluation of field sales performance. Lobby design, point-of-purchase materials, self-service equipment, and window merchandising were main functions in the retail area.

The Office of Consumer Advocate acted as a liaison between the Postal Service and its customers. It handled an average of 500 complaints a week. The Consumer Advocate had the authority to call any postmaster in the country and find out what was right and what was wrong and get any problems seen to immediately.

Organizational Problems. The marketing organization faced some important problems resulting from the overall organization of the Postal Service and from the

---

[2] Henceforth, the term "product" is used in the generic sense to denote service offerings as well as physical goods.

newness of marketing within the Postal Service. These problems were primarily concerned with the interaction of marketing and operations.

The first problem was that all field activities were under Operations and, thus, marketing had no line authority over the "salesforce"—customer service representatives who worked closely with major customers —or the postmasters and their activities. This complicated coordination of all the elements in a marketing program.

Second, individual post offices were treated as cost centers, and thus postmasters resisted any changes which would increase costs. The impact of changes on revenues was institutionally overlooked at this level.

To overcome this institutional inertia, marketing had to go to great efforts—in the form of market research, operations research, and detailed marketing plans—in order to ensure that its recommendations received careful consideration at all levels.

THE OFFICE OF PRODUCT MANAGEMENT

The Office of Product Management had overall responsibility and authority for product marketing within the U.S. Postal Service.

Upon assuming the newly-created position of Director of Product Management on July 1, 1973, Mr. Jordan realized that he had to develop an organizational structure that was appropriate for the Postal Service as a whole and the Customer Services Department in particular:

> Starting from the mandate in the Reorganization Act that said we should provide services based on customer needs, we have asked ourselves: what is the proper business of the Postal Service?
>
> Our answer is that, first, we are in the communications business with our message transfer services like first-class mail. Second, we're in the media business by using the mails to deliver advertising messages. Third, we're in the materials handling business with products and services like parcel post. Fourth, we're in the financial business. We're the number one money order brand in the United States, for example, and have a very high cash flow and a lot of financial expertise. And we run a large retail business. I think the number of outlets is ten times greater than the A & P chain, for example.

Goals, Objectives and Responsibilities. The primary goal underlying creation of the Office of Product Management was the development of an organizational structure compatible with the existing range of services and able to permit appropriate new products and services. A secondary goal was to provide flexibility for the organization to evolve, expand, and contract over time in response to a changing environment and product line. Mr. Jordan particularly wanted to avoid a structure "carved in granite." [3]

A key element of product management is to be as flexible as possible. I change things as the needs of the business require. I do not want the organization to get carved in granite in some kind of civil service personnel department because if the thing works I'll go from two to fifty people and if it doesn't work I'll go from two to zero people. I also need the flexibility to move resources from declining to growing businesses.

He defined the objectives of the Office of Product Management as twofold. First, to increase the technical performance, customer acceptance, and revenue contribution of current postal services and products, except philatelics. And second, to improve service and build revenues through the development and marketing of new postal services and products.

As Director of Product Management, Mr. Jordan had prepared the following written statement of the basic responsibilities of Product Management within the Postal Service:

1. Establish policy, objectives and priorities regarding the development and sales of assigned products and services.

2. Determine customer needs, customer acceptance, and technical performance. Develop new services or standards, or modify existing services and standards as required.

3. Develop and approve marketing plans and programs for assigned products and services. Be accountable for the volume and revenue results of these activities.

4. Develop and approve marketing budgets for assigned products. Be accountable for the net contribution of products assigned.

5. Provide market research services to other Customer Services and USPS organizations.

6. Work closely with others in carrying out the responsibilities of the Office of Product Management. Receive creative and media services from the Office of Advertising. Receive implementation support from the Sales and Retail Divisions. Coordinate with other Headquarters and Regional groups as required. Select, manage, and evaluate the performance of assigned contractors.

Organization. In designing a product management organization which would meet the above objectives, Mr. Jordan drew heavily on his previous experience at Procter & Gamble. Product-related divisions were based on three principles:

1. *Marketing*—The organization should mirror the way the customer views our business and the structure of the markets where we do business.

---

[3] This was *literally* true for the former Post Office Department. At the old Post Office Building on Washington's Pennsylvania Avenue (which the USPS had recently vacated for newly-constructed offices in L'Enfant Plaza) the names of the services offered by the Department were actually carved into the stone frontage of the neo-classical building.

EXHIBIT 4
Organization of Office of Product Management

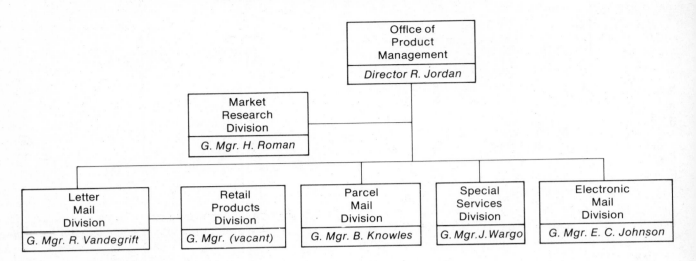

2. *Operations*—The organization should have a natural, common link to the way the Postal Service provides products and services to the customer.

3. *Priorities*—The organization should provide maximum focus against key products.

By October 1974, after several interim designs, the organization had been refined to that shown in Exhibit 4. Mr. Jordan commented:

> ....Taking the results of our analysis, and adding postal nomenclatures with an eye for the need to communicate and be able to relate to the rest of the Postal Service, we came up with this particular array. I could think of about three other ways of doing it, which might be as good or better, but this has worked very well. We'll change it again as the needs of the business require.

The Office of Product Management was structured into six Divisions, titled Letter Mail, Parcel Mail, Retail Products, Special Services, Electronic Mail and Market Research. Each Division was headed by a General Manager and, in some cases, supported by a Group Product Manager. Responsibility for individual products rested with the Product Manager, who would provide technical direction to Assistant Product Managers and Product Assistants assigned to the product. Titles in the Market Research Division differed due to the nature of the business; however, the positions were similar in level and responsibility.

The five product-related divisions were a rational grouping of the numerous USPS products and services. The divisional structure provided an umbrella under which new lines could be added and weak ones phased out. Each division represented a product line, and thus a coordinated effort across a group of products could be effected.

DIVISIONS IN THE OFFICE OF PRODUCT MANAGEMENT

Letter Mail Division. The Letter Mail Division had primary responsibility for First Class Mail, Airmail, and Special Delivery—products producing more than 55% of Postal mail revenues annually. These were the only USPS products protected from competiton by Private Express Statutes.

First Class Mail contributed approximately half the volume and revenue of the Postal Service. It represented the cornerstone of the business. Volume had grown 36% in the last ten years from 38 billion pieces in 1964 to over 51 billion pieces in 1974, putting extraordinary demands on processing techniques. Revenue more than doubled in that period, from $2,109 million to $5,019 million.

Airmail volume was 1,334 million pieces in 1974 and revenue was $234 million. Special delivery volume was 82 million pieces, which produced $52 million revenue in 1974.

These Letter Mail products held a 20% share of the domestic, private-message communications market. Telephone, telegraph services, and, to a very small degree, TWX, Telex, Telegram and courier services constituted the primary competition in this market.

Retail Products Division. In late 1974, the responsibilities of this Division, which some felt might more aptly be titled "Financial Products," were being shared among several other Divisions. The responsibility for Money Orders was placed with the Letter Mail Division, since most were sent through the mail. In FY 1974, the Postal Service sold 165 million money orders which generated fee revenues of $52 million. Registered and

Certified mail were with the Special Services Division. Responsibility for products and product development related to the emerging area of Electronic Funds Transfer was with the Electronic Mail Division. Long-range plans were to form a complete Division devoted exclusively to Financial Products.

Parcel Mail Division. Products under this Division were Parcel Post, Priority Mail, and Express Mail, and other fourth class mail.

Fourth class had fiscal year 1974 revenue of $732 million with volume of 859 million pieces. Over half of the revenue came from Zone Rated Parcel Post, which competed primarily with the service offered by United Parcel Service and, to a lesser extent, with those of other private carriers such as freight forwarders.

Priority mail consisted of First Class mail over 12 ounces, Airmail over 9 ounces, and Air Parcel Post and accounted for $394 million revenue in fiscal year 1974 with a volume of 222 million pieces.

Express mail was a new service designed to provide fast inter-city delivery of information, merchandise, and other materials of 50 pounds or less, with a money-back guarantee if performance standards were not met. This service took two forms. First, Programmed Service was provided to companies, such as banks, which had regularly scheduled needs between specific cities. Special service agreements were individually custom-tailored, typically calling for a 12 hour delivery. Second, Regular Service was provided to those with unpredictable needs at designated counters in specific post offices. This service guaranteed next day delivery by 3 p.m. to the addressee or to a specified post office to be picked up by 10 a.m.

Revenues from Express Mail increased from $1 million in fiscal year 1972 to more than $3 million in 1973, and $6 million in 1974. By October 1974 the network included over 400 cities in the United States and abroad.

Special Services Division. This Division managed products and services which met the special needs of select customers. Organizationally, the Division was divided into the Security Mail Group and the Advertising Mail Group. The Security Mail Group included Registered, Certified, Insurance, and COD mail, as well as a new service, Controlpak. The Advertising Mail Group was comprised of direct mail advertising (first class, third class and fourth class catalogs) and second class mail (primarily magazines).

Security Mail products were additional, value-added options available for the basic requirement categories of mail. These products generated $140 million in postal revenue through 240 million transactions in 1973. Controlpak was a new service designed for the valuable letter market. The service was positioned between Registered and First-Class mail. Controlpak traveled through the Registry system in heat-sealed plastic bags until it reached the office of delivery. At this point, the individual pieces entered the First Class delivery network. By October 1974, more than 50,000 shipments had been made with none lost or stolen.

Advertising Mail was one of the most important revenue producers. In fiscal year 1974, advertisers sent over 22 billion pieces of Advertising Mail, spending over $1 billion in postage to generate an estimated $50 billion in the sale of goods and services. This product, 93% of which was Bulk Rate Third Class, faced extreme and continuing competition. Ad Mail was an important component of the direct mail industry. In 1973, national expenditures for direct mail were $3.7 billion, a 14.7% share of total U.S. advertising expenditures. Major competition was from newspapers, television, radio, magazines, private postal operations, and hand-delivery firms.

Electronic Mail Division. This Division was organized primarily to explore and develop new services in the area of telecommunications. Rather than physically transporting the hard message, these services electronically transmitted the information content of the message to its destination where a hard copy was recreated and delivered. Some of this division's work involved products which were not expected to reach the marketplace until 1980. Others, such as Urgent Message Service and Mailgram, were already operational.

The *Urgent Message Service* provided for electronic transmission of visual images between specified cities. This service made it possible for a customer in one city to transmit the image of, say, an engineering diagram, and have a facsimile copy generated by receiving equipment in a distant destination. There was guaranteed one hour lobby pick-up of four hour door delivery. The average cost per page was $4.

Mailgram, initiated in 1970, was a joint venture between the USPS and Western Union. The service, first proposed by Western Union, involved first transferring a message by WU equipment and then delivering a printed copy the next day through the Postal Service's regular mail network. By October 1974, 450,000 Mailgrams per week were being sent, as compared with an average of 265,000 in the last quarter of 1973. Postal revenues during the first six months of 1974 were $2.9 million, up from $1.3 million during the same period in 1973. By the end of 1974, Mailgram volume surpassed Telegrams.

Market Research Division. In discussing the role of market research, Mr. Jordan noted that the Office of

Product Management had market research responsibility for the entire Postal Service. This had the advantage of insuring that the marketing activities of the regular Divisions took full advantage of research, but required special management skills.

> The Market Research Manager and myself have to insure that other Postal clients get fair, confidential treatment. One of our own product managers can get pretty upset if he or she has to wait for research because someone from another Office or Department was in line first or has higher priority work.

PRODUCT MANAGEMENT STAFFING

Mr. Jordan regarded the Product Manager as "the focal point around which everything turns. He's the guy whose supposed to make everything happen. I'm 'overhead' by comparison."

The Product Manager typically headed a small group consisting of one or more assistants. Some assistants were called Product Assistants, which was the entry-level position. Others were called Assistant Product Managers, more experienced and only one step away from being promoted to manage their own product. The size and composition of one of these groups varied by the requirements of a particular business. They ranged from one to six people, with a group of three being most typical.

There was also provision for a Group Product Manager position:

> We are just beginning to actually fill these positions. On one hand, we favor the idea because it provides additional depth, focus, and opportunities for professional growth. On the other hand, it is not needed until individual product clusters are implemented that are too many in number for the Division Manager to handle well.

Creating an organization on paper and activating it with qualified people were two different things, Mr. Jordan stated.

> We have been able to attract some good people from within the Postal Service, but the talent base is too thin for our needs. There was no marketing in a profes-

sional sense in the old Post Office, so people with the skills and instincts we need are few in number.

> This has made it necessary to recruit heavily from the outside. Before we started, we trained ourselves in interviewing, conducted salary and job surveys, and got help from experts in the private sector. The job is worth doing, very challenging, and, we think, competitive from a compensation view.[4]

> Still, we've had some difficulty. First, there is a general skepticism toward government among people in private companies. Second, few have thought of the Postal Service as a business.

> We're also pretty picky and would rather live with a vacancy than fill it with someone about whom we may have a doubt. Initiative and perseverance are two essential characteristics in good product manager, especially here, since we're creating new programs out of whole cloth. So we tend to look more at the psychology of a person, rather than focus on *years of experience* and the like. A common denominator is that the candidate should demonstrate capacity, fluency, and independence in his or her thinking. Leadership ability, results orientation, communications skills, and goal motivation are some of the things we look at before examining technical skills in detail.

> Candidates are pre-screened by the outside consultant and our own personnel people before being scheduled for an interview. Even with tight requirements and the pre-screening, we don't make offers to the majority of people we interview.

> In net, we've done pretty well so far. Six of the last nine product managers we've hired have MBAs, and two of the last three market research specialists have PhDs. Interestingly enough, two of our more successful managers are attorneys.

> Long term, we hope to get to the position where most of our hires are at the entry-level position, and we promote from within for manager positions.

In November 1974, there were 52 authorized management-level positions in the Office of Product Management, of which 34 had been filled. Only six of the present managerial staff had been employed by the old Post Office Department prior to postal reorganization, the remaining 28 having been hired from outside. Most of these had previous business experience.

---

[4] In late 1974, salary ranges were: Group Product Manager, $25,767–$34,603; Product Manager, $21,500–$28,831; Assistant Product Manager, $16,908–$22,617; and Product Assistant, $13,830–$18,409.

30

Stanford University: The Annual Fund

Christopher H. Lovelock

Richard L. Bennett, Director of Stanford University's Annual Fund, was reviewing the performance of the Fund during 1973–74 and considering what changes, if any, should be planned for the year beginning September 1.

At the time of this review, in June 1974, Stanford was nearing the end of the second year of a six-year plan to double the annual income of the Fund by 1978. In addition to maintaining the momentum of this thrust, by increasing the number of annual donors as well as the size of their gifts, many donors would also be asked during 1974–75 for an additional gift to the highly ambitious Campaign for Stanford.

Although the total dollars raised in 1971–72, and the number of donors had increased by 15%, current year projections showed much smaller growth rates. Mr. Bennett wondered how he might improve the Fund's performance during 1974–75, despite the uncertain economic outlook. He was also concerned with keeping down the costs of fundraising in an inflationary period.

Stanford University, privately endowed and nondenominational, was founded in 1885 by Senator and Mrs. Leland Stanford. The Stanfords built the university as a memorial to their son, Leland Jr., who had died in Italy of typhoid at the age of fifteen. Senator Stanford, a former governor of California, had amassed a considerable fortune in railroading and other investments.

The original endowment was about $20 million, plus the college buildings and vast campus thirty miles south of San Francisco. The 8,800-acre land gift, the senator's Palo Alto ranch (hence Stanford's nickname "The Farm"), was conveyed to a board of trustees in perpetual trust.

Despite some rather shaky early years—occasioned by a period of financial instability for the founders and, more

literally, by the infamous 1906 earthquake which devastated San Franciso and severely damaged buildings on the Stanford campus—the new university generally prospered. While it soon achieved a strong reputation on the West Coast, particularly for its undergraduate program, it was not until after the Second World War that Stanford began to achieve national eminence.

Exhibit 1 charts the progress of the university in quantitative terms between 1953 and 1973. During this period, an extensive construction program was undertaken, many new faculty hired and some of the programs—particularly those of the graduate schools—became internationally known.

In 1973–74, Stanford University had some 11,200 matriculated students, of whom 6,400 were undergraduates. Women comprised about 40% of the undergraduate enrollment and 20% of the graduate students. Approximately half the 4,800 graduate students were enrolled in the Schools of

Christopher H. Lovelock is Associate Professor of Business Administration, Harvard University.

EXHIBIT 1
Stanford University: Key Statistics 1953–1973
(thousands of dollars—years ending August 31)

	1953	1958	1963	1968	1973
Operating Expenses					
Total Operations	$16,482	$ 27,930	$ 73,232	$140,949	$215,308
Instruction	4,620	7,890	19,166	32,689	49,712
Research	3,982	8,133	24,985	40,631	44,382
Libraries	605	1,103	2,014	4,912	7,339
Plant Operations	822	1,305	2,695	4,982	8,230
Stanford Linear Accelerator Center and Stanford University Hospital[1]			5,503	25,658	61,483
Major Sources of Funds for Operations					
Student Tuition and Fees	4,812	6,389	12,465	20,613	32,774
Gifts and Grants	1,396	3,110	7,366	11,054	13,956
Endowment Income	1,925	3,445	5,560	9,436	14,844
Government Projects— Grants and Contracts[2]	3,865	8,263	30,306	57,105	65,698
Gifts					
Total Gifts Received	3,626	8,727	38,505	29,720	46,513
To Endowment Funds	1,333	2,783	13,425	13,277	23,744
To Plant Funds	189	2,770	2,601	2,604	2,324
Student Aid					
Scholarships and Fellowships	614	1,169	3,492	7,980	10,434
Loans to Students	122	198	1,108	2,427	3,379
Endowment					
Estimated Market Value	51,001	106,586	194,071	268,242	356,365
Plant Additions	390	6,402	14,005	17,507	19,873
Students					
Enrollment—Undergraduate	4,785	5,290	5,600	5,917	6,469
Enrollment—Graduate	2,476	3,102	4,340	5,562	4,961
Degrees Awarded—Bachelor	1,105	1,195	1,381	1,515	1,712
Degrees Awarded—Advanced	1,109	1,248	1,574	2,398	2,439
Tuition per Full Time Student	660	750	1,260	1,770	2,850
Faculty and Staff					
Academic Council Members	411	495	735	983	1,096
Staff	1,360	1,863	3,796	5,309	5,880

Source: Stanford University, Annual Financial Report, *1973.*

[1] Stanford University Hospital acquired July 1, 1968 and combined with University financial statements in 1969.

[2] Excluding those designated for Stanford Linear Accelerator Center.

Engineering and Humanities & Sciences; most of the others were in professional programs such as Business, Education, Law, or Medicine. There were over 103,000 living alumni, of whom 58% were resident in California, 15% in the eastern United States, and 5% in other countries.

FUND RAISING AT STANFORD

Unlike many private colleges and universities, Stanford could not boast a long history of individual giving. An open letter to the alumni in the Spring/Summer 1974 edition of *The*

Stanford Magazine by the president of the Stanford alumni commented, in part:

> The plain fact is . . . that Stanford alumni have not supported the University financially nearly so well as have the alumni of comparable private institutions—Harvard, Yale, Princeton, and the like. This may seem puzzling, particularly in light of some hard data in our own Continuing Survey of Stanford Alumni Opinion which suggests that The Farm is extraordinarily near and dear to the hearts of its graduates.
>
> The explanation for this paradox lies in the history of Stanford and the differences between the higher education scene on the eastern seaboard and in the West. We can note a few of these factors:

(1) Leland and Jane Stanford's feeling that this was to be their personal memorial to their son, not one built with the contributions of the many; (2) the original endowment of $21 million —huge for its time—and the freedom from tuition which stamped Stanford as a wealthy institution that needed no help; (3) the absence in the West of private institutions of similar stature, a situation quite unlike that in the east where interschool rivalries provided a strong impetus to giving.* no reunions

The Annual Fund.

The significance of annual giving, Bennett noted, was its potential for yielding a regular source of income free from the restrictions often applied to endowment income. Because endowment income distributed over the years had approximated 5%, $20 million of endowment giving was required to generate the same income received from $1 million of annual giving. For this reason, many institutions referred to annual giving as their "living endowment."

Stanford's first annual solicitation was undertaken in 1936–37 and yielded $34,142. In 1938, a general mail appeal was initiated. Various mail approaches were tried during the next 14 years, including the use of separate professional school funds starting in 1945. Personal solicitation began in 1952. In 1960 the Annual Fund—by then generating some $1.2 million in gifts each year—was put into low profile for the duration of a four-year capital campaign, known as PACE. The PACE campaign had a target of $100 million and succeeded in raising $114 million by April 1964. This success proved the critical variable in advancing Stanford into the major league of American universities.

However, because the Annual Fund had been de-emphasized during the PACE campaign, the tradition of annual giving was weakened. It took several years to re-establish it firmly after the fund was restarted in 1964. In 1967, when annual giving reached $1.7 million, a special "club" was formed to encourage individual yearly gifts of $1000 or more and to provide appropriate recognition to the donors.

In January 1968, a five-year plan was proposed for the Annual Fund, designed to boost giving to $3 million a year by 1970–71. Most of the plan's proposals were implemented but the widespread campus unrest of the late sixties and early seventies, combined with a down stock market and a postal strike in 1969–70, cramped Stanford and numerous other universities. Stanford, in particular, received much unfavorable publicity as a result of campus violence. With gifts totalling roughly $2.4 million in 1970–71, the Annual Fund was well below the $3 million target set in 1968.

The Campaign for Stanford.

Like almost all private universities, Stanford found itself financially hard-pressed at the beginning of the 1970s. Spiraling costs, combined with a decline in federal funding, produced an income gap which could be only partly alleviated by increased tuition charges and more sophisticated financial management. Although the total endowment in 1971–72 had a market value of around $300 million, endowment per student was substantially lower than at many well-known private universities, being less than half the per capita figure for Yale or the University of Rochester, and approximately one-third that of Princeton, Harvard, and the California Institute of Technology. In April 1972, President Richard W. Lyman initiated the largest fund-raising program in American university history: the five-year, $300 million Campaign for Stanford.* 5yr $300. mil.

In sharp contrast to the earlier PACE campaign, where the Annual Fund was limited to a low-profile mail appeal for the duration, it was decided that the Annual Fund should form an integral part of the Campaign for Stanford. In this way, it was hoped that the expertise of the Annual Fund organization could be applied to raising "one-time" capital gifts for Stanford from annual donors, while also continuing the tradition of annual giving to Stanford at an increased rate. The target for the Annual Fund was to obtain $17 million in regular annual gifts and $12 million by asking each prospect to make an "over-and-above" capital gift, in addition to his or her annual gift, at least once during the campaign.

A second objective for the Annual Fund was to double the level of annual giving within six years—from approximately $2.5 million in 1971–72 to $5 million in 1977–78—by getting more alumni and others to make donations and by increasing the size of the average gift. A key ingredient in this plan was the Million Dollar Challenge Pledge. An anonymous donor had established a $1,000,000 pledge fund from which each new or incremental gift of $25 or more (subject to a $25,000 maximum) would be matched on a $1 for $2 basis. Thus, if someone who had not previously given donated $40, this new gift would earn an additional $20 for the pledge fund. Alternatively, if an existing donor raised his or her previous year's gift by $100, this increase would be matched by another $50.

In 1972–73, annual giving at Stanford rose to $3.1 million. Comparative figures for a number of other U.S. colleges and universities are shown in Exhibit 2.

ORGANIZATION OF THE ANNUAL FUND

Fund-raising activities at Stanford University were under the vice president for development, Kenneth M. Cuthbertson. Activities were divided into six categories—Foundations, Corporations, Major Gifts, Annual Fund, Deferred Giving, and General Project—each of which was headed by a director, who could draw for assistance from specialist groups in the areas of communications, legal services, and administrative records (Exhibit 3.) The last-mentioned group maintained

---

*Stanford also lacked the tradition of five-yearly class reunions. The class gifts occasioned by such reunions typically accounted for a significant proportion of total annual giving at many eastern colleges.

*In 1974, Yale University topped this by announcing a three-and-a-half year campaign with an objective of $370 million. As of May 31, 1974, the Campaign for Stanford had raised a total of $154.1 million.

EXHIBIT 2
Comparative Annual Fund Statistics for 24 Selected Colleges and Universities, 1972–73

Note: This is simply a representative selection of institutions and excludes many schools with distinguished fund raising records.

Institution	$ Gifts	No. of Donors	Average Gift	Donors as % of Alumni	No. of Living Alumni	No. of Students
Harvard University[1]	$8,273,388	39,656	$209	23.6%	168,025	14,372
Yale University	5,252,054	33,545	157	36.7	91,476	9,427
University of Michigan	4,090,354	38,705	106	13.5	286,305	41,178
Cornell University	4,008,430	27,820	144	22.0	126,730	16,407
Princeton University	3,955,842	19,742	200	44.8	44,030	5,503
Stanford University[2]	3,606,340	22,369	161	21.7	103,059	11,519
Wellesley College	3,598,617	14,081	256	55.9	25,209	1,908
Ohio State University	3,369,385	35,543	95	20.6	172,400	50,040
M.I.T.	3,183,680	21,796	146	39.0	55,913	7,888
University of Pennsylvania	3,045,689	26,513	115	18.1	146,490	19,375
U.C.L.A.	2,213,404	16,112	137	13.0	123,749	29,630
New York University	1,589,635	31,616	50	19.2	165,000	38,577
University of Chicago	1,311,783	15,671	84	19.1	82,036	9,083
Rice University	970,192	4,592	211	23.0	19,953	3,236
Williams College	921,718	7,313	126	60.3	12,120	1,592
University of California, Berkeley	762,894	10,908	70	5.2	210,000	28,488
Duke University	649,434	13,607	48	29.2	46,612	7,898
Amherst College	632,773	5,905	107	49.7	11,887	1,230
Carnegie-Mellon University	588,665	5,357	111	13.5	39,543	4,285
Northwestern University	500,241	7,985	63	6.2	128,952	14,418
University of Rochester	495,542	11,144	44	28.3	39,410	8,000
California Institute of Technology	347,101	1,816	191	15.9	11,400	1,515
Middlebury College	323,878	5,905	55	45.9	12,878	1,833
Reed College	265,354	2,082	127	35.8	5,816	1,105

Source: Council for Financial Aid to Education, Voluntary Support of Education.

[1] Unlike the majority of other colleges and universities, which had a central fundraising program, Harvard had separately organized and administered drives for Harvard College and several of the graduate schools.

[2] Includes approximately $500,000 in capital gifts to the Campaign for Stanford made through the Annual Fund.

files on alumni and other prospective donors, including a press-clipping service.

The Annual Fund director, Richard L. Bennett, had held the position since 1972, having previously worked in various fund-raising capacities at Stanford since 1966. A Stanford graduate, Bennett's earlier employment also included six years as a Navy pilot and seven years' business experience.

The Annual Fund was effectively organized on a matrix-type basis into two complementary sets of activities, with most prospects solicited being associated with both a *Program* and a *Fund*.

The Programs.
For annual solicitation purposes, Stanford alumni were divided into four groups—"Programs"—based upon their forecast giving capacity and the form of solicitation employed. There were also separate programs for parents and student-initiated fund-raising projects.

The *Inner Quad Program** focussed on 1,100 prospects believed to have a capacity of giving at least $1,000 annually.

*This took its name from the famous double quadrangle complex originally built by the Stanfords as the nucleus of the university.

John Hays, director, had a staff of eight professionals who coordinated the activities of 250 volunteer fund raisers in 16 regions.

The *Quad Program* was similar to the Inner Quad Program and used volunteers for personal solicitation of gifts of $100 or more. Its nearly 8,000 prospects were each estimated to have a capacity for annual giving of $100–$999. The director, Connie Gilliland, and ten staff members oversaw approximtely 1,350 volunteers working in 60 regions across the country.

The *Phonathon* was a telephone solicitation program typically starting in March and running through May. Nine staff members, under the direction of Linda Feigel, worked with over 1,700 volunteers in 27 geographical locations in the United States. These locations, 15 of which were in California, all contained high concentrations of Stanford alumni. The 30,000 prospects consisted of alumni in these locations whose giving capacity fell below Quad or Inner Quad levels and for whom the university had a telephone number.

The *Mail Appeal*, directed by Audrey Berkovitz with the assistance of two staff members, sought to reach all other alumni with known addresses (around 54,000 in number). A

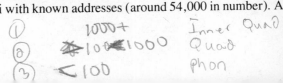

EXHIBIT 3
Stanford University Fundraising: Partial Organization Chart

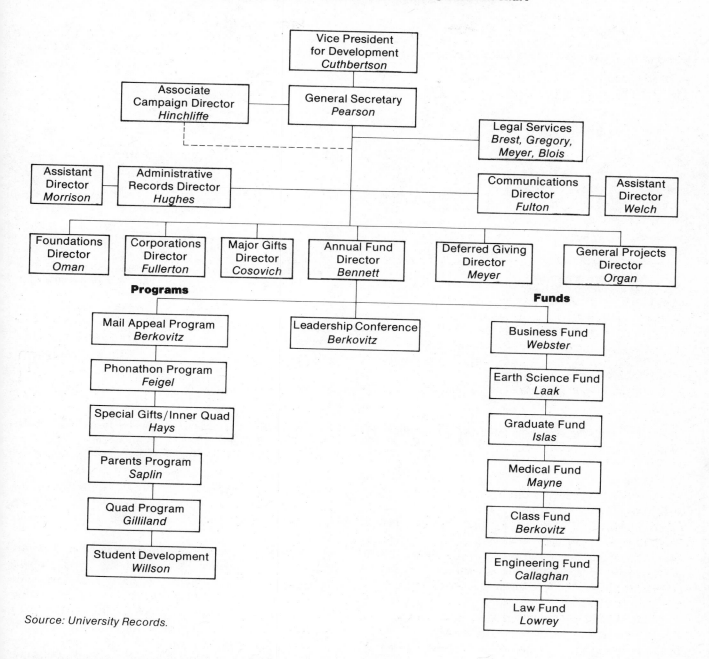

Source: *University Records.*

volunteer Creative Committee reviewed plans each year and evaluated all written material. Mail Appeal prospects were divided into seven categories, based upon their past giving history and level of previous donations (if any), for the purpose of determining the number of mailings sent each individual.

The *Parents Program,* directed by Anne Saplin with one assistant, contacted some 12,000 nonalumni parents of present Stanford students and recent graduates. One hundred volunteers, all parents, personally solicited contributions from about one-fifth of the prospect body in ten different regional areas, while the remainder were solicited by mail.

The *Student Development Program* was under the direction of Janet Willson who worked with about one hundred student volunteers interested in raising money for the university. Activities included the annual Heritage Fund Program to raise scholarship funds from businesses in Los Angeles and the San Francisco Bay area, and participation in the Phonathon Program.

In several instances, directors and staff had responsi-

EXHIBIT 4
Key Statistics for Annual Fund Programs, 1973–74

Program	Principal Activity Period	No. of Regions	No. of Staff[1]	No. of Volunteers[2]	No. of Prospects	Size of Gift Solicitations	Projected Totals			
							Annual Gifts	Campaign Gifts	Direct Expenses	Salaries & Benefits
Inner Quad[3]	June–Dec.	16	8	250	1,100	$1,000 +	$1,215,000	$806,000	$ 31,000	$164,000
Quad	June–Feb.	60	10[4]	1,350	8,000	100 +	776,000	60,000	37,000	
Phonathon	March–May	27	9[4]	1,700	30,000	1–50	229,000	–	35,000	
Mail Appeal	July–May	–	2	70[5]	54,000	1–50	417,000	–	47,000	131,000[6]
Parents (personal) (mail)	Aug.–May Oct.–June	10 –	1	100	{ 2,400 9,600	100 + 1–99	290,000 19,000	5,000	11,000	
Student Development	Oct.–May	–	1	100	not pre-determined	not pre-determined	154,000	–	32,000	
Total			21	3,570	105,100 +		$3,100,000	$871,000	$193,000	$295,000

Source: University Records.

[1] Excluding Director.

[2] Volunteers were typically prospects themselves in the same program for which they were soliciting and are therefore included in the prospect total (for example, 250 of the 1,100 Inner Quad Program prospects were volunteers who were responsible for soliciting the remaining 850 individuals in this category).

[3] The Director and staff of this program divided their time between annual fundraising for the Inner Quad and solicitation of Special Gifts ($10,000–$99,000) for the Campaign for Stanford.

[4] The same staff members were employed in both programs, working for the Quad Program in the autumn and the Phonathon in the Spring.

[5] Members of advisory groups.

[6] Not allocated among different programs.

bilities in more than one program. Exhibit 4 summarizes salient aspects of the six programs.

The Funds. Depending on the course of study which alumni had followed while at Stanford, they would also be affiliated with one or more "Funds." There were seven school-oriented funds: the Class Fund, for those who had attended Stanford as undergraduates in the School of Humanities & Sciences; the Graduate Fund, for those who had undertaken graduate work in Humanities and Sciences or in Education; and the Business, Earth Sciences, Engineering, Law and Medicine Funds. Various rules of thumb were employed for assigning alumni who had undertaken two or more different degree programs at Stanford. The objective was to tailor fund-raising appeals as closely as possible to an individual's probable career path, so that affiliation with progressional graduate programs tended to take priority over undergraduate affiliation.

The strategy was useful for two reasons. First, it was employed to match solicitation communications—personal, telephone or mail—with each alum's past study program. In personal or telephone solicitations, whenever practicable, each potential donor would be solicited by a volunteer with a similar background. With direct mail communications, the content (and authorship) of the letters sent would be matched with the individual's educational program at Stanford. Sec-

ond, gifts could be channeled directly to the area of the university with which the donors had been most closely associated during their Stanford careers. Thus, an alumna of the Law School would either be contacted by a volunteer who was also a law graduate—possibly in her own class—or receive mail appeals on Law Fund stationery; any gift she made would be used specifically for projects associated with the Law School.

At any time, alumni were free to request that their gifts be directed to a different fund, or to change their affiliation. Gifts received from parents were credited to a special Parents Fund and usually applied towards financial aid and scholarships. An additional fund with which alumni might choose to be associated was the Buck Club, intended for support of athletic scholarships. Alumni who were members of the Buck Club were also solicited for gifts to academically oriented funds.

Each fund was supervised by a director who maintained close liaison between the various fund-raising programs and the school associated with that specific fund (Exhibit 3). This job included encouraging faculty-student interaction; assisting in preparation of literature; recruiting new volunteers and working with faculty and administrators on continuing education programs for alumni.

Alumni participation in giving varied sharply by fund affiliation. The highest participation rates in recent years had

EXHIBIT 5
Stanford Annual Fund: Year-End Totals by Fund Category

Fund	1967—68	1968—69	1969—70	1970—71	1971—72	1972—73
Business						
Dollars	$116,037	$108,029	$134,575	$185,312	$219,846	$263,393
Donors	1,031	1,113	1,022	1,377	1,684	2,145
% participation	20%	21%	18%	23%	27%	32%
Graduate						
Dollars	$42,739	$67,823	$51,639	$66,072	$89,786	$109,233
Donors	1,009	1,315	1,038	1,794	2,158	2,580
% participation	6%	8%	6%	10%	11%	13%
Engineering						
Dollars	$255,288	$217,099	$159,690	$150,753	$245,887	$280,579
Donors	1,259	1,381	1,285	1,245	1,946	2,449
% participation	11%	11%	10%	9%	14%	17%
Law						
Dollars	$78,733	$82,677	$66,154	$118,406	$191,165	$244,216
Donors	1,316	1,362	715	1,266	1,604	1,842
% participation	35%	35%	18%	32%	39%	44%
Medical						
Dollars	$87,240	$120,592	$95,132	$69,854	$98,072	$131,531
Donors	807	817	813	881	1,049	1,146
% participation	36%	35%	35%	28%	34%	36%
Earth Sciences						
Dollars	$67,387	$85,195	$38,497	$50,058	$53,663	$99,977
Donors	357	326	327	310	388	490
% participation	21%	19%	18%	17%	21%	26%
Class						
Dollars	$760,529	$789,887	$821,428	$807,415	$1,047,368	$1,108,740
Donors	8,686	8,273	8,254	8,709	9,102	10,874
% participation	17%	16%	16%	16%	17%	19%
Buck Club						
Dollars	$234,291	$257,561	$303,256	$418,042[1]	$483,208[1]	$498,554
Donors	3,465	3,410	3,943	4,537	4,793	4,949
% participation	69%	66%	78%	86%	93%	89%
Parents						
Dollars	$263,889	$301,340[2]	$308,157	$461,122[2]	$408,644	$361,440
Donors	1,277	1,220	909	1,105	1,121	977
% participation	13%	12%	8%	9%	9%	9%
Totals						
Dollars	$1,906,137	$2,030,308	$1,978,532	$2,327,038	$2,837,639	$3,097,660
Donors	19,207	19,217	18,306	21,224	23,845	27,452
% participation	18%	18%	16%	18%	20%	22%

[1] The Stanford football team participated in the Rose Bowl in each of these years.

[2] Less one large donor.

(These figures exclude gifts to the Campaign for Stanford made through the Annual Fund.)

been among graduates of the professional schools, as shown in Exhibit 5. Since affiliation with the Buck Club was entirely optional, membership tended to be self-selecting and participation levels were very high. The Parents Fund, by contrast, did not enjoy wide support. The number solicited varied from one year to another due to a policy of selectively weeding out nongivers and those who asked to be excluded. Among parents who were solicited personally (those who were easily accessible and seen as having a potential for giving $100 or more), participation in 1972—73 had averaged around 16%.

Among those solicited by mail, however, participation was only about 5%.

The Graduate Fund director observed that alumni with a Master's or Doctor's degree from the School of Humanities & Sciences were more likely to identify with their undergraduate shool (which might not have been Stanford). Noting that this school consisted of a broad array of students in many different disciplines who often did not work closely with other students, even those in the same department, he commented:

I think it's very difficult to appeal to "H & S" support for the university. Right now, we're in the process of breaking away the people in the School of Education from solicitation for the Humanities & Sciences Fund. The Ed. School is not as difficult. There is more allegiance to the Stanford School of Education once someone has received a degree. I feel it's because it does give you something towards a career that you want to continue. The giving capacity of the people that get out of the graduate program in H & S isn't what it can be in engineering or in law or in medicine. I've been instilling in the students early the need to support the university. I'm not talking about big bucks, just the willingness to give a couple of bucks a year if that's all they can afford. But I'm not sure what we can do to enhance the experience here and tie that into fund raising.

Discussing the difference between the Graduate Fund and the Engineering Fund, the director of the latter commented:

I think the School of Engineering is a little bit more cohesive a group than graduate H & S, but less so than, say, Business or Law.* We've found that we simply can't rely on engineers to have the same feeling for the School that business students have, because it's a four-, five-, or six-year program that they go through. It's a big school and many of their classes are in departments other than engineering. But on the other hand, they seem to be a much tighter group [than H & S] and they do seem to have some feel for the School of Engineering. We're now trying to do a lot of things here at the school in terms of student involvement—not actually soliciting them, but making a stronger school identification. Faculty get-togethers, etc., so when the students do get out they'll feel closer to the school. Along with that, we're trying to work with alumni a little—meet-the-faculty sessions. It's a really small, informal group where they get chances to talk to faculty, more so than a lecture series.

The Law Fund director believed that his fund had a great advantage when it came to gift solicitation because the 150 members of each entering class got to know each other very well and developed a strong class allegiance. Solicitation for the Law Fund was broken down on a class basis. He noted that 90% of Law School graduates went on to practice law. This made it simpler to track alumni and to ask Law Fund volunteers to identify those prospects with a substantial giving capacity which might not be suspected from their past giving history. A recent graduate of the Law School himself, he theorized that the first impressions made on a student could have an important bearing on willingness to give in the years immediately following graduation.

I've noticed among my classmates and other people who graduated around the same time—they're giving around $10 or $20—that their giving has been affected, first of all, by how their application to the school was processed. Was the reply prompt and courteous or very impersonal? Then, their applications for financial aid are very important. Were these handled very coldly? Was there an effort to try and help the student get financial aid if he or she needed it? Or to get housing, or just to start fitting in as a student? And the extent to which help was received, and the students perceive the school was trying to address their needs, really has affected their willingness to given even a nominal amount.

---

*The Business School's MBA degree involved a two-year program with many required courses and few taken outside the School. The three-year JD program at the Law School was similarly tightly prescribed.

COMMUNICATIONS STRATEGY

Communications between Stanford and prospective donors took two basic forms—printed materials from the university and personal communications. Wherever possible, Stanford preferred that alumni be approached for annual gifts by fellow alumni. Over the years, a substantial volunteer fund-raising organization had been developed, largely at the initiative of interested alumni, but with encouragement and support from the university. An important coordinating role was played by the Stanford Alumni Association, which had offices on campus.

In developing communications strategy and preparing literature and mailings, the Annual Fund was able to draw on the advice and assistance of the director of communications. Additional inputs came from volunteers and the Office of News and Publications. The latter's responsibilities included publication and distribution of the *Stanford Observer*, a monthly newspaper about Stanford mailed to all alumni; this also contained a section entitled "The Alumni Almanac," with news prepared by the Stanford Alumni Association. Since fall 1973, all alumni had received copies of *The Stanford Magazine*, a handsome new color magazine published semi-annually by the Alumni Association. Volunteers associated with the Quad and Inner Quad Programs also received the weekly *Campus Report*, the official internal newspaper of the university (as distinct from student-run publications such as the *Stanford Daily*).

Mail Appeal Strategies. Stanford had become considerably more sophisticated in its approach to direct mail solicitation in recent years. A consultant had helped to develop a system of solicitation which considered the total impact made on a prospective donor. Prospects in the Mail Appeal Program were segmented first by fund (i.e., school affiliation) and then by level and frequency of giving. There were seven groups in the latter segmentation:

A. Last-year, first-time donors of $25 or more;
B. Last-year, first-time donors of less than $25;
C. Last-year donors of $25+ with a previous history of giving;
D. Last-year donors of less than $25 with a previous giving history;
E. Prospects who did not give last year but gave the previous year;
F. Prospects who had given at some time in the past but whose last gift was more then two years ago;
G. Prospects who had never given a gift.

The consultant recommended that the number of solicitations and content of each appeal be tailored to each group. Thus, it was decided to send up to five solicitation letters to Groups "A" through "D," up to four to Groups "E" and "F," but no more than two to prospects in Group "G." Once a gift was received, no further solicitations were sent. Exhibit 6 contrasts the consultant's projections for each group with the actual results in 1972–73.

EXHIBIT 6
Stanford Annual Fund: Results of Mail Appeal Program 1972–73

Group[1]	No. of Prospects	No. of Mailings Sent	No. of Donors	Actual % Partic.	Goal[2] % Partic.	Total $ Received	Direct Costs	Actual Average Gift	Goal[1] Average Gift
A	247	Up to 5	121	49.0%	60%	$ 4,114	$ 805	$34.00	$34.00
B	775	Up to 5	490	63.2%	60%	$ 7,350	$ 1,617	$15.00	$16.00
C	1,539	Up to 5	973	63.2%	75%	$ 35,028	$ 4,491	$36.00	$52.00
D	2,885	Up to 5	2,197	76.2%	75%	$ 32,955	$ 4,126	$15.00	$20.00
E	1,977	Up to 4	1,049	53.1%	20%	$ 20,980	$ 1,392	$20.00	$25.00
F	13,320	Up to 4	1,273	9.6%	15%	$ 36,717	$10,697	$29.00	$20.00
G	33,303	Up to 2	1,156	3.5%	2%	$ 25,933	$ 8,216	$22.00	$16.00
Total[3]	53,429		7,259 (6,977) goal	13.6%	13%	$163,277 ($175,991) goal	$31,344	$22.50	$25.22

Source: University Records.

---

[1] For group characteristics, see text.

[2] Goals for percentage participation and average gift were set by an outside consulting firm. These goals were set without knowledge of group performance.

[3] These figures excluded receipts in the Law, Parents, and Buck Club Funds which employed a different mailing strategy.

Each mailing in the sequence had a different focus. Most were oriented to the prospect's specific fund: one might be an illustrated leaflet discussing student activities; another a personal appeal from a classmate; a third, a letter in brochure format from a faculty member highlighting new course development and research, and the need for supporting funds; and yet another, a letter from the dean.

Some of the other programs also used mailings. All prospects in the Parents Fund who were not solicited personally received up to three solicitation letters each year, at least one of which was written by a fellow parent. Prospects continued to receive such letters annually from their child's initial year at Stanford until two years after graduation. At that point, parents who had made donations were retained on the prospect list, while non-donors were dropped. In the Phonathon Program all prospects received a preliminary mailing advising them that they would soon receive a phone call asking for a contribution. This mailing usually resulted in a number of immediate gifts, thus saving phone volunteer time.

Organization of Volunteers. One of the strongest features of Stanford's Annual Fund, Mr. Bennett believed, was the extent to which it involved alumni volunteers, especially in setting policy and determining program goals and directions.

Paralleling the professional staffing of each of the different funds and programs were extensive volunteer organizations, each headed by its own national chairman. Coordinating the entire volunteer effort was the Annual Fund Council, which consisted of the national chairman of the Annual Fund, the national chairmen of each program and each fund, plus some *ex-officio* members. The council met semi-annually, reviewed plans for individual programs and funds, and sought to develop an integrated, overall plan in conjunction with Annual Fund staff.

An annual leadership conference for volunteers was held on campus each autumn to update them on university activities, involve them in fundraising planning and coordination, and provide a chance to revisit Stanford. The conference also served as a means of rewarding volunteers for their hard work and included a banquet at which awards were presented to outstanding fund raisers.

The Inner Quad, Quad, and Phonathon Programs were all organized on a regional basis, with the volunteer organization having a hierarchical structure. For instance, the Quad Program was headed by a national chairman, under whom were ten national vice chairmen, each responsible for an average of six regional chairmen. The sixty regions were set up primarily by geographic location, but sometimes also by interest group. There were typically four or five captains in a region, each supervising four or five workers, who in turn were assigned about five prospects each. They pyramidal nature of this organization reflected the large number of prospects (over 8,000) and the low prospect to volunteer ratio. Most of those in supervisory positions also solicited prospects themselves. The Phonathon Program, by contrast, had a much flatter organizational structure, despite its 30,000 prospects. This reflected the smaller number of regions (27), the much higher prospect to volunteer ratio, and the fact that the solicitation process was completed relatively quickly.

Staff members assigned to the different funds and programs were responsible for helping volunteer leaders coordinate their activities, including recruitment and training of new workers. Experienced volunteers helped staff to evaluate performance, provided suggestions for new approaches, assisted in development of communications appeals, and reviewed all printed materials for content and tone.

Coordination and regular contact with all volunteers was viewed as a particularly important task, since experience had shown that messages passed down through the chain of command sometimes became distorted. In mid-summer, staff members traveled out to the different regions and met with regional chairmen and captains to discuss goals for the forthcoming year, recruitment and training of workers, etc. Later, in the fall, a staff member would meet again in a group with each regional chairman, captains, and workers.

At this "kick-off" meeting, the regional chairman, aided by staff members, would attempt to motivate volunteers by providing them with helpful information and literature; he or she would also offer suggestions on how to approach prospects, and emphasize the need to mention the possibility of donors' obtaining tax deductions and/or matching gifts from their employers. In addition, the staff member would distribute assignment cards indicating the names of prospects assigned to individual volunteers. These cards provided brief background information about individual prospects and their past gifts, drawn from computerized records. In the Inner Quad Program, assignment cards contained personal, handwritten comments about each prospect, including (where known) information on activities at Stanford of particular interest to the prospect. An instruction booklet was handed out to all Quad volunteers; its contents are reproduced in the Appendix.

The Phonathom Program was likewise quite demanding in terms of staffing. However, telephone solicitation had proved to be a particularly effective way of getting previous nondonors to make their first gift to the university, and in getting small donors to increase their gifts. Staff members worked closely with regional and community chairmen and assisted with each local phonathon; these typically lasted two evenings but sometimes as long as four in the larger areas. Each volunteer worker received printed suggestions on how to ask for a gift by telephone. Computerized sheets provided brief information on prospects to help the volunteer relate to each one individually.

GOAL SETTING AND PERFORMANCE MEASUREMENT

In a sense, goals for the Annual Fund had been set back in 1972, with the decision to aim for doubling its income by 1978. With the aid of both internal staff studies and outside consultants, estimates had been made of how much each program might expect to raise over the five-year period of the Campaign for Stanford (ending in 1977), together with annual goals for the initial year, 1971–73; these indicated target average gift levels and percentage participation rates. New targets were set annually in light of the previous year's experience and prevailing economic conditions. However, there was a feeling among a number of staff members that

such goals were difficult both to set and to relate to, since in any event they would be trying to maximize the total dollar value of gifts.

One practice which complicated goal setting for individual programs was that prospects were frequently transferred from one program to another. Each year a number of new donors were acquired, many previous donors increased their level of giving, and a number of existing donors reduced or ceased giving.

Directors and staff members of the Inner Quad and Quad Programs refined their prospect lists annually. Inner Quad prospects whose giving performance had been disappointing, and whom volunteer leaders felt were no longer good prospects for gifts of $1000 or more, would be transferred to the Quad Program. Likewise, Quad Program prospects who showed potential for gifts of $1000 or more would be "promoted" to the Inner Quad Program. In the same way, Quad prospects who had not lived up to expectations would be "demoted" to the Mail Appeal or Phonathon which, in turn, would yield their most generous donors to the Quad Program. From the prospects' standpoint, all that would happen was that they might notice that one year they were personally solicited and the next they were solicited by mail or phone (or vice versa).

As shown in Exhibit 7, many prospects solicited by the Inner Quad Program made gifts substantially lower than their forecast $1000 capacity, while many Quad prospects gave much less than $100. On the other hand, a number of Quad, Phonathon and Mail Appeal prospects gave more than $1000. By constantly refining the prospect list for each program the fund raisers hoped to use the most cost-effective means of solicitation, devoting the greatest time and effort to those seen as the best prospects. The Inner Quad was the most "successful" of the four programs, with an average gift of $975 in 1972–73 and 95% of all prospects actually making a gift. By contrast, the Quad Program that year yielded an average gift of $122 and could claim 65% participation. The Mail Appeal and Phonathon Programs naturally yielded much lower figures.

No rigid cut-off points were employed for transferring prospects into or out of the Quad and Inner Quad Programs. Instead, a prospect's past giving record was evaluated and volunteers' advice sought to explain a particularly good or poor giving performance. Sometimes, for instance, a Quad captain might know that the reason why a particular individual had not given was that the volunteer worker assigned had failed to follow through in requesting a gift—rather than lack of generosity by the prospect. Anyone giving $50 or more in the Mail Appeal or Phonathon generally became a candidate for personal solicitation the following year.

The university extended various measures of recognition to donors, depending on the size of the gift. All gifts in excess of $500 were acknowledged by a personal letter from the president. Additionally, most of the funds publicized the names of larger donors (unless they had requested anonym-

EXHIBIT 7
Year End Totals for all Programs 1972–1973 vs. 1971–1972

Gift Size	Inner Quad 71–72	Inner Quad 72–73	Quad 71–72[2]	Quad 72–73	Phonathon 71–72	Phonathon 72–73	Mail 71–72	Mail 72–73	Total Annual Fund 71–72	Total Annual Fund 72–73
Over $5,000 Dollars	NA	563,962	641,953	73,780	—	—	28,759	23,596	912,310	884,613
Donors	NA	45	51	8	—	—	2	2	65	63
$1,001–$5,000 Dollars	NA	311,030	437,501	157,061	—	3,500	25,235	35,823	510,689	572,220
Donors	NA	140	204	72	—	3	14	18	226	253
$501–$1,000 Dollars	NA	150,796	186,492	87,442	1,600	5,118	27,189	11,770	235,202	266,056
Donors	NA	179	230	103	2	6	33	15	282	315
$251–$500 Dollars	NA	94,263	180,850	114,272	1,625	14,567	24,935	23,611	218,612	256,915
Donors	NA	222	442	297	4	36	60	59	532	637
$101–$250 Dollars	NA	50,,26	215,233	219,585	2,045	32,910	41,183	44,676	266,082	353,778
Donors	NA	253	1,158	1,332	11	111	224	247	1,434	1,987
$51–$100 Dollars	NA	18,095	212,465	190,230	5,313	27,091	64,384	62,004	288,316	304,103
Donors	NA	192	2,242	2,066	56	294	679	623	3,041	3,302
$26–$50 Dollars	NA	5,311	102,113	101,700	11,305	30,909	64,370	74,056	180,682	214,983
Donors	NA	109	2,121	2,151	268	698	1,422	1,696	3,873	4,716
$1–$25 Dollars	NA	1,869	44,488	43,040	49,246	62,258	132,615	146,956	240,736	257,911
Donors	NA	86	2,225	2,087	3,492	4,220	8,393	9,499	14,392	16,179
Total: Dollars	NA	1,195,755	2,021,083	987,596	71,214	176,354	408,687	422,495	2,837,639	3,097,660
Donors	NA	1,226	8,663	8,066	3,833	5,427	10,827	12,215	23,845	27,452
Average Gift	NA	975	225	122	18	32	37	34	119	113

Source: University Records.

[1] Includes other Annual Fund contributions (over $300,000 both years from some 500 donors) but excludes Campaign for Stanford capital fund gifts made through the Annual Fund.

[2] Inner Quad data not available separately for 1971–72 and are included with Quad for 1971–72.

ity). The Law School, for example, published an *Annual Report of Giving* to the Stanford Law School, with donors of $100 or more designated into one of five groups of "Fellows," depending on gift size. This publication also listed the names of all volunteers, including many photographs; gave a list of all donors by graduating class or other affiliation (e.g., Friend, Parent, Faculty, etc.); and provided summary statistics by class and by region.

Evaluation, Research, and Testing. Every year, efforts were made to increase the effectiveness of the Annual Fund by evaluating past performance and testing new approaches. In the Inner Quad Program, debriefing sessions were held with as many volunteers as possible. The Quad Program used evaluation forms for the same purpose. Supervisory volun-

teers provided staff members with assessments of the performance of other volunteers directly under them. In this way, a promising worker or captain might be promoted to a more responsible position or assigned more difficult prospects. Likewise, a worker who had been unsuccessful might be given different assignments or else tactfully discouraged from participating. New information was often received which would facilitate future solicitation efforts—for example, it might be learned that a particular prospect had developed a strong interest in a current or proposed research study at Stanford.

A continuing concern in this process was to avoid any invasion of privacy. Thus, the Financial Aid Office would not release information concerning parents' confidential financial statements. It was also questioned whether information on donors' and prospects' business affiliations should be included on future computer records, useful though this might be for encouraging donors to seek corporate matching gifts.

The Mail Appeal Program was constantly test-marketing new approaches on matched samples of prospects. For instance, in 1972–73, using an autotyped* letter for mailing #3 to a selected sample had yielded a 41% higher dollar figure and 16% more donors than the same letter in printed format had raised from a similar group of prospects. The higher cost of autotyping was therefore felt to be justified. On the other hand, use of computer-produced vs. autotyped letters for mailing #1 in the 1973–74 program had, surprisingly, produced no significant difference in dollars raised or participation rates among two matched samples. As a result, it had been decided to use only computer-produced letters for this mailing in 1974–75, at an estimated saving of $18,000. A number of other experiments, involving use of different types of envelopes, metered vs. stamped mail, etc., were also being conducted.

Some felt that it might be more important for the Mail and Phonathon Programs to concentrate on maximizing participation rates as opposed to dollars, since small donors represented the seedbed from which larger gifts might be developed. An ongoing study of alumni giving habits over the years indicated that many major donors had a long history of regular giving to Stanford, and had started by making quite small gifts. Once a donor had adopted a habit of annual giving, it was believed that he or she could often be encouraged to increase the gift size gradually. An important goal of the research program was to seek ways of forecasting the future giving potential of new donors, so that the best prospects might be identified early.

Mr. Bennett prepared a monthly report on Annual Fund performance. This highlighted significant events of the past month, as well as listing cumulative performance figures for each program and fund since the beginning of the fund raising year on September 1. Year-to-date program reports

---

*Autotyping involved the use of a typewriter linked to a memory. After typing in the recipient's name and address, plus the appropriate salutation, the typist would instruct the machine to run the text of a letter stored in the memory. In this way, large numbers of typed, personalized letters could be prepared at a fraction of the cost of individual typing.

were computer-generated in a format similar to (but somewhat more detailed than) Exhibit 7. By comparing these data with those for the same period of the previous year, trends could be identified early. Working with staff and volunteers, Mr. Bennett sought to determine reasons for any significant deviations from projected performance.

LOOKING AHEAD TO 1974–75

By early June 1974, Annual Fund solicitation efforts for 1973–74 were almost completed. Between then and August 31, Bennett expected the fund to receive several hundred thousand dollars more in additional gifts as donors made good on earlier pledges or responded to final appeals. Exhibit 4 shows his projections. On June 6, he presented year-to-date results through the end of May. Bennett noted that the stock market slump and solicitation for major gifts ($100,000+) for the Campaign for Stanford were believed to have affected the number and size of large donations. He summarized progress:

> Annual Fund totals reached $2,772,525 and 23,537 donors compared with $2,732,769 and 22,995 at the same time last year. This represents an increase of 1% in dollars and an increase of 2% in donors. The Annual Fund continues to parallel last year's dollar level, maintaining an increase of between 1% and 2%. Our latest forecast is for another $3.1 million year.

In considering goal-setting for the coming year, Bennett was concerned at what effect increased solicitation for the Campaign for Stanford might have on annual giving levels in 1974–75. He also wondered at the impact of continuing inflation in the context of a sluggish economy. Some authorities believed that large gifts might be worse hit in a depressed stock market than smaller ones. Another concern was rising costs. The present expenses associated with the Annual Fund approximated 11% of the value of the gifts. Recent test-marketing programs by the Mail Appeal showed excellent potential for reducing the costs of mail solicitation without adversely influencing giving practices. Could less expensive solicitation approaches be used to reach donors with equal effectiveness? Could prospects for telephone solicitation be segmented in similar fashion to Mail Appeal prospects and receive appropriately different treatments? Indeed, should some Phonathon prospects be solicited instead by mail?

Appendix

Stanford Annual Fund: Instructions for Quad Program Volunteers

Your Job as a Quad Volunteer

Thank you for volunteering to do an invaluable job for Stanford. You have only a few prospects to call on, but they are Quad prospects—a select group chosen for their past generosity to and interest in Stanford—important enough to deserve your personal solicitation. The five sections of this booklet are designed to help you make successful calls.

1. Familiarize yourself with the background material.
2. Complete your calls by the first week in November.
3. Fill out and return staff copy of assignment card immediately after meeting with each prospect.
4. Follow up on each prospect until he gives a gift, signs a pledge, or definitely says no.
5. Thank any of your prospects who make gifts in this fund year, whether or not it was in response to your solicitation.

1
Familiarize yourself with the background material

The following are things you might need to know before making your first call, and some sources of further useful information.

Sound Reasons for Giving to Stanford: Stanford is relatively underendowed compared to the few other universities of its caliber. Furthermore, tuition covers only about 42 percent of the actual cost of a Stanford education. Therefore, the University literally lives on gifts from alumni, parents, and friends.

How Stanford Raises Funds: In addition to seeking endowment and expendable gifts from foundations, corporations, associations, and individuals who are not alumni, Stanford asks *all* its alumni for gifts *every* year.

The $300-Million Campaign for Stanford: Currently Stanford is in the midst of the single largest fund-raising drive ever undertaken by a university. Over the five years beginning April 11, 1972, all alumni, parents, and friends of the University will be asked to make one gift to the Campaign, over and above their regular annual gifts.

The Annual Fund: The Annual Fund's task is to ask Stanford's more than 90,000 alumni for gifts every year. It is divided into four programs—Mail, Phonathon, Quad, and Inner Quad—each of which matches its solicitation techniques to its prospects' expected giving levels. The Annual Fund's goal within the Campaign is to double the level of annual gifts and increase alumni participation.

Your Part—The Quad Program: As a Quad volunteer, you are one of Stanford's most important fund-raisers. 1,300 Quad volunteers divided into geographical regions will personally call on 7,600 selected prospects who have already shown their interest in the university and their generosity.

The Quad's goals are: (1) to call on every prospect, (2) to ask each one to increase his gift over last year.

A Quad *prospect* is any person assigned to a Quad volunteer for solicitation. Prospects normally give between $50 and $500. A Quad *member* is anyone who gave $100 to $1,000 in one fund year—September 1 through August 31. Members' names appear in the Quad Annual Report.

The Professional Funds and Buck Club: In addition to the division by giving level, the Annual Fund is divided into eight funds according to prospects' Stanford affiliation and where their gifts will be used. The funds are Engineering, Business, Graduate, Earth Sciences, Medical, Law, Class, and Buck Club. Whenever possible, volunteers and prospects are matched by fund affiliation to increase the likelihood of successful solicitation.

The Million Dollar Challenge Pledge: An important aid in encouraging your prospects to increase their gifts and meeting the Annual Fund's doubling goal is the Challenge Pledge. Again this year, an anonymous donor will match all new and increased gifts to Stanford, one dollar for two dollars.

The Stanford Staff's Function: The staff person whose card is in the front pocket of this booklet is there to help you. You can count on him or her to: (1) answer any questions and send you any additional material; (2) answer any of your prospects' questions or complaints *with copies to you;* (3) send you biweekly computer reports of your progress, and ensure the accuracy of the reports.

Informative University Publications: As a Quad volunteer, you receive the *Campus Report,* a weekly newspaper for faculty and staff, and the *Observer,* a monthly newspaper sent to all alumni. Both give a comprehensive view of what is currently happening at Stanford.

Two of the brochures in the back of this booklet—"Stanford Facts," and "What You Give Is Stanford," which you may give to your prospects— tell more of the University's story.

2
Complete Your Calls by the First Week in November

You are the Link with Stanford. Remember that as a volunteer for Stanford, you are not begging for money. It is human nature to give, and you are simply directing a portion of your prospect's philanthropy to a cause you both believe in. Your call is one of many which—in total—literally maintain the University.

Give Your Own Gift First. Your gift to Stanford is as important as anyone's, of course, and it will be easier and more natural for you to ask your prospects to increase their gifts after you have increased your own.

Start Immediately. Call on all your prospects within the first two weeks after the kick-off meeting, leaving plenty of time for follow-up. Your prospects have received a mailing telling them of Stanford's needs and including the Quad Donors list, so they are expecting you to call on them. The first call is the most difficult, but once you begin you will take them in your stride. Be positive, make a friend, have fun, and persevere.

The job must be completed early in the fall: first, so that each prospect will have the opportunity to determine the size of his gift with respect to his tax situation, and second, because you will find it difficult to call on prospects during the Christmas rush.

The Approach. There is no one technique for asking for a gift. Think about how you personally operate and what techniques you use from day to day that you are most comfortable with. Generally you will find that being direct, laying your cards on the table, is the best approach. How will the donor know what you want unless you ask for it?

Know Your Prospects and When They Last Gave to Stanford. The assignment card (see Section 3) tells you the prospect's giving record, school affiliation, and other useful information. Some of your prospects may well have given last year's gift as recently as last summer. Note the date of each prospect's last gift on the assignment card and take this into account. He may not want to give again this soon, so encourage him to sign a pledge for this fund year's gift.

Call and Make an Appointment. Call the prospect and identify yourself as a graduate of Stanford. Thank him for his past gifts, and ask for an appointment to see him about Stanford. This is a unique opportunity to meet a new friend with whom you share a mutual interest. The prospect may ask you to discuss his giving over the phone. It is preferable to see him in person, but if he wishes to make a commitment over the phone, let him do so. At least you have let the prospect know that you are committed enough to spend your time with him. This is important to your effort.

Relate to the Prospect. Try to establish a relationship with the prospect on the basis of your mutual interest. If you can establish that you were graduated from the same discipline, do so. Don't be afraid to say "I don't know" when asked question about unfamiliar ground; but be sure to turn the question to a plus by indicating that you will ask Stanford to respond personally—thus letting him know that the University is interested in its alumni.

Tell Him You Have Made Your Own Gift Already.

Ask for a Specific Dollar Gift. Remind the prospect that Stanford literally depends on alumni gifts and that you are there to ask for his gift. It has been proven that asking for a specific dollar amount is the most effective way to raise money. If your prospect is giving below the $100 Quad level, ask for a gift of at least $100. If he is giving $100 or more, ask for a 50 percent increase unless the gift was recently doubled. You should have a specific dollar amount in mind before you make the call. The amount may seem high to you but you cannot make that assumption for the prospect.

You are always in a better position bargaining down to a lower level than bargaining the other way. Once again, the way you ask depends upon your personality, but be as direct as possible. "I would like you to consider a gift of $100 to Stanford this year."

Remember the Challenge Pledge. Remind the prospect that any increase over his last year's gift will be matched one for two by the Million Dollar Challenge Pledge. Then mention exactly how much extra money he can earn for Stanford by making a certain increase over last year.

A few reminders:

Challenge Pledge Money earned by gifts to professional funds—Business, Earth Sciences, Law, Medical, Engineering, Graduate—goes unrestricted to the particular school.

Gifts to the Buck Club earn matching Challenge Pledge money, which goes unrestricted to the Athletic Department.

Get a Definite Reply. Should he agree to give a gift, thank him, ask for the check, and tell him you will make sure it gets to the proper authority. If he cannot pay then, get a signed pledge. If he will not sign a pledge, try to get a clear idea of the amount and the date he is considering, and remember to call again on that date. Should he wish to think about it, ask for a date when you should call back for his decision. Should the prospect decide not to give to Stanford this year, try to get the reason.

The process of learning the prospect's intentions, and following up on them, is what makes our personal solicitation program worthwhile.

Be Generous with Your Thanks. Thank the prospect for his time, interest in the University, and continued financial support. You should thank him in person and send him a letter to reinforce his decision. The University will also write to him, which will be a further stimulus for future gifts.

Look into Corporate Matching Gifts. The companies listed in the brochure "Two Can Give as Easily as One" (in the back of this booklet) match their employees' donations to educational institutions. Check your prospect's employer—from the assignment card or from the prospect—against this list. If his employer has such a program, the prospect has only to get the appropriate forms from the company's personnel department and forward them to Stanford with the gift.

If it does not appear already, note the prospect's business address on the staff copy of the assignment card.

The Challenge Pledge does not match the company's matching gift to Stanford—only the donor's gift.

Point Out the East of Giving Securities. An endorsed stock certificate naming Stanford University as transferee may be sent by registered mail or through the donor's broker to the General Secretary, 301 Encina Hall, Stanford, California 94305.

It may be sent with instructions for Stanford to keep a specified number of gift shares and reissue a certificate in the donor's name for the balance.

Explain the Advantage of Giving Securities. If the stock has increased in value, the donor does not pay capital-gain tax on the appreciation. If he or she has owned the stock for more than six months, its gift to Stanford may be claimed as a charitable deduction.

(If sales of the stock would result in a deductible loss, it will be more advantageous to the donor to sell, take the loss, and make the gift to Stanford by check.)

For further information on giving securities, write to the above address telephone (415) 321-2300, extension 2291.

Critical Dates:

Early October—Prospects received mailing alerting them that volunteers would soon be calling.

Within Two Weeks after Kick-Off Meeting—You call on your prospects.

November 1 through Thanksgiving—Your Quad Captain and Regional Chairman will take the assignment cards of those prospects you did not reach and call on them.

December—You follow up on prospects who are uncommitted.

February—Those prospects who still have not given a gift, signed a pledge, or definitely said no will be sent a follow-up reminder mailing unless you ask your staff member not to send the mailing to a particular prospect.

3
Fill Out and Return Staff Copy of Assignment Card
Immediately after Meeting with Each Prospect

Volunteer Copy. The top of the assignment card, shown below, is your copy on which you may keep all notes of your calls on the prospect.

Staff Copy. The second copy is the staff copy, the back of which is your report to staff on the results of your first meeting with your prospect. The important thing to remember is that it should be filled out immediately after the call and as completely as possible. It is from this information that (1) the staff will derive your computer progress reports, and (2) next year's volunteer will familiarize himself with the prospect's record.

Gift/Pledge Card. The third copy of the assignment card is the gift/pledge card, which either you or your prospect will mail to Stanford with the gift or as a *signed* pledge.

Computer Progress Report. You will receive a computer progress report every two weeks, based on your reports to staff and showing all recorded gifts. From these reports you will know which of your prospects to follow up and which to call and thank for their gifts.

If a progress report is incorrect, please correct and return it to your staff contact.

Assignment Card.

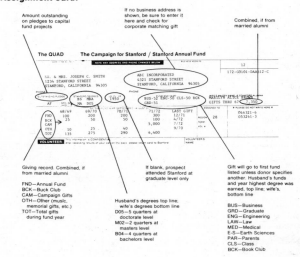

4
Follow Up on Each Prospect Until He Gives a Gift,
Signs a Pledge, or Definitely Says No

Last year we had one out six people still "pending" (intended to give and have not) at the end of the fund year. The goal this year, and your job, is to get definite answers from each prospect about his intentions. If a person does not choose to give or sign a pledge now, he will remain a pending. Be as specific as possible about pendings. Find out the approximate amount they would like to give, and the approximate date, and follow up on that date. If they cannot be that specific, try to get another follow-up date.

Check your computer progress reports against each prospect's stated intentions. If any planned to send gifts and haven't done so, call on them again.

5
Thank Any of Your Prospects Who Make Gifts in This Fund Year,
Whether or Not It Was in Response to Your Solicitation

Write or call each donor to let him know that Stanford is aware of and grateful for his gift in this fund year (September 1, 1973, through August 31, 1974).

Notice of such gifts will come to you on your computer progress reports.

If you see that a prospect made a gift without your calling on him, please be sure to call and offer your thanks. It may be that he wishes to make an additional gift in response to your call.

Thank you for the time and effort you are giving Stanford as a Quad volunteer. Here's to success with every one of your prospects.

Source: *1973 Quad Volunteer Guide*

31
Ethical Problems in Marketing Research

Charles B. Weinberg

Marketing managers and marketing researchers are frequently confronted by ethical problems and dilemmas. Gathering, analyzing, and presenting information raise a number of important ethical questions in which the manager's need to know and understand the market, in order to develop effective marketing programs, must be balanced against an individual's right to privacy. Just as a glass of water may be viewed as being "half empty" or "half full," the emphasis placed on the empirical results of marketing research can alter its interpretation by decision makers.

The following material presents a set of ethical dilemmas that might arise in a market research setting. Your assignment is to decide what action to take in each instance. You should be prepared to justify your decision. Bear in mind that there are no "right" or "wrong" answers; reasonable people may choose different courses of action.

1. As marketing director of a large hospital, you are given the suggestion by the executive director that former patients be telephoned by hospital volunteers under the name of a fictitious market research agency. The purpose of the survey is to help assess the perceived quality of care received by patients, and it is felt that the suggested procedure will result in more objective responses. What action would you take?

a. Approve the procedure?
b. Do not approve the procedure?
c. Other (specify)?

2. You are supervising a study of family planning organizations conducted for an agency of the Federal Government. The data, which have already been collected, include information on race, age and marital status of clients. Respondent organizations have been promised confidentiality. The Federal agency demands that all responses be identified by organization name. Their rationale is that they plan to repeat the study and wish to limit sampling error by returning to the same respondents. Open bidding requires that the government maintain control of the sample. What action would you take?

a. Provide the identified questionnaires to the agency?
b. Provide questionnaires to the organization that is ultimately selected for the follow-up survey?
c. Refuse to provide anyone with questionnaires identified by name?
d. Other (specify)?

These ethical problems have been generated from a number of sources, including C. Merle Crawford, "Attitudes of Marketing Executives Toward Ethics in Marketing Research," *Journal of Marketing* (April 1970), pp. 46–52. The settings chosen here are fictional but are representative of real problems. Charles B. Weinberg is Professor of Marketing, University of British Columbia.

3. You are executive director of a performing arts organization. Your assistant requests permission to use ultra-violet ink in precoding questionnaires on a mail survey of subscribers. He points out that the accompanying letter refers to a confidential survey, but he needs to be able to identify respondents to permit adequate cross-tabulation of the data and to save on postage costs if a second mailing is required. What action would you take?

    a. Approve use of ultra-violet ink?
    b. Refuse permission?
    c. Other (specify)?

4. Your company, along with several other well known market research companies, has been asked to prepare a research proposal to study the trial and repeat rates of buyers of state lottery tickets. The lottery proceeds, which help to support the state's welfare program, have fallen short of the original goals. The director of the lottery is unsure if this is because too few people have ever bought tickets or because not enough of those who try the lottery repeat their purchases on a regular basis. In particular, the director wants to relate geographic and socio-economic factors to lottery ticket purchases. The director claims that the lottery takes revenue away from illegal numbers rackets; others claim that it induces participation from those who can least afford to gamble. Because the state takes at least 40 percent of the total receipts for social welfare programs, many illegal numbers games return more to the bettors than does the state lottery. As president of the company, what do you do?

    a. Prepare a proposal and bid on the project?
    b. Do not bid on the project?
    c. Do not bid on the project and attempt to convince others to do likewise?
    d. Other (specify)?

5. You are employed by a marketing research firm and have conducted an attitude study for a public agency which is trying to promote energy conservation. Your data indicate that energy conservation is not being marketed properly by the agency. This finding is ill received by the agency's administrators. They request that you omit that data from your formal report, which you know will be widely distributed, on the grounds that the verbal presentation was adequate for their needs. What do you do?

    a. Include all data in your formal report?
    b. Exclude the marketing data as requested?
    c. Other (specify)?

6. You are a project director on a study funded by a somewhat unpopular federal agency. The study is on marijuana use among young men in your community and its relationship, if any, to crime. You will be using a structured questionnaire to gather data for the agency on marijuana use and criminal activities. You believe that if you reveal the name of the funding agency and/or the actual purposes of the study to respondents, you will seriously depress response rates and thereby increase non-response bias. What information would you disclose to respondents?

    a. Name of funding agency?
    b. The specific purposes of the project?
    c. Both of the above?
    d. Neither of the above?
    e. Other (specify)?

7. You are employed by a market research company. A state consumer protection agency has retained your firm to conduct a study for them. They wish to know something about how women choose clothing, such as blouses and sweaters, to determine the possible effect on purchase decisions of different labeling programs about the care and durability of clothing. They wish to conduct group interviews, supplemented by a session which would be devoted to observing the women trying on clothing, in order to discover how thoroughly they touch and examine the clothing, and whether they look for and read a label or price tag. The client suggests that the observation be performed unobtrusively by female observers at a local department store, via a one-way mirror. One of your associates argues that this would constitute an invasion of privacy. What action would you take?

    a. Refuse to do the study?
    b. Insist upon telling the women they will be observed?
    c. Do the study as the consumer protection agency wants it?
    d. Other (specify)?

8. You are a study director for a research company undertaking a project for a state agency. A study you are working on is about to go into the field when the questionnaire you sent to the client for final approval comes back drastically modified. The agency official has rewritten it introducing leading questions and biased scales. An accompanying letter indicates that the questionnaire must be sent out as revised. You do not believe that valid information can be gathered using the revised instrument. What action would you take?

a. Run the study as directed?
b. Try to explain to the official what his revisions will probably mean to the value of the study and then proceed as he wishes?
c. Conduct the study using the revised instrument, but qualify the results in the final report?
d. Refuse to continue with the study because you feel it may yield erroneous information?
e. Other (specify)?

9. A well respected public figure is going to face trial on a conspiracy charge brought by the U.S. Justice Department. The defense lawyers have asked you, as a market research specialist, to do a research study to determine the characteristics of people most likely to sympathize with the defendant and hence to vote for acquittal. The defense lawyers have read newspaper accounts of how this approach has been used in a number of instances (for example, the 1974 criminal conspiracy trial of John N. Mitchell and Maurice H. Stans, and the 1976 trial of Joan Little, a Black woman accused of murdering a jailer who allegedly attacked her). What do you do?

a. Carry out the research?
b. Carry out the research, but report the results to the Justice Department as well?
c. Refuse to carry out the assignment?
d. Other (specify)?

32
London Goodwill Industries Association: Used Bookstore

Judith Marshall
David Burgoyne

"Last year our sales exceeded $1,000,000 and we employed 127 handicapped people. We want to continue to grow and to do so we need to consider new ways of expanding sales. Opening a used bookstore may be part of the answer as we have never really paid much attention to books. Some people give us books, we process them, we put them in our existing stores and we sell most of them. The net result is that we create work and sales revenue. What we could do if we were really serious about books is the issue and I've been instructed to prepare a report for our next Board of Directors meeting [September 1981]. At this point I'm not sure we have sufficient information to make such a decision, but on the other hand, I'm not sure what other information could or should be generated."

The above comments were made by Mr. Peter De Gelder, Executive Director of London Goodwill Industries Association (L.G.I.) to the case writer in August, 1981. A board member had requested that Mr. De Gelder investigate the feasibility of opening a second-hand book store as a means of creating additional jobs and increasing sales revenues. Although L.G.I. had no economic ties with other Goodwill Associations throughout North America, ideas and information were exchanged at seminars and conventions. Mr. De Gelder knew that the Toronto Goodwill Association had a very large and recently upgraded store devoted to books adjacent to their plant in the general downtown area. Despite the fact that the store was not located close to many offices or major shopping areas, first year sales amounted to some $75,000 per year. Management felt the space could be reduced and the volume held or increased in future years. Two clients were employed in the book area. Mr. De Gelder was also aware that a number of U.S. Goodwill Associations all located in major metropolitan centres operated second-hand book stores. The Boston group attributed their success to the large university population in the city.

London itself is a city of 250,000 people, located in the southwestern part of the province of Ontario, Canada. Located approximately two hours drive by automobile from Toronto, London is the home of the University of Western Ontario. London has a diversified industrial and commercial base and is regarded as a regional center in Southwestern Ontario. Additional demographic and market data about London are included in the Appendix.

L.G.I.—Background

The goal of L.G.I. was to employ handicapped skills, to provide them with effective work adjustment training and life skills development as a means of preparing them for jobs in industry, and enabling them to lead more personally satisfying lives. An important factor here was taking clients off public assistance and making them self supporting. The

Judith Marshall is a doctoral student and David Burgoyne is Adjunct Professor at the School of Business Administration, University of Western Ontario.

EXHIBIT 1
Client Totals by Handicap
(Not more than three descriptors per client)

Orthopedic 12
Cardio-Vascular 4
Mental Retardation...........................24
Respiratory 3
Visual Defects 1
Speech and Hearing Defects 3
Mental Illness................................63
Socially Handicapped 9
Cerebral Palsy 4
Epilepsy 12
Alcoholism 18
Learning Disability 17
Brain Damage 2
Diabetes 1
Multiple Sclerosis 1
Obesity 3
Dialysis 1
Dwarfism 1
Autism 1

---

handicaps served covered a wide range including physical, mental, social and emotional (see Exhibit 1). Clients' abilities were fairly high when compared to some of the "sheltered" workshops in the area who served individuals whose disabilities were such that there was little or no expectation that they would ever work in industry. L.G.I. also provided a sheltered work environment as not all clients developed to the levels necessary to enter competitive employment. Others developed sufficient work skills and other capacities to handle jobs in industry, but their handicaps (i.e., epilepsy) were such that they were effectively precluded from being hired by many companies.

Clients were paid hourly wages ranging between 70%–110% of the minimum wage ($3.50 per hour as of November 1981). Because of the nature of its operation, L.G.I. had not historically been subject to minimum wage regulations, although there was some pressure from outside groups to change this. Clients entering employment at L.G.I. usually had income sources from public assistance programs such as Disability Pension and Workmen's Compensation, which ranged from less to more than they could expect to earn at L.G.I. Clients were expected to forego these income sources when employed permanently at L.G.I. This represented a major personal commitment to self development, as once clients moved off their assistance programs, reinstatement of their prior assistance source if things did not work out at L.G.I. was not necessarily assured. During their six month probationary period at L.G.I., most clients chose to retain their public assistance funding sources and during this period they were paid token wages of about 50¢ per hour.

Non-handicapped employees of L.G.I. were employed in management, supervisory, professional counselling positions or positions requiring specialized skills such as truck driver, or refrigeration repair technician. They were paid competitive salaries which ranged from $9,500 to $30,000 per year. These individuals were generally fully functioning but, in fact, a number of the store managers by general standards would be considered as having physical disabilities, e.g., leg braces, severe weight problems. L.G.I. employed four counsellors with Social Work degrees who developed special development programs which included weekly counling sessions for all clients. Additionally, all managers, supervisors and other non-handicapped employees were involved to a considerable degree in the client development process as an important, integral part of their responsibilities. L.G.I. skills in client development were such that government agencies sent individuals to them for 3 to 6 month periods for work assessment training, and L.G.I. was paid a fee for these services.

An additional service to the community at large provided by L.G.I. was provision of articles of clothing, furniture and household goods at bargain prices. This was accomplished via their eleven retail outlets, through their special twice yearly sales held in the Progress Building at the London Western Fairgrounds, and through other special event sales such as sidewalk sales and yard sales.

Funding. L.G.I.was incorporated in 1955 as a not-for-profit organization. This status qualified it for funding grants from governments and allowed it to give tax deductible receipts for financial donations but not for donated articles. The founder of Goodwill Industries International had envisioned the organization not as a traditional charity, but rather as "a business with a head and a heart." The founder of Goodwill Industries, a Boston minister, had become disillusioned with the demoralizing effect of giving donated goods to indigent people. He moved to an approach whereby donated goods were sold rather than given away. The funds generated were utilized to pay wages to people with disabilities who would be encouraged to utilize and develop their abilities. Individuals would be expected to function as effectively as they could rather than at some standard level; but, the sum of the efforts had to somehow produce enough funds to keep the operation viable. Operating within this philosophy, L.G.I. strived to operate in as businesslike, self-sufficient a way as possible while recognizing that their goal was to employ and develop handicapped adults (see Exhibit 2).

For the previous few years, L.G.I. had received about 6% of its operating* costs from grants and donations (largely provincial, to some extent municipal and nominally from individuals and groups). The remaining 94% was generated mostly from retail sales. Although the Board recognized that

---

*All financial data refers to operations only. There was also a capital fund which covered all major assets (chiefly real estate with a total value of about $900,000) and for which funding was different (government grants on approved projects were 80% and public campaigns were also held).

EXHIBIT 2
Statement of Operating Fund Revenue:
Expense and Equity (Deficit)

	Twelve Months Ended March 31, 1980	Fifteen Months[a] Ended March 31, 1979
Revenue		
Operations		
Sales of donated merchandise	$ 961,044	$ 907,318
Wiper sales net of related purchases	56,380	
Salvage	49,090	85,988
Training Fees	20,080	21,450
Contract Work	3,910	3,814
	$1,090,504	$1,018,570
Other		
Rentals	4,160	450
Interest	3,162	3,323
Donations	97	572
Miscellaneous	1,249	4,941
	8,668	9,286
	$1,099,172	$1,027,856
Expense		
Salaries, Wages and Employee Benefits		
Handicapped employees and trainees	$ 409,205	$ 403,982
Service and administrative personnel	419,260	403,178
	828,465	807,160
Premises	234,084	270,143
Administration	81,784	64,523
Cartage	67,160	34,437
Production	44,082	51,978
Rehabilitation	8,541	11,812
	$1,264,116	$1,240,053
Loss from Operations Before Grants	164,944[b]	212,197
Grants		
Province of Ontario	92,938	199,819
The Corporation of the City of London	1,627	2,500
	$ 94,565	$ 202,319
Excess of Expense Over Revenue	70,379	9,878
Equity at Beginning of Period	27,347	37,225
Equity (Deficit) at End of Period	$ (43,032)	$27,347

Balance Sheet as at March 31, 1980

Operating Fund
Assets

	1980	1979
Current Assets		
Term deposits	$ 31,500	$ 31,188
Training fees receivable	2,200	1,900
Accounts receivable	20,582	13,786
Receivable from the Province of Ontario	10,088	55,676
Prepaid expenses	8,827	10,901
	$ 73,197	$113,451

Liabilities and Equity

	1980	1979
Current Liabilities		
Bank indebtedness	$ 51,577	$ 15,607
Accounts payable and accrued liabilities	46,256	44,105
Payable to capital fund	18,396	26,392
	$116,229	$ 86,104
Equity (Deficit) in Operating Assets	(43,032)[b]	27,347
	$ 73,197	$113,451

[a]The fiscal year for L.G.I. had previously been on a calendar year basis but the Provincial Government had 'requested' that it be changed to conform to that of the Government.

[b]Application for privincial grants to cover this amount had been approved but would be payable in the next fiscal year.

total financial self-sufficiency was probably not possible in the short run, they constantly strived to attain this goal both as a matter of philosophy and practicality. They recognized that funding from governments was by no means guaranteed in perpetuity; that excessive reliance on this funding source was risky and at times fraught with administrative problems in dealing with the various departments involved.

Therefore, in developing plans and when considering new projects, the Board constantly faced trade-offs between providing employment and development opportunities for clients while striving to attain their goal of operating on a sound financial basis. Although the hourly rates paid to clients were at the minimum wage level and goods were donated, low worker productivity, high supervisory levels (1 to 5 ratio) and the provision of counselling support (1 to 30 ratio) were expensive. The goal of moving out the most productive clients to competitive employment positions in order to replace them with low performing new clients was expensive, and opposite to the goals of most firms who strove to keep their most productive employees.

SIZE AND GROWTH

L.G.I.had been very growth-oriented, particularly during the previous decade. This growth could be measured in terms of jobs created, clients placed in outside employment, number of stores operated and number of customers served (see Exhibit 3). The sales growth had been accomplished by up-grading existing retail outlets, opening new outlets, changing the production system to maximize the sales revenues generated from processed donations, and adding new product lines. Some years previously, the Board and the executive staff had spent considerable time considering a wide range of new product line possibilities (manufacturing; house cleaning, etc.), but had decided to pursue a strategy of continuing to ''do what they were doing only doing it better'' as being most appropriate, at least in the short run.

One recent project of this nature that had been particularly successful was the wiper department. Some of the clothing donated had always been non-saleable (recognized when received or eventually returned from stores) and was baled and sold for about 10¢ per kilogram as salvage. This salvage was now sorted to find those made of absorbent material types, which were then cut into squares, packaged in 15 kilogram boxes and sold to janitorial groups, painters, machine shops, etc. Wipers sold at much higher rates per kilogram than salvage, and sales in 1979–80 amounted to some $56,000 per year and were increasing each month. Most importantly, ten new client positions had been developed, and the type of work created was most desirable from a rehabilitative standpoint as individual production was measurable, and the use of machinery was involved.

Another example of attempting to improve on present business involved the furniture department. A paint stripping facility had been purchased and, in addition to using it on

EXHIBIT 3
London Goodwill Industries Association Growth—Evidence from Selected Years

	Average Number of Workers Employed Daily	Placed in Outside Employment	Number of Stores Operating	Estimated Number of Customers Served	Retail Sales
1980–81	127	6	11	285,191	$1,111,740
1979–80	103	12	10	266,295	961,044
1977–78	82	8	9	183,607	612,875
1976	82	9	9	157,728	526,409
1974	71	14	6	127,479	345,326
1969	38	0	3	59,104	117,136

donated goods to make them saleable and/or improve their resale value, it was also used to do furniture stripping for the general public on a fee basis. As well as adding additional revenues, both from the sales of upgraded furniture and from contract stripping, this expansion also provided additional client positions. The skills required provided a nice complement to the positions in the clothing operation and were comparable to those needed in some "competitive" employment positions.

The overall growth of L.G.I. had been attained by an aggressive stance on the part of the Board who were prepared to take reasonable risks in the interest of growth. Although it was expected that new stores would continue to be opened and the upgrading of stores continued, it was recognized that this form of growth had potential limitations from both a market and donation standpoint. It was also felt that further production system changes to upgrade resale values of the current product mix also had long run limitations. The disturbing factor was the current waiting list of potential clients who wanted to become involved as workers with L.G.I. for whom there were no positions presently available and the recognition that the demand for the kind of services provided by L.G.I. would continue to grow.

Operations. L.G.I. operated 11 retail outlets in the London area (see Exhibit 4 for location and sales data). One outlet sold furniture only, while all the others carried the major lines of men's, women's and children's clothing, as well as shoes, housewares, books and to the extent that individual store space permitted, some furniture and appliances. L.G.I. attempted to achieve between $30 and $50 in sales per square foot in all their outlets.

Although manufacturers, wholesalers and retailers at times made most welcome donations of new goods, 99% of the merchandise processed and sold consisted of used goods donated by householders of the community. Donors could call L.G.I. for home pick-up or place their donations in one of the 50 yellow bins located at convenient locations such as malls, churches, service stations, and factories throughout the area. Most furniture and appliances came from household

pick-ups while clothing, shoes and books, largely came from the yellow bins.

All goods from the yellow bins or from pick-ups were taken to the plant dock and then sorted, prepared for sale (furniture repaired, shoes cleaned, clothing cleaned), priced and then organized for shipment to the stores. Store managers could indicate their preferences for goods to be sent to them, but of necessity, shipments to stores were a function of what was available from donations, which did not neces-

EXHIBIT 4
Retail Store Analysis 1980–81

Location	Total Sales Revenue	Store Area Square Feet	Sales Per Square Foot
295 Richmond London	$198.990	4,020	$49.50
266 Richmond London	97,630	1,790	54.54
615 Dundas London	226,850	4,600	49.52
908 Oxford London	76,380	1,490	51.26
1474 Dundas London	84,420	1,690	49.95
840 Dulaney London	70,720	1,630	43.39
St. Thomas (15 miles from London)	99,910	1,560	64.05
	99,910	1,560	64.05
Woodstock (40 miles from London)	81,530	1,300	62.72
Stratford (40 miles from London)	95,320	1,040	91.65
Brantford (50 miles from London)	9,990	1,540	51.95
aKitchener (60 miles from London)		3,300	
	$1,111,740		

aNew, opened April 1981.

sarily fit a store manager's specific needs at a particular point in time.

Overall donations were sufficient, but tended to be somewhat cyclical (Spring and Fall were particularly heavy) and not consistent with store sales levels. In addition, seasonality was a problem particularly with some clothing. Winter garments were donated in the Spring, and it was necessary to inventory both unprocessed donations and processed goods. There were real limitations to this, particularly with some unprocessed donations which could deteriorate in storage. Other problems included space costs and the double handling costs that were involved.

Donors and Customers. No serious research had been conducted on donors or retail customers. It was believed that they represented two different socio-economic groups within the community. Four years previously home pick-up donors not only received the usual personalized letter of thanks, but were also mailed a gift coupon worth $1 redeemable in merchandise at any of the stores. Less than one half of 1% were ever redeemed, and they were not necessarily redeemed by the original donors.

Although it was believed that the majority of L.G.I. store customers came from lower income groups, recently management had noted an increasing number of customers from other income levels who shopped at L.G.I. stores because of the very real bargains that were available (shirts $1.79 to $3.98; men's suits $5.69 to $14.98; dresses $2.29 to $7.79). The store upgrading approach had been designed to "make it difficult for an individual to realize they were in a second-hand store." The stigma associated with buying second-hand goods (particularly clothing) was felt to be lessening with the tightening economy and the whole phenomena associated with the conserver society and the recycling of goods of all kinds.

Store Personnel. The existing stores operated with a store manager and three to seven clients, depending on store size. The initial assignment for clients at a store involved hanging clothes and straightening up merchandise in the display bins and shelves. Development opportunities involved: (a) learning to operate the cash register (all goods were pre-priced with tags at the plant), (b) making deposits, and (c) opening and closing the store. The hours of operation for all stores had been set at 9:30 a.m. to 5:30 p.m., 6 days a week. Clients working in the stores had their weekly counselling sessions with their counsellors at the store in a small room set up solely for this purpose.

Promotion. L.G.I. currentlly utilized seven methods of promotion:

1. *Regular Media* (radio, newspaper, T.V., billboards, bus signs) which the organization received on a no-charge basis as part of the media's community service. This included regular spots and insertions along with other paying advertisers as well as occasional news and editorial features in newspapers, on radio and on T.V. L.G.I. worked hard to ensure that all media were contacted regularly so they always had updated, appropriate materials for their use on hand. The media had been most generous in slotting in L.G.I. messages when time or space was available (full price $30,000). This promotional approach, of course, did not necessarily result in L.G.I. receiving the slots and times they might have selected themselves. In addition, the message content preferred for use by the media were those stressing the community service provided by L.G.I. and the need for donated goods. The media were most reluctant to use materials which focused on the retail activities, even when L.G.I. felt this was needed. It was felt that to retain this generous support, the purchase of media space from any one particular media source could jeopardize the privileges received from the whole media community.

2. *Classified Ads.* To support new store openings or the development of new product lines (i.e., furniture stripping), small classified ads running for a number of weeks were purchased from time to time.

3. *Public Appearances.* Some 55 speeches (with slides) to service clubs, church groups, etc. were given each year by two of the members of the senior staff of L.G.I. The content stressed the community services provided by L.G.I., the need for donations with some mention of the retail store bargains.

4. *Plant Tours.* Various groups in the community were given plant and store tours each year (20 groups in 1981 involving 260 people) which ended with a talk with slides on L.G.I.

5. *Direct Mail.* L.G.I. issued discount cards to anyone who completed an application form (10% off regular prices when purchases were made at the retail outlets). About three times per year these 30,000 discount card holders were mailed flyers announcing store openings, special sales, etc.

6. *Flyer Distribution.* Once or twice per year, the cooperation of one of the food chains was obtained to distribute flyers at the checkout counters of all their stores in the London area. These usually were used to announce special sales or new store openings. Flyers were also distributed in the general area surrounding any new stores at the time of opening.

7. *In-Store Promotions.* Not only did each store use signs within the store for their merchandise promotions, but also large signs were put up within stores to indicate other store locations, new store openings, special sales, and new product lines.

THE BOOK STORE ALTERNATIVE

Sales of books amounted to about $26,000 in 1981. This included paper back romances, textbooks from all educational levels, hardcovers of various types and vintages, plus 3 or 4 magazines (*Playboy* and *National Geographic* at 50¢ each were popular) with paperbacks being the major sales generator. About 60% of the books donated were paperbacks, 40% were hardcovers. However, during sorting, more hardcover books had to be discarded, as hardcovers from the

30's, 40's and 50's did not sell through the current system. This meant that the mix available for selling was about 75% paperback and 25% hardcover. Sorting and pricing of books was handled by one client at the plant who spent about 75% of his time on this assignment. Although it appeared that other used book stores in London generally priced at one-half of the original retail price, L.G.I priced at one-third of the original price. Other used book stores of course knew values and tempered the general rule of one half of the original retail price with known value and priced collectors' items and other special books at higher prices.* Although L.G.I. had developed skills in pricing any unusual types of donations of clothing, housewares, and furniture, at market value levels, no such capacity currently existed in the book processing department. Paperbacks were priced at one third of the original retail price as shown on the book. Since the same book might have sold for double the retail price in 1981 as it did in 1978, essentially the same title could be priced at different levels. Prices of new paperback fiction books ranged from about $1.95 for Harlequin romances to $3.95 for the typical paperback novel. Hardcover books which rarely had the original retail price shown, were priced on a judgemental basis using easily understood criteria such as physical condition and thickness and not on author, title, vintage or other such factors of potential importance to consumers. The typical selling price of the books sold ranged from 60¢ to $1.25.

Each of the L.G.I. outlets (with the exception of the furniture store) had a set of book shelves (about 6 feet high, 5 feet wide) usually located at the back of the store in the corner, and customers selected their books and took them to the counter. In two of the larger stores there were open bins as well. Books were date coded and when they had been on the shelf for about six weeks and more inventory was shipped to the store, they were either discarded by the store manager or occasionally returned to the workshop for distribution to other stores. It was felt that about 70% of the books received as donations were processed as saleable, and of these, about 75% were sold with the remainder being discarded. Mr. De Gelder viewed the book section as an important part of the product mix in each store as in his view it was important to offer a wide variety of merchandise to generate customer interest.

There were five second-hand book stores in London all located in the general downtown area. Attic Books and City Lights Bookshop carried large selections of hardcover, paperbacks and selected magazines of both the rare and popular types. Attic Books was located in one large room involving about 1,000 square feet on the second floor of an old building in a downtown fringe location. The inventory was well organized and easy chairs were provided for customers to peruse and read any books they might be interested

in purchasing. City Lights Bookstore was on the street level involving about 1,000 square feet, was well organized as well, but with different rooms and sections devoted to specific types and categories of books. Antique furniture, plants and music created a pleasant atmosphere. The staff at both Attic Books and City Lights were pleasant and knowledgeable. Basically Books and G&A Book Exchange and Joke Shop specialized in popular books. G&A carried only paperbacks which were piled around the shop. All of these used book shops usually bought their books from individuals, although Attic and City Lights also purchased from libraries, estates and collectors. Prices paid for these books varied tremendously depending upon the book. Prices for paperbacks could range from zero to the face price of the book. Generally 30¢ to 40¢ was paid for paperbacks. Prices paid for hardcover books varied even more. The judgment of the buyer was critical in determining the price of all books. The locations of these stores is shown on the London map, Exhibit 5.

Second hand books were available from a large number of other types of outlets—including flea markets, garage sales, church bazaars, student book exchanges at the University, Community College, and high schools. The Ladies Auxiliary of a major hospital put on a major book drive in the community each year as a fund-raising activity. Books were donated by households in the community and sold in a three-day long sale.

Mr. De Gelder knew that some of the L.G.I. outlets sold more books than others and he felt that generally sales volume depended on the amount of space devoted to books not on the geographic location of the store.

L.G.I. had experimented previously to a very limited extent with book merchandising. During the winter of 1978–79, one of the bigger outlets, located on a main street among a number of second-hand shops tripled the book section for six months. Extra attention was directed toward the book displays and classified ads were run in the local newspaper and the University Student Press. However, book sales did not increase appreciably and the book section was reduced to its former size to make room for higher volume goods.

Depending on the kind of book store that was planned, the requirements for store staff and for the sorting operation at the plant could vary. For many of the current client group, books were not and had not been a significant part of their lives; however, within the client group, there were a number of individuals who had university degrees both at the undergraduate and graduate levels, and who, prior to encountering their disabilities, had held positions and led lives where books were probably important and utilized to a great extent (law, teaching, etc.) There were also a number of people waiting to become L.G.I. clients who had these attributes.

Mr. De Gelder believed if a used bookstore were to be opened, that a downtown location was probably the most appropriate. Rents varied considerably with location, and were considerably higher than the rents paid for the existing

---

*One of the most valued paperbacks, according to a radio announcer reading from a collector's journal (not subscribed to by L.G.I.) was "Naked on Roller-Skates" at $250.

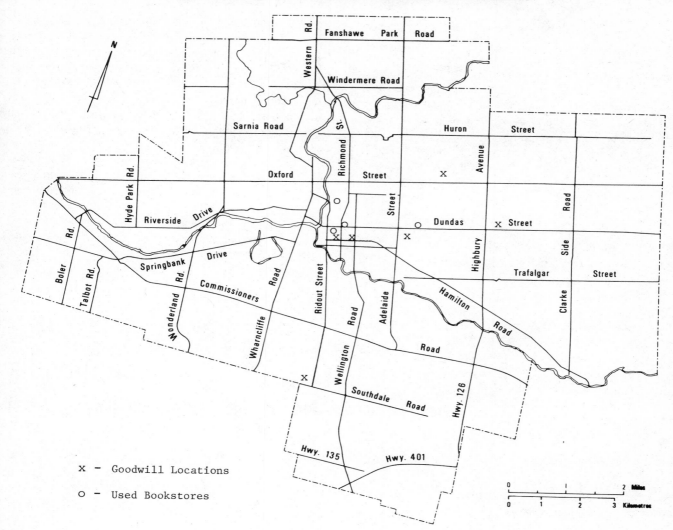

x — Goodwill Locations

o — Used Bookstores

stores (highest $4 per square foot per year net). Estimates obtained from a realtor during the summer of 1981 were as follows:

Locations	Estimated Annual Rental Costs*
Dundas Street Downtown (Main downtown street—high pedestrian traffic)	$15.00–$25.00 per sq. ft. net
Downtown Fringe Areas (e.g., Clarence, Talbot, Dufferin, Queen, Richmond, etc., borders downtown core—fairly high pedestrian traffic)	$5.00–$7.50 per sq. ft. net
Richmond Row (Area of trendy boutiques and shops along Richmond Street)	$12.00–$14.00 per sq. ft. net
Major malls throughout the city located in the surburbs	$20.00–$25.00 per sq. ft. net
Small neighbourhood strip malls	$10 per sq. ft.

*Additional costs, such as municipal taxes, utilities, and insurance (some paid to landlord, others paid directly), amounted to $1.00–$1.50 per square foot.

Precise figures on the amount of inventory required to stock a book store were not available. The Toronto Goodwill Bookstore maintained an inventory of about 3000 hardcovers and 2800 paperbacks on shelves. They also stocked 2000 hardcovers and 600 magazines in bins. One arrangement L.G.I. management examined consisted of floor-to-ceiling shelving units around the perimeter. One hundred twenty books could easily be shelved on a 10-foot shelf and approximately seven shelves could be constructed floor-to-ceiling. Three to five feet of walking space was required between aisles. The existing book stores in London utilized different types of arrangements. A Classic Bookstore (which sold new books) of 2000 square feet carried about 15,000 new books at a time. Generally, there was an attempt for an esthetically pleasing, comfortable, informal arrangement. Although the library type arrangement would allow storage of the largest inventory, it was felt that the atmosphere created by such an arrangement would be unsuitable for book browsers. City Lights had arranged their books by category in small nooks to break up the large space and create a relaxed atmosphere to encourage browsing. For example, history books were shelved in a U-type arrangement separated from science fiction and popular books.

In all cases, leasehold improvements would be the responsibility of L.G.I. but were difficult to estimate precisely without considering a specific site. Prior experience indicated that these costs would probably amount to between $15,000 and $18,00 for a 1,000 square foot location. These costs could be somewhat less for a smaller location. There was the possibility of obtaining government support of 80% to 100% of these expenditures but application for such assistance had to be made *after* the work was completed and approval would depend upon a host of factors (budget, policies, etc.) faced by the government agency involved. Leasehold improvement costs for the last three stores opened had eventually been approved. The length of the lease could vary, but the minimum possible was one year with three and five

years being more common. If a bookstore was to be opened, Mr. De Gelder needed a strategy for location, scale of operations, source and type of books, and promotions—he needed a marketing strategy both to get more books donated and sold. To complicate matters, although he had considerable data on the community of London (see the Appendix), he knew little about potential "used book" consumers. On the basis of library usage, new books sales, magazines and newspaper subscriptions, Londoners appeared to be "readers." From visits to existing used book stores, he felt they tended to serve at least two groups. One group purchased popular type books (paperbacks chiefly) in quantities of 1 to 15 (often returning them as trade-ins on their next purchases), and another group consisted of "booklovers" who tended to purchase hardbacks that appealed to them and rarely traded them in on other purchases.

Appendix

Selected Market and Demographic Data for Metropolitan London

Source: *The Financial Post*, Survey of Markets, 1979, pp. 318–320

Market: 9% Above National Average
Retail Sales, 1978 ....$864,300,000
Percent Canadian Total 1.28
Per Capita $3,120

Income: 10% Above National Average
Personal Disposable Income, 1978 ....$2,019,100,000
Percent Canadian Total 1.29
Per Capita $7,290

Current Growth Rate: 14% Per Decade
Population, June 1, 1978 277,100
Percent Canadian Total 1.18
Percent Change, 1971–78 ....+9.53

Households
Number, 1976 91,770
Average Number per Household 2.9

Population
1976 Census: Total 270,385
Male 131,820
Female 138,565

Age Groups:	Male	Female
0–4	10,005	9,330
5–9	10,795	10,020
10–14	12,600	12,030
15–19	13,075	12,835
20–24	13,550	14,860
25–34	21,515	22,425
35–44	15,210	15,235
45–54	14,430	15,365
55–64	10,965	11,845
65–69	3,720	4,650
70 and over	5,950	9,960

Families: Number 68,740
Average Number per Family 3.3

Employment (1961 = 100)	London	Canada
1973	132.4	135.9
1974	138.5	142.8
1975	132.9	141.1
1976	134.7	144.1
1977	134.7	144.3

Average Weekly Earnings (dollars)

	London	Canada
1973	154.86	160.46
1974	171.57	178.09
1975	193.92	203.34
1976	213.28	228.03
1977	229.99	249.95

Labour Force by Occupation	1971 Census	% of Total
Management, Administration	5,835	4.5
Engineering and Science	3,275	2.5
Law and Social Science	1,485	1.1
Religion	365	0.3
Teaching	6,015	4.6
Medicine and Health	7,415	5.7
Art and Literary	1,230	0.9
Clerical	23,505	18.1
Sales	14,285	11.0
Service	15,130	11.7
Primary	4,105	3.2
Processing	2,725	2.1
Machining	4,290	3.3
Product Lab	10,780	8.3
Construction	7,490	5.8
Transportation Equipment	4,500	3.5
Materials Hand	3,315	2.6
Miscellaneous	13,815	10.7
All Occupations	129,555	100.0

Labour Force by Industry (1971 Census)	Male Number	Female Number
Agriculture	2,470	730
Manufacturing	21,865	7,525
Food and Beverage	3,640	1,705
Transportation Equipment	4,740	605
Construction	7,465	495
Transportation and Communication	6,890	1,360
Trade	12,120	7,825
Retail	8,000	6,515
Finance and Insurance	3,475	4,710
Services	15,605	21,400
Education	5,305	5,650
Health and Welfare	3,250	8,645
Government	5,600	2,015
All Industries	76,395	46,550

Retail Trade (1971 Census)

Total Sales ($000)	478,163
Number of Stores	1,789
Year-End Inventory ($000)	55,801
Number of Employees	9,756
Total Payroll ($000)	51,306

By Kind of Business Group	Number of Stores	Sales ($000)
Food	397	121,591
Groceries, Confection and Sundries	100	5,138
Grocery	104	13,619
Combination[a]	71	90,373
Meat Markets	29	4,413
General Merchandise	92	87,849
Department	8	65,476
General Merchandise	13	9,826
Variety	65	11,935
Automotive	452	132,736
New Motor Vehicle Dealers	36	75,372
Tire, Battery, Etc.	11	1,969
Home and Auto Supply	5	6,554
Service Stations	258	38,567
Garages	51	3,131
Paint and Body Shops	49	2,742
Apparel and Accessories	204	32,229
Men's and Boys' Clothing	33	8,490
Women's and Misses'	42	8,080
Family Clothing	19	4,522
Family Shoe	37	5,227
Hardware and Home Furnishings	234	29,465
Hardware	29	3,101
Furniture	21	4,316
Furniture, TV, Radio, Appliance, Etc.	65	13,248
Other Stores	410	74,291
Pharmacies	56	11,853
Liquor	10	16,067
Jewelery	35	5,280
Sporting Goods	33	3,266

Taxation Statistics (1976)		Percent of Total
Income Class: Under $2,000	22,196	14.1
$2,000–$3,000	10,752	6.8
$3,000–$4,000	9,300	5.9
$4,000–$5,000	9,984	6.3
$5,000–$7,000	15,989	10.2
$7,000–$10,000	24,185	15.4
$10,000–$15,000	32,341	20.6
$15,000–$20,000	16,809	10.7
Over $20,000	15,675	10.0
Total number of returns	157,231	100.0
Total income (thousands of dollars)	1,599,752	
Average income (dollars)	10,175	
Total tax (thousands of dollars)	252,010	
Average tax (dollars)	2,369	

[a] Grocery stores with fresh meat.

33
Rapid Transit in Los Angeles

Christopher H. Lovelock
L. Frank Demmler

''Los Angeles has been a long time reaching the point where it is right now. We're at the crossroads,'' observed Thomas G. Neusom, President of the Board of Directors of the Southern California Rapid Transit District.[1] ''Look at that pale gray coating of smog,'' he continued. ''Look at the price of gasoline! I don't think a lot of people are fully aware of the part a transit system would play in alleviating the problems and in improving the quality of life in the [Los Angeles] basin.''[2]

The RTD directors were commenting on the new Master Plan for public transportation in Los Angeles County approved by them on July 2, 1974. In just four months' time, voters would be asked to approve an increased sales tax to help finance the cost of the proposed transit improvement plan, which included both a new rail rapid transit system and a greatly improved bus service.

Other RTD directors emphasized the importance of the upcoming transit referendum. Said Jay B. Price: "The proposal we have now, the multimode system, is absolutely perfect! This is the way we've got to go, or we're never going to have free highways or clean air around here. . . . We're the largest metropolitan area in the world with no viable mass rapid transit system. If the voters turn this down, we'll never see it in our lifetime. It's now or never!" "If this measure fails," added his colleague Arthur Baldonado, "we'll miss the boat on federal funding." Don C. McMillan concluded: "People

are smart—they aren't going to vote for it unless they know what's going to happen. . . . More and more people are coming to know the RTD Service—that's the key to the whole thing."

With the Master Plan finally adopted, after nearly two years of planning and more than 250 community meetings, attention now turned to the upcoming referendum of November 5, 1974—four months' away. By law, the District was required to inform the electorate of the transit improvement plan but prohibited from actually advocating passage of the ballot measure.

In order to fulfill this obligation of informing the public, the RTD's Public Information Department was given the task of preparing an appropriate communications program. This assignment was in addition to the Department's ongoing responsibilities, and its management recognized that each of their other marketing and communications activities could, if handled effectively, contribute to the chances for success in the November election.

THE LOS ANGELES AREA

In 1974, the City of Los Angeles had a population of 2.8 million and covered 464 square miles. It was

---

Christopher H. Lovelock is Associate Professor of Business Administration at Harvard University. L. Frank Demmler was formerly a Research Assistant at Harvard University.

[1] Henceforth referred to as "RTD" or "the District."

[2] All quotes by RTD Board members are taken from the *Southern California Rapid Transit District Annual Report*, 1973–74.

EXHIBIT 1
Proposed Initial Rapid Transit and Busway System for Los Angeles County

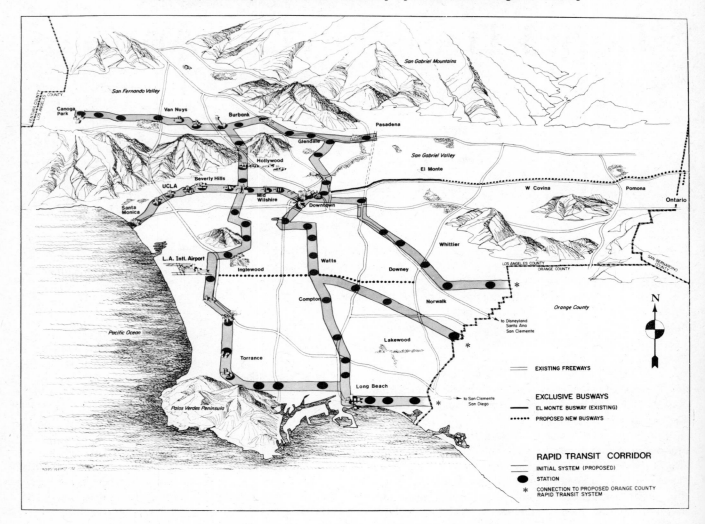

the seat of Los Angeles County which, with over seven million residents, accounted for more than a third of the total population of California.

Greater Los Angeles covered an area of about 40 miles by 40 miles, included portions of four counties and some 200 separate municipalities, together housing over nine million people. Low density urban development sprawled outside the county across three standard metropolitan statistical areas. An extensive network of freeways criss-crossed the region.

Physically, the setting of Los Angeles was a beautiful one. Enjoying a subtropical climate, the city lay in a basin, surrounded by mountains rising as high as ten thousand feet, with the Pacific Ocean forming a boundary to the west and south. Smaller hills separated the suburban San Fernando and San Gabriel Valleys from central Los Angeles (see Exhibit 1).

Employment and retailing locations were much more decentralized than in most cities. However, in recent years significant commercial office expansion had taken place in downtown Los Angeles, which now boasted a growing number of 40–60 story office towers in addition to governmental offices, retail stores, and the cultural attractions housed in the new Music Center.

With a median family income of $10,535 in 1970, Los Angeles ranked sixth among the nation's cities. But incomes were substantially lower for the great majority of the Black and Mexican-American populations. Housing in the mostly Black area of Watts and the Spanish-speaking barrio of East Los Angeles tended to be crowded and often in poor condition, contrasting sharply with the spacious and well-maintained single-family dwellings in white suburbs.

Los Angeles County boasted the heaviest per

capita concentration of automobiles in the world. Critical authors had commented at length on the prevalence of the automobile culture in Southern California. Wrote Curt Gentry:

> The first thing the new arrival . . . noticed was not the scenery, the smog, or the sprawl but the incredible number of automobiles. . . .
>
> In Southern California, one needn't leave his car to eat, be entertained, cash a check, or worship, that area having pioneered drive-in restaurants, movies, banks, and churches. . . .
>
> Over 55 percent of the Los Angeles land surface was dedicated to the auto. This included freeways, streets, driveways, parking lots, gas stations, [and] showrooms.[3]

Popular mythology held that Los Angeles had no transit service at all and it came as a surprise to many people to learn that the RTD had one of the largest bus fleets in the country.

PUBLIC TRANSPORTATION IN LOS ANGELES

The first transit service in the city was a 2.5 mile horsecar route, introduced in 1874 at a fare of ten cents. Between 1887 and the early 1920's, an extensive electric streetcar and interurban rail system was developed, stimulating rapid population growth for both the city and surrounding towns.

During the twenties, the Pacific Electric Railway, the nation's largest electric transit system, operated nearly 1,200 miles of interurban rail service in the region. PE's peak traffic volume of 109 million annual rides was achieved in 1924, when the population of metropolitan Los Angeles was just over one million. After 1930, the rail system began to contract, being replaced by extensive motor bus services. Transit ridership continued to increase until 1947, in which year 575 million passenger trips were made and the region's population stood at approximately 3.5 million people.

Thereafter, transit use declined rapidly, while the new freeway system grew from a mere 45 miles to 260 miles. During this period, atmospheric air pollution—better known as smog—became increasingly prevalent in the Los Angeles Basin. In 1958, three formerly private transit systems were merged into the publicly-owned Los Angeles Metropolitan Transit Authority, which proceeded to replace all remaining local rail and trolley lines by buses. After six years, LAMTA was inself superseded by a new, state-created agency with a broader mandate.

The RTD. The Southern California Rapid Transit Dis-

trict, a public agency created by the California Legislature in 1964, was charged with two legislative mandates: to operate and improve the existing bus system; and to design, construct, and operate a modern rapid transit system.

In 1974, the RTD served an area of 2,280 square miles of Southern California, covering most of Los Angeles County and parts of Orange, Riverside and San Bernadino Counties. The RTD was one of the largest transit systems in the country, with a fleet of 1850 buses which operated a total of 67 million vehicle miles per year. Most routes in the 3,300-mile system ran on city streets, but there were also a number of express services on freeways. In mid-1973, RTD had inaugurated the El Monte Busway, the first "bus rapid transit" route in the nation. In addition to RTD operations, a number of municipalities in the metropolitan area offered their own local transit services.

RTD patronage in recent years had stabilized at around 190 million rides annually, but the introduction of a 25 cent flat fare in April 1974 had resulted in substantial increases in ridership. In July 1974, the system carried some 650,000 riders daily, of which 400,000 were believed to be totally dependent upon RTD, lacking access to alternative transportation.

The District's annual budget totalled $116 million. In fiscal year 1974, farebox revenues of $48.1 million accounted for 51.6% of the $93.3 million operating budget, with most of the resultant deficit being supplied by various tax revenues. The non-operating budget included planning and capital expenditures financed primarily by federal sources, with additional state and local assistance.

RTD employed a staff of 4,480 people, about 85% of whom were represented by organized labor. Approximately $62 million of the annual budget was for unionized employees' wages and fringe benefits.

Governance and Management of the District. The District was governed by an 11-member, non-salaried Board of Directors appointed by elected local government officials. Five members were appointed by the Los Angeles County Board of Supervisors, two by the Mayor of the City of Los Angeles with concurrence of the City Council, and four by a selection committee which represented the other 76 cities in the District.

Day-to-day management of RTD operations and planning activities was in the hands of a salaried, professional staff, headed by a General Manager appointed by the Board.

The executive staff consisted of nine individuals in addition to the General Manager, representing top-level staff positions and five functional areas: operations, control, planning and marketing, engineering, and

[3] Curt Gentry. *The Last Days of the Late, Great State of California.* Putnam, 1968.

EXHIBIT 2
Southern California Rapid Transit District: Organization Chart

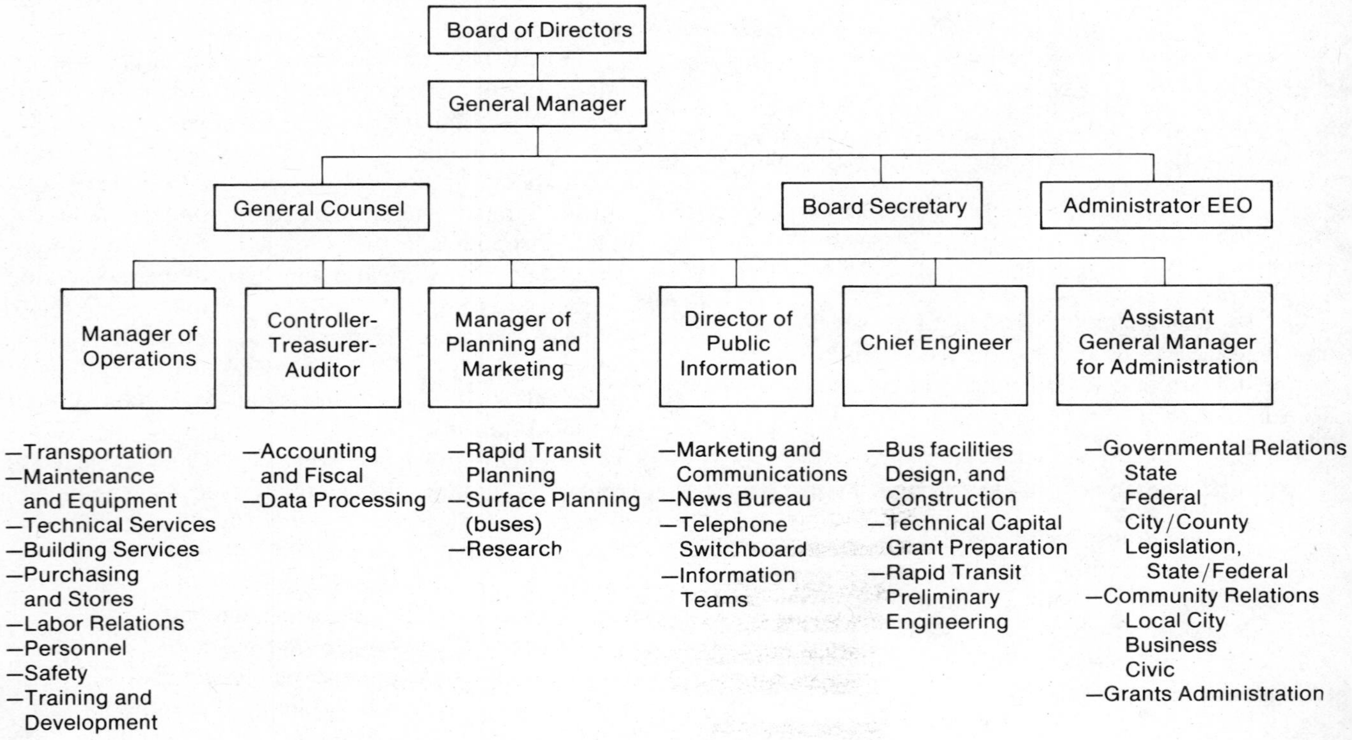

```
                    ┌──────────────────┐
                    │ Board of Directors│
                    └──────────────────┘
                    ┌──────────────────┐
                    │ General Manager  │
                    └──────────────────┘
        ┌──────────────────┐  ┌────────────────┐  ┌──────────────────┐
        │ General Counsel  │  │ Board Secretary│  │ Administrator EEO│
        └──────────────────┘  └────────────────┘  └──────────────────┘
```

Manager of Operations	Controller-Treasurer-Auditor	Manager of Planning and Marketing	Director of Public Information	Chief Engineer	Assistant General Manager for Administration
—Transportation —Maintenance and Equipment —Technical Services —Building Services —Purchasing and Stores —Labor Relations —Personnel —Safety —Training and Development	—Accounting and Fiscal —Data Processing	—Rapid Transit Planning —Surface Planning (buses) —Research	—Marketing and Communications —News Bureau —Telephone Switchboard —Information Teams	—Bus facilities Design, and Construction —Technical Capital Grant Preparation —Rapid Transit Preliminary Engineering	—Governmental Relations State Federal City/County Legislation, State/Federal —Community Relations Local City Business Civic —Grants Administration

Source: SCRTD, July 1974.

administration. Exhibit 2 shows an organization chart summarizing their responsibilities.

The relationship between the Board and the professional staff was described in the 1973–74 Annual Report as follows:

> The Board generally establishes policy; the staff implements it. The Board develops long-range planning; the staff follows that direction in generating various specific programs and the means to carry it out, then presents these programs back to the Board for approval. Because the staff is a fulltime, professional group, a majority of its reports are self-generated, while a smaller number are actually the result of a directive to the staff. . . .
>
> On problems or programs that are agency-wide in scope, various executives are brought together on special standing committees to examine the issues. Many policy recommendations are evolved in this manner, then presented to the Board for approval and adoption as an official policy of the District.

As political appointees and politicians, Board members tended to be sensitive to public opinion, particularly where services in their own communities were concerned. One RTD executive observed:

Anybody can pick up the phone or write a letter and ask why a certain service isn't offered or is unsatisfactory and the Board will demand to know why.

THE PUBLIC INFORMATION DEPARTMENT[4]

This department, which fell within the province of the Manager of Planning and Marketing, had responsibility for most of RTD's marketing-related activities. As the primary information link between RTD management and the public, the Public Information Department (PID) was responsible for informing the public of RTD service offerings, providing promotional support for new services, attempting to improve public opinion of the District, and making newsworthy activities known to the media. At a more subtle level, it was expected to enhance employee morale through its efforts.

_____

[4] Much of the information about the PID and its activities is drawn from *RTD is Going Places: Marketing Activities of the Public Information Department, January–June 1974*, a report published by RTD in mid-1974, and from *Southern California Rapid Transit District Annual Report, 1973–74*. Names of PID personnel have been disguised.

EXHIBIT 3
Marketing and Planning at R.T.D.: Partial Organization Chart

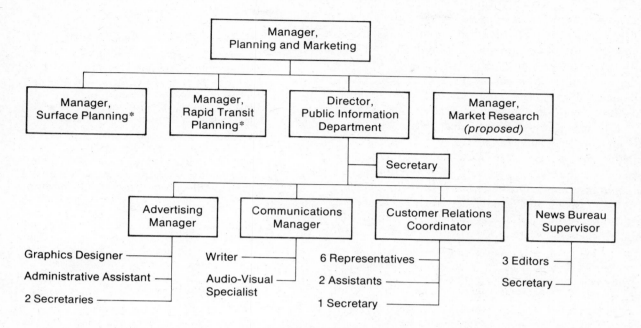

Manager,
Planning and Marketing

Manager,
Surface Planning*

Manager,
Rapid Transit
Planning*

Director,
Public Information
Department

Manager,
Market Research
(proposed)

Secretary

Advertising
Manager

Communications
Manager

Customer Relations
Coordinator

News Bureau
Supervisor

Graphics Designer

Administrative Assistant

2 Secretaries

Writer

Audio-Visual
Specialist

6 Representatives

2 Assistants

1 Secretary

3 Editors

Secretary

*Both of these managers had extensive staff organizations beneath them.
Source: SCRTD, July 1974.

Historically, the PID's activities had reflected an attitude of "We're here to serve those who need us." Advertising and news releases emphasized routes serving public attractions and occasional new services. About five million timetables and literature pieces were distributed each year. However, staffing in the department was thin, precluding the institution of on-going programs requiring public contact. The primary target of PID communications was seen as "transit dependents"—those without alternative means of travel.

When Bruce Fielding was appointed as Director of Public Information in October 1973, this position had been vacant for about a year. Mr. Fielding brought to the District a number of new ideas and goals which he had developed from 20 years' experience in journalism and private industry. Prior to joining RTD, Mr. Fielding had been Manager of Public Relations and Advertising for a large manufacturing firm in Los Angeles.

At the time of this appointment, few of the department's staff had either formal training in communications or relevant work experience outside RTD. The new Director formulated an organizational structure with four positions reporting to him—Advertising Manager, Communications Manager, Customer Information Coordinator, and News Bureau Supervisor—and provided for a greatly enlarged, professionally-trained staff, reporting to these four managers.

One of Mr. Fielding's first moves was to fill the position of Advertising Manager, an existing post which in November 1973 had been vacant for a number of months. Rather than promote a less qualified person from within RTD, the Director offered the position to an outside candidate with extensive advertising experience, Ms. Nancy Moeller.

After graduating with a Masters degree in Advertising from Northwestern University, Nancy Moeller had joined the J. Walter Thompson Company in Chicago. She worked for JWT for two and a half years as an account manager on several consumer product accounts. Subsequently, she moved to California where she started up and ran her own business, a magazine in the San Fernando Valley area of Los Angeles. A year later she took advantage of an opportunity to sell the business at a profit and, intrigued by the marketing challenges facing the District, selected the position at RTD from among several job offers she had received.

A number of additional new appointments were made during the next few months. Exhibit 3 details the organizational structure of the Public Information Department in July 1974 and its relationship to other RTD Planning and Marketing activities.

Objectives and Strategy. The new management moved quickly to establish a more assertive role for

PID. The marketing objectives established for the Department sought to create first, a leadership posture for RTD in the community; and second, an image of initiative and responsiveness for the Department within RTD. Marketing strategy guidelines emphasized frankness and directness in communications to the public; an attempt to gain maximum editorial coverage of the District's activities in local media; and a policy of documenting Department programs and activities for RTD's Board and top management (see Exhibit 4).

PID managers recognized that public transportation in the Los Angeles area faced a formidable competitor in the private car. They believed that if the District were to have any chance of converting non-riders to transit use, it must attempt to convince people that RTD's existing and planned services represented a viable, desirable transportation alternative. Commented Nancy Moeller:

> Only by adopting a winner attitude can we change public attitudes towards us. The payoff is an increase in public ridership sufficient to justify the large capital expenditure that a rail rapid transit system implies.

In formulating a long-term marketing program for the Public Information Department—something it had not previously possessed—management was of the opinion that departmental activities had to be carefully coordinated. Ms. Moeller noted:

> Basically, there are two steps in the selling process: informing potential buyers about the makeup of the product, and then persuading them to buy it. Completing this two-step "sale" must be the overall objective of the entire PID.
>
> I feel that the first step—that of giving out information—should be accomplished by the News, Communications and Customer Relations units of the Department. The new strategies being adopted by these units should eventually enable them to fulfill this task, but in the short-term, paid media advertising will also have to be used for provision of information to the public.
>
> Advertising works best when the necessary educational groundwork has already been laid so that it can move on swiftly to the second, key step in the sale—the "close." In the long-run, the PID should plan on utilizing advertising activities for the kill, rather than wasting these arrows in the early part of the hunt.

Information Dissemination. Information programs and sales promotion activities were designed to maximize RTD's exposure to both existing and potential riders. At the core of these activities was the telephone information service. This was augmented by timetables and brochures, which were continually updated to take account of new services and route and schedule changes. More than ten million pieces of literature were distributed by RTD between January and April 1974.

The general public could obtain RTD information literature from several sources. They were available

---

EXHIBIT 4
Marketing Objectives and Strategy
For Public Information Department

Marketing Objectives of PID

1. To establish a leadership posture for RTD in the community. This leadership posture is vital if RTD is to gain public support for funding, both to operate and maintain its current fleet and to plan and construct a rapid transit system, together with other system improvements.

2. To establish a leadership position for the Public Information Department within RTD. Vital if Public Information is to change its internal image from a low-response "reactive" organization to one of high response and initiative.

Marketing Strategy of PID

1. Reflect a no-nonsense, "straight dope" attitude in all written and verbal public contact, with emphasis on maximum information—about routing, about RTD, about future plans, about what we can and cannot do, and about the funding we are seeking.

2. Utilize budget spending strategy calling for maximum editorial coverage of RTD service changes and route information by the area's media, leaving sufficient budget for a major promotional program for RTD's overall operation, together with stepped-up literature production and distribution.

3. Maximize direct public contact in disseminating ridership information to minimize confusion, mistrust, and bad feeling. This strategy opens up direct lines from the public to the mysterious inner workings of a public agency.

4. Document department programs and activities for management and directors' review. This move strengthens the link between RTD management and the riding public, while assuring proper implementation of public and political policy by the department.

Source: RTD is Going Places. *Marketing Activities of the Public Information Department, January– June, 1974.*

---

from RTD offices, on board the buses, and from literature racks recently placed in 265 Post Offices and nearly 200 Thrifty Drug Stores in the Los Angeles area. Newspaper advertising carried coupons for a free Rider's Kit; on receipt of a completed coupon, RTD responded with a packet of timetables tailored to the travel needs of each individual enquirer, plus various support literature. Over sixty thousand such kits were distributed during the first half of 1974.

In addition, the Customer Relations Coordinator supervised three two-person Mobile Information Teams. These recently instituted teams set up stands in high traffic locations such as office building lobbies, shopping centers, and hospital cafeterias to distribute literature and answer questions from the public about RTD services. When introducing new services, the PID also sought the cooperation of civic groups in appropriate neighborhoods.

The role of the News Bureau was to achieve maximum news coverage of RTD activities on a continuing basis. News releases were employed to inform newspapers and broadcast media of service changes, important Board decisions and progress in rapid transit planning. During the first half of 1974, some 130 news releases were issued; in nearly every case the PID reported that they had been picked up by a majority of area media.

Press conferences and briefings, featuring appropriate public officials, took place to inaugurate significant new service additions and other newsworthy developments. Periodic, off-the-record seminars were being held for area editors to update the media about recent occurrances and strengthen RTD's position in the editorial sphere. Special attention was being focused on those sources of editorial opinion that had been identified as being particularly anti-RTD or that were disseminating incorrect information.

Audio-visual and text materials for various public speaking engagements and presentations had met with increasing demand and a new group, Communications Services, handled that function. Its staff provided materials and audio-visual equipment for use by District presenters.

Advertising Strategy. For advertising purposes, the market for public transportation was divided into three broad categories. *Transit dependents* were residents of RTD's service area lacking access to private modes of transportation. *Transit independents* were those people who not only had public transportation available to them on an adequate and regular basis, but also had their own private means of transport. This group included both riders and nonriders. Finally, *transit impossibles* were those people with no adequate or regular access to RTD services.

Prior advertising, in English and Spanish, had been directed at transit dependents and lower income independents (for example, Exhibit 5). However, the belief at PID was that the former group was already "sold," and the future advertising should focus on transit independents. A 1968 opinion poll presented a profile of the "transit independent" person:

1. Any income group above the minimum level needed to own a car for his/her family status, for example, $5,000/single, $9,000/family of four.

2. Any educational and occupational level, but tending toward the high school and higher educated, blue or white collar occupations.

3. Any ethnic group, but tending toward Caucasian.

4. Any travel pattern, with at least one auto and licensed driver per household.

Additionally, among that very broad group the most likely potential RTD customer was described as:

1. A male or female wage-earner.

2. A regular commuter to a single location and home again.

3. A person whose discretionary spending capability would be strained by a relatively small increase in the cost of goods and services.

4. A person with regular access to just one auto per household.

The advertising program developed by Ms. Moeller, working with a newly selected advertising agency, was built around the theme "RTD is Going Places." Four basic media were employed: radio, newspapers, billboards, and on-bus advertising. Although television advertising had been used in the past by RTD, this medium was not considered cost-effective by the new PID management.

A major radio advertising campaign was initiated in mid-February and scheduled to run four months. Its objectives were: (1) to increase ridership and utilization of RTD services through improved information; and (2) to improve public attitudes towards transit by projecting an honest, confident image of RTD as a desirable alternative to private auto travel. Radio commercials used a pleasant jingle, "Come Ride the RTD With Us," with spoken announcer inserts offering information on RTD services. Both English and Spanish versions were heard 30 times a week on each of 25 stations, reaching 88% of the area's population. One of the radio messages offered the RTD Rider's Kit and by June was generating more than 200 handwritten requests each day.

Between January and June, 20 separate newspaper ads reiterating the "Going Places" theme were run in metropolitan and community newspapers. Each focussed on a particular, opportunistic situation (such as the El Monte Busway, the energy crisis, reduced fares, new service introductions, etc.). Again, both English and Spanish versions were produced. In many instances, the Board provided supplementary funding to finance such advertisements.

Strategically located billboards highlighted the El Monte Busway and the new Park-and-Ride lots. Meantime, the buses themselves carried exterior posters and interior "car cards" promoting various aspects of RTD services.

Marketing's Impact on RTD. Observers saw this new marketing orientation as something of a novelty for RTD initially. They viewed the Board as fairly supportive of PID's efforts, although often anxious to see im-

EXHIBIT 5
Sample Press Advertising for RTD, 1972

Problems you never have with the EXTRACAR RTD

Boiler Maker.

Why get all steamed up? Engine troubles cost money, so when you're faced with big repair bills, remember the easy way out — your ExtraCar, the RTD.

Savings are probably bigger than you realize. The average cost to maintain a second car is $156 a month (not counting catastrophes) — and a one-zone RTD Monthly Pass lets you ride as many times as you like, seven days and nights a week, for only $12 a month. If your daily trips take you farther, additional zones are just $3.50 per month each . . . so even if you ride in five zones, with unlimited privileges, you save $130 a month.

Worth thinking about? It's worth *doing something* about. If you'd like to have your budget increased by $130 a month or more, here's how to get started. Phone 747-4455, or write the RTD, Dept. 4400, 1060 S. Broadway, Los Angeles 90015. Ask for the ExtraCar Rider's Kit. It answers all your questions on schedules, routes and rates.

For me the bus is better!

Even when my husband isn't using our car, I prefer taking the RTD to my job. We live only a couple of blocks from the bus stop. The Extra-Car gets me downtown in about 20 minutes, and lets me off right where I work. I also prefer this way to come downtown on errands over the week end, because it's so easy, and I don't have to pay for parking. All in all, I figure it's good business for me to take the bus for my trips around town. And a pleasure, too.

Elizabeth Bradshaw

ELIZABETH BRADSHAW

Southern California Rapid Transit District
RTD—The people who know how to move people.

mediate results. However, the definitions of success and failure were nebulous and there were no generally accepted guidelines against which to measure performance.

SPECIAL ACTIVITIES IN THE FIRST HALF OF 1974

During 1973–74, RTD initiated or expanded many new projects that the PID was called upon to promote. Perhaps the most dramatic was the $53 million El Monte Busway. Inaugurated in July 1973, the Busway was being opened in stages, with the final section scheduled for completion in late 1974. It consisted of dual, segregated lanes for buses in the median of, or alongside, the San Bernadino Freeway. The busway extended 11 miles from a specially constructed terminal station at El Monte, where extensive parking was provided, to a point near the Los Angeles central business district (Exhibit 1). There were additional stations at California State University and the Los Angeles County-USC Medical Center, plus two intermediate on and off ramps. It was calculated that passengers using the full length of the Busway would save 20 minutes traveling time over drivers on the chronically congested San Bernadino Freeway.

Since the Busway was the area's one true rapid transit development and had high visibility, the PID was seeking to use it to improve public opinion toward RTD, as well as to bring about a significant increase in transit patronage. Using the theme "Fly to Los Angeles," a large campaign had been mounted to promote the Busway through billboards, external posters for buses, media and publicity releases. Between January and July, 1974, daily patronage increased from 3,000 to 11,000 riders.[5]

In January 1974, the RTD Board conceived the idea of "Sample Sunday." To induce the public to test-ride RTD bus services, including the El Monte Busway, all fares were reduced to a dime on Sunday, January 20. This compared with a normal fare structure of a 30¢ base fare plus 8¢ for each additional zone traveled. Under this system, the six-zone Busway fare was 70¢. Financing for the experiment was obtained from the L. A. County Board of Supervisors.

The January 20 trial was supported by PID with print advertising in El Monte and Central Los Angeles (Exhibit 6), as well as with special brochures distributed on all buses. Sample Sunday proved an outstanding success, with patronage increasing from a normal average of 125,500 to almost 230,000. The Board voted, therefore, to offer the Sunday dime fare on a permanent

basis. The continuing program was supported by news releases informing the media of weekly statistics and "Take One" brochures on the buses. After one month, ridership had reached 350,000.[6]

When the full impact of the energy crisis hit Los Angeles in February 1974 and gasoline shortages began to develop, the Public Information Department launched a substantial advertising and public relations drive to let people know what RTD was doing to help. In addition to news releases and press briefings, full page newspaper advertisements appeared, directed primarily at car drivers. These sought to dispel possible misperceptions of transit travel, as well as to provide basic information about RTD services and how to obtain specific details on individual routes. The opportunity was also taken to mention the forthcoming transit referendum.

Buoyed by the success of the dime fare on Sundays, the RTD turned its attention to the fare structure prevailing during the rest of the week. With more than 300 zones in the RTD service areas, fares—which had to be paid in exact change—could range from a 30¢ base up to $1.87, with a 5¢ charge for transfers. Alternatively, patrons could buy a monthly pass for $12.50, plus $3.00 for each additional zone. Apart from the inconvenience to the traveler, the zone system was also complex to police and administer.

Following the initiative of a number of other transit systems in the country, the RTD Board voted a three-month experiment to eliminate all fare zones in Los Angeles County and introduce a flat fare of 25¢. This measure was proposed by an RTD Director who was also an L.A. County Supervisor and was able to persuade the County to provide the necessary funding. It was estimated that $8.7 million would be needed to finance the experiment, although no one was certain exactly what the impact on patronage might be.

To facilitate a change of this magnitude, the PID mounted a major communications campaign. Full page newspaper advertisements explained the new procedures and asked public forebearance of any problems which might result in the preliminary "shake down" period (Exhibit 7).

During the 13-week trial period, ridership grew steadily, resulting in a 19% overall increase and a 24% increase during the last five weeks. It was calculated that the experiment had helped keep an average 31,500 automobiles off the roads each day, saving nearly two million gallons of gasoline during the period of the experiment. Subsequently, the County Board of Supervisors voted to make the 25¢ fare permanent.

Also initiated during April 1974 was the BUS 2 US retail campaign. Deluged during the gasoline short-

---

[5] Most of the increased ridership on the Busway was believed to come from new users. Surveys indicated that almost 90% of new RTD riders either owned cars or had access to one.

[6] It was estimated that approximately half the additional Sunday travelers were new to RTD.

EXHIBIT 6
RTD Newspaper Advertising for Sample Sunday, January 1974

Fly to Los Angeles: 10¢

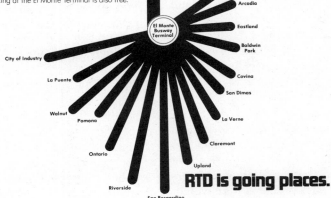

**Reduced from 70¢.
Sunday, January 20, is RTD "Sample Sunday". 5 A.M. to midnight.
A one-day-only opportunity for you to sample the El Monte Busway to downtown Los Angeles.**

Sunday, January 20 is the day you can stretch a dime all the way from the San Gabriel Valley to downtown Los Angeles. And that's quite a stretch. We want you to know just how quick and easy it is to travel on your own private freeway lane, all the way downtown, or as far as Wilshire Boulevard to Western Avenue.

If you commute to work in downtown Los Angeles during the week or want to take an occasional shopping trip to the central city, here's your chance to take a test ride with a dime doing the work of 70¢, our regular daily fare. In fact, if you take a feeder bus to the El Monte Terminal and continue on the same bus to downtown, you still pay only a dime and get the extra local zones free. The only time you part with another dime is when you board another bus. Busway and Monthly Passes remain in effect on "Sample Sunday" as will special senior citizens' fares and fares for the blind. Children under five years ride free, as always. And parking at the El Monte Terminal is also free.

So if you thought this Sunday had to be as dull as the last few, pick up the family, pocket a few dimes and test ride the Busway. Take a leisurely look at the changing downtown skyline.

Stretch your legs a bit and see the sights; the towering new buildings, shopping centers, and restaurants. Also visit some of the older attractions and famous landmarks. We also want you to know that our Sunday service is reduced somewhat and the freeway is less crowded, so you won't actually have the weekday experience of zipping past a crawling mass of motorists. But you should have an enjoyable energy-saving day. After all, when was the last time you got as much mileage out of a dime?

**For Busway Information
From the San Gabriel Valley
Phone (213) 443-1307**

RTD is going places.

THE 25¢ FARE.

It's no good if you don't know how to use it.

By now, you probably know that a flat 25¢ will take you anywhere in Los Angeles County on an RTD bus until June 30.

But there are a few other things you may need to know to make the best use of a bus.

It's really very simple.

Starting April 1st, when you get on a bus, you will pay just 25 cents for the ride, no matter where you get on and no matter how far you ride on that bus in Los Angeles County.

The only time you pay more in L.A. County is if you change buses during your trip. Then it costs you 10 cents for a transfer which lets you change buses 3 times.

Your transfer will be honored on all municipal bus lines in the County.

This nice, easy single fare of 25 cents will be in effect Mondays through Saturdays.

It will be in effect on all our buses. In Los Angeles County only.

It will even be in effect on the new El Monte Busway.

And it will be in effect until June 30th.

About Sundays, senior citizens and students.

Some things will stay the same as before. Sunday fares will still be 10 cents for everyone. On weekdays, senior citizens will now pay just 10 cents, all day long. And student fares will still be just 15 cents with the proper I.D. card. All transfers are 10 cents.

On the former Eastern Cities lines 140, 141 and 142, the 20¢ cash fare is discontinued. The cash fare will now be 25¢.

However, you can still get 3 tokens for 50 cents on these three lines, and transfers between them are still free.

In addition, for the first time you can now get a 10¢ transfer to other RTD or municipal buses when you pay the new 25¢ cash fare.

About monthly passes.

They'll still be issued by the calendar month, but under the new fare system, they'll cost just $10.

You get unlimited transportation throughout the County for a whole month for $10. That's quite a buy. And for senior citizens, they're just $9.

And your pass will also be honored on the Eastern Cities and the former Blue & White buses.

The 10-ride commute card is discontinued in Los Angeles County.

What has changed. And why.

For a long time, we've been trying to make our whole fare system a much simpler thing. So that most rides would be a lot easier and a lot less expensive.

We needed help to do it. Because running a transportation system is expensive, and the fares the RTD receives don't even come close to paying for the full cost of running the buses.

RTD is a public agency, but very little of your tax money goes to it. At least, there's not enough to make bus rides cheaper, or to make our service more often or more convenient in many places.

We've looked for help at the Federal, State, County and local levels. And for three months at least, thanks to our Los Angeles County Board of Supervisors, we've got it. It's a beginning.

Through June 30, the County Board will channel your tax dollars to help make up the difference between the fares you pay and the actual cost of bringing you this flat 25¢ fare.

This is all part of the RTD's plans to bring you better transportation, with lower fares and more buses and added service.

We may get the extra money needed to bring you these improvements, if the 25¢ fare experiment is successful. A lot of agencies throughout the country will be watching. We're going to work hard to make it work. But we'll need your help.

What hasn't changed. And why.

Regular fares and additional zone fares will still be charged in San Bernardino, Riverside, and Orange counties.

This is because the 25¢ fare experiment is only in Los Angeles County because it's only funded by Los Angeles County. If the experiment is successful, we hope to eliminate all of RTD's fare zones. Permanently.

The good part about 25 cents.

There's no need to tell you this is a bargain. You can see that for yourself. But you'll save more than money and gasoline, now. You'll save hassle. With a fare that's easier to understand, bus riding will be easier to take.

So we expect more people are going to take the bus for more than just getting to and from work.

For instance, weekends won't have to be empty just because your gas tank is. You can use the bus for shopping and family outings and short errands.

Of course, the crunch will really come during rush hours.

Which brings us to our biggest worry: you. We're going to need all the good will you've got.

The other side of the coin.

Because we expect more people will be using buses more often, we'll be adding drivers and maintenance people as fast as we can recruit them to service the additional buses we are adding to the fleet.

But we can't get it all done in a week or two. So sometimes you may find yourself on a not-so-new bus.

Sometimes you'll feel like sitting down, but there won't be any seats available.

Sometimes a driver may be too busy to answer all your questions.

And sometimes a bus may be too full to stop and you'll have to wait for the next one. (That wait will get shorter, as we add more buses to the busier routes.)

We're not saying all of these things will happen to you, but some of them are bound to happen to some of you. Please. Don't get too annoyed.

We're trying very, very hard.

We wish we could honestly promise you that everything is going to be just perfect right away.

We can't.

What we can promise is that it will be the very best we can do at the time, and that it will get better all the time.

Because we'll keep on working to get more buses and better buses and smoother schedules and really super service.

How to use the 25-cent fare.

It won't be any good to you, if you don't know how to use the bus. To find out how, you can phone or send in the coupon.

Our special Los Angeles information number is (213) 747-4455. For the number in your local area, please check your directory. Please have a pencil and paper ready to write down all the information.

Next to the telephone company, the RTD switchboard is the largest one around: 99 operators throughout the week. In operation 18 hours a day, 7 days a week.

But with a lot of you calling in, there may be a long wait. If you get a busy signal, it's because a few hundred others have called and are waiting their turn.

For more complete information, your best bet is to use the coupon. You'll get a free Rider's Kit with a comprehensive bus line map, and information about fares, routes and special services.

You'll also get a route custom-tailored to your needs. Or as close as we can come to it. Just give us your starting point, and where you want to go.

We're the first to admit we don't go everywhere. But we try to get as many of you as possible to your destination, as fast as possible.

And at 25 cents, that's the best bargain in town.

Mail to: Southern California Rapid Transit District
Public Information Department
1060 So. Broadway
Los Angeles, California 90015

Please send me the following:
☐ A free RTD Rider's Kit ☐ Information on a route for me:
I want to travel from ___
(closest major intersection or street address/community)
to ___
(closest major intersection or street address/community)
Normal travel times ___ a.m. ___ p.m.
I'm interested in RTD mainly for:
☐ Commuting to work ☐ For shopping
☐ Recreation ☐ Other ___
Name ___
Address ___
City ___ Zip ___

RTD is going places.

age by requests from retailers for promotional materials that would help generate patronage via public transportation, Nancy Moeller developed kits that were mailed to hundreds of businesses located in RTD service areas. This program centered on use of a symbol like a California vehicle license plate, bearing the slogan "BUS 2 US." Included in the kits were ad mats and copy, together with stickers, banners and signs, plus display and merchandising suggestions. Business and retail advertising featuring the BUS 2 US logo had appeared in 20 area newspapers.

On May 1, 1974, five new Park-and-Ride lots were opened, following a successful experience with two test locations, and more were planned. This service provided daytime facilities (typically drive-in theater lots) where patrons could park their cars and commute by express bus to their work locations. The fee, which covered both parking and bus fare, was 75¢ a day or $12 a month if monthly passes were used. Most lots were strategically located close to freeways, but some observers believed that political considerations had played a role in the selection of locations.

PID activities focused on informing the general commuter market. Management had originally planned to promote Park-and-Ride through bus-stop sleeves, posters and handouts in and around office buildings in the central business district, as well as newspaper advertising (Exhibit 8). However, the Board directed that additional promotional efforts be made in the specific geographic areas served by the new facilities. Billboards, theater marquees, news releases to local papers, radio advertising, and mobile information terms were, therefore, being used for this purpose.

Another PID activity at this time involved trying out prototype models of new bus stop signs, which were being developed for the District. The objective of these signs was to provide as much information as possible about each service, including schedules and route schematics.

During the summer of 1973, RTD had initiated what it termed its "Street Fleet"—bus service direct to the beach from various inland communities in the L. A. area. Although management had not planned on repeating this service in 1974, the County Board of Supervisors insisted that it be continued and that two specific lines be included. With this mandate (and the necessary financing), RTD developed five additional lines to provide a more complete route structure.

The PID developed many innovative ideas for this program; these included renovating a number of old buses and decorating them in a submarine design, complete with conning tower and marine graphics. The distinctive-looking Street Fleet service was being promoted through such varied media as posters in area high schools, a special student beach pass, an informational brochure, letters to school principals, "sleeves" over bus stops marking beach runs, and letters to area chambers of commerce and youth groups encouraging them to promote utilization of the service by young people in their communities. Other ways of publicizing this service were also being sought.

Additional projects for the Department in early July included development of publicity materials for five new bus routes due to be introduced in August and preparation of a new system map.

THE RAPID TRANSIT REFERENDUM

For almost two years, the RTD had been preparing a master plan for public transportation in Los Angeles County.[7] In an effort to fulfill its statutory obligations to provide information to the public, and to obtain citizen viewpoints, hundreds of public meetings had been held.

On July 2, 1974, the RTD's Board of Directors adopted a revised Master Plan for Balanced Transportation, containing seven major elements.[8]

1. Mass rapid transit, consisting of a "priority" 145 mile rail system to be constructed over a 10–15 year period (see Exhibit 1 for proposed routing). It was expected to be somewhat similar to BART[9] in conception, with subway, surface and elevated sections. The "ultimate" system proposed an additional 95 miles of expansion to provide a truly comprehensive 240 mile grid system for the 1990's.

2. Personal rapid transit. Small vehicles operating on fixed guideways around congested local areas (such as the L. A. International Airport, downtown L. A. and Long Beach).

3. Commuter rail service. Operation of limited service on existing railroad tracks in cooperation with Amtrak and private railroads.

4. Construction of additional exclusive busways, similar to the El Monte Busway (see Exhibit 1).

5. Immediate expansion of local bus service. By adding 1,000 new, advanced-design buses (including 40 new minibuses) between 1975–77 it was planned to provide a dramatically improved level of local bus service, with new and augmented lines, and innovations such as priority bus lanes on surface streets.

---

[7] Although the RTD's bus service area extended to parts of Orange, Riverside and San Bernadino Counties, the District's area of jurisdiction for rapid transit purposes was confined to Los Angeles County. Orange County was in the process of preparing its own rapid transit plan which would be coordinated with that of L.A. County.

[8] *Transit for Los Angeles County: A Subregional Transit Element of the Transportation Plan.* Prepared for the Southern California Association of Governments by the Southern California Rapid Transit District, July, 1974.

[9] San Francisco Bay Area Rapid Transit, a modernistic new system opened in late 1972.

EXHIBIT 8
RTD Newspaper Advertising Promoting Park-and-Ride Service, May 1974

Ride out inflation.

Now $12 a month parks your car, takes you downtown and back.

If you work downtown, now you can do more than fight inflation. You can beat it. With RTD's Park 'n' Ride.

You just drive to one of our four new Park 'n' Ride lots any weekday morning, board a waiting bus, then read, sleep, work—or congratulate yourself on the money you're saving—all the way to town.

The Freeway Flyer you'll ride doesn't make any stops along the way. So you'll make the same speed you would if you drove yourself.

Meanwhile your car will be basking under the watchful eye of a security guard. It won't be burning any gas, wearing itself out, wearing *you* out, polluting the air or taking up high-priced downtown real estate. And, of course, it'll be waiting for you

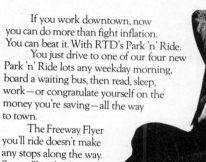

when you ride another Freeway Flyer back after work.

The cost of all this convenience is an incredible $12 a month. (Or 75¢ a day for anybody who'd like to sample the service first.) Which is a lot less than you're paying just to park, isn't it?

The $12 price includes a monthly RTD pass, by the way. So, in case the Freeway Flyer doesn't take you *exactly* where you want to go downtown, you can transfer to another bus that will. For no extra fare. In fact, your RTD pass will get you all the rides you want, even on weekends. Check the schedules below for the best Park 'n' Ride time and place for you. And start cashing in on something unheard of these days. A bargain.

Burbank
San Val Drive-In Theater
2720 Winona Ave.

A.M. INBOUND TO LOS ANGELES
DEPART (San Val Drive-In) / ARRIVE (Olympic & Main)

DEPART	ARRIVE
6:30	7:15
6:45	7:30
7:00	7:45
7:15	8:00
7:30	8:15
7:45	8:30
8:00	8:45
8:15	9:00
8:30	9:15

P.M. OUTBOUND TO SAN FERNANDO
DEPART (Olympic & Main) / ARRIVE (San Val Drive-In)

DEPART	ARRIVE
4:00	4:50
4:15	5:05
4:30	5:20
4:45	5:35
5:00	5:50
5:15	6:05
5:30	6:20
5:45	6:35
6:00	6:50

La Mirada
La Mirada Drive-In Theater
Alondra Blvd. at Firestone

A.M. INBOUND TO LOS ANGELES
DEPART (La Mirada Drive-In) / ARRIVE (Broadway & 5th)

DEPART	ARRIVE
6:10	7:00
6:30	7:20
6:45	7:35
7:00	7:50
7:15	8:05
7:30	8:20
7:45	8:35
8:00	8:50
8:30	9:15
9:00	9:45
9:30	10:15
10:00	10:45

P.M. OUTBOUND TO LA MIRADA
DEPART (Flower & 5th) / ARRIVE (La Mirada Drive-In)

DEPART	ARRIVE
4:00	5:00
4:30	5:30
4:45	5:45
5:00	6:00
5:15	6:15
5:30	6:30
5:45	6:45
6:00	7:00

San Gabriel
San Gabriel Drive-In Theater
140 W. Valley Blvd.

A.M. INBOUND TO LOS ANGELES
DEPART (San Gabriel Drive-In) / ARRIVE (Washington & Olive)

DEPART	ARRIVE
6:30	7:03
6:41	7:15
6:54	7:27
7:04	7:37
7:14	7:47
7:24	7:57
7:34	8:07
7:44	8:17
7:54	8:27
8:06	8:39

P.M. OUTBOUND TO SAN GABRIEL
DEPART (Washington & Olive) / ARRIVE (San Gabriel Drive-In)

DEPART	ARRIVE
4:00	4:35
4:12	4:47
4:24	4:59
4:34	5:09
4:44	5:19
4:54	5:29
5:04	5:39
5:14	5:49
5:24	5:58
5:35	6:07

Van Nuys
Van Nuys Drive-In Theater
15040 Roscoe Blvd.

A.M. INBOUND TO LOS ANGELES
DEPART (Van Nuys Drive-In) / ARRIVE (Hill & 7th)

DEPART	ARRIVE
6:00	6:50
6:15	7:05
6:30	7:20
6:45	7:35
7:00	7:50
7:15	8:05
7:30	8:20
7:45	8:35
8:00	8:50

P.M. OUTBOUND TO VAN NUYS
DEPART (Hill & 7th) / ARRIVE (Van Nuys Drive-In)

DEPART	ARRIVE
4:00	5:00
4:15	5:15
4:30	5:30
4:45	5:45
5:00	6:00
5:15	6:15
5:30	6:30
5:45	6:45
6:00	7:00

RTD is going places

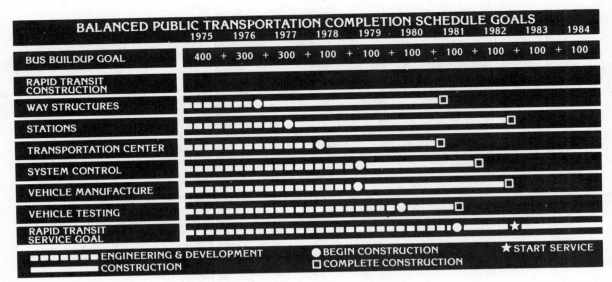

BALANCED PUBLIC TRANSPORTATION COMPLETION SCHEDULE GOALS									
	1975	1976	1977	1978	1979	1980	1981	1982	1983	1984
BUS BUILDUP GOAL	400 +	300 +	300 +	100 +	100 +	100 +	100 +	100 +	100 +	100

RAPID TRANSIT CONSTRUCTION
WAY STRUCTURES
STATIONS
TRANSPORTATION CENTER
SYSTEM CONTROL
VEHICLE MANUFACTURE
VEHICLE TESTING
RAPID TRANSIT SERVICE GOAL

■■■■■■ ENGINEERING & DEVELOPMENT ● BEGIN CONSTRUCTION ★ START SERVICE
━━━━━ CONSTRUCTION ☐ COMPLETE CONSTRUCTION

6. A greatly expanded network of Park-and-Ride lots, served by buses on freeways, to extend fast commuter service to more communities.

7. Additional express bus service on freeways, including special bus lanes and ramps in many locations.

On November 5, 1974, the General Election ballot would include a key referendum item for the RTD.[10] Proposition "A" on Los Angeles County ballots would ask voters to approve a proposed one cent increase in the sales tax (raising the existing tax from 6% to 7% on all retail sales). A simple majority was required for passage. It was anticipated that this sales tax would generate local revenues of $210 million in 1975. One half would be used to finance bus maintenance and operations, plus continuation of the 25¢ flat fare. The other half would finance capital expenditures, going toward purchase of new buses and development and construction of the initial 145-mile rapid transit system. It was anticipated that $4 in matching federal funds would be made available for every $1 of local capital investment. The estimated cost of the initial rail transit system and immediate bus improvements amounted to $4.7 billion (in 1974 dollars). The timetable for these capital improvements is shown in the chart above.[11] Rapid transit construction would begin approximately one year after a successful vote on Proposition "A"; key links in the system would be operational within six years and the full system within 12–15 years.

This referendum was regarded as a critical one. The Urban Mass Transit Administration had set aside federal funds for L.A. pending this referendum vote. If the measure were defeated, this earmarked money would go elsewhere and future availability of similar funds was uncertain. Given the rate of inflation at the time and a trend to curtail federal spending, this vote was seen by many as a do-or-die proposition for rapid transit in Los Angeles.

Los Angeles County had traditionally provided very little tax support for transit. In 1973–74, the average family of four, with an income of $12,000, paid about $23 a year in subsidies to public transportation in Los Angeles, compared to $212 in San Francisco. The additional annual cost of the 1% sales tax in 1975 was estimated to range from $20 for a single person earning $5,000 per year, to $69 for a household with a $25,000 income and consisting of two parents and two children. This extra sales tax would raise the average total family subsidy for RTD to just under $70 a year. By contrast, it was estimated that a one-car family that elected to use public transportation instead of buying a second car could save up to $1,900 a year.

This would be the second rapid transit referendum to be placed before Los Angeles voters in recent years. In 1968, a $2.5 billion, 94-mile rail rapid transit system had been proposed, to be funded by bond issues secured against an increase in local property taxes. There was no federal participation. Strong opposition developed (financed in part by highway interests) and the measure failed in the November 1968 election with 45% voting "yes."

However, it was felt that the environment had changed significantly since then. Extensive federal funding was available, significantly reducing the burden on local taxpayers. The energy crisis was believed to have reinforced an existing attitude trend in favor of public transportation. City and County leaders in Los Angeles, led by Mayor Thomas Bradley, were strong proponents of the Master Plan, and a Citizens' Committee was being

---

[10] Proposition A was one of many state, county and city referenda and was preceded on the ballot by hotly-contested races for Congress, the Governorship of California, and numerous state and local offices.

[11] Source: *Coming Your Way—A Plan for Balanced Public Transportation*, RTD, 1974.

EXHIBIT 9
Availability and Usage of Public Transit in Los Angeles County

Availability

Public Transportation is Available and Used	28.7%
Public Transportation is Available but *Not* Used	47.3
No Public Transportation is Available	24.0
	100.0%

Usage	a % Saying Transit is Available for:	b % Saying Family Members Use Transit for:	Share Using Where Available (b ÷ a)	c % Saying Transit is Not Available for:	d % Saying They Would Use Transit If Available for:	% Share Who Would Use Transit If Available (d ÷ c)
Going to downtown L.A.	63.4%	14.7%	23%	36.6%	13.3%	36%
Local shopping	48.8	11.3	23	51.2	18.1	35
Local trips within and around your neighborhood/community	45.9	10.5	23	54.1	20.2	37
Commuting to more distant spots	42.8	6.5	15	57.2	21.8	38
Recreational activities	30.2	5.3	18	69.8	21.8	31
Visiting friends	26.7	5.6	21	73.3	21.5	29
Getting to work	26.1	6.3	24	73.9	25.7	35
Trips to school	25.6	5.8	27	74.4	13.7	18
NONE AVAILABLE	24.0	24.0				
AVAILABLE BUT DON'T USE	—	47.3				

Source: Dorothy D. Corey Research (commissioned by RTD).

formed to advocate passage of the referendum; but no organized opposition had appeared. Major regional newspapers, such as the *Los Angeles Times,* had endorsed the adoption of the Master Plan and were expected to encourage passage of the referendum measure in November. In the June 1974 primary election, the electorate had voted overwhelmingly in favor of diverting a portion of state gasoline and highway user taxes from highway applications to financing mass transit planning and development.

Market Research Findings. In February 1974, the Public Information Department commissioned an attitude and awareness study among registered voters concerning public transportation in Los Angeles County. In it, 1,501 randomly selected personal interviews were subsequently completed.

Of the respondents, 76% indicated that public transportation was available to them, but only 29% actually used it. Those with access to public transportation were most likely to use it for commuting trips to work or school (unless a lengthy commute trip was involved) and least likely to use it for recreational activities. Many of those lacking transit service indicated they they would use it if available, notably for commuting (Exhibit 9).

Most respondents made negative comments when asked to describe the existing transit system (Exhibit 10a). But when asked how important they considered public transportation to the total needs of Los

Angeles County, 62% replied "extremely important" and 29% "very important."

Although almost all were aware of the Southern California Rapid Transit District, only 8.1% claimed to know a "great deal" about it and 33.4% knew "something." By contrast, 57.7% knew "just a little bit" or had "just heard the name." Residents of central Los Angeles were slightly better informed than those in suburban areas. About one respondent in five felt that the RTD was doing an excellent or good job, with users tending to rate it higher than non-users (Exhibit 10b). People rating the RTD favorably felt that it was doing its best given its present equipment, while those rating it negatively complained about poor scheduling and inadequate geographic coverage.

When asked what they would most miss about not having a car, the convenience of "going where I want when I want" received the most mentions (Exhibit 11a). One third of all employed respondents indicated that it would be difficult or impossible for them to get to work without a car.

Respondents were then shown a card listing 11 features of a rail rapid transit system and asked to rate the importance of each. Key features cited included nearness of station to home or work, dependable schedule, and frequent services (Exhibit 11b).

Finally, respondents were asked how they expected to vote in the November referendum. Of them, 61.2% indicated that they would vote for the transit sales tax, 21.5% were against, and 17.3% undecided. Exhibit

EXHIBIT 10
Attitudes Towards Present Transit System in Los Angeles County
and the RTD's Performance

		By Availability of Public Transportation to the Family		
(A) Present System	**Total**	**Available and Use**	**Available Do Not Use**	**Not Available**
Base: (All respondents)	1501	431	710	360
Percent saying the existing public transportation system in L.A. County is	%	%	%	%
Good/OK/fine/no complaints	7.8	15.1	6.3	1.9
Time schedules are bad/never runs when it's supposed to/no buses when you need them/always late/undependable	10.5	13.2	11.0	6.1
Too time consuming/too slow/inconvenient time-wise/takes too long to get anywhere	15.7	21.3	14.2	11.9
System is inadequate/need to extend system/better planning	24.5	24.4	25.1	23.6
Terrible/poor/lousy/bad/really needs improvement	45.6	41.1	45.5	51.4
(B) RTD Performance				
Base: (Respondents who have heard of SCRTD)	1489	428	705	356
Percent who feel the SCRTD is doing	%	%	%	%
An excellent job	1.9	2.3	1.4	2.5
A good job	17.0	23.6	16.3	10.4
A fair job	35.2	40.9	35.2	28.4
A poor job	25.9	24.1	25.1	29.8
Don't know/unable to rate	20.0	9.1	22.0	28.9
	100.0%	100.0%	100.0%	100.0%

EXHIBIT 11
Key Aspects of Automobile Ownership and Desired Features of
a Rail Rapid Transit System Along L.A. County Voters

(A) Auto Ownership: What would miss most about not having an automobile as a means of transportation.

	Total	Unemployed	Employed	Student	Housewife
Base: (All respondents)	1501	279	762	54	406
Percent saying they would miss	%	%	%	%	%
Convenience/going where I want to go when I want to go	43.3	41.6	40.0	59.3	48.5
Couldn't get to work/transportation too difficult	21.5	8.2	33.3	13.0	9.6
Grocery shopping/carrying groceries	12.9	14.7	8.3	—	22.2
For recreational needs/movies/etc.	10.5	10.8	8.8	13.0	13.3
General shopping/errands	9.3	7.9	6.3	5.6	16.5

(B) Rail Rapid Transit: Important elements/features of a rail rapid transit system.

	Importance of Feature			Most Important (multiples OK)
	Very	**Somewhat**	**Not/DK**	
Base: (All respondents)				
Percent ration	%	%	%	%
Nearness of station to home	80.7	15.1	4.2	33.7
Dependable schedules	95.6	2.4	2.0	33.0
Frequency of service	85.1	10.9	4.0	26.4
Nearness of station to work	72.2	12.8	15.0	20.1
Length of the trip	48.2	28.2	23.6	5.1
Knowledgeable employees	79.5	15.9	4.6	4.0
Comfortable seating	56.6	34.9	8.5	3.9
No standing (seats for all)	55.5	29.4	15.1	3.2
Air conditioning	46.2	29.9	23.9	3.1
Courteous employees	69.7	24.7	5.6	2.6
After midnight service	23.6	26.0	50.4	1.7

Source: Dorothy D. Corey Research (commissioned by RTD).

12 shows voting intentions broken down by different segments of the population.

While this situation provided grounds for optimism that the referendum would be successful, RTD managers and others were well aware that voter attitudes could change. Amongst other things, growing inflation and recession could make voters wary of passing additional tax measures; organized opposition might yet develop; current RTD-Union negotiations over a new labor contract could break down and cause service disruptions; while cynicism over the developing Watergate political scandal could result in a low voter turnout at the polls.

The Communications Program. Recognizing the importance of the referendum, the Public Information Department was putting together a comprehensive communications program. The RTD's responsibilities concerning the ballot measure was specified in California State Assembly Bill 1727, which stated, in part:

> ...the district shall have the obligation to provide appropriate information to adequately inform the voters of the district's purposes for the authorization of a tax ...

At the same time, public information efforts had to be conducted within guidelines that prohibited actual *advocacy* of this program, a task which would fall to the independent Citizens' Committee.

It was intended that the information campaign should highlight both anticipated benefits and negative aspects of the proposed program.[12] These benefits included savings to transit users; enhancement and protection of the Los Angeles environment; provision of improved quality public transportation for the community at large; initiation of a County-wide, grid rapid transit system;[13] greatly improved access to job markets, educational facilities and leisure time pursuits; construction of rapid transit before inflation rendered the program too costly; and insurance against future fuel shortages.

The major disadvantages that had been identified were the additional tax burden upon residents of the area and disruption during construction.

The public information program for the referendum was formulated on the premise that voters would base their decisions on an evaluation of how they would benefit from the proposed rapid transit system. Due to the complex geographic nature of Los Angeles County,

---

[12] *Selected Community Impact Analyses of the Proposed Rapid Transit Program.* Report prepared for RTD by Arthur D. Little, Inc., 1974.

[13] The 1968 proposal had called for a radial system, with lines radiating in different directions from downtown Los Angeles. The grid system would provide better coverage of Los Angeles, and, for most journeys, require less travel than the radial system.

EXHIBIT 12
Profile of Rapid Transit Measure Supporters, March 1974

Total Sample	**61.2%**
Area	
Central	62.8
San Fernando Valley	63.1
San Gabriel Valley	57.3
South Bay	62.5
Whittier/Norwalk	57.7
Race	
White	60.8
Black	56.7
Mexican-American	67.2
Sex	
Male	61.2
Famale	61.2
Age	
30 or Under	67.2
31–60	59.1
Over 60	55.0
Number of Cars	
None	60.1
One	65.7
Two	58.6
Three	60.2
Party Registration	
Democratic	64.2
Republican	55.6
Other	59.6
Labor Union Affiliation	
Yes, Member in Immediate Household	68.2
No Member	59.0
Length of Residence in Los Angeles County	
Under 5 Years	63.8
5–20 Years	62.7
Over 20 Years	59.9
Total Yearly Family Income	
Under $10,000	66.2
$10,000–$14,999	65.2
$15,000–$24,999	56.4
$25,000 And Over	57.7

Source: Dorothy D. Corey Research (commissioned by RTD).

---

the proposed transit improvement plan had to be presented to each community in a manner that related to the area in question. The County had, therefore, been divided into 6 "transit use corridors" for this purpose.

Three additional public opinion polls were to be taken prior to November with the following objectives. First, to determine understanding of the ballot measure and the proposed transit plan via voting intentions —"Yes," "No," and "Undecided." Second, to determine potential problem areas; that is, the system itself, financing, lack of understanding, etc. And third, to analyze public opinion by geographic and demographic market segments.

It was planned to target a variety of different voter subgroups for individualized attention. The identification of appropriate market segments and development of appropriate communications to be targeted at each had become the keystone of the public information effort.

The News Bureau would serve as liaison between RTD and the various news media. It would prepare news releases, arrange press conferences and briefings, prepare rebuttals to unfavorable editorials, and participate in creating special RTD supplements in area newspapers. The employee magazine, *Headway,* had already begun to feature articles concerning the referendum, with an emphasis on the employment opportunities implied by the program.

The communication services group had developed speakers' materials in both audio-visual and script form for presentations by RTD personnel. A film presentation explaining each of the six corridor alignments had been made available. It was also planned to give extensive distribution of the RTD's 1973–74 Annual Report to Los Angeles area decision-makers; this report would feature a separate pull-out section dealing with the Rapid Transit and Bus Improvement project.

A major effort was being devoted to published materials—including envelope stuffers, "Take One's," newsletters, and items for distribution by speakers; plans called for printing more than three million pieces in total. The Mobile Information Teams had responsibility for the distribution of much of this printed material and temporary personnel were to be added to help these teams expand their activities.

The Role of Advertising in the Referendum Program.

As Advertising Manager, Ms. Moeller had responsibility for several specific functions during the campaign. These included the creation and scheduling of newspaper supplement promotions; coordination of market research and analysis; mailing services for rapid transit literature; and graphics preparation.

In approaching these responsibilities, Nancy Moeller was aware of many potential dangers. First the constraints imposed by law severely limited her copy options. Any justified attacks on promotional efforts could seriously jeopardize the referendum's chances of success. The visibility of RTD during this time period made it particularly susceptible to attacks by politicians running for election in November. This was further heightened by the general criticism, often raised against public agencies, that they should not spend taxpayers' money on advertising. Concerning public opinion, Ms. Moeller stated, "Forty pounds of support for the referendum cannot stand up against a whisper against it."

DEVELOPING A PLAN

In early July, the Public Information Department was preparing a detailed proposal for marketing activities at RTD for the period July 15–October 31. While primary emphasis had to be placed on the communications campaign for the transit referendum, it was recognized that promotion of existing and upcoming transit services would also be needed and could serve to reinforce RTD's position. During 1973–74, the PID had spent a total of $1,507,655; the original budget had been set at $915,000, but had been increased several times by supplementary grants from both RTD's Board and the Los Angeles County Board of Supervisors. For 1974–75, the budget, including salaries, had been set at $1,711,000.

PID management was debating how best to coordinate the transit referendum information program with other RTD marketing activities, and wondered which of the latter should receive the greatest emphasis during the next few months. Issues under consideration for the referendum program included identification of voter subgroups, development of appropriate messages targeted at each, selection of the most appropriate media for reaching each group, and establishment of priorities.

34
Strategies for Introducing Marketing into Nonprofit Organizations

Philip Kotler

Marketing is a topic of growing interest to nonprofit organization managers as their organizations confront new, complex marketplace problems. These institution heads are taking their first, tentative steps toward marketing, often confusing it with its advertising and selling sub-functions. Nonprofit institutions can introduce marketing in a number of ways, such as appointing a marketing committee or task force, hiring an advertising agency or marketing research firm, hiring a marketing consultant, or appointing a marketing director or marketing vice president.

In most societies of the world, economic activity is a function of the actions and interactions of a profit sector and a governmental sector. The American economy, however, contains an important third sector made up of tens of thousands of private, not-for-profit organizations ranging from The Society for the Preservation and Encouragement of Barber Shop Quartet Singing in America to major foundations, colleges, hospitals, museums, charities, social agencies, and churches.

This strong third sector constitutes a *middle way* for meeting social needs, without resorting to the profit motive on the one hand or government bureaucracy on the other. Third sector organizations tend to be socially responsive and service-oriented. They specialize in the delivery of social services that are not adequately provided by either business or government.

While Big Business is healthy and Big Government continues to grow, the third sector, unfortunately, is in trouble. Third sector organizations depend upon the support of private citizens and upon grants from the other two sectors. Many colleges, hospitals, churches, social agencies, performance groups and museums are increasingly feeling the pinch of rising costs and stable or declining revenues. Consider the following:

- More than 170 private colleges have closed their doors since 1965, unable to get either enough students or funds or both. Tuition at Stanford and Yale is now over $6,000; if college costs continue to climb at the current rate, the parents of a child born today will have to put aside $82,830 to buy that child a bachelor's degree at one of the better private colleges [Pyke 1977].
- Hospital costs continue to soar, leading to daily room rates of $300 or more in some large hospitals; many hospitals are experiencing underutilization, particularly in the maternity and pediatrics sections. Some experts have predicted the closing of 1,400–1,500 hospitals in the next 10 years.
- The Catholic Church drew as many as 55% of all adult Catholics under 30 years of age to church in a typical week in 1966. By 1975 the figure had fallen to 39% and further declines in weekly attendance were expected.

Philip Kotler is the Harold T. Martin Professor of Marketing, Northwestern University.

- Many performance groups cannot attract large enough audiences. Even those which have seasonal sellouts, such as the Lyric Opera Company of Chicago, face huge operating deficits at the end of the year.
- Many third sector organizations that flourished in earlier years —the YMCA, Salvation Army, Girl Scouts, and Women's Christian Temperance Union—presently are reexamining their mission in an effort to reverse membership declines.

In a word, these third sector organizations have marketplace problems. Their administrators are struggling to keep them alive in the face of rapidly changing societal needs, increasing public and private competition, changing client attitudes, and diminishing financial resources. Board members and supporters are asking administrators tough questions about the organization's mission, opportunities, and strategies. Unfortunately, many administrators are mere "Monday morning quarterbacks" when it comes to strategic planning. At a time when these organizations face uncertain prospects, the lack of management depth poses a serious threat to survival.

Let us examine a major requirement for such survival: third sector administrators must begin to think like marketers. Ten years ago, Sidney J. Levy and I advanced the thesis that marketing is not just a business function—it is a valid function for nonbusiness organizations as well—and that all organizations have marketing problems and all need to understand marketing [Kotler and Levy 1969]. The article created considerable controversy. Many academic marketers attacked it, saying that marketing made sense only in profit-oriented enterprises. However other marketing professors found the idea stimulating and, without necessarily agreeing that it was valid, began to study and experiment with it. Initial interest was confined to academia. The issue was of little concern to businessmen, and was largely ignored by administrators of nonprofit institutions.

More articles followed in the 1970s, reporting applications of marketing technology to such areas as college recruiting, fund raising, membership development, population problems, public transportation, health services, religion, and arts organizations.* Benson Shapiro's article in the September-October 1973 issue of the *Harvard Business Review* elicited many favorable comments, published in the following issue of *HBR*. The only textbook on the subject, *Marketing for Nonprofit Organizations*, appeared in 1975 and has enjoyed a growing readership [Kotler 1975]. Recently Gadedeke [1977] published a book of readings, Lovelock and Weinberg [1977] a book of cases, Lovelock [1977] a bibliography of over 100 cases, and Nickels [1978] a general marketing textbook giving equal attention to business and nonbusiness marketing. It appears that marketing

for nonprofit organizations is an idea whose time has come.

How have administrators of nonprofit organizations responded? Are they interested or aware? Enthusiastic? Do they know how to use marketing? Is it making a difference anywhere? On this tenth anniversary of the idea's launching, we are in a position to supply some answers.

ENTER MARKETING

Of all the classic business functions, marketing has been the last to arrive on the nonprofit scene. Some years earlier, nonprofit managers began to get interested in accounting systems, financial management, personnel administration, and formal planning. Marketing lagged, except where the nonprofit institution experienced a decline in clients, members, or funds. As long as institutions operated in a sellers' market— as colleges and hospitals did throughout the 1960s—marketing was ignored, but as customers and/or resources grew scarce the word "marketing" was heard with increasing frequency, and organizations suddenly discovered marketing or reasonable facsimiles thereof.

Colleges. Colleges provide a good example of this development. By the mid-1970s, they were reading this grim scenario: (1) the annual number of high school graduates would decline from a peak of 3.2 million in 1977 to 2.8 million in 1982–83; (2) the proportion of high school students electing to go to college might decline; (3) a higher proportion of the college-bound students would elect to attend community colleges instead of four-year colleges; and (4) the absolute and relative future level of tuition would deter college-going in general and hurt private colleges in particular.*

What are college administrators doing about this? One group is doing nothing. Either enrollment hasn't slipped, or if it has, the administrators believe the decline is temporary. Many believe it is "unprofessional" to go out and "sell" their colleges.

A second group has responded with "marketing," which in too many cases means aggressive promotion unaccompanied by any real improvements in competitive positioning, teaching quality, or student services. For example:

- The admissions office at North Kentucky State University planned to release 103 balloons filled with scholarship offers.
- The admissions staff of one college passed out promotional frisbees to high school students vacationing on the beaches of Fort Lauderdale, Florida during the annual Easter break.
- St. Joseph's College in Rensselaer, Indiana achieved a 40% increase in freshmen admissions through advertising in *Seventeen* and on several Chicago and Indianapolis rock radio stations. The admissions office also planned to introduce tuition rebates for students who recruited new students ($100 finders fee), but this was cancelled.

---

*A relevant 43-page bibliograhy lists over 600 references. See Rothschild, Michael L. (1977), *An Incomplete Bibliography of Works Relating to Marketing for Public Sector and Nonprofit Organizations*, Second Edition, Boston, MA: Intercollegiate Case Clearing House 9-577-771.

*See *A Role for Marketing in College Admissions*, New York: College Entrance Examination Board, 1976, 54 and elsewhere.

- Bard College developed a same-day admission system for students who walk into their office and qualify.
- Worchester Polytechnic Institute offers negotiable admission in which credit is negotiated for previous study or work experience to shorten the degree period.
- The University of Richmond has spent $13,000 to create a 12-minute film for showings to high school students and other interested publics.
- Drake University advertised on a billboard near Chicago's O'Hare Airport that "Drake is only 40 minutes from Chicago" (if one flies).
- Duke University paid for a supplement in *The New York Times* to tell its story.

Promotional competition has not yet led to premiums given to students for enrollment (free radio, typewriter) or offers of "satisfaction guaranteed or your money back," but these may come.

In equating marketing with intensified promotion, there are several dangers. Aggressive promotion tends to produce strong negative reactions among the school's constituencies, especially the faculty, who regard hard selling as offensive. Also, such promotion may turn off as many prospective students and families as it turns on. Aggressive promotion can attract the wrong students to the college—students who drop out when they discover they don't have the qualifications to do the work or that the college is not what it was advertised to be. Finally, this kind of marketing creates the illusion that the college has undertaken sufficient response to declining enrollment—an illusion which slows down the needed work on product improvement—the basis of all good marketing.

Promotion alone doesn't always work. Briarcliff College, a long-established women's college, faced an enrollment drop from 688 in 1969 to 280 in 1973. The college president scrambled to find ways to "sell" Briarcliff to prospects, including advertising and more high school visits. He personally went on the road to talk up Briarcliff, managing to raise enrollment to 350. But his effort was too little and too late. Briarcliff's finances continued to deteriorate and the college finally closed its doors in 1977.*

A genuine marketing response has been undertaken by a relatively small number of colleges. Their approach is best described as *market-oriented institutional planning*. In this approach, marketing is recognized as much more than mere promotion, and indeed, the issue of promotion cannot be settled in principle until more fundamental issues are resolved. These issues are shown in Exhibit 1. By doing its homework on market, resource, and missions analysis, a college is in a better position to make decisions that improve student and faculty recruitment and institutional fundraising.

As an example, the University of Houston recently completed an intensive institutional audit using several faculty task forces. The final report presented recommendations on

*See "Rest in Peace," *Newsweek*, April 11, 1977, 96.

EXHIBIT 1
Issues in Market-Oriented Institutional Planning Facing Colleges and Universities

Market Analysis

1. What important trends are affecting higher education? (Environmental analysis)
2. What is our primary market? (Market definition)
3. What are the major market segments in this market? (Market segmentation)
4. What are the needs of each market segment? (Need assessment)
5. How much awareness, knowledge, interest, and desire is there in each market segment concerning our college? (Market awareness and attitude)
6. How do key publics see us and our competitors? (Image analysis)
7. How do potential students learn about our college and make decisions to apply and enroll? (Consumer behavior)
8. How satisfied are current students? (Consumer satisfaction assessment)

Resource Analysis

1. What are our major strengths and weaknesses in faculty, programs, facilities, etc.? (Strengths/weaknesses analysis)
2. What opportunities are there to expand our financial resources? (Donor opportunity analysis)

Mission Analysis

1. What business are we in? (Business mission)
2. Who are our customers? (Customer definition)
3. Which needs are we trying to satisfy? (Needs targeting)
4. On which market segments do we want to focus? (Market targeting)
5. Who are our major competitors? (Competitor identification)
6. What competitive benefits do we want to offer to our target market? (Market positioning)

---

the university's mission, strategy, and portfolio. The portfolio section recommended which components of the university's "product mix" (schools and departments) should be built, maintained, phased down, or phased out. The criteria included: (1) the centrality of that academic program to the mission of the university, (2) the program's academic quality, and (3) the program's marketing viability. Thus, a department of women's studies that is marginal to the mission of the school, of low national reputation, and unable to attract an adeqauate number of students, would be slated for phasing down or out. A few other schools such as New York University, Northwestern University, and Kent State University are taking marketing initiatives to bring strategic planning and marketing into their operating frameworks.

Hospitals. Hospitals are beginning to treat marketing as a "hot" topic. A few years ago, health professionals scorned the idea of marketing, imagining that it would lead to ads such as "This week's special—brain surgery, only $195." Hospital administrators also argued that patients didn't choose hospitals, their doctors did; so marketing, to be effective, would have to be directed to doctors.

Thus, it came as a surprise when a single and tentative session on marketing for hospital administrators, sandwiched between several other sessions during the 1975 convention of the American College of Hospital Administrators, drew about one-third of the 2,000 attendees. Perhaps they were tired of hearing panels on rising hospital costs and money collection problems, but more probably they were beginning to sense an opportunity, in marketing, to halt their declining occupancy rates.

As did many colleges, some hospitals rushed into marketing with more enthusiasm than understanding, believing it to consist of clever promotional gimmicks. For example:

- Sunrise Hospital in Las Vegas ran a large advertisement featuring the picture of a ship with the caption, "Introducing the Sunrise Cruise, Win a Once-in-a-Lifetime Cruise Simply by Entering Sunrise Hospital on Any Friday or Saturday: Recuperative Mediterranean Cruise for Two."
- St. Luke's Hospital in Phoenix introduced nightly bingo games for all patients (except cardiac cases) producing immense patient interest as well as a net annual profit of $60,000.
- A Philadelphia hospital, in competing for maternity patients, let the public know that the parents of a newborn child would enjoy a steak and champagne candlelight dinner on the eve before the mother and child's departure from the hospital.
- A number of hospitals, in their competition to attract and retain physicians, have added "ego services," such as saunas, chauffeurs, and even private tennis courts.

Fortunately, some hospitals are now beginning to apply marketing to a broader set of problems. Where should the hospital locate a branch or ambulatory care unit? How can the hospital estimate whether a new service will draw enough patients? What should a hospital do with a maternity wing that is only 20% occupied? How can the hospital attract more consumers to preventive care services, such as annual medical checkups and cancer screening programs? How can a hospital successfully compete in the recruitment of more highly trained specialists who are in short supply? What marketing programs can attract nurses, build community goodwill, attract more contributions?

The marketing naivete of the typical hospital is well-illustrated by a hospital in southern Illinois that decided to establish an Adult Day Care Center as a solution to its underutilized space. It designed a whole floor to serve senior citizens who required personal care and services in an ambulatory setting during the day, but who would return home each evening. The cost was $16 a day and transportation was to be provided by the patient's relatives. About the only research that was done on this concept was to note that a lot of elderly people lived within a three-mile radius. The Center was opened with a capacity to handle thirty patients. Only two signed up!

EXHIBIT 2
Approaches to Introducing Marketing in a Nonprofit Institution

1. Appoint a Marketing Committee
2. Organize Task Forces to Carry Out an Institutional Audit
3. Hire Marketing Specialist Firms as Needed
4. Hire a Marketing Consultant
5. Hire a Director of Marketing
6. Hire a Vice President of Marketing

Not all hospital administrators launch new services without research and testing of market size and interest. An increasing number are now attending marketing seminars to learn more about marketing research and new service development. The Evanston Hospital, Evanston, Illinois, a major 500-bed facility, appointed the world's first hospital vice president of marketing. Recently, MacStravic [1977] published an entire book devoted to hospital marketing, and many articles are now appearing on health care marketing.*

Other Institutions. In addition to colleges and hospitals, other institutions are paying more attention to marketing. The YMCA is taking a fresh look at its mission, services, and clients in order to develop new services and markets for the 1980s. Major charities like the Multiple Sclerosis Society, the American Heart Association, and the March of Dimes are investigating marketing ideas that go beyond selling and advertising. Marketing successes have been reported by arts institutions,† family planning associations [Roberto 1975] and energy conservation groups [Henion 1976]. It is likely that within 10 years, much of the third sector will have some understanding and appreciation of the marketing concept.

IMPLEMENTING MARKETING

The interesting thing about marketing is that all organizations do it whether they know it or not. When this dawns on a nonprofit organization, the response is much like Moliere's character in *Le Bourgeois Gentilhomme* who utters: "Good Heavens! For more than forty years I have been speaking prose without knowing it." Colleges, for example, search for prospects (students), develop products (courses), price them (tuition and fees), distribute them (announce time and place), and promote them (college catalogs). Similarly, hospitals, social agencies, cultural groups, and other nonprofit organi-

---

*See, for example, the special issue on marketing of hospitals, *Journal of the American Hospital Association*, June 1, 1977.

†See, Newman, Danny (1977), *Subscribe Now! Building Arts Audiences through Dynamic Subscription Promotion*, New York: Theatre Communications Group, Inc. This book deals primarily with the use of promotion as a marketing tool rather than with overall marketing strategy.

zations also practice marketing, wittingly or unwittingly; whether they do it well is a separate issue. For institutions which would like to improve their marketing effectiveness, I recommend consideration of the six steps shown in Exhibit 2. The "steps" really represent alternative approaches to the introduction of marketing into a nonprofit institution rather than a rigid sequence of steps.

Marketing Committee. As early as possible, the head of the institution should consider appointing a marketing committee to examine the institution's problems and look into the potentialities of marketing. In a college, for example, such a marketing committee might consist of the president, vice presidents of faculty and development, director of admissions, dean of students, and one or two school deans. The committee should also include a marketing professor and/or a marketing practitioner. The marketing committee's objectives are (1) to identify the marketing problems and opportunities facing the institution; (2) to identify the major needs of various administrative units for marketing services; and (3) to explore the institution's possible need for a full-time director of marketing.

Task Forces. The chief administrator should consider appointing task forces to carry out various phases of an institutional audit. The aim is to discover how the institution is seen by key publics, what its main constituencies want that institution to be, which programs are strong and which weak, and so on. The task force's reports should adduce a consensus on institutional goals, positioning, and strategies. Even when task forces fail to find dramatic solutions, the members usually gain a deeper appreciation and understanding of the institution's problems and the need to work together to solve them.

Marketing Specialist Firms. From time to time, the organization should engage the services of marketing specialist firms, such as marketing research firms, advertising agencies, direct mail consultants, and recruitment consultants. A marketing research firm might be hired to survey the needs, perceptions, preferences, and satisfaction of the client market. An advertising agency might be hired to develop a corporate identification program or an advertising campign. High quality marketing specialist firms bring more than their specific services to the client; they take a total marketing viewpoint and raise important questions for the institution to consider concerning its mission, objectives, strategies, and opportunities.

Marketing Consultant. As a further step, the organization should seek a marketing consultant to carry out a comprehensive *marketing audit* on the problems and opportunities facing that organization. The marketing consultant could be someone affiliated with the institution—such as a marketing professor, or a board member who is a marketing specialist.

However, volunteers tend to give less attention than is necessary to the project, and often lack objectivity. It is usually preferable to engage a professional marketing consultant, one who has experience in that nonprofit subsector of the economy. In education, for example, several consulting firms have emerged specializing in college marketing and management. Alternatively, the institution could seek the services of a general consulting firm. In any event, the institution should make an effort to invite at least three proposals from which to select the best consultant. A contract should be written which specifies the objectives, the time frame, the research plan, and the billing. A liaison person within the institution should be assigned to work with the consultant, arrange interviews, read and comment on the emerging reports, and make arrangements for the final presentation and implementation of proposals.

The marketing consultant will interview representative sets of people connected with the institution. In the case of a college, he or she will interview the president, members of the board of trustees, major vice presidents, directors of admissions and public relations, several school deans, several department chairmen, several professors, several students, representative alumni, and outside opinion leaders. The marketing consultant would seek to answer the following questions for each *academic program* studied:

- What is happening to student size and quality?
- How successful is the program in attracting qualified students?
- What are the main competitive programs and their positions in the market?
- What is the image and reputation of this program?
- What is the mission and what are the objectives of this program over the next five years?
- What budget is needed to accomplish these objectives?
- What fund raising potentials exist in the program?
- What marketing problems face the program and what marketing activities are being pursued?
- What useful services could a marketing director contribute to this program.

On the basis of this survey, the marketing consultant will develop and present a set of findings and recommendations regarding the institution's operations, opportunities, and needs in the marketing area. One of the recommendations will specifically deal with whether the institution is ready to effectively utilize a marketing director or vice president of marketing.

Marketing Director. Eventually the organization might become convinced of the need to appoint a director of marketing. This requires the development of a job description which specifies to whom this person reports, the scope of the position, the position concept, the functions, responsibilities, and major liaisons with others in the institution. Exhibit 3 presents a job description in a university context. The job is conceived as a middle management position, one in which

---

EXHIBIT 3
Job Description: Director of Marketing for a University

Position Title: Director of Marketing

Reports to: A vice president designated by the president.

Scope: University-wide

Position Concept: The director of marketing is responsible for providing marketing guidance and services to university officers, school deans, department chairmen, and other agents of the university.

Functions: The director of marketing will:

1. Contribute a marketing perspective to the deliberations of the top administration in their planning of the university's future.
2. Prepare data that might be needed by any officer of the university on a particular market's size, segments, trends, and behavioral dynamics.
3. Conduct studies of the needs, perceptions, preferences, and satisfactions of particular markets.
4. Assist in the planning, promotion, and launching of new programs.
5. Assist in the development of communication and promotion campaigns and materials.
6. Analyze and advise on pricing questions.
7. Appraise the workability of new academic proposals from a marketing point of view.
8. Advise on new student recruitment.
9. Advise on current student satisfaction.
10. Advise on university fundraising.

Responsibilities: The director of marketing will:

1. Contact individual officers and small groups at the university to explain services and to solicit problems.
2. Prioritize the various requests for services according to their long run impact, cost saving potential, time requirements, ease of accomplishment, cost, and urgency.
3. Select projects of high priority and set accomplishment goals for the year.
4. Prepare a budget request to support the anticipated work.
5. Prepare an annual report on the main accomplishments of the office.

Major Liaisons: The director of marketing will:

1. Relate most closely with the president's office, admissions office, development office, planning office, and public relations department.
2. Relate secondarily with the deans of various schools and chairmen of various departments.

---

the occupant primarily provides marketing services to others in the institution.

A major issue is where this person should be located in the organization and his or her relationships with kindred functions. Specifically, what is the marketing director's relationship to planning, public relations, and fund raising? A good case could be made for locating the marketing director within the planning office and therefore reporting to the vice president of planning. It would not make sense for the marketing director to report to public relations or fund raising because this would overspecialize the use made of marketing. The solution used by a large, eastern hospital consisted of appointing a vice president of institutional relations to whom directors of marketing, public relations, fund raising and planning reported.

Some public relations directors have been uncomfortable about the emergence of marketing directors, out of fear that they may eventually be reporting to the latter. Some public relations directors argue that marketing isn't needed, or that it is being done, or that they can do it. To the extent that marketing is thought to be aggressive promotion, public relations people feel they are best equipped to carry out this

function. To the extent that marketing is seen to consist of market analysis, new services development, marketing strategy, product line evaluation, and so on, public relations personnel are not equipped insofar as their training is basically in the fields of journalism and communications, not economics and business analysis. However, public relations persons can, of course, take courses in marketing and attempt to promote the concept of a combined office of marketing and public relations.

Marketing Vice President. The ultimate solution is the establishment of a vice president of marketing position. This is an upper level management position which gives more scope, authority, and influence to marketing. A vice president of marketing not only coordinates and supplies analytical services but also has a strong voice in the determination of where the institution should be going in terms of its changing opportunities.

The vice president of marketing would be responsible for planning and managing relations with several publics. The person's title may be altered to that of vice president of institutional relations or external affairs to avoid unnecessary semantic opposition. Thus far, only a few nonprofit organizations have gone this route.

The top marketing job should be tailored to the specific institution. Consider the YMCA, often called "the General Electric of the social service business." The YMCA is in not one, but several "businesses": recreation, education, camps, physical fitness, hotels, and so on. Central headquarters must wrestle with decisions on where to build new facilities, what new programs to introduce, what programs to drop, how to promote membership, and dozens of other matters. Were a vice president of marketing appointed, this person would be responsible for defining better ways to serve various constituencies. Reporting to the vice president would be functional marketing specialists (marketing research, pricing promotion, and planning), product managers (recreational programs, educational programs, camps) and market managers (teens, young marrieds, senior adults). These people would design programs and offer services to the various YMCA units throughout the country. There is no question that marketing decisions are being made all the time throughout the YMCA system but they are made, unfortunately, without professional marketing expertise.

Let us assume that an institution decides to hire a marketing vice president. This person's contribution will be carefully scrutinized. The new appointee will have to develop a strategy to make marketing visible and useful.

The marketing executive is not likely to be immediately swamped with requests for services, because many administrators initially will not understand marketing. The marketing executive should spend the first few months meeting various groups within the institution to learn about their problems. For example, Evanston Hospital's new marketing vice president arranged separate meetings with senior physicians, residents, interns, senior nurses, and others. At each meeting he described his job position, explained the nature of marketing, indicated the kinds of problems he could solve and services that he could offer, and then opened the meeting to discussion. He sought suggestions of projects that he might conduct. At the end of two months, he found more than enough useful projects. His problem, in fact, was to set priorities for the many projects, and he did so by rating each potential project using the following criteria (on five-point scales): (1) the importance or centrality of the project to the future of the institution; (2) the magnitude of the improved service or cost savings that it might effect; (3) its probable cost; (4) the difficulty of carrying it out; and (5) the length of time it would take to complete. An ideal project was one that was very important, would effect great cost savings, would cost little to do, could be easily carried out, and could be completed in a short time. It became clear which projects went to the top of the list, and he concentrated his efforts in the first year on these projects.

The marketing executive will be expected to prepare an annual marketing plan listing major projects and a required budget. Much of the budget will go toward buying the services of outside marketing research firms and advertising agencies for needed projects. At each year's end, the executive will prepare a report summarizing levels of accomplishment and savings. Eventually, the nature of this position will become well understood within the organization and easy to assess its contributions toward institutional survival and growth.

CONCLUSION

At the present time, the marketing idea is beginning to attract the interest of administrators in the third sector. This is evidenced by the growing literature on college, hospital, and other third sector marketing, as well as by increased attendance at specialized marketing conferences for nonprofit organizations. Interest is not likely to abate; indeed, it is likely to increase as more administrators come to see their institution's future in marketing terms. For an institution, marketing offers a much richer understanding of what is happening and throws light on new opportunities.

Despite the growing interest in marketing, however, many nonprofit organizations still resist it. Many groups within these organizations see marketing as a threat to their autonomy or power. Eventually, out of necessity, marketing ideas will filter into these organizations. Marketing will initially be viewed as advertising and promotion rather than as a revolutionary new way to view the institution and its purposes. A few institutions will lead the others in developing an advanced understanding of marketing. They will start performing better. Their competitors will be forced to learn their marketing. Within another decade, marketing will be a major and accepted function within the nonprofit sector.

The issue that frightens some observers is not that marketing will be ineffective but that it may be too effective. They see funds and clients flowing to institutions that are willing to spend the largest sums of money on advertising and promotion. They fear that large scale promotional warfare will ruin the smaller institutions that cannot afford marketing, and will create a competitive stalemate among the larger institutions. This fear is based, once again, on the fallacy of viewing marketing as primarily promotional.

The real contribution of marketing thinking is to lead each institution to search for a more meaningful position in the larger market. Instead of all hospitals offering the same services, marketing leads each hospital to shape distinct service mixes to serve specific market segments. Marketing competition, at its best, creates a pattern of varied institutions, each clear as to its mission, market coverage, need specialization, and service portfolio.

Administrators and businessmen who have a stake in the third sector are beginning to recognize the contributions that marketing thinking can make. Marketing will lead to a better understanding of the needs of different client segments; to a more careful shaping and launching of new services; to a pruning of weak services; to more effective methods of delivering services; to more flexible pricing approaches; and to higher levels of client satisfaction. Altogether, marketing offers a great potential to third sector organizations to survive, grow, and strengthen their contributions to the general welfare.

REFERENCES

Gaedeke, R. M. (1977), *Marketing in Private and Public Nonprofit Organizations: Perspectives and Illustrations*, Santa Monica, CA: Goodyear Publishing Co.

Henion, Karl E. (1976), *Ecological Marketing*, Columbus, Ohio: Grid, Inc.

Kotler, Philip (1975), *Marketing for Nonprofit Organizations*, Englewood Cliffs, NJ: Prentice-Hall, Inc.

—— and Levy, Sidney J. (1969), "Broadening the Concept of Marketing," *Journal of Marketing*, 33 (January), 10–15.

Lovelock, Christopher H., ed. (1977), *Nonbusiness Marketing Cases*, 8-378-001, Boston, MA: Intercollegiate Case Clearing House.

—— and Charles B. Weinberg (1977), *Cases in Public and Nonprofit Marketing*, Palo Alto, CA: The Scientific Press.

—— and Charles B. Weinberg (1978), "Public and Nonprofit Marketing Comes of Age," in *Review of Marketing 1978*, Gerald Zaltman and T. Bonoma eds., Chicago, IL: American Marketing Association, 413–452.

MacStravic, Robin E. (1977), *Marketing Health Care*, Germantown, MD: Aspen Systems Corp.

Nickels, William G. (1978), *Marketing Principles*, Englewood Cliffs, NJ: Prentice-Hall, Inc.

Pyke, Donald L. (1977), "The Future of Higher Education: Will Private Institutions Disappear in the U.S.?" *The Futurist*, 374.

Roberto, Eduardo (1975), *Strategic Decision-Making in a Social Program: The Case of Family-Planning Diffusion*, Lexington, MA: Lexington Books.

Shapiro, Benson (1973), "Marketing for Nonprofit Organizations," *Harvard Business Review*, 51 (September-October), 123–132.

35
Should Not-for-Profits Go into Business?

Edward Skloot

To the manager of the not-for-profit organization, the idea of entering into a business venture might seem heretical. The precedent has been set, however, and numbers of not-for-profits are currently earning substantial amounts of income through long-term for-profit enterprises that have continuity with the organization's prime mission. The author of this article cautions managers of not-for-profits that an earned-income venture can be a miserable failure unless the organization meets certain conditions: a product to sell, managerial talent, trustee support, an entrepreneurial spirit, and money or the ability to get it. He then describes nine issues managers should consider before undertaking earned-income projects.

Virtually all not-for-profit organiations, from cultural institutions to social service centers, are in deep financial trouble. Expenses are rising faster than income. Mounting labor and energy costs and inflation continue to take their toll. Most recently, large reductions in government funding undertaken by the Reagan administration are having serious, possibly devastating effects.

Many not-for-profit organizations are particularly vulnerable to reductions in government funding. Since the 1960s, national and state dollars have fueled the growth of their programs. The current economic climate now finds many not-for-profits overextended and unprepared to make measured alterations in their operations.

However vulnerable they may be, not-for-profit organizations must now do two things to ensure their survival: stabilize their budgets and diversify their revenue bases. The diversification can occur by expanding the sources of

Edward Skloot is president of New Ventures, a consulting firm in New York City.

unearned funds or by establishing earned-income ventures. Under the right circumstances, such commercial activity can contribute measurably to the income side of the organization's ledger.

Whether and how to earn income are subjects of growing concern to board members and staff of not-for-profits. Often they are looking not only for new funds but also for a rationale to proceed. Some, faced with considerable shortfalls in revenue, are reviewing what was once an unyielding arm's-length relationship with the private sector.

I suggest that the rationale for commercialism in not-for-profits is historically rooted and easy to come by but that many managers of these organizations need guidelines on how to proceed—a sense of what works and what does not.

COMMERCIAL VENTURES CAN BE A SUCCESS

Contrary to conventional wisdom, not-for-profit earned-income ventures are neither new nor compromising. As early as 1874, for example, the Metropolitan Museum of Art retained a professional to photograph its collections and sell copies of the prints as well. Profits were to go into a fund for enhancing the museum's stock of negatives and then to defray the museum's running costs. The Metropolitan established its first official sales shop in 1908.

Before the end of World War I, three state university presses were already well under way. More recently, various earned-income ventures have sprung up under numerous auspices, from the Girl Scouts to UNICEF, and in numerous forms, from small gift shops to vast real estate developments.

Of course, only a small minority of the nation's 300,000 not-for-profit organizations can and should venture into earned-income projects. For some the financial risks are too great, for others the managerial demands are overwhelming. But for those with the opportunity, the economic climate virtually demands the pursuit of earned income.

Five principles are central in starting or expanding such a venture. Managers of the most successful of the not-for-profits know them and operate by them. They are relevant irrespective of the size of the venture.

Something to Sell.

Many not-for-profit staff members think they have found an earned-income venture when in fact it is merely an attractive idea. Staff or board members often propose schemes that look good in concept but have weak vital signs. The not-for-profit ethic, which values program success and client satisfaction as much if not more than bottom-line results, has shaped their thoughts. Their viewpoint is understandable; for example, fees are often necessarily hard to establish in not-for-profits because programs (such as job training) have no real market price equivalent, or because the organization is committed to keeping prices down at almost any cost, or because the service is subsidized (as is geriatric health care).

Not-for-profit executives must ask themselves four questions before pursuing these enterprises: Have I something to sell? If I do, is there a market niche for it? If there is a market niche, can I fill it? If I can fill it, what are the financial risk and danger to the organization's mission?

In some cases, the Internal Revenue Service makes those risks very clear. For example, a not-for-profit that engages in a business "not substantially related" to the organization's exempt purposes may jeopardize its tax-exempt status, particularly if the income stream is large (20% of total organizational activity is a conservative rule of thumb). Not-for-profits whose exemption is not at issue can pursue a commercial endeavor. If they do, they pay taxes on the unrelated business income according to the going tax rate.

The way for not-for-profit executives to answer the four questions is to investigate their organizations' "natural resources." Many organizations have products to develop and merchandise in an intelligent and serious way. It might be some kind of publishing activity, it might be art, real estate, or the processing or sharing of information. It might be skilled or even unskilled labor. These natural resources

might be turned to advantage to produce a stream of earned income.

Two examples make the point. One is that of the Twyla Tharp Dance Company. Not only does this company sell tickets and therefore market its live performances for money (a common approach of dance companies) but it also recently sold a choreographic work to cable TV. In the fall of 1981, CBS Cable Television presented the company in a one-hour TV special. The choreographic work was the company's natural resource. CBS Cable covered all production costs, which exceeded $300,000. Twyla Tharp kept full artistic control over the product. A satisfactory arrangement was made for future cablecast and nonbroadcast rights and for cassette and disk sales. In addition, CBS Cable also made a modest contribution to the Twyla Tharp Foundation.

Partly as a result of this venture, the dance company has several projects under way, including an examination of archived materials for possible future use on cable or network television. Box office sales for dance companies generally account for 55% of their operating budgets. The Twyla Tharp Dance Company garners about 75% of its budget through its various earned-income activities.

Another example concerns a real estate venture by a modest-sized cultural organization in New York City. In the fall of 1981, the Film Forum constructed two small adjacent movie theaters in lower Manhattan. It programs one of the theaters, which shows the work of independent, often unheralded, filmmakers. For this activity the organization charges general admission.,

The Film Forum leases the second theater, however, to a private exhibitor of similar artistic sensibilities, who pays a monthly rental. The two theaters provide a focus of artistic activity that expands the attendance at each. The Film Forum also runs the high-quality food concessions at both theaters and derives additional revenue from them.

In less than two years, the Film Forum's budget has skyrocketed from $100,000 to $500,000, reflecting program growth supported by earned income. Sixty percent of its income is now earned, and its finances are in much more stable condition.

Critical Mass of Management Talent.

In this time of scarce resources, a not-for-profit must shepherd its human resources with skill. This means searching out enterprises that can flourish over the long haul and that can change direction with the market.

Some not-for-profits regularly come up with one-shot earned-income schemes—"six posters in search of a buying public." Smaller organizations in particular are drawn to these projects which seem to demand so little attention and expertise. But they should be wary. These schemes require an enormous burst of management energy that frequently leaves an organization's bottom line little improved. Put another way, successful earned-income ventures in not-for-profits, as in the private sector, require sustained managerial attention to tasks that have clear financial payoffs. Quick fixes don't work in either sector.

Two examples will help make the point. The Smithsonian Institution is a huge not-for-profit organization that grosses approximately $70 million annually. It runs a publishing company and *Smithsonian* magazine. It sells $9 million worth of food and grosses $7 million in retail sales. It mails between 5 million and 6 million catalogs annually to members and nonmembers, from which it takes in another $7 million in mail order sales.

Concessionnaires run the Smithsonian's food services. As contracts come due, the institution reviews them for both profitability and service to the public—and to see whether the entire operation might be handled in-house. These reviews involve making numerous marketing, sales, and service assumptions, which require considerable management talent and funds.

An example of more moderate scale is the New York Shakespeare Festival Theater, directed by Joseph Papp, which in recent years has become a major producer of commercially successful plays. Although its productions of *A Chorus Line* and *The Pirates of Penzance* have been tremendously successful, a more interesting example for the purpose here is the less ambitious show, *I'm Getting My Act Together and Taking It on the Road.*

Here was a slow-starter. The show ran seven months at the Public Theater and more than two years at the Circle in the Square. The question Papp and his colleagues faced was, could it sustain a road company? Their answer was no.

They decided instead to see if the show could be licensed in large cities hospitable to its message. Papp's general manager went to such cities as Toronto, Chicago, and San Francisco, making a studious effort to seek out local producers who would ensure a quality product. In each city he looked at theaters, tested the acoustics, auditioned available actors who might be in the casts, and interviewed possible investors.

Ultimately, producers in six cities mounted separate productions, each with a separate licensing and royalty arrangement. To date the effort has brought the New York Shakespeare Festival Theater $400,000 in earned income.

As did the Smithsonian, the Festival Theater had enough creative and sophisticated management talent to pursue an unusual earned-income opportunity and to get its natural resource merchandised in the way it wanted.

When the organization doesn't have that talent, it must hire it, rent it, or forget it. Essentially, the decision to proceed is a decision about resource allocation and reveals the entrepreneurial values and analytic capabilities of the not-for-profit organization.

Trustee Support. Having an angel on the board helps; two or three are an invaluable asset. They can do more than donate money; committed trustees can provide essential services in

marketing, law, or accounting, and can make the difference between failure and success of an earned-income venture.

Because they don't work in businesses, staff members—program chiefs, curators, clinicians, and so forth—often are uneasy with earned-income ventures. Trustees can be particularly helpful in educating them. Staff members usually lack familiarity with bottom-line issues and need to become comfortable with commerce at a gradual pace. Thus in some cases, one or several trustees must carry the banner, doing what they do best.

In bringing new plays to the stage, the Kennedy Center in Washington, D.C. has no specific investment policy. The director of the center, Roger Stevens, runs this effort; he and his colleagues get help in financing the plays they want to produce from a separate organization called Kennedy Center Productions, Inc., which has its own board and which makes grants to the Kennedy Center for play production. KCP, Inc. has a line of credit at a local bank that is guaranteed by what Stevens calls "public-spirited citizens."

The Kennedy Center has done extremely well with this fluid, close arrangement. For instance, the Kennedy Center started *Annie* toward stardom; the center will net $4 million to $5 million or more before the road shows close.

Conversely, it is extremely important to avoid trustee hostility. Some trustees have strong feelings against earned-income ventures, and they may actively or passively resist commerical involvement. Some of them see these ventures as unrelated or even destructive to the goals or the operating focus of the organization—and in some cases they may be right. When this sentiment exists, staff and other board members should think twice about proceeding. Only in rare cases is it worth going to the mat with trustees over this issue.

Entrepreneurial Attitude or Tone. Many staff members have far more entrepreneurial spirit than commercial wisdom. They want appealing exhibitions, functioning outreach programs, and comprehensive service networks. Their training (and past government policy) pushes them in this direction. Yet to be successful, organizations must marry program thrust with commercial sensibility. In the most successful not-for-profits, the attitude is entrepreneurial and the approach is strictly businesslike.

For example, about ten years ago the New York City Ballet started its gift bar with only a few posters for sale. Open only during the half hour before curtain time and the two intermissions, the gift bar now carries roughly 200 items. Bloomingdale's even merchandises selected items there.

The gift bar example is important for two reasons. One, it nets a lot of money for its size. The gross is perhaps $125,000, and the net is somewhere between $50,000 and $60,000. Two, and related to the first, the gift bar is run entirely by volunteers, which has positive tax implications as well. Sixty volunteers, nine per night, do the job well and at no cost.

The gift bar is a model of entrepreneurial attitudes harnessed to the benefit of the not-for-profit organization, but numerous others have worked equally well.

Baltimore's South East Community Organization bought a supermarket and leased it to a food store chain. The Monastery of the Glorious Ascension in Resaca, Georgia runs MGA Computer Services, a computerized letter-writing and records service. The Denver Children's Museum has marketed everything from in-flight activity books for children to Frontier Airlines to several million check-out bags with educational messages on them to a national grocery chain. The museum earns a staggering 98% of its income through such ventures.

Cash or the Ability to Get It. Smaller organizations often have little ready money to invest. Larger ones face different issues: How much to invest? Over what period of time? With what risk and potential for return on investment?

A very important way to obtain funds is by joint venturing. Not-for-profits are increasingly successful in getting private sector sources to assist with the idea they want to develop. Bringing in the private sector, preferably as an investor, can lower the risk as well as infuse funds and marketing and management support.

For example, museums often team up with publishing houses to make exhibition catalogs widely available, and to turn a profit. The Museum of the City of New York possesses 3,000 Currier & Ives lithographs, one of the finest collections in the world. In 1978, the museum entered an agreement with the Abbeville Press, which put up funds for a big Currier & Ives coffee table volume to be sold at a hefty price. The museum got a fee and a few smaller benefits.

The book sold well, and the next year the partners went a step further. Abbeville published a paperback volume of the hundred best Currier & Ives lithographs for book clubs and stores. The next year they put out the oversized *Currier & Ives America,* which, at a hundred dollars, sold well too. The public was also treated to a Currier & Ives wall calendar and engagement calendar, both at popular prices. The first joint venture obviously stimulated others.

Numerous other (and sometimes more controversial) examples of joint venturing have also worked well: Massachusetts General Hospital will receive $50 million from Hoechst, the giant West German chemical company, for biological research in exchange for exclusive licenses to develop commerical products from certain research discoveries. Anheuser-Busch and the Children's Television Workshop have developed their first theme park for young people aged 3 to 12 in Langhorne, Pennsylvania, with great success. This year a second park will open in Texas.

If not-for-profits take the initiative, they can ride piggyback on the private sector for money and expertise, to everyone's benefit. Moreover, trustees can be particularly helpful in assisting in the creation of a joint venture. Only in unusual cases should not-for-profits compete head-to-head with the expertise and money available to private corporations.

THE OBJECT IS INCOME

Suppose the not-for-profit organization meets all five criteria—something to sell, management talent, trustee support, entrepreneurial attitude, and money or the ability to get it. What then? The key factor in the success of the venture is treatment of it as a business, not a service: they should use earned income to support program activities, not use the latter to enhance the former.

Executives should also be careful about trying to mix social motives with business considerations. Quite often staff members will try to slip a primary service objective into an earned-income plan—for instance, using a real estate development project to train young people for jobs. Because of their experience, staff members tend to equate program acceptance with market success—a view fostered in the 1960s and 1970s by expanding federal budgets. In earned-income ventures, although a program may have the desired social thrust, a manager must keep it under tight rein or run the risk of compromising the venture and threatening the enterprise.

The most commercially successful not-for-profits have learned to apply private-sector tools to move toward self-sufficiency. They do not fear commercialism; indeed, they use commercial activity to support their charitable, educational, research, and other similar purposes. They write business plans, develop and market new products, construct housing, rent real estate, and license patents. In the 1980s, managers of these organizations will have to seize opportunities such as these to keep the not-for-profit sector healthy.

For the managers of not-for-profits just beginning to contemplate an earned-income venture, the following nine steps are a useful way to structure their thinking:

1. *Review your goals and objectives.* Be sure that your primary mission is clearly defined and that an earned-income venture fits comfortably within it. If it doesn't fit, stop right here.
2. *Gather internal support.* Seek staff and board attention and support, particularly if earned-income activities are new to your organization. One or two senior board members might be especially helpful.
3. *Investigate your "natural resources."* These range from written materials, to art and photographs, to land, to the skills of staff members. If at all possible, marry your natural resources to your earned-income efforts. This will be your strong suit.
4. *Be willing to seek advice.* Even the best program executives are not necessarily shrewd business persons. Make sure the person you ask understands both private-sector and third-sector operations. If you are not going to oversee the project yourself, assign a committed senior staff member to shepherd the entire effort.
5. *Remember the bottom line.* Give good value in the marketplace or your enterprise will not succeed. Articulate the risks you want to take and the payoffs you want to achieve.

6. *Develop the venture prospect.* Think creatively yet cautiously. Research the field relentlessly. Ask yourself: Is there a market niche for a product? If yes, can I fill it? At what financial and organizational cost?

7. *Write a business plan.* Your plan should be comprehensive, literate and ultimately persuasive. Seek experienced business, legal, and financial advice, as may be necessary. The business plan is the most important financial and planning tool you have. Be prepared to spend long hours developing and updating it.

8. *Review your goals and resources again.* Be sure the venture won't demand things of you and your staff (funding, time, or attention) that you cannot, or should not, give.

9. *Implement your business plan.* Move to organize the work, raise the funds, hire the staff, and so on. Be ready to make mid-course corrections based on experience.

36

Marketing National Change: Decimalization in Britain

Christopher H. Lovelock

What happens when an entire country has to change its way of doing things? An analysis of the 1966–1971 program for decimalizing the British currency provides valuable insights into the role of the different elements of the marketing mix in helping to facilitate a major societal change. It also highlights the tasks facing an official change agency in managing and coordinating such a program. Parallels are drawn to current programs for the metrication of weights and measures.

Government organizations are increasingly finding themselves cast in the role of change agencies. In order to achieve social, economic, or environmental objectives, it is sometimes necessary for large numbers of citizens to modify or discard old ways of doing things and to adopt new ones.

Recent examples of dramatic national changes in industrialized countries include the 1967 Swedish switch from driving on the left to driving on the right [3, 6]; the adoption of decimal currencies by Australia, New Zealand, and the United Kingdom between 1966 and 1971 [1, 7, 10]; and current programs in Australia, Britain, Canada, the United States, and elsewhere to replace customary systems of measurement with the metric system [9].

However, even more modest programs may require careful coordination by a central agency to be successful.

Christopher H. Lovelock is Associate Professor of Business Administration, Harvard University.

The assistance of the Central Office of Information and the J. Walter Thompson Company is gratefully acknowledged. Unless otherwise specified, the views expressed are those of the author.

In 1976, the United States Treasury Department attempted to reintroduce the two-dollar bill into general circulation [8]. By replacing half the 1.6 billion one-dollar bills printed annually with an equivalent value of "twos," it hoped to save $35 million in printing costs over a five year period. Yet the two-dollar bill has so far failed to find acceptance in the U.S. This failure reflects the apparent inability of the Treasury and the Federal Reserve System to develop and fund a coordinated marketing strategy for reintroduction, although they had the results of a detailed study of consumers, retailers, and bankers available to guide them [2].

In this article, we shall examine a much more complex task—namely, the replacement of an existing currency system with an entirely new one. Apart from its intrinsic interest, an evaluation of the successful British decimalization program of 1966–71 provides some valuable insights into the planning and management of large-scale changes in established practices. It also highlights the role of an official change agency in facilitating such changes through judicious use of marketing.

THE PROBLEM IN PERSPECTIVE

On February 15, 1971, the United Kingdom officially went decimal. In a program described as "the biggest monetary operation in the history of the world," the old currency of 12 pence to a shilling and 20 shillings to a pound was abandoned for a new decimal currency of 100 new pence to a pound.[1]

Since money is used by almost everyone, this dramatic change affected the daily lives of practically everybody in a nation of over fifty million people. Almost overnight, it seemed, a coinage with a twelve-hundred-year background was replaced with some five billion units of a new one that had a different value and appearance but a similar name. And yet, this seemingly momentous switch came to be referred to as the "non-event of 1971"—confounding the many critics who had predicted chaos.

How was such a smooth and successful operation achieved in the face of significant public antipathy? Many factors contributed, but the key element in facilitating the changeover was undoubtedly the marketing strategy adopted by the official Decimal Currency Board and its advisers.

Most major marketing programs are directed at specific segments within the population, and their originators are generally satisfied to achieve desired changes in attitudes, behavior, or purchasing patterns among only a fraction of the target audience. Consumer goods marketers are often contented with seeing their products purchased by only a small percentage of potential consumers; a politician may be glad to obtain 50.1% of all votes cast in a two-way election race. But for the decimalization campaign to be successful, it had to encourage virtually an entire population to change its behavior. In the long run, there could be no personal choice about whether to work in decimals *or* in the old currency. Everyone had to change sooner or later, since the old coins—and the calculations based on them—were to be phased out. The challenge was to see that the desired adaptation to the new currency took place as quickly as possible, with minimum public confusion or dislocation of business.

THE DECISION TO DECIMALIZE

A feature in the conservative *Sunday Telegraph* on January 3, 1971, just six weeks before "D Day" ("Decimal Day"), reflected the bemusement felt by many citizens concerning the way in which decimalization had finally caught up with them:

There remains to this day a certain mystery about how a nation so [unkindly] disposed to [decimals], a nation moreover habitually accused of excessive attachment to historic institutions such as its own venerable currency, came to acquiesce with apparent calm in the abandonment of pounds, shillings and pence in favour of the decimal system which will invade its life on February 15. . . .

Needless to say, there had been no perceptible demand from the general public for the change. However, the idea took root [in government circles] in a way that it had signally failed to do hitherto, in spite of the efforts of interested minorities during upwards of two centuries to plant it there.

In practice there were several forces at work. In the early 1960s, three major trends combined to bring about decimalization in Britain. Since the Second World War, a growing number of other Commonwealth countries had successfully abandoned pounds, shillings, and pence (£sd) for new decimal currencies, or else had announced their intention of doing so. Another significant development was Britain's growing trade and tourist links with already decimalized countries, particularly in Europe. Tourists especially found the British currency hard to use and to understand. The third major incentive for change concerned the rapid mechanization of accounting and cash handling procedures, which could not be used to their full advantage with a £sd system.

A Marketing Framework for Decimalization. How should one go about introducing a new currency in an economically stable, highly industrialized democracy of some fifty million people? Several major considerations faced the British Government in developing and implementing an appropriate program for change.

The key problem was the need to design a new decimal currency. In a three-tier currency system, where twelve pence equaled one shilling, and twenty shillings equaled one pound, decimalization necessarily involved the disappearance of at least two of the existing units. The unresolved question in the past had always been, which? Once the basis of decimalization had been selected, there were what might be termed "packaging" decisions to be made, relating to the names selected for the new monetary units, the denominations in which coins and bills were to be issued, and the physical appearance of the new currency.

Conversion to decimals would involve financial costs for business and a certain amount of effort and inconvenience for individual citizens. The Government had to decide whether it should pay compensation to businesses and how it could minimize the time and psychic costs to individuals. In part, the answer would lie in judicious use of advertising, personal selling, publicity, and sales promotion. The problem was to design an appropriate campaign, directed at all types of businesses, cash handlers and the public, that would explain the rationale for the changeover and provide each target segment with the information needed to make the change to decimals smoothly and at the appropriate time.

Since money is used so widely, there would be a significant distribution problem in getting the new coins rapidly into circulation wherever money changed hands. A related

---

[1] Under the old system £1 = 20 shillings = 240 pence, and 1 shilling = 12 pence; under the new system £1 = 100 new pence (the pound remained unchanged). At the time of decimalization in 1971, the Pound Sterling was worth $2.40 in U.S. currency. Thus one (old) penny was exactly equivalent to 1¢ and one shilling to 12¢. Under the new system, one new penny was equal in value to 2.4¢. The abbreviation £sd was widely used to denote pounds, shillings and pence and was for years referred to in colloquial speech as "LSD." The use of the £ sign, a fanciful "L," was derived from the Latin "libra" (a pound), while the "d" for penny came from the Latin "denarius," a small Roman coin. With the advent of decimal currency, new pence were designated "p."

problem was to ensure that all coin-operated and accounting machines were quickly converted to decimals. Clearly, market research would be needed to provide insights into these problems and to facilitate evaluation of alternative strategies designed to resolve them.

PRODUCT DECISIONS: DESIGNING THE NEW DECIMAL CURRENCY

In December 1961, the Government announced the appointment of a Committee of Inquiry under the Earl of Halsbury, a distinguished scientist and administrator, to advise on the method, timing, and cost of decimalization. In a very real sense, the Halsbury Committee's principal task was one of product design. As can be seen from Exhibit 1, there are a variety of alternative ways of transforming a £sd

system into a decimal one, and some important considerations involved. The question was, which approach would yield the most enduring benefits, while minimizing the problems of changeover? The table lists the eight most plausible alternatives. In September 1963, by a majority of four to two, the Committee recommended adoption of the £-cent-½ system [11]. The minority recommended a 10s-cent system (as adopted in Australia, New Zealand, and South Africa).

A lengthy delay ensued, due in part to a change of government. Finally, on March 1, 1966, two weeks after successful introduction of a decimal currency in Australia [1], the British Government formally announced its decision to adopt a decimal currency, with the official changeover scheduled for February 1971. The pound was to be retained as the major unit, and divided into 100 "new pence." (The name "new penny" (p) was chosen for the minor unit instead of "cent," since it was felt that the latter would be unpopular because of its foreign associations.) The coins and notes selected for the new system—designated as £p—are listed in Exhibit 2 with their £sd predecessors.

The final product-related decision was taken the following year and concerned the size, shape, and metal of the new coins, as well as their design. Bronze was selected for the new 2p, 1p, and ½p coins, continuing the tradition of the

---

EXHIBIT 1
Some Decimalization Problems

1. Basis of Decimalization

(a) Old System:
12 pennies (d) = 1 shilling(s); 20 shillings = 1 pound (£)

(b) Principal decimal alternatives

	Terminology	Previous adopters
£1 major unit of 200 subunits	£-cent-½	
£1 major unit of 1,000 subunits	£-mil	Cyprus
10s major unit of 100 subunits	10s-cent	Australia, New Zealand, South Africa
8s 4d major unit of 100 pence	100-penny	Ghana
5s major unit of 100 subunits	Crown-cent	
4s 2d major unit of 100 half-pence	100-ha'penny	British West Indies
2s major unit of 100 subunits	Florin-cent	
1s major unit of 100 subunits	Shilling-cent	

(c) Some Considerations

Retention of old upper unit (pound)
Retention of old lower unit (penny or halfpenny)
Easy conversion of old middle unit (shilling) to new system (1s = 10¢ in 10s-cent system)
Extent to which present coins and/or notes can be used
Impact of any change on inflation (size of smallest monetary unit)
Preservation of confidence in the currency
Continuity of record-keeping
Two spaces vs. three spaces after decimal point/avoidance of fractions
Integration of old and new currencies during changeover period

2. Naming the New Currency

Need for public acceptance
Preservation of tradition vs. creation of new tradition
Avoidance of confusion, both domestically and internationally

3. Design of New Coinage

Choice of denominations
Size/shape/design/metal for new coins (identification, handling, acceptance)

EXHIBIT 2
The Old and New Currencies

	New (£p)	Old (£sd)	Name
Notes	£20[1]	—	
	£10	£10	
	£ 5	£ 5	
	£ 1	£ 1	
Circulating Coins:	50p (= 10s)	10s (= 50p)	
	10p (= 2s)	2s6d (= 12½p)	Half-crown
		2s (= 10p)	Two shillings (or florin)
	5p (= 1s)	1s (= 5p)	Shilling
		6d (= 2½p)	Sixpence
	2p[2] (= 4.8d)	3d[3] (= 1.25p)	Threepence
	1p[2] (= 2.4d)		
	½p[2] (= 1.2d)	1d[3] (= 0.42p)	Penny
		½d[3] (= 0.21p)	Ha'penny

[1] This new note was not part of the decimalization program. Its introduction simply reflected the need for a higher denomination banknote.

[2] No exact £sd equivalent.

[3] No exact £p equivalent.

old penny and halfpenny. One innovation was to adopt a weight-to-value relationship for these coins, such that 1p weighed twice as much as ½p and 2p weighed four times as much. In this way, cash handlers could simply weigh a bag of mixed bronze coinage to determine its value. The cupro-nickel (''silver'') 5p and 10p coins were to retain the same weight, size and metal specifications as the equal value 1s and 2s coins they replaced, while a new seven-sided 50p coin was announced in 1968 to replace the equal value 10s note. Higher value notes were unaffected by decimalization and remained unchanged. Like current American coins, the old British coins displayed their face values in words. To simplify identification, especially for foreign visitors, the designs of the new coins incorporated their values in prominent numerals.

FORMATION OF THE DECIMAL CURRENCY BOARD

In 1966, the government established a Decimal Currency Board (DCB) to plan and coordinate the decimalization program. The Board's function was to ''examine in detail, with the institutions concerned, the problems of the change-over, to organize a programme of guidance to the public, and to do everything necessary to promote a speedy and efficient transition.'' [10, p. 60].

The concerns of the Decimal Currency Board were broadly threefold: the logistics of the changeover, the education of people and organizations concerning the switch to decimal currency, and the resolution of any resulting problems. Underlying its work was a continuing program of investigation, consultation, and research.

Named as Chairman of the DCB was Lord Fiske of Brent, a former Leader of the Greater London Council. Lord Fiske's personality, experience and appearance were all well suited to the increasingly exposed role he was to fill. A big, bearlike, avuncular man with a long record of public service, he projected an image of good humor and unflappability.

THE STRATEGY OF CHANGEOVER

The five-year preparatory period prior to D Day emphasized the amount of work that had to be done. The biggest physical task—and one requiring early action by manufacturers—was conversion or replacement of machines. Some 2.3 million business machines and cash registers and 2.7 million coin-operated machines were affected by decimalization. In addition, five billion new coins had to be minted, and some existing coins had to be withdrawn from circulation.

The DCB's strategy was to spread the publicity effort over a three year period, 1968 to 1971. It concentrated first on informing business management about decimalization and encouraging early and systematic planning for the change-over. Then it turned its attention to retail and other cash-handling organizations, emphasizing the need for full and detailed preparations. Finally, it explained the new system

and coinage to the general public, so that people could go shopping with confidence from February 15, 1971, onwards.

In its *First Annual Report* the Board outlined the role it expected to play in the communications effort, noting that

> Many other organisations besides the Board will be issuing publicity and educational material about decimal currency. We welcome this because we cannot alone persuade over 50 million people in Britain to change the money habits of a lifetime. We are always willing to help organisations to prepare publicity and training material. . . . The publicity campaign is a team effort but we are glad to act as coordinators [4, pp. 1–2].

In late 1967 the Decimal Currency Board appointed the London office of the J. Walter Thompson Company (JWT) to handle its advertising account. JWT was to work closely with the Central Office of Information—a Government office which exercised a centralized, coordinating function for all Government advertising—and with the DCB's own Publicity Group.

The advertising agency's main tasks were creation of advertisements and media selection and buying; in addition, its market research subsidiary undertook consumer surveys at various stages in the campaign. The DCB handled its own, very extensive, public relations activity. Looking back some years later, the former secretary of the DCB reflected:

> The early appointment of an agency was important for, although it soon became established policy that the main advertising campaign should be reserved until the final weeks, a good deal of careful forward planning had to be done; there were also general advertising campaigns on several aspects of the Board's campaign for businessmen; and a programme of regular research surveys was carried out so that the Board would be aware of what people knew of and thought about the changeover. The early appointment also ensured that the Board and agency staff . . . were able to build up a close and informal working relationship which was conducive to the interchange of ideas [10, p. 182].

Encouraging Early Planning by Business. The Board moved quickly to establish some priorities:

> The immediate need is to convince management, in the widest sense of that word, that they face problems which they should be seeking to solve now rather than in 1970—not because these problems are great but because, if they are tackled early, they can be solved with comparative ease [4, p. 15].

For decimalization to go smoothly, businesses had to plan well in advance for conversion or replacement of the machines they operated, to draw up new accounting conventions, to develop revised cash-handling procedures, and to retrain certain personnel.

In what was termed the Management Campaign, the DCB emphasized use of publications, particularly reference booklets and newsletters. In all, 11 reference booklets were published between 1968–1970. All booklets had an initial free distribution of about 60,000 copies through trade associations, with additional copies thereafter being sold through government bookstores and retail booksellers. Some 3.75 million booklets were distributed in this way. The DCB *Newsletter* was issued at approximately six—week intervals and by

1970 had a print run of some 275,000 copies, with around 140,000 being distributed to trade and other associations for circulation to their members and the balance going to a subscription list, sent out in response to inquiries, or distributed at meetings.

The Board's most direct contact with the business community was through its extensive program of speaking engagements. These were often reported in local newspapers, which greatly widened their audience. The DCB also participated in many exhibitions and issued news releases with information of interest to business managers.

Marketing Decimals to Cash-Handling Organizations. A second major thrust of the Board's educational and promotional work was directed at retailers, transport operators, and other cash handlers, with 1969–70 being promoted as the "Year of the Retailer." The Board developed close links with trade and professional associations in order to ensure a frank, two-way flow of ideas and suggestions. Formal surveys of management and retailers provided periodic feedback on levels of preparedness for decimalization and indications of problem areas.

Recognizing the problem of reaching small shopkeepers, many of whom were not members of trade associations, a variety of media were employed to convey the Board's message to retailers. Press advertising was done in national and provincial papers and in 52 trade publications; postal franking messages were used to get the attention of those operating small businesses; and 1.6 million copies of a popularly written booklet entitled *New Money in Your Shop* were distributed free through banks to all businesspeople having cash transactions with the general public. A special film about retailing aspects of the decimal changeover was produced for free loan to Chambers of Commerce, trade associations, clubs, and other business groups: it proved very successful. Other audio-visual messages appeared over BBC (the government-owned British Broadcasting Corporation) television. These consisted of four short public-service films of interest to retailers, plus a series of five BBC-TV programs entitled *Decimal Shop,* aimed at helping retailers prepare for D Day. Rounding out the Board's communications with retailers was a series of 12 syndicated articles for the trade press which appeared in about 350 journals. In addition, trade publications ran many articles of their own on issues relating to decimalization, and several books were published on the topic.

Preparing the General Public for the Changeover. In spite of this early managerial focus, the general public was not being neglected in the years preceeding D Day. For both logistical and educational reasons, the DCB had decided on a phased withdrawal of £sd coins and notes and introduction of new decimal coins over a period of several years, as follows:

April 1968—Introduce 5p and 10p coins (exactly equivalent in size, metal and value to the existing one-shilling and two-shilling coins).

Aug. 1969—Withdraw the old ½d (halfpenny) coin.
Oct. 1969— Introduce the 50p coin—equivalent in value to the ten shilling note—and withdraw all 10s notes.
Dec. 1969—Withdraw the half-crown (2s6d) coin.
Feb. 1971— Introduce ½p, 1p and 2p coins, and begin withdrawal, over a period of up to 18 months, of 1d, 3d and 6d coins.

The Board insisted that:

Each coinage change must be carefully presented to the public, through Press advertising and other means, and its relevance to the general operation explained. By adopting this approach, we hope people can accustom themselves to decimal currency in easy stages [4, p. 15].

The general publicity campaign began on February 15, 1968, with the announcement that D Day would be in exactly three years' time (February being selected as a month of low retail sales activity, with a Monday being chosen so the weekend could be used for final preparations). That same day, the Royal Mint released the designs of all decimal coins but the 50p piece. From then on, the Board planned to maintain a steady flow of news, building to a peak in early 1971.

Half-page newspaper advertisements introduced the 5p and 10p coins in April 1968. Special copy was produced for use in children's periodicals. These initial advertisements set the style (described by the Board as "reassuring and authoritative but with a light touch of friendly informality" and by a journalist critic as "faintly patronising") for subsequent Board advertising to the general public. One of these initial advertisements was chosen by the Gallup Field Readership Index as "Ad of the Month," achieving higher reading and noting scores than any other half-page newspaper advertisement in the Index's 21-year history. Similar but smaller advertisements in 1969 announced the introduction of the 50p coin, the withdrawal of the ten-shilling note, and the demonetization of the half-crown.

Two of these changes resulted in public outcries, which the press covered with enthusiasm. The new seven-sided 50p coin was initially very controversial; a newspaper survey reported that 75% of respondents were opposed to what was, for them, a strange-looking coin with a very high value ($1.20). But the government resisted demand for withdrawal of the new coin; after nine months, surveys showed 53% of respondents favoring the new coin and only 7% preferring the old 10s note. Another controversy later arose over the DCB's proposal to withdraw the sixpence, a popular and widely used little coin which converted to 2½p in decimals. Faced with emotional campaigns to "Save the Sixpence" and polls with loaded research questions "proving" that 80% of the population wanted to retain this coin, the government finally overruled the DCB and allowed the coin to stay.

From February 1968 onwards, the DCB made regular use of the British Market Research Bureau's continuous consumer survey. Questions on decimalization were added to the survey every two to four months, revealing long-term trends in public awareness and attitudes. Individual questions were added as needed to investigate specific problem areas.

The Preparatory Campaign. This research confirmed the need for a preparatory advertising campaign to provide basic facts on decimalization and to dispel misconceptions and anxiety. The findings showed that the elderly and less well educated were the least informed segments of the population. It also showed that many women were concerned about prices and shopping.

So between July and November 1970, informative and reassuring advertisements were placed in a wide range of women's magazines, social and welfare publications, and selected religious periodicals. The campaign was supplemented by distribution to local authorities and citizens' advice bureaus of 300,000 posters in four different designs, and of ten million single-page leaflets. Additionally, 500,000 booklets entitled *Decimal Money: Some Questions and Answers* were prepared as a reference source for workers in local welfare departments, women's groups, and welfare-oriented voluntary organizations.

During 1970, a modest level of advertising and publicity was also directed at the general public. A 25-minute color film, *Granny Gets the Point,* prepared by the Central Office of Information, received thousands of showings across the country during the months to D Day, and was also widely shown on television.

THE FINAL CAMPAIGN

The main task of educating the general public on the specifics of the decimal changeover was confined to the period December 30, 1970, to February 24, 1971—beginning less than seven weeks prior to D Day and ending a week and a half after it. The advertising campaign was believed to have been the most concentrated ever directed at the general public in the United Kingdom. There were three good reasons why this final campaign was compressed into a relatively short period.

First, in contrast to machine suppliers and businesses, which needed a lengthy planning horizon, there was no need for the general public to have *detailed* information on decimalization years in advance of the date. Second, it was desirable to reduce the risk that people might forget much of the information contained in the advertising before they had had a chance to put it into practice. And, third, it was important to reach people when they were more likely to be attentive—and therefore receptive—to detailed information about an event which was shortly to affect them, instead of preoccupied with Christmas.

JWT defined the objectives of the campaign as follows:

1. To convey all the information, some elementary and some more complicated, that the general public must have if the switch is to go smoothly.
2. To make the DCB be seen to be giving the lead, to be an authoritative, responsible, sympathetic body providing all the information necessary to complete a smooth changeover.

Advertising's task was primarily one of educating the public, helping them to eradicate the money habits of a lifetime, to learn new habits, and to put these into practice. Since money played such a central role in people's lives, it was vital to maintain public confidence in the new decimal currency throughout the changeover period and thereafter; it was especially necessary to reassure people that decimalization was not a major cause of inflation as many feared. Above all, the changeover had to go smoothly on the first attempt.

Surveys showed a continuing level of significant public resistance to decimalization. As D Day drew nearer, public concern appeared to increase; the percentage of respondents not in favor of the change rose from 39% in July 1969 to 45% in November 1970. Attitudes seemed to be closely related to socio-economic class (Exhibit 3). Worries about confusion over conversion and anxiety over prices and shopping were the major concerns.

The cornerstone of the educational campaign was a free, 24-page color booklet, *Your Guide to Decimal Money,* intended for distribution to every household in the country. This contained all the information necessary for an understanding of decimalization, but its disadvantage as an educational text was that its authors had no control over when it was read, or how much was read at a time, in what order, how often, and so forth.

EXHIBIT 3
Public Attitudes Towards Decimalization

	Favor	Against	Don't Know
(A) All Respondents			
July 1969	48%	39%	13%
November 1969	50%	38%	12%
March 1970	47%	41%	12%
May 1970	51%	39%	10%
July 1970	44%	48%	8%
September 1970	45%	46%	9%
November 1970	44%	45%	11%
January 1971[1]	49%	45%	6%
(B) By Socio-Economic Class			
(1) AB: Professional/Higher Managerial			
July 1969	60%	34%	6%
November 1969	69%	25%	6%
March 1970	64%	28%	8%
(2) C1: Lower Managerial			
July 1969	54%	37%	9%
November 1969	59%	30%	11%
March 1970	54%	37%	9%
(3) C2: Skilled Working Class			
July 1969	49%	37%	14%
November 1969	51%	36%	13%
March 1970	47%	41%	11%
(4) DE: Unskilled Working Class/Pensioners			
July 1969	36%	46%	19%
November 1969	35%	50%	15%
March 1970	36%	50%	14%

(Numbers may not add to 100% due to rounding)

---

[1] National Opinion Poll Survey (all other surveys made by British Market Research Bureau for Decimal Currency Board).

Source: Decimal Currency Board.

To make the learning task as logical and coherent as possible, without confusing the audience with too much information at once, the balance of the campaign was structured into three sequential "lessons."

1. The effect of decimalization on coins.
2. The effect of decimalization on shops and prices.
3. How to handle mixed money (i.e., low denomination old and new coins).

The advertising media employed for the campaign were local and national newspapers, magazines, television, and billboards.[2] The coverage of this total campaign was estimated at 99% of the adult population.

Newspapers carried the basic information about decimalization, with all three elements of the educational program outlined above being dealt with in a series of nine large advertisements commencing in late December. These used a countdown approach, with headlines reading "D Day —7 Weeks to Go," "D Day—6 Weeks to Go" and so on down to "D Day Starts at Midnight" and "Today is D Day." An example appears in Exhibit 4.

Magazines carried full-page advertisements giving practical advice on shopping and cash-handling. Five such advertisements, in continuity form, appeared between January 11 and D Day, February 15, in large circulation magazines. Exhibit 5 shows an example.

Television was used to demonstrate shopping situations and to accustom the eye and ear to the sight and sound of decimal prices and change giving. From the week commencing January 18, a series of six 30-second commercials appeared at both peak and off-peak hours on the Independent Television Network. Altogether, 1,444 30-second spots were shown on TV, one of the most concentrated television campaigns ever undertaken in the U.K. Meantime, the noncommercial BBC television and radio networks broadcast a large number of TV and radio programs and short announcements devoted to decimalization.

Billboards (known as "posters" in Britain) were used on some 10,000 high-visibility urban sites to reiterate key points about the decimal system.

Since research had shown that the elderly and less well educated groups might need additional help, a special advertisement was run in selected social welfare and religious publications—encouraging readers and their families to study the booklet *Your Guide to Decimal Money* and then pass on their knowledge to those who might find some of the points a bit confusing. The Board also supplied information directly to organizations working with these groups.

Weekly surveys were conducted from January 26 to February 22. The objective was to pinpoint any major areas of difficulty so that the content of later advertising could be adjusted accordingly. Speed was essential and a nationally representative sample of 800 adults was interviewed on the

Tuesday and Wednesday of each week, with the results being processed and tabulated for a Friday presentation.

A contingency plan had to be brought into operation when delivery of the booklet was halted by a lengthy postal strike, with an estimated 25% of all British households still to receive a copy. More press advertising was placed, reproducing as much as possible of the information in the booklet.

As the DCB had anticipated, numerous other organizations provided publicity concerning the changeover to decimals.

> The Board were not alone shouldering the task of preparing Britain for D Day. Children were given decimal lessons at school; those who handled money in their everyday work received training courses from their employers; many shops provided information for their customers; there was a growing volume of articles in the general and specialist press, many of them prepared after consultation with the Board or based on Board material; and the broadcasting authorities were very active [5, p. 16].

The banks produced leaflets for all their account holders and bank speakers addressed more than 18,500 meetings with a total audience of nearly 800,000 people. In addition, there were a large number of commercial promotions with a decimal theme, such as decimal games, dishcloth and dress materials with a decimal pattern, and so forth. The DCB itself spent a total of £2 million ($4.8 million) on publicity (including advertising) over a 3½ year period, of which 75% was spent on the final, two-month campaign.[3]

Press Coverage. The editorial role of the press during the decimalization period was viewed with mixed feelings by some of those responsible for the changeover. One J. Walter Thompson executive stated that women's magazines had done an "outstanding" job in preparing their readers for decimalization, but that most of the press had approached D Day with an attitude which he described as "eagerly anticipating disaster."

Newspaper articles in the "popular" national dailies reported the results of their own opinion polls, which showed often sharply different findings from those of the DCB concerning people's preparedness for the changeover. For instance, an article in the *Sun* (a popular daily), on February 1, 1971, began in this discouraging vein:

4 Out of Every 10 Still Don't Quite Get the Point

> Four out of every 10 people are still totally confused about decimal money.
> This startling fact has emerged from a nationwide SUN survey to find out if Britain is ready for the switch to the new decimal currency a fortnight today.
> It means that only a dramatic increase in the public's decimal knowledge will avert chaos in the High Street on D Day, February 15.[4]

---

[2] There were no commercial radio stations in Britain at the time of decimalization. Neither BBC radio nor television carried commercial advertising.

[3] Total advertising expenditures in the U.K., by all advertisers, in all media, were £591 million ($1.3 billion) in 1971.

[4] "The High Street" is Britain's version of "Main Street."

EXHIBIT 4
Newspaper Advertising, Final Campaign, February 1971

DECIMAL CURRENCY BOARD

D DAY-ONE WEEK TO GO

When you go shopping on Monday week, you'll find this information useful

On 15th February, we change to decimal currency. Three new 'copper' coins—the 1 new penny (1p), the 2 new pence (2p) and the new halfpenny (½p)—will join the money we are already using. Some public transport and most shops will switch on that day and the rest will do so as they change their cash registers and other machines to decimal working.

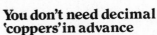

There will be £sd shops and decimal (£p) shops and this is what the new prices will look like

Most shops will start trading in decimal money at once but for a time some will continue as £sd shops. £p shops will mark prices in £p, and the top illustration is how decimal prices under £1 will look. £sd shops will continue to show their prices in £sd. To help you, some shops will show their prices in both £p and £sd for a time. This is called dual pricing. An example is shown in the centre illustration. The selling price is shown in large figures; the £sd amount is a guide to value only. The lower illustration gives an example of how decimal prices over £1 will look.

You don't need decimal 'coppers' in advance

You will be able to go shopping on D Day with your existing money. £p shops will have stocked their tills with the new decimal 'coppers' and you will get them in your change. The shopkeeper can give the right change if you give him a note or silver coins. You can spend old pennies and 3d bits in decimal shops, in lots totalling 6d, which exactly equals 2½p. The shopkeeper can then give you the right change in decimal 'coppers.'

Two ways to simplify shopping

First, as far as you can, use decimal 'coppers' in decimal shops, and old pennies and 3d bits in £sd shops. You may find, at first, that it helps if you keep these coins separate.

Second, if you do not have the exact money handy, do just as you do now—*give more and get change.*

Some examples of shopping after D Day

In a decimal shop. You want to buy a small tin of soup marked 4p.

1. You can pay exactly with decimal coins—for example, with two 2p coins.

2. Or you can hand the shopkeeper a 5p coin (or an old shilling) and get 1p change.

3. Or you can pay with £sd coins by giving, say, two threepenny bits and a sixpence. That equals 1/-, of course, and is the same as 5p. So you'll get 1p change.

In an £sd shop. You want to buy a packet of sweets marked at 1s 2d.

1. You can pay exactly with an old shilling (or a 5p coin) and two old pennies.

2. Or you can also hand the shopkeeper a 5p coin, a 2p coin and a ½p coin. That equals 7½p. And since 7½p is 1s 6d in the old money, you'll get 4d change.

Check with 'Your Guide to Decimal Money'

If you are doubtful about anything, refer to the official booklet, "Your Guide to Decimal Money," which has been sent to every home. Remember, too, that it contains two pull-out copies of the Shoppers' Table to help you check £p prices against £sd prices.

If you need another copy of the booklet, you can get one this month from any Post Office.

Dial-a-Disc

In all towns and cities where the Post Office Dial-a-Disc service is available, you can hear a recorded message about the change to decimal currency by Lord Fiske, the Chairman of the Decimal Currency Board. This message can be heard during the week before D Day and for two weeks after it. Just dial the normal Dial-a-Disc code between 8 am and 6 pm on weekdays.

POINTS TO REMEMBER

From D Day:

- The £ stays the same, but is made up of 100 new pence.
- There will be decimal (£p) shops and £sd shops.
- You can use both old and new coins in either kind of shop.
- In decimal shops, use 3d bits and old pennies in amounts totalling 6d (2½p).
- If in doubt, give more and get change.

From 15th February-think decimal

Cut this out and keep it.

EXHIBIT 5
Magazine Advertising, Final Campaign, January 1971

Mum gets the message

On Monday, 15th February, we change to decimal currency. Let's follow Betty Fisher as she takes her old (and rather crotchety) mother with her to the shops on D (for Decimal) Day.

D Day today, Mum! They say most of the shops will be decimal.

H'm!

It said in the paper that a penny's going to be worth more than 2d. How can a penny be more than tuppence? I ask you!

They're new pennies, Mum. There's only 100 to the £, instead of 240 — so each new penny must be worth more than two old pennies. They're smaller and lighter, too.

Well, I suppose it'll work out in the end!

You'll soon get used to it, Mum. We've already got a 50 new pence coin which we've been using as ten shillings, and we can use the two shilling piece as 10 new pence ...

... and the shilling as 5 new pence! Everyone knows that!

THINKS *Decimals? Easier than I thought!*

A free copy of 'Your Guide to Decimal Money' is now being delivered to every home. It tells you all about shopping with the new money. Read it carefully and keep it by you for reference.

DECIMAL CURRENCY BOARD

The "quality" press was, as always, more restrained, but still voiced fears that things could not possibly go as smoothly as the DCB seemed to be anticipating.

D DAY AND AFTER

The normal financial workings of the U.K. came to a halt on Thursday, February 11, four days before D Day. The banks, Stock Exchange, and Foreign Exchange were all closed for four days to allow a breathing space for the necessary changeover. The banks faced the biggest task, since they could not convert their machines and accounts to decimal until all outstanding £sd items had been brought to account; a massive clearing operation, "Operation Checkpoint," was launched to clear all checks and credits on schedule and then to convert each account to its decimal equivalent. Retailers obtained supplies of decimal bronze coins (½p, 1p, 2p) in advance, so as to have decimal change ready for customers on D Day, but remained open during normal working hours.

British Rail and the London Underground had decided to go decimal a day early, since Sunday was obviously a quieter day for travel than Monday. This went over smoothly, and on D Day the morning newspapers were expressing cautious optimism, already having one decimal success story to report.

Early indications on February 15 were that members of the public seemed to have learned their lessons well. Among retailers, the DCB later reported,

> The general consensus was that customers, although unpracticed, had a good understanding of basic principles . . . elderly customers tended to be slower. Customers appreciated the efforts which retailers had made to help them—for example, by providing special decimal advisers or enquiry points—even though their services were in practice not often called upon. . . . Many people had used up their low-value £sd coins the previous week and others deliberately disposed of them on D Day. . . . There was a general air of calm acceptance and good humour amongst the shopping public; and shop staff on the whole enjoyed the exercise [5, p. 38].

During the morning of D Day a special survey was taken of a representative sample of 1,040 shoppers across the country, with responses being telephoned to London, quickly processed, and released to the press that afternoon. The results showed that 67 percent of those interviewed found shopping easy, 25 percent had difficulty and 8 percent had no definite feelings. When asked whether, once they had got used to the new money, they felt it would be easier, harder, or about the same as shopping in the old money, 73 percent said easier, 6 percent harder and 17 percent about the same. The evening papers reported D Day as a success story, with headlines such as the London *Evening News'* "You're Getting the Point."

Two guidelines which the DCB had sought to put across to the general public were, wherever possible, to give old coins in "6d lots" (since this was the smallest amount converting exactly into decimals, namely 2½p), and when in doubt, to "give more and get change." Many people resorted extensively to the latter approach, often tendering one-pound notes for quite small purchases; this helped them avoid hav-

ing to work in decimals at all, while also serving to get large supplies of decimal coins quickly into circulation. Over 90 percent of all retailers and other traders went decimal during the first week of the changeover, thus quickly driving out the old coins and reducing to a minimum the confusion which inevitably arose from having old and new currency systems in operation together. Compared with other countries that had switched to decimals, Britain came nearer to an overnight change.

Perhaps the most remarkable feature of the press coverage on the morning after D Day was that only two of the ten national newspapers made decimalization their lead story. Although one paper claimed that prices had been rounded up by pubs and restaurants, most papers stressed the smoothness of the changeover. Some coverage was given to last-ditch efforts to persuade the public to resist decimals by a small organization called the Anti-Decimal Group. Most newspapers reported that a London housewife had made her own contribution to putting the new money into circulation by swallowing a 2p coin in the early morning. Perhaps the most telling observation of all appeared in the February 20 edition of *The Economist.* "Lord Fiske [the DCB Chairman] was right," they said, "and the politicians who told Mr. Wilson [the former Prime Minister] not to risk a spring election after decimalization were wrong. It was a non-event."

Within six weeks of D Day, virtually all business in the U.K. was being transacted in decimal currency. Although the duration of the changeover had originally been set at 18 months, it was decided to end the changeover period a year sooner, on August 31, 1971. One month later, the Decimal Currency Board was dissolved, its early dissolution a tribute to its success as a change agency.

AN EVALUATION OF THE CHANGEOVER

Few people would disagree with the contention that the decimal changeover was a remarkable achievement. What was the key to its success? Perhaps a major advantage in Britain's favor was the fact that it was virtually the last country to decimalize its currency. Consequently, it was able to profit from a detailed study of the South African, Australian, and New Zealand experiences, avoiding any mistakes these countries had made and improving upon approaches which had already proven successful.

Several aspects of the Decimal Currency Board's work may be credited for the success of the operation.

1. The very well organized planning of the logistics of the changeover;
2. The carefully researched and sequenced nature of the Board's publicity strategy, concentrating first on business, then on retailing and trading organizations, and finally on the general public;
3. The decision to concentrate the main public communications campaign in the weeks immediately preceding the changeover;
4. The use of regular surveys to monitor progress, followed by appropriate corrective action where needed;
5. The use of each medium of communication to its best advantage, complementing, rather than duplicating, messages in other media;

6. The leveraging effect which DCB publicity efforts obtained through close coordination with businesses and other organizations, so that much of the publicity and educational effort surrounding the change came to people in the course of their day-to-day dealings with retailers, banks, post offices, and transport undertakings;
7. The personality of the DCB's Chairman and chief "salesman," Lord Fiske, who seems to have conveyed throughout an impression of calm, reassuring competence, coupled with good-humored confidence and a pleasing common touch;
8. Early selection of an advertising agency. By involving the agency very early in the planning process, rather than leaving selection until the time came for mass media advertising, the DCB was able to coordinate its marketing communications activities more closely than might otherwise have been the case. The agency's wealth of expertise (its clients included banks, retailers, and marketers of a wide range of consumer and industrial goods and services) provided skills which are not normally found in government agencies.
9. The firm commitment of successive governments to the decimalization program from 1966 onwards.

As a change agency, the DCB and its personnel seem to have possessed most of the characteristics necessary for a change agent's success in securing adoption of an innovation [12, 14]. In particular, the Board was highly "client-oriented"; it developed a program compatible with the needs of both intermediary organizations and the general public; it commanded the support of organizations which might be thought of as opinion leaders in their fields; and, despite periodic carping from critics, it succeeded in maintaining considerable credibility.

What, if anything should have been done differently? The answer is, probably very little. It is possible that additional consumer research concerning the 50p coin might have resulted in a design and an introductory campaign which would have generated less controversy. The argument over whether the £-newpenny-½ system should have been selected over the ten shilling-cent system can still occasionally be heard. A major advantage of the latter was supposedly its easy conversion against the old currency, but this is one area in which consumer input was not sought.

Although the press did not, in some people's view, play a particularly helpful role with its widely voiced fears of "Chaos in the High Street," it was basically supportive of decimalization once the decision had been made. One of the media's problems in this instance was that good news may be no news. After all, there is little journalistic challenge or excitement in reporting the fact that a major change is proceeding so smoothly as to be a "non-event." However, the press may well have contributed to the final success of the changeover by verbalizing people's fears and doubts in the preceding weeks and making it clear to their readers that these fears were being made known to the DCB and the Government. At the same time, the press performed a very useful task with their various "price-watching" services; these watched out for any attempts to cheat the public with fraudulent price conversions or surreptitious price hikes.

As an exercise in change, decimalization was clearly a brilliant success, especially when one considers the extent of opposition among ordinary citizens. But was it worth the effort and expense? Within a matter of weeks, business interests—including banks, retailers, and the accounting profession—were reporting that significant benefits were already being derived from working in the new system. Formal and informal research showed steady gains in acceptance of decimal currency as people accustomed themselves to using it. The following editorial comment in the March 24, 1971, edition of the popular *Daily Mirror* is probably a fairly accurate reflection of public opinion some six weeks after D Day:

> Nobody wanted decimal currency. . . . But now it's here we don't know how we managed so long without it.

INSIGHTS FOR OTHER CHANGE PROGRAMS

For students of marketing and communications, the decimalization campaign in Britain represents what may come to be seen as a classic example of utilizing the tools and strategies of marketing and research to facilitate a major, but initially unpopular, societal change. The nature of the task, persuading the entire population to change the habits of a lifetime, required a sophisticated understanding of communications theory and the potential and limitations of each available medium. It also required the presence of a change agency capable of implementing a marketing program in both industrial and consumer markets.

The coordinating role of the Decimal Currency Board illustrates clearly the leveraging powers possessed by this type of change agency. By far the greater part of the communications and promotional effort was actually carried out by groups such as machine manufacturers, banks, transport organizations, and retailers. These were obviously in much more direct contact with small businesses and the general public than the Board itself. By coordinating such efforts (although it could not *control* them), the DCB succeeded in ensuring that these other communications were both accurate in content and reasonably consistent with its own work.

While it is rare that an entire country faces such sweeping innovations as decimalization, social and technological change will periodically require adoption of new ways of doing things at national or local levels or among specific segments of the population. A clear understanding of the marketing tasks involved is central to facilitating such changes, and it is evident that official change agencies can play important coordinating roles. However, their task is likely to be more difficult in situations where businesses, the mass media, and/or other intermediary organizations are antagonistic towards the change program.

Metrication Programs. One program of national change, which is of current interest in several countries and which poses a number of problems somewhat similar to decimalization, is metrication of weights and measures. Several major industrial nations—including Britain, Canada, Australia, and the United States—are currently engaged in metricating their weights and measures.

Although there are some obvious parallels (including that of unpopularity), metrication differs from decimalization in at least two important respects. First, there is no need for a universal "M Day" comparable to D Day, since metrication can proceed on a sector by sector basis. Second, compulsory use of metric measures by consumers is limited to legislative areas such as highway speed limits, although it may become increasingly inconvenient to "speak" in and use traditional measures. In the case of decimalization, by contrast, the old currency units literally disappeared.

Curiously enough, the success of the decimalization program in Britain has made the task of metrication there harder rather than easier. Many people blamed decimalization for inflation, a claim largely unsupported by economic studies. The fact that inflation accelerated sharply in the United Kingdom from 1970 onwards is a good example of "correlation not causation" where decimalization is concerned, but many Britons became afraid lest metrication should "also" prove inflationary. Concerned, in part, about electoral popularity, successive British governments have been reluctant to take firm stands on metrication with the result that the program is now several years behind schedule. The work of the Metrication Board has been made much harder by the lack of strong Government support and it has been somewhat difficult for this Board to maintain an ongoing, coordinated marketing effort.

Australia and Canada started their metrication programs some years later than Britain, but both are now ahead. By 1978 Australia's program, begun in 1970, was almost 75 percent complete. In part, this success may be ascribed to strong government support for the metrication program, cooperation by the news media in quickly ceasing to use the old units as each metric change was initiated, and a series of legislated cut-off dates after which use of the old units in industry or trade became illegal.

How much has the United States learned from national change programs in other countries? The evidence to date is not encouraging. The Department of the Treasury and the Federal Reserve Board ignored the insights provided by the British decimalization program when they came to implement the much simpler two-dollar bill reintroduction. The result was an embarrassing flop. Although one can argue the merits of the decision to reintroduce the two-dollar bill, once that decision had been made, a serious effort should have been made to ensure success.

In the case of metrication, there is a very real danger that America may be ignoring the lessons of the successful Australian experience and instead drifting into a poorly coordinated program lacking government support and legislated cut-off dates. If public confusion and deceptive practices are to be avoided, then stronger powers will have to be given to the U.S. Metric Board. The Administration's current philosophy, as expressed by President Carter in a recent message to the American National Metric Council, is that,

> It is the intent of the Metric Act that the rate of metrication be governed by the market place, with the U.S. Metric Board playing but a facilitating part in the process [13].

But for metrication to be completed in a reasonable time frame will require a strong, centrally coordinated marketing effort. Reacting simply to the forces of the market place could easily result in a haphazard conversion program lasting fifty years.

REFERENCES

1. *Australia and New Zealand Bank Quarterly Review,* "Decimals— Change After the Changeover." Vol. XVII (October 1967), 12–15.
2. Axelrod, Joseph *et al. The Feasibility of Reintroducing the Two Dollar Bill: A Marketing Approach.* A Report to the Board of Governors of the Federal Reserve System. Boston, MA: Graduate School of Business Administration, Harvard University, 1975.
3. Bjorkman, Johan. *Kortsiktiga Effekter Av Trafikinformation.* Stockholm, Sweden: EFI, 1971.
4. Decimal Currency Board. *First Annual Report, 1967/8.* London: Her Majesty's Stationery Office, 1968.
5. Decimal Currency Board. *Fourth Annual Report, 1970/71.* London: Her Majesty's Stationery Office, 1971.
6. Englund, Anders. "Changing Behaviour Patterns: Sweden's Traffic Switch." *Progress* (The Unilever Quarterly), No. 3, 1968, 26–32.
7. Lovelock, Christopher H. "Decimalization of the Currency in Great Britain," 9-575-101. Boston, MA: Intercollegiate Case Clearing House, 1975.
8. Lovelock, Christopher H. "Department of the Treasury: Reissue of the $2 Bill" (A), 9-576-102, and (B), 9-578-168. Boston, MA: Intercollegiate Case Clearing House, 1975, 1978.
9. Lovelock, Christopher H. "Marketing the Metric System—1978," 9-578-167. Boston, MA: Intercollegiate Case Clearing House, 1978.
10. Moore, N. E. A. *The Decimalisation of Britain's Currency.* London: Her Majesty's Stationery Office, 1973.
11. *Report of the Committee of Inquiry on Decimal Currency.* London: Her Majesty's Stationery Office, Cmnd. 2145, 1963.
12. Rogers, Everett M. and F. Floyd Shoemaker. "The Change Agent," Chapter 7 in *Communication of Innovations.* New York: The Free Press, 1971.
13. *The Wall Street Journal.* "U.S. Metric Board's First Meeting Hears Wide Discord on Outlook for Conversion." April 5, 1978.
14. Zaltman, Gerald and Robert Duncan. "The Change Agent," Chapter 9 in *Strategies for Planned Change.* New York: Wiley, 1977, 185–224.